POLICY AND ETHICS IN BUSINESS

POLICY AND ETHICS IN BUSINESS

BY

CARL F. TAEUSCH

ASSOCIATE PROFESSOR OF BUSINESS ETHICS
MANAGING EDITOR, HARVARD BUSINESS REVIEW
GRADUATE SCHOOL OF BUSINESS ADMINISTRATION
HARVARD UNIVERSITY

First Edition

McGRAW-HILL BOOK COMPANY, Inc.

NEW YORK AND LONDON

1931

THE MAPLE PRESS COMPANY, YORK, PA.

To

NORMAN KEMP SMITH
AND
JAMES HAYDEN TUFTS

PREFACE

In dedicating this book to a former teacher and a former colleague, the author wishes to acknowledge an indebtedness which can never be repaid. It may appear to Norman Kemp Smith, and also to James Hayden Tufts but to a lesser degree, that this work has deviated so far from the field in which their chief interest lies as to be no longer a part, even by implication, of philosophical inquiry. On the other hand, it must be apparent to business men that, however much this work has deviated from philosophy, it has fallen far short of coming to grips with the realities of business. A consideration of these two serious qualifications has at times disturbed and held up the work, but only until it has again become apparent that these limitations would be minimized by honestly admitting them at the outset.

Methodological difficulties of relatively minor importance are discussed throughout the book wherever they have arisen. Those which have presented almost insuperable difficulties must be mentioned here. Chief of these is the absence of records, comparable in the least degree, for example, with those available for legal research. This volume is critical to an extreme of the interference of the Law with Business. And yet, anomalously, most of the evidence for that criticism is found in the legal, and not in business, records. These records, the "law reports," have furthermore been inextricably bound up with the rule of *stare decisis*, a rule which is the basis for much criticism against the law and which has been regarded by students of business as incompatible with the most characteristic feature of business activity, its dynamic character.

The Graduate School of Business Administration of Harvard University has attempted to meet this situation by collecting cases of actual business conduct as the raw material and foundations for a science of business. Some of these cases have been formulated into business problems for classroom work and published in the "Problems" series of case books. Some of these cases in turn have been published, together with commentaries, in the *Harvard Business Reports*. In order to keep inviolate the confidence reposed in the School by business men, who have given generously of their time and who have been frank in disclosing the technical methods successfully employed in business, it has been the policy of the School from the start to disguise the proper and place names of cases and frequently to change the name of the commodity. This process of abstraction has made it difficult for one not conversant with the identity of the company to employ this material for teaching purposes, and even more difficult to use such material for constructing an empirical science of business.

The business case has not gone to the extreme of the hypothetical case spun out by the ancient Druids and woven into an ephemeral legal web that has since been brushed aside by the realities of the English common law. But, on the other hand, the business case does not approach the reality and concreteness of the law reports, which represent an attempt accurately to describe the realities as identified with actual names and places and things. These law reports are also abstractions, at least to the extent that any description is an abstraction in reference to the real event. But there is at least a difference in degree of reality between the legal case and the business case as published in the business problems and reports. The business cases themselves vary in degree of reality, of course, and frequently approach the legal case in concreteness. But the difference in degree also frequently is so great as to become a difference in kind, and this possibility must be constantly kept in mind for the sake of that methodological soundness which lies in critical self-consciousness.

These difficulties have been particularly acute in connection with the study of Business Ethics. For even though the law reports, the *Harvard Business Reports*, and the reports of such agencies as the Federal Trade Commission and the Better Business Bureau have been freely drawn upon for such pertinent facts as are imbedded therein, their methodological peculiarities have laid additional burdens on finding the ethical implications. Ethics shares with its mother subject, Philosophy, the characteristic quality of a reflective study, and is not therefore wholly or even largely dependent on direct access to original materials; but the future collection of original case material must at least supplement the reflective analysis of material already assembled for another purpose. In connection with this task, as so far performed, the difficulties have been discouraging to say the least.

The cases which have not been used in this volume far outnumber those which are presented, and the cases which have been used are frequently and obviously unsatisfactory. It is for this reason that a number of cases retain the real names and places and specify the actual commodities and functions, especially where such of our largest business corporations are involved as can and do withstand particular criticisms by quietly and confidently going about their own business. It is in the hope that such observations will be welcomed or successfully shown to be unfounded or beside the point, that this volume is offered as a modest attempt to contribute to a subject which seems to be of increasing concern to business men as well as to others.

The materials dealt with in this volume fall mainly within the fields of mercantile transactions and business organizations. A thorough-going treatment of this limited material soon necessitated the excluding of matters which are equally connoted by the title of the book; namely, banking and finance, labor problems, accounting, etc. Where such matters could be referred to profitably by way of analogy, they were used to explain the problem illustrated by the more strictly defined "business" activity. But the direct treatment of these additional matters has been deferred to the future.

The author wishes to acknowledge with gratitude the help of colleagues and business men who have aided in this work and the facilities of the Graduate School of Business Administration of Harvard University, which have so generously been placed at his disposal.

CARL F. TAEUSCH.

SOLDIERS FIELD,
  BOSTON, MASS.
    January, 1931.

CONTENTS

xi

POLICY AND ETHICS IN BUSINESS

A. THE LAND, THE PEOPLE AND THEIR IDEAS

An understanding of the problems of Business Ethics obviously presumes a knowledge of business facts. But business facts are not separable from the social texture in which they are woven. And the social texture in turn can be fully appreciated only by an understanding of the physical conditions which support it. How far does it become necessary, therefore, in a study of American Business Ethics, to become acquainted with the background of business behavior—the character of the land and of the people and the context supplied by their social relations and ideas?

The history of a nation and the social pattern of a people are determined to a large extent by physical circumstances: the location of the country, the topography of the land, its climate and natural resources, the racial make-up of its people and their technological equipment. In addition to such factors there are the reflective activities, artistic creations and spiritual strivings of man, which are not only effects but also conditions of a civilization. But systems of law and government and of religion, and even the resultant efforts of scientists and artists, are never free from the influences of their material foundations. It is true that the human mind has often overcome Nature— directly in reclamation projects and flood control, in the facilitation of communication and transportation, and in crop tillage and mechanical invention; and indirectly through migrations, flood warnings or reports of the weather bureau, and statistical knowledge. But the Stoics were probably right, that we "overcome" Nature by studying and obeying her.

Great cultural periods probably cannot be fully explained by material facts—the Ages of Pericles, of Augustus, of Elizabeth, and of Louis XIV are beyond any such analysis. But it is just as true that the winds of the Aegean drove the reluctant Greeks to the attack on the Persian fleet at Salamis, forcing one of the greatest issues in history, and that it was the Aegean winds again

1

almost 2,000 years later that drove two crippled Turkish galleys against a crucial bastion in the walls of Byzantium and paved the way for a turn in the whole tide of European history. Napoleon attributed his defeat at Waterloo to a light rainfall which delayed his artillery, and his Russian campaign was largely thwarted by "Generals January and February." In a broader sense, the then-existing ratio of racial constituents affected to some extent the great periods of Greek and French culture—whether we can determine it exactly or not—and a period of material imperial expansion preceded and vitally affected the great cultural epochs of Rome and England.

These highly dramatic events are not so important for historical analysis, however, as are the more extensive and more persistent conditions so painstakingly worked out by Ratzel, Semple and Huntington, and recognized by most modern scholars as essential to an adequate historical-social interpretation. It is not the purpose of this volume to contribute still further to this excellent body of work, but its importance and significance must be recognized. And it will be necessary to indicate, at least briefly if inadequately, the rôle which the physical elements of the land, and the racial factors constituting our people, have played in the national and local traits of the United States; traits that represent and constitute our character and to a considerable degree explain our individual and social behavior.

A study of the way in which men have written history may present the problem in its proper perspective. Just as in the course of events the political structure wrested certain prerogatives from the religious, so the first serious inroads on the religious and supernatural interpretations of historians were made by the political schools of thought. Within the compass of the last century, however, this dominance of view-point in the writing of history has passed successively from the political interpretation—which in Bancroft is still intermingled with the religious—to the economic, from the economic to the physical, and then back again to the economic and sociological. The significance of this development is centered partly on the place occupied by the physical interpretation of history. It began as a reaction to, or intensification of, the claims of the economists and was sponsored by the scientific and industrial developments of the Nineteenth Century. The physical interpreters of history pointed out that if the economists were going to insist on "basic" considerations, one might as well pursue this policy to the limit and rest historical events on such fundamental conditions as climate and topography. For, however much the economist may insist that the diapasonic factors in which he is interested play a deeper note than the treble of government or law or of religion or art, he must recognize that even the bass notes are determined in part by the mechanism of the organ.

No attempt will be made to connect causally the general physical or racial constituents of America with specific national traits or local behavior or with the details of our social organization. This would be explaining the more by the less. It is also a valid criticism of the materialistic interpretation of history that fundamental physical conditions are too remote from the the final stages of individual expression or social behavior to warrant any inferences of a continuous or determinative causal relationship. The relative location, topography and climate of Greece have changed but little in many thousands of years, and yet there has been but one Age of Pericles; whole races have migrated without successfully carrying with them the integrity of their social organization or the cumulative intellectual achievements of their homeland; while, conspicuously in the case of the United States, a new social order has arisen among immigrants who might even once have been regarded, especially from the European point of view, largely as social undesirables, or at best as dissatisfied minorities in a continent, the accepted social organization of which represented a high degree of civilization. History, perhaps unfortunately, has no accurate laboratory check on its data, and it only partly performs the task of empirical observation. Not only have the migrations of peoples been almost universal, but racial mixtures have been so prevalent as to effect immeasurable material changes in racial constituents everywhere. Therefore, at best, the physical and racial factors, affecting and effecting a people such as those of the United States, can be regarded only as probable and fragmentary causal agencies.

Intermediate to the physical-racial factors influencing any society and the resultant pattern of that society itself, however, are the more cogent elements of social organization and control. The "gridiron" topography of Greece may have been conducive to the development of an individualism that later expressed itself in her glorious period of art and science and government and philosophy, but a necessary step in this process was the intermediate effect of generating many small independent social units which in turn encouraged the development of individual clan leaders.   Greek colonization was necessitated by the relative poverty of the soil; the products of the olive and the grape lent themselves to transportation to far-distant countries and begot a trade that involved much stimulating travel; wealth and leisure later followed the Persian Wars; and, finally, the disastrous expedition to Syracuse was prompted by the need of Athens for an adequate source of grain supplies.

The point need not be labored.   And the illustration of Greece will suffice to indicate the point of view, in spite of the tremendous differences between that ancient commonwealth and modern America.   To discover the economic factors that have contributed to a civilization is as important as to point out the significance of the more fundamental physical and racial elements, and perhaps logically more pertinent and cogent in view of their relatively greater proximity to the social results which are to be explained or illuminated.   Other factors, including the racial and psychological as well as the broader ethnic and sociological views, have made their claims good.   But the economic view of historical explanation is still the strongest in the field.

Inasmuch as the main part of this volume has for its purpose the study of the social control of American business and of the evolution in this country of a justifiable system of Business Ethics, the question may arise: How adequate is an economic analysis itself as an explanation of social behavior and control?   The answer to this question has already been partly anticipated: certainly no one who has weighed the merits of a materialistic interpretation of history, and has found it wanting, would be so presumptuous as to set up as exclusively dependable another single type of interpretation.   A recognition of the limitations of an economic interpretation, even of economic facts, is necessary.   The appropriate weight which is to be attached to business and economic factors, even in determining business behavior and social control, must constantly be kept in mind.

CHAPTER I

THE LAND AND THE PEOPLE

Realizing the difficulties of a materialistic interpretation of social phenomena, especially the difficulty of causal remoteness, we shall nevertheless attempt to discover such physical and racial factors as have contributed to the national and local characteristics of America; characteristics which may in part explain American business behavior, which at least will illuminate what otherwise might appear as a mystery, and which certainly should contribute alike to two important factors bounding the facts of business behavior: an intelligent tolerance of American business activities and such effective social control as may seem desirable.

Geographic Isolation and Foreign Trade

In spite of the tremendous facilitation of communication and transportation during the last century, the United States still remains geographically isolated from Europe and Asia. Whether as effect or contributing cause, our foreign trade has never formed a large portion of our total commercial transactions. A more correct statement of this fact is that our commerce has been chiefly internal—domestic—a condition which has been brought about largely and positively by the diversified nature of the country and of the people. The nation is not only practically self-sustaining because of the great variety of products which can be supplied by one part of the country or another, but the variegated demands of our widely scattered population have made possible a large and diversified market for most of the goods which we ourselves can and do produce. This condition, fostered by a high protective tariff wall, has limited our international dealings. We have, indeed, been more isolated in our business dealings than we have in extending our political ideas. Our insistence on the "open-door" policy and the territorial integrity of China has never been practically followed up by such investments or by such extensions of trade in China

5

as would be necessary to make our political policies effective or even real. Our financial entanglements with Europe have recently become more involved than have our political relations, and have assumed dimensions that approach those of our commercial dealings, but neither has ever been more than a small fractional part of our total financial and commercial activities. Both the political and the military significance of the Monroe Doctrine have been at times subordinated to our commercial interests, but not when weighed against the sound and justifiable trade activities that we have directed toward Latin America. Even our possession of the Philippines has not been warranted by or resulted in a vigorous growth of business relations.

At recurring intervals our foreign policy has been determined by the belief that "trade follows the flag." Without going into the merits of this catch phrase, and however well it may express the situation regarding some countries, it does not apply to the commerce of the United States. Our political ideals, our religious missions, our technological improvements and the migrations of our tourists, all have extended themselves into foreign countries to a far greater extent than have our commercial dealings, especially if one considers the ratio of these external relations to the internal activities of their respective fields. The Report of the Balfour Committee on British Industrial Conditions begins significantly with Foreign Trade; President Hoover's Committee on Recent Economic Changes confines itself, also significantly, largely to domestic market conditions. This relative insignificance of foreign trade, again let it be repeated, must be restated as a condition in which the saturation point in our domestic market has not been reached; the attraction of the home market has engrossed the almost exclusive attention of our business men. The flag has again and again been employed on behalf of our various foreign activities, but it has never seriously encouraged a sufficient expansion of our foreign commerce to disturb the ratio of our foreign and domestic commerce. The proper statement of this fact, as well as the recognition of the fact, must precede any attempt to discover its significance: the self-contained nature which characterizes our business dealings.

We are, in short, business introverts, in spite of our political, educational and religious evangelicism. We have, as a result, intrinsically developed our own business methods and standards. Not only has our tariff wall kept us free from serious foreign competition at home, but the home market has been so attractive as to blind us to the need of competing abroad. Our foreign trade is marked more by amateurism and ignorance than by unfairness or unethical conduct. We have not heretofore had the experience of extensive and diversified business competition on foreign soils, but on the other hand, our business methods and ethical standards have been subject to the intensive criticisms and checks which an exclusively domestic competition, common interests and a common governmental control are bound to effect. In the field of marketing and investments, we have undoubtedly benefited as well as suffered from this situation: for although a general standard of slovenliness, especially in the technique of both, might become prevalent and receive no internal check comparable to that resulting from the meeting of foreign business men on their own or a neutral ground, yet, on the other hand, our general material prosperity, our daring financial ventures and our perfection of marketing technique are in part due to our insulation from old-world control and old-world premises that have closed their dead hand on activities which we think should be more dynamic. We have become highly sensitive to the right and wrong of business dealings, independently of foreign standards; we are nationally self-conscious and self-critical to an unusual degree, our legislative excesses being but symptoms of this condition. Furthermore, whatever the merits of what we do, most of our activities are engaged in spontaneously and speedily and much more thoroughly and intensively than would be possible with world-wide contacts; due to our lack of traditional knowledge and experience, we have at least blundered into mass production and high wages, the chain store and the trade association, the large corporation and the holding company, the investment trust and mergers. All of these forms and activities have materialized at a very rapid rate, whether they arose as immediate necessities, opportunistic policies, or as voluntarily adopted methods, and our social, legal and ethical reactions to these business devices have been no less violent.

To what extent the relative emphasis on our internal trade has controlled and restricted our business ideas may never be calculated, but it is impossible to deny that the great and relatively exclusive development of our domestic commerce has

colored our whole social philosophy. Not only are we establishing, especially by our behavior even if not by our ideology, a
distinctive system of relative social values by giving therein
a prominent place to business; but our intrinsic development of
Business Ethics has become unique and characteristic. Bearing
witness to this statement are the activities of the Department
of Commerce of the United States, the Federal Trade Commission, the Chamber of Commerce of the United States, Better
Business Bureaus and Rotary International. The independent
character of our economic theories and business activities has
apparently approximated more nearly our geographic isolation
than have our political or religious relations.

Internal Diversity: Climate, Topography and Racial Factors

The most outstanding internal characteristic of America—
at least to those who have lived in various parts of the United
States—is its diversity, its variegations and rapid changes. Both
at home and abroad we have the reputation of running to type,
but this is more true of our ideologies than of our behavior,
and our reputation is due largely to the provincialism of the
observers. At home, "100% Americanism" is usually the
generalized hypostatization of certain local desires by people
who have not even traveled, let alone lived, in other parts of the
country, or who have traveled with the spiritual blindness of the
self-content; while those who can afford to travel—at home or
abroad—are not always those who might derive the greatest
benefit therefrom. The impressions that foreigners, especially
Englishmen, derive from observing us are frequently justified
only by the particular cross-sections of American society that
are met here or that are represented by our tourists abroad.
Consequently, generalizations about Americans are as frequent
and unfounded as are a bachelor's observations about babies.
Many delightful people of culture and refinement who are
scattered throughout the United States, and the men and women
who are doing the real business of the country, do not have the
means or the time to be adequately represented abroad; nor are
these more representative people frequently encountered by
such literary lions as come from across the Atlantic to tell us
superciliously what to read and how to live, and who carry back
to their own countrymen an intensified version of their own
preconceived notions of us. The highways and byways of

England and Germany and France, and of other countries as well, contain many people who cannot afford a trip to America and who see only a few of those who travel abroad. Thus most people on either side of the Atlantic are ignorant of each other. Certainly if one wishes to understand the heart-throbs and muscle-plays of a people, one cannot rest content with the superficial observations or behavior of travelers. One must live in various parts of the country to know it and to record the picture accurately.[1] So to know the United States is conducive to a recognition of its highly diversified character.

The United States has a climate that is more nearly like China than any other region, each having been engendered by the dominating presence of a long, broad plain falling gradually eastward from a high western mountain chain. The prevailing westerlies are fairly well stripped of their moisture by the time they have crossed the continental divide and frequently cause severe droughts, intensive electric and wind storms, and extreme variations in temperature. The extensive crippling of lines of communication and transportation and the catastrophic destruction of crops and houses all call for an alertness, adjustability, reorientation, and expenditure of effort which still leave almost as little comparative time for leisure and culture as did the pioneering of the last century and a half. The losses which snow and ice levy on our railroads and overhead wires would lay an unbearable burden on European countries. Long, hard winters and sustained heat spells and droughts tax the patience of our people as much as they develop foresight and industry as cardinal virtues. The smiling fields of France and the drenched farms of England would often have a sadder, browner appearance if subjected to the climate which Americans have learned to expect; a comparison of the implacable workings of a slow destiny in Thomas Hardy's novels with the berserker destructions portrayed by Rölvaag will tell the story. The debilitating effects of a semi-tropical climate are just now being successfully met in the South by suitable diet, clothing and exercise; the psychological effects, although now becoming partly known, are only partly controllable. It would be more difficult to find an Englishman or a Frenchman who has experienced a temperature range of 60

[1] André Siegfried's *America Comes of Age* is one of the few books which have accomplished this. Lewis Mumford's "Supercilious Europe and Indifferent America," in *Scribner's*, May, 1930, is illuminative.

degrees Fahrenheit in his own country than it would be to find an American who has lived through twice that variation in almost any single year, while a little travel or "living around" in America during the course of five years would enable a person to experience almost a triple amount of that variation.   The nervousness and alertness of the Mid-westerner, as well as the thrifty habits, sharp dealings, and daring business ventures of a type such as the New Englander, can frequently be connected very intimately with the climatic conditions under which each lives, as much so as can the tolerance and graciousness and easy-going ways of the Southerner or of the Californian.

Fortunately, the negative effects of such drastic climatic events and such tremendous topographical variations are counterbalanced by the positive results.   Westward waves of migrations meeting the eastern course of climatic changes not only involved tremendous capital gains and losses; this also necessitated and developed an attitude of mind which finally came to expect such immediate gains as a matter of course and to view such losses with fortitude.   Indeed, it developed an attitude of looking forward to newer and better prospects, excluding from the attention all other interest-rivals.   The ability to become oblivious to major economic losses permeated the American mind, and although further migrations and abundance of natural resources and the more benignant character of succeeding seasons more than neutralized all previous losses, it is doubtful whether the potential gains could have been fully realized without the mental attitude which was quick to seize the renewed opportunity.   How much this experience had to do with the phenomenon which ever strikes the European with surprise—our speculative courage, generous wage policies, and managerial flexibility; our willingness to "junk" machines, plants, railroads, plans of all sorts for newer equipment and better ideas—is difficult to say.   But much of this attitude may be explained by recalling the reactions to capital, and not merely current, losses that were necessitated by our earlier experiences with the climate and topography of a highly diversified and variegated country.

If one travels in America from east to west, as most people do, racial variations are not so apparent among the persons one meets, because migrations have followed a similar direction and have divided the country into long east-and-west iso-racial belts. Southerners very early swept westward into Texas and later into Southern California. The ancestry of a group of people now living in Colorado—one of the few remaining frontiers of the country—could be traced from North Carolina during the Revolutionary days, into Tennessee, across into Missouri at the time of the Civil War, then into Oklahoma, and finally to Colorado. North Carolinians also moved into Tennessee and Kentucky. New Englanders traveled almost due west to Iowa and Nebraska, and Iowans now are crossing down into southern California. German settlers came through New York and Baltimore and converged in the Ohio Valley and spread westward from there. Some Germans and Hollanders and many Scandinavians settled in Wisconsin and Minnesota respectively, the latter spreading westward into the Dakotas. New Yorkers went by way of the Erie Canal and settled Northern Ohio, Indiana, and Illinois.

Travel east and west along any of these lines of migration and one finds chiefly topographical differences[2] and variations in humidity; and the westward paths of migration present these as only gradual, almost imperceptible differences. But if the traveler wishes to experience the added shock of differences in temperature and in human traits, let him go from the North to the South or even travel the length of Illinois; or change his locus from conservative Iowa to radical Wisconsin—the very legal systems and social attitudes of which are almost as different as the Latin atmosphere of Louisiana and the Southwest is from the rest of the country. The struggles of New York City and Chicago with the rest of their respective states are political and economic, true enough, but they are accentuated by the fact that the cities and their up- or down-state hinterlands lie in different iso-racial bands. Few of our other large cities have such difficulties, because they lie to the east or to the west of the rest of their states.

Sectional Differences

There was a time when the growing point of westward migration highly accentuated the differences between East and West— witness the successive waves of resentment toward the East that have emanated first in the earlier migration periods from the

[2] For a detailed account of this factor, see Hulbert, Archer B., *Soil. Its Influence on the History of the United States*. New Haven: Yale Univ. Press, 1930.

Middle West, then at the time of the Ballinger-Pinchot controversy from the Rocky Mountain section, then during the period
of the Japanese exclusion demands from California. The
mortgage banker of the pioneer days was generally thought to be
a "slick Easterner," although the general banker was a "city
feller" who soon became identified with the local metropolis.
And although the tariff problem originally split East and West,
and does so again today, it was only when it divided the North
and South that a complete rupture resulted. The railroad
builder intensified these east-and-west iso-racial belts by constructing his railroads in that direction, partly because of the
natural obstacles to north-and-south lines except near the Mississippi River. His earlier accomplishments met with the favor
of the pragmatic Westerner, at least to a sufficient extent to excuse
his ruthlessness, but, when railroad stocks became the backbone
of trading on the New York Stock Exchange, it did not take
long for the Westerner to identify Wall Street with the powers of
evil and to vent his spleen by sending knights-errant to Washington to represent his hostile opinions.

East and West differ in point of view regarding the importance
of a merchant marine and of trans-oceanic commercial dealings,
a difference which generally arises between inland and maritime
regions—the same situation that kept the Middle West apathetic
at the beginning of the World War. The significance of the
export problem is gradually filtering westward, however, the
general direction followed by the great trunk-line railroads and
migrations having facilitated the diffusion of this idea, at least
sufficiently to prevent a break between the highly interested
East and the more apathetic West. Another interesting problem,
which appears to have resulted from the course of westward
migrations, was the conflict over water rights in the arid regions
of Kansas and Nebraska. The common-law rule of riparian
rights was held by judges who came from the eastern part of
the country or were appointed from among the lawyers of the
eastern part of the states west of the Mississippi River. As
the western and more arid parts of this region became populated,
they became more vociferous in demanding what the necessities
of the region demanded and finally were represented in the
judicial offices themselves. Then the greater suitability of
the Spanish rule of "prior right" became recognized. It was
in this way, more even than because of the Latin strains in the

population, that the entire Southwest appropriated much of its land and water law from arid Spain rather than from soggy England.

The Old South is perhaps the largest uniquely differentiable area of the United States. Mountain chains have prevented the construction of many railroads between the South and North, the relative absence of intercommunications accentuating the climatic differences engendered by temperature. The dominance of Cavalier, Huguenot and Emigré racial strains, the presence of great numbers of Negroes, the persistence of agrarian interests long after industrialism had swept westward across the North, the crippling effects of the Civil War, and the diversion of some of the best southern minds into law and politics rather than into business and industry, all have given the South a distinctive character that is little known and less appreciated by the rest of the country. Living as an art and as an end in itself has been further cultivated there than anywhere else in the United States, with the possible exception of the Pacific Coast. Literary and artistic interests have been allowed to compete with commercial, industrial and financial activities, with the result that the latter either have not been so well developed or so highly regarded as in the other parts of the country or have been pursued largely by those who have more recently moved to the South. What the result will be as the younger Southerners awaken to the necessity of meeting this more vigorous competition remains to be seen. Whether the Old South will "lose her soul" or establish the material basis necessary to her own salvation depends on the point of view. The exploitation of the Negro, and more recently of the "poor white," has in the past diverted into a broad social-moral situation most of the energy which in the North and West has, in the free competition among equals, generated the more acute problems of Business Ethics.

Within the South itself a high degree of local differentiation exists. New Orleans and its hinterland, which extends even beyond the boundaries of Louisiana, is a Latin metropolis, with Spanish and French traditions and more recent Italian influences. To understand the business relations of this community one must understand what is meant by the suggestion that the seal of this community include a crayfish rampant on pompano; one must know that Mardi Gras is but the culmination of the carnival season beginning with Twelfth Night, and that all this revelry is less significant of the character of the city than is her somber appearance on All Souls' Day; one must know that New Orleans is always sure of her instincts. No sharper contrasts of the old and new in social-economic life can be discovered anywhere than those presented by the Florida "cracker" under the influence of a land boom, or proud Charleston holding her own against the shopkeeper, the "tar-heel" working in the textile mills of the Piedmont region, or the black belt of Alabama resounding to the racket of the steel mills. The very intensity of these contrasts is accentuated, not only by the peculiar characteristics of a comparatively isolated region such as the South, but also by the variegated nature of this region itself. Social forces are there being subjected to changes in already differing conditions, a situation which presents too many variable and powerful factors to warrant any predictions as to the outcome, and there is not yet apparent a sufficient amount of even relative stability to regard any part of it as permanent. And this is the hinterland of many important commercial and industrial centers, determining indirectly but powerfully, although to an unknown extent, their social-economic policies and their standards of ethics.

Consider the ramifications of the cotton situation alone. Although the cotton-textile situation the world over is in a precarious state of affairs, the development of southern mills has presented New England with an exceptionally difficult problem: drawing away labor and capital and management, forcing old and established New England towns to reconstitute their tax programs, dispossessing the older families of their long-held management and even social control, and affecting all related industries. On the other hand, the change in policy as regards the raising of raw cotton—from a one-crop policy to one of diversification—not only affects mills the world over by inevitably decreasing the supply of raw cotton, but also will probably make the South completely self-sustaining as regards foods, and may perhaps withdraw her as a major source of exports. Texas is thinking in terms of a self-supporting empire, while North Carolina is building a new civilization on the basis of cotton and tobacco. The fact that coffee, sugar, and tropical fruits are being increasingly imported through New Orleans means, on the one hand, the possibility of different Latin-American relations than if trade routes were otherwise, and, on the other, a wholly different emphasis on the problem of inland waterways than has prevailed. In either case the determination of policies by the South, especially by the Latin South, will color such policies. To say that the South, unquestionably the largest distinctive region of the country, cannot affect our social philosophy or our general trade ethics because of its isolation and relatively small economic wealth, can be met by the paradoxical assertion that it profoundly affects the rest of the country by virtue of its very isolation. For this isolation, although largely of the past, has persisted long enough to differentiate the people into a distinctive civilization. And present indications seem to point to the fact that the South will play an increasingly important part in our national commercial and industrial life.

New York City has always played a peculiar part in American history, the extreme features of which were represented by its Toryism during the Revolution, the draft riots during the Civil War, its commercial and financial arrogance, and its leadership in protesting against the Volstead Act. The economic supremacy of the city is not basically due to natural conditions; it began with the selection of that city as a railroad center, and it has been maintained by the personnel of its population. This personnel is largely immigrant and not native. Although quantitatively of much smaller moment than the immigration from Europe or the great westward migrations, qualitatively the migration of capable men and women to New York City from all parts of the United States is perhaps of even greater significance. This sociological phenomenon of population drift from rural to urban regions—a phenomenon which in France was viewed with such pessimism by de la Pouge, especially because of its accompaniments, rural depletion and urban "race-suicide"—has been prevalent throughout the country, but it has contributed particularly to the development of such cities as New York and Chicago. The native population of these cities has supplied its quota of leaders, but one of the chief causal factors of urban leadership there, just as was the case with Athens, Rome, Paris, and London, is the stimulus provided by the influx of some of the very best of our rural and small-city population.

Observations and analyses of the complexity of New York City's population, or of Chicago's, have too frequently stressed only the foreign immigration factor; they have failed to include the reciprocal impact of the migration to these cities of a highly important sociological cross-section of the entire United States. Men who would have been preeminently successful in their native region have here discovered new leverages and have geared up their powers so that they often surprise themselves as well as others with their success. Some who would similarly have succeeded at home have not succeeded in the new environment, and contribute to the tragic undertone that is here ever audible. Coloring the whole attitude of the population of these cities—fortunately, however, with many and important exceptions—one detects a superciliousness toward the rest of the country, bordering on contempt; an attitude more characteristic of New York than of Chicago. This attitude on the part of the native or the foreign population could be attributed to ignorance; on the part of those who have themselves come from other parts of the country, the attitude is most frequently symptomatic of a failure to achieve the dreams of conquest in the metropolis. But the fact that the attitude is a defense mechanism does not allay its power to contribute to that ever-present sociological and economic rupture between town and country. To view New York City as a "foreign city," as many do, is to confuse its admittedly exotic features with its most characteristic quality; the real New York City is a metropolitan reflection of the very quintessence of the social and economic streams of American life.

The location of coal and iron deposits has had as much influence in determining the national power of certain sections of America as it has in England. In this sense, Pennsylvania has been a keystone state, and not merely because of its geographic location among the original colonies. The conservatism of the "Pennsylvania Dutchman," developed during the agrarian period, becomes especially significant when it is remembered that his state contains most of the anthracite in America and that his steel mills and cement factories supply a large bulk of the product. A similar conservatism is discoverable in Michigan and, though to a lesser degree, in Minnesota, the other great states containing iron deposits, states in which the Hollander and the Scandinavian are important racial groups. West Virginia, southern Ohio, Kentucky and southern Illinois contain a great part of the remaining commercially usable deposits of coal in the North; regions which are characterized not only by the legislative and managerial policies there exercised but also by the type of labor they supply—hill-folk, for the most part, provincial and illiterate, and almost as persistent as the Englishman and Welshman in following mining as a vocation in the face of an obvious oversupply of labor. This chronic oversupply of labor, amounting on the average to 200,000 miners out of a total of approximately 700,000, has had as much to do with the difficulties in the mining regions of America as have the stupid and often vicious and exploitative policies of the mine managements. Both conditions are traceable to the type of people that live in these regions.

The development of the automobile industry and its pre-eminence in the economic activities of the country have encouraged the growth of a new type of business leadership and of economic conditions. The consequent shift of the center of industrial activity toward the Middle West, the intensification of mass production, the prevalent incentive to technological ingenuity and inventive genius, the encouragement of a tremendous amount of human transportation, especially of those of moderate means and domestic tourists with a new philosophy of leisure, the adoption of a generous wage policy and a new philosophy of labor, the stimulation of industries such as iron and steel, oil, rubber, glass and textiles, and the establishment of new metropolitan centers, are but some of the effects of this industrial phenomenon. Of practically equal significance are the fact that the owner of a small Midwest bicycle shop should become the most powerful industrial leader in the world and the fact that the scion of a former religious leader of New England should find an outlet for his capacities in a prominent Midwest steel company.

In discussing the diversity of the physical conditions which have undoubtedly affected American life profoundly, attention should not, therefore, be confined exclusively to "surface" phenomena: that is, to climate, topography and soil, and the iso-racial belts, together with the distinctive regionalism of the Old South. Such conditions were primary determinants of the earlier history of the United States, because we were until comparatively recently an agrarian nation. With the development of the more acute activities of mining and manufacturing, however, these "surface" phenomena assumed less apparent importance. But the diversity which already so characterized American life was highly accentuated by the variegated pattern of our abundant subsoil resources. The location of coal and iron, and later of oil and also of the various finer metals, determined to a large degree the location of industrial plants; which in turn presented various parts of the country with different and relatively acute labor problems, directly created local tariff demands, and indirectly produced many American cultures. This situation is so apparent as to need no further elaboration.

Criticism and "Reform" Attitudes

With the discovery of oil and later with the invention of the internal-combustion engine, both culminating in the amazing development of the automobile, the industrial development of America was highly accelerated: the regional and sectional conflicts of former days gave way directly to labor disputes— not so much in these newer, as in the older industries, however— and indirectly to less clearly defined class struggles in which men might have taken sides more definitely and violently if they had known on which side they belonged. The urban workman and the industrialist were clear as to their stand. But the farmer and small merchant, especially of the Middle West, regarded themselves as capitalists as well as laborers, in spite of the fact that they also recognized themselves to be so different in degree from the former as to be practically different in kind. Just enough hostility to big business was generally aroused to produce hostile legislation, but not enough to administer and enforce its full implications. Our national sentiments, so like the French in their earlier emotional make-up, ever fail to display the subsequent realistic French reactions. Like the hunter that Lincoln tells of, who was not certain whether he saw a deer or a cow, we "just sort of aimed" our legislation at business so that if business needed to be hit we would hit it, and if not we would miss it. Legislative acts were regarded as sufficient gestures; their enforcement, a disagreeable superfluity. Coupled with this attitude was the fact that most of the major industries— textiles, sugar refining, flour milling, meat packing—required and bought heavily the products of the soil, so that the farmer and small-town merchant recognized a community of interest in their welfare at the same time that their exploitative excesses were feared. The organization of these industries and their corporate form, furthermore, were sufficiently identical with the lumber and mineral industries, and also with the banks and railroads, to make impossible any restrictive legislation that would not at the same time injure the credit facilities and market outlets of the farmer, and indirectly those of the smaller merchant.

Requiring particular attention, however, is the interesting psychological fact that the various parts of the country, differing so among each other, paid less critical attention to proximate conditions and events than they did to conditions and events that were more remote. Thus, the rural districts, even when they were gradually but unconsciously approaching economic bankruptcy, have directed many of their "reform" energies toward correcting the "evils" of the city and of industry, evils which were criticized as such as well as because they were regarded as almost the sole cause of rural difficulties; while the city dwellers, enjoying few of the things for which cities are noted and steeped in provincialism, failed to perceive what was happening to their own urban civilizations while they were laughingly observing their rural cousins.

Newspapers have contributed much to this unfortunate state of affairs: fearful of telling the truth about local conditions and playing up a jingo patriotism and a regional provincialism, they have drugged their readers and avoided irritating their advertisers by publishing the lurid and ludicrous details of remote events and have thereby directed the attention of each locality elsewhere than toward its own problems. The insularity of our national point of view has been developed by misstatements about foreign countries, especially Latin America, Eastern and Southern Europe, and Asia. The churches have distorted the descriptions of civilizations older and often better than our own in order to secure funds for missionary enterprises: *e.g.*, the footbinding of Chinese women was condemned by well-intentioned American ladies who laced so tightly that the fashion plates of that day would almost pass for a catalog of insects. Chicago newspapers exaggerated the election riots of Mexico! California newspapers relegate the news of droughts and earthquakes to the inside pages, but devote glaring headlines to eastern snow and ice storms—even Los Angeles "tattled" on San Francisco until she received several major quakes herself. New England led the crusade against Negro slavery at the very time that she was imposing an industrial slavery on the immigrants cluttering her manufacturing centers, and today precariously clings to a belief in her intellectual and cultural superiority over the rest of the country. Small-town merchants and bankers diverted attention from their own sharp practices by painting graphic pictures of the "wolves of Wall Street." Midwest provincialism has been caricatured by Easterners who would have experienced the surprise of their lives if they could have sympathetically visited and appreciatively viewed some of those "Olympians in homespun" in former days, and who still might profitably visit the art galleries of Cleveland, Cincinnati, Chicago or Minneapolis, and listen to their symphony orchestras, or examine the domestic architecture of Virginia, Louisiana or California.

This phenomenon, of playing up the shortcomings of others, is not peculiar to America, but it is not by any means absent from our behavior. And the significance of this fact lies in the results: "reform" movements and amateur legislation directed at almost everything except the surgical needs of the home locality, and the cultivation of a complacency that so often accompanies sheer ignorance. In the case of the tariff, "log-rolling" has ironically prevented drastic activities of this sort, unless we except the eastern industrialists' opposition to the McNary-Haugen Bill and to the other demands of the Farm Bloc; but our tariff policy has been maintained by the argument that it would "benefit" the American laborer, a "reform" argument of the positive rather than of the negative type, and therefore even more hypocritical. This very apparent characteristic of American people, to "reform," to "change things," to "improve" them, may superficially be attributed almost directly to the diversity of our land and people. Each locality has become so fixed in its ways as to regard its local customs as desirable universals. In spite of our tremendous domestic commerce and internal tourist traffic, the lack of mutual understanding of the circumstances underlying the behavior of others has induced and then accentuated an endeavor to modify that behavior. But continental Europe is as highly diversified as is the United States, and yet is more tolerant except where political artificialities are accentuated. Perhaps we have not yet matured sufficiently to become mellow; perhaps our knowledge is just little enough to be dangerous. This diversion of the reform attitude toward remote regions has resulted, on the one hand, in a total lack of regional self-criticism and local improvement, and, on the other, in a tremendous amount of self-criticism within the United States as a whole; and also in a generally critical attitude toward non-Americans which is probably harmless in view of the fact that it is due some day soon to have an abrupt awakening.

The Frontier Character of American Life

Finally, there is another element in the diversity of American life that has determined our point of view, namely, the factor of change: every part of our country has at one time been a part of our westward-moving frontier. So important is this single factor that Frederick J. Turner has succeeded in revolutionizing the writing of American history by making the frontier the central theme in interpreting the whole of our history. The westward-moving frontier maintained the shape of a relatively straight north-and-south line until the California gold rush and the Civil War disturbed its general configuration; since then it has encircled a steadily diminishing region west of the Mississippi, until today there are left only a few frontier islands in the Rocky Mountain region. This "growing point" of the greatest colonization movement the world has ever known has always had many of the characteristics of the ancient Greek colonies. There were to be found the more alert, ambitious, lawless, dynamic, adaptable peoples, especially intolerant of any form of "laziness," including leisure, and therefore with little of the riper cultural flavor of Asia or Europe or even of the Old South or of the East of America. There also were to be found the most startling material and social accomplishments, there arose most of the "progressive" legislation that was symptomatic of the developing self-consciousness of a people, a type of legislation that culminated in the laws of Wisconsin.

Just as the more dynamic changes in her colonies again and again shook England from her social-legal lethargy, so did "breezy" western legislation and "radical" social views flow back in an ebb tide upon a startled and highly indignant East, an East that had just finished sighing with relief at losing its more obstreperous citizens. In both cases the effects were postponed by virtue of the fact that both England and the eastern part of the United States—Ancient Greece, similarly— had been drained of the very type of people that characterized the colonies or the West, thus leaving the older communities more resistant to the ideological invasion. But in America this westward movement reached its peak about 1890, when the supply of government lands was practically exhausted. Where, before, the eastern farmer or laborer could express his dissatisfaction with existing conditions by following Horace Greeley's advice to young men to "Go West," after 1890 this alternative was less and less possible or desirable. The labor movements of 20 or 30 years ago are in part due to the fact that the East had finally begun to retain those elements for which the West hitherto had provided a safety valve. The eastward migration of "progressive" legislation, as well as that of ambitious men and women to the large metropolitan centers, highly accentuated this phenomenon.

The ceasing of the major westward migrations affected not only the farmer and the industrial laborer. The predicament became apparent also to the sons and daughters of the more successful business and professional men. Except where the family business or the capital funds were sufficient to provide a financial nucleus for all members of the younger generation, there simply were not places enough "to go around," competition became keener, and problems of legislation and of business and professional ethics as well as of industrial, commercial and financial technique became acute. In the small towns, the lure of the city supplanted for a while the lure of the West, but it was not long until reports came back that the saturation point had been reached there also. The net result is that young people are being thrown back in increasing numbers upon their home communities, to clash with the older, entrenched, generations.

In addition to the diversity of social pattern among various places in America at a given time, therefore, there is the additional diversity presented by the various times in which successive phases of development have occurred in a given locality. Each locality contains people that are not only of different "periods" than others, but the present behavior of various persons in a locality may be dated as accurately as may styles. Some men have never ceased to change with the changing times, and are "modern" even though they have grey hairs. But most men reach a stage of development, in their point of view and behavior, at which they "set" like concrete. In the older civilizations this difficulty is moderated by a caste system. Where the population is highly mobile, however, as in the United States, the more dynamic persons being on the move, the less dynamic consolidating their positions, men of different ages and of different "dates" are constantly being thrown together, and mutual relations must constantly be adjusted. The social and vocational friction so engendered is perhaps greater, although less apparent because it is so prevalent and so universally distributed, than the more acute and more striking frictions developed on our frontier.

Men now living can, or should, remember the halcyon days of their early business careers; the community in which they have achieved success and in which they still live is frequently other than the one in which they were born, and they have shed most of the consequences of their earlier mistakes by moving to their present location from elsewhere. These established and reputable men of a community are asked to join a business club with high ethical ideals because they are the outstanding men of the community; they then sponsor these ideals, often expressed in "codes of ethics," and try to urge or even force them upon the younger business men, whose behavior is perhaps superior to their own early activities, inferior to their present ideals, but necessary today for an ordinary young man to achieve business success. Only a highly mobile people such as ours presents such a situation. Some of the older men have lived through the greater part of the post-Civil War period; they have seen perhaps two successive generations of younger men come upon the scene and have perhaps seen a younger generation move on still further; they have witnessed the successes and failures of strangers who have attempted to gain a foothold in the community; and many of them are keen enough to see that "other times beget other morals." But the frictions are there nevertheless.

Very few of the business giants of the last century have left progeny to carry on a prominent part of the work they once dominated. This startling fact is more apparent among the families whose names are prominently recorded in history, but the same situation extends to practically all persons of moderate means as well. One explanation is to be found in the pioneering character of the country: the pioneers expended so much energy upon the conquest of the natural physical obstacles in their path that their children were given but scanty attention, while the mortality among their wives—in body and spirit—was tremendous. The second generation did not receive their heritage—the developed natural resources of a wealthy country—until late in life, for the older generation was a hardy lot: a situation dramatically and tragically illustrated by the relations between King Edward VII and Queen Victoria. It is only the third generation of Americans that can be said to have enjoyed the riches of the land, in assured income, educational opportunites, and leisure. The psychological effect of this situation is incalculable: repressed and thwarted ambitions were the alternative, of the generation now passing away, to leaving home and starting a new life without the benefit of family help or guidance. A minimum of charity toward the business behavior of these men, as well as toward the ruthless acts of their fathers, would discover extenuating circumstances for the resulting ethical standards.

The difficulty of attempting an historical analysis of American Business Ethics becomes apparent. Most of the diversified sections of the United States have fairly recently gone through at least these three stages of human development: the pioneer overcoming physical nature; the succeeding generation working as hard, but less dramatically and with fewer rewards, and under the domineering attitude of the father; and the third generation, tasting the fruits of inherited funds but remote from the disciplinary experiences that secured them. Even if these people did little thinking, as is so often stated, their behavior patterns alone would be difficult to explain or even to describe. But still further complications were introduced by certain ideological effusions, particularly religious, that have as profoundly determined our national or local characteristics as have the racial or physical conditions.

CHAPTER II

RELIGIOUS AND SOCIAL IDEAS

Gentile Religious Ideologies

The development of religion in America has presented a most extraordinary problem, American religious sects being highly diversified, varying in different parts of the country with type of people and locality. Perhaps the greatest contrast is to be found between the northern and southern branches of the three largest Protestant sects: Methodist, Baptist, and Presbyterian. In the South, these sects have developed among a group of people who have been socially and racially relatively stable, but who have been compelled by the presence of a large Negro population to subordinate the broader humanitarian principles of Christianity, and the relatively democratic views of the founders of the numerically most powerful of these sects, to the more aristocratic doctrine of the elect, a doctrine sponsored earlier in this country by the Scotch Presbyterian, Jonathan Edwards. The chief sectarian representative of this doctrine, the Episcopalian Church, was transplanted to America with the early Virginia settlers and was admirably adapted to the living conditions of the large plantation owners of the Old South. In spite of the fact that its membership has never been large and that its prestige has never fully recovered from the disorganization of the underlying economic-social structure that was brought about by the Civil War, Episcopalianism has set the religious tone of the South. Not only are its members socially and economically more powerful than would be indicated by their numerical strength, but its point of view has received general support in the South, a diluted form of its doctrine of the elect having been incorporated into the other Protestant sects. The exclusion of the Negro from membership in southern churches has not only been general among all denominations but it has perpetuated the rift between the northern and southern branches to this day.

Ineffably bound up with this racial exclusion has been the virtual relegation of manual labor to the realm of inferior values, a point of view which is implicit in any dualistic religion. The only religious group that could possibly have taken an opposing stand on these social-economic taboos was Catholicism. But Catholicism has nowhere in the South, except in Maryland and Louisiana, made any headway, largely because the attitude of most southern Protestants is directly derived from the anti-Jacobin feelings of seventeenth-century England. This attitude has since then been little modified, because the South has not received many Catholic immigrants to change its religious complexion and has never until recently been subjected to the cross-currents of thought, religious and otherwise, that stirred so frequently the religious sediments of the North.

The chief economic accompaniments of this religious-social situation in the South have been the exploitation of the Negro, and more recently of the "poor white," and the development of an agrarian aristocracy. The dignity of physical labor, which was a part of the religion of the Puritan and which by him was made prevalent in New England and then was extended westward by the pioneer over the northern part of the United States, has until recently been absent from the religious-economic motivations of the South. Consequently, one finds conditions in the South very much as they are in England: the best minds have found their outlet in politics and law, and perhaps also in the church and in the army. A great deal of human energy and grace was expended in a social structure that was highly enjoyable to the few who partook of its benefits, but which in the South never has produced a compensatory art or literature—in proportion to its cost—which in England might be cited as its justification. The further difficulty of such a condition is that those who engage in business activities, who are also by implication constantly made to feel the inferior position to which they are relegated, are tempted to compensate themselves by exaggerated money returns. Exploitation is one of the methods to which such men resort; another is patronage, which in the South is so frequently the economic counterpart of a social *noblesse oblige*. In the midst of this situation, the Church has played a sorry rôle, being either brushed aside as a substanceless ideology fit only for solacing the unsuccessful, or exploited as a means of perpetuating agricultural and industrial slavery.

There has been little difference between North and South as regards capitalism and the financial structure; the rift occurred rather in the productive phases of agrarianism and industrialism.

The impression prevailing in Europe, that we are a materialistic nation, is derived partly from the accounts carried back to Europe by visitors to this country and partly from the fact that the doings of a George Babbitt are more widely read than are the thoughts of an Irving Babbitt. The recent award of the Nobel Prize to Sinclair Lewis is typical of the attitude of those Europeans who persist in regarding as characteristic of and best in America such traits as emphasize the assumed superiority of Europe. Much of this European, and especially English, criticism can of course be explained as a Freudian wish generated by a jealousy of our achievements; England herself experienced the same thing a century ago and now views, with little pleasure and less grace, our assumption of a pivotal place in world affairs. And even the admissible truth of this European criticism, that we are materialistic, can easily be converted into the justifiable view that physical labor does and should have a place of dignity in our social attitude and that material well-being is compatible with and perhaps even necessary to the distinctive and justifiable type of culture which we hope to effect. The religious factor which more than any other has contributed to this American attitude has been the Puritan principle of "stewardship," derived from the Calvinistic doctrine which in turn undoubtedly gave rise to capitalism in Europe.[1] This religious principle was intensified by the principle of individualism basic to the Puritan view, a principle which also in southern Europe gave rise to the development of modern capitalism as a break from the preceding guild control.[2]

How did this Puritan attitude, held by only a small group of people in New England, become the prevailing attitude in the greater part of America? It requires a stretch of the imagination to see how the idea of so small a group of people could leaven the large loaf of continental United States and especially how

---

[1] The writings of Weber, Troeltsch and Tawney all point to this conclusion. For a somewhat different interpretation, see Hall, T. C., *The Religious Background of American Culture*, Boston: Little, Brown and Co., 1930, in which the author stresses the English dissenting tradition rather than Puritanism as the origin of our social-economic doctrine.

[2] Strieder, Jacob, "Origin and Evolution of Early European Capitalism," II *Journal of Economic and Business History* 1, November, 1929.

such an idea could prevail against the successive waves of alien immigration that populated the country during the last century. The answer to this problem is partly the obvious one: the idea was vigorous and it did persevere because of the racial continuity of our population.

But the actual situation requires further analysis and explanation. Not only did the Puritan element form only a small part of the total English immigration, but great numbers of other races, especially the German and Scandinavian, later flooded the country. The more recent tides of immigration from southern and southeastern Europe have unquestionably disrupted our previous social heritage, although the industry and thrift of the Russian and Polish Jew, and of the Italian and the Greek, have fitted in with the prevailing American economic doctrine. The attempted restriction of these newer elements of immigration has been motivated rather by the feeling that they cannot readily be assimilated to our social and religious traditions, and by their failure to fit in with our legal and political heritage, especially because these people have congregated in the already congested areas of our cities. But, disregarding this more recent immigration problem, how does it happen that the Puritan view had previously become an essential and perhaps even dominant part of the character-pattern of the distinctive American life? Certainly that pattern was not determined to any degree of completeness by the Puritan element itself.

The answer to this problem is to be found in the character of the American people at about 1890, which may be viewed as a resultant of the Puritan heritage and of the immigrants of the Nineteenth Century. Neither of these factors may be regarded as strictly Puritanic. True, the descendants of the Puritan strain could be presumed to carry on most of the Puritan traditions, and the western migrants of this strain encountered frontier conditions similar to those which their ancestors had faced in New England. But the conditions which these migrating peoples had to meet were different as they moved westward, and varied greatly throughout the country; and not the least of these differences was the relatively richer lands they encountered. Puritanism has always been regarded as admirably adapted to the mastering of "barren and rock-bound coasts" and stony fields; but how would it react to the broad fertile valleys of the Ohio, Mississippi, and Missouri, silted deep and

limed by the Laurentian glacier, fertilized by great herds of
buffalo and deer, amenable to facile and long-range transportation, and capable of supporting a teeming population? Prosperity would be a greater test for the Puritan than poverty had
been, especially for succeeding generations who forgot or were
ignorant of the earlier pioneering difficulties. Puritan and
Cavalier had early encountered conditions in America which
accentuated their differences by intensifying their respective
characteristics. What was to happen when the Puritan met
conditions which were more nearly like the abundant resources
which accentuated the character of the Cavalier of the South?

What actually happened was that people who formerly
expended the maximum amount of exertion to secure the minimum requirements for subsistence, have later and just recently
discovered themselves to be so productive, especially with the
aid of accumulated capital, that they are .afforded a basis for
leisure and for social organizations that must seek an outlet in
activities other than physical labor. The new situation approxi-
mates the bourgeois environment of the English Puritan. The
transitional stages involved many difficulties, not the least of
which was the viewing of the new situation from the standpoint
of the heritage of the old. A failure to appreciate the material-
ism of the Middle West which opened up to the Puritan the
social and economic possibilities once enjoyed by his ancestors
in England, baffled Stuart P. Sherman. The New Humanism,
represented by Irving Babbitt, Paul Elmer More or Norman
Foerster, is probably all the more vigorous because of the
naturalistic environment against which this movement critically
reacts and because of the very difficulties inherent in the transitional stage from realism to a desirable but still remote idealism.

Puritanism was subjected to tremendous strains in its westward
advance, strains so severe and tests so rigorous that two opposing
views have developed regarding its ability to meet them: the
one view is that Puritanism was so vigorous that it withstood
everything encountered in its path; the other, that Puritanism
has become lost in the new situations that it has been forced to
meet. Both of these views emphasize the individual vigor of
the Puritan and the qualities that enabled him to overcome the
difficulties of a barren New England soil. Both fail to indicate
the importance to the Puritan of the "community" spirit,
introduced into his social life by his religious views, and the fact

that the Puritan in England had been relatively well-to-do. It is this latter Puritan type that has again come into its own in the midst of mid-western prosperity, after having gone through the fiery furnace of an intervening New England experience. To discover the basic character of Puritanism one must remember the bourgeois England from which he originally came and the New England communities that he established. Only so can anyone understand the paradoxical statement that Puritanism, so generally identified with individualism, is the cause of most of our social and legislative "reforms," in which may be included governmental restrictions on business. Here again we come to the same situation that can be discovered in the religious attitudes of the South: a fundamental opposition between religious and spiritual views, on the one hand, and economic and business activities, on the other, in spite of the fact that the views and activities are frequently held to support each other.

Puritanism, as well as the most numerous Protestant sects of the United States, is based on the religion of the Pharisaic Hebrew. Superimposed upon this foundation is the theology of the Sadducee, which in the form of Platonism first invaded western Europe through Plotinus and later recurred, under Augustine and Luther, to confound the Church Fathers with its paradoxes and its inconsistencies with the Aristotelian tradition. What might have happened, had southern Europe contributed more to the earlier streams of American immigration, is a fruitless question; we may conjecture, however, that the doctrine of the Catholic Church, attempting since the time of Thomas Aquinas to reconcile these major paradoxes, might have worked out a more consistent dogma in the new country, at least by subordinating the one view to the other. But that phase of the orthodoxy of the Reformation which called for the direct study of the Bible in the vernacular was brought to America and resulted in the attaching of equal weight to the Old and the New Testaments, the perpetuating of the religious-theological paradox being intensified by stressing the Pauline doctrines in the New Testament at the expense of the Book of James.

To regard social forces in the northern and western parts of the United States as adequately explainable on the ground of Puritan tradition alone, however, is to fail to perceive the other racial and religious elements that constitute the population of the United States. One of these, the German strain, was the product of economic and political dissatisfaction in the "Fatherland." The revolutionary elements of the earlier part of the Nineteenth Century were swelled by the "*Acht-und-vierziger*" and by those who later wished to avoid military conscription. Although frequently well-to-do,[3] most of these people were democratic to the point of being political radicals, although it would be difficult to reconcile this fact with their later almost unanimous support of the Republican Party in America. But religiously many of these people were mystical "pietists," strict, almost harsh moralists, highly individualistic, and yet exhibiting a "community" spirit, regarding many of their positive interests, which found an easy transition from the "sense of duty" self-imposed to the imposing of duties onto others. Bred into the pietist's bone was this "sense of duty," universalized in the philosophy of Immanuel Kant and still present in the attitude of officials, and toward them, in the municipalities of Germany. This "*Pflicht-gefühl*" established a sympathetic bond, unconscious but present, between the German mid-western farmer and the Puritan strain in the towns, supplying a motive for industry, thrift and good workmanship on the farm and in the factory that has since been supplanted by the wage appeal. Though these German immigrants, many of them, brought across the water the spirit of tolerance which so characterizes continental peoples in regard to religion and the more intimate moral problems, most of them observed and supported the moral rigors of the Puritan which were directed toward social problems, and neither confined his standards to his own conduct.

The chief source of contention between the German and the Englishman or New Englander, strangely enough, was the feeling on the part of the former that the latter was inclined to shirk work and preferred to live in the towns at the expense of another's labor, while the latter regarded the former superciliously as "dumb" enough to do the work. But how could the first charge be directed against a Puritan or the second charge emanate from him? Obviously because the Puritan had either succumbed to or mastered the conditions which were to test him: he had become at least once removed from direct contact with the soil and also, but more recently, from direct contact with the workman's tool and the machine. These Puritans were finding again

[3] See Hansen, Marcus L., "Revolutions of 1848 and German Emigration," II *Journal of Economics and Business History* 4, August, 1930.

the bourgeois level that they had formerly occupied in England, and were becoming lawyers and, significantly, legislators and local officials, editors of newspapers and the directors and managers of businesses, industries and banks.

If, in addition, it be remembered that Presbyterianism derives its doctrine from Calvinism and emanates largely from Scotland, the name of which country is almost synonymous with "thrift"; that Methodism had its origin among the laboring people whom the Established Church of England contemned or disregarded, and still is the "common man's church"; and that the Baptist insistence on "sanctity of contract" has determined our international dealings; then, the prevalence of the Puritanic view is understandable, not only as a matter of essential vigor, but also as a view which was sympathetically supported by the most numerous racial strains and religious adherents newly flowing into the body of the country. To this list may also be added the Quaker, a highly concentrated Puritan, whose charities so frequently are accompanied by admonitions and whose influence in America has been far more powerful than is indicated by his numerical strength.

Industry, honesty and thrift were means of salvation: materially, as the more successful of the living could testify; and spiritually, as the religiously inclined easily inferred by analogy. And the more fortunate members of society had a double purpose in instilling this religious dogma in the minds of all: not only would the parable of the talents reflect to their own credit, but the hope of eternal salvation would quiet any aspirations or desires of the "have nots" to appropriate property by any other than the long and straight and narrow path of honest labor and thrift. This ideology was supported by the prevailing pioneer psychology, with its annoyance and irritation at indolence. Even the failure to achieve material success would be more than compensated for by the blessings of a happy immortal life.

The social effects of such a doctrine were probably as fortunate as they are evident. Property rights were respected as sacrosanct at the same time that they were practically attainable by most people, a view that certainly could not be challenged so long as there remained a public domain that was continually being opened up for settlement. It is only since 1890 or 1895 that these lands are no longer available; and it was a decade or two later before the effect of that limitation was realized in the increased congestion of our industrial and urban centers. The resulting labor disturbances were met by an ideology of the church which could be expected: let the laborer seek his salvation on this earth by working and by saving, and through his individual and not through his collective strength; at any rate, if he fails to achieve worldly goods, there is eternal salvation to which he may look forward. This view, admirably fitted to an agrarian society and pleasant to contemplate among those who were successful in commerce or industry, failed to convince the industrial worker, whose disaffection from the church was but the beginning of the lost control of society which the church now laments.

The Clash between Religion and Business

This later manifestation of the dualistic religious idea in America contributed much toward alienating the industrial worker. It failed to appear earlier in America because of the practical turn which the Puritan, the Calvinist and the Lutheran, the Catholic and the Jew gave to religion. But this practical turn is constantly suspended between two extremes, either of which may appear with any considerable social change: the wholly functional view which the modernist takes, converting religion into a glorified sociology or humanism; and the fundamentalist view which, when fully aware of its implications and pressed for a decision, must regard all worldly affairs as subordinate to the spiritual, and which as a consequence relegates physical labor and business activities to an inferior position in the scale of values. This latter logical necessity has undoubtedly operated, at least subconsciously, in the minds of many Americans, making some of those who succeed in business uncomfortable and solacing the unsuccessful remainder. "Reform" movements and "blue" laws may frequently be the result of the former of these logical necessities: of honest and sincere efforts to improve one's own condition, and to prevent others from interfering with one's rights and from appropriating by economic force too much of one's available funds. But they also result from a psychological attitude which purposes to "set things in their proper place"; an attitude which, although logically resting on a standard of behavior and a system of values accompanying the more practical religious sects, also is ambiguously implied in the opposing attitude, which regards the things of this world as relatively unimportant or at best as justifiable only when employed as instruments for spiritual advancement.

The basis of the dualistic attitude is Oriental, but its western origin is discoverable in the Platonic attitude toward the actual world of experience, especially as this attitude was developed in the "other-worldly" doctrine of the Mediaeval Church. The dualistic attitude of Plato was concerned with determining the relative values of idea and reality, while his adoption of the idealistic position necessitated a criticism of what had generally been recognized or accepted as real, namely, science and economics. But in science, and especially in mathematics, Plato discovered enough of the universal to enable him to integrate this field with his ideal system. Hence there remained solely the artisan and the shopkeeper to occupy the inferior position, and upon them Plato expended the full force of his contempt when he gave them any consideration whatsoever. The logic of the dualistic view forced the same attitude upon the Mediaeval Church, although the combining of "flesh" with "lucre" made a more comprehensive objective for the attitude.

The attitude of the Mediaeval Church toward certain practical business functions, however, is even more directly traceable to Aristotle. Consider, for example, his statement regarding interest:

> But (of all forms of bad finance) there is none which so well deserves abhorrence as petty usury (interest), because in it it is money itself which produces the gain instead of serving the purpose for which it was devised. For it was invented simply as a medium of exchange, whereas interest multiplies the money itself. Indeed it is to this fact that it owes its name ("tokos" or offspring, our modern "token" or "symbol"), as children bear a likeness to their parents, and interest is money born of money. It may be concluded therefore that no form of money making does so much violence to Nature as this.[4]

Here lies the germ of the ecclesiastical attitude even of modern times; an attitude which was appropriated by law and is still expressed in the form of "usury laws." The basic assumption of Aristotle's statement was the view that economic income from exchange could be justified only in the form of mutually advantageous barter. This assumption had been previously expressed[5]

[4] *Politics*, Book I, Chapter x. (Welldon trans.)
[5] *Ibid.*, Book I, Chapter ix.

in distinguishing between barter on the one hand and retail trade or the production of producers' goods on the other; where the latter carry the situation "beyond the point of satisfying mere requirements," they represent "the bad art of finance," a departure from natural requirements.

Although Aristotle was attempting, in this section of the *Politics*, to define the functions of the household and to set off as distinct from these what he regarded as the functions of "finance" or of the "State,"[6] he labelled the latter "bad" and gave rise to the traditional Church view, a view which still persists and which furthermore has been in large part appropriated by the State. The championing of the consumers' interests by these two powerful social organizations has unquestionably been fortunate. Not so fortunate, however, has been the orthodox persistence of Church and State in a view which was narrow even for the immature state of economic activities of Ancient Greece. The practical outcome has been that the American courts have identified "the public interest" with the rights of the consumer at the same time that they have been accused of listening too sympathetically to the pleas of the large business corporation. But the latter situation may, paradoxically and in part, be attributable to the former; for the judges of our courts are selected from among the ablest lawyers, who frequently have become prominent through successfully representing large corporations in overcoming the "pleader's" attitude of such courts as give a restricted meaning to "the public interest." The defects of our legal system, however, may not be so serious as has been the uncompromising attitude of the Church toward business activities that are the inevitable as well as justifiable accompaniments of our modern complex civilization.

As regards the political field, Plato was able to detect a sufficiently comprehensive organization and unity therein to identify this realm with the ideal. But the Catholic Church has never been able to achieve any greater degree of reconciliation of its doctrine with that of the State than it has with that of Business, although it incorporates the elements of both in its structure and activities and compromises with both in its external relations. Any tendency within the Catholic Church to reconcile itself with these two realms was probably stopped during the Reformation, when Luther identified himself with the nationalist move-

[6] See, *e.g.*, his discussion of "monopoly," *ibid.*, Book I, Chapter xi.

ment and Calvin with the industrial and mercantile. Thereafter the Church could not escape identifying the forces so allied as common objectives of its hostility. This event added a psychological factor which intensified the previously existing logical necessity. Since the Renaissance, the Church has been prevented from becoming reconciled with the concept of the State by virtue of the very practical points of issue between its all-embracing catholicity and the political pluralism, autonomy and independence inherent in the development of national governments. And in spite of the justifiable universal as well as anachronistic Aristotelian elements in the Church, the stressing of the Book of James as against the Pauline doctrines, and the efforts of Aquinas to incorporate these with the Augustinian in a more comprehensive doctrine, the work of Plotinus and Origen was too well done to effect any other outcome than the establishment of a dualistic doctrinal precedent from which the Church cannot now emancipate itself.

In the meantime the psychological attitude of theocratical hostility toward the "things that are Caesar's" has gone on apace in the Western world in spite of its materialistic activities, nor has this attitude been broken down to any appreciable extent by the compromises of Luther with social conditions or by the backward leanings of the Calvinistic doctrines toward economic values. The rich man, for most people, still faces the eye of the needle; and even where the few know that he faces the eye of the gate, he must needs divest himself of his pack and crawl on his knees before he may enter the City. The facilitation of business of every sort is qualified by this deeply lodged emotional attitude, which in turn is basic to the religious ideology we have inherited.

Two further psychological explanations may be offered for this situation. Envy is a well-known human trait, and it is easily conceivable that those who have attempted to succeed in the business world but have failed, would decry the value of what they have not gained. Another group of persons, however, who have succeeded materially in achieving their purposes, have in many cases done so by virtue of methods which have brought business into disrepute. Among these persons are to be found employers who cannot succeed except at the price of underpaid labor, merchants who employ unfair tactics against their competitors, bankers who withhold pertinent information from the investing public, and business men of all types who seek to cover their unscrupulous dealings with their customers by a cloak of charitable and philanthropic activities. All such unethical dealings are justified, consciously or by implication, by the Calvinistic doctrine, which admits of an apologetic distinction between religious behavior and the behavior in the market place. Whereas the first-mentioned psychological attitude, that of envy, is engendered by *the failure to win the game*, this second attitude, of severing various purposes and activities of life from each other, *sacrifices the rules of the game to winning*.

The significance of an analysis of these two attitudes becomes apparent when it is recalled that the United States was populated largely by people who had not made a success of life in Europe. Not only have some of these people and their descendants failed to achieve success in America, but many who have succeeded have done so by the short-cut methods that seem to be necessary to get from a position of poverty to a place of economic importance. The failure to achieve material success in America has particularly embittered the immigrant by the dashing of exaggerated hopes, and even a mediocre accomplishment in a land of outstanding material successes would make the solace of a dualistic religion particularly attractive. It is from this source that much of the criticism of business emanates. On the other hand, the success of the self-made man, an outstanding characteristic of America, is not always an unmitigated blessing: not only could many of his competitors testify to his unfair methods, but it is this type of man who is more frequently guilty of the unfair treatment of his former equals, of his employees, than is the man "born to the purple." Not only, therefore, has much dissatisfaction and complaining criticism arisen from the unsuccessful, but the rapidly successful have given abundant cause for such. We are face to face here with the bald necessity of recognizing our immigrant sources; and although society is not necessarily like water, which cannot rise above its source, yet not too rapid changes in the direction of justifiable standards of business conduct can be expected from our "great American experiment."

There is no gainsaying the survival value of economic and business values. They have persisted in spite of the tremendous hostility of centuries, a hostility to which science and religion, art and politics contribute, even when these activities are the beneficiaries of its largess. It may perhaps even be regarded by some as fortunate that such a powerful agency as business has been held in leash by these overly supercilious attitudes. It is unfortunate, however, that abuses in business have been held by insiders, as well as outsiders, to be necessary accompaniments of business itself.[7] A saner view would be that the recognition of the facts should sober our enthusiasms regarding a sudden new order in American business or in a society dominated by business standards.

The Jewish Religious Ideology

Another religious element that has contributed powerfully to the American attitude is the Jewish, a very numerous element and especially powerful because of its concentration in certain regions like New York City or in certain industries such as the clothing industry. Whatever the origin of the European Jew, whether he is racially homogeneous or the economic product of the Ghetto, he acts in this country on the principle that he is racially as well as religiously homogeneous and he is so regarded by others. These attitudes can no longer be differentiated from facts. But, however his origin be regarded, he is nevertheless a transplanted person, and for the most part he has generally been very much in the minority, except in New York City, and frequently he has been the only representative of his race in the small community. His dislike of certain types of manual labor, especially on the land, has made him unpopular in the rural sections of the country; even the South, which will never forget that the Jews helped finance the Confederacy—the Jews have probably never forgotten this either—shows signs again and again of the smouldering agrarian resentment against the Jewish trader, who so often typifies sharp practices whether in buying cattle or cotton or in selling clothing. Those who know the American Jew wonder at the strength of the Zionist movement: not only is the Jew averse to putting his hand to the plow, but for the most part the country knows him only as an urbanite who fattens on others through the license of his peculiar religion and who would find it inexpedient to live in a community made up largely of his fellows.

[7] This, to my notion, is the chief mistake made by James Truslow Adams, *Our Business Civilization*, New York: Albert and Charles Boni, 1929.

That this criticism is unfair is apparent not only to those who have studied any other racial group—the Pole in Chicago, for example—and have seen the ravages which a new environment can make on the best racial heritages; but also to those who are acquainted with the older Jewish communities of New York or Cincinnati or New Orleans, where a sufficient amount of social-racial-family tradition is present to control the centrifugal tendencies of the young. The unethical conduct of the Jew in business does not lend itself to a simple explanation; it may even be questioned as a fact, although one is struck by the prevalence of Jewish names in the cases prosecuted by the Federal Trade Commission because of unfair trade practices. But any explanation of the fact must take cognizance of additional facts: that the Jew is a man without a country, that his sharp dealings are frequently matched by those of Gentiles—Mortimer Schiff once said to a Presbyterian business associate who wished to pursue a certain course, "Ah, Henry, thou almost persuadest me to become a Christian!"—that the Jew is after all a great imitator—a fact which may explain why there are no good Jewish bankers in a certain large American city—and that few Jews have succeeded in Scotland or New England. And where the Jew has succeeded in business, he is subject to the same resentment that is directed against a successful minority elsewhere—witness the attitude of the Turk toward the Greek or Armenian trader.

Regardless of any apologies for the Jew in business, the fact cannot be denied that he has influenced the conduct of business in the United States. His sharp dealings have contributed as much to the rule of *caveat emptor* as his generosity and benevolence have been conspicuous in the endowment of universities, libraries and hospitals. What has made his influence most effective, however, is the similarity of his religious view with that of the Calvinistic sects, that the ownership and use of property constitutes a stewardship for which a man is held accountable to his God. Whereas the Calvinist adheres to the doctrine of predestination and grace, neglecting the intrinsic business responsibilities, the Jew sees in material wealth the constant index of his favor with God; but the apparently fatalistic attitude of the Calvinist is tempered by the feeling, which the Jew shares, that God will look favorably upon his industrious and thrifty servants. Jew and Protestant have become more closely related, in a Bible-reading America, than have either with Catholic doctrine.

Much of what has been said may not be directly related to business activities in America, especially such as will later be discussed as functions of the business structure. Indeed, religion has done little toward correcting strictly business abuses. It has, it is true, provided us with most of our moral substructure, but its dualism has also provided us with most of our apologetics by which we have rationalized our unethical business conduct. Conversion and revival meetings, Sabbath observance and deathbed repentance, all have been resorted to, and are looked forward to, as expiations of conduct that was at the time knowingly unfair. The wellsprings of our business as well as of our other social conduct have been closely identified with our religious and sectarian beliefs, but the latter have failed to function fully as a social corrective of the powerful forces which they have generated. The Church has been too much inclined to let the resulting forces propel and determine and subsidize it, instead of asserting its own independent values and prerogatives. The more recent result has been a decline in the prestige of the Church and in the personnel of the ministry, partly and perhaps largely because the Church has worked itself into a position where it deals as an amateur with social problems that require an increasing amount of non-religious knowledge and technique. Just as, in its contact with Feudalism and Art during the Middle Ages and the Renaissance, the Church was prostituted into exhibiting some of its greatest powers and was left pregnant with a social hierarchy and cathedral forms but spiritually exhausted and spent;[8] so more recently, in its contact with industrialism and business, has it sold its soul for a wealth of pottage and come into possession of many fair cities and fertile plains by bowing down and worshiping alien objectives, some of which involved the very elements which business, if left to itself, might have been most interested in eliminating.

In its clash with the Church, Business has shown its uglier side. So long as the Church held to otherworldliness as its main interest and objective, friction between the two was at a minimum. But when the Church became more secularized, when it began to develop a social program especially in regard to labor problems, it found itself faced with a hostility that was far deeper seated than any it ever encountered in its clashes with the State. For when the Church program of social, especially

[8] A figure drawn from *The Education of Henry Adams*.

industrial, reform began to be fully appreciated, the crack of the business whip was heard and timorous preachers and athletic-minded Y. M. C. A. workers, faced with the loss of their subsidies, readily concluded that their main business was to hold forth to the laborer the solace of another world as a relief from the tribulations of this, a doctrine which could readily be reconciled with the appropriative and exploitative desires of Industry and Business. This supineness was probably as painful to the more generous type of business man as it was to the more intelligent and courageous cleric. For the otherworldliness to which the Church was now encouraged to devote its energies was not the sincere doctrine which formerly represented its essential characteristic. The resultant Church policy, although practically indistinguishable from the essential objective of the earlier Church, lacks the spontaneity and sincerity of the spirit to be regarded as anything other than a superimposed exotic form. The Fundamentalist-Modernist controversy was not altogether indigenous to religion; it was partly the result of the impact of Business on the Church. The need for industrial reforms and the insistence of management and capital on their own rights have been strong motive powers respectively behind Modernism and Fundamentalism. The outcome has been disastrous to the Church, for the reassertion of its main function has been the result of compulsion, while the endeavor to promote a secular program is more compatible with the function of the State or of Business than with its own and has in many ways been realized by them to a superior degree.

Where the Church has not succumbed to the view of social pragmatism, it has retained ideas of personal immortality and otherworldliness that cannot be reconciled with the behavior of its adherents. The Jewish religion, upon which the Christian doctrine has been erected as a superstructure, has never stressed such ideas to begin with, and this basic fact explains many of the paradoxical and even contradictory views held by the adherents of Christianity in Europe and America; while the essential worth and sublimity of Jesus' own teaching are lost amid the doctrinal superstructures and hierarchical organizations that clutter the representative Christian denominations. The Protestant sects have even departed far from the original and orthodox ideas of the Reformation and have accentuated the paradoxical compromises which Luther later made with social realities; the Catholic Church, which has honestly faced the existence of the paradox, has merely converted the essential contradiction into an ambiguity; while the Jew, although traditionally committed to the doctrine of immanence, has never solved the resulting problem of Job. The American business man too frequently has found an advantage in converting the hybrid views of Catholicism, Protestantism and Judaism into an amphibian opportunism which enables him to wander on the land or take to the sea according to the dictates of the religious-social-economic weather.

The attempt on the part of outside agencies, such as Church or State, extrinsically to control or evaluate business purposes and activities thus leads to two serious results. On the one hand, a mistaken sense of the ability to engage in such attempts is apt to persist long after the ability has ceased to exist, while the superciliousness and even arrogance of regarding their own activities as possessed of superior values is as dangerous to Church and State as it is impolitic in reference to Business. On the other hand, the persistence of such exotic attitudes may result in engendering one of two reactions among business men, neither of which is desirable from a social point of view. The less likely of such results is the cultivation among business men of an inferiority complex, colored by an unhealthy brooding resentment and destructive of that minimum of dignity, self-respect and self-confidence which is every man's due. The more likely result is a sullen resentment that reacts in the form of ruthless defiance and an intolerance of values—religious, political, artistic, scientific—which are associated with the critics of business. Encouragement is thereby given the business man to abuse a discovery that he can easily make—that most of such values, and many of the men who represent them, can easily be bought and paid for and made to act and speak at command. The net result of such a situation is bad from any point of view and leads one to conclude that a new valuation of business, resting on an intrinsic factual basis, developing spontaneously, and generally recognized, is as necessary a prerequisite to a comprehensive social evaluation of business as it is to an adequate social philosophy.

Social Philosophies in America

Whether academic philosophy has made any effective contribution to the determination of the social configuration or even the social theories of the United States is similarly a question; with this difference, that philosophy appeared on the scene much later than religion and therefore is less accountable for the results. But, like religion, our academic philosophy was first transplanted to America from Europe, especially from Germany, England and Scotland, and has only with difficulty made any general impression even on the racial groups from which it emanated. The St. Louis "School" and that located at Cornell bore the deepest imprint of the Hegelian philosophy, in the form, however, of abstract ideologies; these did very little more to Americans than to furnish them with certain educational ideas that soon succumbed to the immediate necessities, and to supply a dialectical verbiage that engrossed for a while the attention of the would-be learned. On this prepared soil, however, there developed a more vigorous growth, the Bosanquetian tradition, sponsored in part at Cornell and Harvard and Princeton and spreading westward through the American-trained teachers of philosophy that now were supplanting the German doctors of philosophy. This Bosanquetian tradition caught up the better elements of Thomas Hill Green and John Stuart Mill with echoes of Cobden and Bright and Bentham and Adam Smith and the English Empiricists, and also, through Lotze and Sigwart the German philosophers. Furthermore, Princeton University developed a very hardy if exotic realism that injected additional Scottish vigor into Presbyterianisn. But these philosophies, like the religious sects that preceded them, were European importations that adapted themselves less to American society than the immigrant himself did to his new environment. And these philosophical currents never approached the religious in vigor or prevalence.

It remained for William James to break loose from old-world tradition and to establish a distinctively American type of philosophy—although he himself said that Pragmatism was but a new name for an old method of thinking, and he attributed the genesis of his views to the earlier work of Charles Peirce. Pragmatism, which briefly holds that that is true which works, was like the Puritanic dignifying of labor: it caught the practical needs as well as the imagination of Americans, it fitted their conditions and problems of life, and it was converted by them into a social attitude and social force that could not be attributed solely to the generative power of an idea. Religions and philosophies had previously emanated from New England—Unitarianism, Mormonism and Christian Science, Transcendentalism and the Brook Farm movement—but none has gripped the nation's common sense or stirred its instinctive reactions as has the pragmatic philosophy of James. The reason for this is obvious: a country that for a century has been growing by extending its frontiers and whose ideas are still colored by the reflections of these frontier experiences on the older parts of the country, has learned the value as well as the necessity of immediate practical solutions. Ideologies that have developed in older societies may be well-worked-out there and may be consistent as programs of final action in a well-settled community; but unless such ideas can be made to *work* in a new community like America, they must be discarded and perhaps had better be forgotten.

To understand the historic background of Pragmatism it is necessary to recall two important stages in the development of science that have profoundly affected philosophy. In the earlier stage, the empirical and experimental methods of natural science gnawed away the greater part of what formerly had constituted the field of philosophical speculation. Cosmology gave way to astronomy, while ontology, with certain exceptions, has been supplanted by the atomic hypothesis of the physical sciences. Pragmatic philosophy virtually led a counter-attack against this movement by appropriating the point of view and method of science, especially in regard to the interpretation of human society. Politics, religion, education, sociology and ethics have all been affected by the pragmatic point of view. The net gain to philosophy by its pragmatic tendencies has been a comprehensive, if not yet adequate, grasp of social problems, at the expense virtually of yielding still more to the inroads of science. For at least the members of the "Dewey wing" of Pragmatism have swung so far to the scientific right as to be faced with the dilemma of stopping short arbitrarily in their tendencies in order to remain philosophers or of going on still further and actually becoming scientists and therefore ceasing to be philosophers.

The later stage of scientific development has qualified this necessity. The difficulties attaching to problems of organization, evolution and emergence in the biological sciences, and the admission by the physical sciences that empiricism and experiment do not always precede but frequently follow intuition and analysis, especially in determining the nature of space and time and order, have tempered considerably the scientific enthusiast.[9] The limitations of scientific method as related to social and other values are being subjected to rigorous self-criticism. Whether this means a breaking-away from the present tyranny exercised by the methods of natural science over the studies of social phenomena, cannot be foretold. The situation may discipline the scientist to the extent of eliciting from him a more sympathetic regard for the student of social affairs as well as for the philosopher and metaphysician. For, although human events may basically be conditioned on solar energy, gravitation, glaciation and natural resources, they occur partly also because of organizations and forces which, upon analysis, are as "real" as the physical elements which usually monopolize the meanings of this term. And whether science or even a philosophy like pragmatism can deal with the additional problem of values is seriously to be questioned. It may well be that the present situation in philosophy and science, characterized as it is by bafflement, reconstructed assumptions, and the willingness to seek new objectives, presents an exceptional opportunity for reconsidering the facts and the values of such "social disciplines" as economics and its applied field, business.

A dynamic society, such as America, when meeting the natural obstacles which an unexploited country constantly supplies to successive waves of settlers, is bound to be characterized by an almost continuous series of balked activities. This social phenomenon is repeated in miniature by numerous individual experiences. At such times situations bristle with possible alternatives, which are tentative and immediate but not necessarily final or adequate solutions of the predicament. The thing to do is to *try* at least one of them at once and to give it up the moment it shows signs of failing; and the resultant activity generally is accompanied by an idea-behavior pattern that involves compromises and perhaps even ideological contradictions. A people such as ours, whose behavior and history had been saturated with experiences of this sort, was ripe for the relatively coherent and facile expression of a philosophical view-point such as James' pragmatism. Our religious ideologies were Platonic, but our behavior and our functional reflections were Aristotelian

[9] See, for example, the writings of Bridgman, Whitehead, Milliken, Eddington and Jeans.

and prepared us for a pragmatic social philosophy. Like the man who was overjoyed at learning that he had been speaking prose all his life, Americans discovered that they had been living a philosophy which when expressed in words they could understand as well as admire. Our apologies for the ruthless treatment of the aboriginal Indians, the social as well as physical makeshifts of the pioneer, our ready acceptance of election results after the most vigorous campaigns, the development of our Federal system and of the independence of the judiciary, our glorification of the "captains" of industry and finance, our opportunistic stumblings onto significant social principles, all present difficulties to one who attempts an ideal and comprehensive justification for them; but the ends attained are felt to have justified the means, while the means themselves attain an added value through their having been instrumental to the synthetic ends achieved.

Peirce's work, to which James attributed the pioneer place in pragmatism, has become academically shunted off in the direction of Logistic, an important tool for Science and Metaphysics, but socially unfruitful. James' work directly, immediately and extensively leavened the social consciousness of America and gave even its unconscious behavior a significance and value. Academically, the idea was taken up in the 1890's by the newly founded university at Chicago, where it not only was invigorated by the emphasis placed on its scientific foundations but also was functionally extended to other fields than philosophy, conspicuously economic and industrial problems and, through its most vigorous present-day exponent, John Dewey, to education. Not only has the Chicago "school" tremendously influenced the West and South through its students, especially of philosophy, but the view was brought to Columbia University by Dewey and now thoroughly penetrates the entire educational system of America.

The leavening effect of Pragmatism on American life through the agency of the public-school system is incalculable. The emotional support of general education in America was early symbolized by the glorification of the "little red schoolhouse" and has more recently been evidenced by the pride which every community has in its school buildings and the high morale of the teaching force. We have been criticized by foreigners for dissipating our educational energies over the whole population, and many Americans have lost heart because the intensive

education of the few deserving students is seemingly being
sacrificed to raising the level of an apparently inert and unap-
preciative mass. But the democratic ideal has been extended
from our political organization to cover every phase of our social
life, and our abiding faith in the experimental possibilities of
universal education is not yet shaken by the delay or absence of
immediate and substantial verifications. And the philosophy
of the American school teacher is the philosophy of Pragmatism.

Partly as a result of the pressure from below, due to this
general system of education, and partly through the generous
endowment of private colleges, higher education has also been
much more generally available in American than elsewhere,
especially since the recent phenomenal growth of state universities. Here also there has been much wasted effort, but it is
becoming more and more apparent that the criticisms leveled at
partial defects are largely irrelevant in view of the general
results. The most striking of these results is the interest of
business men in higher educational institutions and their sustained loyalty to their colleges. In the course of their schooling
they have associated with scholars and professional men at least
four years longer than is the case in other countries, their loyalty
expresses itself in the form of munificent gifts that provide the
material basis for cultural and scholarly pursuits, and the scholar
in turn has been disciplined to a sense of the reality of things
by his collegiate contacts with these future business men. In
addition, the abundance of business schools and graduate
professional colleges has largely supplanted the apprentice training to which even the best business men abroad must resort.
Here, again, we have been criticized by foreigners, on the ground
that education connotes a cultural exclusiveness. But, although
we may have achieved more quantitatively than qualitatively,
there is no denying the fact that we are already reaping the
benefit of the last half-century developments in legal, medical,
teaching and engineering training; and the quantitative restrictions already applied in medical education, with a view to
qualitative improvement, are readily available elsewhere.

Business training of a similar nature has barely passed the
threshold of its possibilities. And if the pragmatic idea has
permeated all other parts of our educational system, it certainly
will find a fruitful field among prospective business men. For
business, more than any other activity in America, has at least

unconsciously been imbued with the pragmatic idea. True, there has been much unjustifiable use of the rule-of-thumb method; but there has been a courageous and intelligent scrapping of obsolescent machinery and plants, and also a similar junking of impracticable though rationally sound management and financial methods. The tests of business policies have been experimentation and the anticipation of their results. The employment of the problem and case methods in business education not only has been necessitated by the circumstances attending business but also will intensify the pragmatic attitude in business and in all social relations by making it a consciously employed method. The increasing number of superior men who are entering business schools will still further intensify the business character of our civilization. To protest against this development as an undesirable shift of values not only blinds one to an overwhelming fact but also fails to exert a proper amount of energy in the direction of recognizing the possible virtues of the situation and of attempting in some measure to control it by imbuing this new social factor with a sense of its social responsibilities and with an appreciation of its highest possible values. Idealism can well await a riper and more mature America before insisting on the recognition of its values.

Pragmatism, especially in so far as it is accompanied by the whole force of self-conscious American business behavior, may be said to be one of the most distinctive and important ideological contributions that America has made to civilization. For pragmatism has back of it the entire material experience of America, gradually coming to self-consciousness during the course of a century, but never before having been coherent enough to be heard. Even aside from the fact that it is more indigenous to America than most of our other ideas, pragmatic philosophy has become a more representative idea of America than has our religious ideology because of its more intensive and more general relation to our actual life. Pragmatism may not represent our national ideological pattern a century from now. As Sir Henry Jones once observed, we may, like Saul, in seeking our father's asses, return with a kingdom. But there is no denying the present prevalence of this philosophical attitude.

It is less certain, but perhaps demonstrable, that pragmatism, as supported by our business behavior, has been more significant, more generally and distinctively expressive of American life than have any or all of the political ideas which have so largely absorbed America in the past. Among these possible rivals of pragmatism for such a title, John Marshall's doctrine of the independence of the judiciary and Hamilton's political and fiscal policies have far less general acceptance in America than has business pragmatism; the chief challenge has emanated from an opposing political idea, the Jeffersonian doctrine of democracy, an idea derived largely from France. True, there is much in common between the dignity accorded labor in France and America, and there is the willingness in both countries to get to work when the occasion demands; but in neither case is the similarity of view due to a borrowing process. Lincoln's doctrine of national unity, which has been extended to our foreign policy in the Monroe Doctrine and in the insistence on the territorial integrity of China, not only had its contemporaries in the policies of Bismarck and Cavour, but also was anticipated by Napoleon, by Ferdinand and Isabella, and even by William the Conqueror. Woodrow Wilson's idea of a league of nations can only with difficulty be subjected to a similar analysis; not only its permanence but even its originality is subject to question.

Business Clashes with the State

It can safely be asserted that the political ideas above enumerated, and others that have presented issues to the American voter, engrossed his interests almost exclusively during the first century of our national life; even an economic question like the tariff being made a political issue. But such is no longer the case. Our traditional political issues, translated into governmental policies and supported by the whole organization of the law, have finally been confronted with the mass weight of opposing individual business enterprises. Business interests are more and more engrossing our attention and being recognized in their true light, while business itself, "the oldest of the arts," is being elevated to the dignity of the professions. The absolute ideology of political doctrines, sustained by the legal rule of *stare decisis* but weakened by the dissensions between the constitutive and administrative functions of government itself, is face to face with the pragmatic behavior of business supported by the whole weight of that part of our legal machinery that functions in support of the rights of the individual. This is indeed a drama in which giants alone can take part, probably even transcending in magnitude the controversy between Religion and Business.

How far back in our history the drama may be traced is a difficult question to answer. It may even be doubted whether the first century of our national existence was dominated by a political ideology, for economic conditions may have determined most political issues. But it must be admitted that the discussion and settling of these issues were effected largely through governmental and legal instrumentalities and with reference to political principles. In short, although business may even then have paid the political piper, the tune the piper played was of his own choosing and he himself played the tune. Whenever business men showed any inclination toward initiative and tried to secure their independence from the political organization of society, their activities were characterized, not by the courage of their convictions, but rather by the attitude of the "artful dodger," a symptom of their relatively inferior position in the social order. The high quality of legal education during the latter part of this period unquestionably perpetuated this dominance of legal-political control: not only did legal counsel always play a large part in the deliberations of business administrators, but their superior training enabled them to abandon in great numbers their strictly professional activities, and to take active part in, and control of, the management of most great business corporations.

The last 30 or 40 years, however, have witnessed a shift in the relative position of the legal-political-governmental ideology in the determination of our social organization. Business has unquestionably become an increasingly important factor in American life. Improvement in the technique of business education and the extension of self-regulatory activities have assumed such a magnitude that the dominance of business in American social life must be regarded seriously as an achieved reality.

The instrument by which Business has effected this revolution is the corporation. The corporation may not be peculiarly characteristic of the economic structure, in that it had its conceptual origin in the Law and applies to Church and State and University as well as to Business. But no one can deny that one of the most powerful social forces of today is the business or industrial corporation. Defined and limited alike as to functions and liabilities, and recognized by the courts as a person, the corporation has within the last fifty years become an integral and characteristic part of the business and social structure. Not only does the immortality which accompanies corporate structures enable business to become rooted in a past and anticipate a future stability—to a degree greater even than that of the family in America, and supplanting the Church as the focus of interest and confidence—but a psychological coloring has accrued to certain corporations, enlisting the personal loyalties of stockholders, managers, employees and even the public as well. "Preserve our good name," "service," and "goodwill" have, for many of these companies, passed the stage of flamboyant slogans and sentimental camouflage, and have become at once ineffable social as well as business ultimates.

The clash between Corporation and State was inevitable, although the actual outcome of such a clash was not and could not have been predicted under the circumstances. The struggle began at a time when the State was in full possession of its powers and when the Business Corporation was but a mere infant. The Sherman Anti-trust Law was as ruthless and decisive as the victory of the old bull of a herd over the bumptious claims of a younger rival. If the Sherman Law be regarded as a legislative curb to the growing abuses of corporate power, then it must be recognized as having done its work well and as having supplied a much-needed corrective. If, on the other hand, the Law be regarded as the assertions of the State against the encroachments of Business on the domain of social organization and control, then the results are questionable, from the point of view both of efficacy and of desirability. For there is little doubt that Business has gone on its way, only temporarily checked, sometimes by indirection and sometimes by virtue of a complexity which the State would find it hopeless to pursue in its intricate details. Just recently, for example, those entrusted with the administration of the Sherman Law have been faced with the anomalous necessity of defending "big" business, as represented by mergers and combinations, chain stores and mail-order houses, against the efforts of the smaller individual local units to cooperate in order to maintain their own very existence.

The fear of restrictive legislation as well as of a public boycott, or "buyers' strike," apparent though it may be, has probably been less potent in the determination of Business Policy, however, than has the intrinsic and positive factor of self-development implied in the pluralistic philosophy which lies at the basis of modern business enterprise. The waning administrative power of the State, especially in its national and state forms and in its personnel, is but an index of the inability of a monistic social philosophy to prevail against a pluralism of intrinsically powerful social values. It is the thesis of this volume that Business has succeeded in securing for itself a prominent place among these social values.

B. BUSINESS AND THE SHERMAN LAW

It may seem like an act of overrefinement to set a date for the origin of Business Ethics in the United States, and yet the year 1890 does serve as a convenient point from which the ethical problems of modern American business may be said to have developed. Not only was this the year in which the Sherman Law was enacted, a law which first represented the awakening self-consciousness of the American people to the broader social problems engendered by our business behavior; but this date fairly accurately fixes the peak of the westward migrations of our people, for it was at this time that the last great tracts of public land were settled. From this time on, excess social, political, and economic energies could no longer expend themselves on a virgin territory, but reacted more and more upon established human communities. It is in such reflective situations that ethical considerations arise; and so they arose in our economic life, first in the form of labor disturbances and agrarian readjustments, and later in the sharper conflicts of business competition. Thomas Beer has characterized the literary and cultural activities of the 1890's as "The Mauve Decade," mauve, in Whistler's phrase, being "pink that is trying to be purple." It is no straining of the point to assert that business behavior was passing through a similar stage during the same period—a stage, shall we say, in which brass was trying to become gold, a process which is always fertile with problems of business ethics.

A description of the Sherman Law or of Federal anti-trust policies by no means tells the whole legal story; a great part is to be found in the records of anti-trust suits in the state courts. Hence the admittedly definitive nature of the present section. Indeed, an adequate picture of the legal symptoms of our social background would have to include the whole of criminal law, or at least that part which has been enacted into the Federal Code; for the more recent development of criminal law has been characterized by its inclusion of business abuses. Another field which would prove fruitful of investigation is the legislative activity which in the 1890's and later undertook to control embezzlement.

53

Similarly, the history of the Federal Bankruptcy Law of 1898 would disclose materials that very properly fall within the field of Business Ethics. Again, the Interstate Commerce Act of 1887 was directed mainly against the chief business abuse of the 1880's, namely rebates. These materials, however, more properly should be included within the field of financial transactions and capital values. The present volume is concerned largely with the ethical problems of marketing and of business organization.

It is admitted that the setting of a date, such as 1890, for the origin of Business Ethics in America, is arbitrary. There is no sharp cleavage between the governmental processes set in motion by the Sherman Law and those which preceded it, the unbroken continuity of the common law and of our political metaphysics being especially apparent in the judicial interpretations of the Sherman Act. Furthermore, the background of our religious ideas, which vitally determined our social, especially our regulative, attitudes toward business, had been in process of development for centuries and were rooted in a remoter past. The still more enduring physical conditions of the United States make the selection of a point of historic origin meaningless. And, although the temporal character of our migrations and racial patterns makes time "of the essence," our national experience, developing our national and regional characteristics, in which individualism and industry and the placing of a premium on material and economic values play so great a part, largely antedated the 1890's. But the force of all these objections to the setting of a relatively definite date for the origin of Business Ethics is minimized by the observation that these various factors determined our business *behavior* more than they developed our business *doctrines*. The *reflective* elements which constitute so large a part of Business *Ethics* are of more recent origin; just as philosophy arose in Greece at a very definite period of time in spite of the indefiniteness of its antecedent and determinative, even if unreflective, human history. Furthermore, practical considerations of convenience would call for the selection of some point of origin, even arbitrarily. And a study of earlier business conditions in America would warrant a charitable drawing of the curtain over many indefensible acts, the reminder of which might cloud the consideration of the more wholesome tendencies of the present.

With this justification for assuming that business ethics had its origin at the time of the enactment of the Sherman Law, we shall proceed in the next three chapters to examine the first thirty years of anti-trust legislation in America as a period in which the ethical problems of business were becoming more and more apparent.   The first chapter of this section will indicate the considerations which prompted the enactment of the law; and will accentuate the significance of this situation by referring to a leading case, then occupying the attention of the English courts, which presents the sharp contrast of the British philosophy of business with our own.   The succeeding chapter will then examine that interesting American phenomenon, unenforced legislation, which in the case of the Sherman Law was effected by the prevailing political metaphysics of our courts, a metaphysics which was apparently oblivious to current American business conditions.   A third chapter will conclude this section of the volume by tracing the functional view which began to dominate our courts and legislators in the early part of this century.   This functional view, first appearing in the courts in 1911 in the decisions of Chief Justice White, found its legislative counterpart in the enactment of the Clayton and Federal Trade Commission Acts and certain legislative exceptions to the Sherman Law.

The present section will deal largely with anti-monopoly legislation.   "Anti-trust" legislation, however, includes within its prohibitions not only monopolies but also restraint of trade and unfair competition, matters which will be more fully discussed in later sections.   Furthermore, monopoly, which in England involved control over territory coterminous with the entire kingdom,[1] might be very effective in only a regional part of so large and highly diversified a country as the United States, without necessarily including the whole nation.   So, e.g., in the purchasing of milk[2] in New England, and of sugar beets[3] in Utah and Idaho.   For the most part, however, the ensuing discussion of the Sherman Law will concern itself with alleged national monopolies; and, except for certain elements in the Packers' Cases, not with monopoly control over the purchasing of raw

[1] See, e.g., Standard Oil Company v. U. S., 221 U. S. 1, 51; also Northern Securities Company v. U. S., 193 U. S. 197, 404.

[2] U. S. v. Whiting Milk Company, 212 Fed. 466 (1914).

[3] VI Federal Trade Commission Reports 390 (1923).

materials. But it must constantly be kept in mind that the problem of business behavior in the United States is complicated by virtue of these territorial as well as functional differences. In the face of such complications the problem of legislative control is particularly difficult.

But if these governmental and legal activities be interpreted as symptoms of a deeper change in social attitudes, their significance for a study of Business Ethics becomes apparent. For Business Ethics, which is basically grounded upon a social philosophy of functional pluralism, had to await this deeper change in social attitudes before it could make its appearance. Grounded, not in the law, but rather in the same social *milieu* that gave rise to anti-trust legislation, Business Ethics, once it began to manifest itself, soon developed into a relatively independent field of human activity and thought, the "domain of the unenforceable."

CHAPTER III

THE SHERMAN LAW: CURE OR SYMPTOM?

The speaker at a recent medical convention threw the members into an uproar by suggesting that the various micro-organisms which are present in diseased bodies are the result and not the cause of the illness: that they can be explained on the assumption that the condition of the blood provides a medium for their existence as well as for the disease, and that any attempt to regard them as the cause of illness might even be placing the cart before the horse. Without entering into the merits of the question as it applies to health and disease, the point of view should be given due consideration. John Stuart Mill, in developing his canons of inductive inference, was always careful to state that the accompanying factors in a causal nexus could be regarded *as either cause or effect*. This warning applies particularly to methods of social diagnosis; the protective tariff, for example, was originally devised because of the relatively higher wages prevailing in America, but in the course of its history it has come to be regarded as the cause of high wages. It will be the purpose of this chapter to subject the Sherman Anti-trust Law to such an analysis as will disclose its historical import: Was it the causal agent it was intended and has been supposed to be, benign or malignant in its control of business conditions as points of view differ, or was it paradoxically the effect or a symptom of the conditions it was intended to control?

The Debate in the Senate

The first obvious step in such an analysis would be to discover what the author of the bill himself had in mind. This may be difficult to discover, and when discovered it may be beside the point. But the following excerpts from Senator Sherman's speech in support of the original bill clearly point to a single objective: that the Sherman Law was intended to extend the anti-monopoly common-law rules, which then were available in state jurisdictions, to interstate and foreign commerce, which was subject only to Federal jurisdiction.

57

The object of this bill, as shown by the title, is "to declare unlawful, trusts and combinations in restraint of trade and production." It declares that certain contracts are against public policy, null and void. It does not announce a new principle of law, but applies old and well-recognized principles of the common law to the complicated jurisdiction of our state and federal government. Similar contracts in any state in the Union are now, by common or statute law, null and void. Each state can and does prevent and control combinations within the limit of the state. This we do not propose to interfere with. The power of the state courts has been repeatedly exercised to set aside such combinations, as I shall hereafter show, but these courts are limited in their jurisdiction to the state, and, in our complex system of government, are admitted to be unable to deal with the great evil that now threatens us.

Unlawful combinations, unlawful at common law, now extend to all the states and interfere with our foreign and domestic commerce and with the importation and sale of goods subject to duty under the laws of the United States, against which only the general government can secure relief. They not only affect our commerce with foreign nations, but trade and transportation among the several states. The purpose of this bill is to enable the courts of the United States to apply the same remedies against combinations which injuriously affect the interests of the United States that have been applied in the several states to protect local interests.[1]

This bill declares a rule of public policy in accordance with the rule of the common law . . . It is a remedial statute to enforce by civil process in the courts of the United States the common law against monopolies.[2]

The statement, that there was no "common law in the United States" although it prevailed in each of the states of the Union, appeared later in the speech of Senator Vest,[3] and also later on in Senator Hoar's reply to Senator Kenna's questions: "Is monopoly prohibited at common law? If so, why does this bill denounce monopoly?" Senator Hoar went on to say:

The great thing which this bill does, except affording a remedy, is to extend the common law principles, which protected fair competition in trade in old times in England, to international and interstate commerce in the United States.[4]

In view of the fact that Senator Hoar was a member of the Judiciary Committee, to which the Sherman Bill had been referred and which reported back the substitute bill which was finally accepted, Senator Hoar practically writing the whole of the sub-

[1] *Congressional Record*, 51st Congress, pp. 2456, 2457, 2459; the argument was amplified in William T. Sherman, *Recollections of Forty Years*, pp. 832–836.

[2] *Ibid.*, p. 2461.

[3] *Ibid.*, p. 2603.

[4] *Ibid.*, p. 3152.

stitute bill, the idea back of this piece of legislation is as clear as it evidently was continuous.

In his endeavor to establish a continuity between the common law and the proposed legislation, however, Sherman became involved in a line of fallacious reasoning. Sherman's argument rested on the fact that the Federal courts obtained jurisdiction by virtue of two conditions: one being the nature of the case, the other being the nature of the parties in a controversy. By stressing the factor of the parties in an agreement or conspiracy, the author of the Sherman Law felt that he had avoided the necessity of discovering in the Constitution the express authority for passing legislation of such substance.[5]

But it remained for Senator Platt to discover the untenability of the position:

> The real difficulty of the bill is that under the Constitution of the United States you cannot reach an *agreement* made between parties residing in different states, no matter for what purpose. It is the *controversies* arising between persons residing in different states, between corporations residing in different states, which can be reached in the courts of the United states.[6]

It seems almost impossible that such a fallacy could be so long sustained in the Senate debate, and yet the statements speak for themselves. They represent the attempt to meet the new dynamic forces of business by resorting to the political metaphysics underlying our Federal system, a metaphysics which was to dominate the reasoning of the courts for 10 years more and which was every bit as rigid as any metaphysics the Church had ever asserted. The argument, that the common-law rules applying to monopoly were being included in a part of the Federal jurisdiction, rather than that the more flexible form of legislation was being used to meet the dynamics of the situation, was met by the frontal attack of Senator Morgan:

> It is very true that we use common law terms here and common law definitions in order to define an offense which is itself comparatively new (*sic*), but it is not a common law jurisdiction that we are conferring upon the circuit courts of the United States. It is a federal jurisdiction, arising under

[5] Senator George had observed that the first draft of the bill was absolute and plenary, that the next four were based on the commerce clause of the Constitution, and that the final draft was based on the parties involved.— *Ibid.*, p. 2600.

[6] *Ibid.*, p. 2607.

the Constitution of the United States.   If it did not arise there we could not confer it.[7]

The Interpretation of the Courts

Furthermore, the view that the Sherman Law was legislative fiat rested on one of the rules derived from our doctrine of judicial review, namely, that the debates in Congress do not determine the interpretation of legislative acts.   In an early case[8] arising under the Sherman Act, the Circuit Court did examine the history of the Law in Congress; and although the court conceded that it could not take the views or purposes expressed in debates in Congress as supplying the construction of statutes, the court did agree that these debates could be referred to, as well as other sources, "in order to determine the history of the evil which the legislation was intended to remedy."   The court pointed out, however, that upon the introduction of the bill into the House, the chairman of the judiciary committee had made the following statement:

Now just what contracts, what combinations in the form of trusts, or what conspiracies will be in restraint of trade or commerce, mentioned in this bill, will not be known until the courts have construed and interpreted this provision.[9]

Justice Peckham still further minimized the importance of congressional debates in affecting judicial decisions:

Looking simply at the history of the bill from the time it was introduced in the Senate until it was finally passed, it would be impossible to say what were the views of a majority of the members of each house in relation to the meaning of the act . . . All that can be determined from the debates and reports is that various members had various views, and we are left to determine the meaning of this act, as we determine the meaning of other acts, from the language used therein.[10]

Later, in 1911, Chief Justice White stated:

The debates (in Congress) show that doubt as to whether there was a common law of the United States which governed the subject in the absence of legislation was among the influences leading to the passage of the act. They conclusively show, however, that the main cause which led to the legislation was the thought that it was required by the economic conditions of the times, that is, the vast accumulation of wealth in the hands of corpora-

[7] *Ibid.*, p. 3149.

[8] *U. S. v. Debs*, 64 Fed. 724 (1894).

[9] *Congressional Record*, 51st Congress, p. 4089.

[10] *U. S. v. Trans-Missouri Freight Association*, 166 U. S. 290, 318 (1897).

tions and individuals, the enormous development of corporate organization, the facility for combination which such organizations afforded, the fact that the facility was being used, and that combinations known as trusts were being used, and the wide-spread impression that their power had been and would be exerted to oppress individuals and injure the public generally. Although debates may not be used as a means for interpreting a statute, that rule in the nature of things is not violated by resorting to debates as a means of ascertaining the environment at the time of the enactment of a particular law; that is, the history of the period when it was adopted.

It is certain that the terms ("restraint of trade" and "monopoly") at least in their rudimentary meaning, took their origin in the common law, and were also familiar in the law of this country prior to and at the time of the adoption of the act in question.[11]

The point of view, that the Sherman Law was to be interpreted literally, was carried to the extreme by Justice Peckham:

> We are asked to regard the title of this act as indicative of its purpose to include only those contracts which were unlawful at common law, but which require the sanction of a federal statute in order to be dealt with in a federal court . . . We are of the opinion that the language used in the title refers to and includes and was intended to include those restraints and monopolies which are made unlawful in the body of the statute.[12]

The title of Sherman's original bill was: "An Act to declare unlawful, trusts and combinations in restraint of trade and production." Later, the title of the enacted bill became: "An Act to protect trade and commerce against unlawful restraints and monopolies." Justice Holmes later refused even to consider the title: "I stick to the exact words used" (in the body of the Act).[13] Justice Lacombe, however, had stated that "although the title to an act cannot control its words, it may furnish some aid in showing what was in the mind of the legislator."[14]

The literal view of the court severs the intent of the legislature as expressed in the published debates, from the enacted legislation; except in so far as the wording of the legislation expresses the intent of the legislature, and also except in so far as the debates in Congress are considered by the courts in connection with other contemporaneous events in order to understand the import of the words of the statute. Thus, the District Court, in the Trans-Missouri case, had considered the following facts:

[11] *Standard Oil Company of New Jersey et al. v. U. S.*, 221 U. S. 1, 50.

[12] *Op. cit.* (note 10), p. 327.

[13] *U. S. v. Northern Securities Company*, 193 U. S. 197, 403 (1904).

[14] *Dueber v. Howard*, 66 Fed. 637, 643 (1895).

A number of combinations in the form of trusts and conspiracies in restraint of trade had sprung up in the country which were dangerous to its commercial interests; for example, the steel-rail trust, the cordage trust, the whiskey trust, the Standard Oil trust, the dressed-beef trust, the school-book trust, the gas trust, and numerous other trusts and combinations, which threatened to destroy the commercial and industrial prosperity of the country. These trusts assumed the absolute control of the various corporations entering into them, directing which of the constituent members of the trust should continue operations and which should cease doing business; how much business should be transacted by each, what prices should be charged for the product, and in fact had the power to direct every detail of the business of every corporation forming the trust. It was to combinations and conspiracies of this sort that the Act of July 2, 1890, was directed.[15]

The decision of this court was reversed, however, by the Supreme Court of the United States, as was also another similar case.[16] Relying upon the wording of the statute, Justice Peckham held that the Sherman Act applied to every contract in restraint of trade, whether reasonable or not. This was directly opposed to the view that the Sherman Act extended the common-law rules to the Federal courts, and clearly showed that judicial decisions may emphasize the fiat character of legislation. A statute might have a history; but once it was enacted, the law was to be interpreted as worded. Especially was this the case with the early interpretation of the Sherman Act.

It was known, at the time that the Sherman Bill was being considered, that the positive authorization of an indictment for such offenses as were listed in the Act, was not a part of the common-law practice. The common-law control over monopolies was not a positive control at all; it consisted largely in the refusal of the courts to entertain suits for breach of contract on the part of those who had made an agreement in furtherance of a monopolistic restraint of trade and who wished to enforce this contract against a member of the agreement who later had breached it. Therefore, if the real purpose of the Sherman Law had been to establish the common-law rule in the Federal courts, the bill should have vested the Federal courts with the power to refuse to enforce contracts in restraint of trade. Indeed, if the Federal courts were, under the Constitution and the Judiciary Acts,

[15] 53 Fed. 440, 455 (1892). Interestingly enough, practically none of these "trusts" were proceeded against during the first 15 years of the life of the Sherman Law.

[16] *U. S. v. Joint Traffic Association*, 171 U. S. 505 (1898).

restricted to the specific powers therein granted, and if there
was no Federal common law, then the very absence of jurisdiction
to enforce such contracts would actually have been equivalent
to the common-law situation.   The theory underlying the common-law rules regarding monopolies and agreements in restraint
of trade was that these organizations could be expected to break
up of their own accord.   The establishment of a monopoly by
agreement, with the materialization of its intent to raise prices,
aside from being liable to attract new competitors to invade the
field, would tempt one or more of the members of the agreement
itself to secure more than his share of the trade by selling at less
than the monopoly price.   Therefore, so the theory went, the
courts could control the situation by refusing to entertain suits
at law against such members as breached their monopoly
agreements.

In the light of this situation, particular interest attaches to
the hypothetical case raised by Justice Harlan in his dissenting
opinion in the Sugar Trust case:

Suppose that a suit were brought in one of the courts of the United States
—jurisdiction being based, it may be, alone upon the diverse citizenship of
the parties—to enforce the stipulations of a written agreement, which had
for its object to acquire the possession of all the sugar refineries in the United
States, in order that those engaged in the combination might obtain the
entire control of the business of refining and selling sugar throughout the
country, and thereby to increase or diminish prices as the particular interests
of the combination might require.   I take it that the court, upon recognized
principles of law common to the jurisprudence of this country and of Great
Britain, would deny the relief asked and dismiss the suit upon the ground
that the necessary tendency of such an agreement and combination was to
restrain, not simply trade that was completely internal to the State in which
the parties resided, but trade and commerce among all the States, and was,
therefore, against public policy and illegal.   If I am right in this view, it
would seem to follow, necessarily, that Congress could enact a statute forbidding such combinations so far as they affected interstate commerce, and
provide for their suppression as well through civil proceedings instituted
for that purpose, as by penalties against those engaged in them.[17]

The interesting point about this hypothetical case is that no
specific cases were cited—probably because no such cases existed!
Even up to the beginning of Roosevelt's administration, that is,
during the first 10 or 12 years of the Sherman Act, only four
cases were so defended; in three of these cases the court allowed

[17] *U. S. v. E. C. Knight Company et al.*, 156 U. S. 1, 38 (1895).

the plea of the defense.[18] Only one of these cases, however, preceded the Knight case. One of three things is implied: either there was no Federal common law, to which the parties to a monopoly-trust agreement could resort in case of breach and in case they desired to sue for enforcement of the agreement; or the formation of trusts and combinations in restraint of trade were so recent that no Federal cases had arisen; or else no need or disposition was felt among business men for recourse to the courts in order to maintain their trade agreements.

This latter alternative must be given due consideration. Whether recourse could be had to the Federal courts or not, business men were held to their agreements through the fear of the economic rather than legal effects of their breach, and aside from the sentimental sanction attaching to a "gentlemen's agreement." This was recognized by Justice Peckham when he stated that "a company desirous of deviating from the rates agreed upon would face a diastrous rate war" and that "under these circumstances the agreement prevents competition."[19] Business, in other words, had discovered a sanction for its agreements, more powerful even than the provision, for example, in the Trans-Missouri Association of a fine in case of breach: the sanction of continued participation in group business profits. And it was the discovery and use of this business sanction which had practically negated the old common-law control over such agreements, a control which relied upon the urge of individual rather than group or trade profits. Hence the provision in the Sherman Law that such offenses be positively indictable. Law had hardly anticipated, by appropriate regulations, the development of the modern business corporation, before it was called upon to face combinations of such corporations, at first in the form of trusts and later in the form of holding companies. The "veil of corporate entity" had become still further veiled in an additional corporate form over which the State no longer could exercise jurisdiction, and for the regulation of which no Federal laws existed. That such business organizations might regulate themselves, in an adequately social manner as well as in a way

[18] *American Biscuit and Manufacturing Company v. Klotz*, 44 Fed. 721 (1891); *Cravens v. Carter-Crume Company*, 92 Fed. 479 (1899); *Delaware, Lackawanna and Western Railroad Company v. Frank et al.*, 110 Fed. 689 (1901).

[19] *U. S. v. Joint Traffic Association*, 171 U. S. 505, 564 (1898).

satisfactory to business, did not occur to Congress—and unfortunately was not properly appreciated by business men themselves. External regulation, which had for a thousand years dominated the attitude of the Church toward Business, was now being appropriated by the State; the rigorous provisions of the Sherman Law were symptomatic of the growing strength of American Business and of the feeling that it should be curbed.

The Mogul Steamship Case

It is of extreme importance to students of the Sherman Law to know that, at the very time the Sherman Law was being debated in Congress, a case was being tried in the English courts which bore directly on the problem of trade restraints. An examination of this case will disclose the common-law status of business combinations in restraint of trade in England in 1890.

The Mogul Steamship Company was an English firm incorporated in 1883 and engaged in the ocean carrying trade, a part of which included the transporting of tea from China to England. The company had by 1885 acquired a controlling interest in certain steamships—including the *Sikh*, the *Afghan*, the *Pathan*, and the *Ghazee*—which had been built for and were employed in the China and Australian trades.

In 1884, the Mogul Steamship Company joined a "Conference" of steamship owners trading in and out of Hankow and joined with the members of the Conference in sending the following circular letter:

Shanghai, 10 May, 1884.
To those exporters who confine their shipments of tea and general cargo from China to Europe (not including the Mediterranean and Black Sea ports) to the P. & O. Steam Navigation Companies, Messagerie Maritime Companies, Ocean Steamship Companies, Glen, Castle, Shire, and Ben Lines, and to the steamships *Oopack* and *Ningchow*, we shall be happy to allow a rebate of 5 per cent on the freight charged.

Exporters claiming the returns will be required to sign a declaration that they have not made nor been interested in any shipments of tea or general cargo to Europe (except the ports above named) by any other than the said lines.

Shipments by the steamships *Afghan, Pathan*, and *Ghazee* on their present voyages from Hankow will not prejudice claims for returns.

Each line to be responsible for its own returns only, which will be payable half-yearly, commencing October 30 next.

Shipments by an outside steamer at any of the ports in China or at Hong Kong will exclude the firm making such shipments from participation in the return during the whole six-monthly period within which they have been made, even although its other branches may have given entire support to the above lines.

The foregoing agreement on our part to be in force from present date till April 30, 1886.

The Mogul Steamship Company's predecessor, Gellatly and Company, had participated in a similar agreement in 1879, the purpose of which was to prevent a large number of ships appearing for tea cargoes at the time of the tea season and thereby taking the "cream" of the traffic away from those steamship lines that operated all the year round. Another member of the Conference was McGregor, Gow and Company. This company and the other members of the Conference asserted that the admittedly large profits obtained from the tea trade alone enabled them to keep up a regular line of communication all the year round between England and China and that without a practical monopoly of the tea trade they would be unable to maintain a continuous traffic between England and China throughout the year.

In May, 1885, the members of the Conference except the Mogul Steamship Company issued the following circular, which had the effect of excluding the Mogul Steamship Company from the benefits of the Conference:

Shanghai, 11 May, 1885.

Referring to our circular dated 10 May, 1884, we beg to remind you that shipments for London by the steamships *Pathan*, *Afghan*, and *Aberdeen*, or by other non-conference steamers at any of the ports in China or at Hong Kong, will exclude the firm making such shipments from participation in the return during the whole six-monthly period in which they have been made, even although the firm elsewhere may have given exclusive support to the Conference lines.

Prior to the agreement of 1884 certain confidential suggestions had been exchanged among the members of the Conference, among which the following memorandum was accepted by them as a statement of the situation: "So long as there is a glut of tonnage at Hankow, whether 'Conference' or not, it is impossible to maintain freights." Out of this memorandum developed the plan to limit the number of Conference vessels loading at Hankow, and also to prevent others from loading there with profit, and then, after driving out such competitors, to maintain the high freights which a free competition would inevitably lower.

The means for accomplishing this purpose were agreed to as follows: if any non-Conference steamer should proceed to Hankow to load independently, any necessary number of Conference steamers should be sent at the same time to Hankow in order to underbid the freight rate which the independent steamer might offer, without regard to whether the resulting rate would be remunerative or not. This agreement, dated April 7, 1884, was renewed in May, 1885. If no non-Conference steamers went up the river to Hankow, then only six

Conference steamers were to make the trip. Each party to the agreement was at liberty to withdraw from the agreement on notice.

After 1883, when the Mogul Steamship Company was incorporated, Gellatly and Company retained their position as shipping agent for the Mogul Steamship Company although they had transferred to the latter company their shipping interests. On May 25, 1885, Gellatly and Company were dismissed as shipping agent by the Ocean Steamship Company, a member of the Conference, after the Gellatly Company had been offered a choice of serving either the Ocean Steamship Company or the Mogul Steamship Company. This action resulted from a series of events that had led to the circular of May 11. On May 1, it had become known to members of the Conference that the *Pathan* was going up the river to Hankow to secure a cargo of tea at the height of the season, and that the *Afghan* was soon to follow. On May 8, three Conference steamers were sent in addition to those already at Hankow. On May 14, the Conference members at Shanghai determined on a general reduction of freight rates at Hankow. Rates immediately dropped from 50 shillings to 25 shillings, a wholly unremunerative rate. The Mogul Steamship Company met the competitive rate and carried the tea from Hankow rather than sail their ships away empty. On May 29, while the *Pathan* had a full cargo at Hankow and was on the point of sailing and while the *Afghan* was taking cargo on board, the Mogul Steamship Company brought action against the members of the Conference, charging them with a conspiracy in restraint of trade.

The case was tried before Lord Coleridge January 30 and 31 and February 4, 1888, and judgment was rendered August 11 of the same year.[20] In the meantime the Conference had come to an end in August, 1885, and in the summer of 1886 the rate of freight from Hankow was determined by free competition in an open market in which the Mogul Steamship Company and the members of the Conference were competing as individuals among one another. The Mogul Steamship Company had asked the court for an injunction and for the damages which they claimed they had sustained in the mutually ruinous conflict in 1885. The amount of the damages was by mutual agreement to be determined by arbitration after the court had decided on the merits of the case.

Lord Coleridge held that "the association, or Conference, formed to keep the tea trade in their own hands and not with intention to ruin trade of plaintiffs or through any personal

[20] *Mogul Steamship Co. v. McGregor, Gow and Co. et al.*, L. R. 21 Q. B. D. 544.

malice or ill will towards them, was not unlawful, and that no action for a conspiracy was maintainable." In the course of his decision, he stated the following argument:

There is a moral and sensible defense for defendant's conduct, whatever legal view be taken of it . . . They confer a considerable benefit on the mercantile community of both countries by running their steamers regularly all the year round . . . This they cannot do at a profit unless they can practically monopolize the carrying trade during the tea harvest. It is the large profit they make by keeping up the rate of tea freights, which enables them to give a regular line of communication during the other months of the year . . . The damage, if any, to plaintiffs was the necessary and inevitable result of the defendants carrying on their lawful trade in a lawful manner.

* * * * * *

The question comes at last to this: What was the character of these acts, and what was the motive of the defendants in doing them? . . . I do not doubt the acts done by the defendants here, if done wrongfully and maliciously, or if done in furtherance of a wrongful and malicious combination, would be ground for an action on the case at the suit of one who suffered injury from them . . . (But) amongst the lawful means (to pursue their trade) is certainly included the inducing by profitable offers customers to deal with them rather than with their rivals. It follows that they may, if they think fit, endeavor to induce customers to deal with them exclusively by giving notice that only to exclusive customers will they give the advantage of their profitable offers . . . It is a bargain which persons in the position of the defendants here had a right to make, and those who are parties to the bargain must take it or leave it as a whole.

. . . As to the motive of defendants, there can be no doubt that they were determined, if they could, to exclude plaintiffs from this trade . . . It must be remembered that all trade is and must be in a sense selfish; trade not being infinite, nay, the trade of a particular place or district being possibly very limited, what one man gains another loses. In the hand-to-hand war of commerce, as in the conflicts of public life, whether at the bar, in Parliament, in medicine, in engineering, men fight on without much thought of others, except a desire to excel or to defeat them . . . Our age, in spite of high authority to the contrary, is not without its Sir Philip Sidneys; but these are counsels of perfection which it would be silly indeed to make the measure of the rough business of the world as pursued by ordinary men of business. The line is in words difficult to draw, but I cannot see that these defendants have in fact passed the line which separates the reasonable and legitimate selfishness of traders from wrong and malice.

. . . The plaintiffs' conduct cannot affect their right of action, if they have it; but it is impossible not to observe that they were as reckless of consequences in regard to the defendants as they accuse the defendants of being in regard to themselves; they were as determined to break in as the defendants were determined to shut out; and they made their threats of smashing freights and injuring the defendants a mode of rather forcible suasion to the defendants to let them into their conference. If they have their right of action, why they have it; if they have it not, their own conduct disentitles them to much sympathy.[21]

Judgment was accordingly rendered for the defendant. The combination, or Conference, was held not to have been wrongful or malicious, nor guilty of a misdemeanor, and the acts of the members of the Conference were held not to have been unlawful.

The case was appealed, and decision rendered on appeal July 13, 1889. Lord Esher, Master of the Rolls, dissented from the opinion of Lord Coleridge.

The Hankow agreement is in restraint of trade, and therefore void as between the parties to it.

The agreements held to be illegal (in cases cited by litigants) because in restraint of trade must have been so held, not because there was any wrong done to the traders who agreed, but because there was a wrong to the public. The restraining themselves from a free course of trade was held to be a wrong to the public. If that be so when parties agree to restrain themselves, it must be much more so when they agree to do acts which will restrain and are intended to restrain another trader from a free course of trade. That restraint is equally a wrong to the public. The present agreement is therefore illegal and void as in restraint of trade on that ground also.[22]

If, Lord Esher now argued, an agreement violates the right of an independent trader by restraining his trade and if there is a sufficient public interest which is also injured, the agreement is an indictable conspiracy. An agreement between two or more traders, who are not or do not intend to be partners, for the purpose of interfering with the trade of another, is not done in the due course of trade and is therefore wrongful against the public. The injury to the plaintiff furthermore, he held, gave the latter a good cause of action. Damages accruing were therefore the difference between the freight ordinarily earned and the amount actually obtained by charging only the 25 shillings.[23]

Lord Coleridge had stated in the original decision:

As to the contention that this combination of the defendants was unlawful because it was in restraint of trade, . . . it was no more so, as that phrase is used for the purpose of avoiding contracts, than if two tailors in a village agreed to give their customers 5% off their bills at Christmas on condition of their customers' dealing with them and with them only. Restraint of trade has in its legal sense nothing to do with this question.[24]

[21] *Ibid.*, pp. 548, 552–554.
[22] *Ibid.*, L. R. 23 Q. B. D. 598, 605.
[23] *Ibid.*, p. 610.
[24] *Ibid.*, L. R. 21 Q. B. D. 544, 553.

This view was elaborated in the appellate decision by Lord Justice Bowen, dissenting from Lord Esher:

. . . I find it impossible myself to acquiesce in the view that the English law places any such restriction on the combination of capital as would be involved in the recognition of a distinction between acts done jointly by a combination of capitalists and similar acts done by a single man of capital. For if so, one rich capitalist may innocently carry competition to a length which would become unlawful in the case of a syndicate with a joint capital no larger than his own, and one individual merchant may lawfully do that which a firm or partnership may not. What limits, on such a theory, would be imposed by law on the competitive action of a joint-stock company limited, is a problem which might well puzzle a casuist. The truth is that the combination of capital for purposes of trade and competition is a very different thing from such a combination of several persons against one, with a view to harm him, as falls under the head of an indictable conspiracy.[25]

The first part of this argument was repeated by Lord Morris in the House of Lords, where final appeal was taken.[26] The significance of this point will be appreciated by those who have observed the employment of the Sherman Law and of the Federal Trade Commission and Clayton Acts against groups of small local merchants who attempted by concerted activities to meet the competition of individual but large mail-order and chain-store businesses. That the exact situation presented by the Mogul case may recur at any time has recently been shown by the invasion of the New York-Havana holiday trade by the Cunard Line. The United States Lines, which operate on this route all the year round, claim a moral right to exclude the Cunard Line from the highly profitable winter traffic, the Shipping Board Act of 1916 exempts steamship lines from the Sherman Law, and the Shipping Board has seriously considered allowing the American lines to adopt a policy of rate-agreements like that of the Hankow agreement.

The Common-law Status of Business in England

The Mogul case, it must again be remembered, was contemporaneous with the enactment of the Sherman Anti-trust Act. The common-law point of view as regards business combinations, as contrasted with the legislative standpoint, is no more interesting, however, than Lord Justice Bowen's discussion of the terms "fair" and "reasonable," which have since so much concerned the Interstate Commerce Commission and the Federal Trade

[25] Ibid., L. R. 23 Q. B. D. 598, 617.
[26] 1892 A. C. 25, 50.

Commission, as well as the courts in their interpretation of the Sherman Law. The statement specifically questions the major assumption upon which the study of Business Ethics rests.

. . . There seems to be no authority or sufficient reason for a proposition which asserts that there is some natural standard of "fairness" or "reasonableness" beyond which competition should not go, apart from fraud, intimidation, molestation, or obstruction of some other personal right. . . . It would impose a novel fetter upon trade.

It is said that a "fair freight" was one which is reasonably remunerative to the shipowner. But over what period of time is the average of this reasonable remunerativeness to be calculated? All commercial men with capital are acquainted with the ordinary expedient of sowing one year a crop of apparently unfruitful prices, in order by driving competition away to reap a fuller harvest of profit in the future.[27]

Applying himself to the issue, Lord Justice Bowen concludes:

The acts of the defendants which are complained of here were intentional, and were also calculated, no doubt, to do the plaintiffs damage in their trade. But in order to see whether they were wrongful we have still to discuss the question whether they were done without any just cause or excuse. Such just cause or excuse the defendants on their side assert to be found in their own positive right (subject to certain limitations) to carry on their own trade freely in the mode and manner that best suits them, and which they think best calculated to secure their own advantage.

. . . The defendants have done nothing more against the plaintiffs than pursue to the bitter end a war of competition waged in the interest of their own trade . . . This commercial motive is not a personally malicious one.[28]

He then summarizes his opinion:

In the result, I agree with Lord Coleridge, C. J., and differ, with regret, from the Master of the Rolls. The substance of my view is this, that competition, however severe and egotistical, if unattended by circumstances of dishonesty, intimidation, molestation or such illegalities as I have above referred to, gives rise to no cause of action at common law. I myself should deem it to be a misfortune if we were to attempt to prescribe to the business world how honest and peaceful trade was to be carried on in a case where no such illegal elements as I have mentioned exist, or were to adopt some standard of judicial "reasonableness," or of "normal" prices, or "fair freights," to which commercial adventurers, otherwise innocent, were bound to conform.[29]

[27] L. R. 23 Q. B. D. 598, 615.
[28] *Ibid.*, pp. 613, 614.
[29] *Ibid.*, p. 620. See also Lord Morris' statement, 1892 A. C. 25, 51: "I am not aware of any stage of competition called 'fair' intermediate between lawful and unlawful. The question of 'fairness' would be relegated to the idiosyncrasies of individual judges."

Lord Justice Frye, concurring with Lord Justice Bowen, pointed out another distinction in reference to combinations in restraint of trade; namely, a distinction between the principal object of such a combination on the one hand, and on the other, the means for carrying out such objects.   Was the principal object of the Conference lawful?   Yes, answered Lord Justice Frye:

> The real object of the agreement was the acquisition of gain by the defendants, and the means by which they sought to accomplish this end was a competition on the part of the united shipowners against all the world, so vigorous as to drive outsiders from the field, and thus to prevent competition in the future.[30]

Second: Were the means employed lawful?   If the immediate competition was severe, the purpose was to exclude competition in the future.   Repeating Lord Justice Bowen's point that no ill will or malice toward the plaintiffs in general had been proved, Lord Justice Frye referred to the distinction, made by Justice Erle in *Regina v. Rowlands*,[31] between combinations positively intended to promote their own welfare and those purposing to hurt another.   Such hurt as specifically fell to the lot of the Mogul Steamship Company was not a net public harm, for it was neutralized by the gain which the Conference members desired to win for themselves.   "Competition exists when two or more persons seek to possess or enjoy the same thing; it follows that the success of one must be the failure of the other."   He therefore, in such a case, "recognized no limits in law to the right of competition in the defendants . . . I am not speaking of morals or good manners. To draw a line between fair and unfair competition, between what is reasonable and unreasonable, passes the power of the courts."[32] Lord Justices Bowen and Frye therefore voted against the view held by Lord Esher, and in favor of the defendants.

Lord Halsbury, L. C., stated the case briefly to the House of Lords, to which the case was finally appealed:

> An associated body of traders endeavor to get the whole of a limited trade into their own hands by offering exceptional and very favorable terms to customers who will deal exclusively with them; so favorable that but for the object of keeping the trade to themselves they would not give such terms; and if their trading were confined to one particular period they would be

[30] L. R. 23 Q. B. D. 598, 622.
[31] L. R. 17 Q. B. D. 671.
[32] L. R. 23 Q. B. D. 598, 625.

trading at a loss, but in the belief that by such competition they will prevent rival traders competing with them, and so receive the whole profits of the trade to themselves.

If this is unlawful it seems to me that the greater part of commercial dealings, where there is rivalry in trade, must be equally unlawful.[33]

The House of Lords decided unanimously that the Mogul Steamship Company had no cause for action, but that the contract itself was void. The Sherman Law would have made the contract illegal, indictable, and actionable by the Mogul Steamship Company.

As Justice Frye pointed out in the Mogul Steamship Company case,[34] the general tenor of statutory development in England had been in the direction of freeing business men from the prohibitions against combination. The older penal statutes against "regrating" ("cornering the market") and similar acts of combination had been repealed early in the reign of George III,[35] thus leaving the common law to its unaided operation. Furthermore, the statutes of 1871 and 1875,[36] enlarging the power of combination among workmen as well as among masters, positively imported the tendency of English law to take cognizance of the fact that industry and business required organization as a method of coping with the new situation.[37] This view was also held by Lord Bramwell in the House of Lords,[38] to which the case was finally appealed, a view which is to be compared with the exemption of labor and agricultural organizations from the operation of the Sherman Bill in its original form and also later in the Clayton Act of 1914 and the Marketing Act of 1929, respectively, and with Senator Sherman's recognition of the useful function performed by the corporation in modern civilization.[39] In brief, the repeal of English statutes against monopoly, which had been practically completed by the beginning of the Nineteenth Century, resulted simply in the condition that monopoly agreements were unenforceable at common law.

This did not mean that agreements in restraint of trade were not subject to positive action. As Lord Coleridge pointed out,[40]

[33] 1892 A. C. 25, 35.
[34] L. R. 23 Q. B. D. 598.
[35] 12 Geo. III, c. 71.
[36] 34 and 35 Vict., c. 31; and 39 and 40 Vict., c. 22.
[37] L. R. 23 Q. B. D. 598, 629.
[38] 1892 A. C. 25, 47.
[39] *Congressional Record*, 51st Congress, p. 2459.
[40] L. R. 21 Q. B. D. 544, 548 ff.

an indictment could be brought by the State if a public
wrong, as defined in the statutes, could be proved, the public
having an interest to interfere whether damages to individuals
could actually be proved or not. He referred to two cases[41]
in which nothing was done in fact but in which conviction
followed the mere entering of the agreement; no one was harmed,
but the public offense was complete. The situation in a civil
action was declared to be otherwise; it is the damage which results
from the unlawful combination itself with which the civil action
is concerned. "If a combination is lawful; or, being unlawful
there is no damage, an action will not lie."[42]

Lord Coleridge's decision was sustained both in the Appellate
Court[43] and in the House of Lords.[44] In the Appellate Court,
however, as will be recalled, a dissenting view held by Lord
Esher, Master of the Rolls, relied largely on the decision of
Justice Crompton in *Hilton v. Eckersley*.[45] In this case Eckersley,
one of a number of masters who had signed an agreement not to
sell except under certain circumstances, was sued for the penalty
attaching to the agreement because he failed to observe the
agreement. Justice Crompton held that the bond was void
and therefore not actionable, and that it was also indictable.
Lord Campbell, an associate justice, agreed that the bond was
void and therefore not actionable, but asserted that it was not
indictable. Lord Esher based his argument on Justice Crompton's decision and on the reasoning in Sir William Erle's *The
Law Relating to Trade Unions*, that "a right involves a prohibition
against the infringement thereof . . . and a prohibition involves
a remedy for the violation thereof."[46] Inasmuch as the case
before Lord Esher was an action for damages, it is difficult to
see why he ruled that the acts of the defendants constituted an
indictable conspiracy, except in so far as the point led instru-
mentally to the conclusion that action would lie and damages
be awarded; the rule of pleading should have confined the argument to the issue at hand. At any rate the two judges who
were associated with Lord Esher, Lord Justices Bowen and Frye,

[41] *The Bridgewater Case* (unreported) and *Rex v. de Berenger*, 3 M. & S.
67, 76, Bayley, J.
[42] L. R. 21 Q. B. D. 544, 549.
[43] L. R. 23 Q. B. D. 598.
[44] 1892 A. C. 25.
[45] 6 E. & B. 47.
[46] Erle, p. 13.

dissented from his opinion and sustained Lord Coleridge's decision.

Lord Justice Bowen, reverting to Lord Coleridge's distinction between actionable and indictable offenses, denied the validity of Justice Crompton's opinion in *Hilton v. Eckersley*, and reasserted the status of combinations, business and others, under the common law. He cited *Wickens v. Evans*,[47] in which a regional distribution of sales territory was held to be not against the public interest because it was expected to fail of its own accord owing to the fact that legal enforcement would be denied the combination. Justice Bowen then said:

> Contracts are not illegal in any sense except that the law will not enforce them. It does not prohibit the making of such contracts; it merely declines, after they have been made, to recognize their validity. The law considers the disadvantage so imposed upon the contract a sufficient shelter to the public.[48]

There now appears the statement by Justice Bowen which becomes highly significant when it is recalled that the Mogul Steamship Company case was contemporaneous with the debates on the Sherman Bill:

> If, indeed, it could be plainly proved that the mere formation of "conferences," "trusts," or "associations" such as these were always necessarily injurious to the public—a view which involves, perhaps, the disputable assumption that, in a country of free trade, and one which is not under the iron régime of statutory monopolies, such confederations can ever be really successful—and if the evil of them were not sufficiently dealt with by the common law rule, which holds such agreements to be void as distinct from holding them to be criminal, there might be some reason for thinking that the common law ought to discover within its arsenal of sound common sense principles some further remedy commensurate with the mischief. Neither of these assumptions is, to my mind, at all evident, nor is it the province of judges to mould and stretch the law of conspiracy in order to keep pace with the calculations of political economy. If peaceable and honest combinations of capital for purposes of trade competition are to be struck at, it must, I think, be by legislation, for I do not see that they are under the ban of the common law.[49]

Social-economic Conditions in America and the Sherman Law

Note the two conditions in England which Justice Bowen held had checked the development of combinations: free trade and

[47] 3 Y. & J. 318.
[48] L. R. 23 Q. B. D. 598, 619.
[49] L. R. 23 Q. B. D. 598, 620. So also Lord Justice Frye, *ibid.*, pp. 626–638.

the absence of statutory monopolies.   In the Senate debate on the Sherman bill, much was made of the first point by Southern senators, who contended that a lowering of the tariff wall would effect the results aimed at by the bill.[50]   One very definitely gathers the impression from the replies of the Northern Republican members that the shot told, and it is not difficult to infer that their support of the Sherman Bill resulted, at least partly, from the fear that the alternative would be an attack upon the sacred tariff.   As regards the factor of statutory monopolies, no such difficulty presented itself in the United States either.   But a trust or combination or agreement in restraint of trade could be based upon a contract as well as a statutory charter, and such was the way in which trusts and combinations were developing in America; in that case the Constitutional provision for the inviolability of contracts and the absence of a Federal common law would work together to create almost ideal conditions for the development of monopolies in interstate and foreign commerce.   If it was this situation which the Sherman Bill was intended to meet, and if it was intended to extend the common-law rules as regards monopoly to Federal-court procedure, the purpose of the bill could have been achieved, as has already been stated, by vesting the Federal courts with the power to declare such contracts null and void.   This still would have left the protective tariff as an additional aid to corporations in the United States and beyond what the English corporation could rely upon in order to achieve or attempt to achieve a monopoly.

But there was still another factor, peculiar to business in the United States as contrasted with England, the existence and significance of which are just now becoming apparent, 40 years after the enactment of the Sherman Law.   Anyone who has carefully observed business conditions in England and the United States during the last 10 years, must be struck by the fact that the grouping and association of business interests in the United States is much more extensive and intensive than it is in England. There have, it is true, been tremendous banking and railroad consolidations in England, and the industries in which Lord Melchett was interested have effected virtual monopolies, while

---

[50] No less than eight bills were introduced in the House of Representatives, 51st Congress, to declare trusts and combinations unlawful.   Six of these bills were introduced by Southern representatives; four provided for importation free of duty of articles handled by trusts or combinations.

Federated British Industries, Incorporated, has achieved a considerable degree of cooperation among its members. But Lord Melchett was never able to interest enough industrial leaders of England to constitute a working majority in British industry, especially in connection with labor problems, and the cooperation among the members of Federated British Industries is not comparable with the actualities achieved in American business or the possibilities opened up by the Webb Act in the United States. Although these possibilities have not yet to any great extent become actual, they are very nearly akin to the continental cartel. English business men in contrast are intensely jealous of their individualism, the administration of even such "associations" as they have formed—equivalent to our "amalgamations"—being highly decentralized. There is very little in England comparable to the extent of our "trade associations,"[51] and the pooling and interchange of trade information engaged in by the latter are not only almost absent in England but are not believed by Englishmen to be existent or even possible. The interrelations that do apparently exist among American business men are condemned in England as undesirable regimentation.

In short, there is a psychology of American business which discloses itself socially in attempts at effecting uniformity and establishing community control, a psychology which is directly traceable to our Puritan-Calvinistic heritage. For this we are much criticized abroad, especially by the individualistic Britisher and Frenchman. The desire of legislators to control business is also criticized by American business men who forget that a similar motive on their part has unquestionably made possible the coercing of small units into the "big" businesses so characteristic of America, and also manifests itself in the attempts of business to control the church, the press, or the universities. The imagination necessary to business achievement is nurtured in part by our background of frontier history and by the opportunities offered by our tremendous natural resources, in part by the spanning of our great distances by accessible lines of communication, in part by the alertness and ambition of most Americans to achieve a striking success, and in part by the fluidity of our population. Very few men in America are denied the chance

[51] See Heermance, Edgar L., "Some Impressions of the British Trade Association," VI *Harvard Business Review* 304, April, 1928.

to succeed, "to do well"; or at least most men think so, and it is this belief, however deluded it may be, which contributes to business imagination.   Closely coupled with this attitude is a form of sociability, of adaptability, and of generosity which exhibits itself in "getting together," in adjusting difficulties, and in pooling resources for a common aim, attitudes and activities that are little understood among foreign politicians or business men.   Trade-association activities and corporation mergers have made the trade and the industry, and not the individual business, the unit of the broader administration of policies: prices are set by business leaders; statistics of production, of stocks, and of sales are freely shared, uniform accounting methods employed, credit information exchanged, cooperative advertising engaged in; and informal meetings of chambers of commerce and business clubs have brought competitors together in the interests of "trade health."   The result is a psychological setting for trade agreements and possible monopolies.   Attitudes such as this do not develop in a year or in a decade.   Now that we see the overt expression of this point of view, there is every reason to believe that it was in process as far back as the time of the Sherman Law.   The framers of that bill may not have been fully conscious of the situation, but subconsciously they may have felt the need of curbing something which they could not accurately define. It is this fact which explains in great measure the deviation of the Sherman Law from the common law, in the clause providing for indictment.

That the Senate was not aware of certain forces in American business life, now quite certainly present and then probably in their incipient stages, is indicated indirectly by its attitude regarding the persons that were to be protected by the Sherman Law.   All through the debate in the Senate, the individual *consumer* or the seller of farm products is regarded as the aggrieved party, the person to be protected against the power and greed of the business monopoly.   Indeed, this point was stressed by one of the most vigorous opponents of the bill, Senator George, of Mississippi.   He held it to be a practical objection to the bill that the consumer, as the injured and damnified party, would be impotent, because of his limited means, to bring suit against a wealthy corporation.[52]   Nowhere in the debate was much attention paid to the purchaser of "producers' goods" or to the com-

[52] *Congressional Record*, 51st Congress, p. 1767.

petitor of "big" business who might be standing in the way of trend toward monopoly. The ruthless disposal of competito by such organizations as the Standard Oil Company and t. National Cash Register Company, was not considered as of sufficient social interest—unless the competitors were very small —to make the preservation of the trade or even of competition the direct or major objective of the bill; in spite of the final title of the enacted bill: "An act to protect trade and commerce against unlawful restraints and monopolies." The metaphysical view of "competition" appearing in the earlier judicial decisions was not prominent in the congressional debates. It was assumed that most business men, especially the larger competitors, could and would look out for themselves; such preservation as was accorded them was incidental to the rights of the consumer to purchase commodities at "fair" prices. Congress had the clear feeling that every business man, big or little, was the potential member of a pool or trust, however unfriendly he might have been to it previously. The prime consideration was the effect of monopoly on prices to the consumer. In this sense the State took exactly the same attitude as did the Church, championing the consumer's interests; as opposed to the psychological attitude permeating American business, the assertion of the rights of the producer.

The early history of the Federal Trade Commission shows exactly the same point of view: an endeavor to protect only the consumer against unfair trade practices. Just within the past few years has the Commission, by means of "trade-practice submittals," taken cognizance of the unfairness of certain practices to the competitor and to the trade at large. But business men had themselves anticipated the adoption of this point of view, partly by joining pools and trusts and partly by forming business organizations that had no legal status. The Better Business Bureau more nearly represents the endeavor of competing business men to maintain their individual as well as group or trade existence by eliminating such practices as encouraged cutthroat competition and eventually led to monopoly control; and yet that individualism has been achieved, paradoxically, through cooperative activities. The forces which have held these business groups together are not legal or governmental, but economic; largely in the case of trusts and other combinations, and almost entirely in the case of trade and business associations.   As Sherman himself pointed out, corporations "have enabled individuals to unite to undertake great enterprises only attempted in former times by powerful governments . . . They had monopolies and mortmains of old, but never before such giants as in our day."   The trade association and other non-corporate business organizations have achieved similar results.   Furthermore, positively at variance with the negative attitude of Church and State, which aims at protecting the individual consumer, is the most outstanding phenomenon of American business life, namely the justification of high wages on the ground of their great purchasing value.

In short, the Sherman Law recognized that a new power had appeared on the social horizon: Business.   The aggregate power had been present in society from earliest times, but it had been scattered among many separate individuals.   Now these forces were converging into organizations which constituted a new kind of major social energy, comparable in size and strength with the State and the Church.   The presence of this rival, with tremendous autonomous possibilities, although but vaguely recognized, was not to be tolerated by the ever-jealous State; the Church had always been perfectly clear in its attitude toward Mammon and lucre.

The possibility of a benign or generous business policy, on the part of an achieved monopoly, did not occur to the framers of the Sherman Act.   Not until 1925 did the Supreme Court of the United States[53] assert that it would no longer assume as a major premise that business men normally were prompted by greed and cupidity!   The autonomous regulation of business— early manifesting itself in organizations which did not disintegrate of their own accord when the common-law sanctions were denied their agreements, and which could be curbed only by the positive statutory provisions of the Sherman Act—has achieved nationwide and even world-wide proportions, with extra-legal functions dominant and characteristic; and now is occupied with the development of policies, ethical as well as economic, which shall not only keep business well clear of legal entanglements but which also are rapidly and intensively developing the self-regulatory functions of Business itself.

From the standpoint of Business Ethics, the most significant feature of the Sherman Law was, therefore, not its purposes or

[53] *Trade Association Cases*, 268 U. S. 563, 588.

its subsequent achievements, but its symptomatic indication of the fact that the Law was viewing with apprehension the growing power of Business.   There is no denying the remedial activities of the law: business itself was not sufficiently aware of the obligations attaching to the development of its social power and needed an external corrective, and the Sherman Law may still be necessary as a potential curb even though its actual employment be considerably lessened.   But its enactment exhibits an attempt to conserve the political values of society as against the encroachments of the economic on the pattern of social values. The repeal of the Sherman Act has been advocated again and again, but its retention could be defended solely on the ground that it be a perpetual reminder to business that freedom from the law can best be achieved by proper self-government.   The Sherman Law need be regarded neither as a cure-all nor as a killjoy; the cure and the joy are to be discovered in autonomous business health, a condition which is amenable to direct attention without the assistance of either Church or State.

CHAPTER IV

THE EARLIER, ABSOLUTE, INTERPRETATION OF THE SHERMAN LAW

It now remains to discover the course taken by the earlier judicial interpretations of the Sherman Act in the United States. To do this thoroughly would be a task far beyond the limitations of this chapter. It has, furthermore, been done quite satisfactorily elsewhere.[1] A brief survey will, however, be attempted.

Prosecutions under the Sherman Law devolve upon the Attorney General of the United States, either by himself or through the Solicitor General. During the first 32 months of the life of the Sherman Act, which constituted the remaining period of Harrison's administration, little was accomplished. Five prosecutions were begun during that time, but four of them were complete failures. In his annual report of December 1, 1892, Attorney General Miller stated: "As was to be expected, it has been found, in all cases investigated, that great care and skill have been exercised in the formation and manipulation of these combinations so as to avoid the provisions of this statute, . . . and these efforts have not been without success." These five cases were tried in equity, the Government asking that an injunction be issued against the companies violating the Act.

Cases Involving Necessities of Life

The one successful prosecution was that against the members of the Nashville Coal Exchange.[2]

The membership of the Nashville Coal Exchange was composed of various coal-mining companies operating mines in Kentucky and Tennessee, chiefly in Kentucky, and of persons and firms dealing in coal in Nashville. Every person, firm, or corporation owning or operating mines who shipped coal to Nashville was eligible to member-

[1] Taft, William H., *The Anti-trust Act and the Supreme Court*, New York: Harper & Brothers, 1914. Walker, Albert H., *History of the Sherman Law*, New York: Equity Press, 1910.
[2] *U. S. v. Jellico Mountain Coal and Coke Co. et al.*, 43 Fed. 898 (1890).

ship in the exchange, as were also all coal dealers in Nashville. A written agreement provided for the establishment, by the exchange, of prices at which coal was to be sold at Nashville. Every member found guilty of selling coal at a price less than that fixed by the exchange, was to be fined 2 cents per bushel and $10 for the first offense, and 4 cents per bushel and $20 for the second offense. Owners or operators of mines were not to sell or ship coal to any person, firm, or corporation in Nashville who was not a member of the exchange, and dealers were not to buy coal from any one not a member of the exchange.

The defendants held that the actual transportation of coal was not engaged in by any of them, but the Appellate Court held that such transportation from Kentucky to Tennessee was a necessary incident to and element in the arrangement, the execution of which would have been impossible without it.[3] The injunction was granted, and the case was not further appealed.

Two other cases against coal-dealers' associations were later— *i.e.*, shortly after Harrison's Administration—successfully prosecuted.[4] The fact that coal was a prime necessity of life contributed to the determination of these cases, again showing that the consumers', rather than the producers', interests were considered as of primary, even exclusive, importance.

The California Coal Dealers' Association, unincorporated, was in 1897 composed of retail dealers in coal who were residents of San Francisco, and of miners and shippers of coal who carried on their business in the same city. Coal was imported by these dealers from British Columbia, Washington and Oregon, to an amount that represented from three-fourths to seven-eighths of the coal consumed in San Francisco. The distance of appreciable amounts of other sources of supply was so great as to make them prohibitive.

A scarcity of labor in the British Columbia mines, due to the Klondike rush at that time, coupled with a lack of vessels, for the same reason, made it difficult to secure enough coal in San Francisco. The situation encouraged a number of dishonest retail dealers to engage in business, who were guilty of short weighting, substitution of poorer grades of coal, and of the failure to pay their bills. To meet this situation and to stabilize trade conditions, the association was formed. It comprised all of the wholesale dealers of San Francisco, who could, combined together, absolutely control the price of domestic coal. A membership

---

[3] *Ibid.*, 46 Fed. 432, 435 (1891).

[4] *U. S. v. Coal Dealers' Association of California et al.*, 85 Fed. 252 (1898). *U. S. v. Chesapeake and Ohio Fuel Co.*, 105 Fed. 93 (1900); 115 Fed. 610 (1902).

fee of $500 was charged, and fines provided—even for non-members—of $10 to $100 for a first offense, and $25 to $200 for a second offense against the association rules. Non-member retail dealers were charged $2 per ton more than members, and effective means adopted to restrain recalcitrant dealers from obtaining coal at all.

The court held that the association constituted a restraint of trade which was "injurious to public interests, against public policy, and therefore unlawful." The case was not appealed. In both cases the courts held that the potential menace to consumers outweighed the obvious benefits to trade health.

The Sherman Law not only provided for prosecution by the Government, but also could be made the basis of private suits as in the common law. Three such suits were brought during Harrison's administration. Only one of these suits was of any importance, the court being asked to appoint a receiver for a company acquired in the process of organizing a bakers' trust. Again the consumer's point of view is given paramount place, and the common-law rule employed. The court declined to aid the claimant "to perfect, and perhaps to enlarge, his combination or trust . . . The attempt to accumulate in the hands of a single organization the business of supplying bread itself to so large a portion of the poor, as well as the rich, people of the United States should not be favored by a court of equity."[5] This particular combination, however, was so limited in its field of operation that the effect of its suppression was not extensive.

The most important case involving non-necessities of life was decided shortly afterward.

The Dueber Watch Case Manufacturing Company, an Ohio corporation, doing business at Canton, Ohio, prior to November 16, 1887, manufactured watch cases throughout the United States and foreign countries; this business involved a profit of $175,000 per year. On November 16, 1887, a number of companies, including the E. Howard Watch & Clock Company, a Massachusetts corporation doing business in New York City and selling watches and cases, mutually agreed "that they would not thereafter sell any goods manufactured by them to any person, firm, association or corporation whatsoever who thereafter should buy or sell any goods manufactured by the Dueber Company." A large number of dealers thereupon withdrew their patronage and ceased to deal in the Dueber Company's goods. Members of the agreement also agreed

[5] *American Biscuit and Manufacturing Co. v. Klotz,* 44 Fed. 721, 726 (1891).

among themselves that they would maintain an arbitrary fixed price for their goods. The purpose of this agreement was to compel the Dueber Company to join in the agreement to fix and maintain arbitrary prices for watch cases. After the Act of July 2, 1890, members of the association ratified, confirmed, renewed and continued in force their agreement.

The Dueber Company sued the Howard Company and others at law,[6] but the case was so poorly pleaded—no allegation being made, for instance, that the goods involved were articles of interstate commerce—that the court refused to sustain the complaint. Two observations of the court are interesting:

No authority has gone to the extent of holding that a transaction, whereby two or more dealers fix an arbitrary price for their goods, in the absence of other facts, is illegal . . .

Many perfectly legitimate reasons might be suggested for an agreement among two or more traders not to deal with those who prefer to purchase the goods of another designated trader in the same business . . . The construction contended for by plaintiff would . . . make unlawful almost every combination by which trade and commerce seek to extend their influence and enlarge their profits . . . It would strike at all agreements by which honest enterprise attempts to protect itself against ruinous and dishonest competition.[7]

The case was appealed to the Circuit Court of Appeals, Second Circuit, where the judgment was sustained.[8] In spite of the obvious deficiencies in the plea, the court, including the dissenting judge, discussed the material situation involved in the case. Justice Lacombe pointed out that gold watches were not articles of prime necessity, as were flour, coal, and other staple commodities referred to in many of the cases cited; and also that the members of the agreement constituted only a small part of the industry and that there was not a limited supply of the commodity as there was, for example, in the case of anthracite coal. He then discussed the general principles underlying competitive business in much the same way that the English courts did in the Mogul Steamship case:

. . . Each one of the defendants had an undoubted right to determine for himself the price at which he would sell the goods he made, and he certainly does not lose that right by deciding to sell them at the same price at which

[6] *Dueber Watch Case Manufacturing Company v. E. Howard Watch and Clock Company et al.*, 55 Fed. 851 (1893).

[7] *Ibid.*, pp. 853, 854.

[8] *Ibid.*, 66 Fed. 637 (1895).

a dozen or so of his competitors sell the goods which they make . . . And it is difficult to see how the public is injuriously affected by any such agreement between the combining manufacturers . . . If they fix the price too high, they restrain their own trade only.

. . . In regard to the agreement not to sell: it did not operate in general restraint of trade, the total amount of purchases and sales remaining constant. But it does not follow that restraint of plaintiff was unreasonable, nor heavier than the interest of the favored party required. An individual manufacturer or trader may surely buy from or sell to whom he pleases, and may equally refuse to buy from or to sell to any one with whom he thinks it will promote his business interests to refuse to trade . . . It is a business device, probably as old as business itself, . . . to treat more favorably those who become exclusive customers . . . And the case is in no way different if half a dozen individuals combine into a partnership or a hundred individuals combine into a corporation and adopt the same method to enlarge their business. If this be so,—and no authority to which we are referred holds to the contrary,—it is difficult to see in what respect it is unlawful for a score of different manufacturers to enter into a like arrangement to push the sale of their own goods, or to secure some business benefit to themselves by increasing the number of their exclusive customers, when there is nothing to show that the parties so combining constitute substantially all, or even a majority of the manufacturers of such goods, even in the half dozen states where their factories are located, and when the field of manufacture is open to all.

. . . The device (used by defendants) is not one in general restraint of trade. It seems to be a reasonable business device to increase the trade of one set of competitors at the expense, no doubt, of their business rivals, who are equally free to avail themselves of similar devices to secure their own trade.[9]

Justice Wallace dissented from this opinion:

No body of manufacturers is justified in combining to coerce a competing manufacturer to join them and sell his goods at a price to be fixed by them, and to destroy his business in the event of his refusal to do so; and it matters not that they propose to destroy his business by peaceful methods of influencing his customers not to deal with him . . . The statute upon which this action is founded discriminates between combination and conspiracy, and it not only makes both criminal, but it makes contracts in which there is no element of a conspiracy or combination also criminal if in restraint of trade. It is therefore quite immaterial whether the acts charged in the complaint are sufficient to constitute a criminal conspiracy at common law. It suffices if the combination set forth is oppressive in its nature, and mischievous in its effects.

I do not question the right of the defendants to combine for their own protection against unfair competition, and in that behalf, their commodity not being one of prime necessity, to agree not to sell to those who do not buy exclusively of them, or who buy of the complainant or some other

[9] *Ibid.*, pp. 644–646.

obnoxious competitor; but I repudiate the doctrine that they can combine to induce the customers of a rival manufacturer not to deal with him unless he will join their combination.[10]

Metaphysical Doctrines of the Courts

The first case of major importance to be tried by a Federal court under the Sherman Act was decided August 4, 1892.[11]

Greene *et al.*, of Ohio, Illinois and New York, owners of the Distilling and Cattle Feeding Company, a corporation organized February 11, 1890, had obtained control, by purchase, renting and leasing, of some 70 distilleries in the United States, producing 77,000,000 gallons of spirits, which constituted 75% of the production in the United States. These various distilleries had previously been competing among each other; by means of the control exercised by the Distilling and Cattle Feeding Company, prices were fixed, resale prices controlled and maintained, and exclusive markets secured by a rebate of 5 cents per gallon. The Government charged the company with violating the Sherman Act, on the ground that the parties involved had effected a combination in restraint of trade.

Justice Jackson, Circuit Judge of the Southern District of Ohio, Western Division, delivered the opinion of the court. He began by pointing out that there were no common-law offenses against the United States, the Federal courts being unable to resort to the common law as a source of criminal jurisdiction. Crimes and offenses cognizable under the authority of the United States were therefore such, and only such, as were expressly designated by law; hence Congress must define these crimes, fix their punishment, and confer the jurisdiction to try them.[12] When Congress, in the exercise of powers conferred by the Constitution, adopted or created common-law offenses, continued Justice Jackson, the courts might properly look to that body of jurisprudence for the true meaning and definition of such crimes, if they were not clearly defined in the Federal act creating them.[13] Thus the continuity between the common law, alien to Federal law, and the Sherman Law, was clearly established, but on a totally different basis than that on which Sherman had relied in his argument before the Senate.

[10] *Ibid.*, pp. 651, 652.

[11] *In re Greene*, 52 Fed. 104.

[12] *Ibid.*, p. 111.   Cited: *U. S. v. Hudson*, 7 Cranch. 32; *U. S. v. Coolidge*, 1 Wheat. 415; *U. S. v. Britton*, 108 U. S. 199, 206.

[13] Cited: *U. S. v. Armstrong*, 2 Curt. 446; *U. S. v. Coppersmith*, 4 Fed. 198.

Justice Jackson then went on to say:

The act of July 2, 1890, in declaring that contracts, combinations, and conspiracies in restraint of trade and commerce between the states and foreign commerce were not only illegal, but should constitute criminal offenses against the United States, goes a step beyond the common-law, in this: that contracts in restraint of trade, while unlawful, were not misdemeanors or indictable at common law.   It adopts the common-law rule in making combinations and conspiracies in restraint of the designated trade and commerce criminal offenses, and creates a new crime, in making contracts in restraint of trade misdemeanors, and indictable as such.   But the act does not undertake to define what constitutes a contract, combination, or conspiracy in restraint of trade, and recourse must therefore be had to the common law for the proper definition of these general terms, and to ascertain whether the acts charged come within the statute.[14]

It is very certain that Congress could not, and did not, by this enactment, attempt to prescribe limits to the acquisition, either by the private citizen or state corporation, of property which might become the subject of interstate commerce, or declare that, when the accumulation or control of property by legitimate means and lawful methods reached such magnitude or proportions as enabled the owners to control the traffic therein, or any part thereof, among the states, a criminal offense was committed by such owners.[15]

This case is important, not only because it was one of the earliest cases to arise under the Sherman Act, but also because it was referred to by the United States Supreme Court in the first case arising under the Sherman Act to come before it for review.   This case, known as the "Sugar Trust Case," first arose in the Circuit Court of Pennsylvania, Eastern Division.[16]

By March 4, 1892, the American Sugar Refining Company, of New Jersey, had obtained control of all of the refineries in the United States, except the Revere Company of Boston, manufacturing 2%, and four refineries located in Philadelphia—E. C. Knight, Spreckels', Franklin, and Delaware Sugar House—refining 33% of the sugar refined in the United States.   The American Sugar Refining Company purchased the stock of the four Philadelphia companies, paying therefor by the transfer of an agreed equivalent of its own stock.   The contract of sale left the sellers free to engage in a similar line of business elsewhere.   After the sale had been made, the Delaware and Spreckels' plants were combined in order to effect more economic operation, as were also the Knight and Franklin plants.   Subsequent to these transactions an increasing amount of sugar was refined at Philadelphia, and although the price

[14] 52 Fed. 104, 111.
[15] *Ibid.*, p. 115.
[16] *U. S. v. E. C. Knight and Company et al.*, 60 Fed. 306 (1894).

of refined sugar was advanced slightly, the price was lower than it had been for some years previously. At the time this case was tried, about 10% of the sugar refined in the United States was being refined by companies other than the American Sugar Refining Company; and additional sugar, but not much, was being bought in Europe for sale in the United States.

The Circuit Court, and the Circuit Court of Appeals, Third Circuit of Pennsylvania, to which the case was appealed,[17] based the arguments of the decisions largely on a distinction between commerce and manufacturing, and asserted that the Sherman Law applied to the former and not to the latter. The Government had contended that a monopoly in the refining of sugar virtually secured a monopoly of the commerce in that article.[18] The courts held however:

> The alleged control of refining does not of itself secure such commercial monopoly; and at present none exists. The most that can be said is that it tends to such a result . . . Whether it would or not depends on their (defendants') ability with this advantage to control such commerce. They have not tested this ability by attempting to control it, nor shown a disposition to do so . . . It is the stream of commerce flowing across the states, and between them and foreign nations, that Congress is authorized to regulate.[19]
>
> The utmost that can be said is that the American Sugar Refining Company has acquired control of the business of refining and selling sugar in the United States . . . The Commerce Clause and the Sherman Act apply to commerce . . . Manufacturing and commerce are two distinct and very different things. The latter does not include the former; commerce includes buying and selling, intercourse and traffic.[20]

This distinction between commerce and manufacturing was maintained by Chief Justice Fuller, who read the majority decision of the Supreme Court of the United States, to which final appeal had been taken.[21] Justice Fuller also referred with approval to the definition laid down by Justice Jackson, who had said:

[17] *Ibid.*, 60 Fed. 934.
[18] An obviously unsound, or misdirected, plea, and one based on facts which concerned only a part of the company's business. Even Justice Harlan's dissenting opinion took issue with the majority opinion on this point, instead of indicating its lack of cogency.—Walker, *op. cit.* (note 1, this chapter).
[19] *Ibid.*, 60 Fed. 306, 309.
[20] *Ibid.*, 60 Fed. 934.
[21] *Ibid.*, 156 U. S. 1 (1895).

Commerce includes, not only the actual transportation of commodities and persons between the states, but also the instrumentalities and processes of such transportation. It includes all the negotiations and contracts which have for their object, or involve as an element thereof, such transmission or passage from one state to another. Such commerce begins, and the regulating power of Congress attaches, when the commodity or thing traded in commences its transportation from the state of its production or *situs* to some other state or foreign country, and terminates when the transportation is completed and the property has become a part of the general mass of the property in the state of its destination. When the commerce begins is determined, not by the character of the commodity, nor by the intention of the owner to transfer it to another state for sale, nor by his preparation of it for transportation, but by its actual delivery to a common carrier for transportation, or the actual commencement of its transfer to another state.[22]

Chief Justice Fuller then went on from this business and economic distinction, to indicate the political problem involved: the relation between the Federal and the state governments. The residual powers left to the states by the Federal Constitution were not to be unduly encroached upon by Federal legislation, which must find its justification in the powers specifically granted to the Federal legislature by the Constitution. The Federal Government was vested with the power to control commerce among the several states, this power "furnishing one of the strongest bonds of union." But the police power of the several states is independent of this and "is essential to the autonomy of the states." Therefore, inasmuch as the police power of the states included the power to regulate manufacturing, the economic distinction between manufacturing and commerce was accentuated by the political distinction between the Federal jurisdiction over interstate commerce and the police power of the states over manufacturing.

Doubtless the power to control the manufacture of a given thing involves in a certain sense the control of its disposition, but this is a secondary and not the primary sense; and although the exercise of that power may result in bringing the operation of commerce into play, it does not control it and affects it only incidentally and indirectly. Commerce succeeds to manufacturing, and is not a part of it.[23]

[22] *In re Greene*, 52 Fed. 104, 113. Cited: *Pensacola Tel. Co. v. W. U. Tel. Co.*, 96 U. S. 1; *Brown v. Houston*, 114 U. S. 622; *Coe v. Errol*, 116 U. S. 517–520; *Robbins v. Taxing District*, 120 U. S. 497; *Kidd v. Pearson*, 128 U. S. 1.

[23] 156 U. S. 1, 12.

It seems almost ironical that this early decision, which was based on a functional interpretation of business—a view which was held in abeyance during the next 10 years—and which refused to accept "existence" or "tendency" as *prima facie* evidence of wrongdoing or illegal acts, should at the same time have become involved in two other metaphysical doctrines. One of these doctrines was basic to the political theory underlying the American Federal System and maintained the reality of political boundaries which for business had practically ceased to exist. The other doctrine distinguished between commerce and manufacturing, a distinction which is practically impossible in a case such as the one under discussion, where the producing company controls its distribution channels even only so far as the wholesaling function.

Justice Fuller quoted Justice Bradley, in *Coe v. Errol:*

> There must be a point of time when goods cease to be governed exclusively by the domestic law and begin to be governed and protected by the national law of commercial regulation, and that moment seems to us to be a legitimate one for this purpose, in which they commence their final movement from the State of their origin to that of their destination.[24]

He then affirmed the decisions of the lower courts:

> In the act of July 2, 1890, Congress did not attempt to assert the power to deal with monopoly directly as such; . . . what the law struck at was combinations, contracts, and conspiracies to monopolize trade and commerce among the several States or with foreign nations.[25]

Justice Harlan delivered a dissenting opinion, which is important because its opposition to the narrow construction of the Sherman Act later became the prevailing opinion of the Supreme Court. Although lengthy and at times too passionate to constitute a judicial view, Justice Harlan's opinion did include a logic which finally prevailed. He cited an impressive number of cases in which the state courts had held similar transactions to be monopolies or conspiracies illegal under the common law.[26]

[24] 116 U. S. 517, 525.
[25] 156 U. S. 1, 16, 17.
[26] *Morris Rim Coal Co. v. Barclay Coal Co.*, 68 Penn. St. 173; *Arnot v. Pittston & Elmira Coal Co.*, 68 N. Y. 558; *Central Ohio Salt Co. v. Guthrie*, 35 Ohio St. 666; *Craft v. McConoughy*, 79 Ills. 346; *People v. Chicago Gas Trust Co.*, 130 Ills. 269; *India Bagging Ass'n. v. Kock*, 14 La. Ann. 168; *Santa Clara Mill & Lumber Co. v. Hayes*, 76 Cal. 387; *Richardson v. Buhl*, 77 Mich. 632; *Texas Standard Oil Co. v. Adone*, 83 Tex. 650.

This extended reference to adjudged cases relating to unlawful restraints upon the interior traffic of a state was made "for the purpose of showing that a combination such as that organized under the name of the American Sugar Refining Company has been uniformily held by the courts of the states to be against public policy and illegal because of its necessary tendency to impose improper restraints upon trade."

Not only was the American Sugar Refining Company organized, to quote the charter, "for the purpose of buying, manufacturing, refining *and selling sugar in different parts of the United States*," said Justice Harlan, but the court itself recognized that contracts to buy and sell were part of interstate trade or commerce, and these may even precede the actual manufacturing process.

It is said that manufacturing precedes commerce and is not a part of it. But it is equally true that when manufacturing ends, that which has been manufactured becomes a subject of commerce; that buying and selling succeed manufacturing, come into existence after the process of manufacturing is completed, precede transportation, and are as much commercial intercourse, where articles are bought to be carried from one state to another, as is the manual transportation of such articles after they have been so purchased.[27]

The treatment of this case by the courts indicates clearly the struggle going on between legal-political theory and business realities, and the reluctance with which the former was yielding to the latter. Whatever may be the merits of this political-economic-metaphysical problem of determining exactly where manufacturing ceases and commerce begins, and therefore where state jurisdiction ended and Federal jurisdiction under the Sherman Law could become effective, the outstanding business fact was apparent that a monopoly had been achieved at a point in the process from raw material to finished product, a matter which had been of grave concern to the mediaeval guilds as a business problem and which apparently was of chief interest to the framers of the Sherman Law, however little it could be entertained by the courts. The peculiar structure of the Federal system established a neutral zone of sufficient ambiguity so as to enable those who were attempting to monopolize a certain business to avoid Federal jurisdiction and to rely on the relatively ineffective state governments not to prosecute, a neutral zone, the

[27] 156 U. S. 1, 35, 36.

presence of which for years enabled courts to hold up much remedial legislation, both state and Federal; conspicuously, for example, legislation for improving labor conditions.

Whether "commerce" could be defined so as to include even the "intent" of the parties attempting to establish a monopoly, still further divided Justice Harlan from the rest of the court. According to the former, the intention was disclosed on the very face of the transactions; the court, however, had referred to a number of cases in which the state governments had asserted their jurisdictions up to the shipment of the article to its destination outside the boundaries of the state. None of these cases, Justice Harlan pointed out, had any but a remotely analogous bearing on the problem of restraint of trade: they involved problems of taxation or of the prohibition of the manufacture or sale of liquor; the court held that the admitted differences were only of degree and that the cited cases afforded a sufficient and objective basis for distinguishing between Federal and state jurisdiction, but Justice Harlan maintained that the cases differed in kind. Justice Harlan then extended the meaning of "commerce" to include the very *existence* of combinations capable of such functions. It was this definition of the object of the Sherman Law—and not the view that the Law was aimed at unfair business or socially dangerous *functions* and *activities*—that soon came to prevail.

The mere existence of a combination having such an object and possessing such extraordinary power (control of 98% of the sugar refining business) is itself, under settled principles of law a direct restraint of trade in the article . . . (Otherwise) interstate traffic . . . may pass under the absolute control of overshadowing combinations having financial resources without limit and an audacity in the accomplishment of their objects that recognizes none of the restraints of moral obligations controlling the action of individuals; combinations governed entirely by the law of greed and selfishness—so powerful that no single State is able to overthrow them and give the required protection to the whole country, and so all pervading that they threaten the integrity of our institutions.[28]

"The doctrine of the autonomy of the states," concluded Justice Harlan, "cannot properly be invoked to justify a denial of power in the national government to meet such an emergency, involving as it does that freedom of commercial intercourse among the states which the Constitution sought to attain." These three

[28] *Ibid.*, p. 44.

metaphysical issues—of existence *versus* function, of commerce *versus* manufacturing, and of Federal *versus* state jurisdiction— were made matters of material import by the Supreme Court, in the face of dynamic business relations which could not be resolved to such absolute concepts.   Business itself was to blame for this situation, at least inpart, by not having formulated commensurate positive doctrines, expressive of its own behavior and socially justifiable.

Cases Involving Labor Unions and Railway Associations

One of the most striking facts connected with the early history of the Sherman Law is the number of cases prosecuted in the courts against labor unions and railroad companies, neither of which probably was intended by Congress to become the objective of "anti-trust" legislation.   This perversion of the original purposes of Congress exhibits again and strikingly the metaphysical and absolute character of legal thinking.   The courts had done the same thing before with the Fourteenth Amendment to the Constitution, the purpose of which was to complete the emancipation of the Negro; the phraseology of the amendment was actually used, however, to protect business corporations against state legislation which was aimed to curb and control them.   Disregarding the pragmatic justification for such a procedure, the situation itself is anomalous.   Similarly with the Sherman Law: the wording of the statute was used by the courts as the expression of a metaphysical-legal doctrine, and its application was directed toward business and economic organizations that were not intended to come within the province of the Law, while the business organizations that were uppermost in the minds of the 51st Congress were left practically untouched.

Of the 10 cases prosecuted on behalf of the United States for violation of the Sherman Act during Cleveland's administration, five were brought against men as alleged participants in labor strikes; four of these cases were successfully prosecuted.   This is to be contrasted with the fact that only two of the remaining five cases were brought against industrial "trusts."[29]   This situation is rendered more striking by the fact that during the same period the only two successful civil litigations—out of the eight instituted by private parties under the Sherman Act—were decided against the labor organizations.   Hence it is easy to

[29] One of these has just been discussed: the Sugar Trust case.

understand the feeling, then and even yet to some degree prevalent among labor unions, that the courts were prejudiced against them.

One of these five labor cases[30] involved the question as to whether labor unions were guilty of conspiracy "in restraint of trade" if they interfered with the flow of commerce on the railroads.

During a dispute between the Pullman Palace Car Company and its employees, the latter "struck." The American Railway Union, of which Eugene V. Debs was president, attempted to compel an adjustment of the dispute by creating a boycott against the company. To make this effective, they interfered physically with trains running in and out of Chicago. Intimidation and open violence were resorted to by some of the strikers, who also took forcible possession of some of the railroads, interfering with transportation of passengers and goods and preventing the passage of trains carrying the United States mails. Railroad property was destroyed and persons in the employ of the railroads were attacked by the strikers, many persons being injured and killed.

The Supreme Court decided against Debs and the unions on the ground that any interference with the mails could not be tolerated and also on the ground that the acts of the strikers constituted a nuisance. The court "entered into no examination of the act of July 2, 1890, upon which the Circuit Court relied mainly to sustain its jurisdiction. It must not be understood from this that we dissent from the conclusions of that court in reference to the scope of the act . . . "[31] The Circuit Court, Northern District of Illinois, had examined the history of the Sherman Law in Congress. Although the court conceded that they could not take the views or purposes expressed in debates in Congress as supplying the construction of statutes, these debates could be referred to, as well as any other sources, "in order to determine the history of the evil which the legislation was intended to remedy."

In this instance it is perhaps apparent that the original measure, as proposed in the Senate, "was directed wholly against the trusts, and not at organizations of labor in any form." But it also appears that before the bill left the Senate its title had been changed, and material additions made

[30] *In re Debs, Petitioner*, 158 U. S. 564 (1895).
[31] *Ibid.*, p. 600.

to the text; the exemption of agricultural associations and labor unions from its provisions was not adopted[32] . . .

The most decisive civil case successfully sued against a labor union was known as the "Danbury Hatters' Case." The local union of hat makers, of Danbury, Connecticut, was a branch of the United Hatters of America, which in turn was affiliated with the American Federation of Labor.

In 1903 Loewe and Company, with a capital of $130,000, were operating a hat factory at Danbury, with annual sales of $400,000. They employed approximately 230 persons, and at the time had some 150 dozen hats in process. The hatters' union, through its officers, had been for some time trying to compel Loewe and Company against their will to unionize the factory. The union had previously succeeded in their purpose in some 70 of the 82 factories throughout the United States, and were "parading" their successes before Loewe and Company and threatening to coerce them in similar fashion into yielding to their demands.

Union members withdrew from Loewe and Company's factory and succeeded in preventing others from working there. With the help of their associates in the larger bodies of union labor with which they were affiliated, they declared a boycott upon hats made by Loewe and Company, particularly among the retail dealers of California and Virginia. Loewe and Company contended that these activities limited and restrained their interstate trade in hats, resulting in an alleged loss of $80,000.

Inasmuch as there was no allegation that Loewe and Company's product had been touched, handled, obstructed, or in any manner physically interfered with, nor that the unions were themselves engaged in interstate commerce, the District Court refused to find in favor of Loewe and Company.[33] The Supreme Court, however, held the union to be a combination in restraint of trade, by virtue of their obstruction not only of the manufacturing process but also of the retail selling of hats in other states. The suit being at law, damages of three times the amount of the injury proved were awarded.[34] The court evidently slurred over

[32] *U. S. v. Debs*, 64 Fed. 724, 747. Cited: *Congressional Record*, 51st Congress, p. 4089. This same view had been held in *U. S. v. Workingmen's Amalgamated Council*, 54 Fed. 994 (1893). Labor unions were later exempted from the operation of the Sherman Law by the Clayton Act, Section 6, but the unions were soon to find that this apparent victory was illusory.

[33] *Loewe and Company v. Lawler et al.*, 148 Fed. 924 (1906).

[34] *Ibid.*, 208 U. S. 274, 292, 300 (1908).

the fine distinctions between commerce and other allied acts which it had made in the Knight case.

The case is cited to complete the record of early decisions as regards labor unions under the Sherman Act. The decision in this case and in the Debs case effectively settled the status of labor unions under the Sherman Act. The discussion of the merits of these labor cases properly belongs elsewhere. It is apparent to anyone, however, that the courts were much less uncertain in their determination of labor cases than they were in handling the cases of business organizations which undoubtedly were the objectives of the Sherman Law.

It is equally doubtful whether railroad companies were intended to come within the jurisdiction of the Sherman Act. And yet, of five cases prosecuted during Cleveland's administration and not directed against labor unions, two were directed against railroad associations.

The decisions in these latter two cases definitely brought railroad companies within the scope of the Sherman Act, in spite of the fact that the Interstate Commerce Act of 1887 had given full regulating powers to the Commission which it had created. Whether the courts acting under the Sherman Law, or the Commission acting under the powers granted it by the Act of 1887, should have jurisdiction over railroads, is a political problem[35] and is not within the scope of this chapter. But the courts not only applied the Sherman Law to these railroad association cases but decided them on the basis of principles which in turn were later applied to all business companies.

On March 15, 1889, a "memorandum of agreement" was drawn up by 18 competing railroads west of the Missouri River, which formed the Trans-Missouri Freight Association. By the terms of this agreement, the association controlled the competitive traffic of a large region. The member railroads gave the association the power to establish and maintain rules, regulations, and rates, and to punish by fine any member that reduced the rates fixed by the association. Subsequent to the formation of this association, a number of eastern railroads formed the Joint Traffic Association, with a board of nine managers, one being appointed by each of the following railroads: Baltimore & Ohio, Chesa-

---

[35] See Dickinson, John, *Administrative Justice and the Supremacy of Law*, Cambridge: Harvard University Press, 1927. The Transportation Act of 1920 restored to the Interstate Commerce Commission a great part of the administrative jurisdiction that it lost in these cases.

peake & Ohio, Erie, Grand Trunk, Lackawanna, Lehigh, Pennsylvania, Vanderbilt, and Wabash; with similar purposes in view.

Justice Peckham, who had previously read the dissenting opinion in the Sugar Trust case, now delivered the opinion of the Supreme Court in each case, the opinion representing a bare majority; and the two situations were treated as similar. Justice Peckham held that the language of the Sherman Act included every contract, whether reasonable or not,[36] thus setting a new standard for the Supreme Court and reversing the decisions of the lower courts, which had held that only unreasonable restraints of trade were condemned by the Sherman Act.[37]

The question as to whether the Sherman Act applied to common carriers involved the possibility that its general provisions had superseded or abrogated the specific provisions of the Interstate Commerce Act of February 4, 1887. This was denied by Justice Peckham, who asserted that "both statutes stand, as neither is inconsistent with the other.[38] . . . We are unable to see that the railroads were not intended to be included in this legislation."[39] His argument was not only that there were many points of agreement between railroad corporations and trusts,[40] but also that to exclude the railroads from the jurisdiction of the Sherman Act would make "its applicability so limited that the whole act might as well be held inoperative"![41] Justice White held that it was not the intention of the Act of 1890 to interfere with the Act of 1887.[42] This had been the view of the lower courts which had handled these two railroad cases,[43] a view which was supported by the argument that "a general will not repeal a special statute unless there be a clear implication unavoidably resulting from the general law that it was so

---

[36] *U. S. v. Trans-Missouri Freight Association et al.*, 166 U. S. 290, 312, 328 (March 22, 1897); *U. S. v. Joint Traffic Association*, 171 U. S. 505 (October 24, 1898).

[37] *U. S. v. Trans-Missouri Freight Association et al.*, 53 Fed. 440, 449 ff. (November 28, 1892); 58 Fed. 58, 70 ff. (October 2, 1893). *U. S. v. Joint Traffic Association*, 76 Fed. 895, 897 (May 28, 1896); 89 Fed. 1020 (March 19, 1897). So also *In re Debs*, 64 Fed. 724, 747.

[38] 166 U. S. 290, 314. Concurred in by Justice White, pp. 357 ff.

[39] *Ibid.*, p. 319. See also 171 U. S. 505, 571.

[40] *Ibid.*, p. 322.

[41] *Ibid.*, p. 326.

[42] *Ibid.*, p. 360.

[43] 53 Fed. 440, 455; 58 Fed. 58, 74; 76 Fed. 895, 897.

intended"; [44] and that the railroads, in their capacity of quasi-public corporations, subject to the rate regulations of the Interstate Commerce Commission, differed so much from private business corporations as to put them in a class by themselves, over which the Sherman Act could exercise only a redundant jurisdiction. [45]

The argument which sustained this adverse view is interesting because it is similar to that which prevailed in the Mogul Steamship case and has since become more and more prominent.

The Interstate Commerce Law imposes several important restrictions upon the right of railway companies to do as they please in the matter of making and altering rates, and Congress has thereby expressed its conviction that unrestrained competition between carriers is not, at the present time, and under existing conditions, most conducive to the public welfare, but that other things are quite as essential to the public good.

(According to the published reports of the Interstate Commerce Commission) it was the purpose of Congress to place important restraints upon competition; (the Commission held) that uncontrolled struggles for patronage by railway carriers are frequently detrimental to the public welfare, that rate wars are especially injurious to the business interests of the country and contrary to the spirit of existing laws, that the Interstate Commerce Act invites conferences between railway managers, and that concert of action in certain matters by railway companies is absolutely essential to enable it to accomplish its true purpose. [46]

This argument is made even broader in District Judge Riner's decision:

It cannot be said that the public is benefited by competition when that competition is carried beyond the bounds of reasonable prosperity to the parties engaged in it. [47]

Thus the issue was clearly established between business practice, on the one hand, attempting to control ruinous competition and sustained by the common law so long as the restraints which inevitably resulted were "reasonable"; and, on the other hand, the curbing of business combinations by a restraining act, interpreted by the court to be absolute in its intent and applying to all combinations whether in reasonable restraint of trade or not. How this issue had come to a head is indicated by an

[44] 116 U. S. 290, 357.
[45] 58 Fed. 58.
[46] *Ibid.*, pp. 74, 75.
[47] 53 Fed. 440, 452. Cited: Christiancy, J., in *Beal v. Chase*, 31 Mich. 521.

observation made by Justice Peckham, that "a company desirous of deviating from the rates agreed upon would face a disastrous rate war," and that "under these circumstances the agreement prevents competition."[48] Business, as has been stated before, had discovered a sanction for its agreements, more powerful even than the provision of a fine.[49] And it was the discovery and use of this sanction which practically negated the old common-law control over such agreements; for the reliance of the common law on the inherent weakness of business combinations to effect their dissolution was no longer adequate. Hence the provision in the Sherman Law that such offenses be positively indictable. When this fact of business development is coupled with the view of men like Justice Peckham, that business power would be abused unless curbed from without, the explanation of the situation as so far developed becomes complete. The only answer to this argument, that business then had or would soon develop a sense of social responsibility commensurate with its economic power, did not appear in either word or deed.

The Holding Company: The Northern Securities Merger

In spite of the fact that railroad cases assumed a greater relative prominence under the administration of the Sherman Act than Congress probably had intended, the court decisions regarding them assumed great importance in regard to industrial combinations because of the general principles involved and stated. Thus, it was the railway-association case, just referred to, which elicited from the court the statement that all combinations in restraint of trade, whether reasonable or not, were in violation of the Sherman Act. So also, as the following case will show, it was a combination of railroads that first presented to the Supreme Court of the United States the problem of the "holding company." Although this case was decided in Roosevelt's Administration, it is dealt with here to complete the discussion of the relation of the Sherman Law to railroad companies.

The Northern Pacific Railway Company, a majority of the stock of which was owned by James J. Hill and J. Pierpont Morgan, and the

[48] 171 U. S. 505, 564.

[49] Provided for in the Trans-Missouri Association; also, *e.g.*, in the California Coal Dealers' Association, 85 Fed. 252, and in the Watch Dealers' Association, 55 Fed. 851. See notes 4 and 6, *supra*.

Great Northern Railway Company, controlled by Mr. Hill through the ownership of one-third of the stock and proxies for much of the remaining stock, owned respectively parallel and competing lines of railroad extending from Duluth, St. Paul, and Minneapolis, across the continent to Puget Sound. In the spring of 1901, they united in purchasing about 98% of the entire capital stock of the Chicago, Burlington and Quincy Railway Company, par value $107,000,000, paying therefor in joint bonds of the two purchasing companies; and became joint sureties for the payment of bonds of the Burlington Company. Since the Burlington system so purchased had a railway extending from Minneapolis and St. Paul to Chicago, and railways covering large portions of the states of Illinois, Iowa, Missouri, and Nebraska, and connecting again with the Northern Pacific at Billings, Montana, the Burlington system, though still managed by its own directors and officers, afforded to the two purchasing railroads the needed mutual extension to transport their trains of lumber from the Pacific Northwest to desirable markets in the Middle West, and to carry return traffic, in coal, iron, steel, cotton and other commodities.

The Union Pacific Railway, largely owned by E. H. Harriman, extended from Omaha to Ogden and, by its connection with the Central or Southern Pacific, to San Francisco. Much of the freight gathered by the Burlington system and bound for the Pacific Coast passed over the Union Pacific. Hence the purchase of the Burlington by the Great Northern and Northern Pacific led the managers of the Union Pacific Company to fear a diversion of traffic from their lines. Harriman requested Hill and Morgan to permit the Union Pacific to join and share with them in the purchase of the Burlington system, but his application was denied. He then began rapidly and quietly to purchase the stock of the Northern Pacific Company. By May, 1901, he had succeeded in obtaining approximately $37,000,000 of the outstanding $80,000,000 common stock and $41,000,000 of the outstanding $75,000,000 preferred stock of the Northern Pacific. J. P. Morgan and Company thereupon purchased $15,000,000 of the common stock of the Northern Pacific, which, with their previous holdings and those of Hill and other associates, gave this group the control of more than $41,000,000, or more than a majority, of the common stock.

The preferred stock had the same voting power as the common, but the company, by the action of its directors, was empowered to retire and pay off at par any or all preferred stock on the first day of January, of any year beginning with 1902. As it was known that the board of directors of the Northern Pacific, dominated by Morgan and Hill, would insist upon the payment and retirement of the preferred stock on January 1, 1902, Harriman and his associates abandoned their attempt to obtain the control of that company.

This attempt of Harriman and the Union Pacific Company to obtain the control of the Northern Pacific, and through it of the Burlington system, so alarmed the managers and stockholders of the Northern Pacific and Great Northern Railroads that they conceived the design of forming a "holding" company which should purchase or secure, in exchange for its own stock, a majority of the stock of the two systems. To this end the stockholders, on November 13, 1901, formed a corporation under the laws of the state of New Jersey with capital stock valued at $400,000,000 par, which corporation was to buy at least the greater part of the stock of the Northern Pacific and Great Northern Companies. The Northern Pacific stock was purchased at $115 per share, the Great Northern at $180, both being paid for with Northern Securities stock at par value.   The final result of this transaction was that the Securities Company became the owner of 96% of the stock of the Northern Pacific, and through this, of the Burlington, and also of 76% of the Great Northern stock.   Mr. Harriman received something more than $82,000,-000 of stock in the Northern Securities Company and about $8,000,000 in cash for his holdings.

The Northern Securities Company was prosecuted by Attorney General Knox, and a decree of dissolution entered by the Circuit Court for the United States,[50] in spite of the admission of the court that such a "consolidation of parallel and competing lines of railroad, taking a broad view of the situation, is beneficial to the public rather than harmful," that "it may be that the motives which inspired the combination were wholly laudable and unselfish," and that the combination, "if carried out as it was conceived, would prove to be of inestimable value to the communities which these roads serve and to the country at large."[51]   The case was appealed to the Supreme Court, where the decision of the lower court was affirmed by a vote of five judges to four.   Justice Harlan delivered the opinion of the Court, Justices Brown, McKenna, Day and Brewer concurring. He reiterated the statement made in the lower court, and repeated his dissenting opinion in the Sugar Trust case, that all contracts in restraint of trade, whether reasonable or not, were forbidden by the Sherman Act, and that railroad carriers engaged in interstate or international trade were embraced by the act.[52]

In his dissenting opinion, in which Chief Justice Fuller and Justices Peckham and Holmes concurred, Justice White held that

[50] *U. S. v. Northern Securities Co.*, 120 Fed. 721 (1903).

[51] *Ibid.*, p. 730.

[52] *Northern Securities Company v. U. S.*, 193 U S. 197, 330 (1904).

the power of Congress to regulate commerce did not include the power to regulate the ownership of stock in railroads,[53] a power which, he held, was reserved to the states. Justice Harlan had pointed out how anomalous the system of state incorporations had become: in the present case a corporation formed in New Jersey would control two railroads, one incorporated in Wisconsin, the other in Minnesota, and both owning and operating property remote from New Jersey and extending to the Pacific Coast. This view, however, in spite of his general agreement with the minority, Justice White held would result in a situation whereby Congress could abrogate every railroad charter granted by the states, a situation which would be equally anomalous. Business had outgrown state boundaries, true enough, but it was, in its defense offered to the court, attempting to restrict regulatory powers to these outgrown political units.

Without holding a brief for or against the Sherman Law, it is apparent to anyone that, if it was to effect its purposes, a "holding" company could not be allowed to hide behind its "veil of corporate entity." For, however Englishmen have succeeded in maintaining the autonomy of management in the subsidiary plants of their joint-stock companies, no such divorce of management from stock ownership has prevailed in America. If, on the other hand, the holding company and ownership of stock were held to be beyond the jurisdiction of the Sherman Law, then the latter is shorn of its power and becomes a mere symptom of business conditions, a gesture without effect. Such, it is the contention of this and the preceding chapter, it had been from the very start.

To return to the Northern Securities case, the issue was succinctly stated by Justice Holmes:

> The question to be decided is whether under the Act of 1890, it is unlawful at any stage of the process, if several men unite to form a corporation for the purpose of buying more than half of the stock of each of two competing interstate railroad companies, if they form a corporation and the corporation buys the stock.[54]

Relying largely on the decision in the Sugar Trust case, Justice Holmes dissented from the majority opinion of the court which held that the purchase was illegal. In this dissenting view he was supported by Justice White:

[53] *Ibid.*, p. 368. So *In re Greene, cit. supra,* note 15.
[54] 193 U. S. 197, 401.

The only premise by which the power of Congress can be extended to the subject matter of the right of the Securities Company to own the stock must be the proposition that such ownership is within the legislative power of Congress, and if that proposition be admitted it is not perceived by what process of reasoning the power of Congress over the subject matter of ownership is to be limited to ownership by particular classes of corporations or persons. If the power embraces ownership, then the authority of Congress over all ownership which in its judgment may affect interstate commerce necessarily exists . . . If the control of the ownership of stock in competing roads by one and the same corporation is within the power of Congress, and creates a restraint of trade or monopoly forbidden by Congress, it is not conceivable to me how exactly similar ownership by one or more individuals would not create the same restraint or monopoly, and be equally within the prohibition which it is decided Congress has imposed . . . It would in effect hold that, although a particular act was a burden upon interstate commerce or a monopoly thereof, individuals could lawfully do the act, provided only they did not use the instrumentality of a corporation . . . [55]

It may not be doubted that from the foundation of the government, at all events to the time of the adoption of the Anti-trust Act of 1890, there was an entire absence of any legislation by Congress even suggesting that it was deemed by anyone that power was possessed by Congress to control the ownership of stock in railroad or other corporations, because such corporations engaged in interstate commerce. On the contrary, when Congress came to exert its authority to regulate interstate commerce as carried on by railroads, manifested by the adoption of the Interstate Commerce Act, it sedulously confined the provisions of that act to the carrying on of interstate commerce itself, including the reasonableness of the rates to be charged for carrying on such commerce and other matters undeniably concerning the fact of interstate commerce . . . No assertion of power in Congress under the Act of 1890 to control the ownership of stock was ever knowingly made until first asserted in this cause.[56]

This is an especially obvious bit of legal sophistry. Of course no such legislation or judicial interpretation had occurred before because there was no occasion for it: corporations of great size and particularly holding companies were innovations and required new forms of social control if there was to be *any* social control. The question was, *what* form of control was to be exercised. Self-control they were not themselves exhibiting to any marked extent, therefore the inevitable legislation followed. The courts had the opportunity of applying this new legislation to the current situation. Too close an adherence to precedent would have practically vetoed the law, too free an interpretation

[55] *Ibid.*, p. 371. This same point was made in the Mogul Steamship case by Justice Bowen. *Cf. supra*, p. 70.

[56] *Ibid.*, pp. 374–376.

would have meant judicial legislation, and too strict an interpretation of the wording of the statute would have encouraged additional legislation. But to balk at the simple fact that stock ownership involved a control of management seems like mere chicanery. And yet basically this functional view is socially preferable to the absolute view of the majority of the court. There does seem to be an anomaly in denying to a corporation what a natural person would be allowed to do; but practically no natural person could achieve the control effected through a pyramiding of holding companies, especially when coupled with the American practice of exercising control over management; and even if he could, serious consideration could then be given to the social desirability of preventing it. As Justice Holmes pointed out, that very provision constituted section 2 of the Sherman Act.[57] Justice Brewer, who concurred with the majority of the court, but held with Justice White that the purchase of the stock of a competing corporation was not in itself illegal, stated that:

A corporation, while by fiction of law recognized for some purposes as a person and for purposes of jurisdiction as a citizen, is not endowed with the inalienable rights of a natural person.[58]

But Justice Holmes' point, in which he agreed with Justice White, was that the Sherman Law did not apply to stock ownership as distinguished from management:

I accept (the Joint Traffic and Trans-Missouri) decisions absolutely, . . . but the provision (of the Sherman Act) has not been decided and, it seems to me, could not be decided without perversion of plain language, to apply to an arrangement by which competition is ended through community of interest—an arrangement which leaves the parties without external restriction. That provision, taken alone, does not require that all existing competitions shall be maintained. It does not look primarily, if at all, to competition. It simply requires that a party's freedom in trade between the states shall not be cut down by contract with a stranger. So far as that phrase goes, it is lawful to abolish competition by any form of union . . . It is impossible to say that the phrase "every contract in restraint of trade" forbids one man or corporation to purchase as much stock as he likes in both . . . Every railroad monopolizes, in a popular sense, the trade of some area. Yet I suppose no one would say that the statute forbids a combination of men into a corporation to build and run such a railroad between the states.[59]

[57] *Ibid.*, p. 404.
[58] *Ibid.*, p. 362.
[59] *Ibid.*, pp. 405–407. This view he repeated in the Shoe Machinery case, *infra*, p. 156.

The issue again narrowed itself down to the distinction between the *ownership* of stock and the *existence* of a corporation, more *capable* because of its size of restraining or controlling trade, on the one hand; and, on the other, the actual commission of an *act* of restraint by the *controlled* management of a company. On this ground, reason seems to be with the functional views of Justices Holmes and White, as opposed to the metaphysical view defending competition as such.

There is no attempt (in this merger) to monopolize . . . and there is no combination in restraint of trade, until something is done with the intent to exclude strangers to the combination from competing with it in some part of the business which it carries on . . . To suppress competition in connection with a contract with a stranger is one thing, to suppress it by fusion is another.[60]

Whether the Sherman Law as a matter of public policy should apply to stock ownership, rests in the last analysis upon two questions: Do the owners control the management of the company? And if, as the pragmatic character of American business seems to indicate, they do, are their acts socially justifiable?

The State of Minnesota also prosecuted the Northern Securities Company in the Federal courts. This case arose partly under the Minnesota Anti-trust Act of 1889, which was almost identical with the Sherman Act. The court agreed that the Act applied to railroads, but adopted the *functional* view by asserting that contracts which did not directly and necessarily affect transportation, or rates therefor, were not in restraint of trade, or within the statute, even though they might remotely and indirectly appear to have had some *probable* effect in that direction.[61] Relying largely on the argument in the Sugar Trust decision, the Court held that the ownership of stock of the two competing railroads by the Northern Securities Company did not violate either the Minnesota or the Federal anti-trust acts.

The Northern Securities Company is merely an investor in and owner of a majority of the stock of each of the two railroad companies. It is not a railroad company, and has no franchise or power to manage or operate or direct the management or operation of either railroad in respect to rates or charges for transportation, or otherwise; and there is no scintilla of evidence that it has sought to control or interfere in respect to any of these matters . . . No director of the Great Northern Company can be a director of the

---

[60] *Ibid.*, p. 409.
[61] *Minnesota v. Northern Securities Company*. 123 Fed. 692, 701 (1903).

Northern Pacific Company. The directors of each railroad company will appoint its managing and other officers, and control its business and policy.[62]

The case would not be different if one natural person with abundant capital should invest in the majority of the stocks of one of these companies, and another like person should invest in the majority of the stocks of the other company. The interest of the two, if they chose to act in harmony, would be the same as the interest of one person owning the whole.[63]

The crux of the situation, the court held—and thereby agreed with Justices Holmes' and White's view—was the effect on railway rates, and this matter was under the control of state regulations. Rates had to be fair, reasonable, stable, and uniform, otherwise they were subject to action by state officials; and their publication, with no changes before ten days' notice, gave shippers accurate and sufficient information to safeguard their interests. Furthermore, untrammeled competition between rival railroads, resulting in rate wars, sporadic struggles for particular contracts or consignments, as well as all rebates, open or secret, were eliminated by prohibitions carrying heavy penalties. The *formation* of the Northern Securities Company did not presume violation of the law. When or if the latter should specifically occur in *acts*, then the railroad corporations would be amenable to prosecution and appropriate legal or equitable proceedings.[64] This functional view was opposed, however, by the prevailing metaphysical view of the Supreme Court of the United States.

When this case was appealed to the Supreme Court of the United States, it denied that the Federal courts had any jurisdiction in the matter.[65] It was unfortunate that such an excellent judicial decision had thus to be disposed of. The fact that railway companies are quasi-public corporations, subject to rate regulations, should have eliminated them from the provisions of the Sherman Law. Including railroads within the Sherman Act grossly interfered with the major regulatory powers of the Interstate Commerce Commission.

The proof of the pudding is in the eating thereof. The Supreme Court, in the case which it did review, decided that the Northern Securities Company was an illegal combination and ordered it to be dissolved. The company thereupon allocated to each stockholder an amount of stock in each of the constituent

[62] *Ibid.*, p. 701.
[63] *Ibid.*, p. 705.
[64] *Ibid.*, p. 707.
[65] *Minnesota v. Northern Securities Company*, 194 U. S. 48 (1904).

companies in proportion to the shares which such stockholder held in the Northern Securities Company.

Thus, Harriman, who held 820,000 shares of the Northern Securities Company, out of a total of 4,000,000 shares, and who had received an additional $8,000,000 in cash when he exchanged his Northern Pacific holdings for these shares, received $32,000,-000 in Northern Pacific and $24,500,000 in Great Northern stock. He protested that the Great Northern stock was not the equivalent of the Northern Pacific stock which he had transferred to the Northern Securities Company, which he claimed merely held the railroad stocks in trust. This conformed to J. P. Morgan's testimony that the holding company was merely a custodian of the stock and did not own it.[66]   Harriman carried his case to the courts, and obtained a preliminary injunction in the Circuit Court, District of New Jersey.[67]   The judge was doubtful of the solution temporarily allowed, however, and permitted an appeal. The Circuit Court of Appeals, Third District, reversed the temporary decree;[68] and this latter decision was upheld by the United States Supreme Court.[69] The court held that the transaction between Harriman and the Securities Company was one of purchase and sale, and not of bailment or trust, and that the adjudication of a previous case[70] disentitled Harriman to the restitution of his original stock. Chief Justice Fuller held that the Securities Company had only two alternatives, distribution in cash or in kind, and that the former was probably inadvisable because the necessity of selling the stock in the open market would too much affect its value adversely.

Thus arose the application of the phrase, "the impossibility of unscrambling eggs," to the attempt to establish the *status quo ante* of corporations which had become members of holding companies which they were ordered by the court to dissolve. Justice White noted the ineffectiveness of such a "dissolution":

The decree, whilst forbidding the use of the stock, by the Northern Securities Company, authorizes its return to the alleged conspirators, and does not restrain them from exercising the control resulting from the owner-

---

[66] *U. S. v. Northern Securities Company*, 193 U. S. 197, 354.
[67] *Harriman et al. v. Northern Securities Company et al.*, 132 Fed. 464 (1904).
[68] *Northern Securities Company v. Harriman et al.*, 134 Fed. 331 (1905).
[69] *Harriman v. Northern Securities Company*, 197 U. S. 244 (1905).
[70] 193 U. S. 197.

ship. If the conspiracy and combination existed and was illegal, my mind fails to perceive why it should be left to produce its full force and effect in the hands of the individuals by whom it was charged the conspiracy was entered into.[71]

Justice White's remarks were in the form of an *argumentum ad absurdum*. As such, they fail to take account of the alternative of the restitution of the original stock. The method of dissolution employed by the court was later repeated—conspicuously in the Standard Oil case. Of the two major objections to it, the one, that holding companies would be formed to entice and later mulct the minority stockholders of a strong corporation by combining it with a number of weak companies, is met by the basic principle of *caveat emptor* and the rights of such stockholders in courts of equity. The other objection, that such a dissolution does not dissolve, has interestingly recurred recently: the Rockefeller-Stewart controversy can be basically explained in part by the real rivalry which seems since to have developed between the managements of the former New Jersey and Indiana subsidiaries of the Standard Oil Company. On the other hand, the contemplated merger of the New York and Vacuum subsidiaries seems to show the persistence of a common interest.

Résumé of Cases Prior to Roosevelt's Administration

Of the 18 cases which were brought and prosecuted by the United States for alleged violation of the Sherman Law prior to President Roosevelt's administration, ten were successful and eight were not. Of the successful ten cases, four concerned labor unions, and two, the railroad associations already discussed. Three combinations of coal dealers were restrained. The remaining case was that of the Addyston Pipe and Steel Company. The practical effect of this latter case upon business was quite limited, inasmuch as industrial corporations were subsequently guided by their lawyers into other and more effective, and yet legally immune, methods of suppressing or eliminating competition. But Justice Taft's masterly decision in this case definitely marked a radical change in the judicial interpretation of the Sherman Act, a change which will be especially noted in the following chapter. During the first 11 or 12 years of its existence, therefore, the Sherman Law was not effectively employed to suppress any of the combinations at which it was

[71] 193 U. S. 197, 373.

primarily aimed.   How much of this may be attributed to the
disinclination of the various Attorneys General to prosecute
business organizations, or to their inefficiency, especially in
making their pleas, is a matter that must be left to judgment
and inference.

At the time of President McKinley's death, practically no
suits were pending against existing business combinations, not-
withstanding the fact that it was during this administration
that hundreds of "holding" companies were organized as state
corporations, their purpose being to associate competing corporations under the control of a few men.   These holding companies,
of which the earliest and best examples were the Standard Oil
Company and the United States Steel Corporation, supplanted
the previously existing "trusts," all of which had been dissolved
by the end of the Nineteenth Century.   Not one of these trusts
or holding companies had been successfully prosecuted prior to
Roosevelt's administration.   Hence, the evidence as to the judicial status of the Act at the beginning of Roosevelt's administration is confined practically to such decisions as have already been
discussed in this chapter.

In addition to these 18 prosecutions there were, prior to
Roosevelt's administration, 18 suits by private parties for alleged
violations of the Sherman Law by other private parties, and four
cases in which individual litigants based their defense on the
ground that the Sherman Law disentitled the plaintiffs to
recover judgments therein.   These four cases were perhaps the
only cases, of the total of 40 in all, that would have arisen under
the common law; three of these defenses were upheld by the
courts; the situation arising in the remaining case will be dealt
with in subsequent pages.   Of the 18 suits brought by private
parties under the Sherman Law, only two were successful, one
involving a labor dispute.   Most of the failures are attributed
by Walker[72] to the errors committed by the attorneys who
prosecuted the cases.

The general impression which one has after reviewing this
earlier period in the history of the Sherman Law is that Government and Law presented a sorry spectacle in this attempt to check
or control the development of American Business.   Much of the
situation, of course, was due to the fact that the ablest lawyers
were employed by business corporations to defend them against

[72] *Op. cit.*, note 1, this chapter.

prosecutions or to avoid litigations, while many of the lawyers who were engaged in prosecuting cases under the Sherman Law were characterized by muddle-headedness and inefficiency. The law, in short, either proved to be incapable of handling the situation or prostituted itself by aiding business to dodge the consequences of the Act. Regardless of the justification of business itself in this situation, the law clearly became at this time a subordinate factor in the pattern of American social forces and values. The only qualification of this severe statement lies in the fact that during this period the law was chiefly successful in performing one of its major functions, the protection of the individual against social aggression. But in playing this rôle, it became largely a negative factor; the positive impulse toward this assertion of individualism came from business itself.

When we examine the course of business conduct itself during this period, especially from the standpoint of social values, the greed and cupidity that propelled its individualistic activities go far to lessen any claim that business might make to its championing of a social ideal, namely, individualism. But the history of morals may be said to consist largely of the problems presented by the continual warfare which the individual makes against social inertia and coercion, and moral ideals frequently arise from the effective assertion of individual rights and values against what after all prove to be unjustifiable social hindrances. Especially is this true where social interests have developed a "cake of custom" that needs breaking in order that a proper balance of values may be achieved. The attitude of the courts, where they did permit the Sherman Law to curb business development, is a case in point: the metaphysical view that size and existence and even "potentiality" warranted legal restraint, now appears to have been imaginatively barren and socially undesirable. The persistence of the courts in this view over a period of 20 or 30 years subsequent to the enactment of the Sherman Law definitely enabled business finally to topple the legal-political structure from its central position in the hierarchy of American social values.

Several factors, however, prevented the immediate consummation of that social reorientation. Chief among these was the hesitancy among business men themselves in adopting socially justifiable values and in assuming enough self-regulatory functions to control them. Another important factor which per-

petuated a large measure of political-legal control over business
was the enactment of legislation which functionally supplemented
the Sherman Law, such as the Federal Trade Commission Act
and the Clayton Act, or which made desirable exceptions, such
as the Webb-Pomerene Export Act and the Marketing Act of
1929.   A third factor was the anticipation of the functional
character of these legislative acts by the Federal courts themselves.   The insertion of the "rule of reason" and the shifting
of the attention of the court away from the *existence* and *capacities* of business corporations to their *behavior* and *specific acts*,
represents a point of view which more and more characterizes
the dynamic, functional and real social values of business.   Before
dealing directly with the development of self-government and
ethics in business, therefore, it is necessary to examine the judicial
symptoms of the social point of view which underlies the phenomenon of Business Ethics.

CHAPTER V

THE LATER, FUNCTIONAL, INTERPRETATION OF THE SHERMAN LAW

Once having accepted the Sherman Act as the initial phenomenon in American Business Ethics, the early history of the judicial interpretation of this law, including the first 10 to 15 years of its existence, can be set off as an interesting phenomenon in the struggle between administrative law and business for supremacy in the American social order. The record of this struggle, from the point of view of law itself and evidenced by the court records dealt with in the preceding chapter, shows clearly how futile the legal-metaphysical doctrine was. What is not shown by the records is the tremendous amount of business activity, large-scale and small, that succeeded, during this period, in avoiding judicial cognizance altogether; a welter of activity that was only partially indicated later by the zealous governmental activities characterizing Roosevelt's administration. It was during this later period of the history of the Sherman Law that the courts began to take the functional rather than an absolute view toward business activities and to insist on confining the prohibitory incidence of the law to such specific modes of behavior as constituted unreasonable restraint of trade.

The Changing Attitude of the Courts

In discussing the problem of trusts and combinations,[1] Watkins quotes with approval the statement of the Supreme Court of Ohio, that "It was the danger to the public interest from the existence of the power, not the evils from its abuse, which constituted the reason for the rule"[2] against monopolies. Watkins goes on to say:

[1] Watkins, Myron W., "The Change in Trust Policy," XXXV *Harvard Law Review* 7 and 8, May and June, 1922.

[2] *State v. Standard Oil Company*, 49 Ohio 137, 186 (1892).

The public interests will be far better safeguarded in these cases (of subterfuge to effect the purpose) by holding the tendency of such arrangements generally to prey upon public well-being a sufficient ground for condemning them. These considerations seem to have been appreciated by judges in early cases, and were wisely made the basis of a majority of their cases.[3]

Such views very clearly typify the earlier attitude of the Law toward large business corporations. Whether this attitude was justified by the actual menace of business combinations or was merely a metaphysical reaction to a situation which might better have been dealt with functionally, is a matter of judgment. At least the judicial attitude is clear.

It can be made equally clear that the judicial attitude changed completely during the first decade of this century—the second decade in the life of the Sherman Law. Watkins, while recognizing that there was then no legal basis for distinguishing between "good" and "bad" trusts, attributes much of the admitted change in judicial attitude to the changed policies of corporations, conspicuously represented by the International Harvester Company and the United States Steel Corporation. Here again, however, whatever the *cause*, the *fact* seems to be that the courts were becoming more discriminative in discovering the kinds of business behavior which were to be regarded as condemned by the Sherman Law. This may in part be due to the fact that the courts were beginning now to view the Sherman Law as its authors intended: as an enactment which incorporated the common law into the fabric of the Federal legal system. This change in the *quality* of judicial decisions is to be distinguished from the further characteristic of the administration of the Sherman Law during the first decade of the present century: the *quantitative* increase in the number of prosecutions. Much of this latter change can be attributed to the fact that the courts were beginning to sense the public attitude which was being stimulated by Roosevelt's vigorous anti-trust activities.

[3] *Op. cit.*, p. 828. In a recent publication, *Mergers and the Law*, edited by Watkins, the statement is made (p. 25), in reference to a series of anti-trust decisions, that "there was nothing in these cases to negative the current assumption that a reasonable, prudential sort of restraint of trade might be lawfully effected by corporate combination." This statement is too broad; the functional view to which it refers did not appear in the earlier cases and, as this chapter will show, developed only by a slow process of some 15 or 20 years.

"Restraint of trade" as forbidden by the Sherman Act undoubtedly had a broader meaning than it then had in the common law.[4] The opposition of the Sherman Law to any restriction of such competition as was indulged in by those who aimed to control the market, while anticipated by many state decisions in the United States, was not apparent in the common-law rules in England after the Eighteenth Century, for contracts in restraint of trade have been allowable under certain circumstances, especially if they were "reasonable." Although the doctrine of "reasonableness" appeared sporadically in American courts, in the majority of American jurisdictions the conditions or consequences of "restraint of trade" were not regarded as mitigating or crucial circumstances. The reason for this is probably to be found not so much in the tradition and logic of the law as in the prevailing American social attitudes on closely related subjects. Thus, the general American attitude toward "monopoly" was largely derived from the hostility of seventeenth-century England to the royal prerogative to grant exclusive privileges, an attitude that culminated in the Puritan Revolution. England herself outgrew this attitude in less than a century; we in our isolation and slower economic development persisted in it. Later, this same American attitude of hostility, directed toward the end accomplished, was intensified by the reaction to the methods employed, which generally amounted to a "conspiracy." This attitude of hostility persisted in the United States up to the close of the Nineteenth Century, the changes in the English method of dealing with the situation having little effect on us after the American Revolution. Thus the repeal of certain English statutes[5] led to the necessity, on the part of the English courts in 1800, of finding a remedy in the old common-law rules against "engrossing," a remedy which was not available to the American Federal courts. The whole course of this part of common-law history in America was as completely independent of English developments as was the Government of the United States. Thus, America was practically

---

[4] Watkins: *op. cit.*, note 1, *supra.*

[5] Conspicuously that of 5 and 6 Edw. VI, c. 14, by 12 Geo. III, c. 71, in 1771. This point has already been discussed in Chapter III in connection with the Mogul Steamship Case. Watkins' analysis of "anti-trust policies" into those directed against "restraint of trade," "monopoly," and "unfair competition" clears up many points which cannot be dealt with here.

unaffected by the development of Manchester liberalism, especially in regard to labor legislation; and, although we behaved in the same basic spirit of *laissez faire* which led to the ruling doctrine of Manchester, our common-law development was untouched by such an event as 7 and 8 Vic., c. 24, whereby, in 1844, prosecutions of labor unions for what had previously constituted certain common-law offenses were prohibited.

Still another social-legal factor in America was the doctrine of "free competition." Although this doctrine undoubtedly had for its purpose the welfare of the individual trader, it had relatively a more negative meaning than did the term *laissez faire* and it came eventually to refer to *competition as such* regardless of its instrumental value to the welfare of the trade, the individual competitor, or even of the consumer through its probable lowering of prices. It was this turn given to the social attitude by legal metaphysics that made the doctrine of "free competition" compatible with the legislative regulation and administrative supervision of freedom of competition, a situation which on its face appears to be a contradiction in terms. In addition to this doctrine there developed the doctrine of "unfair competition," an elaboration of the law of fraud. That this negative interpretation of "free competition" was inadequate, from the point of view of business health, is evidenced by the fact that trade piracy was controlled largely through the protection accorded trade-marks and trade names, the control of disparagements was confined largely to the application of the law of libel, while there was no bar to such practices as espionage, price discrimination, exclusive sales contracts, or cutthroat methods of competition.

The refusal of Justice Peckham in the Trans-Missouri traffic case to seek a definition for the terms of the Sherman Law in the common-law rules effectively determined the earlier, metaphysically absolute, interpretation of the Anti-trust Act. The narrowing effect of the previous decision in the Sugar Trust case had made the Act largely innocuous. But Justice Harlan's dissenting opinion in the latter case eventually prevailed, thus extending the jurisdiction of the Act sufficiently to bring it in contact with the major part of business activity. And the opinion of Justice Taft in the Addyston case led the way to incorporating the common-law rules into the judicial interpretation of the Act.

The Addyston Case

Although the direct effects of the decision in the Addyston case were limited, nevertheless this case heralded a distinct change in the point of view of the courts and in the material considerations contained in the decisions. True, "reasonable" as well as "unreasonable" restraints of trade were still regarded as violating the Sherman Law, but the common-law principles now began to be woven into the fabric of interpretation of the Act. The masterly decision of Justice Taft, then of the Circuit Court of Appeals, Sixth Circuit, particularly illustrates this. Furthermore, this case, and those which were prosecuted in Roosevelt's administration, concerned themselves, not so much with the business structures themselves, or with the *existence* of corporations capable of menacing trade; but rather with the particular *functions* which involved unfair trade practices. It is as if the governmental attitude were now determined more by the Aristotelian, rather than, as formerly, by the Platonic point of view. This stressing of functions rather than of structure anticipated the later enactment of the Federal Trade Commission and Clayton Acts.

We shall now examine the cases which were prosecuted during the Roosevelt and Taft administrations, beginning, however, with the Addyston case which was decided during McKinley's administration.

Six corporations, the only manufacturers of cast-iron pipe in a large territory, formed the Associated Pipe Works, the executive committee of which was composed of one representative of each component corporation. These corporations agreed not to compete among each other: a bonus was to be charged upon all work done and pipe furnished within the territory in which these companies operated; this bonus, $3 to $9 per ton, was added to the real market price of the pipe sold and to that extent increased the price to the purchasing public. When bids were advertised for by any municipal corporation, water company, or gas company, the executive committee determined the price at which the bid was to be put in by some company in the association; the question as to which company was to receive the contract was settled by the highest bonus which any one of the companies, as among themselves, would agree to pay or bid for the order. When the amount was thus settled, the successful company sent its estimate or bid to the city or company desiring pipe, the bids of all other companies being made slightly higher. Settlements were made by distributing the bonus among the pipe companies, largely by offsets at regular intervals.

The aggregate annual output of the six companies was 220,000 tons; the daily capacity, 650 tons. There were nine other companies within the designated territory, with a daily capacity of 835 tons. Ten other companies outside this territory had a daily output of 1,550 tons. All corporations doing business with the six companies forming the Associated Pipe Works declared by affidavit that prices were reasonable, although prices were higher than prior to the formation of the association, when reckless and ruinous competition prevailed. The uniform phraseology of these testimonies, however, aroused the suspicion of the court as to their independent and voluntary character.

The Circuit Court for the Eastern District of Tennessee, Southern Division, held that the Sherman Act was inapplicable, and dismissed the case.[6] This decree, however, was reversed by the Circuit Court of Appeals, Sixth Circuit,[7] this judgment being affirmed by the Supreme Court of the United States.[8] This latter decision was governed largely by political considerations, involving the relations of the states to the Federal Government. The court held, however, that the facts set forth showed conclusively that the effect of the combination was to enhance prices beyond a sum which was reasonable, and that the agreement or combination, in contrast with that considered in the Knight case, did interfere with the flow of interstate commerce.[9] In the main, however, the court virtually sustained Judge Taft's decision in the lower court.

Justice Taft's argument follows:

If the contract of association which bound the defendants was void and unenforceable at the common law because in restraint of trade, it is within the inhibition of the statute if the trade it restrained was interstate.

Contracts in unreasonable restraint of trade at common law were not unlawful in the sense of being criminal, or giving rise to a civil action for damages in favor of one prejudicially affected thereby, but were simply void, and were not enforced by the courts . . . The effect of the act of 1890 is to render such contracts unlawful in an affirmative or positive sense, and punishable as a misdemeanor, and to create a right of civil action for damages in favor of those injured thereby and a civil remedy by injunction in favor of both private persons and the public against the execution of such contracts and the maintenance of such trade restraints.[10]

[6] U. S. v. Addyston Pipe and Steel Company et al., 78 Fed. 712, 723 (1897).
[7] Ibid., 85 Fed. 271 (1898).
[8] Addyston Pipe and Steel Company v. U. S., 175 U. S. 221 (1899).
[9] Ibid., p. 238.
[10] 85 Fed. 271, 278, 279.

In recent years, even the fact that the contract is one for the sale of property or of business and good-will, or for the making of a partnership or a corporation, has not saved it from invalidity if it could be shown that it was only part of a plan to acquire all the property used in a business by one management with a view to establishing a monopoly. Such cases go a step further than those (in which restraints are usually enforceable if commensurate only with the reasonable protection of the covenantee in respect to the main transactions affected by the contract). In them the actual intent to monopolize must appear.[11]

Upon this review of the law and the authorities, we can have no doubt that the association of the defendants, however reasonable the prices they fixed, however great the competition they had to encounter, and however great the necessity for curbing themselves by joint agreement from committing financial suicide by ill-advised competition, was void at common law, because in restraint of trade, and tending to a monopoly.[12]

(The cases referred to in the Knight case do not control—*Coe v. Errol*, 116 U. S. 517, and *Kidd v. Pearson*, 128 U. S. 1.) The subject of the restraint here (in the Addyston case) is not articles of merchandise or their manufacture, but contracts for sale of such articles to be delivered across state lines, and the negotiations and bids preliminary to the making of such contracts, all of which do not merely affect interstate commerce, but are interstate commerce . . . The error into which the circuit court (below) fell, it seems to us, was in not observing the difference between the regulating power of Congress over contracts and negotiations for sales of goods to be delivered over state lines, and that over the merchandise, the subject of such sales and negotiations. The goods are not within the control of Congress until they are in actual transit from one state to another. But the negotiations and making of sales which necessarily involve in their execution the delivery of merchandise across state lines are interstate commerce, and so within the regulating power of Congress even before the transit of the goods in performance of the contract has begun.[13]

The presumption created by this decision enabled the city of Atlanta, Georgia, to recover from the Chattanooga Foundry and Pipeworks and others, the difference between the enhanced price of pipe, due to the combination, and the market price.[14] It is interesting to note that this was one of the two successful cases, of a total of 11 litigations during McKinley's administration, by which private parties attempted to invoke the Sherman Law as a means for remedying the wrong suffered through a violation of the Act; several of these cases being dismissed because

[11] *Ibid.*, p. 290.

[12] *Ibid.*, p. 291.

[13] *Ibid.*, p. 298.

[14] *City of Atlanta v. Chattanooga Foundry and Pipeworks et al.*, 127 Fed. 23 (1903). Affirmed, 203 U. S. 390 (1906). See also *Manion & Co. v. Chattanooga Foundry and Pipeworks et al.*

2 cases

they were improperly brought in equity. In two cases, the defendants succeeded in relying on the common-law principle to absolve them from their contractual obligations. In one of these, a combination of woodenware manufacturers agreed to restrict production, and by contract agreed to guarantee a certain sum to the owner in consideration of his closing his factory for a year. When the owner sued for the amount, $9,000, he was refused recovery by the court, which relied directly on the common-law rule that the contract was void.[15]

The Packers' Cases

During the course of the Senate debates on the Sherman Act, specific mention was made of the unfair practices of the large meat-packing houses, directed against stock-raisers. And yet the earliest case of any significance prosecuted against those engaging in this industry was first decided in a circuit court in 1897,[16] and then finally failed of its purposes. Hopkins and others were members of the Kansas City Live-stock Exchange, a voluntary unincorporated association of commission merchants, having a fixed minimum rate of commission and other restrictions intended to protect the members against the excesses of competition. Persons attempting to do business without joining the exchange were systematically blacklisted and boycotted. The Circuit Court of the District of Kansas, First Division, held that the association was an illegal combination to restrict, monopolize, and control that class of trade and commerce.

The crying complaint of today, and the great menace to the welfare of the people, is the tendency of wealth to monopolize and control, by trusts and combinations, the products and industries of the country; and it must be confessed by every thoughtful observer that many of the so-called stock and produce exchanges are among the most potent instruments for the accomplishment of these purposes by speculators and adventurers.[17]

This view of the court was unquestionably in harmony with the purpose of many senators who supported the Sherman Act. The Circuit Court of Appeals, Eighth Circuit, on appeal,[18]

[15] *Cravens v. Carter-Crume Co.*, 92 Fed. 479 (1899).
[16] *U. S. v. Hopkins et al.*, 82 Fed. 529.
[17] *Ibid.*, p. 536.
[18] *Hopkins et al. v. U. S.*, 84 Fed. 1018.

allowed the cause to be removed to the Supreme Court on writ of *certiorari*, where, however, the decree of the lower court was reversed and the bill dismissed, on the ground that the business and occupation of the several members of the association were not interstate commerce.[19] The court held that "where the live stock came from or where it may ultimately go after a sale or purchase, and procured through the services of one of the defendants at the Kansas City stockyards, is not the substantial factor in the case. The character of the business of defendants must, in this case, be determined by the facts occurring at that city."[20]

In a similar case,[21] decided the same day, the Supreme Court found for the appellant, Anderson. In the Hopkins case, the defendants were commission merchants who sold cattle upon commission; Anderson, however, was a purchaser of cattle in the market, but the cattle, of the class known as "stockers and feeders," were not intended for any other than the local market. Although the court held that the acts complained of were not interstate commerce, it held that even granting that they were, the purpose of the association was the better conduct of the business. Any possible violation of the Sherman Act was only incidental, and the court refused to agree that the evidence showed that violations of the law followed from the adoption and enforcement of the rules of the association.

While these cases were being tried, the Spanish-American War was being waged. Subsequent disclosures, dramatically intensified by Upton Sinclair's *The Jungle*, created a great amount of ill will against the meat packers, especially those located at Chicago. Theodore Roosevelt's "trust-busting" activities later included prosecutions of various large corporations, and the packers were made to feel the effects of a vigorous policy of enforcing the Sherman Act. Here, as in the preceding cases, can be seen the change in the attitude of the Government as well as of the courts: size and degree of control are still regarded as pertinent factors, but specific acts that constituted unfair business behavior are being singled out. The functional interpretation of the Sherman Law is becoming apparent.

[19] *Ibid.*, 171 U. S. 578 (1898).
[20] *Ibid.*, p. 588. The similarity to the view in the Knight case is apparent.
[21] *Anderson v. U. S.*, 171 U. S. 604, certified to the Supreme Court by the Circuit Court of Appeals, Eighth Circuit, 82 Fed. 998, decision not reported.

Seven corporations—including Swift and Company—, one copartnership, and 23 other persons, controlling 60% of the trade and commerce in fresh meats in the United States, agreed among themselves to refrain from bidding against each other when making purchases of live stock. They furthermore agreed to "bid up," through their agents, the prices of live stock for a few days at the stockyards, thereby inducing shippers to make large shipments; and then, refraining from bidding on such live stock as arrived at the stockyards, succeeded in purchasing such live stock at relatively low prices. This practice was specifically mentioned in the debates in Congress as necessitating the Sherman Law. This agreement among the packers furthermore extended to the fixing of prices to dealers, by conferences and by controlling and curtailing the output of the respective packing houses. Penalties were provided for violations of these agreements and of such as involved uniform credit arrangements with customers. Rebates were also obtained from railroads, in order to enhance the competitive advantages otherwise obtained.

Suit was brought by the United States in the Circuit Court of the Northern District of Illinois, Northern Division.[22] Judge Grosscup granted a temporary injunction, the purchase, shipments, and transportation of meat animals and sales of meat to principals or through agents being regarded as commercially interdependent and as constituting in this case interstate commerce. "Restraint of trade" was held to be not dependent upon its "reasonableness" or "unreasonableness," nor to be tested by the prices that resulted from the combination. "Indeed, combination that leads directly to lower prices to the consumer may, within the doctrine of (adjudged) cases, even as against the consumer, be restraint of trade;[23] and combination that leads directly to higher prices, may, even as against the producer be restraint of trade." This view is a reversal to the metaphysical object of the Sherman Law, a strange doctrine that can be matched only by that which raised "competition" as such to a fetish:

The statute, thus interpreted, has no concern with prices, but looks solely to competition, and to the giving of competition full play, by making illegal any effort at restriction upon competition. Whatever combination has the direct and necessary effect of restricting competition, is, within the meaning of the Sherman Act as now interpreted, restraint of trade.[24]

[22] *U. S. v. Swift & Co. et al.*, 122 Fed. 529 (1903).
[23] The French law of 1926 is directed, among other things, at any artificial raising or *lowering* of prices.
[24] *Ibid.*, p. 534.

The case was appealed to the Supreme Court of the United States, where the decree of the lower court was modified, but affirmed.[25] The case was distinguished from the Knight case, in that sales of commodities were involved; and from the Hopkins case, in that the agreement involved a closed membership. The modifications of the decree of the lower court were largely in the direction of a functional interpretation of the Sherman Law: informing the packers "as accurately as the case permits, what they are forbidden to do," especially as regards the securing of favorable railroad rates, for the court recognized that "it is obvious that no more powerful instrument of monopoly could be used than an advantage in the cost of transportation." This case, finally decided in 1905, may be said to be the first important case successfully prosecuted through the Supreme Court of the United States against a combination in restraint of trade as originally intended by Congress to be prohibited under the Sherman Act. And it is highly significant that this case should, at least at the hands of the Supreme Court, receive a functional interpretation.

The Standard Oil and American Tobacco Decisions

Following these important "packers' cases" came the decisions of the Standard Oil and American Tobacco cases. Inasmuch as these cases were being tried at approximately the same time and were decided in the Supreme Court of the United States almost simultaneously, the successive decisions in each case depended to some extent on the status of the other case. No attempt will therefore be made to separate the two series of events; the cases will be taken up in the order in which the various court decisions were given.

In March, 1892, the Supreme Court of Ohio entered a decree against the Standard Oil Company and others, adjudging the trust agreement of the Standard Oil Trust to be void, as in restraint of trade and constituting an unlawful monopoly. The Trust thereupon at least gave the semblance of dissolving by transferring the stocks it held in 64 companies to some 10 separate companies, conspicuous among which were the Standard Oil Company of New Jersey, to which were transferred the stocks of 23 companies, and the Standard Oil Company of New York and the Anglo-American Oil Company, to each of which were transferred the stocks of 11 other companies. The Trust, how-

[25] *Swift & Company v. U. S.*, 196 U. S. 375 (1905).

ever, retained its stock ownership of 20 of the principal companies, which
in turn held stock in the 64 transferred companies. Each holder of
the trust stock, a total of 972,500 shares, received his fractional share
in all of the companies formerly constituting the Trust. Seven stockholders held a controlling interest in the 20 principal companies.

In 1899, the Standard Oil Company of New Jersey succeeded the
19 other principal companies as a holding company, and by 1907 it
controlled three-fourths of the crude oil manufacturing of the country,
one-half of the tank cars, four-fifths of the illuminating oil, four-fifths
of the exports of oil products, four-fifths of the naphtha production, and
nine-tenths of the lubricating oil used by the railroads. Out of a total
of 5,000 stockholders, seven held control by the ownership of one-third
of the stock, the board of directors consisting of 15 persons. The
company had the power to fix both purchasing and selling prices and
transportation rates. Unfair methods resorted to by the company
were various: securing of preferential rates, restrictive contracts, pseudo-
independent company transactions, espionage, and price-cutting. And
yet, in spite of the listing of such acts, and evidence supporting them,
the court preferred to stand on more general grounds in curbing the
action of the trust and its subsidiaries.

The immediate occasion for Federal prosecution was the
allocation of the trade territory comprised in Missouri between
the Standard Oil Company of Indiana and the Waters Pierce
Oil Company, each corporation agreeing not to market petroleum
products in the district of the other. The Waters Pierce Company and the Galena Signal Oil Company between them controlled 90% of the business of furnishing lubricating oil to the
railroads. The court issued a decree enjoining the Standard
Oil Company of New Jersey from voting the stock it held in
these subsidiaries, and the subsidiaries were enjoined from
paying any further dividends to the New Jersey company; all
of the defendants were enjoined from entering any trust or other
agreements.[26] Note the basis of the court's decision:

> The power to restrict competition in interstate and international com-
> petition, vested in a person or an association of persons by a contract or
> combination, is indicative of its character; for it is to the interest of the
> parties that such a power should be exercised, and the presumption is that
> it will be.[27]

In a concurring opinion, Justice Hook refused to give any weight
to the arguments that monopolies reduced the prices of products
and effected economies in operation.

[26] U. S. v. Standard Oil Company of New Jersey et al., 173 Fed. 177 (1909).
[27] Ibid., p. 188.

It is now almost universally believed that the ultimate, if not the immediate, effect upon the development of trade and commerce is detrimental, and that belief, so generally prevalent and enduring, has been embodied in legislation, the policy of which is not open to question in the courts.[28]

The case was appealed to the Supreme Court, as was also that of the American Tobacco Company.

The formation of the original American Tobacco Company antedated the Sherman Act. Subsequent to the Act, a merger was consummated between this company and 60 others, controlling approximately 80% of the tobacco business of the United States, except the cigar business. Evidence of unfair competition or of improper practices was not submitted, nor was there any indication of an increase in the price of tobacco products to the consumer, although the Court expressed suspicion regarding these matters. New enterprises, in competition with the American Tobacco Company, were started and thrived, "although parties with moderate capital and desiring to enter the field would have found it difficult to do so against the opposition of this combination." The price of leaf tobacco, during this time, steadily increased until it nearly doubled, and an additional acreage was constantly being devoted to tobacco crops.

And yet the court held that each of the purchases of existing concerns was a contract and combination in restraint of a competition existing when it was entered into, sufficient to bring it within the ban of the Sherman Act.[29] An enormous sum of money had been used to acquire plants, which on being purchased were not utilized but were immediately closed. Those plants which had not been closed were shown to have been under the absolute domination of the supreme central authority, everything directly or indirectly connected with the manufacture and sale of tobacco products, including the ingredients—as regards purchase of raw materials, the company was buying three-fourths of all the Burley and Virginia sun-cured tobacco in the United States—, the packages, the bags and boxes, being controlled by it. Although many of the associated corporations joined the combination voluntarily, "many preferred to do so rather than face an unequal trade war in which the odds were against them." The enormous inherent and collateral power

[28] *Ibid.*, p. 196.

[29] *U. S. v. American Tobacco Company*, 164 Fed. 700, 703; 164 Fed. 1024 (1908).

of the American Tobacco Company outweighed, in the minds of the court, the fact that their record was remarkably free from acts of oppression or coercion. The question was one of "the existence of power, not its exercise."[30] The court, still clinging to the metaphysics of the 1890's, ordered the company dissolved.

The case came before the Supreme Court, Chief Justice White delivering the opinion. After an exhaustive analysis of the whole history of the tobacco industry and of the interrelations in stock ownership and management of the constituents of the American Tobacco Company, Justice White concluded that the company existed in violation of the Sherman Act.[31] The following considerations were regarded as "overwhelmingly" establishing this conclusion: (a) that the first combination was impelled by a previously existing trade war, evidently inspired by one or more of the minds which brought about the combination; (b) that acts subsequent to the combination indicated an intention to use the power of the combination further to monopolize the industry, by trade conflicts and coercion of competitors; (c) the use of indirection—purchase of stock, organization of new companies—to obscure the real purpose to monopolize; (d) the absorption of control over all the elements essential to the successful manufacture of tobacco products; (e) the expenditure of millions of dollars in buying out plants and the subsequent closing of them; (f) the binding of many persons by contract not to engage in the business; all these acts being legal, individually, but "portentous when viewed in their entirety."[32]

The great difficulty which the court faced was the remedy. To restore the *status quo ante* was impossible. Forbidding stock ownership by one part of the combination in another part was felt to be inadequate. To grant a permanent injunction restraining the combination or its constituents from further engaging in interstate commerce would have inflicted a great amount of injury upon the public through the limitation of supply and the enhancement of prices; similarly would the granting of a receivership for dissolving the combination. The court therefore directed the Circuit Court to consult with the members of the combination in order to work out a plan which would create a condition in the tobacco industry not

[30] *Ibid.*, p. 720.
[31] *American Tobacco Co. v. U. S.*, 221 U. S. 106 (1911).
[32] *Ibid.*, pp. 182, 183.

repugnant to the law. The significance of this remedial view and solution are highly significant for business.

The Circuit Court, Second District of New York, accordingly issued a decree November 16, 1911, which virtually created or recreated 14 corporations, each to do business only under its own name and none to hold stock in any other corporation; nor was the stock of any company to be held by a "holding" company which also held the stock of another tobacco company. The independence of the managements of these corporations was secured by prohibiting agreements among them, by guarding jobbers against such agreements in regard to sales, by prohibiting joint sales agencies for five years, and by prohibiting "interlocking" directorates, together with other provisions securing the purpose of the court.

The most important effect of this decision, and that of the Standard Oil case, was the avowed departure from previous tendencies in the courts to condemn all contracts in "restraint of trade," and the insertion of the "rule of reason" in the interpretation of the Sherman Act. In the Standard Oil case, it was held that, since the statute had not defined the words "restraint of trade," it became necessary to construe these words, a duty which could be discharged only by "a resort to reason."[33] The ambiguity of the two phrases, "reasonable interpretation of 'restraint of trade'" and "the interpretation of 'reasonable restraint of trade,'" enabled Justice White to assert that the doctrine now announced in the American Tobacco and Standard Oil cases was "in accord with all the previous decisions of this court, despite the fact that the contrary view was sometimes erroneously attributed to some of the expressions used in the Trans-Missouri and Joint-Traffic Association cases."[34] Justice Harlan testily objected to this view and to what he regarded as aspersions cast on his previous decisions, and declared that Justice White was guilty of judicial legislation.[35] But Justice White's view prevailed.

Just as in *Marbury v. Madison*, where the upholding of the President's power to appoint judicial officers seemed on the surface to give the Executive Department of Government priority over the Judicial, the very fact that the case was decided by

[33] *Standard Oil Company et al. v. U. S.*, 221 U. S. 1, 58 ff. (1911).
[34] *Ibid.*, p. 179.
[35] *Ibid.*, p. 192.

the courts established the more basic doctrine of judicial review; so in the Standard Oil and American Tobacco cases, the basic doctrine of the "rule of reason" was established in a case in which the court declared that the acts of the companies involved were not within the limits established by the rule. Business, in other words, was emancipated from the absolute interpretation of the Sherman Law by two decisions in which the companies involved were held to have violated this liberal interpretation of the Law.

Asserting that the context of the Sherman Act indicates that the statute was drawn in the light of the then-existing practical conception of the law of restraint of trade, Justice White gives the common-law meaning of the words employed in the Act. His argument then is: "*undue* restraint" was intended by the Law to be prohibited; the lack of an express definition of such terms calls for judgment setting a standard, hence the standard of reason of the common law. The rule of "reason" and the rule of "direct," as opposed to "indirect," effect of restraint—as interpreted in the railroad cases—amount to one and the same thing.[36]

Applying the rule of reason to the construction of the statute, it was held in the Standard Oil case that as the words "restraint of trade" at common law and in the law of this country at the time of the adoption of the Anti-trust Act only embraced acts or contracts or agreements or combinations which operated to the prejudice of the public interests by unduly restricting competition or unduly obstructing the due course of trade or which, either because of their inherent nature or effect or because of the evident purpose of the acts, etc., injuriously restrained trade, the words as used in the statute were designed to have and did have a like significance. It was therefore pointed out that the statute did not forbid or restrain the power to make normal and usual contracts to further trade by resorting to all normal methods, whether by agreement or otherwise, to accomplish such purpose. In other words, it was held, not that acts which the statute prohibited could be removed from the control of its prohibitions by a finding that they were reasonable, but that the duty to interpret which inevitably arose from the general character of the term restraint of trade required that the words restraint of trade should be given a meaning which would not destroy the individual right to contract and render difficult if not impossible

[36] 221 U. S. 1, c. 66. The weak link of Justice White's argument is the ambiguity of the phrase "of reason," which may be interpreted as either a subjective or an objective genitive, an ambiguity which is also present in the adjective "reasonable." Justice White's fallacy was more successful however, than was Sherman's fallacy regarding "parties," in establishing the continuity of the common law and the Sherman Act.

any movement of trade in the channels of interstate commerce—the free movement of which it was the purpose of the statute to protect. The soundness of the rule that the statute should receive a reasonable construction, after further mature deliberation, we see no reason to doubt. Indeed, the necessity for not departing in this case from the standard of the rule of reason which is universal in its application is so plainly required in order to give effect to the remedial purposes which the act under consideration contemplates, and to prevent that act from destroying all liberty of contract and all substantial right to trade, and thus causing the act to be at war with itself by annihilating the fundamental right of freedom to trade which, on the very face of the act, it was enacted to preserve, is illustrated by the record before us. In truth, the plain demonstration which this record gives of the injury which would arise from and the promotion of the wrongs which the statute was intended to guard against which would result from giving the statute a narrow, unreasoning and unheard of construction, as illustrated by the record before us, if possible serves to strengthen our conviction as to the correctness of the rule of construction, the rule of reason, which was applied in the Standard Oil case, the application of which rule to the statute we now, in the most unequivocal terms, reexpress and reaffirm.[37]

The two great decisions, dissolving the Standard Oil and American Tobacco companies, were regarded by some persons as pyrrhic victories. For although the decisions were actually adverse to these large business corporations, the inclusion of the "rule of reason" as a standard was felt to be a recession from the previous position of the court. William Howard Taft, however, in answer to this point of view, and to the further criticism that the meaning of the Sherman Act was even less clear than before, stated that there was no longer any difficulty in interpreting the statute:

If what [the business] man is dealing with is interstate commerce, if what he is going to do is to reduce competition and gain control of the business in any particular branch, if that is his main purpose and reduction of competition is not a mere incidental result, if except for that purpose he would not go into the arrangement, then he must know he is violating the law, and no sophistry, no pretense of other purpose need mislead him.[38]

This statement seems at first glance to be a reversion to the absolute position of the earlier court decisions, but not when it is recalled that the context of Taft's statement implies the common-law rule of "reasonable restraint," which governed all later decisions. The test of the remark lies in an examination

[37] 221 U. S. 106, 179, 180. The involved sentences are unfortunate; they probably resulted from the fact that this remarkable decision was given orally by the Chief Justice, without manuscript or notes.

[38] *The Anti-trust Act and the Supreme Court* (1914), p. 96.

of some of the cases which the courts were later called upon
to decide, conspicuously the cases involving the National Cash
Register, United States Steel, and International Harvester
companies. The last two cases presented a situation in which
the courts attempted to distinguish between "good" and "bad"
trusts on the basis of what had actually been done, and in which
it was discovered that there was such a thing as a "good" trust.
In the National Cash Register case, the Court became bogged
in technicalities, but did see fit to examine closely the specific
acts which constituted the behavior of this monopoly.

The National Cash Register Case

In June, 1912, the National Cash Register Company, its officers,
and certain other companies, formerly competitors, were overruled[39] by
the District Court, Southern District of Ohio, Western Division, as
regards their demurrer to an indictment charging them with conspiracy
in restraint of trade and with being a monopoly. Among the specific
charges of the grand jury which had investigated the company was the
circumstantial evidence that the National Cash Register Company had
during the course of 20 years increased its control over the cash-register
business from a percentage of 80 to that of 95, largely at the expense
of the 32 competitors named in the indictment, who were induced by
one method or another to join the company or go out of business.
Among the specific practices charged against the company were: bribery
and espionage, disparagements of competitors to their bankers and
customers, price-cutting, inducing the customers of competitors to
cancel their contracts, marking competitors' cash registers as "junk"
and displaying them in conspicuous show-windows, trade piracy, threats
and harassing suits directed against competitors, and enticing from
them their agents and employees. Veritably, a rogue's gallery of
business practices! There was also submitted evidence as to the use
of fisticuffs, but this the court ruled out.

The case was decided by this same court[40] in February, 1913,
the court concerning itself largely with answering the defense
of the company, which was that its actions were the result of a
policy of defending itself against the infringements of its patents.
The Circuit Court of Appeals later recognized the validity of
this countercharge in some instances. The National Cash
Register Company had been the first company in the field and
could normally have expected to be at least one of the leading

[39] *U. S. v. Patterson et al.*, 201 Fed. 697 (1912).
[40] *Ibid.*, 205 Fed. 292 (1913).

companies, and it had acquired extensive patent rights. But the District Court had already pointed out that the proper defense against such infringements was an action for damages or an injunction in the courts,[41] and refused to accept the company's plea as a valid defense.

Any one may, as a matter of right, go into the cash-register business and make his products the subject of interstate commerce, and may continue to do so until he is restrained by a court of equity, upon the fact being established that he is an infringer; and even after the establishment of such fact, he is amenable only to the court issuing the injunction, or may be subject to the payment of damages or profits, or both; but he is not, figuratively, an outlaw, to be brought in dead or alive, and his business confiscated by a patentee who is unwilling or afraid to pursue him by lawful methods, and who would destroy his business, interstate though it is, by unlawful means.[42]

This point was sustained by the Circuit Court of Appeals,[43] which also held that the charge of the "malicious prosecution" of competitors by the company was proved. The decision of this appellate court, of the Sixth Circuit, Judge Cochrane reading the decision, is a marvel of legal ingenuity founded upon a basis of social principle and expediency that cannot be denied. After an involved argument regarding the legality of the plea, the court held that the indictment did not mention specifically the competitors injured and their injuries, hence that most of the counts were void because of their uncertainty;[44] and, second, that the statute of limitations barred all those charges included in the list except those which had occurred during the preceding three years. "The Government's evidence brought the conspiracy down almost to the door of the three-year period; it remains to consider whether it entered that door."[45] Very few of the Government's charges were found to withstand both of these tests.

The general policy of the National Cash Register Company was formulated without much fear of government prosecution because the company was not dealing in a necessity of life, a point which the courts had already recognized.[46] That the

---

[41] *Ibid.*, p. 298.

[42] *Ibid.*, p. 300.

[43] *Patterson et al. v. U. S.*, 222 Fed. 599, 646 (1915).

[44] *Ibid.*, p. 623.

[45] *Ibid.*, p. 637.

[46] 55 Fed. 851 (1893), where the commodity was gold watches.

company was emboldened to adopt extreme policies and, by implication, severe measures to achieve those policies is indicated by the following samples of the evidence. In a letter dated May 1, 1892, the company made the following statements to a part of its executive and sales force:

If the opposition knew what was in store for them, they would not waste any more time and money staying in the business.   They are all beginning to realize that there is no hope for them.

It is only a question of whether we propose to spend the money to keep down opposition.   If we continue, it is absolutely certain no opposition company can stand against this company and its agents.   If necessary, we will spend five times as much money as we have already done, in order to down opposition.   If they really believe this, they will throw up the sponge and quit.

We are receiving overtures to buy out opposition.   We will not buy them out.   We do not buy out; we knock out.[47]

In an address at a convention of the district managers of the company July 22, 1897, President John H. Patterson discussed the methods by which the company was "going to absolutely control the competition of the world . . . The first thing we aim to do is to keep down competition." He then significantly added:

I asked the Standard Oil Company what was the secret of their success, and they said this question could be answered in a very few words.   Men, nothing but men; men well organized; they will keep down competition and make things succeed.

This attitude unquestionably was basic to the philosophy of big business in America during the latter part of the Nineteenth Century. And the court rightly recognized that where competition was excluded by efficiency, neither the law nor public policy could be expected to prevent the growth of individual companies.[48] But the employment of unfair means to achieve this prominence was treated by the court in the following surprising manner:

In the case of a monopoly brought about by monopolizing through a "combination by fusion" or "corporate combination" the monopolizing exists as long as the combination continues to exist.   It can at any time be dissolved, and its constituent elements restored to existence.   But in the case of a monopolizing by wrongful means, as here, the monopolizing ceases whenever the pugnacious competitor ceases to fight.   It is not possible

[47] *Patterson et al. v. United States*, 222 Fed. 599, 633.
[48] *Ibid.*, p. 619.

to resurrect the competitors who have been slain in the contest and restore to them what they have lost. Such competitor does not continue to monopolize, within the meaning of the statute, in holding onto the spoils of victory. It is never to be lost sight of that actually doing business, no matter how large, is not monopolizing. It is excluding from the opportunity of doing business that is. If it is thought that this is an evil condition of things, which should not be allowed to continue, the answer is that things should not have been allowed to get in that condition. The competitors attacked should have called upon the courts to protect them whilst they were being attacked.[49]

In short, both the National Cash Register Company and its competitors were exhorted by the courts to refrain from handling their business difficulties by the direct methods they had employed and to resort to the courts for a redress of their grievances. But the National Cash Register Company discovered in the courts that its methods, which it knew to be effective, were not subject to legal liability because of the statute of limitations; while the competitors of this company had the solace of the sympathy of the court for their demise, and learned that it took the courts three years at least to provide legal redress, if any.[50] According to the records, this gave ample time to "knock out" a competitor completely. The last of the competitors of the National Cash Register Company to go out of business ceased to exist November 1, 1906. Evidently, according to the courts, these competitors—failing the help of the Government in prosecuting the company under the Sherman Law—should have sought redress in the courts; employing, possibly, injunction proceedings, with all their hazards; and using the relatively more certain method of a suit, for redress and damages; with impaired financial strength, however, against a competitor that was ready and willing to fight the case through the long, hazardous and expensive processes of the courts.

It is doubtful whether any department of government has ever been subjected to a greater single test and found so wanting, as were the courts in this case; and they themselves freely supplied the evidence—in the court reports—for their condemnation. Not only did the manifest delays and technical intricacies of the courts explain in great measure why "big business" could so

[49] *Ibid.*, p. 625.

[50] The case was given a preliminary hearing on June 26, 1912. Previous to this the case had to be prepared by the Government. The Circuit Court of Appeals gave its decision March 13, 1915, and the Supreme Court denied the petition for a writ of *certiorari* on June 14, 1915.

flagrantly violate the ordinary rules of social and business decency and could go ahead with its own ruthless methods, but they also show the serious need of the broader legislation which shortly followed. Business itself was to be condemned for not showing that it did not need police surveillance, and the Attorney General's office bungled the case unmercifully. But a great judge or a court with vision would have swept these matters aside and penetrated the fog of evidence and claims and pleadings, rather than add to the confusion and muddle by pronouncing an apostolic blessing upon business misdeeds on the ground that they had been effectively accomplished.

Here is the American philosophy of Pragmatism at its worst. And one wonders how much the other circumstances of the case contributed to the final decision of the courts. The World War had come on, a fact which was given consideration in the International Harvester case; and John H. Patterson had endeared himself to the people of Dayton, Ohio, by his behavior during and after the great flood of 1913. Throwing himself and all his resources into the situation with the same vigor that had characterized his previous treatment of competitors, he helped restore the material well-being and morale of that stricken city. Query: What are the relative merits of such an achievement and the previous and subsequent economic welfare of such a community when weighed against the many mortalities of competitors, the mute evidence of which was exhibited to future victims in dramatic fashion by a visit to the "morgue"—a mound of broken and scrapped competitors' cash registers gathered from all parts of the country?

The net legal effect of the National Cash Register Company case was that the Court of Appeals remanded the case to the lower court for retrial; after barring all evidence of acts prior to three years preceding the indictment, all charges directed against the manufacturing departments, and all counts except those relating to certain proved specific instances of the following practices: disparagement of competitors, piracy, inducing competitors' customers to cancel their contracts, and enticing employees and agents away from competitors to learn their trade secrets.[51] The District Court had noted that "the charges are general so far as the naming of particular instances is concerned, but are all very specific as describing a course of con-

[51] *Ibid.*, p. 639.

duct."[52] But the appellate court insisted that the charges in the indictment, except those mentioned above, failed specifically to make a case.[53] The court agreed that the statute of limitations did not apply merely because an agreement had been discontinued, if its effects remained. "A conspiracy continues so long as the partnership in a criminal purpose continues."[54] But it declared inept most of the evidence as to an existing conspiracy. And this view, together with the elimination of the attribute of "monopoly," practically withdrew the case from the jurisdiction of the Sherman Law.

Are There Any "Good" Trusts?

The International Harvester Company was organized August 12, 1902, with a capitalization of $102,000,000. It included the following companies, which previously had been operating independently since the date stated: McCormick Harvesting Machine Company, 1849; D. M. Osborne and Company, 1860; Warder, Bushnell & Glessner Company (Champion), 1869; Deering Harvester Company, 1875; Milwaukee Harvester Company; Plano Manufacturing Company, and several smaller concerns. The stock of these various companies was transferred to the "purchasing company" in return for a due proportion of the International Harvesting Company's non-assessable stock. The combined production capacity of the newly formed company was about 80% to 85% of all binders, mowers, reapers and rakes made in the United States.

The Federal Government prosecuted the company in the District Court of the District of Minnesota. The court held that this combination suppressed all competition among the five companies, "which is as illegal as destruction of competition among them without combining";[55] a view directly at variance with the following earlier opinion:

The prohibition (of the Sherman Act) was suggested by the trusts, the objection to which, as every one knows, was not the union of former competitors, but the sinister power exercised or supposed to be exercised by the combination in keeping rivals out of the business and ruining those who already were in. It was the ferocious extreme of competition with others, not the cessation of competition among the partners, that was feared. Further proof is to be found in Section 7, giving an action to any person injured in his business or property by the forbidden conduct. This cannot

[52] U. S. v. Patterson et al., 201 Fed. 697, 718.
[53] Patterson et al. v. U. S., 222 Fed. 599, 623, 628.
[54] Ibid., p. 631.
[55] U. S. v. International Harvester Co., 214 Fed. 987, 994 (1914).

refer to the parties to the agreement and plainly means that outsiders who are injured in their attempt to compete with a trust or other similar combination may recover for it. (*Montague & Company v. Lowry*, 193 U. S. 38.) How effective the section may be or how far it goes, is not material to my point. My general summary of the two classes of cases which the act affects is confirmed by the title, which is "An Act to Protect Trade and Commerce against Unlawful Restraints and Monopolies."[56]

The court which heard the Harvester case further held that the size of the constituent companies of the International Harvester Company and their combination accentuated the illegality![57] In a concurring opinion, Justice Hook asserted that the combined organization was not the result of normal growth of the fair enterprise of an individual, a partnership or of a corporation, and stressed the fact that it controlled more than 80% of the field. "All else is detail."[58] The company was ordered to dissolve into at least three companies, but the advent of the World War caused the Government eventually to drop the suit for fear of disturbing too much the already unsettled economic situation.

This conclusion seems all the more startling when Justice Hook shows that the company had a clean bill of health:

In the main the business conduct of the company towards its competitors and the public has been honorable, clean and fair . . . Specific charges of misconduct were made in the government's petition, which found no warrant whatever in the proof.[59]

Such a state of affairs warranted Justice Sanborn's dissension from the majority opinion of the court. Not only, said he, was the International Harvester Company not excluding its competitors from their share of the business, but its proportion of the trade had during the preceding 10 years been decreasing in respect to theirs.[60] Justice Sanborn then went on to apply the functional test which had been raised in the Standard Oil case: (1) Were prices to consumers raised? (2) Was production limited? (3) Was the quality of the product deteriorating? (4) Were wages decreased? (5) Were prices of raw materials lowered? And (6) Was there unfair or oppressive treatment of

[56] *Northern Securities Case*, 193 U. S. 197, 405.

[57] *U. S. v. International Harvester Company*, 214 Fed. 987, 1000.

[58] *Ibid.*, p. 1001.

[59] *Ibid.*, p. 1002.

[60] *Ibid.*, p. 1007. One wonders what has become of the increased efficiency promised prior to so many amalgamations; but that is not the question here.

competitors?[61] The negative answer to all these questions, which the evidence presented, satisfied Justice Sanborn that the Sherman Law did not apply. But the majority of the court insisted on the absolute interpretation which had prevailed in the previous decade.

The intent of a statute at its passage must continue. It does not automatically adjust itself to the variations of the public pulse, and a judicial adjustment would be an usurpation. In our National Government such things are for Congress alone.[62]

Is it any wonder that a dynamic force such as business would break or avoid such a "cake of custom," characterizing alike the fundamentalism of Law and Religion? It required approximately 10 years for the functional interpretation of the Sherman Law to develop from a dissenting opinion to the majority view of the United States Supreme Court, and even longer than that for the judicial news to reach the courts throughout the country.

The United States Steel Corporation was organized in 1901 and comprised the following companies organized respectively in the dates following their names:

Federal Steel Company	1898
American Tin Plate Company	1898
American Steel and Wire Company	1899
National Tube Company	1899
National Steel Company	1899
American Steel Hook Company	1899
American Sheet Steel Company	1900
Carnegie Steel Company	1900
Carnegie Company of New Jersey	1900

The latter, as a holding company, controlled the Carnegie Steel Company of Pennsylvania. The organization of the United States Steel Corporation did not include the following companies which were competitors during some or all of the 10 years following the organization of the United States Steel Corporation:

Bethlehem Steel Company, South Bethlehem, Pennsylvania
Inland Steel Company, Indiana Harbor, Indiana
La Belle Company, Wheeling, West Virginia
Jones and Laughlin Company, Pittsburgh, Pennsylvania
Cambria Steel Company, Johnstown, Pennsylvania
Colorado Company, Pueblo, Colorado
Republican Iron and Steel Company, Youngstown, Ohio
Lackawanna Steel Company of Buffalo, New York
Pennsylvania Steel Company of Harrisburg, Pennsylvania

[61] *Ibid.*, p. 1010.
[62] *Ibid.*, p. 1002.

The relative production of the products of the United States Steel Corporation and of its competitors was as follows: in unfinished rolled products, a basic supply excluding pig iron, steel castings, and ingots, the total production in the United States in 1901 was 13,000,000 tons, of which the United States Steel Corporation produced slightly more than 50% and the competitors slightly less than this amount. By 1911, however, out of a total of 19,000,000 tons produced in the United States, the United States Steel Corporation produced 8,700,000 tons while its competitors produced 10,300,000 tons or 54% of the total, and indications were that this latter percentage was increasing.

The total production of steel ingots in the United States in 1901 was 13,000,000 tons, of which the United States Steel Corporation produced 8,500,000 tons or 66% while its competitors at that time produced 4,500,000 tons. In 1911 the total production had reached 24,000,000 tons, of which the United States Steel Corporation produced 13,000,000 tons or 54% while its competitors produced 11,000,000 tons.

The production of pig iron in the United States in 1901 totaled 16,000,000 tons, of which the competitors of the United States Steel Corporation produced 9,000,000 tons or approximately 57%. In 1911 the production of pig iron amounted to 22,000,000 tons, with the competitors producing 12,000,000 tons or approximately 55%.

In 1901 the competitors of the United States Steel Corporation produced approximately 80% of the wire manufactured in the United States. In 1911 these competitors were producing 78%. The greater part of the increase in production by the United States Steel Corporation could be attributed to foreign trade. In 1901, a total of 9,000,000 kegs of nails was produced in the United States of which the United States Steel Corporation produced two-thirds and its competitors one-third. In 1911 the total production of nails amounted to approximately 14,000,000 kegs, the production being equally divided between the corporation and its competitors.

In structural steel the corporation in 1911 produced 33% of the output, a smaller percentage than in 1901. In 1901 the corporation produced 1,700,000 tons of steel rails, its competitors producing 1,100,000 tons. In 1911 the corporation was producing 1,600,000 tons of rails while its competitors were producing 1,200,000 tons of rails.

The seaboard competitors of the United States Steel Corporation had in 1911 an ore supply independent of the Lake Superior source, these supplies being located in eastern Pennsylvania, Sweden, Cuba, Brazil, and Chile. Among the independent companies which obtained their supplies from the Superior districts was the Youngstown Sheet and Tube Company which had free home and foreign markets for its goods, especially the marketing of steel ingots, a primary product.

The seaboard competitors of the United States Steel Corporation had substantial freight advantages in regard to the securing of their supplies. The supplies from which steel was made and the basic articles into which it was turned were of such bulk and weight as to localize or restrict their markets. The bulk of the mill production of the United States Steel Corporation was centered near Chicago and Pittsburgh. Furthermore, the company adopted the policy of not receiving rebates from railroads or other transportation companies.

A further evidence of the freedom of competition in the steel business was offered by the fact that Mr. Charles Schwab, who helped organize the United States Steel Corporation, later organized and built up the Bethlehem Steel Company, an independent organization. Competitive trade wars in the localized regions dominated by the independents were difficult because the competitors or the customers of steel companies would soon discover the fact of lowered prices and thus necessitate general price reductions.

The possibility of an agreement in regard to prices or of the control of prices by any single company was remote. This situation was supported by the policy of the United States Steel Corporation in maintaining its prices above the average during depressed times and below the average in prosperous times. The theory back of this policy was to prevent speculation in iron and steel products and to keep prices relatively uniform. One of the effects of this policy was the elimination of delivery premiums and of attempts to postpone the delivery of orders until such time as lower prices prevailed. One of the practical effects of this policy was that buyers tended to give orders to the United States Steel Corporation during prosperous times and to its competitors in depressed times.

The policy of the Carnegie Steel Company prior to 1901 had been to keep the mills running at maximum capacity no matter at what price. This policy resulted in a furious trade war in which the prices of steel rails were forced down to a point below the cost of manufacture. A further effect was the elimination of competitors, the Scranton Company being among those forced out of business. Wages were, as a consequence, forced down and the effect was particularly felt by the wholesalers who had to write off large amounts because of the fall in prices. The policy of the United States Steel Corporation not to sell at lower prices when prices dropped and were low resulted in relatively stabilizing the price of iron and steel products.

The United States Steel Corporation was prosecuted by the Government in the District Court of the District of New Jersey, the decision being given June 3, 1915.[63] Asserting that the construction of the Sherman Law had been settled by the United States Supreme Court, especially in the Standard Oil and

[63] *U. S. v. United States Steel Corporation*, 223 Fed. 55 (1915).

American Tobacco cases, Circuit Judge Buffington held that the case now under consideration was one of business facts and of the application of the settled law to those facts. The question which the court set itself was whether the formation of the United States Steel Corporation "prejudiced the public interests by unduly restricting competition or unduly obstructing the course of trade." Taking into account the facts already presented, the court came to the conclusion that, following upon the cutthroat competition which characterized the industry at the close of the last century, the formation of the United States Steel Corporation and its first 10 years of existence had resulted in a more general division of business among all competitors, the minimizing of the shutting-down of plants in times of depression, and the withdrawing of steel products from speculative markets.

These significant figures prove that mere size, or bigness of business, is not necessarily a monopoly of business at the expense of all others engaged in it.[64]

The court found the foreign-trade methods of the company similarly free of charges of unfairness.[65] Similar conclusions were reached regarding the motives back of the original amalgamation and of subsequent purchases of additional plants.[66] More significant than the conclusions of the court was the point of view with which the court approached the case, namely, to see what the company had *done* to warrant its subjection to the prohibitions of the Sherman Law. The functional point of view had finally become established in the court.

With the further development of the judicial interpretation of the Sherman Act we are not here concerned. Once the attitude of the court had veered away from the idea that the mere bigness of a business corporation presumed its violation of the act, and after the court had begun to examine the effects of business organizations, the cases arising under the Sherman Law became matters of technical information, valuable to the lawyer and his business client in clearing up uncertainties but of interest to the student of social philosophy only when a concrete case again raises a problem of major public policy. In short, the controlling cases arising under the Sherman Law,

[64] *Ibid.*, p. 96.
[65] *Ibid.*, p. 114.
[66] *Ibid.*, pp. 142, 144–150.

most of which have already been discussed, bid fair to set the standards for the courts for some time to come; the cases which are now being decided are largely concerned with the refinements of application of these general standards to the particular border-line cases which will continually recur. Of more concern to the student of Business Ethics are the legislative enactments during the early part of the Wilson administration, which dealt more analytically with business evils. Before discussing the Federal Trade Commission and Clayton Acts, however, it is necessary to break away completely from considerations of legal and governmental policy, in order to discover the status of American business itself, its structure, its functions and its peculiar and distinctive organization.

C. THE STRUCTURE AND DYNAMICS OF BUSINESS

A detailed study of the legal status of the Sherman Law should not blind one to the significance of the Law from the standpoint of Business Ethics. Not only must one keep in mind the point already stressed, namely, that the Sherman Law and its interpretation were symptomatic of a developing and critical self-consciousness of business, an attitude which may also result in business self-government, but one must also constantly evaluate the actual external regulations of the Law, as indicated by the history of the Sherman Act, with the potential internal control that might have been exerted by Business itself. This challenge has been met by the assertion of the Chamber of Commerce of the United States that "business should render restrictive legislation unnecessary through so conducting itself as to inspire and deserve public confidence."[1] An intensive study of legal-business relations is as necessary to a thorough understanding of the relative social values of Law and Business as is a similar study of the relation of religion to business[2] in order to determine the relative social values of Business and the Church. Such studies would indicate that there has been an emancipation of Business, at first from the Church and more recently from the State, which should enable Business to work out its own problems, ethical as well as others, in its own peculiar and unique way. On *a priori* grounds, such a condition of functional pluralism is philosophically and logically defensible. Its ethical justification, however, is a separate problem which must be determined positively and pragmatically.

The empirical study of Business Ethics, however, although it would rule out the extrinsic factors that have hitherto been applied by Church and State, must take account of underlying social forces. Not the least of these are the structure and relations of Business itself, and the dynamic activities constituting business behavior. Just as the morals of a community are affected by physical conditions, programs of sanitation and health, or technological changes; so is Business Ethics conditioned

[1] *Principles of Business Conduct*, XV.
[2] As, for example, Tawney's *Religion and the Rise of Capitalism*.

by business organization and modifications of business technique. Here, again, the woods must not be lost sight of for the trees. A study of business technique or of business policy is not to be confused with a study of Business Ethics. But the latter is very definitely and very intimately related to the former, especially in the sense that Business Ethics cannot be understood apart from a knowledge of business facts. Indeed, the existential value of the latter is such as to warrant the presumption that tried business behavior and cumulative business experience are the determinants of a sound system of Business Ethics. This is not to say, with Hegel, that "Whatever is, is right," or that the prevalence of a type of behavior is socially or ethically justifiable. But it is to say that the "existing order of things" must be recognized, that Schopenhauer's dictum that "Whatever is, is wrong" is an absurd form of cynicism, and that any values which Business Ethics would assert as a desirable departure from the present state of affairs must carry the burden of proof and justify themselves.

In the following five chapters an attempt will be made to describe the structure and functions of the business organization with a view to discovering therein the factual basis for a system of Business Ethics. No attempt will be made to give a complete picture of the business drama that has been unfolding itself in America in recent years, but an endeavor will be made to picture the situation by singling out certain significant factors for concrete and detailed analysis. The growth of corporation activities will be indicated by referring to their vertical extensions, at first in the direction of the source of raw materials and then later in the direction of marketing activities, through full-line forcing, the horizontal extensions of functions, and mergers. Next will be considered the responsibilities which such integrations and expansions have thrust upon shareholders, directors and managements, and the ethical problems that consequently arise. Finally, consideration will be given to the business doctrine of "legitimate channels of trade" through which such forces find their outlet; and to certain horizontal relations among independent businesses that have been intensified by trade-association activities.

CHAPTER VI

FULL-LINE FORCING

Division of Labor and Specialization of Function

One of the earliest, and yet most comprehensive of social theories was developed in Plato's *Republic*. The essence of this theory was that society is at its best when each person is working at the limit of his capacity in that particular field of activity for which he is best fitted. Society, as Plato ideally conceived it—and Plato had in mind the economic as well as the political functions of society—is an organism in which the individual is regarded, not as an end in himself, but as instrumental to the welfare of the state. Thus both Plato and, later, Aristotle accepted slavery as a necessary part of a successful society; just as many men today, who have thought out the implications of our industrial society and are honest in their opinions, would regard industrial slavery as a possible price of the resulting civilization. Both Plato and Aristotle pointed out the necessity of specialization in order to achieve such an organic state. Plato's system of education provided for a gradual separation of the rulers of the state from the artisans and shopkeepers on the basis of their proved respective abilities, his observation being that the trouble with most states was that many of the rulers should be cobblers—and perhaps plumbers!—while many men who might with proper encouragement have developed into good rulers had been relegated to inferior jobs through circumstances. Without going too much into details, most of which referred to possible improvements in the conditions in Athens at that time and are not strictly applicable to modern conditions, Plato's general principle was that specialization and intelligent vocational guidance, definition of functions and organization, were necessary to the welfare of any society.

The attitude of certain business men generally and of trade associations in particular, that business functions should be defined and that only a limited group of commodities be handled by each business, follows, in general, Plato's idea; it is also

145

quite similar to the attitude developed by the Mediaeval guilds. Both craft and merchant guilds derived their character, however, not so much from the process or function performed, as more exclusively from the type of commodity handled.   The following excerpt from the *Book of the Prefect* will indicate the situation. This *Book* contains the trade ordinances of Constantinople during the Tenth Century, which supplemented the great legal compilations of that day.[1]

II. The Jewelers

1. We ordain that the jewelers may, if any one invites them, buy the things that pertain to them, such as gold, silver, pearls, or precious stones; but not bronze and woven linens or any other materials which others should purchase rather than they.   However, they are not hereby prevented from buying anything they wish for private use.

Similar provisions applied to: IV. The Silk-garment Merchants; V. The Dealers in Syrian Silks; VI. The Dealers in Raw Silk; VII. The Silk Spinners; VIII. The Silk Weavers; IX. The Linen Merchants; X. The Perfume Dealers; XI. The Candlemakers; XII. The Soapmakers; XIII. The Victualers; XIV. The Leathercutters; XV. The Butchers; XVI. The Pork Dealers; XVII. The Fishmongers; and XVIII. The Bakers.   Violation of this rule of specialization subjected the guilty person to be "scourged, shorn, and banished," or to suffer a substantial fine.

The principle of specialization is exhibited today in many of the professions.   The education of a doctor is so highly specialized, and the definition of his functions by his professional organizations so rigid, that relatively few men can become members of the profession, while those who do become doctors would find it difficult to do anything else.   And self-government in the medical profession has developed proportionately with the limitation of membership and with the definition of professional functions.   Specialization is also characteristic of engineering and law, but to a lesser degree, for many lawyers and engineers have become successful business men by attending to the financial or management, manufacturing or commercial dealings of the companies to which they had formerly given independent professional advice.

Business itself has not achieved anywhere near the degree of vocational distinctiveness or specialization as have the pro-

[1] See Boak, A. E. R., "The Book of the Prefect," I *Journal of Economic and Business History* 4, August, 1929, p. 597.

fessions. True, a business man cannot extend his activities to include the practice of law or of medicine; but this is due, not so much to any positive requirements of business that he attend strictly to business, nor even to his inability to practice law, but rather to the fact that he is prevented from so doing by doctors and lawyers themselves. Thus the statutes of the State of New York prevent a business corporation from furnishing free legal advice to its clients, a service which many banks and trust companies at one time attempted to perform;[2] and although anyone can give remedial medical treatment to a person, most states forbid the charging of a fee for such purposes other than by licensed practitioners. Engineering and teaching, to a lesser extent than law or medicine, have defined their professional functions and prevent the amateur from practicing them indiscriminately. Even some engineers, however, agree with the prevailing notion that "anyone can build a bridge," while there is considerable agreement with G. B. Shaw's statement about teaching, that "those who can, do; those who can't, teach." But business has not been even so well defined as has engineering or teaching, while only in recent years has there been any recognition of the need for business training other than such as might be implied in a loosely regulated apprenticeship.

Whether, in addition to defining its own province, Business can achieve an internal social organization at all comparable to that already achieved by Church or State or the professions, is a question that must be determined largely by examining the present social status and organization of Business. Two factors which have made the present organization of State and Church possible are the clear definition of internal functions and of the organic relations among them so as to achieve a virtual social unit. In the case of the Catholic Church and certain Protestant churches, such as the Methodist, these functions and relations have become relatively more stabilized than they have in the case of the State; at least in the United States, the division of powers among the three major departments and between the Federal and the state governments is still in a considerable state of flux. But such fluidity is even more prevalently the case among the various activities of Business.

[2] See *Trust Companies*, August, 1930, for several articles dealing with the situation as it developed, *e.g.*, in the states of Washington and Missouri and in the cities of Buffalo, Cleveland and Chicago.

It may be that the institutionalizing of Business commensurate with that of Church or State is undesirable, especially if this would involve any interference with the dynamic character which is so often regarded as one of the chief, or at least most distinctive, qualities of Business. But the value of a social institution often lies in the momentum resulting from its organic strength, especially when it comes in conflict with another social organization. So it was with the Reception of the Roman Law in northern Europe during the Renaissance: the systematic code made havoc of the more adaptable and better fitted *coutumes* of France and municipal law of the German States because the latter had not been sufficiently institutionalized. The deadening results of institutionalism should be avoided, but certainly not at the risk of losing the survival value inherent in organization. If Business is successfully to cope with Government and Church, it may find its lack of organization to be a handicap. This is as much a problem of personnel as it is of structure and functions. Martin Littleton once said, in reply to the suggestion that more business men be elected to Congress, that the resulting mess would require the untiring efforts of lawyers for half a century to unravel.

President Lowell and Dean Donham have frequently referred to business as the "oldest of the arts and the youngest of the professions." This attempt to class business with the professions represents somewhat the same point of view as that of the late Judge Parker, who was largely responsible for drawing up the *Principles of Business Conduct* of the Chamber of Commerce of the United States. The most significant of these principles deals with the relation of business to law. Its assertion that "Business should render restrictive legislation unnecessary through so conducting itself as to secure and deserve public confidence," is a veritable declaration of independence of business and an assertion of its peculiar province. But the emphasis of the Chamber of Commerce, and of Rotary International, on "Service" as a primary function of business illustrates the extreme length to which the fallacy can be persisted in, of identifying business too closely with the professions. The phrase, "Business is business," although formerly connoting some of the worst features of business practice, especially the resentment of business men toward legitimate governmental regulations, may be reexamined, from the standpoint of the principle of identity, as justifiably defining and characterizing business as a distinctive vocation, and not merely as an imitator of the professions.

Not only has the principle that "the shoemaker should stick to his last" not been positively observed as regards the choice of business as a vocation or as regards the performance of business activities, but, as has been shown in the preceding chapters, most of the broader determinations of business policy and conduct have been determined by such outside agencies as the Law and the Church. Furthermore, within business itself there has not been that degree of specialization which is implied as a desirable state of affairs in Plato's ideal commonwealth and which has been found desirable and necessary to professionalism. True, individual corporations are highly organized as regards their internal relations and specialized as regards their products. It may be the very nature of business in general to be otherwise, however, and a highly dynamic set of relations may be preferable to the caste system implied in the degree of specialization achieved by the other social groups. At least, whatever values we may attribute to specialization and whatever explanations may be made of the lack of it in business, the fact is that business in the United States is not a well-defined activity and that it is not, in this country, to any appreciable extent differentiated within itself into specialized activities.

The principle of division of functions which Adam Smith pointed out in his *Wealth of Nations* as characteristic of economic society during the Industrial Revolution, applied largely to manual laborers in manufacturing enterprises. But nothing is so characteristic of American labor today as its mobility, a characteristic which differentiates the American laborer from the European and which indeed may be one of the most important reasons for our relatively greater industrial prosperity. The jurisdictional dispute represents an attempt on the part of organized labor to establish industrial specialization, but the social values of such attempts are often questionable. The suggestion has been made at times to license bankers, whose activities have achieved a considerable degree of distinctiveness in business; for we have not yet passed the stage in which otherwise successful business men and retired farmers regard themselves as fully capable of organizing and operating a bank, although the past 10 or 15 years have seen the elimination of many of these ambitious amateurs through the operation of a veritable "economic law." But the operation of such a law, like that of the "law of nature," while ruthless in the long run, is not immediately intelligent, or at least is not consciously imposed as are some of the professional restrictions. And the distinctions among various kinds of bankers—investment, commercial, trust, etc.,—are becoming less rather than more clear, especially since the era of bank mergers. But bankers do not view with favor the suggestion that they be licensed; they prefer to retain their present mobility, and can justify their position by accepting the responsibilities involved. Accounting has become a profession, especially by providing for certification; as regards the definition of accounting functions, however, the unwillingness of some accountants to accept the responsibility for physical inventories, although professional in spirit, is probably unfortunate from the point of view of business. In brief, not only do the facts seem to disclose the absence of specialization in business, but there is much to be said against the value of specialization where it actually occurs.

Within business itself, specialization of functions performed and of commodities handled presents a fundamental problem. A London sugar merchant once complained of the conditions he found in America on his successive visits to this country at intervals of four or five years. "Men that I formerly had business dealings with, had gone from sugar to soap or to banking, and those now engaged in the sugar business had previously been something else. I've been a sugar man for 30 years; my father was a sugar man before me; and my grandfather before that. As a consequence, I know sugar." The fluidity of capital is a well-known fact; the fluidity of American labor has previously been mentioned; but neither is perhaps greater than the fluidity of American management or the rapidly shifting emphasis on various phases of corporate activities. Whether certain functional activities of business—wholesaling or retailing or manufacturing—can be kept distinct and can be made to observe their place in a business hierarchy will be discussed in a succeeding chapter. For the present we shall confine ourselves to the question as to whether the principle of specialization is valuable enough to preserve against an obviously contrary tendency, the extension of business activities to commodities and services that were not originally, or would not normally be conceived to fall within the strict province of the business.

Unquestionably, flexibility has had a considerable survival value. The amoeba is practically shapeless and yet it can flow about hard obstacles and completely assimilate the relatively more rigid diatom. Certainly 40 years of anti-trust legislation and litigation in America have done little to interfere with the normal development of business, and largely because of the flexibility of the latter's activities. A greater rigor in business organization might have jeopardized the formation of larger business units and might even conceivably have definitely subordinated Business to Law in a well-defined social hierarchy.

Vertical Extensions and Horizontal Diversification

Inasmuch as specialization of function, exact definition of internal relations and organization of structure have characterized such social institutions as Church and State, it might be profitable to examine Business from this point of view. Just what is the institutional status of Business? Has it an organization in fact that would afford a social basis for determining its values in comparison with Church and State? Is there a sufficient structural basis to provide adequate sanctions for self-government? How far can the field of a business company's operations justifiably be extended? What obligations does a business owe to the trade or to competitors in determining such a policy? Granted a nucleus of particular operations, what additional commodities can a business justifiably handle and what additional functions or services can a business profitably perform?

The vertical extensions of corporate activities have arisen as a matter of normal growth out of the situations already dealt with; these extensions have frequently been in the direction of the sources of raw materials. Such developments in themselves presented tremendous problems to law and government during the first 20 years of the life of the Sherman Act, but they are relatively simple in comparison with the more recent business developments, in which corporate growth has been horizontal and diversified, extending to new commodities and new functions, with businesses resorting to "full-line forcing" and engaging in extensive "mergers" that carry the issue into the marketing field. If the relatively simple corporation, handling a restricted set of commodities, caused so much difficulty in business circles and to society as is evidenced in the preceding chapters, what must be the situation under the more recent circumstances?

The Sherman Law was directed at a comparatively simple type of business corporation, namely, one that was engaged for the most part in the manufacture and sale of a fairly distinctive or well-defined group of commodities. The combinations at which government prosecutions were directed because of their alleged monopoly control, at least during the early part of the present century, were identified respectively with such products as steel, sugar, tobacco, shoe machinery, whiskey, cash registers, meat, and the like. In very few of these cases, furthermore, was much attention paid to the expansion of a company's business in the direction of securing an adequate supply of raw materials. On the other hand, the sales activities of such companies, which were for the most part the activities that were feared by their competitors and which were being subjected to criticism in the courts, were largely such as would normally be necessary to dispose of their products; that is, they consisted in selling to merchants or fabricators and did not involve a control of the entire marketing activities necessary to convey the commodity to the ultimate consumer. And in practically none of the earlier cases was there evident the extension of functions and diversification of interests that characterize the present-day business corporation, holding company and chain store.

The most obvious justification of the diversification of commodities handled, and of the extension of business functions into allied fields, lies in the fact that business stability is thereby effected. A company which has its plants and trade outlets located in various parts of the country, and which perhaps also engages in foreign trade, reflects the same principle that governs wise individual investment policies: a depression may affect one locality or may exist in a certain field of business, but the chances of a general or universal depression are much less. Any losses, temporary or local, that a company with geographically diversified activities might be forced to meet would be more than compensated for elsewhere or at another time. And the same argument applies to a diversification of functions and of commodities. Opposed to this consideration is the undeniable fact that mergers have not in the past, as a matter of fact, effected the economies they promised through large-scale production and the elimination of duplications; in fact, experience has shown that the resultant earnings are frequently less than the previous or anticipated combined earnings of their constituent businesses, and largely because of overhead, especially promotional, expense.[3]

Furthermore, it is doubtful whether a single business organization can successfully perform many diversified functions, not only because of the different managerial skills which they may require, but also because of certain inherent contradictions which they may imply. How, for example, can a bank or a trust company justifiably combine with an investment house? If the former either markets or holds the security issues of the latter, how can the charge of double agency be avoided? And if they do not, what will the investment house tell the companies whose securities it is promoting? One wonders what sort of a board of directors will control the recent bank merger, in Berlin, of the conservative Disconto-Gesellschaft, which had been financing the heavy industries of Germany, and the Deutsche Bank, which had been engaged in the romantic venture of foreign loans. Certainly when the Postum Cereal Company combines with Maxwell House Coffee, much of the disparaging advertising capital of the former will have to be written off; just as when the Royal Baking Powder Company bought the "alum" baking-powder companies of Canada, against which it had been waging a tremendous advertising campaign.

Full-line Forcing of Closely Allied Products

That such mergers and extensions of business activities must be studied, in order fully to understand the basic problems of Business Ethics, is apparent when one observes the intensive competition that is engendered by an "interloper" in the newly invaded field with those businesses already intrenched. This situation becomes particularly acute in view of the fact that a company, so extending its functions, is at least initially an amateur in the new field. Where this situation is accompanied by the fact that a company, already strongly intrenched in the marketing of a particular line of commodities, attempts to force its customers to buy all of the commodities the company handles, including new lines of goods, competition becomes

[3] Dewing, A. S., *Financial Policy of Corporations*, New York: The Ronald Press Company, 1926 ed., Book IV, Chapter III, "Industrial Combinations," especially pp. 684, 685.

highly intense.   The development of this movement in business has become particularly accelerated through company mergers, which frequently result in the handling of a highly diversified line of commodities, a situation which particularly tempts a company to essay the forcing of all of its goods upon the customers of its previously independent constituent companies.

It will be the purpose of this and succeeding chapters to present a number of cases illustrating the extension of business functions beyond what normally would be regarded as their distinctive sphere.   These cases range all the way from those presented in this chapter, in which the business extensions may be warranted by the basic function or commodity involved, to cases in which the justification can be discovered only by a stretch of the imagination, and even to such cases as involve unwise public policies and economic and business contradictions that must seriously affect the earning capacities of the extended or combined businesses.   The first of these cases, involving the formation of the United Shoe Machinery Company, presents an apparently logical culmination of previous developments, and yet one that seriously jeopardized the interests of the few remaining competitors.

The United Shoe Machinery Company was incorporated in New Jersey, February, 1899, with an authorized capital of $25,000,000, and with powers under its charter to manufacture, operate and deal in all kinds of machinery, tools and equipment connected with the manufacture of boots and shoes.   The constituent companies were four in number, the percentage of their respective output to the total output in the United States being as indicated: Goodyear Shoe Machinery Company, 10% of the lasting, 80% of the welt-sewing and 80% of the outsole-stitching machines; Consolidated and McKay Lasting Machine Company, 60% of the lasting machines; McKay Shoe Machine Company, 70% of the heeling and 80% of the metallic-fastener machines; and the Eppler Welt Machine Company, which made welt-sewing and outsole-stitching machines.   Of these companies, those manufacturing the lasting, welt-sewing and outsole-stitching machines were already intimately related in 1899; the remaining company, however, was then independent.

Some 13 separate kinds of machines were necessary to equip a shoe manufacturer, most of these being engaged in a continuous series of processes to which each shoe was subjected.   This interrelation of mechanical processes argued strongly in favor of the amalgamation of the various shoe-machinery companies in 1899, especially in view of the keen competition which some of them faced at the time; and this amalgamation was then achieved. By 1915 the situation had developed to a point where the United Shoe Machinery Company supplied practically all of the 13 or more machines necessary to boot- and shoe-making. The greatest amount of independent competition was in outsole-stitching machinery, where competitors supplied 758 machines while the company supplied 2,676; in welt-sewing machines, where the competitors furnished 142 machines to the company's 2,527; and in the eyeletting machinery, where the competitors furnished 150 to the company's 4,472.

The advantage, which the company had in being able to supply boot and shoe manufacturers with a complete line of machines, was accentuated by the fact that machines were leased, and not sold, to boot and shoe manufacturers. The schedule of rentals which the company charged was so arranged that it was much more advantageous economically for the lessee to obtain all of his machines from the company, than to buy from other companies. Although the price differential was not prohibitive, it was sufficiently great to make it highly unwise for any shoe manufacturer to secure his machines separately from independent competitors.

The attention of the public was attracted to the situation when Thomas G. Plant, an inventor, in 1910, sold his patents on shoe machinery to the company for $6,000,000, half of which he received in cash and the other half in stock in the company. Plant had earlier perfected some patents on individual machines, but had found it impossible to market his patents or machines because the individual machines could not be leased by shoe manufacturers without their being subjected to the higher rates for leasing only the remaining part of the United Shoe Machinery Company's entire series of machines. Plant then set to work to improve the entire series so as to be able to produce a series of machines, all of which would be protected by patents. When he had practically accomplished his purpose, he alleged, his bank credit was suddenly curtailed, his banking houses being controlled by the same men that were heavily interested in the United Shoe Machinery Company. His patents and machines were declared by technical experts to represent a distinct improvement in the entire series of machines. The company alleged that he offered to sell his patents and machines to them but at an exorbitant price. He did finally sell to them.

Individual members of the company had previously been indicted under the Sherman Law, the case being tried in the District Court of the District of Massachusetts.[4] The court argued, however, that "admitting that each group (all the

---

[4] *U. S. v. Winslow et al.*, 195 Fed. 578 (1913).

machines were grouped in four "groups") was controlled by a separate organization without any cross-holding, it would have been clear that the result (of combination) would have been simply a union of four different industries, not competing but supplementing each other."[5]   In other words, the court would have similarly held that a person attacked or menaced by four persons at one time would have been under no greater danger than if he had come upon them separately at considerable intervals of time!   Continuing this line of reasoning, the court held that, inasmuch as the Government admitted that each of the four groups controlled monopolies within their field prior to their amalgamation, monopolies which themselves were not illegal, then the combination of these groups into a single organization could not be regarded as illegal.   Even Justice Holmes, in reviewing this case, fell into the same erroneous line of reasoning:

> We see no greater objection to one corporation manufacturing 70% of three non-competing groups of patented machines collectively used for making a single product than to three corporations making the same proportion of one group each.[6]

Such an attitude of the court is to be criticised on two counts. In the first place, it represented a reversion to the earliest attitude of the courts, that mere size and capacity to engage in monopoly control was the criterion, and not the unfairness of the acts of the company.   And in the second place, the court rejected in an illogical manner the evidence which would, as a matter of fact, have answered in the affirmative the *a priori* judgment which they were seriously considering as pertinent.   In other words, the court regarded as unproved a proposition which they held to be pertinent; whereas, as a matter of common observation, the evidence clearly proved a proposition that should have been regarded as non-pertinent.   The real test of this case should have been the actual results of the activities of the United Shoe Machinery Company since its formation.

When the court turned to the economic and business situation involved, they were on more certain ground:

> This combination, then formed, was purely an economic arrangement, not in violation of any rule in restraint of trade at common law, or which has been announced by the Supreme Court . . .

[5] *Ibid.*, p. 591.
[6] *U. S. v. Winslow*, 227 U. S. 202, 217 (1913).

It seems to be impossible to deny that the combination of various elements of machinery, all relating to the same art and the same school of manufacturers, for the purpose of constructing economically and systematically, and of furnishing any customer, the whole or any part of an entire system, is in strict and normal compliance with modern trade progress . . . [7]

But in the remaining part of the sentence the court falls into the same "fallacy of composition" previously cited by asserting that a command of the entire market of a whole set of processes and machines, such as the company had achieved, was not different from separate controls of limited parts of such a series. Returning to the business point of view, Justice Holmes agreed with the previous contention of the court:

On the face of it, the combination was simply an effort after greater efficiency . . . The machines are patented, making them a monopoly in any case, . . . and it may be assumed that the success of the several groups was due to their patents having been the best . . . As they did not compete with one another, it is hard to see why the collective business should be any worse than its component parts . . . It is as lawful for one corporation to make every part of a steam engine and to put the machine together as it would be for one to make the boilers and another to make the wheels.[8]

The District Court had found in favor of the defendants, and this judgment was affirmed by the United States Supreme Court. Sound and justifiable developments in business were thus fortunately sanctioned by the courts, in spite of their faulty reasoning.

In a later case, in which the same company was again prosecuted, the court recognized the validity of the Government's contention that the organic combination of a number of monopolies in related businesses required separate consideration in addition to that which the court might direct toward the several component parts.[9] This change in the attitude of the court was effected by two previous decisions,[10] where it was recognized that "whatever we may think of the elements separately, when taken up as distinct charges, they are alleged effectively as elements of a scheme."

[7] *U. S. v. Winslow*, 195 Fed. 578, 592.

[8] *U. S. v. Winslow*, 227 U. S. 202, 217.

[9] *U. S. v. United Shoe Machinery Company of New Jersey et al.*, 222 Fed. 349, 355 (1915).

[10] *U. S. v. Reading Company*, 226 U. S. 325, 358; and *Swift and Company v. U. S.*, 196 U. S. 375, 396.

We agree with the United States in the proposition that whether or not the conduct of the respondents is in fact in restraint of trade does not depend on the effect of any element considered singly, so that every element considered singly may be wholly innocent; but the question of an existing monopoly, or an intended monopoly, is to be determined by the effect of all the elements which are in fact combined.[11]

Having rid itself of the persistence in an obvious fallacy, the court then shifted the issue from the metaphysical basis on which so many of the earlier court decisions relied and proceeded to examine the activities of the company. The case under discussion thus becomes especially significant as typifying the change in the judicial attitude toward monopolies and restraint of trade, in the direction of a functional test of the actual operations of corporations upon their competitors and customers. In this case the particular problem which concerned the court was: What effect had the formation of this company on its dealings with customers? Not only did the evidence seem to the court to show that the United Shoe Company did not enforce its leases in any arbitrary or unreasonable manner,[12] and "that there was nothing in the terms of the leases justifying any allegation indicating a purpose to enhance the cost of the machines to the users thereof, to wrong or oppress the public, or to impose any arbitrary, oppressive or unreasonable terms," or "to destroy or cripple competitors"; but the court further pragmatically held that:

The fact that the United Shoe Company has acquired so large a percentage of the business of the country to which it devoted itself comes so largely from the use of extraordinarily competent methods as to shut out from the eyes of the impartial investigator suggestions of other methods.[13]

Finally the court held that:

. . . (The company) constitutes an organization so successful in its operations, continuing so long a time, and so harmonious in its major parts, that anything which would bar out provisions in the leases and licenses necessary to the maintenance thereof must be admitted to be injurious to the manufacturers of shoes, as well as to the manufacturers of machinery, with regard to what each justly desires to accomplish.[14]

The above cases arose in Massachusetts under the Sherman Act. A similar case was brought against the same company a

[11] *U. S. v. United Shoe Machinery Company*, 222 Fed. 349, 356, 357.
[12] *Ibid.*, p. 353.
[13] *Ibid.*, p. 357.
[14] *Ibid.*, p. 361.

few months later in Missouri, significantly another shoe-manu-facturing center, but this case was prosecuted under the newly enacted Clayton Act, which expressed more of a functional view than had the courts. The charge brought by the Government rested upon certain clauses which were included in the United Shoe Machinery Company's leases; to the effect that the lessee "shall not use the machine in the manufacture or preparation of footwear which has not had certain essential operations performed upon it by other machines leased from the lessor" and "shall use exclusively the leased machine for the class of work for which it is designed." The result was, as the court stated, that the "prin-cipal" machines could not be operated profitably without the use of some, if not all, of the "auxiliary" machines, and that the latter were of no practical value except as they were used in connection with the "principal" machines. "It is hard to see how the ingenuity of man could have devised a scheme that would more effectively create a monopoly than the scheme set forth in the bill in this case."[15] The court ordered a temporary injunction and a later motion to dismiss the case was denied.[16]

A considerable part of the defense of the United Shoe Machin-ery Company rested on the fact that its machines were patented and that the patent rights implied a justification of monopoly control. This, of course, is the situation as regards patent rights and cannot be questioned from the ethical point of view because of the broader social benefits derived from thus encouraging mechanical invention. The legal problem was to determine the extent to which such implications of a patent right could be allowed. When later[17] the company tried to include in such implications the right to insist on the exclusive use of its own supplies for its machines—*e.g.*, tacks—the courts denied this contention.

The business problem involved in this situation was a com-plicated one. Here was a company which had enlarged its business through efficient methods, and which had extended its operations to include a number of closely related lines. Some

[15] *U. S. v. United Shoe Machinery Company*, 227 Fed. 507, 511 (1915).
[16] *Ibid.*, 234 Fed. 127 (1916).
[17] *United Shoe Machinery Company Corporation v. U. S.*, 258 U. S. 451, affirming 264 Fed. 138 (1922), decided on the basis of the Clayton Act. An earlier decision, *U. S. v. United Shoe Machinery Company of New Jersey*, 247 U. S. 32 (1918), which had sanctioned the company's practice, was decided on the basis of the Sherman Law.

of these lines were more profitable than others, therefore a generous price concession could be made to such customers as purchased exclusively from the company—or, putting it the other way, isolated sales bore charges that were greater than the proportionate charge on those isolated units in a combination sale. It is from this point on that the question of business policy and of business ethics becomes crucial. Shall the customer be forced to take the entire line or output of a company, with the alternative of receiving none? Obviously this is unfair to the customer as well as to the smaller competitor, especially if the latter produces only a part of the entire output. Furthermore, although it is unreasonable to ask of any business that all of its parts show an equal percentage of profit, it is not necessary, to avoid this absurdity, to go to the opposite extreme of contractual full-line forcing; a price differential is the more justifiable alternative. And it may easily be that such a check on the operating efficiency of the various parts of a business, as is offered by competitors who do not produce a full line, is wholesome from the point of view of the business itself. Such would certainly be the case in regard to the sale of supplies, even more than in the sale of related operating machines.

Block-booking and Full-line Forcing of Supplies

A similar situation is presented by the practice of "block-booking" in the motion-picture industry. The strict meaning of the term "block-booking" is that a producer or distributor refuses to sell individual picture films separately and insists that an exhibitor buy "all or none" of his products. Producers are thereby permitted to unload inferior films onto customers who desire to purchase certain other films that have a large sales appeal. The question is by no means one-sided, for the risk involved in the production of pictures is large. The issue is as to the acceptance or apportionment of the risk. The producer and distributor should recognize that a part of the justification for their existence and profits lies in the risks they assume; to pass these risks entirely over to the exhibitor reduces this justification. The risk can be apportioned by schedules of prices in which discounts may be offered for the purchase of groups of films. The Supreme Court in 1917 reversed the position it previously had held in regard to tying contracts, a position no longer tenable because of the Clayton Act, and held against the practice of "block-booking" in its extreme form.[18] Later the Federal Trade Commission issued a "cease and desist" order in the following case.

The Stanley Booking Corporation[19] was a New York corporation doing business in Philadelphia. It exhibited, leased, licensed, booked and dealt in moving-picture films. Its activities consisted, as a booking agency, in procuring and booking moving-picture films, by means of contracts with various exhibitors of films, on a commercial basis. The films were purchased and leased from producing companies and film exchanges and were then distributed, together with advertising matter, among exhibitors.

For three years prior to February, 1918, the Stanley Booking Corporation, among other activities, made contracts for the lease and sale of films only on the condition, agreement or understanding that the lessee or purchaser should not exhibit, use or deal in moving-picture films produced, handled or dealt in by any of its competitors.

By threats and intimidations the Stanley Booking Corporation induced owners and operators to pay them 10% of the cost of all moving-picture films booked directly from producers, in case they did not purchase their films from the Stanley Booking Corporation itself. By threats of withdrawing their patronage the Stanley Booking Corporation induced producers to cease supplying any of the Stanley Booking Corporation's competitors with films.[20]

An interesting point arises here, however: what if the company declares, and even believes, that the quality of the supplies used is necessary to the satisfactory operation of the machine? Such a situation arose in the following case.

For several years preceding December, 1916, A. B. Dick & Company engaged in the manufacture and sale of stencil duplicating machines, stencil paper, stencil ink and other duplicating-machine supplies. During the year 1915 A. B. Dick & Company controlled in the money value of sales approximately 85% of the commerce in these machines, 88% of the commerce in stencil paper and 80% of the commerce in stencil ink. Their products were selling at prices substantially higher than those quoted by their competitors and such sales were being made at a large profit.

On the Rotary Mimeograph Neostyle manufactured by A. B. Dick & Company appeared substantially the following statement:

[18] *Motion Picture Company v. Universal Film Company*, 243 U. S. 502.
[19] I F. T. C. D. 212 (1918).
[20] See Lewis, Howard T., "Arbitration in the Motion Picture Industry," 1929, printed separately by the *Harvard Business Review*.

This machine (this Neostyle) is sold by A. B. Dick & Company and purchased by the user with the expressed understanding that it is to be used only with the stencil paper, ink and other supplies made by A. B. Dick & Company.

This statement was further augmented by similar statements, and endorsements thereof in agreements which were contracted by A. B. Dick & Company with its dealers. Similar restrictions were made as to the exclusive use of stencil papers and of ink on mimeographing machines. Certain parts of the machines and the stencil papers were covered by letters patent.

In this case, the Federal Trade Commission issued a "cease and desist" order,[21] although the Supreme Court of the United States had previously, prior to the Clayton Act, held to the contrary.[22] Regardless of the legal points involved, the business situation again resolves itself, as in the case of the International Shoe Company, to a question of fairness to customers and to competitors as well as of business expediency. Where the efficient operation of the machine is dependent on the quality of parts and supplies, especially of the former, the right of the manufacturing company to insist on "tying contracts" seems to be justified. The ethics of the situation depends, however, on the facts in each particular case. Tacks, ink, and paper, respectively, would seem to afford increasing right to the company's arguments. That the burden of proof rests on the company is evidenced by the fact that a complicated system of tying contracts is apt to delude a company into a false sense of its business efficiency; the check of competition of various parts of a company's operations is wholesome, and the sales department frequently profits only at the expense of the purchasing or production department of the company itself.

An outstanding case of the same sort is presented by the policies of the Gillette Safety Razor Company. In the early days of this company's existence, the holder was sold under an implied contract, whereby the purchaser agreed to use only Gillette blades and not to resharpen the blades. The former requirement was fairly thoroughly maintained by the company through its patents and by means of exclusive distribution channels; the latter requirement was little observed. The experience of the company showed that the sale of blades offered a larger source of income than the sale of holders, hence the

[21] I F. T. C. D. 20 (1917).
[22] *Henry v. A. B. Dick Company*, 224 U. S. 1 (1912).

price of the latter was reduced considerably, a highly questionable practice, especially in view of recent developments, particularly the insistence by the bankers on the downward revisions of Gillette's earnings statements for the past five years. But even so, other blades and resharpening considerably interfered with the company's efforts to tie the use of Gillette blades to the purchase of the patented holder. If the company's efforts had been completely successful, it is doubtful whether they could have been justified ethically, for the temptation to lower the quality of parts, the profits on which depended on large sales through rapid replacement, would have been too great a strain on human nature. The piracy of Gillette blades, in itself unjustifiable ethically, probably contributed the competition necessary to check objectively the quality of the product. And the attempt of the Gillette Company to control absolutely the sale of blades set the pace for the industry, a pace which however was met more successfully by Gillette's most powerful competitor.

Finally there arose the "leading" case, in which an attempt was made to "tie" together the sales of different commodities.

Warren, Jones & Gratz, a copartnership located in St. Louis, were distributors of jute bagging, used for covering and wrapping bales of cotton, and of steel ties, used for binding cotton bales.

Warren, Jones & Gratz were sole distributing agents for the Carnegie Steel Company which made and sold approximately 75% of all the steel ties in the United States. The Carnegie Steel Company sufficiently dominated the cotton-tie situation to enable it to fix and control the prices of such ties throughout the country. About 45% of the jute bagging used in the United States was at this time manufactured by the American Manufacturing Company; about 20% was manufactured by the Ludlow Manufacturing Associates; the remaining 35% of jute bagging required for the cotton crop was at that time made up of second-hand bagging and so-called "sugar-bag cloth." All of these firms were competitors among each other for the sale of jute bagging. Warren, Jones & Gratz were the distributing agents for the American Manufacturing Company.

On a number of occasions prior to January, 1917, merchants, jobbers and dealers in bagging and ties throughout the cotton-growing states were unable to procure ties from any firm other than Warren, Jones & Gratz or their two agents, P. P. Williams, of Vicksburg, and C. O. Elmer, of New Orleans. Warren, Jones & Gratz, having virtually a monopoly of the cotton-tie business, forced the would-be purchasers of ties to buy also a proportionate amount of the jute bagging manufactured by the American Manufacturing Company. Warren, Jones & Gratz refused to sell ties unless a corresponding amount of bagging was purchased at the same time.

The Federal Trade Commission ordered the Gratz Company to "cease and desist" their practice,[23] but this order was reversed by the Circuit Court of Appeals, Second Circuit, partly on the ground that "the public interest" was not sufficiently involved and that the Federal Trade Commission Act did not contemplate unfair methods of competition between individuals!

That the Commission did not find sufficient proof to sustain the second count in the complaint, *viz.*, that the method of the respondents found to be unfair violated section 3 of the act of October 15, 1914, known as the Clayton Act, which makes unlawful any condition, agreement, or understanding that may lessen competition or tend to create a monopoly shows that the method found to be unfair must have been unfair in certain individual transactions. And we discover no evidence to support the finding in paragraph 2 that the respondents "adopted and practiced the policy of refusing to sell steel ties to those merchants and dealers who wished to buy them from them unless such merchants and dealers would also buy from them a corresponding amount of jute bagging." It is the natural and prevailing custom in the trade to sell ties and bagging together, just as one witness testified it is to sell cups and saucers together. Such evidence as there is of a refusal to sell is a refusal to sell at all to certain persons with whom the respondents had previous unsatisfactory relations and a refusal to sell ties without bagging at the opening of the market in 1916 and 1917 when there was fear that, owing to scarcity of ties and the prospect of large crops, the marketing of the cotton crop might be endangered by speculators creating a corner in ties. The evidence is that with these exceptions the respondents sold ties without any restrictions to all who wanted to buy and indeed made extraordinary efforts to induce the manufacturers of ties to increase their output so that all legitimate dealers and all cotton raisers should get enough ties and bagging at reasonable rates to market their cotton. It is only these exceptional and individual cases, which established no general practice affecting the public, that can sustain the findings in paragraph 4.[24]

The significance of this case lies in the fact that certain elements were thrown into confusion which must be cleared up before the field of Business Ethics can be properly appreciated. In the first place, as has been stated before, the legal points involved are not necessarily the important business points: most of the business objection to "tying clauses" consists in the probability of a business deluding itself into believing that additional business inevitably results in increased profits. In

[23] I F. T. C. D. 249 (1918).
[24] *Gratz v. F. T. C.*, 258 Fed. 314; affirmed, 253 U. S. 421 (1919).

the second place, by "public interest" the courts, following the traditional attitude of the Church, mean "consumers' interests"; the point of view developed in this volume is that the "competitors'" and the fabricating "purchasers'" interests, as well as the "producers,'" must also be considered in connection with business ethics. If the courts refuse to regard these latter interests as sufficiently great to be included in "the public interest," then the law definitely represents the consumer as opposed to the business interest. But Business Ethics has a broader conception of the situation; namely, that the producer and the competitor have an interest which must be taken into account before an adequate ethical judgment is rendered. These interests do not exclude the purchaser-consumer interests, but they have an ethical right to be heard and to be considered in proportion to their social value. It is fortunate that Church and State have protected the rights of the consumer; but they have both become special pleaders, even extreme advocates, against interests and rights which should in justice be recognized. The problems of business ethics that arise beyond this elementary point are too numerous and too important to warrant resting content with an arbitrary solution of a moral-social issue that inadequately represents the sum-total of the situation.

Full-line forcing is objectionable, therefore, even from the vendor's point of view, because of the danger that the weaker parts of the business may become a drain on the stronger parts. Like the buttresses which were added to Lincoln College to prevent the further weakening of the building, the building may eventually have to support the buttresses. Where each new line or function does strengthen a business by being profitable and attractive, it seldom requires the artificial support of the rest. And if it does require such support, then the competitors and the customers have a just cause for complaint. Instead of pursuing the argument further from the producer-vendor's point of view, therefore, it may be profitable to consider the whole matter from the standpoint of the purchaser-consumer.

The Problem of the Customer

The problem of "full-line forcing" may well be studied from the point of view of the buyer, especially if he faces the predicament of purchasing something which he is not particularly desirous of having, and if, on the other hand, he desires to maintain the goodwill of the company from which he has been buying satisfactorily in the main.   And inasmuch as the problem is not necessarily confined to the buying and selling of commodities, it might be well to examine a case involving the marketing of securities.

In March, 1923, Wald and Jamson,[25] an investment-banking firm with offices in New York and Boston, was offered a participation of $75,000 in a syndicate formed by Larson and Company[26] to sell an issue of $4,500,000 Ludwig Railroad Company[26] 5½% equipment trust certificates issued under the Philadelphia plan.[27]   The amount of the participation did not exceed that usually accepted by the firm, but a divergence of opinion existed among the partners as to the advisability of accepting the offer.   The proceeds were to be used for the purchase of new equipment, the wisdom of which was not questioned either as a matter of policy or in regard to detailed items.   The merits of the situation might, however, be questioned in themselves.   The issue was to be secured by approximately $6,500,000 of equipment, including the proposed purchases and a certain amount of new equipment already in use.

The Ludwig Railway Company had been in the hands of a receiver since late in 1921, when it had defaulted on the interest of its first and refunding mortgage bonds.   The gross income for 1922 was $5,688,458, to be applied to interest charges, rentals, and hire of equipment amounting to $6,060,925, leaving a deficit for that year of $372,467.   The funded debt of the Ludwig Railroad Company in 1923 was:

Improvement Mortgage 5s 1928.............	$ 8,335,000
First lien on 1,647 miles	
Cumulative adjustment income 7s 1932.......	10,000,000
Second lien on 161 miles, third lien on 325 miles, fourth lien on 2,058 miles	
Interest in default since Sept. 1921	
Consolidated Mortgage 4s 1936..............	34,125,000
Consolidated Mortgage 4s 1936..............	6,382,000
First lien on 1,647 miles	
First and refunding mortgage 5s 1955........	31,114,000
First lien on 161 miles, second lien on 325 miles, third lien on 2,058 miles	
Interest in default since Dec. 1921	
First trust mortgage 4s 1939...............	15,190,000
First lien on 411 miles	
First consolidated mortgage 4s 1944.........	15,080,000

[25] *I Harvard Business Reports* 515.   Fictitious name.
[26] Fictitious name.
[27] See Dewing, *Financial Policy of Corporations*, rev. ed., pp. 190–192.

First lien on 316 miles, second lien on 417 miles

Also secured by deposit of $10,000,000 capital stock of Cressona Light & Power Co.

Equipment trust 5½% certificates, 1924–1938 —this issue............................. 4,500,000

$124,726,000

The Ludwig Railroad Company also guaranteed the interest on:

Antioch and Western First Mortgage 4s 1940.... $4,510,000
Antioch Junction Railway First Mortgage 5s 1939   2,000,000

The dividend warrants and maturing certificates of the proposed issue were to rank ahead of the $31,114,000 first and refunding mortgage bonds and the $10,000,000 cumulative adjustment income bonds among the receiver's obligations. Hence, of the gross income of $5,688,458, applicable to interest charges, rentals, and hire of equipment, the dividend warrants of the new issue were junior only to two items; $3,279,740 senior interest charges and $525,485 rentals and hire of equipment. Annually from 1924 through 1938, $300,000 of certificates of the new issue were to mature. Equipment was to be leased to the receiver at a rental equal to certificates and dividend warrants as they matured. Principal and dividends were guaranteed unconditionally by endorsement of the receiver. Provision was made for the assumption of these obligations to the new issue by any new company subsequently formed.

One partner of Wald and Jamson believed that the firm should not participate in the syndicate, because the certificates were likely to be difficult to sell, and therefore the participation would be unprofitable. At the price fixed by the terms of the syndicate agreement, the certificates were to be sold to yield 5⅝%. Numerous firms, among them Wald and Jamson, were offering other equipment-trust certificates with equal or greater security at the same yield, and it was evident that the new issue should return a higher yield than equipment of railroad companies with well-established credit, in order to appeal to investors. It was also maintained that participation in a syndicate whose securities were difficult to sell should carry with it the possibility of a substantial profit. The members of this syndicate, however, were allowed a profit of only 1½%. This partner pointed out also that the condition of the bond market was not favorable to the purchase of securities which might have to be sold after the close of the syndicate.

The other partners, however, believed that the decision should be based, not on the merits of the securities themselves, but on the reputation of Larson and Company, which was one of the leading originating firms in the United States. Participation in its syndicates was valuable.

In January, 1923, it had formed a syndicate to sell an issue of Jackstone Manufacturing Company[28] bonds but had not offered participation to Wald and Jamson. When the latter asked the reason for this, the originator intimated that Wald and Jamson's refusal to accept participation in a less desirable syndicate, formed a short time previously, was responsible for the omission. These partners were convinced that the gain from participation in the profitable syndicates formed by Larson and Company was much greater than the loss from those which were not successful, and that it was important therefore to remain on this originator's syndicate list. Larson and Company were specialists in railroad financing and could be depended upon to bring out securities which were safe investments. Since title to the equipment remained with the trustee until the certificates were paid, the credit of the railroad company was a factor of less importance than if the issue had been of debenture or mortgage bonds. The firm decided, therefore, to subscribe for $75,000 of the certificates.

The problem confronting Wald and Jamson is obviously that of assuming a temporary disadvantage for the sake of the larger and broader advantages accruing from their continuance as customers of Larson and Company. The problem is presented from the customer's point of view in order to give an adequate picture of the "full-line forcing" situation. The customer's predicament is a part of the situation, and if this predicament involves giving the customer no choice at all other than economic ruin—as would be the case if a monopoly in one product should be used to drive the competitors in an allied product out of business or to sell products to customers at prices above the market—then business should cease the practice. Otherwise the interference of a law such as the Clayton Act can be fully justified. We are here on the borderland of ethics; for the business policy regarding full-line forcing should not be determined wholly by the threat of legal action or even by immediate economic considerations, but rather by maintaining a nice distinction between attractive price schedules and unfair economic pressure to secure the full and continued patronage of customers. And if in addition there must be included the indefinable factor of "fairness" to effect a just resolution of the situation, business must recognize that such a consideration is inextricably bound up with self-government and ethics in business.

The merit of a full-line forcing policy lies in the fairness with which it is administered. The urge toward fairness on the part

[28] Fictitious name.

of the vendor consists in the desire to maintain a relatively permanent clientele. This attitude recognizes the potential threat of competition but is not to be confused with the immediate and direct activities connected with competition itself. Furthermore, to uphold competition as such as preferable to a full-line forcing policy, is to forget that competition also entails unfair business practices; an effect such as excessive price-cutting may not only be unfair to the vendor, but it may also have so disastrous an effect upon him as to drive him out of business, thus depriving the buyer of his source of supplies. It is upon this broader basis of the mutual long-time interests of both buyer and seller that the ethics of full-line forcing is to be determined.

CHAPTER VII

EXTENSION OF FUNCTIONS AND MERGERS

The preceding chapter dealt with certain cases in which companies extended their sales activities to closely allied commodities, especially by means of tying contracts and through policies of full-line forcing. The present chapter will deal with a similar situation, amplified however by the fact that the list of commodities handled by a company is much more diversified, either through an extension of the company's activities into other fields or through its merging with other companies which have handled other lines of commodities. In a number of cases this tendency involves the consequent intensification of competition in the invaded field. Those companies which have previously occupied the invaded field assume that they have a vested ethical right to that field and base their plea for "business ethics" on that claim. It will become apparent, however, that the ethical problems involved in the situation are not so superficial as such a claim makes them appear to be, and that the merits of the claims must be tested by the more basic social-economic movements of which they are symptoms.

The following situations have been selected as representative of some of the most crucial ethical problems arising from the recent tendency to extend business functions and to effect mergers. None of the cases are disguised, the information in all cases having been secured from published material and being generally known. The activities engaged in by these various companies are not peculiar to them, the general record of these companies can well stand the test of public scrutiny, and other companies have become involved in similar situations. But "it is the plug hat that draws the snowballs," and the prominence of these companies is the excuse for using their experiences as illustrative material.

The Packers' Case

On February 27, 1920, the Attorney General of the United States filed a bill of complaint against Armour and Company, Swift and Company, Morris and Company, Wilson and Company, and the Cudahy Packing Company, known as the "Big Five" Meat Packers, alleging violations of the anti-trust laws.

The contention of the Government was that these companies, avowedly engaged in the packing of meat and meat products, were extending their functions so widely as virtually to create a monopoly of food products. The five packing companies were enjoined from engaging any further in the ownership and control of public stockyards, stockyard terminal railways, and stockyard market journals; in the selling of meat or milk and cream at retail, of holding an interest in cold-storage plants, or of using branch houses, refrigeration cars or motor trucks for other than the specific functions connected with the packing of meat. These meat-packing companies were furthermore enjoined from dealing in the following food products: fresh canned fish, vegetables, and fruits; confectioneries, syrups, soda-fountain supplies, grape juice, molasses, honey, jams, jellies, preserves, spices, sauces, condiments, and relishes; coffee, tea, chocolate, and cocoa; nuts; flour, sugar, and rice; bread, wafers, crackers, biscuits, cereals, and grain; and 25 other classes of miscellaneous products.[1]

The packers' case was complicated by the fact that on April 19, 1922, the California Cooperative Canneries filed a petition to intervene, on the ground that the injunction against the packers afforded Armour and Company a ground for cancelling a contract they had with the California Cooperative Canneries to purchase 52% of the latter's output, amounting approximately to $4,000,000. The cooperatives asserted not only that their interest in the effect of the injunction should allow them to intervene, but also that the injunction virtually created a monopoly in canned goods on the part of the Wholesale Grocers' Association. Indeed, the Southern Wholesale Grocers' Association and the National Wholesale Grocers' Association had applied for permission to intervene on behalf of Armour and Company. The intervention of the cooperatives and wholesalers had the effect of making the legal problem approximate more nearly the actual complex business situation.

Wholesale grocers deal largely in "canned goods," this being the largest single item in their business. So interested are they in this phase of their business that they have made especial efforts to retain it by financing the growers and in some cases the canners. Consequently, the wholesalers must have viewed with considerable alarm the extension of the activities of meat packers to include the sale of general food products in their business.

The suit resulted in a "consent decree," whereby the packers agreed to restrict their operations. By 1928 the entire marketing situation had changed with the advent of "chain" grocery stores, many of which

[1] *California Cooperative Canneries v. U. S.*, 299 Fed. 908; *Swift and Company v. U. S.*, 276 U. S. 311, 316.

erected packing houses to supply them with meat sold at retail. The packers therefore undertook to have the consent decree annulled in order that they might compete throughout with distributors of foods that were competing with them in the meat-packing business.

The extension of the activities of the meat packers, following the vacation of the "consent decree," might take either one of two directions: the handling of various lines of food products besides meat, or the taking-over of the retail distribution of meat. It is conceivable, of course, that both kinds of extensions are contemplated, but the distinction between the two is sufficiently important to warrant considering them separately.

To begin with, the vacation of the consent decree has, through recent business developments, practically come to be a right which can no longer be denied the packers as a matter of justice. Not only are the chain stores establishing their own packing plants; but many small packers, that are not large enough to attract the limelight of public or governmental attention, are engaged in handling the various food products which the large packers have been prohibited from handling. But this right, moral as well as legal, which might be secured by an extension of the government prohibition to all packers and perhaps even to the chain stores, is not to be confused with the business expediency of engaging in such activities as are legally permitted or morally justified.

Undoubtedly the retail distribution of meat offers an attractive field to the packers. Out of every dollar paid for the original animal, the farmer receives 63 cents, the packer receives 13 cents, while the retailer receives 24 cents. It would seem that economies in retail distribution would make possible a reduction of costs, especially in view of the fact that the chain stores have reduced this item to 20% or less. According to Julius Klein, the annual waste in distribution in the United States amounts to some $8,000,000,000, and it seems reasonable to suppose that a large and efficient organization could profitably enter such a field of activity and perhaps even reduce the cost to the consumer. Furthermore, the recently developed "quick-freezing" process might enable the packers to cut and wrap meat centrally and distribute it with great efficiency and economy. Opposed to this possibility of entering the retail field is the outstanding fact of corporation experience in the United States that, although expansion other than in mere size has been in the direction of acquiring sources of raw material, very little of this expansion has until recently been in the direction of retail outlets. Not only is there a presumption that the experience of unforeseeable expenses in marketing activities has deterred expansion in that direction, and that the $8,000,000,000 of "waste" referred to by Klein must be regarded as "necessary and inevitable expense" until experience shows the contrary; but the endeavor to expand in the direction of marketing, by price reductions or whatever means employed, has encountered and stimulated the determined and united opposition of the distributors already engaged in such functions.

This opposition of many smaller units in a field that was being invaded by a large corporation has in the past raised crucial problems of social policy and of Business Ethics. The resulting situation has been much the same as was felt by laborers when labor-saving machinery was first introduced, and the human values unquestionably cannot be wholly brushed aside as inconsequential in relation to the material economies undoubtedly involved. The sociological problems involved in this larger problem will be considered more fully in a succeeding chapter. The packers, however, in this particular case, have to face in addition the business predicament of making their first advances in the retail distribution of meat at the expense of the packers' best customer, the independent retailer. That is, the independent retailer will probably be much more vitally affected by the initiation of the contemplated policy of the packers than will the packers' competitors themselves, and many will probably be eliminated before the real issue is joined with the chain store; thus every initial gain of the packers will be neutralized by a corresponding loss of retail outlets.

The other direction in which the packers' business may be extended, namely, the handling of other food products, more particularly involves the problems with which this chapter is concerned. Here the case seems clearer for the packer, for he is already possessed of facilities—refrigerator cars, packing machinery, and distribution organization—to warrant the belief that many economies could be effected by a fuller and more extensive use of such facilities; while the diversification of products would undoubtedly stabilize the business. Furthermore, the social menace and public suspicion of a group of such large food-distributing corporations is less than it was 10 years ago, because of the advent, in the meantime, of chain stores and other large food distributors—such as General Foods and Standard Brands—affording relatively equal and therefore effective competition.

Socially and ethically there is much to be said for an organization of specialized business activities. This is the attitude developed among the professions, which have learned by long experience that a man, who is improperly trained or insufficiently equipped to perform professional functions properly, inevitably brings the profession into disrepute; while any attempts on the part of a professional man to extend his functions very far beyond the lines of demarcation which his profession sets up, either make him neglect his own functions or effect an undesirable course of behavior in his newly assumed functions in which he is, after all, merely an amateur. The situation, in the packers' case, is that the wholesale grocer, who is the most vociferous opponent of the proposed policy, has not apparently been performing his own functions efficiently or economically; by his own admissions he is losing ground. Therefore, it would seem, even on the basis of the broader and more abstract principles involved, that the meat packer is not unduly extending his own justifiable functions when he handles allied food products —this part of the Consent Decree has been vacated—especially when he invades a field that would have difficulty in defending its record on the ground of efficiency and economy, matters which are important from a social and ethical point of view.

Financial Operations of Merchants

The objection of the wholesaler to the packers' invasion of the distribution field is particularly interesting in view of the fact that the wholesaler himself has begun to extend his activities beyond the performing of strictly wholesaling functions. What the "wholesalers' functions" are, will be dealt with in a later chapter. But it is pertinent here to raise the question whether the wholesaler is justified in extending his activities to banking, for example, which seems only indirectly or remotely related to the wholesaler's activities.

It is of course obvious that one of the primary functions of the wholesaler is to maintain a stock of merchandise, sufficiently large to require a substantial investment. In most cases the investment is greater than the investment of the retail outlets which are served.   In addition to this investment in plant and merchandise, the wholesaler is called upon to extend credit to the retailer.   In the grocery business,[2] for example, as much money is tied up in accounts receivable as in merchandise; in the coal business, the figures are even higher; hardware wholesalers as a rule credit to dealers about 50% of their stocks; seasonal lines, such as wall paper, sometimes run as high as 75%.   The financial statements of various wholesale dry-goods firms disclosed the following results:

Invested Capital	Per Cent Assets in Accounts Receivable
Less than $250,000.......................	37.1
$250,000 to $500,000......................	41.8
$500,000 to $1,000,000.....................	41.7
$1,000,000 and over.......................	34.5

When it is remembered that interest on accounts receivable is seldom charged, and that some losses must be written off due to bad debts, it becomes evident that the wholesaler has become to a large extent a banker.   And in so far as the wholesaler allows accounts receivable unduly to increase, or advances money to growers or manufacturers, he has allowed his wholesaling functions to be supplanted by banking activities.

Now, banking is a business which requires especial skill; it is not successfully performed by all men who undertake it even to the exclusion of other functions.   Therefore, the wholesaler, who tries to strengthen his main business by adventures in credit and loan activities, may be jumping from the frying pan into the fire.   The actual result is that the wholesaling business comes to consist in the selling of terms instead of the selling of goods and services, with sales of doubtful net value being made by the business which is most lenient in its terms.   Little effort is made to enforce sales terms, the outstanding violation by buyers being the taking of unearned discounts.   The extent to which merchants have become bankers is indicated by the following conclusions of the Committee on Credits, Sales Terms and Collections at the National Wholesale Conference of 1929.

1. The tendency toward the taking of unearned discounts is one of the serious credit problems wholesalers face.   Only united effort will

[2] See *Report* of Committee IV on "Credit, Sales Terms and Collections," National Wholesale Conference, 1929, auspices Chamber of Commerce of the United States.   The Louisville Survey has, of course, become classic.

prove effective in defending the sanctity of the contract which exists when goods are sold on clearly stated terms of sale.

2. Competition should be based on the quality of the goods and the efficiency of the service, rather than upon the elasticity of the sales terms.

3. Bad debt loss percentages of well-defined wholesaling groups, combined in average percentages for the group, are of great value to credit managers.

4. The practice of clearing credit information through some central trade or credit agency is a valuable form of cooperation.

5. A working arrangement between the credit and sales departments of a wholesale house is of primary importance in maintaining good credit and collection conditions.

6. The development of standard sales terms in well-defined trade groups is necessary for the common interest.   Such a development and adherence to established terms insures against the present marked tendency toward "terms grabbing" on the part of the buyers.

7. The development and persistent use of effective collection machinery by the individual wholesaler is a distinct aid to better wholesaling conditions.

8. The use of trade acceptances in settlement of accounts on extended terms is on the increase and is believed to be a worth-while tendency.

9. The charging of interest on past due accounts is a logical corollary of the cash-discount privilege and is approved in principle.

Wholesalers have been engaged in extending their functions into the field of banking, not only as regards credit terms offered to customers, but wholesale grocers have also been financing the growers of fruits and vegetables, commodities which form a large part of the trade of the wholesaler.[3]   When one inquires into the reasons why the growers have been seeking their financial support from the wholesalers, three reasons in particular are mentioned: it has become a custom and tradition in the trade, funds can be thus obtained with relatively less obligation in the form of security, and money can be obtained at a lower rate of interest.   Obviously, the last two factors are sufficient to make the whole situation a questionable one, for the security of the loans is less than what a banker would require, and the low interest rates evidently make impossible the building up of a reserve against losses.   This situation is typical of the extension of a business-man's activities beyond the field in which he is an

[3] French, Earl R., "Six Years' Experience of New York Distributors in Crop Financing," a paper read before the New York Food Marketing Research Council, October 23, 1928.

expert into a field which has been occupied by others who could be presumed to know how to conduct it; but the intruder, an amateur, fails to take into account the necessities imposed on those who wish to retain a permanent tenure of the field, and his shortsighted policies not only jeopardize his own interests but also menace the field of his extended activities by undermining it with reckless competition.

The advances of the wholesaler to the grower are often in the form of seed, fertilizer and supplies, rather than directly in cash; the collateral accepted for such advances is little more than the moral obligation of the grower to sell his products to the wholesaler, who then can repay himself before remitting the amount due; and interest charges are not levied on approximately half the loans, the remaining half carrying an interest charge of 6%. Seed companies which make advances to growers feel that the practice is justified in that it makes possible the profits on their sales; wholesalers and other distributors find a similar justification in thus assuring themselves of their commissions. But both fail to see that a double function is receiving but a single return. The abuse of the system can be expected. One grower stated that a grower with a fair reputation for honesty and enterprise could thus obtain sufficient funds to produce a crop, including the rent on land, the grower contributing only the supervision of the requisite labor. Twenty-five years ago a single New York commission house had loans amounting to $32,000 outstanding in the Georgia district; other firms were similarly committed, and the system of fruit and vegetable credits has continually expanded since then. It may be a case of having hold of the bear's tail without being able to let go, but the situation is bound to decrease the returns of both banking and commission houses.

As to the extensiveness of the practice, the following figures cited by Mr. French are significant. The outstanding 90 of the 200 commission houses in New York were interviewed regarding advances to growers; two-thirds of them stated that they had been engaged in the practice for at least five years. Thirty-four of these firms advanced annually a total sum in excess of $1,000,000, advances fluctuating with prices obtained the previous year. Mixed vegetables, grapes, apples and tomatoes were the commodities which secured two-thirds to three-fourths of these loans; California, Florida, Virginia and Cuba were the regions most favored; and 90% of the loans were in the form of cash.

As regards security, approximately one-half was represented by personal notes, one-quarter additional having no security at all; the remaining one-quarter was largely in the form of two or more securities, only 7% of the entire total being in the form of warehouse receipts or mortgaged crops or real estate. Only 40% of these contracts were written, this part representing two-thirds of the dollars advanced, both percentages declining in recent years. It is not intended to convey the impression that tangible collateral is a better risk than knowledge of the borrower. The test, however, of any loaning policy lies in the amount of loss. In the situation under discussion, the loss over a period of more than five years has been over 8%, due largely to crop failures, spoilage and deterioration because of plant diseases and unfavorable weather conditions, overproduction, and maladjustment at terminal markets. These losses do not include "unpaid balances" which frequently are converted later into losses. The net result is practically a reduction of commission charges by one-seventh to one-fifth. It is highly questionable whether the extension of the wholesaler's and commission merchant's activities into the banking field is wise. Not the least of the evil effects resulting are the encouragements offered to unscrupulous growers to take advantage of the situation and the possibility of rapidly developing overproduction.

But the outstanding fact in the whole situation is that the wholesaler has engaged in functions that are distinct in kind from wholesaling. There is no absolute reason for his not doing so; at least society has not seen fit to separate the functions of wholesaling and banking by licensing either, and the necessary implications of wholesaling may include banking operations. The assumption of banking functions by wholesalers is sufficiently greater in degree than the extensions which the meat packers proposed, however, so as practically to amount to a difference in kind. Not only, moreover, do these different functions require a different kind of skill, placing on the wholesaler the burden of proving that he is not afflicting bankers with the unfair competition of amateurs; but it is highly probable that confusion as to the wholesaler's functions results in concealing the inefficient and uneconomical factors in wholesaling itself.[4]

[4] A series of advertisements of the John Wanamaker store, in the *New York Times* during 1929, evidences the reaction of an individualistic store toward mergers and extensions of functions. See especially No. 10 of the Series, *New York Times*, November 7, 1929.

One of the most far-reaching developments analogous to the extension of mercantile functions into the banking field is the policy of corporations of lending money on the call market. This policy reached its peak just prior to the market crash of October, 1929. The amount of money so loaned "on call" for the account of "others" reached at that time the stupendous sum of $4,000,000,000. Its sources were chiefly four: investment trusts, corporation funds, foreign balances awaiting investment, and wealthy individuals or groups of individuals. Of chief interest were the loans of surplus funds by corporations, a new development in finance. In former years the development of a surplus was regarded by a railroad, manufacturing or mercantile company as the occasion for further expansion of the business or for the retirement of outstanding high-rate obligations. Where a large surplus of liquid funds was necessary for the purchase of raw materials or other corporate purposes, these funds were allowed to accumulate in the banks and drew a rate of interest that varied from 2% to 2½%. With "call money" offering attractive rates of from 6% to 12%, and being secured by readily marketable paper, the temptation offered to corporations was a great one. As far back as 1927, when the cash accounts of many corporations began to swell, the item "assets in cash or call loans" began to creep into the balance sheets, individual amounts ranging from $500,000 upwards. At one time the Delaware and Hudson Railroad had "on call" $24,000,-000, the proceeds of the sale of a subsidiary. In some cases, corporations issued new stock or bonds at a rate that enabled them either to retain their money on the call market or to place additional funds there. The whole situation developed into one in which corporations that had in the main been manufacturing companies were diverting their management activities toward lending money and were deriving therefrom a great part of their income.

This situation differed from that of the commission merchants, previously described, in which an outstanding feature was the relative insecurity of the loans. Call loans are made on quickly marketable stock with a margin which is sufficient to prevent a loss even in such a rapid break as occurred in the latter part of 1929. Not a dollar has ever been lost by lending "on call" in the New York stock market. The principal objection to the practice came from the bankers, who declared that such loans were to be characterized as "irresponsible"; the lenders having no interest in the call-money market or its welfare other than its desirability as a vehicle for the temporary investment of funds. The bankers predicted that, in case of strain, these companies would not be likely to remain in the market as would those which were more permanently interested in the banking business. This prediction came true when the market broke in the late fall of 1929, many additional sales contributing to the debacle because of the high interest rates and shortage of funds resulting from the tremendous decline in loans "for others." Loans "for the account of others" declined more than $2,000,000,000, or more than 50%, by the end of 1929; the $1,000,000,000 thrown into the breach by the New York banks did not even neutralize the withdrawals by out-of-town banks.

The social and business results of this intrusion of mercantile, manufacturing and railroad companies into the banking field are undeniably unfortunate. The speculation preceding the crash was undoubtedly stimulated by the increased funds available[5] as much as the speculative fever itself attracted the funds; and the intensity of the crash was undoubtedly due in part to the rapid withdrawal of funds, the consequent increase in rates, and the unwillingness of these banking amateurs to reduce margins in the interest of financial stability. The difficulty is that the situation differs from the financing of growers in another respect than that of the safety of the loan: the individuals so extending their functions by entering the "call" market are not penalized, as are the lenders to the growers when they withdraw from the field, for their individual corporate interests at times of financial crises are at variance with the general business interests. The banker, in order to remain permanently at his job, must then conduct himself in such a way as would be temporarily to his disadvantage, a mode of behavior which is economically and socially justifiable in view of the profits accruing to permanent bankers "in the long run." The whole situation resolves itself to this, that amateurs temporarily entered the

---

[5] From the middle of 1927 to the peak of 1929, call loans increased from $3,000,000,000 to $7,000,000,000; "others" accounted for $3,000,000,000 of the increase, out-of-town banks $1,000,000,000, while the accounts of New York banks remained constant until the market broke, when they were increased practically 100%. By the end of 1930, "loans for others" had declined to less than half a billion dollars.

banking field without jeopardizing their own interests but with unfortunate financial consequences; and without assuming the responsibilities of a permanent form of competition that might otherwise prove to be a corrective of current banking methods.

The cases we have thus far been discussing have for the most part involved the question as to the expediency of extending business activities into allied fields. This question must be approached by any business from the point of view of the capacity of its management, especially where great diversification is involved. Up to the limit of that capacity, however, diversification of production or sales may be justified by the ability thereby to achieve a high degree of business stability. Thus the Union Pacific ownership of large blocks of New York Central, Illinois Central, Chicago and North Western and Baltimore and Ohio stock may be preferable to retiring its own bonded indebtedness or to the intensive development of its own property. But such a policy of diversification requires that its management have financial as well as operating ability, even though all its holdings be in railroad property; while the ability by such means to attract additional traffic may not be so lucrative in the net results as might appear on the surface. The Standard Oil Company of New Jersey has become heavily interested in the chemical industry, especially through its alliance with "I. G." Farbenindustrie, the German dye trust. Like the United States Steel Corporation, the company owns its sources of raw material and transportation facilities, and has in addition extensively developed its distribution outlets. E. I. du Pont de Nemours & Company has carried its diversification probably further than any other company in this country, it being interested in dyestuffs, paint, lacquer, rayon, coated textiles, industrial alcohol, fire extinguishers, motion-picture film, and chemicals; in addition, its investment policies have given it influential interests in General Motors Corporation and United States Rubber Company.

That there is a limit to such diversification and extension of functions in business has already been indicated. The following case shows strikingly the extremities to which such a policy may be pursued, and also incidentally that the problem is not peculiar to American business.

The Marconi Wireless Telegraph Company

The Marconi Wireless Telegraph Company was an English company, originally organized for the purpose of developing the wireless telegraph as a means of communication. By 1920, however, the company had invested large sums of money in 56 other companies—engaged in foreign banking, lumbering and slate quarrying, and in manufacturing tin plate, carbon products, *etc.*—twelve of which had no connection with the original business of the Marconi Company and many others of which were only remotely related to the main business of the company. Syndicates and other ventures outside the "generally understood objects of the company" began to form so large a part of the activities of the company that the capacity of the management was severely tested. By 1927 conditions in the company had become serious, the auditor's report for that year disclosing "a lamentable record of financial and commercial incompetence, of failures, and of improvident risk of shareholders' money."[6]

During the five years 1920–1924 inclusive, the company had announced profits and declared dividends as follows:

	Profits	Dividends
1920	£297,682	15%
1921	275,361	15%
1922	302,948	15%
1923	172,543	10%
1924	225,600	10%

That during this time the position of the company had been wholly misunderstood by the general body of shareholders and by the general investing public seemed to be evidenced by the fact that at the 1927 meeting of the shareholders, on March 15, accumulated losses of over £6,000,000 were disclosed, and a drastic reorganization plan was proposed.

Evidently this is an instance of a company, originally intended to engage in a particular business, but successively extending its field of operations into other fields, some related, others not, until the directors and management had far exceeded their abilities to control the situation; and a major capital loss ensued. Whether the mismanagement of the more exotic activities involved unfair competition by ruinous price-cutting is not disclosed. Any possible benefits so derived by customers would have been counterbalanced by the disruption of business in those fields. Such seem to be the inevitable accompaniments of amateur extensions of business functions.

But the case turns on the effects which such policies produce, and introduces another phase of the general problem of business organization: the internal structure of a business company and

[6] *London Times*, March 5, 1927, p. 18.

the allocation of responsibility among the share owners, directors and managers for the policies which the company pursues.

The auditors' reports had for five or more years included qualifications of their general certification. The chief qualification, made by Cooper Brothers and Company—and endorsed by Messrs. Garnsey, a branch of Price Waterhouse and Company—was to the effect that they "were unable to form an opinion as to the value of the company's interests in the associated companies." This raises the question as to such responsibility of accountants and auditors—and for the physical check of inventories, an issue that has been a bone of contention between accountants and bankers for years. The bankers, of course, insist that accountants should be responsible for a check of physical inventory, while many accountants insist that they cannot "go back" of the reports of subsidiary companies and company agents but must proceed on the assumption that such reports are reliable. In support of this latter view, one might cite the impossibility of making an inventory of large timber claims; although, in the case of a large woolen manufacturing company a final crash would probably have been averted by only a minimum of investigation into millions of dollars of inflated stock-inventory items. Inasmuch as specialists can be hired to make physical inventories, such a function would appear to be merely a pragmatic implication of the admitted functions of auditors. Responsibility for the correctness of statements of subsidiaries is a separate problem.

Be that as it may, the auditors of the Marconi Company declared, in their report for 1925, and in addition to another repetition of their previous qualifications: "We have obtained all the information and explanations we have required. In our opinion such balance sheet is properly drawn up so as to exhibit a true and correct view of the state of the company's affairs according to the best of our information and the explanations given to us and as shown by the books of the company."[7] One of the two firms of auditors was dismissed, at the annual meeting, not because of a "belief that they had failed to do their duty," there being no specific allegations; "but from a desire to mark dissatisfaction with the wording of the certificate, which was considered to be inadequate to meet the circumstances."[8] In this same editorial it was noted that the directors had been warned by auditors as far back as

[7] *London Times*, March 15, 1927, p. 21d.
[8] *London Times*, March 16, 1927, editorial, p. 17c.

1920 that the values stated in the balance sheet needed revision, and the auditors had repeated their warnings every year since then. Furthermore, Messrs. Garnsey and Cooper were not appointed auditors until July, 1926.

During a period of seven years, 1920–1927, the directors of the company had drawn over £500,000 as remuneration. A number of these directors had resigned; the directors who were still holding office in 1927 had drawn over £100,000 of this amount, in which however were included the salaries of Signor Marconi as technical advisor and Kellaway as manager of the company. The previous managing director, Godfrey Isaacs, had resigned in November, 1924, after having drawn a large part of the half-million pounds noted above; and his death occurred prior to the 1927 meeting. At the 1927 meeting, five of the directors resigned and five new directors were elected. The question as to the responsibility of the directors for this state of affairs rests on the problem as to how much more apparent the auditors' qualifications should have been to the directors than to the uninstructed shareholders.

June 3, 1924, a finance committee had been appointed by the board of directors "to inject intelligence into the subsidiary activities." In November, Isaacs resigned. In February, 1925, a prospectus of new shares was issued, shares being offered at 27s. 6d., from the sale of which £663,000 were realized. This issue of securities had been "made by the board after a careful examination of the figures prepared for them by the then financial director . . . The figures were accurate according to the information then in possession of the financial director. The board acted on the information available at the time and on expert advice in the same way as any other body of business men would have acted."[9] The result of this situation was that for several years the position of the company had been wholly misunderstood by the general body of shareholders and by the general investment public. It is doubtful, not only whether the directors actually did know the real or the whole situation, but also whether any group of men could be expected to know so much.

The Garnsey proposal in 1927 called for writing off £2,766,168 from the capital assets shown for 1925; approximately £3,000,000 of the capital assets was written off as of 1924 and 1923. This was to be accomplished by the writing-off of the entire trading profit for 1925, less the preference dividend, and an additional writing-down of the ordinary shares from £1 to 10s. The result of this reorganization scheme was to retain the 250,000 £1 7% preference shares; to convert the former 3,750,000 £1 ordinary shares to 499,935 10s. ordinary shares; and to issue 3,250,092 new ordinary shares at 10s. The scheme was finally adopted by the shareholders.

[9] "Annual Report for 1925," *London Times*, March 7, 1927, p. 22d.

Not only does a policy of wide diversification and extension of functions involve problems so complex as to reach the quantitative limit of human knowledge and control, but such a policy is bound to develop at times into a situation that presents a company with a fundamental contradiction and inconsistency in policy.

The Attempted National City-Corn Exchange Merger

The National City Bank,[10] of New York City, had, at the close of 1928, capital resources of $217,000,000, exclusive of the $100,000,000 capital and surplus of the National City Company; the National City Bank having a total of $1,300,000,000 in deposits. The National City Bank organization had attained distinction through its diversified activities, departmental banking having been intensively developed. These collateral activities operated as business feeders for the bank and, incidentally, contributed to earnings.

A few years ago, the bank opened a compound-interest department, depositors at the close of 1928 numbering 250,000, with deposits of approximately $60,000,000; counting foreign-savings depositors, the number was 420,000 with $110,000,000 of deposits. In the spring of 1928 the bank instituted a personal-loan department, for making loans from $50 to $1,000. During less than eight months' operations, loans were made to some 28,000 men and women in amount aggregating $8,500,000. The bank has been loaning an average of $300 to more than 4,000 new applicants a month. In 1928 the bank expanded its local branch-banking system, opening nine new offices in addition to a previous total of 21; the deposits at the close of 1928 aggregated $260,000,000. These branches were in addition to the 89 direct and subsidiary foreign branches in 23 countries.

The most significant recent departure of the National City Bank from strictly commercial-banking activities had been the acquisition of the $220,000,000 Farmers' Loan and Trust Company, with its old established trust accounts. Although the National City Bank had maintained a trust department for several years previous to 1928, the plan has been to develop the Farmers' Loan and Trust Company as a separate corporate entity and to build up an extensive trust department along lines similar to the administration of the National City Company.[11]

[10] This information has been obtained from the monthly letters publicly circulated by the National City Bank and from items appearing in the *Boston News Bureau.*

[11] A recent decision of the Supreme Court of the United States (*Worcester County National Bank v. Massachusetts,* May 13, 1929), upheld a decision of the Supreme Court of Massachusetts, that a national bank which had merged with a trust company could not exercise the latter's trust and fiduciary powers—from which national banks are excluded in Massachusetts—without new and express appointment by the Probate Court.

The National City Company engaged in the marketing of bonds exclusively until recently.   In 1926 and 1927 the National City Company led all other companies in the United States with total new bond-syndicate offerings of $873,000,000 and $1,590,311,000 respectively; in 1928 it was third on the list, with total offerings of $896,796,000.   Early in 1928, the National City Company made a notable departure of branching out into stock or other equity interests, thus taking advantage of the more popular interest in the stock market.   In the latter part of 1928, the National City Company instituted a system of real-estate financing by means of stock issues, forming, in cooperation with the United States Realty and Improvement Company, the United States Realty Management Corporation.

Commenting on the policies of these allied institutions, Charles E. Mitchell has said: "Through the cooperation of all units of the institution, including the National City Company and the domestic and foreign branches, new business has flowed in in a volume which assures for the future earnings far in excess of what we have been able to look forward to in the past."   An indirect benefit of these departmental activities has been to extend the connections and personal contacts of the bank.   The splitting-up of stock in 1928 was partly for the same objective—"an institutional policy to increase the number of personal contacts and to make such contacts continually effective through service and proprietary interest."

The National City Bank presents an excellent illustration of the present tendency among banks to extend their functions. The situation which follows will illustrate, however, a particularly crucial problem that is involved in any contemplated merger.

On October 25, 1929,[12] Mr. Mitchell, who had just arrived from a trip abroad, made public a statement to the effect that the "break" in the New York stock market, which had just then begun, was no reflection of business conditions in this country: that earnings of corporations indicated a state of prosperity, that the fundamental condition of industry and business was sound, and that the economic values of investments were not to be judged by any losses exhibited in stock quotations.

At this time the National City Bank had become the largest banking institution in the country, and it was at this time engaged in a plan whereby it would be merged with the Corn Exchange Bank Trust Company; the result would have been the largest bank in the world. At the time the merger plans had been formulated, National City Bank stock was selling at approximately $500 per share, and Corn Exchange

[12] These items were taken from the *New York Times* from October 25 to November 8, 1929, and from the December letter of the National City Bank:

Bank Trust Company stock was selling at approximately $400 per share. Accordingly, the merger plan provided for an exchange of four-fifths of a share of National City for one share of Corn Exchange stock; with an additional clause providing for the payment of $360 a share in cash by the National City to such holders of Corn Exchange stock as did not care to make the stock trade. The decline in the prices of all securities, following the market break of October 24, 1929, included bank stocks, Corn Exchange stock reaching a low of $160, and National City a low of $250 per share. Not only did this throw the ratio of the stock quotations out of line with that established in the terms of the merger, but the cash alternative was at one time $200 higher than the Corn Exchange stock could be purchased for on the open market. Inasmuch as there were 605,000 shares of Corn Exchange stock outstanding, the National City Bank was faced with the prospect of paying $121,000,000 more in cash for the Corn Exchange stock than the latter was selling for on the market. Inasmuch as the Corn Exchange stockholders had agreed to the merger unanimously—82% of the stock having been voted in favor of the merger—and were all contemplating taking the cash alternative, the National City Bank would have had to furnish a total of $217,860,000 in cash to effect the merger.

As the situation became evident to National City stockholders, large numbers of them began to ask for the return of their proxies in order that they might vote their stock against the merger agreement. On the day on which the National City Bank was to vote on the merger, November 7, 1929, the proxy committee found in its hands proxies for only 2,624,000 shares; the number needed to pass the merger agreement was 3,666,667 shares, or two-thirds of the total 5,500,000 shares comprising the capital stock of the bank. The proxy committee voted these shares in favor of the agreement, as it was mandatory upon them to do. With 125 shareholders present, 18,000 shares were voted against the proposal, while 162,000 shares represented at the meeting were not voted.

The situation has been described in detail in order to provide a proper setting for the particular problem in which we are at present interested, namely, extensions of functions and mergers. The whole situation has, of course, not been given; to do that would require a volume in itself. But a number of seemingly irrelevant factors have been included in order to give a more concrete picture than would otherwise be possible, and some of these apparent irrelevancies do have a bearing on the case.

Certain other factors must also be mentioned. To begin with, the National City Bank was clearly within its *rights*, in refusing to sanction the merger, for no agreement of this sort may be said to be completed until final ratification is agreed to by all the parties.   In this sense, the market crash gave the National City stockholders an unusual opportunity to see the worth of the Corn Exchange tested by fire, in spite of any declarations as to the inability of declining market values properly to assess the essential worth of American industries.   Pointing in this same direction is the item which probably was the main reason for rejection of the plan by the National City Bank: the cash alternative.   For the event certainly does lead one to believe that the fixing of a cash price at a certain sum, rather than at a ratio to the market price, was a case of business oversight.   But this observation is partly invalidated by the fact that it is a matter of hindsight; foresight must be judged at a time when the event has not yet occurred, and such judgment should be recorded and published before the event itself makes easy the criticism of the bystander.   Furthermore, the stockholders of the Corn Exchange on their part attempted to "stand pat" on the agreement and lost the whole apparent value of the merger by failing to make a counter-proposition, in respect to the cash alternative, which would have more nearly represented the state of affairs.

But the really significant element in the whole situation was yet to appear.   On Friday, November 8, 1929, the day after the merger plan was rejected by the National City Bank, the following full-page advertisement was inserted in the *New York Times* by the Corn Exchange Bank Trust Company:

IN KEEPING WITH THE SOUND PRINCIPLES OF BANKING

For three-quarters of a century the policy of the Corn Exchange Bank Trust Company has been one of individual service to its customers, and of complete protection to their money.   This individual service begins first with our Board of Directors and is made available to each customer through our Officers and Employees.

The Corn Exchange Bank Trust Company has always been a leader in adding those features of service which will be appreciated by its customers, and in opening additional branches as fast as the growing needs of individual sections of our Greater City require superior banking service.

The Corn Exchange Bank Trust Company stands for safe and conservative management of its depositors' funds; by this is meant that those funds will be invested only in the securities of, or loaned to conservative and well-established concerns, and for promoting legitimate business, and will not be loaned in speculative enterprises, even though this could be done at greater profit to the bank.

This dignified statement is characterized by an assertion of individuality and character. It may be regarded as referring solely to the market situation; but the date is too significant for any such simple explanation, and the specific reference to the policy of lending money in speculative enterprises points clearly to the avowedly more progressive policies of certain other banks, among which the National City might be included. The merger of these two banks would probably have entailed no more acute problems of mutual adjustment than were faced by the merger of the conservative Disconto-Gesellschaft and the romantic Deutsche Bank. But the whole tone of the above advertisement points toward the virtues of a distinctive bank, virtues which must have been lost, in part, by a merger. And one wonders, as in the case of the change in attitude on the part of the National City Bank toward the significance of market prices, whether the Corn Exchange Bank Trust Company did not change its attitude, regarding the benefits of merging, after the plan had fallen through; and why this event was necessary in order to convince the stockholders and directors of the wisdom of independence and individuality.

In this connection the statements appearing recently in financial advertising are highly significant. On February 10, 1930, the Corn Exchange Bank Trust Company itself advertised in the *New York Times:*

The Corn Exchange Bank Trust Company has no securities to sell, nor is it affiliated with any investment company. It, therefore, is in a position to give investment advice to its depositors with no possible incentive except to benefit those who seek financial safety.

The Guaranty Trust Company of New York stated among other things, in an advertisement[13] under the caption, "A Statement of Facts regarding the Investment of Trust Funds":

It is illegal for a trustee, whether an individual or a corporation, to profit either directly or indirectly from the purchase or sale of trust investments. The Guaranty Trust Company of New York in the purchase or sale of investments for estates or trusts does not buy from or sell to itself or any affiliated company, nor does it make or share any commissions derived from the purchase or sale of investments for its estates or trusts.

The Central Hanover Trust Company advertised as follows:

[13] *New York Times*, May 13, 1930.

"NO SECURITIES FOR SALE"

Whenever we are called upon to invest money for our clients, we are free to choose securities from the whole investment field. Only with this freedom, we believe, can we choose the securities that best suit the needs of each individual client.

This is the reason Central Hanover has "no securities for sale."[14]

The implied double agency attributed to combinations of investment houses, commercial banks, retail distributors and trust companies, is a charge which many banking houses must face. That the situation is complex and involved, however, is indicated by the whole history of banking in America. H. Parker Willis and Jules I. Bogen, in their recent volume on *Investment Banking*,[15] stress the fact that the various functions of banking—investment, commercial, mortgage, trust—which we have become accustomed to look upon as separate functions and even as requiring houses that are mutually independent of each other, as a matter of fact were all once performed by the same banking house; differentiation was a later development, investment banking most recently having become independent, and is still in process. This broader view would indicate that individuality among banks is increasing; but no one can deny that the recent merger movement, and the establishment of chain and group banking, is temporarily, at least, a movement in the opposite direction. And if in the main the whole banking situation may be viewed optimistically from the ethical standpoint and especially with regard to the problem of double agency, at least it must be recognized that the present merger movement involves serious ethical problems of a particular nature.

The very fact that many of our largest banking houses have maintained the confidence and respect of their clients and customers, who know the *potential* dangers of inter-company and inter-subsidiary transactions,[16] shows that bankers have recognized and met the responsibilities attaching to business

---

[14] *New York Times*, January 14, 1930.

[15] New York: Harper & Brothers, 1929.

[16] One large investment house specifically declares in its circulars that its directors shall be permitted freely to buy from or sell to the trust-company affiliate the securities which in their judgment may be so handled. The prospective purchaser is thus warned and agrees that the stricter legal safeguards are waived.

freedom.[17] And it would be contrary to the whole spirit of this volume to stress the *a priori* factors at the expense of these functional and actual eventualities. It is so obvious as to need mere mention, that a house which initiates an investment issue knows more about the situation than does anyone else. Furthermore, the competition within a company among the managers of the various departments can be relied upon to safeguard departmental interests; witness the hostility and jealousy that frequently arise between sales manager and purchasing agent of the same company. But the formation of separate subsidiary corporations for handling matters that are otherwise incompatible with their independence cannot satisfy the more acute observers; especially where financial power overrides management independence. The whole situation narrows down to the point that the extension of business functions and corporation mergers can be and has been carried so far as not only to destroy the identity of distinctive companies but also to include incompatibilities and inconsistencies that put a tremendous strain on human ability and honesty.

International Paper and Power Company

A case of a somewhat different type is that of the purchase, by the International Paper and Power Company, of a group of newspapers, ostensibly for the purpose of stabilizing the sale of paper. Beginning as the International Paper Company, owning timber tracts and manufacturing pulp paper, the company soon undertook the manufacture of electric power and, as the International Paper and Power Company, distributed power throughout New England. The old paper company several years ago had outstanding approximately $150,000,000 in bonds and $30,000,000 in preferred stock, the equity being represented by 250,000 shares of common stock. The new paper and power company, which became a holding company in 1929, had outstanding some $235,000,000 in bonds and about $100,000,000 in preferred stock, the equity being represented by 4,500,000 shares of common stock of different classes. The value of this equity, on the basis of quotations on the New York Stock Exchange, ranged from $65,000,000 to $91,000,-000 in 1928, from $75,000,000 to $150,000,000 in 1929, and in the early months of 1930 was approximately $80,000,000. Whether such valuations are accurate indices of the worth of the company is difficult to

[17] See on this point "Ethical Problems of the Modern Trust Department," by Harold A. Rockwell, in *The Ethical Problems of Modern Finance*, New York: The Ronald Press Company, 1930.

determine,[18] as this valuation is determined in part by the actual earning power and in part by the anticipated growth of the company. The financial houses which were alleged to be behind the company in 1929 were Harris, Forbes and Company, the Chase National Bank of New York, and the First National Bank and Old Colony Trust Company of Boston.

The extension of this company's interests in allied fields was typical of the period of corporation growth and mergers. But the act which occasioned considerable public discussion was the acquisition, by the company, of a number of newspapers, among them the Boston *Herald* and *Traveler*. Two problems at once presented themselves: Was the International Paper and Power Company justified, on a strictly business basis, in entering the field of newspaper publishing? and, Could public policy tolerate the ownership of newspapers by public-utility interests, especially at a time when rates and valuations were matters of prime concern to public regulating commissions? The latter question raised such a storm of public disapproval that the company was forced to relinquish its stock ownership of newspapers.

This the company did by selling all its stock in newspapers to a group of bankers acting with the management of the newspapers, and the public was given an opportunity to purchase the stock. "Thus ends," stated an editorial announcement in the *Herald*,[19] "by friendly agreement, an episode which caused an amount of comment all out of proportion to the plain business involved in it." The editorial went on to acknowledge that many other publications, and apparently all other local papers, had "professed to regard with apprehension" the ownership of the *Herald* and *Traveler* by a newsprint company having public-utility affiliations. The policy of the paper was declared to be "never to advocate any policy which in our judgment runs counter to the welfare of the people of New England . . . We believe in encouraging private enterprise. We favor proper public control of utilities; but we are opposed to public meddling at the behest of the political agitator . . . " In an editorial, the *New York Times* stated that "the International's ill-judged venture" could be described as that part of a tragedy which in this instance came between the defense offered by the company for its control and the announcement by the bankers of the divesting of that control: "revelation of the fact that reputable business men of large affairs are unable to see the excellent reason why a company owning public utilities should not own newspapers also."

All's well that ends well, and there will be no disposition on the part of press or public to be unfair hereafter to the International because of its bad

[18] The annual report for 1929 declared the book assets, as of December 31, to be $661,001,400.

[19] September 21, 1929.

judgment and obtuseness in this particular piece of business. That it has retired from the newspaper field is good news. It is all that could be asked of the company. In all likelihood the lesson has been well learned, and the scheme will not again be attempted. It is with the tone of the statement (issued by the Boston purchaser) that press and public can hardly agree. That tone is found in the following extract from the public announcement:

"Thus ends . . . an episode which caused an amount of comment out of all proportion to the plain business involved in it."

The comment referred to was uttered almost unanimously by that great preponderance of American newspapers in which the International owned no stock. These newspapers, understanding the paramount necessity of keeping the well-springs of information free even from the taint of suspicion, naturally saw more than "plain business" in the control of newspapers by a company owning public-utilities franchises. They saw public distrust of the news columns of these particular papers which would grow into suspicion of all. They noted the effort of the International to keep its purchases secret, and felt justly that this course proved the inherent ill judgment of the purchases. They sounded the alarm, in the public interest, against the practical application of an industrial theory that newspapers are mere business enterprises like chain grocery stores. Public opinion swiftly supported the warnings, and, in exact proportion to the gravity of the "plain business involved," the pressure proved sufficient to retire the International from the newspaper field.[20]

The irony of the situation can be appreciated by noting the fact that at almost the same time the Hearst newspaper syndicate, which had been most vociferous in condemning the International policy, was reported to be organizing a company with a capitalization of $71,000,000 to take over timber and power holdings in Newfoundland to produce newsprint for the Hearst newspapers.[21] Issuance of a grant on large timber areas in Labrador on a 99-year lease was also being sought, the land containing 20,000,000 cords of pulpwood, for which the company was offering to pay $1,000,000 in cash plus $1.50 an acre. Plans were announced for a $12,000,000 dam and the erection of a 1,000-ton mill with provisions for expansion. This project was to be completed in five years, when it was hoped that all the Hearst papers could thereby be supplied with newsprint; contracts with American and Canadian companies now supplying newsprint to the Hearst publications expire in 1935. The property involved in the negotiations had been held under option by the International Paper Company, but the option lapsed owing to the inability of the interested parties to agree on a satisfactory price. The

[20] *New York Times*, September 23, 1929.
[21] *Boston Herald*, September 24, 1929.

significance of this situation lies in the fact that it again illustrates the historic tendency of American corporations to reach back into the source of raw materials, a tendency which has become so prevalent as to arouse practically no opposition, public or otherwise, at least when compared with the attempt on the part of any producing company to expand into the field of distribution.

The case has thus far been discussed with reference to the broader public interests involved, a situation which rests, however, upon the basic fact of extending a company's activities into fields other than its primary purpose. The question still remains whether the extension of the International Paper and Power Company's business into the publication of newspapers could be justified from the business point of view.

On September 25, 1929, a banking group consisting of Tucker Anthony and Company, Eastman Dillon and Company, and the First National Corporation of Boston, made a public offering of 182,328 shares of no-par common stock of the Boston Herald-Traveler Corporation at $39.50 per share. What price the International received for its holdings was not, of course, stated; but it was understood to be greater than the price originally paid by the International, thus showing that the investment was a good one for the International. The question, however, is: How would the newspaper companies have fared as business organizations, aside from public opinion that they aroused?

The ostensible purpose of the purchase of newspapers by the International company was to provide a better outlet for the sale of newsprint. This obviously was a recognition of the fact that the International was not selling as much newsprint in the competitive market as it hoped to sell by eliminating competition through the purchase of newspapers. If this is true, then obviously the owners of stock in the newspapers so purchased could expect a decline in earnings due to the higher price which was to be paid for newsprint.[22] This statement must of course be qualified: the cost of newsprint might form only a small part of the cost of newspaper publishing, the new management might be sufficiently superior to the old to overcome any price differential, and the stabilization of the price of newsprint might be mutually advantageous to paper company and newspaper. But if the case be narrowed down to a situation in which a company, which for each of four successive quarters had shown a deficit of over $1,000,000, after payment of dividends, a

[22] The annual report for 1929 stated: "These investments were acquired in connection with the sale of newsprint paper, and the prices already realized indicate that final liquidation of these investments will net a substantial profit in addition to the distinct sales advantages which have accrued from them."—*Annalist*, April 11, 1930, p. 809.

deficit totaling for 1929 to over $4,800,000, attempts to buy another
company with earnings gradually increasing for five years until a total
net, after all charges, of over $1,000,000 was reached for the year ending
June 30, 1929; and the purchase was for the announced purpose of
increasing the sales of a commodity of the first company to the second;
then it may reasonably be asked whether economies are to be effected
for the whole consolidated group or merely so that an advantage be
gained for a part of that group at the expense of another part.   The
pertinent questions are: Could the International Paper and Power
Company go so far outside its particular field as successfully to run a
newspaper; and, Was it operating efficiently even as a paper company
if it had to buy its customer outlets in order to sell to them its newsprint?[23]   It is this feature of mergers and amalgamations, of using the
corporate strength of a company to enter a new and unknown particular
field, that raises questions not only of public policy, as in this case, but
furthermore of business soundness—a question which would presume
that every major part of a business should be able to justify itself by
earnings; otherwise the company can be suspected of introducing into
that new field of business activities an element of unfair business practice, the only possible justification of which could be the temporary
price concessions to consumers.

The problem of extending business functions and of consum-
mating business mergers can thus be presented by developing
a series of cases, ranging from those situations in which the new
activities appear to be a direct and justifiable implication of the
former business activities of a company to situations in which
the resulting diversification of interests appears to be too great
for a single managerial capacity. Long before this point is
reached, however, the situation has developed serious competitive
problems, in which the ethical points raised by competitors are
justified to the extent that the invading company is adopting
amateur tactics—underpricing, over-servicing, and the like. The
test, in short, is a functional test; mergers cannot be condemned
as such, as Mr. Henry Ford's expression would imply: "No
lamp-posts have been provided for weak or overstimulated
businesses to cling to, and so they are apt to cling to one another.
The embrace is called a merger." It is this kind of attitude
which has characterized the Church's criticisms of business, and
until recently those of the Law.

[23] The implied problem of "reciprocity" purchasing is discussed in a
succeeding chapter.

There is no inherent ethical objection to the extension of business functions and to business mergers[24] that cannot be met by pointing out the obvious social as well as business advantages of diversification and resulting stability. The problem for business to determine is the drawing of the line between justifiable and unjustifiable business conduct, whether this happens to be connected with mergers or not. Where a company uses its entrenched position in order to force the buying of commodities of an invaded field, the customer and the competitor are unfairly treated and the soundness of the company itself is being jeopardized. Such extensions of business activities can be justified only if the invasion is a permanent one and if the activities in the invaded field can become self-supporting; there being nothing unethical in the winning of a game, for then the economic advantages of diversification as well as of legitimate competition make their appearance. Where such diversification involves business contradictions, especially the factor of double agency, or where it interferes with sound social and public policy, the extension or merger cannot be justified even though it may result in increased company profits. For, although the game is being won, it is being won by a violation of the rules which are necessary to give full play to competitive efficiency and business freedom.

[24] For the legal phase, see *Mergers and the Law*, prepared by Myron W. Watkins for the National Industrial Conference Board, and published by them. New York: 1929.

CHAPTER VIII

THE CONTINENTAL TRADING COMPANY

The preceding chapter has dealt with some of the more important ethical problems that arise from the modern tendency in American business corporations to extend their functions beyond a limited field, to handle additional products, and to merge with other corporations that have previously engaged in a different line of business. One of these problems, that of "double agency," has been referred to. This problem, however, is of sufficient ethical importance to warrant fuller treatment; and the recent so-called "Stewart-Rockefeller controversy" presented the problem so dramatically as to justify selecting this situation as a typical illustration. At the same time the activities of the parties involved extended to other allied and implied situations and problems that are of interest to students of the broader phases of Business Ethics. Conspicuous among these problems are the public relations and responsibilities of business, especially to governmental agencies, the relations between the board of directors and the management, and the responsibilities of shareholders for company policies.

Operations of the Company

The Continental Trading Company, Limited,[1] was a Canadian corporation, organized November 17, 1921. Inasmuch as the Dominion (of Canada) Companies Act does not require a list of the stockholders or stock-warrant holders to be filed, the records of the Department of the Secretary of State for Canada contained no list of the stockholders of the Continental Trading Company, Limited. The five original incorporators of the company, each holding one share of stock of a total of 100,000 shares at $5 each, were: G. M. Huycke and N. E. Strickland, barristers at law, and T. Delany, J. J. Huggard, and M. H. Bruels, students at law, all associates or employees of H. S. Osler, a barrister of Toronto, who acted as president of the company. The same day it was organized, the Continental Trading Company, Limited,

[1] Sources: *Senate Report*, 70th Congress, 1st Session, on Senate Resolution 101; *New York Times;* published letters of shareholders.

acquired certain contractual rights from G. E. Atwood of Toronto, for 99,994 shares of the capital stock of the company.

The same day it was organized, the Continental Trading Company, Limited, bought 33,333,333 barrels of crude oil, at $1.50 per barrel, from the Mexia Oil Company, a Texas corporation owned and controlled largely by A. E. Humphreys; and then immediately sold this oil to the Prairie Oil and Gas Company and the Sinclair Crude Oil Purchasing Company at $1.75 per barrel. The Prairie Oil and Gas Company was at the time owned by the National Transit Company, a subsidiary of the Standard Oil Company of New Jersey; James E. O'Neil signed the Continental contract as president of the Prairie Oil and Gas Company. Robert W. Stewart and Harry F. Sinclair signed "for the directors" of the Sinclair Crude Oil Purchasing Company, one-half of the stock of which was owned by the Standard Oil Company of Indiana, of which Stewart was chairman of the board of directors. There was also present at the meeting H. M. Blackmer, chairman of the board of directors of the Midwest Refining Company, which was controlled by the Standard Oil Company of Indiana.

Robert W. Stewart was born in 1866; he began his career as a lawyer in Pierre, South Dakota, about 1890. He served two terms as state senator, became a major of the Rough Riders in the Spanish-American War, and served as a colonel in the State Guard of South Dakota for 18 years. About 1905, the Standard Oil Company—this was before its dissolution—lost a suit in a South Dakota court; Stewart reopened the case and won it. In 1907, he was retained as counsel by the Standard Oil Company of Indiana. He became general counsel in 1915, and in 1918 was made chairman of the Board of Directors.

A. E. Humphreys, of Denver, was a very picturesque figure in the oil industry and was known, according to Stewart, as a "wildcatter." He had been associated with Blackmer for several years prior to 1921, and was one of the old stockholders of the Midwest Refining Company. This stock he had later exchanged for stock of the Standard Oil Company of Indiana, and he was interested in exchanging his Mexia properties for stock in the Standard Oil Company of Indiana. After several unsuccessful efforts to effect such a deal he made a number of overtures, in the summer of 1921, to Blackmer, O'Neil, and Stewart in regard to the sale of crude oil from the Mexia fields. During this time he sold 50% of his oil to the Pure Oil Company, following which his negotiations with the Standard Oil Company of Indiana were with reference to selling the remaining 50% for stock in the Standard Oil Company of Indiana. Stewart was unwilling to entertain this proposition because it "was too big a gamble. If we exchange stock with you, that would be a liability upon the firm of paying dividends during the life of the company. If we pay cash for your oil and we lose, or pay cash for the properties and lose it, we only lose the money." Humphreys persisted in his notion all summer, during which time a number of companies were trying to buy the oil: Standard Oil Company of New Jersey, Magnolia Oil Company, Prairie Oil and Gas Company, and Sinclair Consolidated Company.

From March, 1920, up to January, 1921, the price of crude oil, according to Stewart's statements, was $3.50 a barrel.[2] There were times when the Standard Oil Company of Indiana was not able to get enough oil to run its refineries on a 100% basis or to satisfy the needs of the consuming public. During this time Stewart discussed Humphreys' proposition, to exchange his properties for Standard of Indiana stock, with members of the board of directors of the Standard Oil Company of Indiana, but none of those with whom Stewart talked were disposed to favor the transaction. Humphreys had met O'Neil during this period, and they achieved a great liking for each other and became great personal friends. Stewart therefore figured that O'Neil could help him in the negotiations; he thereupon "tried to throw in with O'Neil to tie up this oil." O'Neil, however, was as unwilling to purchase oil with his company's stock as Stewart was with his. The wells were costing Humphreys $60,000 to $75,000 each to develop, pipe lines had to be laid, and storage facilities had to be provided at a cost of approximately 50 cents a barrel.

In the fall of 1921, Stewart went to Blackmer's rooms in New York City and there learned that the oil would not be sold to the Standard Oil Company of Indiana. Stewart was told that Humphreys wanted to sell to the Sinclair Crude Oil Purchasing Company and to the Prairie Oil and Gas Company, and "that was the direction he was told to travel if he wanted it." Mexia oil was then selling at $2 per barrel, and Stewart was told that the Mexia oil would cost him $1.75 per barrel. In these negotiations, Blackmer did not represent the Standard Oil Company of Indiana; he gave the impression to Stewart of representing Humphreys.

Until these contracts were ready to be signed, on November 17, 1921, the officers and attorney of the Mexia Oil Company had never heard of the Continental Trading Company, Limited; which, in fact, had been chartered the same day. The Mexia officials, up to that time, had supposed that the purchasers were to be the Sinclair Crude Oil Purchasing Company and the Prairie Oil and Gas Company. About one-half of the Sinclair Crude Oil Purchasing Company stock was owned by the Standard Oil Company of Indiana, the other half being owned by the Sinclair Consolidated Company; each appointed four directors to the board. Humphreys' counsel, ex-Senator Thomas of Colorado, was present at the meeting of November 17, 1921; and when he learned that the purchaser of the oil was to be the Continental Trading Com-

[2] Referring probably to Mid-continental crude; Mexia crude was selling for much less.

pany, Limited, about which he knew nothing, he suggested to Humphreys that they had better inquire into the power of this company to enter into a $50,000,000 contract. Humphreys replied, "Oh well, I have got the whip hand. If these people refuse to pay, I will simply shut off deliveries and there you are, so you need not bother about that." When Thomas expressed his feelings to the other men present at the meeting, O'Neil offered to guarantee the contract and signed the guarantee as president of the Prairie Oil and Gas Company, and H. F. Sinclair and R. W. Stewart signed the guarantee as "directors" of the Sinclair Crude Oil Purchasing Company, although the latter two men did not occupy such positions.

Public Relations

The Continental transaction was publicly disclosed by an investigation, begun late in October, 1923, by a Senate committee, Senator Nye being chairman. This committee was appointed to inquire into the administration of certain oil lands belonging to the United States Government. On May 31, 1921, the administration of these oil lands had been transferred from the Navy Department to the Department of the Interior, of which Albert Fall was then secretary. April 18, 1922, the Department of the Interior announced the leasing of the Teapot Dome Reserve, a part of government lands, to Harry F. Sinclair, a director of the Mammoth Oil Company, and of the Elk Hills reserve to Edward Doheny. At the same time Secretary Fall dismissed certain proceedings which had been brought to cancel the sale of certain California lands to the Standard Oil Company. The Senate investigating committee discovered that in 1921 and 1922, Sinclair had transferred to Fall certain Liberty bonds, which bonds had been bought with the profits of the Continental Trading Company, Limited. It was later discovered also that in 1922 Sinclair had contributed $75,000 of bonds, similarly obtained, to the treasury of the Republican Party, which had had a deficit in 1920 of $1,600,000. A block of these Liberty bonds amounting to $233,000 was traced to Fall, who had received them from Sinclair. The Supreme Court of the United States finally ordered the cancellation of all these oil land leases issued by Fall.

In connection with these facts, it may be stated that what Sinclair had attempted to do was to contribute a substantial sum to the funds of the Republican Party, without giving the appearance of doing so. The method employed was as follows: Sinclair contributed this sum in the form of Liberty bonds purchased with his share of the profits of the Continental Trading Company, Limited. These bonds were then divided into smaller amounts and distributed among a number of men with the request that a check for an equivalent amount be made out and sent to the treasurer of the Republican Party. Thus Sinclair's contribution would appear to have been made by others and in comparatively small amounts. One such proposal was made to Andrew Mellon, who refused to enter into such an arrangement. A block of $25,000 of the bonds was sent to James Patten, of Chicago, who subscribed that amount to the Republican Party. After receiving the bonds, however, and after considering the proposal a few days, Patten became quite angry at having been approached in regard to the matter, and donated an equivalent amount to a Chicago hospital.

The Senate committee discovered that $3,000,000 in Liberty bonds, a part of the lot into which the profits of the Continental deal had been converted, had been deposited in a Canadian bank. O'Neil, the former president of the Prairie Oil and Gas Company, had left the United States when the Senate investigation began. In September, 1923, O'Neil's doctors told him that the condition of his health was such that he could live only about 18 months longer. O'Neil returned from Europe to Montreal, where he turned over to a representative of the Prairie Oil and Gas Company $800,000 in Liberty bonds, representing a part of the profits of the Continental deal, stating that they "rightfully belong to the stockholders of the company." Most of the coupons which had fallen due had not been cashed; and an amount, in stocks and other securities, was supplied by O'Neil to make good such coupons as had been cashed. O'Neil requested, however, that no further coupons be cashed so long as the Teapot Dome investigation was on. These bonds, to the value of $800,000 were transferred by the Prairie Oil and Gas Company to the Prairie Pipe Line Company in payment of a note which the latter held against the former.

On February 23, 1928, Karl C. Schuyler appeared before the Senate investigating committee and testified that Blackmer had, in July, 1926, turned over to him about $750,000 of Liberty bonds representing Blackmer's share of the profits of the Continental Trading Company, Limited. Blackmer informed him that he had been advised that his right to the bonds might be questioned and that there was a strong probability that the Midwest Refining Company would bring an action against him on the theory that he was supposed to devote his entire time to the interests of the company, and that anything earned by him in outside activities belonged to that company. Blackmer had also heard that there was a strong probability that the Standard Oil Company of Indiana might bring an action against him on the theory that the connection between that company and the Midwest Refining Company was a mere corporate fiction and that in equity he was a servant of the Standard Oil Company of Indiana. Blackmer furthermore felt that to convert the bonds to his own use might jeopardize the good faith of his position in not returning them for income tax, so he kept the bonds intact awaiting developments. Blackmer therefore turned the bonds over to Schuyler in trust to be held pending the determination of the right and title thereto and for delivery to the successful claimant in case of litigation.

The Question of Double Agency

During the investigation of the Senate committee, Stewart was questioned regarding Blackmer's participation in the Continental profits. He stated:

If Mr. Blackmer was making a commission out of this proposition, he had a perfect right to do it. He owed no duty of any kind or character to either the Standard Oil Company of Indiana or the Sinclair Crude Oil Purchasing Company or the Prairie Oil and Gas Company of any kind or character. He was not an officer or director of these companies . . . and the Standard Oil Company of Indiana was at that time only a minority stockholder in the Midwest Refining Company . . . although this may practically have constituted a controlling interest . . . I do not see why he could not take a commission, morally, legally, and every other way . . . In my opinion, he was trying to land this proposition for the Humphreys.[3]

The Standard Oil Company of Indiana had bought a majority of stock of the Midwest Refining Company in November, 1921, at which time Blackmer offered to resign but was urged and prevailed upon by Stewart not to do so.

Senator Cutting. When Blackmer told you that you could not get the oil for less than $1.75, did you make any attempt to verify that from Mr. Humphreys?
Mr. Stewart. No, sir, I did not.
Senator Cutting. You took Mr. Blackmer's word?
Mr. Stewart. I took Mr. Blackmer's word.
Senator Cutting. And you thought that Blackmer was acting as Humphreys' agent?
Mr. Stewart. I thought Blackmer was friendly to me and to Mr. Humphreys and that he was trying to see that this deal went through.

Later the Senate investigating committee asked John D. Rockefeller, Jr.'s, opinion on this matter. The record of this testimony follows:[4]

The Chairman. Senator Walsh has outlined in a very splendid way to you, and in a brief way, the history of the case as the committee has encountered it thus far. He overlooked, however, a little revelation of the attitude of Mr. Stewart when he was on the stand with regard to Mr. Blackmer. He repeatedly prevailed upon this committee to believe that he, personally, had very little faith in Mr. Blackmer, in so far as this Humphreys oil deal was concerned, so repeatedly that he felt that Mr. Blackmer was really an agent for Mr. Humphreys, and when he was confronted with the suggestion that this was rather strange, in view of the fact that Mr. Blackmer was

---

[3] *Senate Report, cit. supra,* Part I, p. 206.
[4] *Senate Report, cit. supra,* pp. 311 ff.

president of the Midwest Refining Company at that time, over which the Standard Oil and he himself had a reasonable measure of control, he did not think that made much of any difference. Does it not strike you as rather strange that a man in Colonel Stewart's capacity would play along, so to speak, and tolerate a subordinate who was playing with those who, were indirectly attempting to get the better of the Standard Oil Company of Indiana? Does it not seem at least passing strange to you that that would be the case?

Mr. Rockefeller. No officer of any company would have any right to make a profit out of a company which he was paid to protect the interests of.

The Chairman. Certainly not. Then in view of the fact that Mr. Stewart felt that Mr. Blackmer was not playing fairly with the interests of the Standard Oil Company, really he ought to have taken steps to have rid the companies of Mr. Blackmer's services, ought he not? Would not that have been the ordinary procedure?

Mr. Rockefeller. If Mr. Stewart felt that Mr. Blackmer was not acting absolutely within the interests of the company, he should have.

The Chairman. Mr. Stewart told the committee repeatedly that he constantly felt that Mr. Blackmer was playing Mr. Humphreys' game rather than acting in the interests of the Standard Oil Company of Indiana.

Mr. Rockefeller. Mr. Blackmer, I understand, has not been an officer of the Midwest for some years.

The Chairman. Oh, I understand that; but during this entire proceeding, when so many millions and so much oil were at stake, Mr. Stewart nevertheless testified that he tolerated Mr. Blackmer holding the position which he did, as head of the Midwest Refining Company, while saying at all times that he was satisfied that Mr. Blackmer was serving the interests of Mr. Humphreys. I merely wanted to call that to your attention, and I wish you would take that testimony and give thought to that particular phase of it, along with the suggestions which Senator Walsh has given you.

Mr. Rockefeller. I want to say, Mr. Chairman, that I completely agree with your position. A man cannot serve two masters at the same time. If Mr. Blackmer was working in the interest of some one else and taking pay from or acting as an officer of the Midwest Company, he was not a fit servant of that company.

I regret to believe that there are times in business in these days when men have felt themselves justified in making profits when they were in a company. Personally I never would stand for it. I do not believe in it.

The Chairman. You mean an individual official making profits?

Mr. Rockefeller. Yes.

The Chairman. While he was accepting pay and expected to be serving a company?

Mr. Rockefeller. A profit, not at the expense necessarily of his company, but because of the position of his relation to the company. I think that is a very dangerous line to approach, and I have no sympathy at all with any who believe in that kind of thing.

* * * * * *

Senator Walsh. It appears, Mr. Rockefeller, that the Standard Oil Company of Indiana had acquired all of the stock or practically all of the stock—there might have been a few shares outstanding—of the Midwest Refining Company. At the time these transactions took place in November, 1921, Mr. Blackmer had been continued as chief executive of the Midwest Refining Company. Colonel Stewart told us that the entire force, through Mr. Blackmer, had agreed to resign, and Mr. Blackmer particularly had offered to resign at any time that Colonel Stewart desired he should, and that he did not desire that they should resign, and they were continued as officers and directors of the corporation, and that was the position that Mr. Blackmer occupied when the occurrences that I have attempted to relate to you took place.

I would like to inquire of you whether under those circumstances you would feel that Mr. Blackmer could either legally or morally act as the agent for Mr. Humphreys in the sale of this oil, and get a commission out of it?

Mr. Rockefeller. Not under the circumstances as you relate them, Senator.

Blackmer and Osler had left the country in 1924, shortly after the beginning of the Senate investigation, and they still remained beyond the jurisdiction of the Senate committee in 1924 and 1925. Stewart and Sinclair, therefore, were the only guarantors of the Continental deal who remained in the country in 1924. Stewart saw O'Neil and Blackmer in Paris in 1924 or 1925.

Public Disclosure of Confidential Information

Previous to the appearance of Stewart before the Senate Committee, John D. Rockefeller, Jr., wrote the following letter to Stewart at his Chicago address, the letter being dated January 24, 1928.

Because of the complete confidence which I have always had in your integrity, based on a business acquaintance extending over many years, the assurance which you gave me several years ago when the transactions of the Continental Trading Company were first questioned satisfied me that your record was quite clear.

The situation has now reached such a stage, however, that nothing short of the fullest and most complete statement of all of the facts relating to the Continental Trading Company can clear the skirts of those who, like yourself, have no improper connection with the transactions in question, and remove the cloud of suspicion which hangs over the entire oil industry.

You owe it to yourself and to your associates in the management of the company, to your stockholders and to the public to help bring these transactions in the fullest light that can be thrown upon them. No desire, however praiseworthy, to protect those who may have been guilty of wrongdoing justifies the withholding of any slightest fact that will help to clear up the situation.

While I read in the newspapers that you were in Washington a few weeks ago waiting to appear in the case then being tried in connection with these matters and while I have understood that when obliged to leave the country on business you have in advance advised the interested authorities of your plans and whereabouts, I urge you with all the influence that I possess not to wait for an invitation from the Senate Committee which has been appointed to look into this matter, much less a subpoena to appear before it, but to wire Senator Walsh at once, offering to put yourself at the disposal of the committee to tell all you know about this matter.

That your own high sense of honor and duty will prompt you to act immediately upon this suggestion, if in fact you have not already taken such a step, thus justifying to the public the confidence which your many friends and business associates have in you, I firmly believe.

Awaiting your reply by return mail, I am

Very sincerely,

(Signed) John D. Rockefeller, Jr.

The above correspondence followed a letter from Senator Walsh, dated January 16, to John D. Rockefeller, Jr., asking him for information and assistance. To this letter, Rockefeller had replied to Senator Walsh in part, on January 19:

Only by bringing all the facts to light can those who acted uprightly be protected and those who are guilty receive the public condemnation which they deserve.

After receiving these communications, Stewart returned to the United States and presented himself before the Senate investigating committee. After making a number of assertions including those already mentioned, he refused to testify on two points: as to the disposition of the Continental bonds, and whether he had ever discussed the bonds with Harry Sinclair. Stewart took the position that he was then under subpoena to testify in regard to the criminal conspiracy case of Fall and Doheny, and that he would reserve his information for the judge and jury in that case. "I do not think this line of investigation is within the jurisdiction of the committee or that the questions asked are pertinent to this inquiry . . . The court is the place to give the information." Later, when the questions were repeated, Stewart said: "Again, with the greatest reluctance and with great respect for the committee, and for the reasons I have already given and others, I will have to respectfully decline to answer that question . . . I am just as regretful as I can be, but in view of my feelings in my mind and in my heart, I just cannot come out and tell."

In refusing to testify before the Senate Committee, Stewart held that the line of interrogation pursued by the committee was not within its jurisdiction under the laws of the United States. He asserted that he was a witness in a case then pending in the courts, in which the issues now raised by the Senate Committee were going to be tried; that he had, in fact, been interrogated in regard to these subjects by the counsel appointed to represent the United States in that case. Stewart held that, with reference to the pending court case, "the government and defendants are entitled to ask me such questions as they desire upon the trial of the case, and it is left to a judge learned in the law to determine the question of the relevancy, materiality, and competency of the testimony; and they have a right to cross-examine and reexamine, and it seems to me, with all due deference to the committee, that there is the place for me to give this testimony." Senator Walsh replied that it was the position of the committee that the United States Senate took a contrary opinion. "We are here to elicit the facts for the use of the Senate . . . and the Senate of the United States does not admit at all that it cannot inquire into matters that may happen to be involved in some other litigation."

Upon being asked why he was so solicitous about the Government on the one side and the defendants on the other, in a trial yet to be held, Stewart replied: "As a citizen of the United States, I believe in a fair and impartial trial, which is accorded to everybody, to every citizen of the United States, and I think when these stories go in they ought to go in before a judge and a jury trying the case . . . I doubt very much, in my opinion as a lawyer, whether the Senate has the right to go into this proposition. I do not think the Senate was elected for the purpose of acting as a court and a jury in these matters."

This attitude subjected Stewart to contempt proceedings. The situation was somewhat analogous to the previous case of Mal Daugherty, president of the Midland National Bank of Washington Court House, Ohio, who had been ordered by the Senate to produce evidence in regard to his brother Harry. In such cases the Senate has two courses open to it: (1) It may vote a person in contempt, whereupon the Sergeant-at-Arms would be directed to arrest the person and retain him in custody until he should answer. (2) It may refer the matter to the District Attorney of the District of Columbia for grand-jury action. On February 4, Stewart was arrested by the Sergeant-at-Arms of the Senate and held for contempt. On February 3, John D. Rockefeller, Jr., had written Senator Walsh in part as follows:

Colonel Stewart's testimony before the Senate Committee as reported in today's newspapers covered all the information which he has given me and confirmed his statement to me previously referred to that he did not personally profit by the transactions in question.

I have not felt that Colonel Stewart failed in his duty to his stockholders, but I am sorry that he did not answer all your questions, for the situation calls for the fullest disclosure of the facts : . .

Management Relations

According to E. G. Seubert, who became president of the Standard Oil Company of Indiana in 1927 after 35 years of service with the company, "crude oil of like character, at the time of the Continental deal, was selling at $2 per barrel and in some instances called for a bonus of 25 cents or more. It was not unusual for a bonus of this amount to be paid for oil, and Colonel Stewart informed us that $1.75 was the best price obtainable." Shortly after November 17, 1921, the board of directors of the Standard Oil Company of Indiana approved the Continental contract, "without much investigation or discussion." According to Stewart, the Continental deal "meant a lot of money" to the Standard Oil Company of Indiana, and "the deal was a good one." When questioned regarding the guarantee of the Continental purchasing contract by O'Neil, Stewart, and Sinclair, and asked: What would have happened if the Continental had not paid the Humphreys Company? Seubert replied that there was a chance of that happening but that it could happen for only one month. When further asked what his company would have done under such circumstances, he replied that his company would have had to make good the amount due the Humphreys Company.

When asked, before the Senate investigating committee,[5] whether the board of directors of the Standard Oil Company of Indiana made any inquiry of Stewart as to why the Continental got the oil and he did not, Seubert stated that the board was satisfied with Stewart's statement that $1.75 was the best price the Sinclair Crude Oil Purchasing Company could get. "My associate directors and I all had implicit confidence in Colonel Stewart, and when he tells us: 'Here is a contract, if you wish to approve of it at a certain price,' we feel he is giving us the facts. We have the utmost confidence in our Chairman, Colonel Stewart."

Senator Walsh. What is the use of your board of directors; what do you have a board of directors for?

Mr. Seubert. To handle the affairs of the business.

Senator Walsh. Well, but if you just take Colonel Stewart's word for everything, you might as well let him run the business.

Mr. Seubert. Yes; but speaking for myself as a director of that company, I was satisfied that that was the best deal the colonel could make.

* * * * * *

Senator Walsh. In the ordinary course of your business, what would become of the letters and telegrams . . . passing between Mr. Blackmer and Mr. Stewart?

Mr. Seubert. I think that they would be kept by Mr. Stewart or his secretary.

Senator Walsh. They were, as a rule, addressed to Mr. Stewart as chairman of the board . . . Do not letters of that kind go on the files of the Standard Oil Company?

Mr. Seubert. I presume they are on the files of the person to whom they are addressed. They are his files and not the files of the general secretary of the company.

[5] *Senate Report, cit. supra,* pp. **127** ff.

Senator Walsh. Are we to understand that the Standard Oil Company of Indiana and the officers in charge of it have not any control over the letters written to Mr. Stewart, the chairman of the board, in relation to business of the company?

Mr. Seubert. If there are matters in those letters pertaining to subjects that are of general concern to the board, those letters would be available, but where they are addressed to any one of the directors—

Senator Walsh (interposing). The making of a $50,000,000 purchase would be of some concern to the board, would it not?

Mr. Seubert. Yes, sir.

Senator Walsh. Why have you not got those letters . . . addressed to Mr. Stewart, the chairman of the board, in relation to these matters?

Mr. Seubert. The letters were not addressed to me. They were addressed to Mr. Stewart and were in his files and are his letters.

In Osler's testimony taken as deposition in Canada on the Teapot Dome case, he stated that in April or May, 1923, the anticipated general shortage of crude oil and consequent anticipated rise in price had not taken place; that instead of crude oil running short and "Mexico drying up," there was a flood of oil from all directions, new discoveries being made; and the price of crude oil, instead of going up very largely above the $1.50 or $1.75 price, had fallen below it, "so that the contract had become an onerous contract as regards these purchasing companies." A great many threats of litigation from the Humphreys Company against the Continental Trading Company, Limited, arose, and claims were made that the purchasing company was not carrying out the contract. Osler furthermore testified that the production of the Mexia Oil Company had declined considerably at this time and that there was little probability that anything like the stipulated amount of oil would be gotten out of the property. He advised the sale of the contract by the Continental Trading Company, Limited.[6]

The Continental contract was purchased June 1, 1923, by the Sinclair Crude Oil Purchasing Company and the Prairie Oil and Gas Company for $400,000, although only approximately one-third of the oil had yet been delivered. Lewis Samuel and Harold E. Boston signed for the Continental Trading Company, Limited; N. K. Moody for the Prairie Oil and Gas Company; and H. L. Phillips and K. Porter for the Sinclair Crude Oil Purchasing Company. In answer to Senator Walsh's question: "Isn't it unusual that a contract representing a clear profit of $5,000,000 could be purchased for $400,000?" Stewart replied: "In my opinion it was a very fine deal." In its decision, *Mammoth*

[6] Osler, in regard to most questions asked him, took refuge in the plea of privilege of counsel. Persisting in his refusal to answer, he was committed for contempt, his plea being overruled. He sued out a writ of *habeas corpus*, but again was held liable to answer. From the judgment thus rendered against him he appealed and departed on a lion hunt to South Africa.

Oil Company v. United States,[7] the United States Supreme Court stated that "the creation of the Continental Company, the purchase and resale contracts enabling it to make more than $8,000,000 without capital, risk or effort, the assignment of the contract to the resale purchasers for a small fraction of its probable value, and the purpose to conceal the disposition of its assets, make it plain that the company was created for some illegitimate purpose." August 9, 1923, the charter of the company was surrendered to the Canadian government for cancellation, "all debts and liabilities having been distributed, all property parted with, and all assets divided ratably among its shareholders." All books, records, and papers of the Continental Trading Company, Limited, were destroyed in January or February, 1924.

The following testimony was given before the Senate investigating committee by W. S. Fitzpatrick, Chairman, Board of Directors, Prairie Oil and Gas Company.[8]

Senator Walsh. With whom did you deal in the matter (of buying the Continental Contract for $400,000)?

Mr. F. I don't know. I think the Sinclair people conducted the deal. We conferred with them and agreed that we would do it, and from then on I don't know how it was carried out.

* * * * * *

Senator W. Who gave you the information that they were willing to sell for $400,000?

Mr. F. The first I heard of it was when Mr. O'Neil told me that was true and that they had talked to the Sinclair people about it.

Senator W. Was it your understanding that the Sinclair people were treating with somebody representing the Continental Trading Company?

Mr. F. Yes, that was my understanding.

Senator W. And they represented to you that $400,000 was the price at which you could get it. Now this was a $200,000 transaction to your company, and how did you come to let the Sinclair people handle your business to that extent?

Mr. F. My dear sir, that is not uncommon at all . . . When I started in as an attorney for the Prairie Oil and Gas Company, the first time they came to me and wanted me to write up a contract for the transfer of a piece of property they were paying $350,000 for, I had buck ague and then I happened to think that it did not make any difference what amount was involved so that the principle was the same, and I went ahead and wrote the contract and have been doing business that way ever since.

Senator W. I can understand that perfectly well, Mr. Fitzpatrick . . . but I cannot understand how you . . . would let Sinclair Consolidated go out to make a deal with the other fellow without your ever coming in contact with the other fellow to find out whether that was really the price or whether you could do any better than that.

[7] 275 U. S. 13, 47–50.
[8] *Senate Report, cit. supra,* pp. 247 ff.

Mr. F.   Well, perhaps you cannot, but when a deal comes along in our business, it is very often a proposition of either take it or leave it and that is the way it struck me . . .

Senator W.   But apparently you were obliged to put explicit confidence in the Sinclair people to carry out a contract in which you were to participate to the extent of $200,000.

Mr. F.   I held that confidence in the Sinclair people, and I have had lots of business with them, millions.   I bought 72 tanks of oil from Mr. Sinclair on an exchange of words and had no difficulty over settlement, over measurements, or anything else.   We had that kind of confidence in the Sinclair people.

The status of Stewart on April 1, 1928, was that he had been arrested by the officers of the Senate for contempt; had sued out a writ of *habeas corpus*, which had been quashed; and was then at large, pending an appeal from the order remanding him to the custody of the Sergeant-at-Arms of the Senate; and he was then under indictment for refusing to answer the questions of the Senate investigating committee and stood in peril of a jail sentence.

April 20, 1928, the Senate investigating committee announced that it had discovered, from the records of the Continental and Commercial Bank of Chicago, a deposit slip for $13,903.75, made out by Stewart and for his account as of December, 1923, covering coupons of the same issue of Liberty bonds as those purchased by the Continental Trading Company, Limited, and equivalent to a principal amount of approximately $750,000.   On April 24, 1928, Stewart admitted before the Senate investigating committee that he had been allotted $759,000 in Liberty bonds, the securities into which the profits of the Continental deal had been converted.   He stated, however, that he had not personally accepted these bonds but had turned them over to Roy J. Barnett, of the tax department of the Standard Oil Company, who held them in trust in the vaults of the company until April 21, 1928, when they were shown to the directors of the company by Stewart.   At this time they were voted by the directors of the Standard Oil Company of Indiana into the treasury of the Sinclair Crude Oil Purchasing Company, of which the Standard Oil Company of Indiana was half-owner. Stewart asserted that this disclosure to the Standard of Indiana board was made as soon as he returned from Washington after being called as a witness in the Sinclair trial.   Sinclair was acquitted of the charge of conspiracy on April 21, 1928.

These bonds had been delivered by Osler at various times to Stewart, who transferred them intact to Barnett, by whom they were opened. No record was kept of the amounts or of the dates of delivery, nor were any receipts asked for or given by Osler, Barnett, or Stewart. The only evidence of the trusteeship was the trust agreement drafted November 26, 1921, by Stewart in "indelible" pencil and signed by

Barnett; and Stewart and Barnett testified that Louis L. Stephens, general counsel for the company, had been informed of the facts "sometime in 1924." This document, until April 21, 1928, reposed in the safety-deposit box held by Stewart in the Continental and Commercial Bank of Chicago.

On the day the above testimony was offered by Stewart, *i.e.*, April 24, 1928, he answered the two questions which he had previously refused to answer, for which he was at this time held in contempt. Stewart stated that now that his testimony in the Sinclair case was in, he felt free to answer these two questions. As to the disposition of the bonds representing the proceeds of the Continental deal, the information cited above was given. As to whether he had discussed these matters with Sinclair, Stewart answered "No." In consequence of Stewart's having answered these questions, the Senate investigating committee recommended the dismissal of the warrant for Stewart's arrest for contempt.

The question now arose as to whether Stewart was guilty of perjury. On his first appearance before the committee, Stewart had testified that he had no knowledge as to the distribution of the bonds or as to who received them. At this second appearance before the committee, he explained that what he intended to convey by his remarks was that he did not know anything as to the source of the bonds delivered by Osler. As to his statement, at the time of his first appearance, that he did not know anything as to who received these bonds, he explained that he thought the question referred to those bonds which had been transferred to Fall by Sinclair. Senator Walsh's question had been: "What do you know about the Continental Trading Company bonds; did you have anything to do with them?" Stewart's answer had been: "I didn't know anything about it." The Senate Committee decided to prosecute Stewart for perjury. Again the question of procedure arose. Senator Walsh advised calling the matter directly to the attention of the Senate; Senator Nye advised that the matter be referred to the District Attorney. On April 26, the Senate Committee adopted the latter course. In the fall of 1928 Stewart was acquitted by a jury of the charge of perjury.

Duties of the Shareholder

John D. Rockefeller, Jr., on February 11, 1928, was questioned by the Senate investigating committee. After stating the amount of the Rockefeller holdings in the Standard Oil Company of Indiana, he said:

If my holdings in this company had chanced to be only 100 shares, my sense of responsibility and of obligation to do everything in my power in uncovering this unfortunate situation, this national scandal which this committee is seeking to uncover, would have been exactly the same. It is not a question of my stockholdings. I, with great appreciation of the work that this committee is doing in the public interest, am more eager, more anxious than you gentlemen can possibly be that this whole situation be uncovered in all of its details.

I have in view the important public interests which are at stake here. But more than that I have personally, as well as in other ways as an officer in these funds, a large investment in the oil industry.   More than that, my father was one of the pioneers in the development of the industry.   The family name has for over 50 years been connected with the oil industry. I have those additional reasons for being more eager than you gentlemen can be to do everything in my power to bring to light all the facts in this unfortunate matter.

Will you allow me to thank you, gentlemen, right here for the opportunity which you have given me of coming here before you this morning that I might assure you in person of my complete cooperation and my desire in every way possible to be of service to you in this public service which you are rendering.

This situation, Senator, and gentlemen of the committee, is far-reaching. It affects certain individuals, but far beyond that it affects the whole oil industry.   The oil industry is under suspicion because of the facts that have been brought to light and more particularly because of the facts that have not yet been brought to light.   The business structure of the country is under suspicion for these reasons.   The cynic is saying: "Is there any such thing as basic integrity in business?"

All of these are reasons which make me keenly anxious to do everything in my power to bring to light the facts in this matter, for, as I have stated to you gentlemen in correspondence, it seems to me that only as all of the facts are brought to light can the suspicion which has grown up be dispelled and can the cloud which has gathered over the oil industry and business generally be dispelled.

*   *   *   *   *   *

I believe in the business of the country.   I believe that business can be run on a sound, high, fair basis.   As a stockholder in any company I want no profit derived from compromise with right.   I want no officer in any company in which I own stock, whether he be high or low or an employee, to do anything that I would not myself be willing to do.   I have given the greater part of my life to philanthropic endeavors.   I am not an active business man.   I have never been actively engaged in the management of any business.   I am a stockholder in many corporations.   I am desirous always of using my influence in the support of able and trustworthy management, and I am prepared at any time to withdraw support from management that no longer justifies the confidence that has been put in it.

May I just say in closing that perhaps after all the greatest contribution that my father may have made during his life is not his philanthropies, but in the investing of large sums of money in businesses well organized that render useful service to the public at fair profit, with adequate wages to their employees, with proper living and working conditions, and with the insistence upon those relations between employer and employee which recognize one as a fellow-man quite as much as the other.

*   *   *   *   *   *

Senator Walsh. It would be a very reasonable thing, would it not, for a stockholder of a company, owning at least a substantial share of the stock, to interrogate an officer of the company who carried out as big a transaction as this, concerning the details of it?

Mr. Rockefeller. Thoroughly within his right I presume.

Senator Walsh. An officer of the company, representing him as a kind of a trustee, would ordinarily be expected to disclose the full nature of the business transaction which he attempted to carry out for the company?

Mr. Rockefeller. I hardly think that, Senator, because both in the foundation and personally we have investments in a great many companies. We are not managing stockholders. We are simply investing stockholders. The number runs into hundreds. It would be utterly impossible for us to follow the transactions in any company.

Senator Walsh. I appreciate that thoroughly, Mr. Rockefeller, but having followed them, and having conferred with an officer about a transaction which had some extraordinary if not suspicious features about it, I inquire whether under those circumstances a stockholder might not very properly expect the officer of the company to tell freely and frankly the whole story of the transaction.

Mr. Rockefeller. Very rightly.

Senator Walsh. All I desire to ascertain, Mr. Rockefeller, is whether you feel that you have exhausted every means of securing information from Colonel Stewart?

Mr. Rockefeller. I will be very grateful to you, if you could suggest any means. I have not been able to think of any way of getting at those facts.

Senator Walsh. But, would not a simple recital of the story as it has been disclosed here before the committee, to Colonel Stewart, force some kind of a statement from him?

Mr. Rockefeller. I was not in possession of the facts in detail when I talked with him, but although I tried in both interviews to get him to discuss the situation, he stood on this statement that I have made here, and I felt that, with the experience of the years that I had had with him, with the reputation that he had, the confidence that he had always been entitled to by his stockholders and his business associates, and with the results that he had obtained as chief executive officer of his company, I could not go farther than I did. In any event, it was not possible to elicit any further discussion from him.

After Stewart had testified before the Senate investigating committee, John D. Rockefeller, Jr., publicly declared that he had lost confidence in Stewart's leadership. At the same time he wrote Stewart asking him to fulfill a promise to resign upon request. This Stewart declined to do. This particular situation resulted from the fact that John D. Rockefeller, Jr., declared that Stewart had promised to resign at his, Rockefeller's, request; whereas Stewart declared that his promise depended on the request of a majority of the stockholders. The issue had been drawn before the annual meeting of March, 1928, but had not been pressed. The Rockefeller interests sent in their proxies to the management committee as usual, but subsequently withdrew them and contented themselves with refusing to vote their stock for Stewart. Of the 9,000,000 shares outstanding, over 6,000,000 were represented at the meeting, of which about 22% represented the holdings of the Rockefeller interests. At this meeting, the entire board, including Stewart, was reelected.

January 2, 1929, the following letter was sent by John D. Rockefeller, Jr., to the stockholders of the Standard Oil Company of Indiana:

Gentlemen:

At the annual meeting of the stockholders of the Standard Oil Company of Indiana to be held on March 7, 1929, members of the Board of Directors to serve until the annual meeting in 1930 will be elected. I understand that Colonel Robert W. Stewart, now a member of the Board and its Chairman, will be a candidate for reelection.

On April 27, 1928, I wrote Colonel Stewart as follows:

"Your recent testimony before the Senate Committee leaves me no alternative other than to ask you to make good the promise you voluntarily gave me some weeks ago that you would resign at my request. That request I now make."

At the same time I stated publicly that this letter had been written because of my loss of confidence in Colonel Stewart's leadership and my belief that the interests of the Standard Oil Company of Indiana would best be served by his resignation. More than eight months have passed and Colonel Stewart has not replied to my letter. I am therefore asking the stockholders of the Company to join me in opposing his reelection.

Under the loyal and devoted leadership of the President of the Company, Mr. E. G. Seubert, who has been with the Company for more than 30 years, backed by the whole-hearted support of the other members of the Board, most of whom have also been connected with the Company for many years, the interests of the Company will be fully protected and its business well handled without Colonel Stewart.

Definite assurance has already been given me by stockholders representing a substantial amount of the stock of the Company that they are opposed to Colonel Stewart's reelection. If this is your position, please sign the enclosed proxy running to John D. Rockefeller, Jr., Winthrop W. Aldrich and/or William Roberts and send it promptly to Mr. Lyman Rhoades, in care of the Equitable Trust Company, 11 Broad Street, New York City, in the enclosed stamped envelope. This proxy will automatically supersede any other proxy you may have already given for this meeting. It will be voted with the purpose of terminating Colonel Stewart's connection with the Company, and, in so far as may be compatible with that result, for the reelection of all of the present Directors except Colonel Stewart.

Very truly,

(Signed) John D. Rockefeller, Jr.

P. S.   The enclosed proxy should be dated and signed by the stockholder personally and by the witness, who should add his address. The proxy also covers any other meeting or meetings which may be held in 1929 for the election or removal of Directors.

January 15, 1929, official notice of the annual meeting to be held on March 7 following, was sent to the stockholders. The notice contained a proxy blank, authorizing R. W. Stewart, E. G. Seubert, and F. T. Graham or any one of them to vote the shares held by the signer of the proxy. The following statement was included:

Chicago, Illinois,
January 14, 1929.

To the Stockholders:

The undersigned, being all of the members of the Board of Directors of the Standard Oil Company (Indiana), except Mr. Robert W. Stewart, feel that it is necessary and proper at this time to inform the stockholders that on May 23, 1928, Mr. John D. Rockefeller, Jr., by letter requested that the resignation of Robert W. Stewart, Director and executive head of the Company, be demanded by the Board.

Being fully informed of the facts, and having no doubts whatever as to Mr. Stewart's honesty and loyalty to the Company, the Board, by unanimous vote, were of opinion that there was no justifiable reason for such action and so advised Mr. Rockefeller under date of May 31st.

The members of the Board feel that they are in the best position to judge Colonel Stewart's actions and value to the Company, and are still of the opinion stated above. They believe that his retirement would be detrimental to the welfare of the Company.

(Signed) E. G. Seubert

Beaumont Parks	Amos Ball
Allan Jackson	Robert E. Humphreys
R. H. McElroy	L. L. Stephens
E. J. Bullock	C. J. Barkdull

The notice of January 15 also contained a complete statement of the Third Employees' Stock Purchasing Plan, to become effective April 1, 1929. This plan was in furtherance of the policy of extending the privilege of owning stock to the employees. During the preceding 10 years the number of stockholders in the company had increased from 4,622 to over 57,000, many (15,000) of the latter being employees intensely loyal to Stewart because of his liberal labor policies. This loyalty also marked the management holders of stock and a number of smaller stockholders, a loyalty which was probably intensified by a 50% stock dividend early in 1929; which dividend stock, however, did not carry voting privileges as regards the forthcoming annual meeting. The phenomenal growth of the Indiana company under Stewart's chairmanship—with assets in 1928 amounting to almost half a billion dollars, and earnings before taxes amounting to over $80,000,000—was indicative of his business ability. An element of uncertainty as regards the outcome of the election of directors was also introduced by the fact that any proxy is revocable by the signing of another proxy at a later date. Another feature of the situation was that the contending parties confined themselves largely to securing proxies, no appreciable buying of stock being apparent.

The Case of the Management

February 20, 1928, Stewart sent a letter to the stockholders of the company. A part of this letter follows:

. . . The following is the question asked by Senator Nye, which I declined to answer, and because I declined to answer it, was arrested and tried for contempt:

"The Chairman (Senator Nye). Colonel Stewart, do you know of anyone who received these bonds that the Continental Trading Company is purported to have dealt in?"

In declining to answer that question, I said:

"I am a witness in a case which is now pending between the Government of the United States and some defendants. I have been interrogated in regard to these propositions by the counsel appointed to represent the United States in that case. From their interrogation of me, I am of the opinion those are the issues which are going to be tried in that case, and I do not think that the line of interrogation here by this committee is within the jurisdiction of the committee under the laws of the United States."

Later—

"The Chairman—You would not desire to say you did or did not know?"

"Mr. Stewart—No; I will have to content myself with this statement, by saying that personally I have never made a dollar out of this transaction; and second, that I have never given any bonds of any description to any representatives of any political party, or to any public officer of the United States, or of any State or Territory or any municipality inside of it."

Several times afterward I was asked to answer whether I knew of any one receiving Continental Trading Company bonds. Each time I refused to answer. I was indicted for contempt of the Senate for these refusals and was promptly acquitted. I was then indicted for perjury on the ground that I had untruthfully answered that I did not know of any one who had received Continental Trading Company bonds and was again acquitted. The utter ridiculousness of such a situation must be apparent even to a child.

I was questioned by Senators at length about bonds supposed to have gone to Secretary Fall, and I testified that I knew nothing of it.

I testified that I knew of no bonds going to any public official of any kind or to any political party, and further than that, I declined to testify on that subject.

I believed, and still believe, first, that the Senate Committee was conducting an illegal investigation; and second, that a court of justice where there could be orderly examination and cross-examination before a judge learned in the law and a jury, was the place for such testimony.

That the Senators understood me, is shown by the fact that one after another urged me to answer the questions as to my knowledge, and some even abused their privilege to insult me for not doing so.

"Senator Walsh: . . . If you know anything, you decline to tell?"

"Mr. Stewart: That is the position I take very reluctantly, Senator."

On the afternoon of February 3, certain Senators, members of this committee, made a report to the United States Senate asking for my arrest because I had refused to answer what I knew concerning these bonds.

On June 1, 1928, in the Supreme Court of the District of Columbia, Senator Nye testified as follows:

"*Q.* Can you state substantially what that question was?"

"*A.* Well, in substance it was: 'Do you know anyone who was the recipient of any of these bonds in which the Continental Trading Company dealt?'"

"*Q.* What was Stewart's reply to that question?"

"*A.* He declined to answer."

Senator Walsh, on the same day, when asked what questions had been asked me, testified as follows:

"One was with reference to what he knew about the disposition of bonds of the Continental Trading Company."

In testifying to my reply to that question, Senator Walsh said:

"If my recollection now serves me, he made some reply which Senator Nye answered was not responsive to the questions. Thereupon the witness said, in effect, that he had been subpoenaed as a witness, or expected to be subpoenaed as a witness, in a case about to come to trial in the Supreme Court of the District of Columbia, that he had been interrogated with respect to the matters concerning which he was expected to testify, and that, as he gathered, the question at issue was quite the same, or somewhat the same, as that under inquiry by the committee, and that under those circumstances he felt that he ought not to be called upon to answer the question. Senator Nye insisting, however, on an answer to the question, he said that he declined to answer."

In a subsequent trial, in November, 1928, again in the Supreme Court of the District of Columbia, on a charge for having testified falsely as is stated in the Aldrich summary, it was overwhelmingly proven that I never testified that I had no knowledge of any of these bonds. At that time Senator Walsh on the witness stand was forced to admit that he had reported to the United States Senate that I had refused to answer on this point and had induced the Senate to order me arrested for such refusal. When asked why he had made such a report to the Senate, if I had really answered the questions, he said:

"Oh, I can't tell you."

When the jury who heard of all of that testimony brought back their verdict of "not guilty," some press reporters, who believe in sensationalism rather than truth, proclaimed, "Acquitted on a Technicality." Every juror has signed a written statement refuting that charge.

* * * * * *

I have been criticised for choosing Mr. Barnett as trustee of the bonds received, referring to him as a "subordinate employee." Mr. Barnett is anything but a subordinate employee. He is now, and has been for many years, tax commissioner of the company, and there is no position in the company through which more highly confidential matters are handled. To whom was it more natural that I should have turned in seeking a trustee than this man already trusted with matters of much greater importance?

It was also stated that Mr. Barnett kept the bonds in a safe to which I had access. Was this said with sinister intent? Of course, I had access to that safe. As chief executive of this company, I have access to every safe it owns, in the general office, in the refineries, in the sales fields, anywhere.

"On April 20, 1928," it has been said, "Stewart called together the directors of the Standard Oil Company (Ind.) and told them of the fact that he had in his possession the Continental Trading Company bonds," etc. That is a positive untruth. It was not I, but Mr. Barnett, the trustee, who had the bonds. He presented them to the directors and asked for instructions as to their disposition. They instructed him to turn them over to the Crude Oil Purchasing Company, which he did, thereby discharging faithfully his duty as trustee and justifying the confidence I had reposed in him, just as he has for years justified the many confidences the company and its officials have reposed in him.

The trustee knew it; later, a General Attorney of the Standard Oil Company of Indiana knew it. It was sufficiently public to protect the companies. The whole reason and purpose of the trust was that it should not be a public matter other than was necessary to protect the company's interests.

At the time I was advised that I would receive some profits from the Humphreys Oil deal (November 26, 1921) this company was in desperate need of this crude oil to keep its refineries running at capacity. It was obvious from the two contracts which had been handed to me, and which had been submitted by me to our Board of Directors, that a brokerage was being made by someone. I did not know either the amount, if any, which would be given to me, nor the reason therefor. If I had turned such profits over to the company immediately on receipt, it would have been necessary to record the matter in the books of the company, and this would probably have resulted in some publicity. The proposition to me was not an ordinary one, and after telling my informant that I would not myself take any profit, I concluded that publicity might seriously jeopardize our company securing this oil, or at least some of it. The company was getting a highly profitable contract, and my immediate concern was to see that this contract was carried out, and that the company was protected to the extent of receiving every dollar that came out of the transaction. The Trust Agreement was thereupon created after a discussion with the Trustee, an official of the company, and was immediately accepted by him. Thereafter, as profits were handed to me, I immediately handed them to the Trustee.

* * * * * *

To you, the stockholders of the company, let me say that I ask no personal vindication at your hands. That has already been given to me by two courts and two juries; but more than all that, by the loyal support and sturdy championship of my associates on the Board of Directors of this company, and by the employees of the company, and by the overwhelming votes of the majority of the stockholders here in the territory where we transact our business. What I do ask of you stockholders is that you vote for the good of the company and your own good. Do not be deceived into injuring this wonderful, loyal, effective organization that has for so long loyally served you and the company and the public it serves.

Respectfully yours,

ROBERT W. STEWART,

Chairman of the Board of Directors, Standard Oil Company of Indiana.

At the annual meeting, March 7, 1929, William M. Burton, a former president of the company, was elected to succeed Stewart by a vote of 5,510,313 shares to 2,954,986 shares. Melvin A. Traylor, president of the First National Bank of Chicago, was elected to succeed Louis L. Stephens, the latter, however, being retained as general counsel for the company. Seven thousand, nine hundred and one out of 7,918 employee stockholders voted for Stewart, as did also 31,337 out of a total of 46,541 stockholders of the company. At the meeting of the board of directors, E. G. Seubert was reelected president. The position of Chairman of the Board was not filled.

Summary

The events connected with the operations of the Continental Trading Company brought to the attention of the general public, as never before, the evidence of an awakening consciousness of business men of large interests to the necessity of controlling or correcting current business activities. The issue was joined on the matter of intra-company activities that had developed out of inter-company affiliations. The description of the events is sufficient to indicate the problems involved, without much additional comment. Especially is this true regarding the main problem of double agency. It should be noted that Mr. Stewart opposed Mr. Rockefeller's position in this matter, not only by his actions but also in his defense, before the Senate committee, of Mr. Blackmer's activities. The reader has, therefore, been given both views of the situation.

Certain other matters, however, may be brought out more distinctly by a brief summary.

The obligation to testify before a governmental investigating body, whether judicial or otherwise, is governed by the fundamental common-law rule that "The State is entitled to every man's testimony." During the course of the development of the "Law of Evidence," however, certain exceptions to this rule have prevailed. A lawyer, for example, cannot testify in a court regarding the confidential communications made by his client; a somewhat similar exemption has been granted to husband and wife. A priest is not called upon to testify regarding confessions, not because of the tolerance of the Law but because the priest has courageously insisted upon his religious and ecclesiastical independence. The status of the doctor is complicated,[9] but in the main is governed by the common-law

[9] See "Should the Doctor Testify?" *International Journal of Ethics*, July, 1928.

rule in New England and in the South, and elsewhere by opposing statutory exemptions. Mr. Stewart, as a lawyer, was acquainted with the status of privileged communications, as is indicated by his attitude. What is liable to be neglected by the public generally, and by business men in particular, is the fact that some degree of privilege is essential to individual liberty and freedom. The justification for keeping confidential communications inviolate—in the church, in law, in medicine—is the very important practical consideration that only so will penitent, client, or patient feel completely free in disclosing all the facts. And the disclosing of all the facts is necessary to proper professional attention. Can this consideration be equally applied to confidential business dealings?

Business and the State have not yet confronted each other on this issue. In minor business matters, the courts have obtained testimony, but the largest and most important business dealings are never subjected to public or official scrutiny. Many business men prefer to yield a point or to forego their legal rights rather than bring the matter to the attention of the courts. This is but a phase of the essential independence of business values, an independence which can be as fully justified as can the professional prerogative. A bank which is approached by the income-tax department for information regarding depositors may well insist that such knowledge should remain confidential; or at least that, if disclosed, it be not publicly disseminated. A trade association, possessed of figures indicating production, stocks and sales, which are given out even to members only in totals or averages, may well protest against disclosing individual figures to the Federal Trade Commission. This is not a justification of deceit or trickery; it is the assertion of a social value that may well be conserved even in the face of the obvious advantages of full publicity. It is for this reason that many banks prefer not to list their stocks on the New York Stock Exchange; and that investment trusts adopt a similar policy in order not to give wide publicity to their portfolio holdings. There is no absolute solution of the general problem—the confidence in the New York Stock Exchange is enhanced by its policy in regard to this matter. But the problem is implied in every business transaction, and the solution in each case depends on the circumstances.

The third major problem presented by the Continental Trading Company case is that of shareholders' and directors' responsibilities. This problem was anticipated by the Marconi case in the preceding chapter. The balance is very nice and subtle between director control, especially in important transactions and for the sake of preserving the goodwill toward and public respect for the industry, on the one hand, and, on the other, the maintenance of the freedom of management necessary to imposing management responsibility. The solution of such problems rests largely with the director and the large shareholder; the small shareholder too frequently allows his selfish interests to prevail and he frequently is helpless in the face of circumstances that he cannot control. The significance of this point cannot be stressed too much. And not only does this place the responsibility for ethical conduct upon business leaders, but, in the case of the Continental Trading Company, the responsibility was evidently more clearly appreciated by men of wealth, the larger stockholders, than it was by the man of ordinary means. Aside from the practical effects—frequently the smaller businesses must and do follow the leadership of their larger competitors in business practices, good as well as bad—it is not too much to ask and expect business idealism from those who have been most blessed with worldly goods. To see this expectation fulfilled is to witness a sign of the ethical soundness of business.

CHAPTER IX

LEGITIMATE TRADE CHANNELS

The hierarchy of our Federal Government is a matter of common information, even among children, who devote a considerable amount of attention to the study of civil government. It is not so well known that there is an analogous structure of Business, with interrelated functions so complex and so important as to effect a social system commensurate in size and value with the political organism. To understand this business structure and organization is to discover some of the basic sources of many ethical problems, the merely superficial examination of which cannot properly evaluate them.

Is There a Business Hierarchy?

The preceding chapters have dealt with certain aspects of the centralization of business power and the ethical problems to which this tendency has given rise, both directly and by implication. Given this size and high degree of centralization, is it not possible that the organization of business similarly provides the non-ethical groundwork for the development of situations that are pregnant with ethical problems? The ignorance of the business structure is so prevalent as to account alike for many misguided governmental policies affecting business and a public support of restrictive measures which is not always discriminative. On the other hand, the consideration of Business Ethics even among business men cannot proceed superficially with a consideration of the ethical problems as such; they must be recognized as having their roots in the very fabric of business itself, much of which is a technical field of activity which is ethically neutral.

One of the purposes of this volume, therefore, is to discover the structure and working of Business as an organization analogous to that of the State or the Church, especially in order to clarify the ethical issues. It will be the purpose of this chapter to indicate to the reader just how far this analogy can be pursued.

Consider, for example, the status of the wholesaler. The attempt of the wholesaler, at present, to insist on the preservation of his peculiar functions, his definition of these functions and their distinction from the functions of the manufacturer on the one hand and of the retailer on the other, and the organization of wholesalers' trade associations to secure his position and these relations, are indicative of the recognition by some business men of the desirability of a well-defined business structure. It may be discovered, on further inquiry, that a business "hierarchy" does not as a matter of fact exist, and the attempt to establish such a hierarchy may be simply a ruse on the part of certain businesses—conspicuously the wholesaler—to preserve themselves against the inevitable and highly dynamic movements of other agencies in the business order. But there it is, a social fact. For social facts include even the mistaken notions which prompt men to act. Hence the necessity and desirability of a study of Business as a working structure, comparable to Church and State.

Aside from the structure and organization of business there is the important element of personnel. Again we resort to the political analogy. Andrew Jackson once told John Marshall himself to enforce the latter's interpretation of the Constitution, an episode which is indicative of the fact that the center of gravity of political power has shifted among the three major departments of government as the personnel of these departments changed. Thus, during the early days of the Government, the presidency, held by a series of outstanding men, was the outstanding department of government. Jackson himself was the only president who qualified the succeeding dominance of the Supreme Court, especially during the chief justiceships of John Marshall and Roger Taney. Then, for a number of years prior to the Civil War, the "war hawks" of Congress raised that branch of government to a predominant plane, the House of Representatives at times rivaling the House of Commons of England in appropriating the legislative power from the upper house. The Civil War and Lincoln's personality restored the presidency again to its former pristine place—as did the World War and Wilson's abilities later; in the interval, only Cleveland and Roosevelt achieved a like result, while since the World War no such commanding position has been achieved by any president. In the interval between Lincoln and Roosevelt, the Supreme Court and the

Senate at times assumed an ascendency, but not for long.   In the main, however, it is apparent that strong personalities, aided at times by conditions, determined the real hierarchy of the various departments of the United States Government.

Similarly, as Bryce has pointed out in his *American Commonwealth*, the supremacy of the Federal Government is in part due to the fact that it has attracted the best men away from the state governments; partly because of the relatively greater "pyrotechnical displays" attaching themselves to national problems, and certainly with the effect of still further accentuating the relative recession of the power of state governments. These two factors interact upon each other, it being as difficult to discover which is cause and which effect as in the similar problem of the hen and the egg; but it cannot be denied that the supremacy of the National Government has in part resulted from the relatively superior abilities of its personnel.

An interesting corollary now arises: within the past few decades, Business has begun to attract better men from politics, from the Law and from the Church, and their training in business is approaching in quality that of any of the professions.   Will this tendency result, not only in a better organization of business, but also in appropriating from religion and from government and politics the center of gravity of social interests?   It is a conspicuous fact that judicial opinions have been colored by the point of view of large business corporations, largely because the judiciary has been recruited from outstanding members of the bar, who in turn have achieved success largely through their ability to defend business corporations against the law.   Might not a further effect result from the increasing ability and training of business men: the organization of a relatively independent structure of business, separate from government, outwitting the increasingly inferior type of man that is engaging in political and governmental activities, and settling its own disputes without recourse to law?   The proposition is a tempting one, to say the least.

Similarly, within business itself, the center of gravity may be determined by the personnel of various parts of the business structure.   Consider, as an example, the tremendous amount of interrelationship which lodges in the very organization of a business: there is first the banker who has perhaps supplied the greater part of the funds temporarily to get the business started, and who holds a mortgage which may persist for some time as an index of his relatively permanent financial aid. Then there are the bondholders and stockholders, preferred and common, and sometimes classified even further; the "owners" of the company, secondary to the bankers, but whose votes control the policies of the business. Then, often partly separate from *ownership*, and in a sense prior to it, is the function of financial *control* represented in the board of directors, and frequently in only a part of that board. Finally, there is the management, with responsibilities and duties running all through the personnel of the operating company and related even to its customers; and, on the other hand, inadequately remunerated— in comparison with the owners—and frequently subject to dictatorial control that not only violates all sense of self-respect but also and frequently jeopardizes the welfare of the company. Certainly the problems and relations here involved are as intricate and important and independent as are those of political government, and perhaps sufficiently so to attract an increasing number of the very best men to business; and within business itself, the struggle between banker and manager may be determined by the same factor. Inasmuch, however, as this phase of the business structure pertains to the major and capital values of business, its problems, so far as this volume is concerned, will have to be represented by the discussion in the preceding chapter.

More immediately related to the present volume, and basic to the considerations involved in this chapter, is the hierarchy which assumes the business organization just described and which is subsidiary to it: the hierarchy which begins with the ownership factor, and then includes serially the manufacturer, the jobber, the wholesaler, the retailer, and finally the purchaser-consumer. Complicating this hierarchical arrangement is the fact that many purchasers are in turn vendors or manufacturers— of a class of goods known as "producers'" as opposed to "consumers'" goods; with the result that any policy or principle involved is handed backward or forward one stage in the hierarchy—such that the cancellation of an order for fabricated goods, for example, gives a ground for the cancellation of orders for raw materials in turn, or price-cutting practices lead to price-maintenance policies.

A further complicating factor arises because the successive functions in business, even though they are performed by different companies, may not be performed by companies that vary correspondingly in size. A political analogy can again be cited: New York City has far less power in the Federal Government —especially in the Senate—than any state, many of which have a smaller population and less wealth. Thus, similarly, a retail store may do a larger volume of business than a wholesale house handling the same commodities: shall the former be obliged to buy from the latter, or, if it buys from another wholesaler, pay a higher price than the "wholesale" purchaser of a smaller quantity of goods? Suppose a group of consumers or a group of retailers effect an organization for the purpose of buying commodities in larger quantities than is possible in single units, and in the expectation of receiving more favorable prices or quantity discounts: shall they be classified still as consumers or retailers and charged accordingly, even though they may have become incorporated in order to set up an entity distinct from any of the constituent members? Is it socially "right" or "ethical" to establish mail-order houses or chain stores, which eliminate the wholesaler or the small local retailer, and which may even extend the operations of the chain store or mail-order house to the manufacturing of the commodities they sell? Many business men answer this question in the negative. Is there a hierarchy of business functions, the defining of the latter and the relating of the parts of the former making possible the stabilizing and "legitimizing" of "trade channels"? This is the problem which we wish to consider in this chapter.

We have thus far treated the corporation as the essential unit or factor in business. Cutting across this warp of the business fabric, however, is the trade-association woof. The broader significance of the trade-association movement of recent years is to be found in the business structure which it implies. The trade association consists, as a rule, not only of businesses dealing in a particular commodity, as did the Mediaeval guild, but also of certain types of businesses in a narrower and more exclusive sense than did the guild: manufacturing, wholesaling, retailing. This means that there arises, with the development of a trade association, the necessity of defining the functions of its members. Especially has this problem arisen in regard to the distinction between wholesalers' and retailers' functions and between the functions of the manufacturer and of businesses included under the indefinite term "jobbers."

Practically what has happened is that certain groups in the marketing of goods have been faced with declining sales because of the encroachments of other groups upon what are called "legitimate" hierarchical functions, which have been regarded as "vested" rights. Conspicuously, the wholesaler has been confronted on the one hand with manufacturers who are more and more inclined to sell direct to retailer and consumer, and on the other hand by chain stores, mail-order houses and retailers' cooperatives which endeavor to purchase directly from manufacturers. The situation is very closely analogous to jurisdictional disputes among labor groups, and arises for very much the same general reasons: changing conditions have enabled some groups to enlarge and extend their functions at the expense of others, and the latter attempt to safeguard their activities by organizing themselves and by defining what they regard as their "legitimate" functions. In some cases, as in the following National Harness Manufacturers' case and Federal Electric case, involving harness and coal respectively, the crisis has been partly brought about by a declining use of the commodity and by a tremendous struggle for the remaining business. In others, as in the cases involving groceries, the situation has been made acute by the development of new marketing devices: chain stores and mail-order houses. Whatever the cause, the purpose of these trade-association organizations seems to be to insist on a business hierarchy, with manufacturer or grower supplying the jobber, the goods then being sold through wholesaler and retailer successively to the ultimate consumer.

Direct Sales

The following three cases illustrate the changes which have occurred recently, especially in the direction of "direct sales."

During the decade from 1912 to 1922,[1] a change appeared to have taken place in the hosiery trade. Prior to that time durability and economy in price were said to have been the principal motives in the purchase of most of the hosiery manufactured by the Drury Hosiery Mills. By 1922, however, there apparently was a much greater demand than formerly for stylish silk and woolen hosiery. In 1922 and 1923, hosiery colors were subject to rapid changes in popularity, such style preferences appearing in the purchase of low- and medium-price stockings as well as in the purchase of high-grade hosiery.

[1] I *Harvard Business Reports* 277. Fictitious name.

In 1923 the company produced about 30 styles of hosiery in approximately 25 colors; for women there were several grades of soft-combed cotton stockings, hard-twisted cotton lisle, mercerized cotton, pure fiber silk, pure silk and fiber mixed, fiber silk and wool, and silk and wool.   There were styles made of similar materials for men, and four styles of standard durable hosiery for children.   The company did not produce hosiery in fancy patterns.   Changing styles, however, had a marked effect on colors.

The Drury Hosiery Company had been selling durable, low-price hosiery for men, women, and children for more than a generation.   65% of the domestic sales were made to wholesalers; 29% to chain stores, mail-order distributors, and buying syndicates; and 6% to retailers. The executives of the company were dissatisfied with this policy of distribution and contemplated attempting to increase substantially the sales made directly to department stores in important buying centers, in addition to its established distributers.

In order to cope with the existing situation, the sales manager of the company proposed that it undertake to make as many sales as possible directly to department stores.   There were several objections to this method of distribution.   Retailers customarily purchased more frequently and in smaller quantities than did wholesalers; the number of customers also would be greater; and hence important changes in the sales organization would be necessary.   In selling to wholesalers, furthermore, the company had not carried finished hosiery in stock. Hosiery was knitted and carried in the gray, but was not dyed until after orders had been received.   Sales to department stores would entail the carrying of dyed stock ready for shipment.   The estimate of the average stock that would be required eventually was 200,000 dozen pairs of stockings per year.   The establishment of warehouses at several central points also would be essential to national distribution; but this step was unnecessary for several years.   A serious risk was involved, also, in carrying finished stocks, since the color preferences of consumers apparently changed with rapidity.   The company filled wholesalers' orders with cases, each of which contained hosiery of only one style and color.   A case ordered by a department store had to be made up of hosiery in assorted styles and colors.   If a policy of selling to department stores were to be adopted, the executives of the Drury Hosiery Mills did not expect to accept orders for less than case lots. Hence, the volume of sales to wholesalers was likely to remain fairly substantial.

In the period following the depression of 1921, department stores had increased the proportion of their purchases from wholesalers in order to secure a rapid rate of stock-turn.   In 1923 it was not entirely clear whether or not this was a permanent change in the buying methods of department stores, but caution in the estimating of future requirements was expected so long as the memory of the experiences in 1920 and 1921 remained fresh in the minds of business men.

The company concluded, however, that it could secure the largest sales volume by selling directly to department stores in important buying centers, and decided to develop that method of distribution. The distribution of low-price Drury hosiery to rural retail stores and retail merchants outside the principal shopping centers in urban communities was to continue through wholesalers.

* * * * * *

The Leon Shoe Company[2] produced men's and women's shoes of medium and high quality and sold them through retail stores which it owned, and through exclusive retail agents. The company's annual sales volume averaged about $5,000,000. As a result of the business depression in 1921, a marked decline occurred in the company's sales in that year, and at the beginning of 1922 it became evident that if sales were to be increased some change in policy was necessary. The proposal was made to the president that the number of styles manufactured be reduced and a single retail price established for all the shoes.

The company reduced the prices of its shoes in 1921 so that the average retail price was about $8.50 per pair. No increase in sales resulted, however, and it became evident to the president that sales could be increased only by a further reduction in price without a corresponding reduction in quality. This could be accomplished only by a reduction in the costs of manufacture and distribution. The plan proposed to secure these results provided for a reduction in the number of styles from 2,500 to 100, all the styles to be of approximately the same quality. Those styles were to be retained which had been the most popular in the past. The plan provided also that, as a means of effecting further economies of operation in selling, the company adopt a single-price policy for its retail stores. A price below $7 per pair was recommended as one that would appeal to the large class of purchasers of medium quality shoes. The plan called for an increase of 50% in the advertising appropriation for the remainder of 1922. The advertising was to feature the single price, and the new policy was to be characterized in the slogan "One Profit, One Quality, One Price." No direct efforts were to be made to induce exclusive agents to sell at a single price.

The chief objection made to the adoption of the plan was that it probably involved loss of sales to exclusive agents. The agents wanted a large number of styles from which to select, so that they could order styles which represented their conceptions of what could be sold most readily to their clienteles. It was likely that the agents would find it impossible to secure the desired variations among 100 styles. Even if the agents continued to order from the reduced number of styles, they

[2] II *Harvard Business Reports* 144. Fictitious name.

were likely to object to the one-price retail selling policy. The company's trade-mark was well known throughout the United States, and the agents would have difficulty in securing a higher price than that asked by the company's own stores.

The president decided to adopt the proposed plan, and it was made effective in March, 1922. The exclusive agents refused to continue to sell Leon shoes under the changed policy. Sales in the company's retail stores increased, however; by November, 1922, the company's rate of sales was equal to that of January and February, 1922, that is, sales of the retail stores increased approximately 100%. No increase in the stores' expenses accompanied this increase in sales. Consequently, the company's percentage of selling expense was reduced one-half, sales were doubled, net profits were increased, inventories were reduced 25%, and the ratio of current assets to current liabilities was increased from 1.79 to 5. Sales continued to increase, and the president was convinced that the new policy was highly satisfactory.

* * * * * *

The Federal Electric Company[3] had a large manufacturing plant in a city of 50,000 population where it employed a relatively large number of men with respect to the population of the town. For a number of years preceding June, 1927, the Federal Electric Company followed the practice of selling coal in five-ton lots or less to its employees for domestic consumption, the company being able to procure coal for its employees at times when the regular dealers could not. The rate charged for this coal was slightly above cost but below the retail price which was prevailing in the community and which was necessary for the proper conduct of the retail coal business. It thus became impossible for any of the local retailers of coal to extend their business to supplying the employees of the Federal Electric Company with coal for domestic consumption even though the retailers were able to secure the coal.

Furthermore, persons not connected with the company and unable to take advantage of the prices given out by the Federal Electric Company tried to secure coal from dealers at less than the price necessary to secure a profit in the retailing of coal. Other firms, learning of the practices of the Federal Electric Company, similarly secured coal for sale to their employees. In one case a grocery store and in another a trucking company received several car loads of coal for distribution during the summer months.

This situation was reported by the retail dealers to the local Coal Dealers' Association, an organization having a membership of several hundred retail dealers in a number of adjoining states in the United States. The membership in this Coal Dealers' Association constituted the greater part of the retail dealers in the territory.

[3] Fictitious name.

The situation in modern business is apparent from these typical cases. Effective selling methods are cutting across the former boundary lines which separated the successive marketing functions, the one from the other. As a result, the businesses which are being eliminated are being forced to justify their own existence. The first justification that occurs to such men is that of their vested interests, a plea which is followed up by the very practical device of establishing a trade association to protect their alleged prerogatives, as in the following case of the harness makers. Here one finds an attempt, on the part of the members of a trade which is suffering from the declining use of horses, to safeguard the business that is left and to maintain its traditional marketing channels.

Trade-association Attempts to Establish a Business Hierarchy

The Wholesale Saddlery Association[4] was a voluntary unincorporated association with a membership comprising the greater part of the wholesale saddlery trade of the United States. The membership was composed of persons, firms, copartnerships, and corporations located in various states of the United States and engaged in the business of distributing and selling at wholesale harness and saddlery goods. Members of the association purchased raw materials and finished articles from the manufacturers of saddlery accessories and sold to retailers, both members and non-members of the National Harness Manufacturers' Association.

The National Harness Manufacturers' Association was an unincorporated association, its members consisting principally of city and district associations located in various cities throughout the United States. The members of these local or subsidiary associations purchased the majority of their supplies from wholesalers, including members of the Wholesale Saddlery Association.

During the years immediately preceding and including 1917, there was a tendency among wholesalers of saddlery accessories to sell direct to the large consuming trade without the services of the retailer, and there also was a tendency for the manufacturers of accessories to sell direct to the retailers without the services of the wholesaler. At this time, furthermore, conditions in the trade had worked toward a situation in which the wholesale and retail saddlery business was conducted as one operation. Many of the members of the Wholesale Saddlery Association were originally retailers, having later entered into the combined wholesale and retail business.

[4] I F. T. C. D. 335 (1919).

The Wholesale Saddlery Association at this time had declared its established policy to be as follows:

It is the policy of this association to promote trade and commerce in the saddlery line in the time-honored and regular channels, namely, through sales of goods by the manufacturer to the wholesaler, by the wholesaler to the retailer and by the retailer to the consumer, thus maintaining the stability of business and contributing to the prosperity of all in their respective situations.

This policy was at variance with the tendencies and conditions stated in the preceding paragraphs. The efforts of the Wholesale Saddlery Association to establish this policy originally met with strong opposition on the part of both manufacturers and retailers, but for a number of years prior to 1905 the manufacturers were associate members of the Wholesale Saddlery Association and were thereby committed to selling only to those concerns recognized by the Wholesale Saddlery Association as legitimate wholesalers.

Upon the abolition of the associate membership in 1905, both wholesalers and manufacturers announced that such action involved no change in their relations, and a large number of manufacturers continued until 1917 to act in harmony with the declared policy of the Wholesale Saddlery Association. Specific instances of discussions, in the joint convention of the manufacturers and of the Wholesale Saddlery Association, as to the status of disputed wholesalers, occurred as recently as 1916.

As the result of the objections made by the Wholesale Saddlery Association, the accessory manufacturers were accustomed to refuse the various competitors of the members of this association recognition as wholesalers, with the result that these competitors were forced to purchase goods from the members of the Wholesale Saddlery Association and, therefore, to pay prices which were higher than those charged by the manufacturers to the recognized wholesalers.

With the declared policy of the Wholesale Saddlery Association there was connected the assumption that the association could determine what concerns were wholesalers, and for a number of years prior to 1917 only those concerns which were members, or were eligible to membership in the Wholesale Saddlery Association, were recognized by it as legitimate wholesalers entitled to buy as such from manufacturers. After 1911 the Wholesale Saddlery Association required that applicants to membership be engaged exclusively in the wholesale business, although its own members were allowed to continue doing both a wholesale and retail business. The association, after 1911, classified all concerns as retailers who were doing a combined wholesale and retail business regardless of the amount or proportion of their wholesale business.

The association, until 1907, compiled and circulated wholesalers' lists containing the names of the wholesalers whom the association recognized as "legitimate." This list was discontinued in 1907, after which time there was circulated, with the same purpose in view, the "membership list" of the association. The association, furthermore, for a number of years preceding January, 1916, censored the list of wholesalers published and circulated among manufacturers by certain trade papers.

For a number of years, including 1914, the Wholesale Saddlery Association notified its members of the names of manufacturers which were not in harmony with the policy of the association as evidenced by their selling to the "retail" trade, including in that term concerns doing both a wholesale and retail business. In 1916 the association urged its members to report for the purpose of publication the names of manufacturers who sold to the retail trade, while the manufacturers who were in harmony with the association policy were given favorable publicity among its members. The result of these activities was to induce the members of the association to withhold and withdraw their patronage from the first-mentioned class of manufacturers and to confine and prefer their patronage to the last-mentioned class. The full purpose and effect of the association policy was to hamper and impede the business of concerns which did not carry a full and complete wholesale stock, to make more difficult the entrance of competitors into the wholesale field and to prevent lower prices to retailers resulting from the economies of direct shipments.

The policy of the Wholesale Saddlery Association was influenced in part by the overtures of the National Harness Manufacturers' Association which cooperated in establishing the principle that a combined wholesale and retail business was not a legitimate wholesale business. The two associations thereby came to an agreement on what constituted a so-called legitimate wholesaling business. The cooperation of these two associations resulted in a refusal on the part of their members to sell to mail-order houses, general stores, hardware stores and other competitors not recognized as legitimate.

The Federal Trade Commission charged the Wholesale Saddlery Association and others with conspiracy[5] against certain of their competitors, and with unfair methods of competition, and ordered them to cease and desist from such conspiracy and combination whereby they induced or coerced manufacturers to refuse to sell to such competitors. The commission furthermore ordered the association to cease continuing or establishing tests or standards of what constituted a "legitimate" jobbing or

[5] I F. T. C. D. 335, 359 (1919).

wholesaling business, "whether based upon eligibility to membership or actual membership in said association, the amount of business done, the stock carried, or the proportion of business which is wholesale"; also to desist from compiling, censoring, and distributing lists of "legitimate" jobbers, or from giving notices to manufacturers to that effect, and from circulating among their own members the names of manufacturers "not in harmony" with the association policies, and from withdrawing their patronage from them or from inducing them not to sell direct to retailers.

The "cease and desist" order of the Commission was furthermore directed against any combination or conspiracy, between the Wholesale Saddlery Association and the National Harness Manufacturers' Association, which effected similar restraints on accessory manufacturers, and against the National Harness Manufacturers' Association in connection with similar tactics toward their competitors.

The National Harness Manufacturers' Association appealed the case to the Circuit Court of Appeals, Sixth Circuit,[6] on the grounds that the Federal Trade Commission Act was unconstitutional, that the Commission had no jurisdiction in this particular case, and that the Commission order was not supported by the evidence. After denying the first two contentions, the court examined the evidence and found that the conditions adduced were sufficient to justify the Commission's order.

That the problem of maintaining "legitimate trade channels" is not confined to industries which are handling commodities with declining sales is indicated by the following cases illustrating the situation in the hardware business.

The Southern Hardware Jobbers' Association[7] was a voluntary unincorporated association with a membership of 150 hardware jobbers doing business in the southeastern part of the United States. Its membership constituted approximately 90% of all those doing a jobbing or wholesale business in hardware in this territory. The members of the association were engaged in distributing and selling hardware at wholesale to retail dealers. About 90% of the members of the association were engaged in the sale of hardware at retail as well as at wholesale.

According to the by-laws of the association the members of the association consisted of wholesale hardware firms doing business in the

---

[6] 268 Fed. 705 (1920).

[7] IV F. T. C. D. 428 (1922).

southern states. Any firm or corporation whose sale of hardware at wholesale constituted 75% of the gross sales of a minimum of $250,000 per year was entitled to membership provided certain other requirements were met. The membership of the association was further restricted to those wholesalers whose policy it was to distribute their goods and merchandise through the so-called regular channels of trade, that is, from manufacturer to wholesaler, from wholesaler to retailer and from retailer to consumer. The members of the association refused to purchase from manufacturers who sold to non-members, the association conducting a system of espionage upon the business of the wholesale hardware trade in the southern states in order to follow up this policy.

Members of the association communicated to such manufacturers, as were found to be selling to non-member customers, the information that such transactions were known to the association and were disapproved by it, the imputation being that such manufacturers must choose between selling to the members of the association or selling to non-members. The list of members of the association was distributed among hardware producers and manufacturers, including particularly the members of the American Hardware Manufacturers' Association, to give information in regard to customers who "were justly entitled to purchase hardware on the legitimate jobbers' terms and conditions."

The American Hardware Manufacturers' Association comprised approximately 500 members, including the principal manufacturers of hardware in the country. In deference to the expressed desires of the Southern Hardware Jobbers' Association, the members of the American Hardware Manufacturers' Association endorsed the practice of distributing its fabricated articles from manufacturer to wholesaler, from wholesaler to retailer, and from retailer to consumer. In some instances the members of the manufacturers' association sold hardware direct to the retail trade, but never on the same terms and conditions that it sold like goods and quantities to the so-called legitimate jobbers or wholesalers. This practice insured that the manufacturers charged the retailer just as much for the goods as if the retailer had bought them from the jobber. No objection was made by the members of the Southern Hardware Jobbers' Association to such sales provided the price differential was maintained by the manufacturer. In the territory covered by the Southern Hardware Jobbers' Association, however, there were many consumers and retailers whose requirements were sufficiently large to make it practicable and profitable for the manufacturers to sell direct to them and on the same terms and conditions as they sold to the members of the Southern Hardware Jobbers' Association.

The American Hardware Manufacturers' Association and the Southern Hardware Jobbers' Association were in the habit of holding their annual meetings at the same time and in the same place, and the executive committees of the two associations held additional meetings together.

In July, 1919, certain retailers of hardware, to the number of about 300, doing business in Georgia and adjoining states, organized two corporations, obtaining charters under the laws of Delaware. The object of these corporations was to act as purchasing agents for the members and to deal directly with the manufacturers and secure the benefits of direct and large purchases on the same terms as the jobbers or wholesalers. By the resultant saving, these retailers expected to compete successfully with mail-order and catalog houses and with the retailing of hardware by the so-called regular jobbers. One of these corporations sought membership in the Southern Hardware Jobbers' Association but was informed that its selling policy did not meet with the approval of the association, and the application was refused on the ground that the requirements for membership had not been met. After these corporations had succeeded in purchasing goods from various manufacturers on the same terms as were extended to legitimate jobbers, the Southern Hardware Jobbers' Association made overtures to the manufacturers and to their associations protesting against such business relations and asserting that such practice would eliminate, in part at least, the services of the jobber in hardware. It represented to the manufacturers that such acts and sales would be regarded as unfriendly acts to the Southern Hardware Jobbers' Association and would be regarded as a sufficient reason for the jobbers to refuse to deal any longer with such manufacturers. As a result, a large number of manufacturers refused to complete orders for hardware supplies, which many of them had already accepted from the retailers' corporations and partly filled, and they proceeded to return these orders unfilled. Great difficulty was experienced by the retailers' corporations in getting manufacturers to complete their orders or to accept others.

The Federal Trade Commission ordered these practices to be stopped.[8] The case was appealed to the Circuit Court of Appeals, Fifth Circuit.[9] The court recognized two kinds of dealers whose activities would be restricted by the association policies: jobbers and wholesalers selling direct and sharing their profits with retailers, and those retailers who do not also do a jobbing or wholesale business. These restrictions were regarded by the court as sufficient to warrant the Commission's order; inasmuch as these restrictions were established by an agreement among a number of independent businesses, they therefore constituted a conspiracy in restraint of trade.

[8] IV F. T. C. D. 428, 442.
[9] 290 Fed. 773 (1923).

Cooperative Buying Groups

The most acute problems related to "legitimate trade channels" have arisen in the marketing of groceries. The advent of the chain store and mail-order house not only introduced direct and disastrous competition in the retailing trade, but its repercussions were felt among the wholesalers and manufacturers as well.

A number of corporations[10] doing business under the laws of Illinois and located in Cairo were engaged in buying and selling wholesale quantities of groceries and similar products. The Interstate Grocery Company was a corporation organized under the laws of Illinois and was also engaged in the business of buying and selling wholesale quantities of groceries and similar products but doing a smaller amount of business than any of the wholesale grocers previously mentioned. The capital stock of the Interstate Grocery Company was owned and held by retail grocers to whom it sold groceries at wholesale at prices equal to cost plus 5% to cover the cost of doing business. The Interstate Grocery Company also sold to nonstockholding retailers at higher prices but sold no groceries to consumers.

In 1917 a number of wholesale grocers, including the Interstate Grocery Company, entered into separate contracts for the purchase of certain amounts of condensed milk with a manufacturer's agent in the city of St. Louis. After this milk had arrived at the railroad station in Cairo, the wholesalers, whose aggregate purchases of milk far exceeded the amount purchased by the Interstate Grocery Company, refused to accept the condensed milk purchased by each of them unless the St. Louis agent should break his contract of purchase and sale with the Interstate Grocery Company and withhold delivery of the condensed milk from them. Similar practices were engaged in by these wholesale grocers with reference to goods supplied by the Postum Cereal Company of Battle Creek, Michigan, and these wholesalers also protested to the Kellogg's Toasted Corn Flake Company against its selling its products to the Interstate Grocery Company.

The wholesalers of this territory had, during the year 1918, agreed among themselves that the Interstate Grocery Company was not conducting its business in accordance with certain tests and standards fixed and established by the wholesalers. These wholesalers agreed and conspired among themselves to make representations to this effect to various manufacturers and their agents. By such means the wholesalers induced the manufacturers of groceries and food products not to deal with the Interstate Grocery Company upon the terms and at the prices offered and charged to the wholesalers. The Interstate Grocery

[10] III F. T. C. D. 87 (1920).

Company was thereby compelled to purchase its supplies from and through the wholesalers, who were its competitors. The prices which the Interstate Grocery Company was thus compelled to pay were higher than those charged to its competitors and others engaged in similar businesses.

* * * * * *

The Los Angeles Grocery Company[11] was a corporation organized under the laws of California and having its place of business in Los Angeles. It was engaged in the business of purchasing in wholesale quantities goods and commodities such as were generally carried by wholesale grocers and selling the same in wholesale quantities for profit to its customers. The company sold to the retail-grocery trade only and did not sell to consumers. The company had about 80 stockholders, most of whom were retail grocers. It did not, however, confine its selling to such retail grocers as were stockholders. The business of the Los Angeles Grocery Company was separate and distinct from the business of any of its stockholders; it never owned, controlled or had an interest in any retail grocery and never conducted a retail business. In the course of its business the Los Angeles Grocery Company bought from a large number of manufacturers and was in competition with a number of so-called wholesale jobbers in buying and selling in wholesale quantities.

The jobbers located in this territory included a number of corporations whose purpose it was to buy and sell groceries in wholesale quantities. About January, 1918, these jobbers had certain secret agreements among themselves with reference to the Los Angeles Grocery Company. They conspired among themselves to report to various manufacturers and their agents that the Los Angeles Grocery Company was not conducting its business in accordance with the tests and standards fixed and established for the trade by the jobbers. They, furthermore, attempted to induce manufacturers to refuse to deal with the Los Angeles Grocery Company upon the terms they were at that time enjoying and with the purpose of compelling the Los Angeles Grocery Company to purchase its supplies from jobbers. Such representations were made, for example, to the Californian and Hawaiian Sugar Refining Company.

A number of firms, known as brokers, were engaged in this locality in selling the products of various manufacturers of groceries and food products. These firms had organized an association known as the Southern California Association of Manufacturers' Products. These brokers, induced by the persuasion of the jobbers, agreed and conspired among themselves to refuse to sell to the Los Angeles Grocery Company upon the terms and at the prices offered and charged to the jobbers and others engaged in similar business. They recommended to their

[11] II F. T. C. D. 151 (1919).

respective principals not to sell to the Los Angeles Grocery Company upon such terms and at such prices as were offered to jobbers, and conspired to compel the Los Angeles Grocery Company to purchase their products from and through these jobbers.

The Western Sugar Refinery Company and the Californian and Hawaiian Sugar Refining Company were corporations existing under the laws of California and were engaged in the business of manufacturing cane sugar. These refiners, acting together with the brokers, refused to sell sugar to the Los Angeles Grocery Company upon the terms and at the prices offered and charged to its competitors, the jobbers. The jobbers at various times threatened the manufacturers' agents with boycott and the withdrawal of patronage in case they sold to the Los Angeles Grocery Company upon such terms and at such prices as were enjoyed by the jobbers. When these jobbers discovered, however, that the manufacturers' agents had, in spite of this agreement, secretly sold sugar to the Los Angeles Grocery Company at the prices enjoyed by the jobbers, the latter refused to continue to handle a certain product sold by the broker engaged in this practice.

The brokers, then, during January, 1918, and succeeding months, insisted that the Los Angeles Grocery Company should purchase its commodities through the jobbers, who rendered no service in connection with the distribution or handling of the commodities so sold but merely rendered bills to the Los Angeles Grocery Company for such commodities at prices higher than the Los Angeles Grocery Company had been paying to the manufacturers or their agents. These jobbers, furthermore, at various times sold and offered to sell to the retail customers of the Los Angeles Grocery Company products and commodities at prices lower than those charged by the jobbers to the Los Angeles Grocery Company for similar products and commodities.

One of the brokers sent to its principal, the Western Sugar Refinery Company, a letter stating that all of the wholesale grocers of southern California had been interviewed and that they objected to the sales of the Western Sugar Refinery Company to the Los Angeles Grocery Company. Such sales were then discontinued by the refinery. Similar action was taken by the Californian and Hawaiian Sugar Refining Company. Other manufacturers were similarly approached by the wholesalers and told that direct sales to the Los Angeles Grocery Company would affect the relations of such manufacturers with the wholesale grocers of southern California.

As a result of these activities the Los Angeles Grocery Company was compelled to purchase approximately 38% of its products and commodities from its competitors, the jobbers or wholesalers, and to pay for such products and commodities prices higher than those regularly charged by the manufacturers to those firms engaged in similar business. The Los Angeles Grocery Company, as a result, lost to its competitors, the jobbers, a large volume of business, especially through its inability to obtain sugar from the Western Sugar Refinery and the Californian and Hawaiian Sugar Refining Companies.

In spite of their understandings with the jobbers of southern California, the brokers, at various times subsequent to January, 1918, met secretly and agreed to permit the Los Angeles Grocery Company to purchase commodities directly from the manufacturers at the prices regularly charged to its competitors and others engaged in a similar business. The usual method employed was to pay to the Los Angeles Grocery Company a rebate on the purchase price paid by the company for goods ordered by it from the brokers and billed through and charged for by the jobbers. This rebate generally amounted to the difference between the price paid by the Los Angeles Grocery Company to the jobbers and the price charged by the brokers for such goods to the jobbers. Such rebates were kept secret from the jobbers for fear that the latter would withdraw their patronage from the brokers and their principals. In some cases direct sales were made to the Los Angeles Grocery Company when the brokers believed that the jobbers would not learn of such transactions.

This case, together with other cases of the same type and involving the sale of groceries, was called to the attention of the Federal Trade Commission,[12] and in each case the members of such combinations were ordered to "cease and desist" their practices. The Western Sugar Refinery Company, and other firms and persons against whom the Commission order was directed, carried their case to the Circuit Court of Appeals, Ninth Circuit.[13] The court pointed out that where several persons were charged with illegal acts or, as in this case, with unfair practices, it was necessary to prove the charges against each person named in the suit. Observing this rule, the court excepted the Western Sugar Refinery Company and the Californian and Hawaiian Sugar Refining Company from the Commission order on the ground that their policy toward the Los Angeles Grocery Company was the result of "a concurrence of opinion as to the classification to be given to the Los Angeles Grocery Company" and not of "any actual understanding or agreement between them or with the Los Angeles jobbers."[14] Similarly the one broker who joined in this appeal to the court

[12] II F. T. C. D. 151 (1919); III F. T. C. D. 87 (1920), 109 (1920); IV F. T. C. D. 466 (1922).
[13] 275 Fed. 725 (1921).
[14] *Ibid.*, p. 741.

was excepted from the order of the Commission. "So long as the classification was the individual opinion and action of the refiners, it could not be made the basis of a finding of conspiracy or combination between the two refiners, or between them and the jobbers, or between them and the brokers." With respect to the Los Angeles jobbers, however, the court held the findings of the Federal Trade Commission to be sustained. The line was thus drawn between the act of an individual and the same act made unlawful by reason of its being the joint or combined act of two or more persons.

The jobbers, in their plea before the court, made much of the point that the Los Angeles Grocery Company was merely a retailers' buying organization and not a wholesaling company. As the court pointed out, this question is subordinate to that of the conduct of the jobbers in dealing with the Los Angeles Grocery Company.[15]

The significance of this attitude of the court lies in the recognition of a business hierarchy composed of grades of members with well-defined functions, and of the right and expediency of protecting these functions against such activities as direct sales. Whether such a view of business structure can prevail against opposing economic forces—such as the economy of direct sales—without some organization consciously directed toward this purpose, it is difficult to see. The law has definitely set itself against business men combining or conspiring to effect such a purpose. The only other basis for its possible success is the concurrence of many individuals in the point of view. But they will constantly be subjected to temptations to depart from this point of view in order to take advantage of an immediate prospect of profitable business.

Wholesalers' Functions and Services

The main problem of "legitimate trade channels" was studied and discussed by the National Wholesale Conference, held in May, 1929, under the auspices of the Chamber of Commerce of the United States. One of the committees dealt with the problem of wholesalers' functions and services. The conclusions of this committee are interesting, not only because their content is an elaboration of the definition of "wholesaler," but also because these "conclusions" may be regarded as a program of

[15] *Ibid.*, p. 733.

good behavior promised by the wholesaler if the public will again restore him to the position which he once held but which he has lost through his failure to realize the necessity of adapting himself to the conditions of the times.

WHOLESALERS' FUNCTIONS AND SERVICES

Conclusions

THE COMMITTEE reached these conclusions as to functions and services which wholesalers perform:

1. There are certain fundamental functions and services of distribution that must be performed in getting goods from producers to consumers.

2. The *efficient* independent wholesaler can perform the functions of distributing merchandise from the manufacturer to the retailer satisfactorily and economically for most merchandise, by proper cooperation among the three essential parties in interest.

3. The great bulk of merchandise in the United States is distributed through the manufacturer-wholesaler-retailer system of distribution. This system is fundamentally sound because the groups can coordinate their special activities to complement each other.

4. It is a primary function of the wholesaler to purchase goods in large quantities and to distribute in smaller units.

Efficient wholesalers make careful studies to determine the number of units that can be packed and carried most economically and advantageously for distribution to retailers, and also to determine the units most advantageous for consumers.

5. The wholesaler maintains an adequate stock of merchandise, selected as to quality, quantity and seasonal needs of his customers, and has these stocks available as required. In performing this function, the wholesaler makes a substantial investment, which relieves the manufacturer, producer and retailer of a costly and burdensome necessity which would be imposed upon them if they performed the distribution function for themselves.

6. The wholesaler necessarily extends credit accommodations to retailers. The manufacturer or producer would have to carry this financial burden himself if the wholesaler did not assume it.

Proper scrutiny of credits to avoid unnecessary losses is more practicable in the smaller areas in which wholesalers operate than in the wider area which manufacturer or producer must cover.

7. Advances by wholesalers to manufacturers or producers are not a proper part of the wholesalers' function.

If this banking function is assumed, it should be undertaken as any other independent investment opportunity might be undertaken by any individual, whether wholesaler or not.

8. The wholesaler functions as a sales agent for the manufacturer and as a purchasing agent for the retailer. As such, the sound interests of both manufacturer and retailer must control these operations and be reconciled.

9. Consumer demand and preference is the ultimate controlling factor in merchandising and, therefore, producers, wholesalers, and retailers should unite to study this subject.

10. It is a function of the wholesaler to introduce desirable new articles of commerce, and advise and aid manufacturers in such matters.

11. Warehousing at strategic points is essential to the proper rendering of service for the benefit of consumers.

12. The wholesaler endeavors to find the most effective means of rendering essential service to the retailer—not merely by supplying him with merchandise under acceptable conditions, but also by assisting him to sell goods, and in various ways helping him to establish his store as a permanent institution. The wholesaler exists wholly because of the economies he effects for others.

Some of these conclusions have to do with problems allied to, but distinct from, that of preserving legitimate trade channels. Some of these problems, such as credit accommodations and advances and the rendering of customer-services, have been dealt with elsewhere. Other problems, concerning types of wholesalers, within particular industries or differentiated according to type of commodities, we shall not concern ourselves with: most of the criticisms directed against such trade movements are merely the querulous complaints of the inert against the radical changes which have characterized recent distribution methods. These new methods do not eliminate any distribution functions; they do however skip the old-line wholesaler and "make the distance, which was formerly covered in three jumps, in two." The mortality among wholesalers has been tremendous, and unless the remaining 100,000 wholesalers in the country cease to regard themselves as necessary and indispensable parts in an immutable economic order, the mortality will continue. Considered as part of the tremendous distribution changes which are also profoundly affecting the small-town retailer, this mortality of wholesalers may be viewed as a sociological as well as economic catastrophe, comparable to the unemployment engendered by the introduction of labor-saving machinery. The larger ethical justification for the change is similar in both cases, however: an achievement of economy in production and distribution, to which the individual problems must be subordinated—and solved by proper adjustments. The opportunity for adjustment and for discovering methods and functions by which wholesaling activities may be salvaged is certainly still present.   Much of this waste is being eliminated by direct selling methods; but much of it also can be absorbed by efficient wholesaling and can thereby be converted into a service for which the beneficiaries would be most willing to pay.

The Problem of the Individual Dealer

The preceding cases have dealt largely with the attempts of certain types of business, performing certain functions, to effect a business hierarchy and establish legitimate trade channels by organized and concerted association efforts.   In contrast with this, the following cases will indicate the attempts which individual businesses have made to solve the same problem.   These cases present the more acute problems faced by those individuals whose business is being seriously invaded by direct selling methods, as well as the administrative problems which confront the larger manufacturers in determining what the business organization shall be in order to secure the best distribution methods.

Raymond Brothers-Clark Company was a Nebraska corporation engaged in the wholesale-grocery business at Lincoln.   It bought groceries from manufacturers in various parts of the United States, and resold these to customers in Nebraska and neighboring states, its business amounting approximately to $2,500,000 per year.   The company competed with various groceries, including the Basket Stores Company, located at Lincoln.   The Basket Stores Company engaged partly in wholesaling, with warehouses at Lincoln and Omaha; but 90% of its business consisted in the operation of a chain of 72 stores, 18 of which were located at Lincoln.   The annual volume of the Basket Stores Company's business was approximately $2,500,000.

The Snider Company in September, 1918, sold its products to a number of groceries in Lincoln, and consigned these to Raymond Brothers-Clark Company in a "pool" car, which was unloaded by the latter as follows: its own commodities were placed in its warehouse, those consigned to dealers outside Lincoln were reconsigned to them by local freight, and other purchasers in Lincoln were notified of the arrival of their goods, except that the Raymond Brothers-Clark Company failed to notify the Basket Stores Company of the arrival of its goods until a month or more had elapsed subsequent to the arrival of the goods.

Prior to the arrival of the consignment, and after receiving from the Snider Company a list of the consignees, the Raymond Brothers-Clark Company wrote the Snider Company, protesting against the sale direct to Basket Stores Company, and asked for the allowance of the regular jobbers' profit on the sale. The Snider Company did not reply to this letter. Later the Raymond Brothers-Clark Company again wrote the Snider Company, referred to their previous unanswered letter, and referred to other matters connected with the transaction. In response to a request from the Snider Company for payment, Raymond Brothers-Clark Company refused until reply was made to their previous letters and until allowance was made for the jobbers' commission on the sale to the Basket Stores Company.

The Snider Company finally suggested that Raymond Brothers-Clark Company remit, taking credit for amounts claimed, and explaining fully the reasons therefor. Raymond Brothers-Clark Company complied, deducting, among other amounts, the sum of $100 as commission on the sale to the Basket Stores Company. This deduction, among others, the Snider Company refused to allow; the remittance was returned. December 16, Raymond Brothers-Clark Company wrote the Snider Company, insisting upon the allowance of the commission, protesting against the action of the Snider Company in selling direct to the Basket Stores Company, and threatening the Snider Company with the cessation of their business and the return of all Snider goods then in stock if the commission were not allowed and if the Snider Company continued direct sales to the Basket Stores Company. In January, the Snider Company sent a representative to Raymond Brothers-Clark Company to interview the president, but he was not successful in obtaining a settlement of the controversy. Raymond Brothers-Clark Company thereafter refused to purchase goods from the Snider Company.

The case was called to the attention of the Federal Trade Commission, which found that Raymond Brothers-Clark Company had unduly hindered competition and that it had pressed the Snider Company to a selection of customers in restraint of trade. Raymond Brothers-Clark Company carried the case to the Circuit Court of Appeals, Eighth Circuit, which reversed the findings of the Commission[16] on the ground that Raymond Brothers-Clark Company was not guilty of unfair trade practices and did not combine with others to affect the trade of the Basket Stores Company. The court held that Raymond Brothers-Clark Company had a positive and lawful right to select any particular merchandise which it wished to purchase, and to

[16] III F.T.C.D. 295 (1921); 280 Fed. 529 (1922).

select any person or corporation from which it might wish to make its purchase, whether any reasons were assigned or not. This decision was later affirmed by the Supreme Court of the United States.[17]

A much more extensive policy than that pursued by the Raymond Brothers-Clark Company was adopted by the Mennen Company. Although the discussion of this case anticipates a succeeding chapter on Price Policies, the whole situation involved fits in with the general problem of "legitimate trade channels."

Prior to January, 1917, the Mennen Company[18] allowed the same prices and discounts to all customers who bought the company's products in identical quantities, the quantity purchased being the only basis for discrimination. After January, 1917, however, the Mennen Company adopted a new plan for the allowance of trade discounts and classified its customers into groups. It classified as "retailers" cooperative and mutual corporations, organized as corporate entities, which bought from manufacturers or importers in wholesale quantities, maintained stocks of manufacturers' products, and distributed the products in wholesale quantities to retailers. These corporations, about 50 in number, sold neither at retail nor to ultimate consumers. The growth of such cooperative organizations had been rapid and extensive, and in 1922 they were distributing a substantial percentage of all the drugs and kindred products made in the United States.

The classification "jobbers" or "wholesalers" included about 275 customers of the Mennen Company who controlled most of the company's distributing trade. The new Mennen policy, by which an additional trade discount was allowed these "jobbers" and "wholesalers" on purchases in lots of 10 gross or more, was adopted after protests of the National Wholesale Druggists' Association had been made against the policy pursued prior to January, 1917. The new policy was approved by the "wholesalers" and was said to have served as a basis for an understanding between the Mennen Company and the "jobbers" and "wholesalers," that the latter class "should make more vigorous efforts to sell the Mennen Company's products than those of other manufacturers who refused to follow a similar policy of discrimination." In the entire drug and sundry trade in the United States, however, less than six manufacturers discriminated in price when quantity and quality were the same. There was no evidence that it was more expensive for the Mennen Company to sell to "retailers" than to "wholesalers" or "jobbers."

[17] 263 U. S. 565 (1924).
[18] I *Harvard Business Reports* 287.

The Federal Trade Commission, on March 3, 1922, after investigations and hearings, decided[19] that the Mennen Company had adopted a discount policy which "was an unfair method of competition in interstate commerce." The Commission thereupon entered an order to the Mennen Company to cease and desist "from discriminating in net selling prices upon the basis of a classification of its customers as 'jobbers,' 'wholesalers,' or 'retailers,' etc." The Mennen Company then petitioned the Circuit Court of Appeals, Second Circuit, to review the order of the Federal Trade Commission.

The court reasserted the principle previously declared in the Gratz case,[20] that "if real competition is to continue, the right of the individual to exercise reasonable discretion in respect of his own business methods must be preserved." It then employed the definition of "wholesaler" and "retailer" laid down in the Atlantic and Pacific case,[21] that "whether a buyer is a wholesaler or not does not depend upon the quantity he buys. It is not the character of his buying, but of his selling, which makes him a wholesaler." The court then held that the Mennen Company was within its rights in classifying the cooperatives as "retailers," and that the facts were not sufficient to support the Federal Trade Commission's conclusions of law. "The Mennen Company is not shown to have practiced 'unfair methods of competition in commerce,' and the order to cease and desist is reversed."[22]

The Mennen Company was quite within its legal rights to make the discrimination it did between "wholesalers" and "retailers." In the Atlantic and Pacific case referred to by the court, it was stated:

We had supposed that it was elementary law that a trader could buy from whom he pleased and sell to whom he pleased, and that his selection of seller and buyer was wholly his own concern.[23]

The court referred here to Cooley on Torts:

[19] IV F. T. C. D. 258.
[20] *Federal Trade Commission v. Gratz*, 253 U. S. 421.
[21] *Great Atlantic and Pacific Tea Company v. Cream of Wheat Company*, 227 Fed. 46, 49.
[22] *Mennen Company v. Federal Trade Commission*, 288 Fed. 774.
[23] *Great Atlantic and Pacific Tea Co. v. Cream of Wheat Co.*, 227 Fed. 46, 48.

It is a part of a man's civil rights that he be at liberty to refuse business relations with any person whomsoever, whether the refusal rests upon reason, or is the result of whim, caprice, prejudice, or malice.[24]

The court in the Atlantic and Pacific case then added:

Neither the Sherman Act, nor any decision of the Supreme Court construing the same, nor the Clayton Act, has changed the law in this particular. We have not yet reached the stage where the selection of a trader's customers is made for him by the government.[25]

Why, if a company chooses to decide and make announcement to the trade that for reasons sufficient to itself it would sell only to wholesalers, it could not make such a rule and adhere to it, we are at a loss to understand.[26]

There should then be no misunderstanding of the legal situation: the conclusion of the Circuit Court, that the Mennen Company was within its legal rights as regards the acts under dispute, simply prevented the mutual and cooperative corporations from utilizing governmental agencies and legal sanctions for their contentions. A later attempt, on the part of the Federal Trade Commission, to force the seller to grant equal terms to buying corporations, was not sustained by the court.[27]

A second reason for eliminating the Commission from consideration is that its order was invoked against the Mennen Company rather than against the Wholesale Druggists' Association. True, it was the act of the Mennen Company which precipitated the situation, but, as the court pointed out, this act, a declaration and pursuit of policy, was wholly within the right of the company. From the point of view of social policy, the incidence of the Commission's restraining order should have been at least partly upon the Wholesale Druggists' Association, because the pressure obviously was exerted from this quarter: the policy of the Mennen Company subsequent to January, 1917, "was approved by the 'wholesalers' and served as a basis for an understanding between the Mennen Company and the 'jobbers' or 'wholesalers' that the latter class should make more vigorous efforts to sell the Mennen Company's products than those of other manufacturers who refused to follow a similar policy of discrimination,"[28] an "understanding"

[24] Cooley, p. 278.   See also *Greater New York Film Co. v. Biograph Co.,* 203 Fed. 39.

[25] At page 49.

[26] At page 48.

[27] *National Biscuit Co. v. Federal Trade Commission*, 299 Fed. 733 (1924).

[28] IV F. T. C. D. 258, 278.

that comes perilously near to being a "conspiracy in restraint of trade." But the failure of the Federal Trade Commission to apply its ruling to the Druggists' Association makes it unnecessary to consider the expediency of such a policy in this particular case, while the attempt to restrain the Mennen Company was effectively stopped by the court.

In making a further analysis of the material facts of the case, viewed sympathetically from the standpoint of the Mennen Company, a commentator says:

The cooperative associations could not provide complete wholesale distribution for the manufacturer; only a small percentage of the retail druggists in the United States are members of such associations, and the limitations of these associations in granting credit and in providing traveling salesmen for receiving orders render it improbable that that type of association will soon supplant the independent wholesale merchants. The Mennen Company needed to have its products available for sale in a large number of retail drug stores. Hence, it would have been unwise for the company to undermine its wholesale distribution by discouraging wholesale merchants from handling its products.[29]

Whatever speculations we may indulge in here, the fact was that the whole matter, of the trade association *versus* the cooperative buying group, was submitted to the Mennen Company, a private corporation, for adjudication. Only incidentally did the two legal-political bodies enter the case, and both were led away from the main problem by the red-herring trail opened up by a trade group, the cooperatives, complaining against a practice of the Mennen Company which was secondary to the main and prime source of the situation, the overtures of the Wholesale Druggists' Association to the Mennen Company. The Mennen Company obviously chose to safeguard its major interest in the face of a fact which must have given it considerable concern; namely, the growing purchasing strength of mutuals and cooperatives. It is seriously questionable whether the promises of the "wholesalers," "to make more vigorous efforts to sell the Mennen Company's products than those of other manufacturers who refused to follow a similar policy of discrimination," constituted a sufficient ground for the change in business policy. Such an intangible and indefinite return for what amounted to restricted sales in other quarters does not strike one as a proper appeal to the hard-headedness of the

[29] 2 H. B. R. 480, 481.

reputed "good" business man. Furthermore, the decision of the Mennen Company was contrary to the trade practices of all but six of the manufacturers in the United States.

The burden of the argument points to the preferability, from the point of view of business policy, of the practices of the Mennen Company prior to January, 1917. The advantages of this policy are discoverable in its objectivity and measurability. Contrast the attempt of a manufacturing company to discover the sales methods of its customers, with the simplicity and definiteness of its knowledge as to their buying power. Furthermore, adjustments in prices and discounts can always be made with fine discrimination if quantity of goods purchased be the basis for price or discount. Whereas a classification of customers into "wholesalers" and "retailers" admits of only the two schedules, "quantity of goods purchased" admits of any number of schedules. Furthermore, to change the classification of a buyer from "wholesaler" to "retailer" is not only to subject him to the dangers of arbitrary judgment, affected often by prejudice, but the change from "black" to "white" is abrupt and much less to be preferred to changes in gradations of "grays." And the latter will be determined almost entirely by the customer, for his classification would be based on the amount of his purchases, a matter under his own control. If we desire individualism and personal responsibility in our business relations, let this last consideration have the attention it deserves.[30]

The preceding discussion is not intended to defend quantity discounts even by implication. The discussion of this problem will be deferred to the section devoted to "Price Policies." The present discussion is confined to the problem confronting the Mennen Company: to persevere in its quantity-discount policy or to classify its customers into "retailers" and "wholesalers," a problem which is central to the establishing of "legitimate trade channels."

The possibility of effecting a hierarchical structure in business has been more or less in the minds of business men in all of their endeavors to regulate their own or others' business. But the actuality of such a structure has nowhere in business reached the degree of unification achieved in governmental or ecclesiastical organization, partly because there has never been developed a business doctrine at all commensurate in scope with political or

[30] Reprinted in part from VI *Harvard Business Review* 401, July, 1928.

religious doctrine. Attempts at formulating such a doctrine have been illustrated in this chapter, but they have been largely opportunistic, arising in response to very rapid, cataclysmic business changes that called for self-protection; they have been only fragmentary, with no attempt at organization; and the doctrine has seldom gone beyond a behavioristic stage. And yet the situations so generated and the doctrines so imperfectly worked out have given rise to a flood of problems in Business Ethics. Some of these problems are but pleaders' protests, but some have been recognized by business leaders as of sufficient importance to warrant serious consideration. The fact that policies pursuant to the formulation of business doctrines have arisen independently and spontaneously among many business men would lead one to believe that they make up in reality for an obviously deficient unity and breadth. From it all has come a relatively well-defined business doctrine, of "legitimate trade channels," which must yet, however, stand the test of more direct business activities.

CHAPTER X

TRADE-ASSOCIATION ACTIVITIES

One of the outstanding phenomena of American social-economic life in recent years has been the so-called "trade-association movement." Hundreds of trades have been organized on state and national lines, with large and more or less complete memberships of individuals interested in a particular type of business; engaging in meetings, direct discussions of common problems, delegation of committee duties and dissemination of pertinent and valuable literature; and formulating policies of "trade health," at first in the form of "codes of ethics,"[1] later in connection with problems of simplification and standardization of commodity types and units, in collaboration with the United States Department of Commerce, and more recently in the form of "trade-practice conferences" and "submittals" in cooperation with the Federal Trade Commission. Nothing comparable to this development in magnitude or significance has occurred since the decline of the Mediaeval guild. It represents the most distinctive tendency in America toward self-government in business, with the possible exception of the integrated activities of the older business corporation.

General Significance of Trade Associations

The decline of the Mediaeval guild may be attributed in part to the development of capitalism, which encouraged a more intensive individualism than was possible under an institutionalized guild system; but also in part to the development of political nationalism, which provided the basis for common-law systems extending over considerable territories united under one government. The absorption or elimination of local governments involved likewise the political control of social activities, many of which had been intimately connected with business and artisan activities. The culmination of this nationalistic movement, at least so far as Europe and America were concerned,

[1] See Heermance, Edgar L., *Codes of Ethics*, 1924, Burlington, Vt.: Free Press Printing Company.

was during the sixties and seventies of the last century, when Germany and Italy were finally amalgamated, and when the Civil War in the United States gave a preponderance to the theory of national unity over that of states' rights. The Interstate Commerce Act, the Sherman Law, and the Federal Reserve Act may be regarded as the outstanding subsequent legislative acts representative of this tendency in the United States.

There has been, since the Civil War, some political recession from the principle of national sovereignty in the United States, but a more significant development has been the growth of self-government in business. The more subtle phase of this development has consisted in the spontaneous and agile activities of business men themselves, outdistancing legislative restrictions and protecting themselves against these through the agency of the courts. Another phase of this development has arisen, however, because of the relative simplicity of any national legislative acts or common-law rules that could apply to so large and highly diversified a country as ours: local political initiative and functional business autonomy are required to supplement national or even state-wide regulations.[2] While the country was relatively new and undeveloped, "artful dodging" was the dominant phase of business activity. More recently, however, there has arisen the recognition of a need to supplement the broader and more general principles of law and government with activities and policies more particularly suited to a restricted group of men. Hence the apparent need for the trade association to pool the interests peculiar to its membership: discovering and furthering their common interests, engaging in concerted action where the activity of individuals would be ineffective or where it would be unfair to depend upon them, and acting as an economic business group rather than relying upon the political or legal machinery to perform such functions.

What are these trade-association activities or functions? Some, like association advertising, are largely or purely matters of positive business policy. Others, like price agreements or agreements to curtail production, are violations of the existing law and require a definite determination of association policy: whether to accept the law as in conformity with

[2] This point has been elaborated in "The Social Philosophy of the Professions and of Business Groups," Chapter X of the author's *Professional and Business Ethics*.

business standards and therefore to obey it, or whether to condemn the law on the ground that it violates defensible business principles and therefore either to disobey the law, change it in the desired direction, fight it in the courts, or comply with it. Other problems, such as commercial arbitration, call for the formulation of a policy either of independent development or of cooperation with law and government. The trade association, as an organization formed for the purpose of self-government, is an essential factor in the determination of these problems.

"Knowledge is virtue," said Socrates. By this he meant that if men fully realized the consequences of their acts, they would as a rule follow the line of good conduct rather than bad. And by "good" conduct he meant that enlightened type of self-interest which is compatible with social welfare. Aristotle and Kant turned Socrates' phrase into the proposition that knowledge was a prerequisite to moral conduct; by which they meant to assert that moral responsibility cannot be imposed on men who act in ignorance of the situation. This implied stressing of the motive factor is an important element in the act of judging moral behavior, and is employed by the law to determine the degree of an offense; but it cannot be given much consideration in the field of business ethics, which is largely concerned with the objective effects of ethical or unethical conduct. Business ethics follows more nearly the legal modification of the Aristotelian and Kantian principle, whereby the law asserts that a certain minimum of knowledge and intelligence can be presumed of every man, whether he has it or not as a matter of fact. It is this ethical principle, that knowledge not only is conducive to ethical conduct but also is an ethical obligation, which affords the philosophical background for regarding the pursuit of information by research and in the form of honest accounting methods and statistical information as an important element in Business Ethics. It has frequently been said that a stupid competitor is worse than a "crooked" one. At least it may be asserted that ignorance breeds a large part of our ethical problems, especially where a good but misguided motive lacks the very essential quality of an intelligent good intent.

Research

The value of industrial research has been demonstrated by the laboratories of such corporations as General Electric Company,

American Telephone and Telegraph Company, and DuPont de Nemours & Company, while the large appropriations of these companies for such purposes is an indication of their faith in the value of research to their respective businesses. Chemical research in Germany has become a dominant interest in the industry. In England, the value of research was indicated in an act of Parliament, 1917–1918, giving to a committee of the Privy Council jurisdiction over the efforts of trade associations to summarize technical information in the trade, to provide for translating foreign articles and for answering technical questions, and to recommend subjects for research and to conduct such research at cost. By 1927, some 24 trade associations had availed themselves of the opportunities provided, and were spending approximately one million pounds annually for research purposes.

In the United States, in the same year, over 70 trade associations were spending over thirty-five million dollars for industrial and commercial research.[3] Industrial-research projects included such matters as elimination of waste and utilization of by-products, *e.g.*, in the manufacture of dyes, cottonseed oil and lumber; improvement of processes, as in laundries and the nitroglycerine and paper industries; packing and refrigeration, problems in which the railways are very much interested, especially because of losses due to pilferage; and the discovery of new and improved uses of commodities such as gypsum, lumber, cement, and coffee. Commercial research has as its objectives the collection and dissemination of statistical and other trade information, the promotion of the trade or industry by publicity programs, and protection of the trade or industry at large, as well as individual members, against unfair practices and competition. Illustrations of commercial-research programs fostered by trades or trade associations are the reports of the Bureau of Business Research of the Harvard Business School on operating expenses in retail jewelry and shoe stores, department stores, and in the retail and wholesale grocery business.

The following example will illustrate the sort of research programs which are being sponsored by trade associations:

The programs of research activities of the American Bakers' Association and the American Institute of Baking are distinct, but for

[3] See *Trade Association Activities*, U. S. Department of Commerce, 1923; also 1927 edition.

Bakers Institute [handwritten]

present purposes can be dealt with together.[4]   The Institute maintains laboratories for the analysis of flour and other ingredients, for making tests and for conducting scientific investigation and research.   The department is in charge of a special committee of men who combine technical education with practical experience.   All research programs are placed in the hands of a special committee which first determines whether the proposed study if solved will be of service to the baker; which, second, directs such research; and which then, third, interprets it to the industry.

For example, nutritional facts, especially the part played by bakers' products, are studied, and the results are then disseminated among bakers and the general public.   The Association, cognizant of the effects of anti-white bread campaigns, has diagnosed the source as threefold: food fakers, "those without scientific background who use white bread as a ballyhoo," food hobbyists, "who may themselves be sincere but are deluded," and the modern vogue for the slender figure. To combat this campaign the Association set itself the task of making a complete study "of what has been said, who said it, and through what media it reached the consumer."   The Association proposed to submit these statements to competent nutritional authorities and "through all legitimate means" to have the refutation of such facts "reach the eyes and ears of the ultimate consumer and the proper educational, scientific and medical authorities."   Unfortunately such a research program can never win the confidence of people that could be gained by a disinterested study, conducted, for example, by an independent university.   The temptation of an interested trade to stress desired results rather than to observe scientific impartiality in methods and conclusions, would be suspected even if it did not exist.   But the safe-guarding of the interests of the trade is preferable to a failure on the part of the trade to state its case.

A further, and broader and more positive, proposal of the Association was to conduct a nation-wide survey as to consumer demand for bakery products.   This is more strictly a program of commercial research, conducted for the information of the baker to plan his selling intelligently and, second, to be the basis upon which a coordinated or cooperative national campaign might be considered.   One of the major facts recognized in this program is the decrease in wheat consumption in the last twenty years.   The three major factors contributing to this condition are: first, increased use of machinery and shorter hours of labor mean less physical work and therefore less need of food; second, the larger variety of food now available to the housewife—conspicuously fruits and vegetables—creates a diversification of attention detrimental to what formerly were regarded as the staple foods; third, the prosperity of

[4] *The Journal*, American Bakers' Association and American Institute of Baking, Chicago, Feb. 15, 1928.

the country has made a market for the more expensive foods, to the detriment of an economical food such as bread. The plans for such a survey show how broadly the program of the Association is built as regards policy.

The scientific and industrial phase of the research program is further illustrated by the maintenance, on the part of the Institute, of a "bread-scoring" department. The object of this department is to create an interest and to assist in maintaining bread quality, by scoring, according to an approved form, such bread as may be sent to it by members or others. The score not only reveals the numerical value given but makes suggestions for the correction of apparent errors. Plans of the Institute also include a cake laboratory and the erection of an experimental cake bakery to conduct experiments in cake production and to make a scientific investigation of cake ingredients and practices.

For the purpose of practically applying and furthering the results of the research program, the Association provides three trained men, who are at the disposal of bakers' organizations and who are prepared to organize meetings on any subject that is deemed to be of value to the bakers of a territory. Salesmen also are provided to promote a better knowledge of bread sales and distribution, to combat anti-bread propaganda, to assist in the making of further surveys, and to provide other forms of service. The Association also has a separate bureau for disseminating and applying research discoveries and conclusions among retail bakers. The Institute conducts a school and extension courses for bakers, and home-study courses for employees.

The Louis Livingston Library of Baking, maintained by the Institute, is the largest and most comprehensive library on the subject of fermentology and baking in existence. It is in constant use by students, by the industry and by scientists. Provision has been made to keep it up-to-date and to promote its greater use. The Association publishes a quarterly journal, containing a résumé of the activities of the Association and of the Institute, together with such practical and technical articles as may be of value and interest to bakers. It contains no advertising and is not operated for profit. Finally, the Association has a trade-relations committee which consults with governmental agencies, and considers trade practices as they arise: "whether they are illegal, unethical, or all right, and what to do about it," in order that relief may be afforded to aggrieved individuals and to the industry and its association.

Much broader in its purposes and in its territorial extent is the International Wheat Institute, located at Rome, Italy. This Institute was founded by David Lubin in order to establish the facts as to production figures and stocks on hand. The information so gained serves to stabilize the wheat market and to provide a basis for intelligent world marketing. A world census of agricultural resources is now being taken by the Institute. The American Institute of Food Distribution endeavors to perform the same function for a number of food products, including sugar, canned vegetables, canned and dried fruits, nuts, fish, cereals and cereal products, butter, dairy and poultry products, meat and meat products, coffee, tea, and spices, and certain fresh fruits and vegetables. Figures are given in most cases for the five-year average, 1921–1925, and subsequent years, of production, imports and exports, and stocks on hand. Such surveys contribute as much to business ethics by stabilizing the market, as is a health survey conducive to improved personal morality. Neither is sufficient completely to solve the problem, but both are essential to such an objective.

The most significant fact regarding trade-association activities in such fields as industrial and commercial research is the social education which the members of such associations receive. American individualism has been discussed and asserted as a theory much more thoroughly than it has been studied as a fact. There are those theorists who, on the other hand, viewing the regimentation so prevalent in factories or business offices, deny that our modern society any longer retains even the vestiges of individualism. The chief difficulty of both views consists in an inability to distinguish between observations of fact and judgments of value. The persistence of individualism in America as a direct heritage from the virtual anarchism of the Puritan or the pioneer, can still easily be detected throughout the farming regions of the country. The real-estate developments in the small town or in the large city are conspicuously devoid of "city planning," even where the community has not been blighted by the influx of the "retired farmer." And so also with the great bulk of small businesses: the inertia which is met by any attempt at trade organization, and its highly volatile character once it is formed, are outstanding characteristics.

The event, however, which more than any other single factor has encouraged the formation of the trade association has been the advent of trade—or industrial—as opposed to individual competition. The use of structural steel and cement in the building industry has confronted the lumber interests with a problem of self-preservation; changes in food habits and the more aggressive tactics of new food businesses have faced the older staple-goods concerns with the problem of rapidly declining sales; style changes ruthlessly affect the use of textile goods; luxuries and amusements, such as the automobile, the radio and phonograph, and the "movies," are contending with former necessities for a place in the family budget; gas, oil and electricity are encroaching on coal both as domestic and industrial fuels. Secondary only to these major commodity changes are the functional changes introduced by such radical movements as direct selling by manufacturer and by chain-store distributors, hand-to-mouth buying and its accompaniment, reduced inventories, and the direct and indirect effects of mass production, installment selling and greatly modified credit arrangements.

In the face of movements of such magnitude, the smaller individual merchant is helpless, and even when his business is benefited, this is due to no efforts on his part and may be only temporary. In most cases he realizes that something is happening seriously to menace his business. If this menace consists in the competition of larger business organizations, he succumbs either to absorption or to elimination entirely. Where the menace is one of a competing industry, he may be driven by fear into a trade-association organization. Bank mergers or the formation of bank groups, buying associations and trade groups are conspicuous today because of their prevalence. Without evaluating such movements from the social point of view, particularly as they affect the great number of men who hitherto have maintained their business independence and individuality, the fact is apparent to anyone that business is becoming organized, in addition to its corporate structures, to an extent which hitherto has been achieved only by political and religious bodies. The social significance of this fact transcends even the problem of the elimination of the individual business man, for the challenge which business thereby is afforded the opportunity of issuing to Church and State may necessitate a complete reorganization of our present social values.

The practical problems presented by the formation of trade associations, however, are more particular and restricted. Chief among these may be mentioned the attempts to improve the state of business knowledge and information. We have already indicated the increased interest in business and industrial research, common to both the corporation and the trade association. Closely allied with this activity is the increased attention now being paid to cost accounting and statistics. Among trade associations particularly, the endeavor to establish uniform cost-accounting methods has come to be a matter of paramount importance.

Cost Accounting

It may seem strange to some people that so matter-of-fact a business problem as cost accounting should be included in a study of business ethics. It is necessary to recall the point, however, that business ethics attempts to discover the competitors' interests and rights as well as the consumers'. And competitors are interested in the manner in which any member of a trade figures his costs, for the price-cutter is most apt to be the very person who is ignorant as to the real costs of doing business. Some of the commonest mistakes in cost accounting are due to ambiguities and confusions as to costs of materials and labor or capital charges as distinguished from running expenses. Most farmers and small storekeepers calculate their income simply by deducting expenses from receipts—they generally neglect to deduct the interest on capital investment, or overhead, including salaries and wages. And even where the consumption of farm products or store stocks by the family is set off against the labor supplied by the wife and children, the facts disclose that the farmer or storekeeper, if he charges himself a fair wage is securing no return on his investment or *vice versa*.

Even where such simple facts are known and taken account of, many business men fail to take into account, adequately or at all, such items as depreciation, obsolescence, or depletion of plant or equipment or stocks. The result is that many businesses may be drifting toward bankruptcy without knowing it. Such ignorance is usually indicative of poor management throughout, and the business can be expected to disappear in time. But the difficulty is that in the meantime it is selling goods at prices which are ruinous to competitors as well as to themselves. And it will not do to say that the eventual liquidation of the business will correct the evil; for not only have such businesses sometimes a remarkable amount of vitality, but their liquidation may involve a forced sale of plant and equipment at bankrupt prices, thus setting up a competitor with an overhead approximately equal to the mistaken conception of the liquidated business. It is this situation which justifies what appears to be an inter-

ference with another man's business: the insistence of the trade
that every man know his costs and govern himself accordingly.

The members of a trade, or of an association in that trade,
have a justifiable interest in encouraging every member to
conduct his business on sound economic lines, especially in his
charging enough for his goods and services so as to return a fair
profit on his investment above all expenses, including fair wages.
The Chamber of Commerce of the United States has published a
pamphlet, entitled "What a Cost System Should Do for You,"
with this purpose in mind. One method of furthering this purpose is the development of uniform systems of accounting among
the various trades and businesses. The Federal Trade Commission has issued two pamphlets—"Fundamentals of a Cost
System for Manufacturers" and "A System of Accounts for
Retail Merchants"—and many trade associations have sponsored
such uniform systems as apply to their own particular industries.
Such cost forms may be developed from within the industry,
as in the case of the National Coal Association and the Tanners'
Council, or by means of outside checks, as in the case of United
Typothetae of America or the Millwork Cost Bureau.

The best argument which can be advanced to show the need
of strictly frank and honest cost-accounting methods is to state
the actual figures for certain typical businesses which have
been compiled by the Bureau of Business Research of Harvard
University.

Thus among building-material dealers, net profits of some
300 firms reporting for 1928 ranged as follows: mason materials,
0.5%; mason materials and coal, 0.6%; lumber, 0.8%; lumber
and coal, 1.6%; and lumber and mason materials, 1.6%. Similarly, 138 lumber firms in 1928 reported net profits as follows:
Cleveland, Chicago and St. Louis, 2.5%; Boston, New York and
Philadelphia, 0.5%; Richmond, Atlanta and Dallas, 0.0%;
and Minneapolis, Kansas City and San Francisco, a loss of 1.5%.[5]
Similar variations were discoverable for size of firms, and of
course much greater variations appear when individual firms
are compared. One hundred sixty-two department stores,
each with net sales over $1,000,000, reported a net profit for
1928 of 1.5%; 251 department stores, each with net sales less
than $1,000,000, reported a loss of 0.2% for the same year.[6]

[5] *Bulletin* 81, Bureau of Business Research, Harvard University,
November, 1929.

[6] *Bulletin* 78.

Marketing expenses of grocery manufacturers[7] vary considerably with the product handled: 9 meat packers report a marketing expense of 7.0%; 13 firms which can and bottle foods, 17.0%; 14 firms handling cereals, crackers, macaroni, salt and preserves, 26.9%; and 11 firms dealing in soaps, cleansers, polishes and disinfectants, 37.2%.

These illustrations show that comparisons of cost items are highly illuminating, and especially so when made by individual firms engaged in the same kind and size of business and in the same locality. It is just such comparisons that the trade association is interested in making, first, as a service to the individual members of the association, but second, in order to show certain members that they may be engaging in practices and methods which are harmful to the trade as a whole. Particularly is this the case in connection with the many "services" which businesses are now rendering, and such items as "entertainment." Frequently such items, when expressed in percentages and set beside net profits, are discovered to be all out of proportion to what they should be; and even more frequently, they are discovered to be wholly absent from the cost sheets of businesses that engage in such services. In either case, individuals are competing on a service basis which is seriously costly in proportion as it is not calculated in figures, and such forms of competition encourage a prevalence of the practice throughout the trade, often with disastrous consequences.

The collection of the figures showing members' costs, their compilation, and their dissemination throughout the trade, is a trade-association problem which is of subordinate importance to that of educating the members to discover their own costs. Therefore the difficulties therein encountered need not be regarded so seriously as some association executives seem to think they ought. Business men are jealous of their figures and supply them grudgingly and only when they know that their information will remain confidential. Some trade associations have, for this reason, employed as executive secretaries men who are amateurs in the trade, in order to avoid the suspicions that would be directed toward a man actively engaged in the business. Furthermore, associations have been careful to disseminate only the average figures; where individual figures are sent out, the names of the firms are withheld, and even then the figures of

[7] *Bulletin* 77.

conspicuously large firms in the trade can only with difficulty be prevented from being identified. The chief benefit derived from disseminating cost figures among the members of a trade association lies in the disclosure to members of items which they have not been calculating at all, or at least have not been calculating with sufficient accuracy to disclose unsound factors in their business activities. There may be some question, for example, as to whether inventories should be carried at cost or at market or at "whichever is lower"; but unless all the members of a trade employ the same basis, general trade-cost figures are unreliable and individual businesses may be insolvent without knowing it. So also with regard to including the item of "supplies" among capital rather than current items. It is the function of the trade association to educate its members in proper cost-accounting methods and to attempt to secure a maximum of uniformity therein.

The legal difficulties which a trade association may face in connection with uniform cost-accounting methods are similar to those met with in connection with statistical information.[8] Uniform cost-accounting methods may be adopted by an association but they cannot be forced upon unwilling members, nor can they be made the basis for any agreements in regard to price schedules. Furthermore no member of a trade can substitute the average cost figures of his industry for the actual costs under which he is operating. Some members of trade associations, whose cost figures, actually or as calculated, were below the average for the industry, have seized the opportunity of substituting the average figures for their own actual figures in their corporation reports to the Government, thus showing smaller earnings than their own books actually would have disclosed. It may not seem necessary to point out such misconceptions of the use of uniform cost-accounting methods, but the situation has arisen a number of times.

It will be interesting to see what will happen, once uniform and honest cost accounting becomes a prevalent practice. A major question which business will have to face is one which has for some time been held in abeyance. That question is, What is a fair profit? This question will supersede the two questions

[8] See on this point Jones, Franklin D., *Trade Associations and the Law*, New York: McGraw-Hill Book Company, Inc., 1922; Kirsh, Benjamin S., *Trade Associations; the Legal Aspects*, New York: Central Book Co., 1928.

which formerly were matters of deep concern, especially to the Church in the Middle Ages and later: What is a fair price? And is usury justifiable? This latter question has been resolved into a social-economic endorsement of the "current" interest rate, which now has come to be regarded as a necessary fixed capital charge on all businesses, to be deducted from gross earnings in order to determine net earnings. The problem of a fair price is partly answered by the social-economic acceptance of the competitive "market" price as basic, with such modifications as circumstances might justifiably warrant. Too often the consumer's interest alone is considered. But a "fair" price in addition should be conceived as that price which will enable a business to earn a fair profit. Therefore the question of a fair profit becomes the dominant consideration.

One might calculate the annual increase in economic values—including appreciation of capital as well as net income—in the United States, for a sufficient period of time to discover the percentage annual increase. This figure would then have to be modified to take care of the fact that a part—and perhaps the major part—of the increase is due to increased capital values rather than production profits, and the question must then be raised as to whether the increase found its way into capital values or into current earnings and dividends. This would afford a broad basis for determining the average increase in economic values, but it would give no indication of the figures that would apply to particular industries, differentiated by their peculiar conditions: raw materials, inventions and improved processes, management skill, labor morale, market and consumption changes. But at least such a basic figure would be superior to the "current interest rate" from which to figure a "fair" profit, because the latter is obtained after the fixed charges have already been deducted from gross income. To confuse a "fair" profit with current interest rates is to indicate particularly the need for cost-accounting methods. The prevailing attitude today is that a "fair" profit should approximate the current interest rate. It is extremely doubtful whether general productivity is great enough to support that view.

The practical outcome of an attempt to discover what constitutes a "fair" profit has been anticipated by the resort to no-par common-stock shares. Debentures and preferred stock are now calculated, together with other borrowings, as involving a fixed charge on the industry. By issuing additional common stock with no par value, all additional earnings above fixed charges, and obtained through good management and other factors which are difficult to control, become evident in the value which is placed on the no-par stock. And this value is checked by quotations and transactions in the stock market. So long as this value is freely sensitive to changes in net earnings, the problem of a "fair" profit has to a considerable extent been solved. Whenever, however, an attempt is made by a public-utility corporation or some other monopolistic business, to reverse this process and to make the quotations or dividends on no-par common stock the basis for modifying earnings or rates or prices upwards, then the situation has reverted to the condition of a common stock with par or fixed value, with all the evils attending a "vested interest" in such capital values. Any attempt on such a basis to argue for increased prices or rates in order to secure a "fair" profit, reduces the problem of a "fair" profit to the Mediaeval conception—the conclusions, of course, being just the opposite—or to certain absolute factors which should not find a place in so dynamic a field as that of business activity.

However the problem of a "fair" profit be resolved, whether into stock-market quotations of no-par stock or into some approximation to "current interest rates," the likelihood is that empirical comparisons and relative values will have more to do with the solving of the problem than will absolute or ideal conceptions. The most important result of wide-spread attention to cost accounting, especially as sponsored by trade associations, will probably be the factual determination of what prevailing profits in business are. And the likelihood is that the percentage so discovered will be less than that which is commonly held to be the case. If so, then one of the fundamental causes of price-cutting, universally recognized among business men as unethical conduct, will be disclosed.

Statistics

The collection and dissemination of statistics, as regards production, stocks on hand, and sales, are vital to business success. The questions which this obvious proposition raises are two: What agency shall perform this function? and, How intricate and detailed shall the information be?

The first question involves the problem of the relation between Government and Business. This is not a merely academic question, for the Government, especially the Department of Commerce, has been most active and efficient in securing and distributing valuable trade information; hence the question is whether trade groups themselves are actually able to compete with the Government in obtaining for themselves this vital information. A mere recital of the degree to which the Government has pursued this project—functionally, geographically, and as regards detail—will indicate the task confronting a trade group which proposes to undertake anything more valuable.

Two bureaus in the Department of Commerce have been particularly active in this matter,[9] the Bureau of Foreign and Domestic Commerce and the Census Bureau. In the commerce bureau there are four regional, or geographic, divisions and five technical divisions, the latter consisting in foreign tariffs, commercial law, commercial intelligence, research, and statistics. In addition there are seventeen commodity divisions, to which others are being added: agricultural implements, automotive, chemicals, coal, electrical equipment, foodstuffs, leather, industrial machinery, iron and steel, lumber, paper, petroleum, rubber, shoes, specialties, textiles, transportation, finance, and motion pictures. The very range of these divisions shows to what an extent the Department of Commerce has engaged in statistical service.

The Census Bureau in addition reports on a number of problems, such as capacity figures, *e.g.*, for structural steel or folding boxes; shipments, distributed geographically or according to classes of purchasers; stocks on hand, *e.g.*, of silk, wool, leather, petroleum, etc.; orders, unfilled and current; and even prices, where such figures have been achieved through "open-price" associations. Production figures have laid stress on the importance, in all statistical work, of the choice of an appropriate unit. Figures in regard to production of shoes or tires are meaningless so far as mere totals are concerned; a proper choice of significant and important grades is essential to intelligible as well as intelligent reports. The machine hour has particular significance in reference to production figures of cotton and wool goods. Employment facts are best stated in hours. Although individual figures are undesirable and often dangerous,

[9] See *Trade Association Activities, cit. supra.*

mere totals and averages can be meaningless. The employment of a proper fiscal unit also presents a difficult problem. Although most business men are agreed that our present calendar units frequently vitiate comparisons—as when months of unequal length are compared, especially when the number of Saturdays varies—not all businesses are agreed as to the best unit. Semi-annual reports seem best for commodities such as fertilizer and paints and varnishes; quarterly reports have found favor in tobacco, fats and oils, and wool stocks; and monthly reports in cotton, wool, leather, sugar, steel, and building materials. It is significant that the *Survey of Current Business* is published monthly, showing that at least this minimum is desirable but that any shorter unit is not generally important.

The great problem facing business as a whole, as well as its functional groups and individuals, is that of gauging production so as to meet demand. Obviously statistical information is a necessary and important instrument in effecting that purpose, whether the latter demands increased or restricted production. Increased production, as well as the cultivation of increased customer demands, can safely be left to individual or group initiative; and there is no objection, economic or otherwise, to the exercise of individual judgment in regard to curtailing production. The difficulty arises when undue limitation of production results from monopolistic control or concerted action; whatever the economic merits of such activities, we have in America placed legal and legislative restrictions on the practice. The result is periods of overproduction—a relative term—and consequent economic depression or even business disaster. It would seem reasonable to suppose that business men should in some measure be allowed to protect themselves against such eventualities, at least short of "combinations in restraint of trade" and "price agreements." It remained for the Supreme Court of the United States, however, to draw the distinctions between illegal group activities and such as were permitted. Whether all of the latter are worth while as a matter of business policy is a separate question. But at least the permissible method has been indi-cated. As exhibited in the following cases, this method of con-duct consists in the obtaining of figures on production, stocks on hand, sales, prices and costs of completed transactions, and the disseminating of these facts among the members of a group or publicly; but only such reactions of producers and vendors are legally permissible and socially justifiable as would result from such independent, voluntary judgments in regard to future policy as were individually made on the basis of the facts available. Legally, as well as from the point of view of business, the major purpose of business statistics is to supply information rather than to provide opportunities for concerted attempts to secure trade advantages. The latter purpose, after all, is the concern of the business executive, and is a matter of individual judgment; to him, trade information as conveyed in statistics is instrumental. But such business judgments or predictions are outside the scope of statistical analysis strictly conceived.

The Cotton Textile Institute, Incorporated, was founded in an endeavor to guide more intelligently the ratio between production and demand than is possible where ignorance rather than knowledge prevails among producers. Approximately 200 manufacturers, forming a large part of the producing capacity of the entire trade, belong to the Institute. Realizing that any attempt to control the ratio between production and sales may approach the problem through either factor, a part of the function of the Institute has been to promote the use of cotton goods by discovering new uses, creating popularity for styles by extensive trade advertising and by concerning itself with major trade policies.

The other factor of the ratio is production. The Institute first set itself to the task of discovering the facts. The following chart shows, for example, the type of information which is requested of members regarding sheetings, 40 inches and narrower.

Additional information regarding sheetings of 40-inch width and narrower is asked for for "Class B," that is, yarn numbers 16s to 2/s inclusive, seven constructions; and for "Class C," that is, yarn numbers above 2/s, 16 constructions. The amount of detail of information is indicated by recalling that these questions apply to only a limited part of production; other information blanks are sent out for the remaining products. Approximately 90% of these requests are complied with. This information is then compiled by the Institute and the composite figures sent to the members confidentially. Each manufacturer thereupon can judge as to production requirements and may voluntarily regulate his own individual production accordingly. A restriction of his output does not involve any social unfairness so long as this restriction is not the result of concerted action, coercion or agreements. Just what action the Institute takes regarding a manufacturer who persists in producing more than is required or who increases production when sales are obviously declining, is of course not known. Such action might be taken directly, or indirectly through the other members of the

Mill_____

Location_____

Total No. of Looms_____

Signed by_____

Official Capacity_____

Date_____

<table>
<tr><td></td></tr>
<tr><td>For</td></tr>
<tr><td>Week Ending</td></tr>
<tr><td>Saturday_____
(Date)</td></tr>
</table>

THE COTTON-TEXTILE INSTITUTE, Inc.
320 Broadway, New York.
SHEETINGS
40″ & Narrower
Class A (Yarn Nos. up to 15s inclusive)

Construction			Looms Oper- ating	Yards		
				Week's Produc- tion	Stocks* On Hand	Unfilled Orders
36″/37″	40/38	3.90				
36″/37″	40 to 44 38 to 40	3.50				
36″	48/44	3.25				
36″	48/48	3.00				
36″	48/48	2.85				
40″	48/44	3.00				
40″	48/48	2.85				
40″	48/48	2.50				
All Other Constructions not included above						

* At end of week.

Please send these reports to us
on TUESDAY of each week.

Institute; in either case, the law is violated, social interests are jeopardized and questionable business practices are engaged in.   But so long as exactly the same result is achieved by individual voluntary "cooperation," the members of the Institute are fully within their ethical as well as legal rights.   To deny voluntary and intelligent conduct in business would be indefensible.   The further method available to the industry, namely, consolidation of mills, is advocated by the president of the Institute.[10]

* * * * * *

The Maple Flooring Manufacturers' Association was an unincorporated trade association.   Its members, most of whom were located in Michigan, Minnesota, and Wisconsin, sold maple, beech, and birch flooring.

In 1922, of the 58 non-member manufacturers of maple, beech, and birch flooring in the United States, 17 were located in Illinois, Michigan, Minnesota, and Wisconsin.   In that year 38 non-members reported a manufacturing capacity of 238,000,000 feet while 22 members of the association reported a capacity of 158,000,000 feet.   In that year the members of the association actually produced 70% of the entire supply, this being a diminishing amount during the preceding five years.

In March, 1922, the association was formed and engaged in cooperative advertising and in the standardization and improvement of flooring products.   The association also distributed information in regard to average costs, to the association members, of all dimensions and grades of flooring, freight-rate schedules, statistics as to quantity and kind of flooring sold, prices received for the same, and the amount of stock on hand.   This information was summarized and distributed among the members without revealing the identity of the businesses.   The association also held meetings at which its members discussed the problems of the industry.

There were no agreed fixed prices, although the association's activities had a tendency to bring about a uniformity of such prices.   Furthermore, prices were not unduly increased, the prices of members of the association usually being lower than those of non-members.

The Maple Flooring Manufacturers' Association was prosecuted by the United States Government and a decree obtained from the District Court for the Western District of Michigan,[11] enjoining the association from engaging in the practices enumerated.   The case was appealed to the Supreme Court,[12]

[10] Speech at Richmond, Virginia, May 17, 1928.   See also Learned, E. P., "Mergers in the Cotton Industry," *Harvard Business Review*, July, 1930.

[11] *U. S. v. Maple Flooring Manufacturers' Association*, 294 Fed. 390.

[12] *Maple Flooring Manufacturers' Association v. U. S.*, 268 U. S. 563 (1925).

where the decree of the lower court was reversed, Justice Stone delivering the majority opinion of the court. The case is significant for a number of reasons, not the least of which is that the court made an exceptionally sympathetic attempt to discover what constitutes sound business methods; Marshall, Hobson and Irving Fisher were actually referred to in a footnote![13] The chief practical value of the decision lay in the fact that it clearly defined what a trade association could do and what it could not do. Previously, business groups had been permitting the discussion of problems in a way which subjected the members to government prosecution, while, on the other hand, many innocuous subjects were tabooed at such meetings under the misapprehension that they violated the anti-trust laws.

The court recognized that circulating data as to the average cost of flooring among the members of the association, when combined with a calculated freight rate plus an arbitrary percentage of profit, *could* have been made the basis for fixing prices or for an agreement for price maintenance so as to constitute a violation of the Sherman Act. But the court held that the record was barren of evidence that the figures *were* so used by the association. Justice McReynolds, in his dissenting opinion, voiced the opinion of many people who are suspicious of business, an opinion which in the earlier history of the court decisions based on the Sherman Law led to the condemnation of businesses because of their *capacity* to engage in unfair practices:

It seems to me that ordinary knowledge of human nature and of the impelling force of greed ought to permit no serious doubt concerning the ultimate outcome of the arrangements. We may confidently expect the destruction of that kind of competition long relied upon by the public for establishment of fair prices and to preserve which the Anti-trust Act was passed . . .

Pious protestations and smug preambles but intensify distrust when men are found busy with schemes to enrich themselves through circumventions. And the Government ought not to be required supinely to await the final destruction of competitive conditions before demanding relief through the courts.[14]

To this statement Justice Stone opposed the view which marks a turning point in the attitude of the court:

It was not the purpose or the intent of the Sherman Anti-trust Law to inhibit the intelligent conduct of business operations . . . Sellers of any

[13] *Ibid.*, p. 584.
[14] *Ibid.*, p. 587.

commodity who guide the daily conduct of their business on the basis of market reports would hardly be deemed to be conspirators engaged in restraint of interstate commerce. They would not be any more so merely because they became stockholders in a corporation, or joint owners of a trade journal, engaged in the business of compiling and publishing such reports. We do not believe that the members of trade associations become such conspirators merely because they gather and disseminate information such as is here complained of . . . [15]

The following statements give an accurate description of the activities of the flooring association:

At the time of the filing of the bill, members reported weekly to the secretary of the Association on forms showing dates of sales made by the reporting member, the quantity, the thickness and face, the grade, the kind of wood, the delivery, the prices at which sold, the average freight rate to destination, and the rate of commission paid, if any. Members also reported monthly the amount of flooring on hand of each dimension and grade, and the amount of unfilled orders. Monthly reports were also required, showing the amount of production for each period and the new orders booked for each variety of flooring. The Association promptly reported back to the members statistics compiled from the reports of members, including the identifying numbers of the mills making the reports, and information as to quantities, grades, prices, freight rates, etc., with respect to each sale. The names of purchasers were not reported, and from and after July 19, 1923, the identifying number of the mill making the report was omitted. All reports of sales and prices dealt exclusively with past and closed transactions. The statistics gathered by the defendant Association are given wide publicity. They are published in trade journals which are read by from 90 to 95% of the persons who purchase the products of Association members. They are sent to the Department of Commerce, which publishes a monthly survey of current business. They are forwarded to the Federal Reserve and other banks, and are available to anyone, at any time, desiring to use them. It is to be noted that the statistics gathered and disseminated do not include current price quotations; information as to employment conditions; geographical distribution of shipments; the names of customers or distribution by classes of purchasers; the details with respect to new orders booked, such as names of customers, geographical origin of orders; or details with respect to unfilled orders, such as names of customers, their geographical location; the names of members having surplus stocks on hand; the amount of rough lumber on hand; or information as to cancellation of orders. Nor do they differ in any essential respect from trade or business statistics which are freely gathered and publicly disseminated in numerous branches of industry producing a standardized product such as grain, cotton, coal and oil, and involving interstate commerce whose statistics disclose volume and material elements affecting costs of production, sales price, and stock on hand.[16]

[15] *Ibid.*, p. 583.
[16] *Ibid.*, pp. 568, 569.

As regards the general business effects of such activities, Justice Stone stated:

It is the consensus of opinion of economists and of many of the most important agencies of government that the public interest is served by the gathering and dissemination, in the widest possible manner, of information with respect to the production and distribution, cost and prices in actual sales, of market commodities, because the making available of such information tends to stabilize trade and industry, to produce fairer price levels, and to avoid the waste which inevitably attends the unintelligent conduct of economic enterprise. Free competition means a free and open market among both buyers and sellers for the sale and distribution of commodities. Competition does not become less free merely because the conduct of commercial operations becomes more intelligent through the free distribution of knowledge of all the essential factors entering into the commercial transaction.[17] General knowledge that there is an accumulation of surplus of any market commodity would undoubtedly tend to diminish production, but the dissemination of that information cannot, in itself, be said to be restraint upon commerce in any legal sense. The manufacturer is free to produce, but prudence and business foresight based on that knowledge influence free choice in favor of more limited production. Restraint upon free competition begins when improper use is made of that information through any concerted action which operates to restrain the freedom of action of those who buy and sell.[18]

The conclusion of the court particularly illustrated the *functional* view now taken toward the Sherman Law, as opposed to the *absolute* view earlier held:

We realize that such information, gathered and disseminated among the members of a trade or business, may be the basis of agreement or concerted action to lessen production arbitrarily or to raise prices beyond the levels of production and price which would prevail if no such agreement or concerted action ensued, and those engaged in commerce were left free to base individual initiative on full information of the essential elements of their business. Such concerted action constitutes a restraint of commerce and is illegal, and may be enjoined, as may any other combination or activity necessarily resulting in such concerted action as was the subject of consideration in *American Column & Lumber Co. v. United States*[19] and *United States v. American Linseed Oil Co.*[20] But in the absence of proof of such agreement or concerted action having been actually reached or actually

[17] See a suggestive analysis of the competitive system by various economists, collected and commented on in Marshall's *Readings on Industrial Society*, 294, 419, 479, 498, 935. See Hobson, *The Evolution of Modern Capitalism*, 403, 405; *Elementary Principles of Economics*, by Irving Fisher, 427 *et seq.*

[18] 268 U. S. 563, 583.

[19] 257 U. S. 377.

[20] 262 U. S. 371.

attempted, under the present plan of operation of defendants, we can find no basis in the gathering and dissemination of such information by them, or in their activities under their present organization, for the inference that such concerted action will necessarily result within the rule laid down in those cases.

We decide only that trade associations or combinations of persons or corporations which openly and fairly gather and disseminate information as to the cost of their product, the volume of production, the actual price which the product has brought in past transactions, stocks of merchandise on hand, approximate cost of transportation from the principal point of shipment to the points of consumption, as did these defendants, and who, as they did, meet and discuss such information and statistics without, however, reaching or attempting to reach any agreement or any concerted action with respect to prices or production or restraining competition, do not thereby engage in unlawful restraint of commerce.[21]

The general purport of the decision in this case is to the effect that the securing and dissemination of business information, particularly as practised by the association in question, did not violate the Sherman Law. It would indeed be a travesty on law if such activities, prompted by the desire to conduct business more intelligently, were condemned by legislation. Whatever individual reactions to such information resulted, especially in the form of voluntary curtailment of production or of stocks on hand or of increased efforts to dispose of stocks, must be accepted not only as the essential right of any business man, but also as a necessary means to stabilized business in general. The public interest would be jeopardized by any concerted effort, on the part of the members of a trade association possessed of such knowledge, to curtail production for the purpose of raising prices. But the functional view of the court recognized that such activities must be disclosed by positive evidence, thus reverting to the basic common-law rule that the burden of proof initially rests with the prosecution or the plaintiff.

So long ago as April 12, 1922, the Attorney General, replying to a question proposed by Herbert Hoover, then Secretary of Commerce, stated that he could see nothing illegal in such activities—where the data were compiled and distributed in certain ways prescribed by the Department of Commerce— "*provided always* that whatever is done is not used as a scheme or device to curtail production or enhance prices and does not have the effect of suppressing competition."

[21] 268 U. S. 563, 586.

Other Activities

A number of other trade-association activities might be mentioned.[22]   The problems of limitation of production, advertising, standardization of products and commercial arbitration, all fall within the province of trade-association activities, but these subjects are dealt with at length in other chapters.   Collective purchasing is not strictly a function of trade associations.   Labor relations are generally taboo—no subject being more liable to cause a disruption in a trade-association meeting.   Joint sales agencies and attempts at price regulation, while frequently brought up in the earlier days, are so generally recognized now as legally dangerous that they no longer are discussed, at least in open meeting.   Similarly with regional distribution of markets, whether by exclusion for failing to join an association[23] or for engaging in obnoxious practices[24] or price-cutting.[25]   Direct apportionment of territories by agreement is, of course, forbidden by law.[26]

The function of exchanging credit information did not originate with trade associations, but has been taken up by a number of them.   Competitive business has seemingly inevitably led to unwise extensions of credit, particularly in periods of inflation, and some form of credit information would seem to be necessary as a preventive.   The National Wholesale Druggists' Association has sponsored an exhaustive information analysis for its members. The Tile Manufacturers' Credit Association shows what a small, compact organization can accomplish.   The National Wholesale Lumber Dealers' Association has shown what can be done for members who serve only limited territories.   Two types of information are sought by associations: the "ledger experience," including amount of purchases, frequency and stability of custom, and liquidity of accounts; and the "assembly" type, including character, capacity, responsibility, resources and liabilities of customers.   Inquiries regarding questionable purchasers

[22] The important activity entitled "Trade Practice Conferences" will be dealt with in connection with another section of this volume.

[23] *Montague v. Lowry*, 193 U. S. 38 (1904).

[24] *Harelson v. Tyler*, 219 S. W. (Mo.) 908 (1920).

[25] *Nives v. Scribner*, 147 Fed. 927 (1906), and *Loder v. Jayne*, 149 Fed. 21 (1907).

[26] *U. S. v. E. I. DuPont*, 188 Fed. 127 (1911); *U. S. v. Cowell*, 243 Fed. 730 (1917); *Morey v. Paladini*, 203 Pac. (Cal.) 760 (1922).

are handled by the Association of Ice Cream Supply Men and by the National Boot and Shoe Association.

The circulation of "delinquent lists" borders on the realm of debatable practices, the danger of libelous acts as well as of accusations of libel being present.[27] The legality of refusal of credit will be dealt with later in discussing the Cement Manufacturers' case. The Tile Manufacturers' Credit Association became similarly involved.[28] Inasmuch as competition in terms is as important as competition in prices, no association may, of course, adopt uniform rules as to terms or agree not to deal with delinquents.[29] Members of trade associations may take reasonably fair actions to protect themselves.[30] The equity rule that men must approach the court with clean hands has its ethical analog.

As regards traffic regulations, the trade association has found it advisable in a number of cases to supplement the work of the Interstate Commerce Commission, which in its public capacity represents their court of appeal from rate schedules, by representing the shippers before the Commission and by taking advantage of such arrangements as frequently are not otherwise known to the individual members. The National Lumber Manufacturers' Association[31] and the American Drug Manufacturers' Association,[32] *e.g.*, have standing committees for this purpose. Trade associations become particularly effective in this respect where the construction of rate schedules shows regional variations, such as the "basing-point" system in the South, the "percentage-tariff" system of the East, or in regard to such matters as "fixed differentials in relation to rates at river crossings" in the Middle West, or the "blanket" rates of westbound and the "graded-zone" rates of eastbound traffic on transcontinental lines. "Mixed-car privileges" present a bone of contention between the packers and the wholesale grocers, the interests of the latter being handled by their association.

[27] *Gibbs v. McNeelay*, 102 Fed. 594 (1900); *Denney v. Credit Association*, 55 Wash. 331 (1909); *Jack v. Armour*, 291 Fed. 741 (1923); *U. S. v. Gypsum Association*, U. S. Dist. Ct., S. D. New York, Eq. No. E 25–215 (Jan. 3, 1923).

[28] *U. S. v. Tile Manufacturers' Credit Association*, U. S. Dist. Ct., S. D. Ohio, Eq. No. 26 (Nov. 26, 1923).

[29] Especially in utilities cases. See LXIX *Pennsylvania Law Review* 365, May, 1921.

[30] *U. S. v. King*, 229 Fed. 275 (1915).

[31] See their 1922 Report.

[32] See their 1921 Report.

Demurrage has been made a matter of particular study by the American Wholesale Lumber Association. Transportation difficulties, such as embargoes, car shortages, freight congestions, priorities, and changing rates, have been studied by various associations, among them the National Automobile Chamber of Commerce, the Rubber Association of America,[33] and the Silk Association of America.[34] The National Association of Farm Equipment Manufacturers has given considerable attention to the matter of adjustments and overcharges.[35]

Whether the trade association is ever to assume a position of importance and strength in the business structure, comparable at least to that now occupied by the corporation, is doubtful. That these two most important business organizations are sufficiently complementary to guarantee a permanent place to both, is unquestionable. But the relatively greater legal difficulties which the trade association constantly faces because of the incompatibility of its effective methods with the persistent social-economic metaphysics of the courts—clustering around the concepts of "competition," "restraint of trade" and "conspiracy"—give the trade association an artificial handicap which up to the present has prevented a real test of its business or economic capacity. It is doubtful, however, whether the removal of such a handicap would permit the trade association to supplant the corporation as the vital unit in the business structure. Membership must remain voluntary unless the trade association wishes to hazard a repetition of the experience of the Mediaeval guilds; information and policies cannot be entrusted to any member or group of members without creating suspicion among the rest, the amateur association executive seeming to be the best practical solution; and geographic or regional differences have in the United States proved to be a more effective bar to national integration than is the case with the corporation. Furthermore, the latter has the opportunity of securing a better personnel, especially in its higher executive offices. But there are enough functions in which trade associations have become proficient, to warrant them a permanent and increasingly important position in the business structure. The greatest test of their longevity will be their ability to adjust

[33] See their December, 1922, Report.
[34] *Silkworm*, February, 1921.
[35] Report, Traffic Department, 1923.

themselves to changing business conditions, by relinquishing functions that become useless or that are appropriated by government or corporation activities and by constantly being alert to the current problems of a highly dynamic situation.

D. THE ETHICS OF PRICE POLICIES

American business companies have been characterized, as we have seen, not only by a tremendous growth in size, but also by the extension of their activities beyond the performance of a single well-defined business function or the handling of a restricted and related group of commodities. In the earlier period of this development, businesses extended themselves in the direction of the source of their raw materials; recently this growth has been more in the direction of acquiring distribution and sales outlets. In both cases, the competition in the invaded fields has been intense, but the earlier and "backward" extensions as a rule met with less violent opposition than have the later, "forward" extensions, largely because the raw-material fields were not so well organized or so highly developed as are the distribution channels. Growers and producers as a rule were not so alert to business events, and to their significance, as distributors and merchants have recently shown themselves to be. In both cases, however, competition has manifested itself in price wars, with price discrimination and price-cutting—and its analog, bidding up of prices for raw materials—of the most violent cutthroat type.

In most of the cases already cited, emphasis has been placed largely on the structural and functional adjustments that were being made in business, these adjustments being basic to some of the most crucial ethical problems of recent years. These ethical problems become particularly acute, however, when the situation develops into a price war, which after all is the most obvious symptom of the disturbance. So with the Mennen case, for example: a problem which involved the broadest relationships between business and government and the most vital relations among the various parts of business itself, but which expressed itself in the last analysis in a relatively small discrimination in the scheduled prices of the Mennen Company. The case was fought out and discussed, however, largely on the ground of business policy and in relation to the business structure and the functions of business. In the present section, the ethical

279

problems of price policies will be dealt with directly and on their own merits, as far as this possibly can be done.

A discussion of the ethics of price policies necessitates a brief discussion of the underlying philosophy of business profits. So much has been said recently of the "service" motive in business that a critical examination of the relative merits of "service" and "profits" as prime business objectives is in order. A comparison of professional and business activities will probably serve to illuminate the problem.

There is a fundamental difference between business and professional activities, and the clarifying of this distinction will serve to correct many misconceptions held alike by professional and business men. The objective of professional activity is and should be service, whereas the objective of business is and should be profit. The abruptness of this distinction might be smoothed off by prefixing to "profit" and "service" some such term as "justifiable," but this would still further cloud the issue which we are trying to clarify. It is no more necessary to qualify the term "profit" than it is to qualify the term "service." If a doctor amputates an arm or a leg of a patient in three successive stages, he is performing a "service" in the strictly technical sense of the word, but not according to the meaning which the profession attaches to the word, which implies "justifiable." And so with "profit": the term has too frequently been identified with the connotation, "unjustifiable," and then compared with "service" with the assumed connotation, "justifiable." The result has been the attaching of an inferior value to business activities in contrast with professional values.

Indeed, business men themselves have been attracted to the word "service" and have even asserted this to be the chief function and purpose of business. More careful attention to economic theory and business facts would have disclosed the untenable character of this point of view. In an ordinary exchange of goods, one of the parties can easily perform a "service" by giving more than the exchange value; but this is not business. Conversely, what one gains in a business deal is not necessarily lost by the other party; both may profit, just as both may serve. A clothing merchant or a baker who gives his goods to the poor is performing a service, but that is not business. A bank, which extends its functions to include all sorts of expensive "services" to its customers without charge, may justify its policy on the score of increasing its future business and profits, but certainly not by asserting such services to be its major objective. Indeed, if services have been increased until the balance sheet shows a loss, the company no longer has a right to continue its existence, and will not continue to exist after the fact is known. The test situation is one in which a corporation reduces its profits by extending its "services": conceivably, the decreased capital values could jeopardize the interests of investors, a social value, more than society would gain by participating in the "services"; and if bankruptcy follows, the consumers will have lost the source of their supply of goods or services. The social value of stabilized investments and, more indirectly, of an assured source of goods to the buyer and consumer is as much conserved by the instrumental value of stabilized business profits as is the social value of health or of the protection of individual rights conserved by the instrumental value of the professional services of doctor or lawyer. Business profits, on this ground, are socially and ethically as justifiable as is the professional ideal of service.

Thus business cannot subscribe to a "service" principle which involves the company in a net loss. On the other hand, it is prevented by competition and by governmental regulation from achieving an infinite or an excessive profit. The argument therefore reduces itself to the question as to what amount of profit is justifiable in the range from nothing at all to infinity; this amount will probably approximate the general average profits of business plus the amount achieved by good management plus the amount necessary to take care of the risk element, and the resulting amount may be greater than that now set by governmental regulation. And in individual businesses, Justice Brandeis' statement should hold: "There is no profit too great to be approved, if it is the result of the exercise of brains and character under conditions of industrial liberty."[1] Certainly any business, which shows a relatively low profit as the result of performing services which cost money but do not return a direct or indirect profit, is justified in eliminating such services. Not so a doctor or a lawyer, who must minister to the needs of patient or client without waiting to see whether a large or sufficient fee can be obtained for the services or whether the man's last bill has been paid. A teacher or a minister or an officer in

[1] *Hearings*, Senate Committee on Interstate Commerce, p. 1245, 1911.

the army who measures his services by the salary he receives is not worthy of his profession. But the profits of a business are not only the incentive to business activities, whether directed toward increased sales or greater economies or better organization, but these profits are also a measure of the justification for the continued existence of the business. And this justification not only takes account of the consumer-purchaser's interest, but also gives adequate recognition to the rights of the stockholder, the laborer, the management, the dealer, and the competitor.

The failure of business men to clarify their objectives has not only led them astray into an unwarranted imitation of the professions, but it has unfortunately given the professional man an added reason for looking superciliously at business. The question is not one of practical activities: many professional men are more directly concerned about their income than are some business men, and many a business man has actually practiced the "service" principle to such an extreme that he can be said to be no longer in business. Many a professional man has devoted himself too exclusively to performing his services and has not given enough attention to the collection of his bills, just as some business men might increase their earnings by extending their services or might spend their earnings for better purposes. This is not the issue. The question is one not of ultimate social ideals, but of objectives, of the qualities which are intrinsic to business and to the professions, qualities which are instrumental to the general social good. The business man who loses sight of the profit objective is like the jackdaw, in Aesop's Fables, that painted himself white and tried to associate with the doves: the doves soon found him out, and when he returned to the jackdaws, they would have none of him either. The most difficult competitor the business man has to contend with, and the greatest social as well as economic menace, is the man who is making too small a business profit or who does not know that he may even be operating at a loss. His stupidity as a competitor is outweighed by his undermining of a common interest in general trade health. He is like a football player who runs too slowly toward the goal or who carries the ball to the wrong goal line. For fear that this figure will be misconstrued by the observation that it does not hold when the ball carrier is on the opposing team, let it be said that one of the most mistaken notions of business is that a competitor in the same field is on the opposing team. The figure applies to the common interests of competitors, among which is a reasonable profit.

Profits—sales and prices—costs. That is the order in which business objectives must be arranged on the basis of importance. Volume of sales formerly held the almost exclusive attention of business men, until they learned that sales income and net profits are not necessarily correlative. The same experience showed the fallacy of excessively high or low prices. So, also, basing the selling price on costs once seemed a logical method of securing a profit until business men learned that this was putting the cart before the horse. The change in attitude effected by the Austrian school of economics has been no less revolutionary in economics and business than was Copernicus' observation that the center of the solar system was in the sun and not in the earth. Costs thereby no longer are regarded as fixed, but are viewed rather as the sales price of the business which supplies the materials; the whole structure being based, not on some intrinsic value of raw materials at the beginning of the productive process, but on the psychological value at the sales end of the business transaction, the value judgment of the ultimate consumer, and the ability of the vendor to supply this demand with available goods at a profit. Services which do not result in profits through increased sales thus become resolved to unjustifiable costs. Functions which are very expensive, such as advertising, may nevertheless justify themselves if they are more than compensated for by increased profits through increased sales.

It is this orientation of business to its chief objective which constitutes a part of the philosophy of business and which gives importance to a consideration of price policies in a book on Business Ethics. As has already been pointed out, the traditional connotation of "fair price" as evolved by the Church and as perfected by the Law in its doctrine of the "public interest," has become virtually identical with "low price," a supposedly unquestionable advantage to the consumer, but a no less questionable pleader's doctrine. This one-sided doctrine, sponsored by such powerful social organizations, was undoubtedly beneficial to society so long as Business was unaware of the harmful business as well as social effects of unduly inflated prices. But it would be difficult to determine which of these two opposing views has been more harmful to society in the long run. Both are extremes. Although business arrogance has undoubtedly led to inflated prices, the denial to business of the intelligent safeguarding of profits by preventing underselling has unquestionably intensified and extended periods of business depression. The policy of stabilizing prices, for example in the steel business and especially as sponsored by Judge Gary in the United States Steel Corporation, is much more defensible from an ethical or social point of view than is either of the other extreme policies.

Relatively high prices may be justified on the ground of their finding their way eventually into the wage envelope, although the route is too long and too precarious to be given much serious consideration. But, even granted the fact, the interest of workmen is not so much in the size as in the stability of income; and stability of prices would effect this result if the argument is sound that high prices effect high wages. Fluctuating prices may be desired by the gambler in business; even the wind of declining prices blows some men good. But gambling involves such a large element of appropriation and acquisitiveness that it cannot be ethically justified in the face of the alternative of relative price stability. For the implied relative business stability does not mean business lethargy, especially because individual differences among the abilities of business men can always be depended on to effect differences of achievement and success. A relatively stable condition, particularly of prices, places a premium on business intelligence and capacity rather than on mere agility and luck. The determination of ethical price policies must, therefore, be based on a doctrine of relative stability of prices.

If such a doctrine cannot be absolutely maintained in the face of apparently uncontrollable price cycles, then business men must meet such a situation by the same methods that most intelligent people employ toward the forces of Nature: by acquiring more knowledge of the situation and by proper adaptations. But where the price situation is not an inevitability, where it is subject to manipulation, then obviously the problem resolves itself to intelligent methods of control. It is this latter problem that we propose to discuss in the three chapters constituting this section on Price Policies.

CHAPTER XI

RESALE-PRICE MAINTENANCE AND PRICE DISCRIMINATIONS

Price policies involve a number of particular problems, conspicuous among which are those of resale-price maintenance, discriminating price schedules and price-cutting. Although it is readily apparent that these problems are interrelated and are seldom practicably separable, we shall deal with them in sequence so that their ethical significance may be dealt with analytically.

Genesis and Logic of the Policy

The following case is particularly significant because it illustrates the genesis as well as the logic of a price-maintenance policy. It has often been asserted that the emphasis of the classical economists on costs as determining price had at least the virtue of being realistic. But here is a case which shows that the Böhm-Bawerck point of view, which by implication emphasizes price rather than costs, can also be realistically validated. To hold both views at the same time would obviously be impossible, and yet business has attempted to do this, with resulting confusion. The following cases will be more clearly understood if the reader assumes the theory of the economics of price which was developed in the preceding pages.

Pritchard and Constance, Incorporated,[1] was in 1923 a New York corporation operating in New York City. Since 1912 it had been engaged in the manufacture of cosmetics and toilet articles, and in the sale of these products to jobbers and retailers throughout the United States. At first Pritchard and Constance, Incorporated, had sold only to retailers, but as business developed it included jobbers among its customers.

The price lists of the Pritchard and Constance, Incorporated, products were made out in reference to the prices to be paid by the ultimate consumer. In selling to retailers and jobbers, Pritchard and Constance,

[1] VI F. T. C. D. 244 (1923).

Incorporated, computed prices by allowing certain discounts from the prices shown on these lists.

In 1913 those retailers who had agreed to maintain the resale price determined by Pritchard and Constance, Incorporated, were offered a discount of 25% and 10% in more than dozen quantities, 5% additional on invoices over $75 net, plus 2% for cash in 10 days, net 30 days. After April, 1922, a flat discount of 33⅓% was allowed retailers. In order to secure the cooperation of retailers, bonuses of free goods were offered.

During 1920 and 1921, the following statements were included in letters to retail customers:

While this bonus reduces the cost of our merchandise to you, we wish to emphasize the fact that it is intended as a payment on our part for price maintenance. Price-cutters will not receive bonuses until we have their written assurance that they will maintain the prices of Amami perfumery products.

Whenever Pritchard and Constance, Incorporated, received information that any retailer was reselling its products at less than the prices fixed by it, Pritchard and Constance, Incorporated, addressed the following form letter to the price-cutter:

Dear Sir: We have received a letter from one of your neighbors this morning to the effect that you sell our Amami Shampoo at 10 cents per envelope, whereas Amami Shampoo retails at 15 cents an envelope or $1 per carton.

There are so many manufacturers who don't care much whether their goods are cut or not that we feel sure that you would be willing to cooperate with us in maintaining the prices of our articles.

If at any time you feel that you cannot dispose of any of our items at the nominal prices, we shall be glad to exchange same for more salable items.

We enclose a stamped, addressed envelope. Will you kindly let us know whether or not you are willing to cooperate with us in price maintenance?

With compliments, we remain, *etc.*

Ten per cent of the amount purchased was awarded in goods to those dealers who had maintained the designated resale prices and whose purchases exceeded $30 monthly.

In selling to jobbers, up to and including September, 1920, a regular discount of 15% off the dealer's price was allowed, and in addition the following quantity discounts: 10% and 2% off for 5-gross lots, 10% and 5% off for 25-gross lots.

In April, 1920, Pritchard and Constance, Incorporated, discovered that jobbers were underselling among their retail customers. After circularizing the trade asking that this practice be discontinued, and after having this letter of request ignored by certain jobbers, Pritchard and Constance, Incorporated, on September 1, 1920, announced that the discounts allowed jobbers thereafter would amount only to 15% and 2%, if their requests for price maintenance were further ignored.

Pritchard and Constance, Incorporated, however, did, after this date, allow certain favored jobbers an additional discount of 10%, after the latter had assured Pritchard and Constance, Incorporated, of their cooperation in maintaining the scheduled resale prices. Pritchard and Constance, Incorporated, through informing salesmen, attempted to induce other jobbers to agree to the resale-price schedule. They did not attempt to refuse to sell to price-cutters, only one instance of such having been reported.

In view of the fact that Pritchard and Constance, Incorporated, had started their business in a modest way and had at first dealt only with retailers, it is easy to understand the principle of their basic price policy: *viz.*, to fix the price to the consumer, and then to offer to the retailer a discount from that price. Later, when jobbers were added to the customer list, Pritchard and Constance persisted in their price policy by offering jobbers' discounts in addition to retailers' discounts. Their effort to establish resale-price maintenance thus became a simple matter: they merely needed to withhold certain discounts from such dealers as refused to cooperate with them.

Up to this point, the problem is one solely of business policy. When Pritchard and Constance, however, went further and asked dealers to promise to maintain resale prices, the agreement virtually constituted a conspiracy; and in so far as the dealers were prevented from obtaining the Amami products without entering into the agreement, there resulted an illegal restraint of trade. The ethical point is a neat one. On the one hand, there is the producer or large distributor of goods, who may, as in this case, have developed from a small-distributor status and who, originating as a direct vendor to the ultimate consumer, may have constantly held in mind the sales price throughout the distribution process—a perfectly sound economic policy. On the other hand, however, there are the successively smaller distributors who have a basic right to the independent management of their own business without being told at what prices they shall sell their goods and even what profits they shall make. Some of the dealers, however, abused their right to independence by cutting prices, thereby competing unfairly against the other distributor outlets of Pritchard and Constance and also jeopardizing the prestige value of the latter's goods.

The significance of the business doctrine of "legitimate trade channels" now becomes accentuated. If the hierarchy of channels of distribution is to be established, then it becomes incumbent on business men to determine the functions which each member of the hierarchy is to perform. This general problem has been presented in preceding chapters. But the introduction of the further question as to the right of each member to determine the price at which he sells goods involves additional ethical considerations. The right of any member of the hierarchy, especially of the manufacturer, to determine the final sale price to the consumer, is basically justifiable on the ground of maintaining not only a constant sales volume but also the prestige of "distinction" goods and also on the ground of protecting each distributor against excessive price competition; but this right directly conflicts with the right of each distributor to the independent determination of his sales prices in order to safeguard the continued and successful operation of his own business. The abuses of both rights, namely, direct sales and price-cutting respectively, frequently carry the issue beyond the problem of resale-price maintenance. Where such abuses are not involved, the maintenance of resale prices can in the main be justified, especially if the manufacturer is alert to the necessity of permanently maintaining his outlets by allowing distributors satisfactory profits.

The factor of agreement in maintaining a price policy arose in the following case, the court refusing to accept any subterfuges as extenuations of the fact that contracts were the sanctions of the policy.

Dr. Miles had a secret but unpatented formula for a proprietary medicine. He distributed his products by engaging in consignment contracts[2] with customers—including some 400 wholesalers and 25,000 retailers—making the latter agents, and prohibiting them from selling at other than a specified price. By the contract, title to the goods remained in Dr. Miles' possession until they were sold by the distributor; but jobbers paid a fixed price without privilege of return, and title was retained by Dr. Miles Medical Company even after the price was paid or "advanced."

John D. Park and Sons Company was a wholesale drug company which sold Dr. Miles' products at other than the specified resale price. Suit was brought by Dr. Miles Medical Company for breach of contract. The court[3] held that the contracts, although ostensibly of agency or

[2] See Appendices A and B, *op. cit. infra*, pp. 807–809.

[3] *Dr. Miles Medical Company v. John D. Park and Sons Company*, 164 Fed. 803 (1908).

bailment, were "mere subterfuges," that they were actually sales contracts, hence were illegal both at common law and under the Sherman Act. It was on this ground that the Dr. Miles Medical Company was prevented from securing enforcement in the courts. The court referred to Coke on Littleton (paragraph 360) in asserting that "a free right of alienation is an incident to the general right of property in articles which pass from hand to hand in the commerce of the world."

Dr. Miles Medical Company argued that the right of a patentee[4] to establish resale prices applied to medicines made by a secret formula. The court, however, pointed out two distinctions: the monopoly extended to an inventor has a limitation of a few years, and to obtain it the inventor must put his invention on record. Not so with the monopoly enjoyed by a proprietary medicine. The court referred to a previous similar case[5] in which such contracts were illegal and could therefore not be enforced in a court of equity. "No legal, economic, or moral reason exists for regarding contracts in respect to the vast and ever-increasing commerce in proprietary medicines as either outside the mischief intended to be remedied by the Federal statute against monopoly or the rules of the common law, or within the statutory protection afforded by the patent and copyright statutes."

The court then distinguished between patents and copyrights in order to show that the latter do not extend so far as was claimed for proprietary medicines by Dr. Miles Medical Company. The copyright statute does not create a right to impose a limitation at which a book shall be sold at retail by future purchasers with whom there is no privity of contract.[6]

The case was appealed to the Supreme Court.[7] Justice Hughes gave the majority decision, affirming the decision of the lower court, and for much the same reasons. The court further held that Dr. Miles' argument, that confusion and damage resulted from sales at less than the fixed prices, concerned the dealers and not the manufacturers. This attitude of the court, which is quite to the point, presents, however, a serious difficulty to the distributors. Agreements among dealers to fix prices are injurious to the public interest and therefore illegal and void. And the view of the court was that "the public is entitled to whatever advantage may be derived from competition in the traffic subsequent to manufacture." It may be questioned whether such a denial of all interests or rights of the distributors in trade

[4] *E. Bement and Sons v. National Harrow Company*, 186 U. S. 92.
[5] *John D. Park and Sons Company v. Hartman*, 153 Fed. 24 (1907).
[6] *Bobbs Merrill Company v. Straus*, 210 U. S. 339.
[7] 220 U. S. 373 (1911).

stability, except such as survive the rigors of competition, is a fair or adequate analysis of the situation. The attitude of the court, which undoubtedly is supported by consumer opinion, requires a considerable amount of initiative on the part of dealers to neutralize, and the subtleties necessary to avoid violating the law by the necessary methods of procedure have not yet been approximated by trade groups.

Right of a Company to Maintain Prices

Colgate and Company, a New York corporation engaged in manufacturing and selling cosmetics and toilet articles, had a price-maintenance policy. Colgate and Company issued price schedules after consulting with their customers and after these customers had indicated that the price schedule, including the resale price, was fair and reasonable. After distributing these uniform resale-price lists, Colgate and Company urged dealers to adhere to the schedule and refused to sell to such dealers otherwise. Colgate and Company furthermore requested its customers to furnish information of sales at other than the scheduled resale prices and discovered such practices itself; the company then investigated all such sales which it so discovered or which were reported to it, placed such dealers on "suspended" lists, and requested promises in regard to future behavior before any further sales were made to such customers.

The Department of Justice instituted action against Colgate and Company on the ground that its practices violated the Sherman Act. There was no charge of monopoly, or of action in concert with other manufacturers; nor was Colgate and Company charged with making agreements with its customers or agreeing with distributors in regard to the maintenance by the latter of resale prices among their customers; nor was there evidence offered as to any exclusive buying contract demanded of customers. The sole charge was that Colgate and Company had entered into an arrangement with its customers whereby the latter were to maintain the scheduled resale prices if they wished to continue as customers of the Colgate Company.

This action was brought as a criminal action and became involved in procedural difficulties. In the first place, the action was brought against Colgate and Company as conspirators, but the distributors were not named but merely referred to as dealers in a certain territory in the United States. In the second place, all the cases cited by the Government to support its position were civil cases which had been brought by distributors against manufacturers or wholesalers. Hence the case, as a legal case, was a flimsy structure.

The court, however, did[8] discuss the merits of the case. It asserted that a manufacturer or distributor might refuse absolutely to sell at any price or might sell at a named sum to a customer with the understanding that the resale price be maintained, and that he might refuse to sell unless such arrangements were complied with. In the case at hand, there was no contract; the manufacturer merely had refused to sell to those who did not comply with his price-maintenance policy.

Price-cutting, the court further went on to declare, would result in reducing Colgate and Company's business in a given community exclusively to those engaged in that practice, and would deprive it of the patronage of the great body of wholesalers and retailers engaged in what they themselves and Colgate and Company believed to be a fair and legitimate conduct of their business. Once the price-cutter had appropriated the business, there would be no check to his raising his prices to the normal level or even to a higher point. The court therefore decided in favor of Colgate and Company.

Whether the court was right in its analysis of the ultimate effect of price-cutting, is difficult to say. From a business point of view, this effect would hardly be possible in view of the fact that a monopoly did not exist in the product. The greater harm would arise even earlier: a demoralization of the distribution channels, a matter of prime concern to Colgate and Company. Especially is this true in regard to the nature of the product, which required, as a part of its market standing, that the price be maintained. People will buy more expensive articles on the assumption that the price is an index of quality. Hence there was a subtle reason for Colgate and Company's interest in its price-maintenance scheme.

The Department of Justice carried its case to the Supreme Court on appeal.[9] Justice McReynolds gave the majority opinion, confirming the decision of the lower court. He called attention to the difference between this case and the Dr. Miles case, in that contracts or agreements were absent, and reasserted the right of a distributor freely to do as he wished in his sales

[8] *U. S. v. Colgate*, 253 Fed. 522 (1918).
[9] *U. S. v. Colgate*, 250 U. S. 300 (1919).

Colgate Co.

activities. Such a distributor, the court pointed out, could exercise his independent discretion as to the parties with whom he will deal, and might announce in advance the circumstances under which he would refuse to sell. By implication, the freedom of the retailer consisted in his right to refuse to handle goods which had to be sold at a fixed price determined by the manufacturer; this freedom might amount to no more, however, than that of a laborer under the "freedom of contract" doctrine.

B.-Nut

The Beech-Nut Packing Company[10] was a New York corporation located in 1919 at Canajoharie, and was engaged in the manufacture and sale of chewing gum and food products. It customarily marketed its products principally through jobbers and wholesalers in the grocery, drug, candy, and tobacco business, who in turn sold to the retailers in these commodities.

All wholesale dealers were selected by the Beech-Nut Company on the basis of:

   a. Good credit standing.

   b. Willingness to resell at prices suggested by the Beech-Nut Company.

   c. Their willingness to refuse to sell to those who were not willing to maintain such resale prices.

   d. Those who were good and satisfactory in other respects.

The Beech-Nut Company sold in a few instances directly to large retailers who were selected on the same basis as the wholesaler. The customers of the Beech-Nut Company included the greater portion of the grocers in the United States, and a large portion of the drug, candy, and tobacco trades.

The "Beech-Nut policy" aimed to provide a profit which should be arbitrarily fixed, and to obtain the support of distributors in pushing the Beech-Nut products and in eliminating sales at lower prices. The company issued circulars containing the resale prices, insisted on compliance with these and on the refusal to sell at other prices, and it threatened to withdraw its business from those who refused to accept its policy. The latter consisted chiefly of mail-order houses and retail price-cutters.

The Beech-Nut Packing Company had a force of specialty salesmen in the field and, through this organization and by means of key numbers on packages and its card records, maintained a system of espionage whereby the Beech-Nut Company was able to detect any deviations from its policies. This system of espionage was further supported by securing the cooperation of distributors in reporting all distributors who failed to adhere to the resale-price schedule.

[10] I F. T. C. D. 516 (1919).

The gross-profit margins allowed by the Beech-Nut Company were so adjusted as to induce a large number of jobbers, wholesalers, and retailers to handle the Beech-Nut products. These margins were greater than were necessary to enable the more efficient dealers to resell at a lower cost and still make a profit. Hence the Beech-Nut policy resulted in a protection afforded to relatively high-cost and less efficient merchants.

The following table will show the range of costs of wholesale and retail dealers who were handling the Beech-Nut products at that time, in comparison with the gross-profit margins allowed under the resale prices suggested by the Beech-Nut Company and excluding cash discounts:

Class of dealer	Range of cost of doing business on gross sales, *per cent*	Percentage gross-profit margin allowed under resale prices suggested by the Beech-Nut Company
Wholesale		
Grocery	5 to 9	14¼
Drugs	12 to 12½	20
Candy	10 to 16	20
Tobacco	5 to 9	20
Retail		
Grocery	12 to 20	37
Drugs	25 to 30	40
Candy	20 to 30	40
Tobacco	20 to 30	40

Cases involving the problem of resale-price maintenance have arisen in a great diversity of products—cleansing powder,[11] drugs and medicines,[12] toilet articles and razors,[13] candy and canned goods,[14] pianos and sheet music,[15] water heaters,[16] watches,[17] electric switches,[18] dress patterns,[19] furniture[20] and

[11] I F. T. C. D. 199.
[12] *Ibid.*, I, 149 and 442.
[13] *Ibid.*, VI, 244 and 291; I, 418.
[14] *Ibid.*, II, 1 and I, 452.
[15] *Ibid.*, III, 124; I, 149 and V, 465.
[16] *Ibid.*, I, 530.
[17] *Ibid.*, IV, 17.
[18] *Ibid.*, V, 376.
[19] *Ibid.*, VI, 310.
[20] *Ibid.*, I, 499.

footwear.[21]   In all of these cases, the Federal Trade Commission has condemned the practice of resale-price maintenance as unfair, so far as was compatible with the exceptions which the courts insisted on in the Beech-Nut case.

It is to be noted that the Beech-Nut Company did not require its customers to enter into an explicit agreement to maintain resale prices, although certain implications to that effect were noted in the Supreme Court decision discussed below.   The Federal Trade Commission, however, ordered the Beech-Nut Company to cease and desist from "securing the cooperation of its distributors in maintaining or adhering to its system of resale prices, or carrying out its policy by any other means." The Beech-Nut Company admitted that it had refused to sell to such dealers as refused to maintain prices, but denied that it had entered into an agreement with its customers requiring resale-price maintenance or had qualified the customers' title to the articles purchased, or had restricted their freedom either to sell to any one or to charge any price they chose.   The Beech-Nut Company took its case to the Circuit Court of Appeals.[22]

The court stated that the legal ground taken by the Commission was that the method was unfair because it stifled competition and so restrained trade, and that the obvious purpose of the Beech-Nut Company was to prevent any competition as to the resale prices among the purchasers of the Beech-Nut products.[23] Referring to the Dr. Miles case, previously quoted, the court observed that where such a method was founded upon an agreement between a manufacturer and his customers, the practice violated the Sherman Act.   The court pointed out further that the same result was attained by acquiescence and cooperation even though without express agreement.[24]

But the Colgate case was now cited to show that a similar, but less drastic, method of sale constituted merely the exercise of a man's right "to do what he will with his own," and was not obnoxious to the Sherman Act.[25]   Instead, however, of inquiring further into the merits of the Beech-Nut case as presented, the court briefly reversed the order of the Federal Trade Commission.

[21] *Ibid.*, I, 506.

[22] *Beech-Nut Packing Company v. Federal Trade Commission*, 264 Fed. 885.

[23] At page 889.

[24] *Eastern States Retail Lumber Association v. U. S.*, 234 U. S. 600.

[25] *U. S. v. Colgate and Company*, 250 U. S. 300.   See also *U. S. v. Trans-Missouri Freight Association*, 166 U. S. 290.

One of the concurring judges distinguished between the Sherman Act, upon which the decision was based, and the Act establishing the Federal Trade Commission, under which this action was brought. The Sherman Act was directed against combinations in restraint of trade already effected; the Federal Trade Commission was empowered to issue orders to cease and desist from practices which *might lead* eventually to an unlawful combination in restraint of trade, and the Act also forbade all unfair methods of competition. Furthermore, Congress had in mind the *prevention* of acts which amounted to unfair competition at their very start. This reversion to the judicial metaphysics of the 1890's is all the more anomalous in view of the functional spirit of the Federal Trade Commission Act.

The concurring judge also pointed out that there was no essential difference between the tacit understanding in the Beech-Nut case and the written agreement in the Dr. Miles case; but that the latter was different in this respect, that the title to the goods was retained by the seller, a factor which introduced an element of coercion which was absent in the Beech-Nut case.[26] Reverting to the Colgate case, the court pointed out that there the problem concerned solely the Sherman Act. In the Colgate case, said the court, the judgment had held that, in the absence of any purpose to create or maintain a monopoly, the Act did not restrict the right of a trader or manufacturer, engaged in an entirely private business, freely to exercise his own independent discretion as to the parties with whom he would deal. The only way in which the distributor was affected by such a resale-price policy was that he might incur the displeasure of the manufacturer, who could refuse to make further sales to him, as he had an undoubted right to do.

This argument, seemingly leading to a dissenting opinion, but relying merely on previous decisions and stopping short of an examination of the facts of the Beech-Nut case which might indicate whether the working-out of the resale policy actually constituted an unfair practice, resulted in the judge's concurrence with the majority opinion of the court, that the order of the Federal Trade Commission be reversed.

Methods of Enforcing the Policy

The case was next brought before the Supreme Court of the United States upon a writ of *certiorari*. Justice Day delivered

[26] See also *Boston Store v. American Graphophone Company*, 246 U. S. 8.

Court

the opinion of the court.[27]   After pointing out that, under the Sherman Act, a trader was not prohibited from refusing to sell, but that he was not permitted to contract with others not to sell to certain individuals, the court declared that the Beech-Nut case arose, not under the Sherman Act, but under the Act establishing the Federal Trade Commission. In that Act, what constitutes "unfair" methods of competition was left without specific definition. Who then should define the term? "The Federal Trade Commission in the first instance," said the court, "but subject to judicial review." The court then quoted from the decision in the Gratz case:

> It is for the courts, not the Commission, ultimately to determine as a matter of law what the words "unfair method of competition" include. They are clearly inapplicable to practices never hitherto regarded as opposed to good morals because characterized by deception, bad faith, fraud or oppression, or as against public policy because of their dangerous tendency unduly to hinder competition or create monopoly.[28]

Having thus determined and clarified the law relating to the situation, the court now turned to an examination of the facts in the Beech-Nut case, an additional example of the functional tendencies in recent court decisions.   This the Circuit Court of Appeals had not done; it had rested content with assuming that the decision in the Colgate case covered all cases in which there was no contract or agreement to maintain resale prices.   The Supreme Court ruling continued with the following statements in regard to the Beech-Nut case:

> The system here disclosed necessarily constitutes a scheme which restrains the natural flow of commerce and the freedom of competition in the channels of interstate trade which it has been the purpose of all the Anti-trust Acts to maintain.   In its practical operation it necessarily constrains the trader, if he would have the products of the Beech-Nut Company, to maintain the prices "suggested" by it.   If he fails so to do, he is subject to be reported to the company either by special agents, numerous and active in that behalf, or by dealers whose aid is enlisted in maintaining the system and the prices fixed by it.   Furthermore, he is enrolled upon a list known as "Undesirable—Price-cutters," to whom goods are not to be sold, and who are only to be reinstated as one whose record is "clear" and to whom sales

[27] *Federal Trade Commission v. Beech-Nut Packing Company*, 257 U. S. 441.

[28] *Federal Trade Commission v. Gratz*, 253 U. S. 421, 427.   This statement, like the similar statement in the *Mogul Steamship* case (p. 71), clearly fails to recognize the distinction between the unfair practices which arise in a dynamic set of activities such as business, and the practices condemned by such a social laggard as the law.

may be made upon his giving satisfactory assurance that he will not resell the goods of the company except at the prices suggested by it, and will refuse to sell to distributors who do not maintain such prices.

From this course of conduct a court may infer—indeed, cannot escape the conclusion—that competition among retail distributors is practically suppressed, for all who would deal in the company's products are constrained to sell at the suggested prices. Jobbers and wholesale dealers who would supply the trade may not get the goods of the company, if they sell to those who do not observe the prices indicated or who are on the company's list of undesirables, until they are restored to favor by satisfactory assurances of future compliance with the company's schedules of resale prices. Nor is the inference overcome by the conclusion stated in the Commission's findings that the merchandising conduct of the company does not constitute a contract or contracts whereby resale prices are fixed, maintained, or enforced. The specific facts found show suppression of the freedom of competition by methods in which the company secures the cooperation of its distributors and customers, which are quite as effectual as agreements, expressed or implied, intended to accomplish the same purpose. By these methods the company, although selling its products at prices satisfactory to it, is enabled to prevent competition in their subsequent disposition by preventing all who do not sell at resale prices fixed by it from obtaining its goods.

Under the facts established we have no doubt of the authority and power of the Commission to order a discontinuance of practices in trading, such as are embodied in the system of the Beech-Nut Company.

We are, however, of opinion that the order of the Commission is too broad. The order should have required the company to cease and desist from carrying into effect its so-called Beech-Nut policy by cooperative methods in which the respondent and its distributors, customers and agents undertake to prevent others from obtaining the company's products at less than the prices designated by it—(1) by the practice of reporting the names of dealers who do not observe such resale prices; (2) by causing dealers to be enrolled upon lists of undesirable purchasers who are not to be supplied with the products of the company unless and until they have given satisfactory assurances of their purpose to maintain such designated prices in the future; (3) by employing salesmen or agents to assist in such plan by reporting dealers who do not observe such resale prices, and giving orders of purchase only to such jobbers and wholesalers as sell at the suggested prices and refusing to give such orders to dealers who sell at less than such prices, or who sell to others who sell at less than such prices; (4) by utilizing numbers and symbols marked upon cases containing their products with a view to ascertaining the names of dealers who sell the company's products at less than the suggested prices, or who sell to others who sell at less than such prices in order to prevent such dealers from obtaining the products of the company; or (5) by utilizing any other equivalent cooperative means of accomplishing the maintenance of prices fixed by the company.

The judgment of the Circuit Court of Appeals is reversed, and the cause remanded to that court, with instructions to enter judgment in conformity with this opinion.[29]

[29] 257 U. S. 441, 454–456.

a) The situation is thus left by the courts: that a resale-price-maintenance policy is permissible as between any manufacturer or distributor and his immediate customers, so long as the customer is not requested or obligated to agree to the policy other than as he fears that he otherwise will be deprived of the goods. *)* But no manufacturer or distributor may induce a wholesaling or jobbing customer to adopt the resale-price-maintenance scheme as regards the latter's customers. This means that a business company may adopt a resale-price-maintenance policy, but a company is virtually forbidden to adopt some of the most effective methods for enforcing the policy.

The proposed Capper-Kelly Bill[30] to validate resale-price contracts extends this privilege greatly so far as the manufacturer is concerned. The bill illustrates, however, the inability of the law to meet or anticipate the more crucial business problems. Not only does the title of the bill wrongly give the impression that the bill deals only with articles of standard quality, but it also fails to disclose the fact that it grants the privilege of resale-price maintenance to producers only and does not extend the privilege to articles sold under "private brands." The bill furthermore, in consequence, deals solely with the problem of the first resale price and does not touch the much more complicated problem of the resale-price policies of distributors.

But such limitations of a bill should not blind one to the fact that business men themselves have not worked out a doctrine of resale-price maintenance. The adoption or rejection of such a price policy on the ground that its full logical consequences have been taken into account, particularly as regards a second or third resale of an article, requires a threshing-out of the whole problem of the hierarchy of business and the validity of the concept of "legitimate trade channels." To deny such doctrines implies a basic denial of the validity of a policy of maintaining resale prices; to affirm them implies an inevitable acceptance of the policy of resale-price maintenance. In the meantime the law through the courts has defined a part of the policy by permitting it to a certain extent. But the mistake must not be made, however, of assuming that because it is legal to adopt

[30] S. 240, H. R. 11.   See address of Charles Wesley Dunn, delivered at the annual meeting of the Associated Grocery Manufacturers of America, Inc., Atlantic City, October 22, 1930. See also Tosdal, H. R., " Price Maintenance," VIII *American Economic Review* 1 and 2, March and June, 1918.

such a policy, it would be a justifiable policy from a business standpoint. The question still remains essentially what it was before the courts took cognizance of the practice, except that certain methods of enforcing the policy are denied to those firms adopting the policy. This limitation alone may of course be crucial to the problem.

The strongest argument in favor of a resale-price-maintenance policy is that it prevents predatory price-cutting, which is an evil if it results from ignorance as to selling costs. But this argument is weakened by the fact that a price-maintenance policy must be so worked out as to secure a profit to the least efficient, highest-cost distributors. This means that the most efficient, lowest-cost distributors secure an abnormal profit per unit but may not be securing the maximum total profit because of fewer sales at the higher prices. Some of these lost sales are distributed generally over the trade, because any effect of high prices would affect all distributors; and this effect in turn would react upon the Beech-Nut Company itself. Therefore it could be assumed that it would be to the interest of the trade, and particularly of the Beech-Nut Company, to eliminate this element in the fixed price. Whether any such modification would conflict with the price minimum at which the high-cost distributors could do business, would have to be determined separately.

But some of the lost sales of the low-cost distributors, due to high or equal prices among all distributors, would be suffered especially by the low-cost distributors themselves; and this loss would be the gain of the high-cost distributors. It is difficult to see how the Beech-Nut Company can satisfy its low-cost, efficient distributors on this score. Furthermore, the policy of the Beech-Nut Company represents an infringement on the independence and functions of the distributors. The latter could be expected to resent such interference with their own business. This interference of a seller with a buyer's method of conducting his business is more serious than the raising of the price to the ultimate consumer. Both, of course, are qualified by the fact that a check is offered by other competing goods, and this again throws the burden of justifying its policy back upon the Beech-Nut Company. Furthermore, it is true that unless certain links in the distribution chain are awake to their responsibilities, other links will encroach upon their functions. This has been conspicuously true of the wholesaler in certain trades in the last few years.   But the concentration of business responsibility has the danger of accentuating mistakes in business judgment.   The denial by the court, to distributors, of effective methods of enforcing resale prices, means that the policy cannot uniformly be carried out.   Theoretically, therefore, the maintenance of resale prices may be condemned; practically, it may be necessary until certain distributors awake to the desirability of correcting their business methods.

Price Discriminations

Price discriminations may be effected in various ways.   Haggling, for example, may be regarded as a form of discrimination, in which various buyers obtain goods at different prices, largely according to their dependence on the article in question or to their ability to haggle.   The practice has been fairly well eliminated from retail dealing in the United States, not so much because of its unfairness to the purchaser or due to his protests as because of the self-recognized effect on the merchant who permits it.   Once a merchant becomes known as a haggler, he is subjected to the haggling tactics of customers in such a way as to necessitate an unusually high mark-up of his goods; this in turn is so detrimental to merchandising that the "one-price policy" inaugurated by John Wanamaker as long ago as 1878 has been found to be expedient by most stores in the United States.   The practice has by no means been completely eliminated in this country, however, especially among unscrupulous small business men.   The term "price discriminations" as used in this chapter, however, does not refer to such variations in prices as result from haggling, but rather to the practice of quoting different price schedules to different customers or classes of customers.

Another form of price discrimination, strictly speaking, is the "trade" or "quantity" discount.   This practice, also, from the point of view now being developed, is not to be regarded as a form of price discrimination.   The practice of quantity discounts, whereby lower prices per unit are offered for greater quantities purchased, at least does not discriminate among purchasers as such: under a quantity-discount schedule, any customer may take advantage of the lowest prices.   The justification of the practice by the vendor is, of course, that those customers who by large purchases enable the vendor to anticipate and plan the greater bulk of his business should be recognized by price concessions. But the danger of such a policy often lies in the fact that the vendor may fail to see that the bulk of his business comes from the many small buyers who patronize him, whose business is often jeopardized by the price advantages allowed their larger competitors through the quantity-discount schedules.[31] Where a company succeeds in maintaining the resale prices of its goods, the quantity discount accrues to the customer of the company in the form of profits; but a resale-price-maintenance policy is not only difficult to maintain, but may itself be questionable. Thus the quantity-discount method may be condemned on its own account or because the avoidance of that criticism may entail another questionable practice.

Where a "quantity discount" is allowed certain buyers as a cloak for favoritism and discrimination, the practice is a plain case of misrepresentation, which is another problem. Unfortunately, this practice has become too prevalent among business firms. The terms "quantity discount" and "price discrimination" as used in this volume are used in their strict sense; as such, they present a distinct problem for Business Ethics, without confusing them by including other complicating matters.

The following excerpts from a letter written by a foreign manufacturer[32] present the borderline problem:

An organization of chain stores, with a price range similar to the 5-, 10- and 25-cent stores in the United States, has recently been formed in this country and has requested us to furnish them with our products. These products are to be sold at the chain stores' characteristic prices but under those prevailing among our distributors, and we are asked to make them certain price concessions because of the quantities they propose to buy.

We are convinced that the chain stores will provide us with better distribution facilities than we now possess through the independent retailers.

The problem is a delicate one for us, for if we do not accede to the request of the chain store, we destroy an important possible sales outlet; and if we furnish the chain store with our products, we risk alienating our retail clientele.

This company is obviously trying to eat its cake and have it too, and is probably not so certain regarding the possibilities of the chain store as the letter indicates. What this company faces is the necessity of deciding which outlet is the better one and then

[31] See Learned, Edmund P., "Quantity Buying from the Seller's Point of View," VIII *Harvard Business Review* 57, October, 1929.

[32] The name cannot be disclosed.

of managing its sales accordingly. If the chain store appears to be the better outlet, then the company needs to figure whether sales at the requested prices will be profitable to the company; and also whether the company wishes to rely fairly exclusively on such a sales outlet, which may at any time itself go into the manufacturing business. On the other hand, if the independent retailers are regarded as affording the largest and best sales outlets, then the company should maintain their goodwill by selling to them at prices which at least do not discriminate between the two kinds of stores. It may be necessary for the company to limit its sales to any one distributor to such an extent as will prevent the company from suffering a severe loss when such a distributor decides to purchase elsewhere or to go into the manufacturing business. Furthermore, it may be necessary, as in the Mennen case, for this company to maintain its sales channels exclusively through the independent wholesalers and retailers. But the far-reaching consequences of a discriminative schedule of prices is apparent, even when it is arranged on a strictly quantity-discount basis, and when it also observes the value and the rights of the older distributors.

Price discriminations arise as the result of the attempt wholly or partly to control distribution channels or to extend sales outlets. Thus, price discriminations, strictly speaking, consist in quoting one price in one territory and another in another territory where no considerable difference in the cost of doing business is involved; or in quoting one schedule of prices to one class of customers and another schedule to another class, aside from differences as to the quantity, quality or unit size of the goods sold. The following case will make the matter clear.

The Cudahy Packing Company[33] was a Maine corporation located at Chicago and engaged in the manufacture, sale, and distribution of Old Dutch Cleanser, a powdered cleanser. The Cudahy Company sold principally to jobbers, but also to a limited extent to certain other selected dealers. Both jobbers and dealers were known as distributing agents, there being some 4,000 in all. The Cudahy Company also sold to other dealers in the same quantities but at "general sales-list" prices, which were higher than prices quoted to the distributing agents.

The Cudahy Company had a price-maintenance plan in pursuance of which, however, it also discriminated among its customers, making sales to jobbers, wholesalers, and cooperative retail associations at both

[33] I F. T. C. D. 199 (1918).

general sales-list prices and distributing-agents' prices. The Cudahy Company sold to retail organizations at distributing-agents' prices, general sales-list prices, and at special prices. The effect of this price policy was to eliminate the competition in price among the jobbers and other dealers. The resale-price policy involved the attempt to make the jobbers quote the general sales-list prices to their customers. As a sanction for this policy, the Cudahy Company threatened the withdrawal of their price privileges from such jobbers as refused to maintain the wholesale prices.

The Cudahy Company maintained over 100 specialty salesmen to solicit from the retailers orders which were then turned over to the jobbers and to other wholesalers for delivery. Where jobbers had not maintained the resale-price policy, the Cudahy Company refused to hand over to them such "turnover" orders. This class of jobbers included such as had accepted the pooled orders from the retail dealers. By employing a system of key symbols for identifying cases of Old Dutch Cleanser, the Cudahy Company was able to trace the source of goods where price-cutting had been reported. The Cudahy Company was able by such methods to induce wholesalers to push these goods. Trade associations had endorsed the price-maintenance policy.

The costs of grocery jobbers and wholesalers selling by mail were at this time in some instances as low as $4\frac{1}{2}\%$ of the price to the jobber. Among cooperative grocers, jobbers, and wholesalers this cost was sometimes as low as 3% to $3\frac{1}{2}\%$ of the selling price of the goods. The total cost of jobbers and wholesalers using the customary methods of doing business ranged from 6.3% to 10.7%, the common figure being 8%.

The gross profits of these dealers ranged from 7.7% to 17.2%, the majority falling between 10.5% and 13.4%. The rate of stock turn ranged from 1 to 12. The Cudahy Company allowed a gross profit of 11% to 14% according to the quantity purchased. Such margins were greater, therefore, than were necessary to the low-cost and efficient jobbers and wholesalers to resell and make a profit. Therefore, the effect of the Cudahy policy was to protect the high-cost and less efficinet jobbers who constituted the majority or bulk of the trade.

The Federal Trade Commission, before which the case was tried, did not lay much stress on the relations between the Cudahy Company and its retail customers, but it did assert that an agreement in restraint of trade arose when the Cudahy Company attempted to secure the cooperation of the jobbers in maintaining among their retail customers the prices which the Cudahy Company was maintaining among its own retail customers.

In its "cease and desist" order, the Federal Trade Commission made two provisos. The Cudahy Company was not prohibited from issuing price lists or printing prices in its advertising or upon containers so long as the Cudahy Company refrained from recommending or requiring the resale of its articles at such prices. And the Cudahy Company was not prohibited from selling directly to retailers at the fixed prices or at any other prices fixed by them in agreement with the parties through whom such orders were filled.   But the Cudahy Company was prohibited from insisting on an agreement from their wholesale customers that resale prices would be maintained among the direct customers of such wholesalers.   Obviously the legal prohibition of the practice of resale-price maintenance involves only a fractional part of the trade relations in which the question as to the policy may arise.   The major part of the question is left to the decision of business companies.

Price discriminations represented only a minor factor in the Cudahy case, although it is obvious that the problem is implied in any case of resale-price maintenance.   It is possible, however, to consider the problem of price discriminations as distinct from the other problems with which it is frequently combined.

Price discriminations are specifically forbidden in Section 2 of the Clayton Act, in the following words:

It shall be unlawful for any person engaged in commerce, in the course of such commerce, either directly or indirectly to discriminate in price between different purchasers of commodities, which commodities are sold for use, consumption, or resale within the United States . . . , where the effect of such discrimination may be to substantially lessen competition or tend to create a monopoly in any line of commerce:

Provided, that nothing herein contained shall prevent discrimination in price between purchasers of commodities on account of differences in the grade, quality or quantity of the commodity sold, or that makes only due allowance for difference in the cost of selling or transportation, or discrimination in price in the same or different communities made in good faith to meet competition;

And provided further, that nothing herein contained shall prevent persons engaged in selling goods, wares, or merchandise in commerce from selecting their own customers in bona fide transactions and not in restraint of trade.

The first decision of the United States Supreme Court upon the meaning and application of this section, and one of the most recent cases involving this problem of price discriminations, is represented in the so-called Van Camp case.[34]   The American Can Company had been furnishing cans to the Van Camp

[34] *George Van Camp and Sons Company v. American Can Company and Van Camp Packing Company*, 278 U. S. 245 (1929).

Packing Company at a schedule of prices that was lower than that quoted to George Van Camp and Sons Company. The difference in the quotations amounted approximately to 20%, with the further fact that machines for sealing the cans were furnished free to the Van Camp Packing Company but were rented to George Van Camp and Sons Company. Both the direct and indirect forms of price discrimination were declared by the court to be forbidden by the Clayton Act, thus overruling in part the previous decisions given in the Mennen and National Biscuit Company cases. The act of the American Can Company was held to have lessened competition substantially and to have tended to create a monopoly in the line of commerce involved. The incidence of the court's decision was on the American Can Company only, and not upon the joint defendants, the Van Camp Packing Company; the buyer who induces or compels the discrimination being held liable only where a conspiracy charge could be proved, a principle retained from the Mennen and National Biscuit cases. The discrimination practiced was held to have effected an unreasonable restraint upon competition, the court holding that strict uniformity of price was not intended by the Clayton Act and that quantity discounts were permitted under the law. The price discriminations forbidden in the Clayton Act were held to be only such as substantially and unreasonably affected competitors differently.

The practice of price discriminations must be viewed primarily as an attempt to secure additional sales through encouraging what the distributor believes are the best sales outlets. Therefore, this practice has a great deal more in common with the policy of maintaining resale prices than at first appears on the surface. Both policies represent efforts, on the part of the producer or wholesaler, to secure and stabilize the best distribution channels, however misguided certain forms of such policies may be in practice. The bogey which all of these distributors are facing is the bogey of price-cutting as practiced by certain distribution outlets. This is directly the case with companies attempting to establish resale-price policies. And although it may appear to be a contradiction in terms to assert the same thing in regard to price discriminations, the major fact is that such discriminations are motivated primarily by the desire eventually to stabilize outlets; although it is true that manufacturers are thereby doing the very thing that they object to on the part of retailers, this fact is of only secondary importance, for the manufacturer is in a much better position to control a general price policy than is the retailer, who in most cases is governed merely by opportunism.

In April, 1930, the Federal Trade Commission broadened its policy regarding price discriminations, together with other items listed as unfair trade practices. In its approval of the trade-practice rules of the knitted-outer-wear and of the metal-lath industries, the Commission took the view that secret rebates, price discriminations, sales of goods below cost and other practices declared to be unfair, would be held so only in case it were proved that the practice in question substantially lessened competition or created a monopoly. The exact wording of the point in the knitted-outer-wear code is:

> The secret payment or allowance of rebates, refunds or unearned discounts, whether in the form of money or otherwise, or secretly extending to certain purchasers special services or privileges not extended to all purchasers under like terms and conditions, with the intent and with the effect of injuring a competitor, and where the effect may be to substantially lessen competition or tend to create a monopoly or to unreasonably restrain trade, is an unfair trade practice.

One difficulty with this principle is that it is not objective but must be determined in each particular case by an act of judgment—and the judgment of a company may lead it to do what a court would later condemn. Another difficulty is that business men may think that the implied permission of the Commission and the agreement of the trade sanction the business act; whereas, it still may not be good business policy to engage in discriminatory price arrangements.

The most conspicuous factor that appears in the presentation and analysis of the foregoing cases, involving resale-price maintenance and price discriminations, is that of the desirability of trade stability and trade health. This element and this point of view are to be contrasted with the traditional emphasis on the right of the consumer-purchaser to a "fair" price, which generally is interpreted to be the lowest price which the immediate situation would warrant. This consumer attitude undoubtedly was fostered by the mistaken opposing belief of business in the past that high prices connoted large profits; and the consumer's defense attitude was early sponsored by Church and State, which in turn became virtual pleaders against any attempts on the part of Business to assert the right to maintain prices at a level which would insure business stability. This broader, objective view of business has developed out of the increasing size and complexity of business activities and relations, whereby individual opportunistic advantage had to give way to considerations of permanent and general trade health. High prices, under such circumstances, become as dangerous as low prices are stupid; and the chief business concern becomes directed toward price stabilization. Indeed, Mr. Walter Gifford has taken the position that a business corporation which has reached the size now attained by the American Telephone and Telegraph Company is socially as well as economically obligated to adopt a policy of stabilized earnings. It is from this prime consideration of price and profit stabilization that policies involving price discrimination are to be condemned; and the sanctions for effectively following up such condemnations are much stronger than a mere consumer resistance based on his alleged moral rights to a "fair price." The necessity of thinking in social or trade terms, instead of in terms of an individual business or a single transaction, is apparent. The problem of resale-price maintenance is more complicated; but the same point of view—of trade health and business stability—enables one to discriminate more intelligently between the policies which are justifiable and those which are not.

CHAPTER XII

PRICE-CUTTING

It is generally admitted that the cutting of prices is necessary to liquidate a business or to dispose of excessive stocks. The ethical factor enters in only when price-cutting is predatory or persistent. Morally, no blame can be attached to the practice of "cutting" prices in order to meet competition, especially in view of the fact that the consumer-purchaser is directly and immediately benefited. Legally, likewise, there is no opportunity of redress; on the contrary, any agreement to maintain prices or to prevent "cutthroat" competition, is regarded as illegal, the Sherman Anti-trust Act having condemned all such "conspiracies in restraint of trade." Business ethics, on the other hand, may find price-cutting, as it is generally practiced, to be a trade evil, and the effects may assume such a magnitude as to make the practice socially undesirable. Whereas morality or law may discover an evil motive in conspiracies or agreements to maintain prices, ethics calls attention to the fact that price-cutting is frequently the result of ignorance and may have seriously detrimental effects on trade and society at large. Where price-cutting is necessitated by overproduction or overbuying, it may temporarily be justified, but there is a prior ethical obligation of preventing overproduction and overpurchasing to begin with. Where such necessities for price-cutting do not exist, the price-cutter frequently does not know his costs; he especially does not know how to charge against his business such items as overhead, obsolescence and depreciation. Hence he is deluded, by a false calculation of profits, into believing that his low schedule of charges is warranted.

Where price-cutting is apparently due not to ignorance but rather to superior management and large-scale transactions, as in the case of chain stores, the merits of the case are not yet certain. The chain store has not yet been thoroughly tested: rents have been admittedly lower than they will be in the future, wages have been relatively less than among independent stores, fixed financial charges will be increasingly felt, services are expanding, and buying methods have not been free from coercions that cannot persist indefinitely. Hence the effects of price-cutting by chain stores cannot yet be fully determined. The problem of price-cutting can be more certainly studied if it be confined initially to the practices of those many business men who have proceeded to formulate price policies without fully knowing their costs.

Agricultural economics is particularly characterized by this type of thinking. A farmer regards an income of $1,500 as "doing pretty well." If his land is worth $20,000 and his buildings and live-stock $10,000 more, he could sell his farm and place his money on interest to yield $1,500 without doing any work. If it be objected that he "gets his living" from the products of the farm, it may be countered that the labor of his wife and children are a set-off to that item; an inquiry in Vermont recently disclosed that this labor value is $350 per farm per year. An investigation by the Ohio Agricultural Experiment Station in 1913 disclosed that the net wages of farm owners, after interest on investment had been subtracted from earnings, were $250 per year; the wages of farm tenants, similarly figured, were $450. The point was that the owner, by confusing wages and interest, was deluded into believing that both were satisfactory; whereas, as a matter of fact, if either were calculated at current rates, the other ceased to exist. But the tenant did not have an interest income to fall back upon: his wages had to be sufficiently high to enable him to live off them.

Similar situations prevail in the small store. The result has been a tremendous mortality in the form of business failures. And it is reasonable to presume that most business failures have been preceded by years of "lingering on," with poor management, excessive inventories, overly-supplied markets, and a consequent underpricing of goods, all of which are detrimental to the trade or industry. Although price-cutting may be merely a symptom, and not a cause, of such unhealthy conditions, it has characterized the sick business the persistence of which prevents the healthier and sounder competitor from realizing on his own good management and from being encouraged by an honest facing of costs to charge a fair—*i.e.*, a higher—price. And the further difficulty is that the matter is not solved by a "survival of the fittest" because the "fittest" may go out of business when the danger marks begin to show, whereas the ignorant, and those who have inherited a farm or a business and who do not charge themselves interest, may linger on indefinitely. It is for this reason—that the difficulty does not cure itself—that price-cutting becomes a major problem of business ethics.

Professional Fees and Charges

The problem of charging a fair price in business may be approached in various ways. One method, which at least has the virtue of introducing certain naive factors, is to make a comparison between the fixing of prices on commodities and the determination of professional fees and charges. Among the many symptoms displayed by professional codes of ethics and indicating conscious attempts to control professional policies, is the relatively definite, objective, and measurable criterion they afford as regards the manner in which the professional man secures his income. Just what are the principles underlying professional fees and charges?[1]

We shall assume at the start that the professional man is to be distinguished from the amateur by virtue of his superior ability and training in a particular field of activity. This superiority entitles him to charge for his services. This prerogative is granted and secured to him not only by law, but by the public as well in its recognition of the desirability of seeking his services. What then differentiates the professional man from the business man? Clearly the priority of rendering services to the assurance of fees and charges. A business man does not lose caste if he refuses goods or credit to a purchaser when the latter cannot guarantee payment. A professional man in similar circumstances is obligated to render his services and to subordinate considerations involving payment.

This does not mean that professionalism is obligated to a sentimental and absolute idealism in its ethical conduct. It does not, for example, preclude a man from considering the financial possibilities of various professions before entering one as a life-work. Furthermore, a successful professional career, in the sense of the performance of services, should entitle a man to a relatively superior income. But this superior income

---

[1] See *Professional and Business Ethics*, by the author, New York: Henry Holt and Co., 1926, Chapter VII; also XXXV *International Journal of Ethics* 4, July, 1925: "Fees and Charges as an Index of Professionalism."

is to be measured over a considerable period of time; the principle which justifies such an income does not apply to every particular professional service rendered. It may be said that some business men are far-sighted enough to stand temporary losses in order to secure more permanent and more extensive gains. In such a case, and in this respect, the business man cannot be distinguished from the professional man. Professionalism demands that service be prior to payment, and that the amount and quality of services should not be measured by the amount of the prospective fee or the certainty of collecting it.

The published schedule of minimum professional fees is the logical implication of the principle of charging for services. It includes a number of intangible factors, chief among which is the matter of overhead. Into this factor enters not only the more obvious item of availability of services, but also the expense of college preparation, the earlier "lean" years of apprenticeship, intermittent periods of inactivity, charity cases, and the failure to collect fees. Any professional man who fails to take all of these items into account in his charges and fees is a menace to his profession, and conceivably to the economic order. It is here that an apparent conflict arises between professional interests and the welfare of society. Individuals and society are interested in preventing overcharging; often this interest fails to acknowledge the indeterminable items which should enter into the making of rates, and the public regards price-cutting as a boon. The professional as well as the business man will not, on the other hand, if he is wise, tolerate price-cutting; the published schedule is a minimum scale, but professionally and ethically permits of increased charges. Given the privilege to practice thus, the professional man by implication is obligated to guarantee his individual services as rendered, and those of his group; otherwise, he cannot be expected to be so obligated. On the other hand, if society demands of the professional man such a guarantee, by implication it should allow him to control his fees without legislative or social interference. And the published schedule of minimum fees is the inevitable conclusion of such an arrangement. This permits of higher rates for qualitative superiority, another important intangible factor. Two alternatives thus are open to professional men who achieve distinction and thereby attract a large clientèle: either to establish an organized group or firm of practitioners, large enough to accommodate the clientèle, or to increase rates so as to reduce the clientèle. Either is ethically justifiable; the latter especially if accompanied by a considerable amount of charitable work.

One test of a profession is the attitude toward such gratuitous work as it does, especially in connection with charity cases. The indigent prisoner, the poor patient, and the unfortunate student, all call for the same kind and degree of professional skill as is exercised in behalf of those who are able to pay generously. Many such cases are now taken care of by organized efforts. The public defender is in many places at the service of persons confronted with lawsuits involving less than certain specified amounts. Certain medical associations— of a county, for example—assume the obligation of caring for the poor. The work is fairly apportioned; and the amount granted by the county—which is about one-third of the scheduled charges—is used as a fund for the professional advancement of the organization. Where, however, there is no such organized handling of gratuitous services, each professional man is obligated to perform services needed, when approached by client or patient. In no case is a professional man warranted in refusing services because of the inability of the client to pay. The loss occasioned thereby, however, should enter as an overhead factor in the published schedule.

It is now apparent why underbidding the accepted or published schedules of rates is unprofessional and antisocial. It shifts the competition from quality of service to amount of fee, thereby encouraging the "quack," the "shyster," and the "fly-by-night" merchant. The publication of minimum fee schedules by doctors has never been questioned by the courts. At present it is illegal for business men to organize for the purpose of fixing prices; social and business intelligence has not yet developed to the point of recognizing a sound and fair principle. A candid examination of the economic and professional relations involved forces one to the conclusion that the enforcement of a minimum published fee is the only ethical course for the professions to pursue. The same may be said for the stabilizing of prices in business if the principle is not abused. The conflict between these two social forces presents an interesting problem to philosophy; a problem which is rendered difficult by the turbid ignorance, especially on the part of the professional clientèle and the consumer-purchaser, of the exact issues and interests involved.

The following statements appear in *Principles of Medical Ethics* under the title CONTRACT PRACTICE:

It is unprofessional for a physician to dispose of his services under conditions that make it impossible to render adequate service to his patient or which interfere with reasonable competition among the physicians of a community. To do this is detrimental to the public and to the individual physician, and lowers the dignity of the profession.[2]

The Committee on Professional Ethics of the New York County Bar Association was asked:

Is it proper for a lawyer, at the request of a social club, to agree with the club to grant a special discount from his fee to its members for any service which he may be called upon to perform for them?

There is to be no solicitation, but the name is to appear upon a list including other lawyers whom the club deems it proper to recommend, and upon application by any member for the recommendation of an attorney he will be informed that any chosen from such list would make a special concession from his fees to him, or members may in general be informed that any attorney they may select from the list would be willing to make a special allowance from his fees.[3]

In the opinion of the Committee, the question presented no excuse for the arrangement, and the arrangement was to be condemned because it virtually amounted to an indirect method for the systematic solicitation of professional employment for the lawyer.

A, an engineer in good standing in the American Association of Engineers, was employed by an engineering firm, X. B, an engineer also in good standing in the American Association of Engineers and unemployed, offered to fill A's position at a smaller salary. The result was that X cut A's salary, who thereupon resigned.

The Practice Committee of the American Association of Engineers, to which this situation was referred, and in reply to the question, "Was the action of B ethical?" stated:

A fundamental rule of personal ethics and therefore of professional ethics is that it is unethical for any engineer to seek or solicit a position occupied by another engineer, thereby displaying a tendency to displace him. Initiative for such action should, and most properly does, rest with the employer, who will exercise it in the ordinary course of administrative duties.[4]

[2] Chapter II, Article V, Section 2.
[3] Case 177.
[4] Case 21, American Association of Engineers.

It is apparent from these cases that the professional attitude toward fees and charges is very definitely opposed to any under-cutting of schedules or underbidding of competitors. Does this situation prevail in business? If profits are a legitimate and necessary purpose of business activity, and if profits are dependent on large or increasing sales, does it not follow that price policies which increase or even maintain existing sales might warrant such price inducements as price-cutting, rebates, prizes and gifts, generous credit terms, resale guarantees, leasing of equipment at less than cost, and other indirect forms or equivalents of price reduction? What ethical objection can there be to price-reduction policies when the benefit to the purchaser is so obvious and certain? Here again, as in most business situations, only an examination of actual business situations can afford an answer; and that answer may be not a single general principle but many and variant according to particular conditions.

Direct Forms of Price-cutting in Business

The analogy between professional and business practices cannot, of course, be made to "walk on all fours." Professional men have discovered the virtue of a schedule of minimum fees, but the persistence of business men in cutting prices may well be presumed, because of its prevalence, to be justifiable until proved otherwise. Certainly, however, the practice must have something to do with the fact that approximately 80% of all men entering the field of retail business fail. The unwillingness to charge a price which affords an adequate profit is the worst form of dishonesty—dishonesty to one's self—where it is not attributable to ignorance. The business man who knows his costs and who sets his prices according, has a justifiable griev-ance against the man who does not. The law prevents him from entering into price agreements or from coercing price-cutters into conforming to minimum price schedules. But he can exert his influence in trade groups and associations in the direction of gathering and disseminating informative figures on production, stocks on hand and sales, together with average cost sheets obtained from the majority of the members of the trade group. Each member can then gauge his own purchases or production and stocks on hand, as well as prices, with greater accuracy and judgment than is possible otherwise. This voluntary regulation of one's own business on the basis of accurate and sufficient knowledge is not only permissible under the law but is ethically justifiable, if self-respect be ethical; and it is a necessary and intelligent method of conducting one's business in the interests of trade health.

Price-cutting illustrates better than most unfair business methods just where the incidence of the injury of unfair trade practices lies. The consumer is in this case directly and immediately benefited and is much interested and perhaps justified in patronizing the price-cutter. It is the competitor, however, who is injured and who now may even appeal to the Federal Trade Commision to order the price-cutter to cease and desist from his practice.[5] For the ultimate purpose of price-cutting may be to effect a degree of monopoly which is unfair to competitors during the process of achieving it, and generally involves unfair price policies as regards the purchaser if and when it is achieved.[6] To gamble on the chance of achieving a monopoly is indefensible, first, because gambling is not good business in spite of the fact that many business men think otherwise, and second because the law condemns monopolies unfairly achieved and can prevent them to the extent of proceeding against businesses with such a purpose in mind. The only form of price-cutting that can be justified—aside from forced sales—is that which is engaged in temporarily to effect a better strategic position in the business. Such a policy cannot be justified or condemned in general, but must be studied in so far as it has been pursued in particular cases.

One of the most dramatic cases of price-cutting is presented by the openly announced policy of Macy and Company of New York to sell all goods at six per cent less than any of its competitors. Macy's argues that selling goods for cash, instead of on credit, and in large quantities enables them to pass on the resulting saving to their customers in the form of lower prices and to the extent of six per cent. The lower prices in turn are alleged to effect larger sales, which factor still further makes possible the price reduction. This policy has aroused some of Macy's

---

[5] For the effect of price-cutting and lowering of quality of goods on competitors, see *Royal Baking Powder Company v. Federal Trade Commission*, 281 Fed. 744, 750 (1922).

[6] This practice was formerly prevalent in the tobacco industry. See *People's Tobacco Company v. American Tobacco Company*, 170 Fed. 396 (1909), and *Ware-Kramer Tobacco Company v. American Tobacco Company*, 180 Fed. 160 (1910).

competitors to the point of conducting advertising campaigns against
the Macy policy.   Gimbel Brothers have met the challenge by advertising that they will sell goods at prices as low as any competitor.   Obviously both cannot be accurate in their statements.   A comparison of the
earnings of these two stores[7] and disregarding size or investment, would

	(In millions of dollars)			Profit per $100 capital
	Net sales	Net profit	Capital	
Macy's				
1929	$98.7	$7.9	$63.0	$12.48
1928	90.6	8.4	37.9	19.94
1927	58.3	7.0	39.3	14.83
Gimbel's				
1929	$124.6	$0.8	$85.2	$0.94
1928	121.1	0.9*	63.9	1.42*
1927	123.6	1.5	60.9	2.45

* Loss.

lead one to conclude that Macy's seems much better able to effect large
earnings than Gimbel's.   Granted that both equally follow their own
advertised price policies, the Macy policy can therefore be justified
more readily than can Gimbel's; there is no objection to a low price
policy so long as the company adopting it can earn large profits.   The
ethical objection to low prices or price-cutting centers on the usual
consequence, a reduction of earnings to a point which jeopardizes the
business and the shareholders' interests, and the resulting predicament in
which the policy unfairly places competitors.[8]

John Wanamaker of New York attacked the Macy policy from a
different angle.   In a series of advertisements published in the *New
York Times* in 1929, John Wanamaker's said:

Is it true, as someone tried to convince me, that another store consistently sells merchandise at least 6% less than in your store?   No!
Absolutely not!   Thinking men and women realize that this is manifestly
impossible.   As far back as 1868 John Wanamaker announced: "As to
our prices, we guarantee them 10 per cent lower than the lowest elsewhere,
or cash handed back if shown to be otherwise," but he later abandoned this
guarantee as competition made it impossible for any store to substantiate
such a claim.   Today all stores at times undersell each other.   We undersell

[7] Figures taken from *The Annalist*, p. 373, August 29, 1930.

[8] An attempt on the part of a book-publishing firm to protect its dealers
against Macy's price-cutting policy was blocked by the courts.   See *Bobbs
Merrill Company v. Straus*, 210 U. S. 339.

the market probably as often as, and maybe more than, we are undersold. And we don't lower quality to do it.[9]

In reference to the Macy argument that selling for cash enabled them to maintain their price policy, John Wanamaker called attention to the Macy policy of handling "store deposit accounts" for the convenience of customers who did not care to carry enough cash with them for possible purchases at the store; a check on this deposit account would be accepted as cash payment. The question whether a department store can justifiably engage in banking operations belongs properly to a preceding chapter.[10] Wanamaker's discussed the practical situation:

What is the difference between a store deposit account and a store charge account?

The only difference is that in a deposit account the store has the use of the money, while in a charge account the customer has it on deposit in his bank, usually at not less than 2 % interest until the bill is paid.

Furthermore, Wanamaker's pointed out, *selling* for cash was not essential to economies effected by a store in *paying* cash for goods:

The Wanamaker business pays cash for 90 % of its purchases . . . would pay cash for 100 % if it could get cash discounts on the remaining 10 %.

The Wanamaker advertisement also pointed out additional economies which it had in low rental (one-third of uptown rentals) and low overhead.

The situation rapidly developed beyond the individually competitive phases here indicated, however. A number of merchants doing business in the uptown department-store district protested to the New York Better Business Bureau against the advertising policies of Macy's. The Bureau, following its usual custom in such cases, sent shoppers to Macy's and to its competitors to buy identical goods and to compare the prices to see whether Macy's advertisements were accurate. *The Record*[11] lists 244 articles so bought from December, 1925, to April, 1926, for which Macy's prices were the same as, or higher than, elsewhere. Unfortunately these figures have little significance, for *The Record* does not disclose how many articles were purchased altogether, and does not indicate prominently how many articles Macy's handles. A Macy advertisement in the *New York Times*, May 3, 1930, stated that Macy's had made 356,986 shopping expeditions in 1929 to check its

[9] No. 9 of the 1929 series of advertisements, *New York Times.*

[10] See Chapter VII, especially p. 174. A further point to be noted in this connection is that Macy's purchase of Bamberger's involves them in operating a store which sells for credit, a difficulty which is typical of recent mergers.

[11] See *The Record*, published by the Better Business Bureau of New York City, June, 10, 1926.

prices with those of competitors, and found Macy's prices to be at least 6% less in 91% of these cases. The figures do show, however, that Macy's advertised assertions were not absolutely accurate; the Bureau claimed that the discrepancy was sufficient to warrant calling these assertions "misleading."

The Bureau suggested to Macy's that, instead of asserting that their prices were 6% less than competitors, Macy's insert a phrase such as "aims to" or "proposes to"—qualifying their broad and absolute claim. Macy's earlier replies to the Bureau took the form of announcing price modifications on the articles reported by the Bureau to be selling at prices which did not conform to the advertised policy. The Bureau pointed out that it was not their function to assist Macy's to maintain their policy, but to see that their advertising was strictly accurate; and reported that a re-shopping of the 244 articles disclosed that:

61 articles were out of stock at Macy's or at competitors and could not therefore be compared.

29 articles had been repriced by Macy's so as to conform to their advertised policy.

6 articles were lower in price at Macy's but not to the extent of 6%.

148 articles continued to be, at Macy's, the same in price or higher than prices at Macy's competitors.

Unfortunately there developed a difference, between the management and the president of the Bureau, as regards the exact policy and suggestions to be directed toward Macy's, a difference which appeared in the independent correspondence of these two officers of the Bureau with Macy's. And Macy's held that the Bureau was interfering unduly with their business management and resigned from the Bureau. These facts, although not pertinent to the case in hand, do throw light on the complexity of the situation. As regards the issue, however, it is significant that a Macy advertisement in the *New York Times*, January 25, 1930, complies with the original contention of the Bureau and with the rigid standards of accuracy in advertising, by stating the policy as follows:

It is Macy's policy to sell for cash only—and to endeavor to sell day by day for at least 6% less than the marked prices of those competitors who do not sell for cash only.

The caption of this advertisement is:

Remember, Macy's Men's Clothing aims to be at least 6% less twelve months out of the year!

* * * * * *

The Feldthal Distilling Company[12] was an Ohio corporation, located at Cincinnati; it manufactured and sold compressed yeast. For more

[12] Fictitious name.   I F. T. C. D. 119.

than one year prior to April, 1918, it sold compressed yeast to operative bakers on the basis of a schedule of prices which varied solely with reference to the amount of yeast purchased. Bakers using under 25 pounds per week were charged 25 to 25½ cents per pound; with increasing quantities purchased, the price was successively reduced. Bakers using 200 to 300 pounds per week were charged 18 to 19 cents per pound, while those using 500 pounds or more were charged 16 cents per pound. A few customers who used from 4,000 to 12,000 pounds per week received discounts of from 2% to 5% of this price. These figures applied to the territory of the United States east of the Rocky Mountains.

Owing to competition in various localities, the Feldthal Company deviated at times from such basic prices in order to retain the patronage of customers. By reducing its prices to them it met the prices of its competitors in that field. Where even such reductions in price did not result in retaining the business of such customers, the Feldthal Company reduced its prices still further to a point below that offered to customers by their competitors.

In a number of cases where customers, as the result of the lower and reduced prices of competitors, abandoned their contracts entered into with the Feldthal Company to purchase yeast, the Feldthal Company still further reduced its prices to such customers in order to regain their business.

Indirect Forms of Price-cutting

The following situations provide a basis for considering various phases of the problem of indirect forms of price-cutting.

The Serl Baking Company[13] was a New York corporation with its main factory located in New York City. It was one of the largest manufacturers and sellers of bread and cake in the United States, its branches being located in various other states. Its financial resources were large.

In May, 1917, the Serl Company conducted a "free-bread campaign," daily giving to the purchasers of its bread an additional quantity equal to the amount daily bought and paid for. The purpose and effect of this policy was to stifle and suppress competition. In addition, bakery products were sold at a price less than the cost of production.

* * * * * *

The United States Hortmann Machinery Corporation[14] was organized in January, 1922, in Delaware with the purpose of conducting its business in New York City. This corporation took over the business of the United States Hortmann Machine Company which had been

[13] Fictitious name. I F. T. C. D. 388.
[14] Fictitious name. V F. T. C. D. 439. See also VI F. T. C. D. 290.

organized in 1913, and which, previous to January, 1922, had been manufacturing and selling 85% of the garment-pressing machines in the United States.

The terms of sale offered by the Hortmann Company to the purchasers of its machines were in part as follows: payment could be made by cash or by notes. In the latter case the title and ownership of the machines by contract remained with the company until complete payment had been made.

This company had since May, 1921, employed the following methods of competition.

1. Espionage among competitors in order to discover sources of supply and the names of customers.

2. Offering inducements to purchasers of competitors' machines already installed to breach their contracts and to install the machines of the Hortmann Company.

In order to carry out this second method the Hortmann Company allowed such purchasers to count as part payment on the Hortmann machines such sums of money as had already been paid on contracts with Hortmann's competitors. Hortmann also furnished such purchasers with the services of attorneys to defend them in the courts, and aided them in the framing of letters that were to be sent to the competitors whose contracts were being breached.

The Hortmann Company ceased to exist in January, 1922, but the same officers organized the Hortmann Corporation at that time and the corporation continued the company's practices.

* * * * * *

The Brarker Company[15] was an Illinois corporation located at Chicago. For the four years just prior to 1918 it was engaged in the manufacture and sale of horse-clipping and sheep-clipping machines and parts. It sold its products to 493 out of 603 jobbers and wholesalers in the United States.

In 1918 the Brarker Company sent a letter to its customers in which the following appeared:

We respectfully advise that on shipments made during the year beginning August 1, we will pay the premium named below on your paid purchases of our horse-clipping machines and sheep-shearing machines and the parts thereof providing you shall have complied with the conditions named below. The continuation of all business relations is not dependent upon your complying with the conditions named below, but your right to receive the premium is dependent upon your strict compliance with those conditions. Whether you win the premium or not is therefore wholly optional with you.

One of the conditions named in this premium offer was as follows:

[15] Fictitious name.   I F. T. C. D. 181.

That during neither of the periods of six months named below you shall have bought, sold, received or quoted either directly or indirectly any horse-clipping machines, sheep-shearing machines or parts thereof made by any other manufacturers.

The premium offered customers consisted of a payment of 7% in cash on all paid purchases during the specified six-months' period, such payments to be made on January 15 and June 15 of each year. The Brarker Company, during a period of several years, paid out in premiums cash amounting approximately to $50,000.

* * * * * *

The Legana Signal Oil Company[16] was a Pennsylvania corporation intimately related with the Legana Oil Company, engaged in the manufacture and sale of lubricating oils, and with the Signal Oil Company, engaged in the manufacture and sale of signal and valve oils. The Legana Signal Oil Company sold its products to railroads which operated approximately 74% of the mileage in the United States.

During a period of four years prior to 1920 the Legana Signal Oil Company contracted with these railroads for the sale of all lubricating oils, greases, compounds and signal oils. The railroads in their turn agreed to purchase all such commodities from the Legana Signal Oil Company, the contracts consisting of uniform printed forms containing the following statement:

The Legana Signal Oil Company agrees that should a reduction be made to any other railroad in the invoice prices named in this contract for the same oils or greases during the period governed by this contract, the second party (the railroad company) hereto is to receive the benefit of a like reduction for the remaining period of this contract.

In certain of these contracts special forms were added differing in certain particulars from the general standard established. The Legana Signal Oil Company guaranteed to the railroads so contracting a certain maximum price or cost per 1,000 miles of operation of locomotives, passenger cars and freight cars respectively. These guaranteed costs, which were dependent on the purchase by the railroads of all the commodities from the Legana Signal Oil Company, were not uniform. The oil company agreed to refund to certain railroad companies the difference if any between the total cost of lubricating and other oils at the uniform invoice prices and the total guaranteed cost. The payment of these refunds by the Legana Signal Oil Company resulted in varied costs to the railroads.

The quantity of lubricating oils used varied per thousand miles for different railroads. But the refund arrangement, in the Legana Signal Oil Company's contract, resulted in a cost to certain railroads not only

[16] Fictitious name. II F. T. C. D. 446.

of less than the invoice price but even of less than the cost to other roads consuming an equal or smaller quantity per thousand miles.   Furthermore, the Legana Signal Oil Company agreed with some roads that any saving of oil cost in one class of equipment—locomotive, passenger cars, or freight cars—should be set off against the excess costs in others.

In many of these contracts it was expressly provided that in case the actual cost of the uniform invoice prices should fall below a certain figure termed the "measure figure"—usually the actual cost at invoice prices—the guaranteed cost specified in the contracts should be further reduced upon a sliding scale, usually measured by one-half the difference between the measured figure and the actual cost.   The ratio between the guaranteed figure and the measure figure substantially varied in the case of different railroad companies.

Cash discounts or trade discounts for quantity purchases are not to be confused with price-cutting.   The Feldthal case shows, however, how easily the two practices merge into each other. Where the trade discount is tied up with an exclusive contract, the problem becomes more complex, as is shown by the Brarker and Legana cases.   If the Brarker Company's offer of a trade discount actually prevented them from making a satisfactory profit when all of their customers complied with the requirements, then the Brarker Company was engaging in a trade-discount policy which bordered on unjustifiable price-cutting.   If the Brarker Company expected some customers to fail to comply with the conditions for obtaining the discount, and therefore expected these extraordinary profits to compensate it for such discounts as it finally did pay, then a degree of uncertainty and discrimination entered the situation which would make the practice questionable. Only the keeping of accurate records could determine the ratio of fulfilled to unfulfilled contracts, and the determination of this ratio was essential to the adoption of the Brarker policy.

The Hortmann case more clearly presents the possibility of self-delusion, although an examination of the figures of the company alone could determine whether the policy could be justified.   The trading-in of old used cars on the purchase price of new automobiles is a similar case in point, much greater, however, in magnitude.   The problem is not so much: How is the purchaser or consumer affected?   As a rule he is immediately and temporarily benefited by a lower price.   The question is: Can any field of business activity afford to let some merchants cut prices, directly or indirectly, ignorantly or with studied purpose, to such an extent as to make it impossible for others in the same field further to sell at a reasonable profit? Until the percentage of business failures ceases to be as high as it has been, the presumption is that many good and efficient men are forced out of business. And too many price-cutters persist in business, because of factors other than their own efficiency, to warrant the conclusion that their survival or relative staying quality is a function of their business efficiency.

Disguised Forms of Price-cutting

In the following two cases, trade discounts—or price-cutting, as they may be—were disguised under the form of selling or leasing equipment at less than cost. Although the form of the practice differs, the substance remains the same.

The H. C. Kannenberg Company[17] was located in Baltimore and for six years prior to 1914 had been engaged in the buying and selling of coffee, tea, cocoa, and sugar. It loaned coffee urns to proprietors of cafés and restaurants in various states upon the expressed or implied condition, without consideration, that these proprietors would purchase approximately all supplies of coffee from the Kannenberg Company.

The title to the urns remained throughout with the Kannenberg Company. Where the proprietor of a restaurant failed to pay his bills or purchased his supplies elsewhere, the Kannenberg Company reserved the right to repossess itself of the urns. The proprietors who used these urns agreed to pay the Kannenberg Company the cost of replacing damaged or broken parts and of all necessary repairs.

* * * * * *

The Rubel Oil Company[18] was an Ohio corporation located at Cleveland. It refined crude petroleum and bought and sold refined oil and gasoline. The Rubel Oil Company also loaned and leased oil pumps and other devices for filling stations. These pumps and devices, which the Rubel Oil Company did not manufacture, were leased for the purpose of containing, storing, and vending its own products exclusively. The rental or lease charge provided for in such contracts was a nominal sum which did not afford the Rubel Oil Company a reasonable profit. No other consideration was involved.

A large majority of the retailers and distributors to whom the Rubel Company sold oil and gasoline required and used only a single pump outfit. Many of the competitors of the Rubel Company were not engaged in selling or leasing pumps or devices and, as a result, they lost

[17] Fictitious name. II F. T. C. D. 399, 403, 407.
[18] Fictitious name. III F. T. C. 68.

a number of their customers because of the practices introduced by the Rubel Company. A small number of the retail dealers, to whom the Rubel Company leased its pumps and devices, as a matter of fact handled similar products of the Rubel Company's competitors.

The matter of leasing equipment at less than cost became such a disturbing factor in the gas and oil supply field, that several cases were called to the attention of the Federal Trade Commission and "cease and desist" orders obtained.[19] The Commission based its action on the ground that the practice tended toward monopoly, citing a part of Section 3 of the Clayton Act: "It shall be unlawful for any person engaged in commerce . . . to lease . . . machinery . . . or other commodities . . . for use . . . on the condition . . . that the lessee . . . shall not use or deal in the goods . . . of a competitor . . . of the lessee, . . . where the effect of such lease . . . may be to substantially lessen competition or tend to create a monopoly in any line of commerce."[20] Several of these cases were carried to the courts, which were quick to point out that there was "no contract, agreement or understanding by which any retailer is prevented from selling any brand of oil, and he can own and lease as many pumps as he likes or can use."[21] This legal point is wholly different, however, from the problem we are discussing, which is the practice of price-cutting by direct or by indirect methods. But the substance of the case, dealt with in a particular way by the law, affords the material for illustrating and analyzing the business problem.

This the court sensed in its statement of the facts:

Every pumping station is an advertisement; each bears the name of the oil producer whose gasoline is supplied therefrom, if the retailer honestly observes his bargain. (The court later recognized the unfairness and dishonesty of giving out from a pump bearing one brand another maker's products.) The system is a great convenience to the public; it has increased enormously the ease with which motor drivers may obtain "gas" even in remote and thinly settled districts. It is the only method known or suggested, of keeping before the consuming public the oil manufacturer's trademark, and it has largely succeeded the system of distributing oil in barrels, which barrels bore the maker's trade-mark and were practically loaned to the vendees, to be returned empty.

[19] II, F. T. C. D. 26, 46, 127, 346; III, 68, 77, 78, 86 (the last citation includes 13 cases).

[20] 38 Stat. 731.

[21] *Standard Oil Company v. Federal Trade Commission*, 273 Fed. 478, 481.

The choice between owning and leasing pumps depends upon the extent of the retailer's business and the amount of his capital. The majority of small dealers have small capital and therefore lease rather than buy. It is perfectly possible to buy from the same manufacturers who supply to the oil dealers the pumps leased by the latter. The competition between the various oil-selling persons and corporations is and has been very keen; each is desirous of extending the sale of its own brand, and the system of leased pumps, each bearing the trade-mark or trade name of its lessor, is regarded by many, though not all, wholesalers as a profitable form of advertisement.[22]

This last statement gives the nub of the business situation. The zeal of the vendor has produced a highly competitive situation in which he indirectly cuts his prices. If price-cutting be classed with such practices, how far can it go without passing from the inevitable requirements of a healthy competitive situation to one in which some vendors set a pace which cannot be followed by the prudent and the intelligent? The problem is not easily solved; it is frequently not even known to exist. The purpose of introducing the preceding cases is to present concrete illustrations of situations on the borderline—the more obvious cases arising, for example, in "cut-rate" drug stores and the like, are not mentioned—in order that a distinction may be made between justifiable and unjustifiable practices.

In the Sinclair case,[23] the court held to the basic principle that "the price which one may put upon that which he has to sell or lease is a matter wholly his own." The court saw that the Commission deemed the real trouble to be "that the monetary considerations received by the vendor did not represent reasonable returns upon the investment in such devices and equipment . . . ," but held that there was nothing in the law "which indicates that it is illegal for one competitor to do that which is beyond the financial ability of another competitor." The question that next arises, however, involves two additional points: Is it unfair from a *business* point of view for one competitor to do that which is beyond *his own* financial ability if he knew the facts?

In partial justification of its view, the court described competition in a way which is worthy of repetition:

[22] *Ibid.*, p. 480. This opinion was accepted in similar cases, *Canfield Oil Company v. F. T. C.*, 274 Fed. 571, and *Sinclair Refining Company v. F. T. C.*, 276 Fed. 686.

[23] 276 Fed. 686, *cit. supra.*

Competition is not an unmixed good. It is a battle for something that only one can get; one competitor must necessarily lose. The weapons in competition are various. Superior energy, more extensive advertising, better articles, better terms as to time of delivery, etc. Expense attending the use of any weapon, the foolishness of it, the fact that a method is uneconomical, or that the competitor cannot meet any method or scheme of competition because it will be ruinous to him to do so, have not ever been held unfair. Such things are a part of the strife inherent in competition . . . The vendor said: Here is a container and a pump; you may take and use them for the storage and pumping of gasoline bought from us; if you wish to use them otherwise, you may and must buy them.

In kind, that is nothing more than loaning a barrel with a faucet in it. The fact that the tank and pump are much more expensive does not make the transaction different nor unfair. If that is not true, then the law must mean that the Commission is set as a watch on competitors, with the duty and the power to judge what is too fast a pace for some and to compel others to slow up; in other words, to destroy all competition except that which is easy. We are of opinion that Congress did not intend to bestow any such power, and that it did not intend to do more than to eliminate the almost infinite variety of fraudulent practices from business in interstate commerce.[24]

No one can take exception to this strictly legal point of view. The argument, however, is directed solely against governmental or legal control of the situation. A separate issue arises if we ask: Should business control the situation? A part of the problem consists in the extension of all sorts of services to customers beyond the particular functions which a business is primarily intended to perform, "services" that range all the way from the broadcasting of musical programs by rug merchants to the giving of free legal advice by banks. This problem has already been discussed.[25] The problem which concerns us here is the indirect factor of price-cutting, in the form of services at less than cost. We have seen concretely what the problem is, and we have seen what the attitude of the law is. What does business have to say on the matter? The following is significant of the situation.

The Grocery Trade Conference at Chicago, October 24, 1928, was attended by over 500 representatives of retail and whole-sale-grocery stores and grocery-specialty manufacturers. This conference adopted eighteen resolutions as the basis of trade practices to be submitted to the Federal Trade Commission in an attempt to do away with unfair methods of doing business.

[24] *Ibid.*, p. 688.
[25] See Chapter VII.

Of these eighteen resolutions, the following six dealt with the problem of price-cutting:

1. Terms of sale shall be open and strictly adhered to; secret rebates or secret concessions or secret allowances of any kind are unfair methods of business; as is also price discrimination that is uneconomic or unjustly discriminatory.

2. Free deals, operating to induce merchants to purchase beyond their economic sales requirements, automatically reduce values . . . Those which are uneconomic or unjustly discriminatory are unfair methods of business.

3. Offering premiums, gifts or prizes by the use of any scheme which involves the elements of chance, misrepresentation, or fraud, is against the trade and public interest.

5. Selling an article at or below delivered cost, except on special occasions for recognized economic reasons, is an unfair method of business.

14. Any deviation from the original agreement with respect to discount for cash terms is an unfair method of business.

17. Any diversion of brokerage resulting in uneconomic or unjust price discrimination is an unfair method of business.

Although the heads of a number of chain stores were present at the meeting to represent their national association, they did not vote affirmatively on the proposals adopted at the conference. They felt that "they were not closely enough in touch with the discussions and did not have sufficient command of the opinion of their trade, especially in view of the very recent formation of their association, immediately to give full approval to the resolutions." After the formal action by the conference, however, the chain-store leaders approached the representatives of the Federal Trade Commission and the committee that had prepared the resolutions and gave assurances of their full spirit of cooperation.

This situation must be read in the light of the fact that distribution and marketing in groceries, as in other trades, are undergoing revolutionary changes; and the trade-practice conference referred to was motivated in part by the desire of some grocers of the old order to protect their *status* against the vigorous encroachments of the mail-order house and chain store. But their proposals must be regarded as a business point of view, as opposed to the legal and to other business points of view. The strength of the conference point of view lies in the questions which are implied throughout the problem: Who pays the bill? Does he know it? Can he be expected to know it? If the ultimate purchaser does pay the bill, he certainly does not know it, but he may receive services that justify his paying the bill. If the dealer pays the bill, in the form of added prices to the wholesaler, the whole argument of the court is unsound; especially if the dealer faces smaller sales as the result of passing the added price on to the consumer, for then we revert to the question as to whether the consumer gets in full what he pays for. If the dealer's competitor pays the bill through lost sales, there has been no net gain to society and there may be losses concealed in view of the preceding considerations. If the manufacturer or his competitors pay the bill, then the trade is saddled with an additional cost and if this cost is passed on to the consumer, we are where we were before; if it is not passed on, then we have a rational explanation of the reason why the grocery trade-practice conference tried to rid itself of the situation. The likelihood is that most businesses engaging in direct or indirect price-cutting are deluding themselves into the mistaken belief that they can pass the resulting cost on to someone else.

The situation calls for extreme wariness on the part of a competitor. The following situation, which is of international interest, narrows the situation considerably and enables one to see that the incidence of a policy analogous to price-cutting may be in an unexpected quarter.

The Hay-Pauncefote Treaty was entered into by the British and American Governments in 1901. This treaty, among other matters, contained a renunciation of any rights which the British Government might have to any part of the Panama Canal Zone, but stipulated that the United States Government should not discriminate in rates charged vessels using the Canal which it was contemplating constructing at that time.

After the Canal had been built, the Congress of the United States was debating a bill which provided that all vessels owned by American citizens or corporations be allowed to use the Canal free of toll-charge. The Ambassador of the British Government represented to the United States Government that the proposed legislation might jeopardize the rights of the British Government and its citizens as defined in the Hay-Pauncefote Treaty.

The British Ambassador asserted that if the proposed legislation went into effect, any attempt on the part of the Government of the United States to operate the Canal with a profit might lead the United

States Government to expect that profit to consist in the difference between actual receipts and expenditures. The British Government expressed itself as satisfied with any arrangement whereby the United States Government remitted to the American users of the Panama Canal the whole or any part of the schedule of tolls. But it insisted that the Hay-Pauncefote Treaty implied the right of the British Government to such a system of accounting as would calculate a reasonable profit if all vessels using the Canal paid the same fees without discrimination. It asserted that the United States Government was prevented by the Treaty from increasing the charges on foreign vessels to an extent necessary to effect an actual profit, while allowing American vessels to use the Canal at reduced rates or free of toll-charges, by regarding such profit as the difference between actual receipts and expenditures.

A very common form of indirect price-cutting consists in the giving of prizes with commodities purchased. In the following case, the objection of the Federal Trade Commission was not to the prizes as such but to their unequal value and to their distribution by lot or chance. The prevalence of such practices in business may become an incubus—as, *e.g.*, in New Orleans, where it was termed "lagniappe"—as insidious and subtle as a similar form of commercial bribery.

The Universal Mercantile Company[26] was an Iowa corporation located at Sioux City and engaged in the roasting and selling of coffee.

The Universal Company gave and offered to customers and prospective customers, as an inducement to buy their products, papers, coupons, or certificates redeemable in prizes or premiums. These prizes or premiums were of unequal value and their distribution was determined by chance or lot.

Each 50-pound lot of coffee, consisting of one-pound packages, contained a coupon in each of 45 packages calling for a bar of candy valued at 10 cents; coupons in each of two packages calling for one package of jell powder valued at 10 cents; coupons in each of two packages calling for one can of baking powder valued at 25 cents; and one package contained a coupon calling for a four-pound package of pancake flour valued at 35 cents. These coupons were redeemed by the merchants in the goods specified and then were sent in to the Universal Company to be redeemed in cash.

The giving of prizes or premiums can be justified only with difficulty. Certainly someone must pay for the premium. If the merchant actually does pay for the premium, he is cutting prices on his goods and thereby afflicting the trade with ruinous

[26] Fictitious name. III F. T. C. D. 60 (1920).

competition. If he is not actually paying for the premium, he is lowering the quality of goods, in which case he again introduces an unfair element into business and misrepresents his goods to his customers. Perhaps the customer should be more intelligent than to think he can have something for nothing, but the task of educating the public beyond a certain minimum operation of the rule of *caveat emptor* is an impossible task. A much more practicable scheme would be to teach the more limited number of merchants in a trade to avoid suicidal trade policies.

The most recent form of premium sales is that of giving shares of stock away free under the ostensible plan of selling stock and giving away merchandise. The following letter is a case of this sort:

NEMCO

Boston, Mass.

From the Sanitary
Daylight Plant of the
World's Finest Ginger Ales:

Dear Friend:

You use Ginger Ale. Everyone does. It is a healthful, thirst-quenching beverage. Thousands of customers have told us that our products are second to none, for taste and purity.

Therefore our business has steadily grown—and we are in a position where user-shareholder advertising should be our best means of even faster advancement, with its accompanying profits. Briefly, here is our plan:

We ask you to purchase one share (at one dollar) of our Fully-Participating Preferred Stock, and we will *give* you absolutely free, delivery charges paid by us, *ten* bottles of our Ginger Ale (five bottles of Golden and five bottles of Pale Dry), and two bottles of our Citrate of Magnesia (acknowledged by thousands as the very finest and most pleasant to take). (Total retail value, $2.50.)

After trying our products, should you not feel satisfied in *every* way, your dollar will be returned *immediately*, without question.

Isn't that fair? Just enclose a dollar bill, money order or check to the order of the New England Magnesia Corporation in the enclosed envelope. No stamp is necessary as the postage will be paid by us.

Very sincerely yours,

NEW ENGLAND MAGNESIA CORPORATION

(Signed) M. W. Robinson

President

In some cases these "combination stock-merchandise" sales are nothing but ruses to obtain a "sucker list" for further exploiting; the share of stock is used as an entering wedge for the unloading of a lot of worthless stock on the unsuspecting "investor." The Universal Locktip Company and Page and Shaw have resorted to this method of selling stock and merchandise. In the latter case a company with an established reputation for the excellent quality of its goods has permitted its name to be used for wholly indefensible financial manipulations that were the inevitable aftermath of a concealed form of price-cutting. Where the situation does not involve fraud and misrepresentation, as it usually does, it implies an insidious form of price-cutting that presents a major trade problem. The only business methods of meeting the problem are to stoop to the same type of practice, or by concerted trade efforts to eliminate it from the trade.

Whatever may be said in general of the price-cutting activities of sellers, applies with equal force to the purchasing of commodities by businesses at prices that are above the market price or above a price established by competitive bidding. A company which purchases its raw materials by offering unusual price inducements is to be placed in the same category as the company which sells in the same manner. The problem assumes particular importance when the policies of the purchasing department are determined or modified appreciably by considerations advanced by the sales department. Frequently the difficulty is concealed by the complex circumstances attending reciprocity buying.

Overbidding in Purchasing

The Union Rendering Company[27] was one of a number of corporations organized and doing business in the neighborhood of Philadelphia, engaged in the purchasing and refining of animal fats and in the selling of the resulting products. For a number of years prior to September, 1915, the individuals connected with these corporations had been holding meetings in Philadelphia for the purpose of fixing and maintaining prices to be paid butchers for fats, suet, and similar materials. They also agreed upon the various divisions of territory in which there would be no competition in the purchase of raw materials. These corporations then refused to accept customers from each other's territory and they succeeded in maintaining practically the same prices for the various materials purchased. The general effect of such agreements was to keep down the price of raw materials.

In 1912 the Burne Company[28] was organized as a corporation in New Jersey with its principal factory and place of business at Trenton. The president of this company was a member of a firm of hide dealers in

[27] Fictitious name. III F. T. C. D. 284.
[28] Fictitious name.

Philadelphia.   The company carried on a business of rendering fats, bones, suet and kindred materials, securing its raw materials from butcher shops located in Trenton and surrounding New Jersey territories.   In September, 1915, the Burne Company decided to increase its volume of raw materials by sending a wagon into Philadelphia, to purchase from butcher shops located there.   They thereby succeeded in acquiring some 70 new customers.

The corporations above mentioned then held a meeting and decided to unite their efforts against the Burne Company to compel it to cease buying in the Philadelphia market.   After the Burne Company had refused their request, they organized a corporation called the Union Rendering Company with a capital stock of $10,000.   An equal amount of this stock was subscribed for by each of four of the above-mentioned corporations.   One other corporation did not subscribe to any stock, but agreed to pay one-fifth of any loss accruing to the Union Rendering Company, provided that the amount did not exceed $2,000.   The officials of this Union Rendering Company were officers of the various rendering corporations.

After attempting once more unsuccessfully to dissuade the Burne Company from entering the Philadelphia market, and after trying without success to purchase a controlling interest in the Burne Company, the Union Rendering Company began purchasing materials in Trenton with the aid of a former employee of the Burne Company. Other customers were secured in the period following until in December, 1916, the owners of the Burne Company were forced to sell their stock because of continued losses.   The materials purchased by the Union Rendering Company were sold to its member corporations at auctions at prices in excess of those prevailing in Philadelphia.

Similar tactics were employed by the Union Company against the Falave Company,[29] a large part of the stock in which was held by stockholders of the Burne Company.   These tactics ceased after the stockholders had sold their holdings in the Burne Company and had paid the Union Company $5,000 for a horse and wagon.

When the Burne Company was sold it was purchased by Patrick Casey[29] who thereupon was approached by members of the Union Company and offered $35,000 in cash and the exclusive privilege to the Trenton territory in return for an agreement to remain away from the Philadelphia market.   Upon Casey's refusal the Union Rendering Company raised prices in Philadelphia, causing a loss of $30,000 to the Burne Company in the five months following December 1, 1916.   Following this experience, Casey sold his stock in the Burne Company.

The Federal Trade Commission ordered the Union Rendering Company to "cease and desist" its price tactics, and this view

[29] Fictitious name.

would be generally accepted. We have become so accustomed to viewing any combination of dealers to control prices as a menace, that we do not distinguish between those which are unwarranted or even vicious and those which may be justified by their insistence on stabilized fair prices. In the Union Rendering Company case, the fact that a loss was sustained in the competitive purchasing operations, afforded circumstantial evidence that the prices offered by its competitors had been too high. Regardless of this fact, it cannot be emphasized too strongly that concerted efforts at stabilizing prices at a fair level are ethically justifiable; and that the unethical phases of concerted efforts abnormally to raise selling prices or to lower buying prices include the evil effects on the trade itself, and not only the unfairness to the customer or supplier of goods.

Reciprocity Buying

The following case illustrates the practice of "reciprocity," the purchasing of goods from a customer of one's own company, a situation in which the possibility of an insidious form of paying more than the market price is apparent.

The purchasing agent of the Herkimer Steel Company,[30] in 1922, received a requisition from the superintendent of the company's Smithtown plant for 10 3-ton trucks to be used for the transportation of employees from the plant to the town. In accordance with the usual procedure, the purchasing agent sent out requests for quotations on these trucks to 15 leading manufacturers. The following quotations of prices and deliveries were received:

Company[31]	Price f.o.b. Smithtown plant	Time of delivery
Burroughs Company	$39,500	3 weeks
Bonner Company	41,000	2 weeks
Burwell Company	43,250	1 week
Cutler Company	38,500	2 weeks
Weyburn Company	40,750	4 weeks
Bliss Company	37,400	6 weeks
Stabler Company	42,000	4 weeks
Finder Company	46,500	5 weeks
Humphreys Company	39,500	4 weeks
Heddon Company	38,000	2 weeks

[30] Fictitious name. III *Harvard Business Reports* 360.
[31] Fictitious names.

Since the time of delivery was of secondary importance, provided the trucks could be obtained within a month, the decision turned on relative prices and quality. Each of these manufacturers had a reputation for making good trucks—some, of course, better than others —but the purchasing agent largely had eliminated the question of quality in selecting the companies to which requests for quotations had been sent.

In determining where to place the order, the purchasing agent's first step was to eliminate from consideration all quotations over $40,000. The quotation of the Bliss Company, although lowest in price, was unsatisfactory, because the purchasing agent had learned that after a recent change in management in the plant the quality of that company's trucks had been lowered; the company also was unable to give prompt delivery. Of the four companies remaining, there seemed to be little choice except on price quotations. All four, in the opinion of the Herkimer Steel Company's engineers, would furnish trucks that would give satisfaction. Because of higher prices, the Burroughs Company and the Humphreys Company were not considered further.

The decision of the purchasing agent then rested between the purchase of Cutler and Heddon trucks. The Herkimer Steel Company had in operation at one of its other plants a fleet of 15 Heddon trucks which had been in service 3 years. The Herkimer sales manager had sent a memorandum to the purchasing agent to the effect that the Cutler Company recently had placed a large order for steel and the day before had written to the sales manager saying that it understood that the Herkimer Steel Company was in the market for trucks and hoped that the Cutler bid would be given careful consideration. The sales manager requested that, if it were possible, the order be placed with the Cutler Company, for he was desirous of cementing the relations between this new customer and the Herkimer Steel Company. The purchasing agent never had bought Cutler trucks but knew from their reputation that in quality they were equal to Heddon trucks.

It had been the policy of the Herkimer Steel Company to have the purchasing and sales departments work in close cooperation. Whenever the sales department obtained a large order, the purchasing department was notified so that it might have this additional information to use when placing orders; and whenever the purchasing department placed an order, the sales department was notified so that it might use this as a further argument in making sales. Although the Heddon Company had made the lowest bid, it had bought no steel from the Herkimer Steel Company for five years.

The purchasing agent of the Herkimer Steel Company had to decide whether to give the order for the 10 trucks to the Cutler Company, despite the price differential of $500, or to the Heddon Company.

On the forms on which another steel manufacturer, the Madison Tube and Sheet Company,[32] sent out requests for quotations, the following statement was made:

It is understood that all material manufactured by ourselves or any of our allied companies must be bought from said companies for this work and prices obtained from the nearest district sales office. Alternative bids may be submitted based on material obtained elsewhere.

The following clause was incorporated in the order blank used by the Madison Tube and Sheet Company:

In accepting this contract the contractor agrees to specify Madison Tube and Sheet Company materials where possible.

The commentary on this case presents the argument against reciprocity.

Inasmuch as the company was operating a fleet of 15 Heddon trucks at one of its plants, some slight gain might have been expected, perhaps, in purchasing the same make of trucks for the Smithtown plant. The advantages of standardizing such accessory equipment between plants, however, were less than the gains from standardization at a single plant. Even though a plan of standardization of accessory equipment throughout the company's various plants were adopted, moreover, the standard selected necessarily would be subject to change when circumstances warranted it, and the situation presented in this case might have been occasion for changing to Cutler trucks as standard equipment. The date when the fleet of Heddon trucks would have to be replaced was approaching. Under these circumstances, the fact that the company previously had purchased Heddon trucks for another plant was not to control the decision. The purchasing agent, according to the case, was convinced that the two makes of truck were of equal quality. The problem thus resolved itself into one of reciprocity in purchasing at a price differential.

The Heddon Company offered the lower price. The Cutler Company was a customer. The steel company naturally desired to retain the favor of all its customers, and the differential involved in this transaction was small, less than 1½% of the price of the trucks. Therein lay the strength of the case for reciprocity in purchasing in this instance. The question was one, however, which should have been looked at from the standpoint of general policy. If reciprocity with the Cutler Company were to have been practiced at a differential of 1½%, then the same practice should have been followed in making other purchases, perhaps at higher differentials. The effect of that policy would have been to increase the Herkimer Steel Company's cost of production. The effect was likely to become cumulative, with a tendency for the sellers to take advantage of their preferred positions.

The Herkimer Steel Company would have expected to receive reciprocal treatment, of course, in selling to customers from which it bought equipment or materials at price differentials. It was not in that direction that the

[32] Fictitious name.

most serious objection to the policy was to be found.   The chief snag was the fact that the company had many potential customers from whom it could not make reciprocal purchases.   To these customers, it would have been necessary to charge higher prices, because of the higher costs incurred through differential reciprocity, or the Herkimer Steel Company would have had to sacrifice profits.   Sooner or later the prosperity of the steel company would have suffered.   Hence reciprocity in purchasing at a price differential was unsound economically and also would have encouraged laxity in business standards.[33]

A considerable part of this argument, however, has to do not with the case in hand but with further extensions of the policy. If it be granted that the possible extensions of the policy are to be condemned, this does not necessarily condemn reciprocity in this particular case. The danger lies, as the commentator points out, in increasing production costs either unduly or unconsciously. Therefore every case should be decided only after an accurate estimate has been made of the actual costs and advantages of the alternatives to the company. The Herkimer case does not present enough facts upon which to base a decision: the total amount of sales to the Cutler Company are not stated, nor is there an estimate of the profits of that business, and it would be very difficult to estimate the future advantages or disadvantages of a reciprocity policy to the Herkimer Steel Company. But where such facts are available, it may be that a restricted policy of reciprocity could be shown to have its advantages.

The principle underlying reciprocity can be defended. This principle is that profits must be calculated from two points of view: from that of the whole of the company's business and from that of the various branches of the company, and that, in case there is a conflict between the two, the major consideration is that the company as a whole shall do a satisfactorily profitable business. In most cases the profitable management of the separate branches will contribute to that major purpose. But it frequently happens that some parts of a business cannot achieve even the average profitable return without paradoxically harming the business as a whole, and sometimes branches must be conducted at a loss, temporarily and especially in their earlier development. Examples may be cited from railroad rate-making, combination orders, differential trade discounts, and service departments of banks. Certainly, many businesses delude

[33] 3 H.B.R. 362.

themselves by employing such methods, and this may be true in the case of reciprocity; and the purchasing department of any business should not become a mere appendage or tool to sales promotion. But such questions are to be decided by a careful examination of the figures and facts and not merely on general *a priori* principles.

The most recent development in the problem of reciprocity buying has been the investigation of the Interstate Commerce Commission in Chicago to find out to what extent railroad purchases are made to attract traffic, and to what extent shippers decide on traffic routes to force purchases. The Federal Trade Commission had previously conducted hearings on the "reciprocal" buying of a draft gear in which Swift and Company were interested; these hearings related to the plea of the packers that their Consent Decree be vacated. The traffic manager of Swift and Company stated in a letter dated January 16, 1929, to the Lehigh Valley Railroad[34] that Swift and Company "expected" the carriers whom they "patronized liberally to reciprocate by using the gear and centering devices." The Lehigh Valley Railroad bought 200 of the gears. The Interstate Commerce Commission's investigations have disclosed that the practice has been so prevalent as to constitute a trade custom, and railroad men have testified that reciprocal buying has been increasing markedly the last five years. The evils and abuses range from small favors "to friends" to veritable racketeering.

As has been stated in commenting on the Herkimer case, it is conceivable that reciprocity buying can be justified if the quality of the goods is satisfactory and if the price differential does not unduly invade the total net profit to the business. But in the gear-sales case, mechanical officers of the railroads rated this particular draft gear as of questionable merit and generally recommended against it.[35] Furthermore the evidence at the hearings disclosed that purchases by the railroads were controlled by an overweening desire to get more business or to retain what they had. In view of the relatively large capital investments of railroads, they are faced with a much more acute problem than are other businesses with a lower fixed overhead, because additional railroad business does not entail corresponding overhead expenses. But even so, the indiscriminate participation in reciprocity buying practically amounts to a slashing of rates

[34] See *Railway Age*, October 4, 11, 18, and 25, and November 1, 1930.
[35] See *Business Week*, October 18, 1930.

that is not only in violation of published schedules but also of sound business methods. And it cost the railroads from 25% to 35% of their meat bills for dining-car service, long-term unfavorable contracts for ice and correspondingly high prices for other supplies.

The case cannot, of course, be decided here accurately or adequately, because of the absence of sufficiently correct and detailed information. But it can be asserted with confidence that the decision of the railroads to engage in the practice is equally unfounded. Other companies than Swift and Company have been involved: Armour and Company, Grigsby-Grunow Company and the Forsyth Company. Other commodities involved in the investigation are: oil, lumber, paint, ice, coal, milk, and cement. Amid all this diversity and prevalence of the practice, the outstanding effect of reciprocity buying seems to be the absence of any net increase in railroad traffic. The gain of one road is solely at the expense of another, an acquisitive and appropriative type of business activity that can be condemned on the same grounds as can gambling; a net balance of gains and losses, with merely a reapportionment of money or goods among the participating individuals, is not worth the time and energy expended. As the colored woman remarked to her son as he finished riding on the merry-go-round: "You've been travelin' for ten minutes, but where's you been?"

In conclusion, the thesis of this chapter is that, in price-cutting as in price discriminations, there is a point beyond which the desire to sell goods leads to unjustifiable trade practices. Price-cutting usually accompanies an ignorance of costs that puts a premium on poor management and handicaps the intelligent merchant who knows when he is not making a fair profit: to continue in business a man must sell goods, and to sell goods a man must compete with the low-price appeals of his competitors. The inevitable results are the elimination or qualification of services that good business can well afford to perform, the deterioration of the quality of goods supplied, and the bankruptcy of companies which may as a matter of fact be sounder than some of their ignorant competitors who may for a while survive.

It matters little whether price-cutting or overbidding for supplies is direct or is achieved through such indirect methods as discounts, selling or leasing equipment at less than cost, or prizes and premiums. And such false price-cutting methods as "mark-down" sales, combination orders, "reciprocity" or "credit terms," face the dilemma of being unfair on the face of things, or of being as little justified as the honest but misguided cut-rate policies themselves. To sell only at a profit, to refuse to sell below cost, "takes the strain off the balance sheet and throws it to the cost sheet" where it belongs.[36]

The logical conclusion of the opposition here disclosed to price-cutting would seem superficially to be a policy of price fixing. This latter, however, is not the only alternative; another and more justifiable remedy would be increased individual business intelligence. To begin with, price-fixing agreements are contrary to law, and Attorney General Mitchell has stated in no uncertain terms[37] that the law would be enforced. President Hoover probably expressed a maxim when he said to the German Textile Delegation, in 1927: "The establishment of international price-fixing machinery would never be considered by the people of the United States . . . The United States is more pledged to open competition than any other nation in the world. It has become a social as well as an economic principle with us." This statement applies unquestionably to general legal or governmental policies. Of equal importance is the factor of business policy. Price-fixing agreements are constantly subject to breach, it being doubtful whether the ability to maintain them is as great today as it was when the Sherman Law was enacted; the Law has unquestionably contributed to the breaking-up of a growing business phenomenon. But even granted the immediate efficacy of such agreements—and the practice is still indulged in to a considerable extent in spite of the law[38]—the ultimate economic benefits are questionable; the encouragement to substitutes and to purchase other commodities sometimes is fatal to an entire industry. The establishment of this fact would require evidence that is not available and that could not be presented here if it were; but the statement of the situation regarding price-fixing agreements is necessary to complete the discussion of the policy and ethics of price-cutting.

[36] Quoted from *Weekly Bulletin*, Ernst and Ernst, July 2, 1929.

[37] Annual meeting, American Bar Association, October 25, 1929.

[38] Statement of L. F. Boffey, former secretary, National Association of Purchasing Agents and author of *Scientific Purchasing*, reported in *New York Times*, c. August 10, 1929.

CHAPTER XIII

COMPETITIVE BIDS AND COMMERCIAL BRIBERY

Are competitive bids ever justified? Business answers "Yes," the professions answer "No." A professional man, conspicuously the lawyer or doctor, cannot maintain his professional standing by engaging in competitive bidding for clients or patients; and those who do try to compete with others in fees and charges, rather than in the quality of services rendered, bring the profession as well as themselves into disrepute. It will be the purpose of the first part of this chapter to question the ethical justification of competitive bidding.

The main attack on this problem will be made on the ground that the abuses of competitive bidding are such as to warrant condemning the practice; and the major abuse will be discovered to be the failure of so-called "competitive bidding" to be what it purports to be. A proper definition of the term might denote practices which are ethically justifiable, but it would at the same time limit very much the denotation of the term. The field of engineering practice affords abundant illustrations of the problem, not only because "competitive" bidding is generally practiced therein but also because engineering is on the borderline between business and the professions.

The Professional Attitude toward Competitive Bids

Is the engineer a professional man or a business man, and can he in either capacity justifiably engage in competitive bidding? These two questions are so interrelated as almost to answer one another. The answer to both must therefore be sought elsewhere, and is to be found in the question: Does the engineer furnish goods or services to his customers or clients? The difficulty with engineering is that its functions are ambiguous. The architect and the consulting engineer have attempted to define their functions so as to be free from all interests in materials and supplies, and these men have come nearest the professional ideal of eliminating competitive bids by establishing a fixed minimum schedule of charges.

340

D. B. Steinman, a former president of the American Association of Engineers, has for years taken the position that a minimum-fee schedule is necessary to the professional self-respect of engineers and to their economic stability. The hard facts are, however, that in an actual case, in reply to an invitation to submit bids for drawing the plans and specifications for an $800,-000 bridge and for supervising the work, three bids, for $40,000, $10,000, and $1,500 respectively were submitted. The lowest bid was rejected because the company did not satisfy the county board in regard to credentials and bonds; but the highest bid was rejected because it involved a greater expense than the board felt like meeting. And yet this bid represented only 5% of the total cost, which is probably the minimum charge at which proper engineering services can be performed. It is difficult to determine whether the greater blame for such a situation attaches to the public, which is unwilling to pay adequate fees, or to the engineering firm which entered a bid of $10,000. Certainly the latter cannot call itself a professional organization; and, on the other hand, if this firm attempts to supply at all adequate services, it will discover that it is not a good business firm. The inability adequately to figure overhead and other expenses places most engineering firms beyond the pale of good business as well as of good professional conduct. And in the endeavor to meet such competitive conditions, most of the other professional engineers are seriously affected.

The only justification for a bid lower than a certain percentage, which can be figured to be necessary to the continued existence of an engineering firm, is the advertising value which a new firm derives from securing and completing a conspicuous job. This situation is really the heart of the professional difficulties of the engineer: the younger men are resorting to methods of obtaining work which the older men cannot afford to use unless they violate the best traditions of the profession. This means that strictly professional engineering societies must either be limited, as regards their membership, to a degree which will exclude most of the younger men; or they must recognize at least two sets of rules, one for the younger men and another for the older men. The difficulty arising from restricted membership is that it may, if carried too far, result in shifting the center of equilibrium from the older to the younger men by virtue of the sheer weight of numbers of the latter. This situation is becoming a serious problem in the medical profession, in which stricter standards have effected a decrease in the number of practitioners but have also encouraged an increase in the number of osteopaths and chiropractors.

The other alternative, of having at least two grades of membership in engineering societies, has virtues as well as defects. Analogies are not wanting. The American College of Physicians and Surgeons has a membership of 2,000 in contrast with the membership of 90,000 of the American Medical Association. The American Association of University Professors, in considering the ethical aspects of the resignation from a teaching position late in the year, has differentiated between those men who are assistant professors and of higher rank on the one hand, and those of lower rank on the other. In England the Association of Consulting Engineers has a much more restricted membership than any other engineering society, partly because of the peculiar functions of its members but also partly because of its rigorous standards. The possibility of differentiating those engineers who would refuse to submit competitive bids for services or who would maintain a minimum schedule, from those who would not, would shift the attention of engineering societies from technical to professional problems, a change which is probably impracticable.

The problem of competitive bids, therefore, as we have said, raises two questions. First, are they justified at all? And second, if so, under what conditions? The first question is answered differently by business and the professions. No profession can theoretically tolerate competitive bids, however much the principle may practically be violated by individual practitioners. For the objective of every profession and of every practitioner is the performance of the best possible professional services, and the basis for professional reputation and advancement is the quality of services rendered. Such an objective implies that professional competition should be based on quality of services, and such an objective and basis is incompatible with any competition based solely or largely on the amount of fees or charges.

Business has not gone so far as to eliminate competitive bids, because it deals largely in goods rather than in services. Indeed, the practice of employing competitive bids, in the strict sense of the term, is quite defensible in business, and affords one basis for distinguishing between business and the professions.   Bidding on securities and commodities on the exchanges, for example, makes possible an objective, fluid and accurate market price, which is essential to business stability.   Price is as important a consideration in business deals as is quality of goods, and competitive bids are as effective in checking the economic efficiency of the seller as they are in protecting the buyer against exorbitant charges.   It may be that a profession such as engineering finds it difficult to decide whether it ought to condemn or sanction competitive bidding.   But this is because the profession is ambiguous as regards its chief function: the handling of materials is integrally bound up with the rendering of strictly professional engineering services.   Where the latter are clearly defined, as among architects and consultants, competitive bidding is either condemned or raises very troublesome questions.

Competitive Bids in Business

Where, however, the major consideration is the supply of goods rather than services, as is the case in most business and many engineering transactions, competitive bids are generally resorted to.   But here we confront the second consideration raised above: If competitive bids are justified, under what conditions are they so?   Clearly, on the basis of accurate and detailed specifications and reasonably complete information. If bids are requested for construction work or for supplies, such bids as are submitted will not apply to the same thing if the bidder adds to or modifies the specifications or is given much discretion in regard to them.   The Salt Creek and Blampton cases, which follow, clearly illustrate this.   Furthermore, competitive bids imply secrecy and independence among the bidders.   If there is collusion among the latter,[1] or if the bids are disclosed by the receiving company to any one of the bidders, as in the Stockport case, then a different form or kind of competition has been introduced, of which the bidder should become highly suspicious.

The United States Government[2] called for bids for a contemplated five-year lease of what were known as the Salt Creek oil lands.   This

[1] An imposing set of cases was cited by Justice Taft in the Addyston case to show that agreements among bidders are fraudulent.   85 Fed. 271, 293 and 294.   See also 175 U. S. 211, 244.

[2] See *New York Times*, October 15–25, 1928.

land was owned by the Government, which proposed to lease for a short period the rights to the oil deposits which were known to exist in that district.

Six bids were received, the lease being awarded to the Sinclair Oil Company, the highest bidder. The bid of the Sinclair Oil Company had attached to it the proviso that the company be given an option to renew the lease for an additional five years after the expiration of the original five-year lease.

When the original lease expired, the Government allowed the Sinclair Oil Company to exercise its option and the lease was renewed. Six months later the Attorney General of the United States declared the renewal illegal.

* * * * * *

The British Government, in collaboration with the Blampton[3] harbor authorities, asked for bids on hoisting apparatus, including a number of heavy cranes, which was to be erected on the docks under construction in the harbor of Blampton. The notice for receiving bids stated the maximum load which the harbor authorities considered possible during the daily operations about the docks. The daily hoisting load varied from nothing at all up to this maximum amount. Firms which contemplated bidding were given considerable discretion in regard to the matter of placing the hoisting units and in regard to the number and size of such units as were to be erected.

Seven bids were submitted. The highest bid was made by the Genner[4] Company, a highly reputable engineering firm, which provided in its bid for hoisting apparatus of sufficient size to handle the full maximum load in a comparatively short period of time, two or three hours. The lowest bid was made by the Halstead[4] Company, which provided a smaller number of units but so arranged as to handle the maximum load over a period three times as long as that provided for by the Genner Company. The bid was awarded to the Halstead Company.

After the hoisting machinery had been installed, it was discovered to be insufficient to handle the peak load expeditiously, and additional apparatus had to be installed. The final cost to the Blampton harbor board was approximately equal to the original bid submitted by the Genner Company.

* * * * * *

The Council of the city of Stockport,[5] England, called for bids for the erection and equipment of an electric generating plant for the city. Among the bids received was one from a Swiss firm, whose tender was

[3] Fictitious name.
[4] Fictitious name.
[5] See *Manchester Guardian*, February 17, 1928.

33⅓ % lower than the lowest British bid. The Council decided to accept the Swiss bid and made arrangements to offer them the contract. The Borough Engineer, though convinced of the superiority of the British equipment, did not consider that it justified an addition of £18,000 to the price offered by the Swiss firm.

The British Manufacturers' Association protested strongly against the decision of the Council and one of the British firms which had made an original bid offered to undercut the previous lowest British tender by some £10,000. The Council of Stockport thereupon decided to give the British manufacturers a second chance of obtaining the contract by calling for new bids.

In the Salt Creek case the bidders were not bidding on the same thing. As some of the unsuccessful bidders pointed out, it was easily conceivable that the addition of the optional clause in the specifications might have elicited a bid higher than that of the Sinclair Oil Company. The conditions presented by the Blampton case, in which the vagueness of the specifications and the discretion allowed the bidders virtually destroy the competitive feature, have led the Association of Consulting Engineers of England to prepare standard Conditions of Contract for use of the members in connection with electrical and mechanical engineering contracts—a separate form being made out for export orders—and to urge upon the national and municipal governments the necessity and desirability of accurate and detailed specifications.

The Stockport case arose as the result of the efforts of British manufacturers and associations exclusively to control the home market. The alleged depressed condition of British trade has encouraged the slogan "Buy British Goods." The merits of this campaign are questionable but cannot be discussed here. The Stockport case was simply one symptom of the movement which appeared elsewhere in the protest against awarding large ship-building contracts to German firms. The action of the Stockport borough council in calling for new bids was an innovation in English practice, and was regarded by many as undermining the confidence in competitive bidding which has been successfully built up in England only after many years of strict observance of the spirit of the system.

It is unfair to carry an argument to its absurdity, but the Stockport case differs only in degree from one of the worst abuses in competitive bidding. This abuse, appallingly prevalent in America in purchasing municipal supplies, consists in opening the bids and then allowing a bidder whose figures are higher than the lowest figures an opportunity to revise his figures downward until they equal the lowest bid. The objection to this method is that the lowest bidder may easily have failed to take proper account of costs and it may entail inferior services especially of a younger and less experienced firm. To ask another bidder to meet the lowest figures jeopardizes the quality of the services to be rendered or unfairly places upon the bidder the task of supplying goods and services below cost or at an unfair profit. It is this practice which opens the way to commercial bribery, a festering sore in most of the dealings between engineers and municipalities.

A still more reprehensible practice which follows from competitive bidding consists in falsely stating to the lowest bidder that he was not the lowest bidder but that a downward revision of his bid would increase and perhaps even assure his chances of securing the bid. The following case is an exact description of such a performance.

The Heller Coal Company,[6] together with other coal companies, submitted a bid for supplying coal of specified quality and at specified delivery dates, to the Amworth Electric Light Company.[6] The amount involved was in the neighborhood of $300,000, and the bid of the Heller Coal Company was figured very closely to net the company a profit of 3% net after deducting all charges. The Heller Coal Company knew that the competition was keen and, after taking all things into consideration, decided to submit a figure which netted them less than their usual profit. The securing of the contract would give the Heller Coal Company its largest single piece of business.

John Heller,[6] the president of the company, was a personal friend of Henry Edelman,[6] purchasing agent for the Amworth Company.[6] Heller received a telephone call from Edelman to come to the latter's office, where Edelman informed Heller that he had the lowest bid but one, the lowest bid being submitted by a rival coal company, the Warsom Coal Company.[6] Edelman intimated to Heller that he would like to give the latter the contract, for personal reasons especially, but that the contract would go to the lowest bidder. "What did Warsom bid?" asked Heller. "Well," said Edelman, "that would be telling." At the same time Edelman wrote a figure on a piece of paper in a very ostentatious manner, said "Excuse me a minute, John," and on getting up from his desk to leave the room, let the piece of paper fall on the floor near Heller's chair. After Edelman left the room, Heller picked up the paper and discovered a figure which was lower than his bid, but on

[6] Fictitious name.

later analysis showed a net profit to his firm of 1%. After Edelman's return, the two men chatted a while and Heller left.

After returning to his office and figuring carefully, Heller called Edelman and offered to meet the Warsom figure. Heller received the contract.

Later Heller happened to meet Warsom and discovered that his original bid had been lower than Warsom's by $8,000. Further inquiry disclosed to Heller that his original bid had been lower than any other bidder that he was able to question regarding the matter.

The problem of finding an ethical justification for "competitive bids" thus resolves itself to a definition of the term. Certain prevalent practices closely identified with competitive bids cannot be tolerated by business men who wish to play fair; they simply represent the methods employed by the unscrupulous and overly zealous competitor. Furthermore, it is doubtful whether there is any such thing as competitive bidding except where tangible goods are to be supplied and where exact specifications are possible—as, *e.g.*, B.M.T. units in coal, or the standards now accepted in the cement industry. Otherwise, as in the case of price-cutting, real or false, successful competitive bidding usually results in a subsequent lowering of quality of product or of services below the standards originally intended by the parties to the contract.

Although it is not the purpose of this volume directly to include financial operations in the subject-matter to be studied from the point of view of Business Ethics, such operations can be studied, by way of analogy, as fruitfully as can professional practices. Competitive bidding is now the rule in the purchase of municipal bonds. The result is such a decrease in rate and in profit as to confront financial houses with the problem of weighing reduced earnings against the prestige accruing to the handling of what amount practically to guaranteed securities. Some houses have ceased to handle such securities; others continue to handle them in the face of their undesirability, and trust to the remaining business to offset the reduced earnings. Here again, as in the problem of price-cutting, the business loss seems to be compensated for by a corresponding public gain; in this case, in reduced financial charges on municipalities. But any such social advantage is neutralized by the fact that many sound investment houses have either withdrawn from the competitive purchasing of such securities or engage in the practice only exceptionally.

The relation which the financing house prefers is the professional relationship in which the client seeks the bank, rather than *vice versa*, and in which all the financing of a particular business unit is done through a single financial house. This would eliminate competitive bidding for securities in the initial stages of financing and until such a time as the security has become sufficiently "seasoned" to be safely listed on a stock exchange. To inquire into the merits of this problem is not within the province of this volume. For purposes of analogy, however, it may be pointed out as a case in point. The professional relations between a bank and its borrowing customer permit of potentially greater profits to the bank and of potentially greater services to the customer. Competitive bidding implies dealing "at arm's length," a situation which is not objectionable as such in business; but which does require extraordinary alertness on the part of the successful bidder to insure the minimum of fair profits, and, on the part of the buyer of goods or of funds, to insure quality of goods and services.

So closely is the nefarious practice of commercial bribery associated with the successful obtaining of a competitive bid that the two problems can be dealt with together. It is not the intention of this chapter to employ against price-cutting and competitive bidding the *argumentum ad absurdum*, but the reader may judge for himself how the three subjects, price-cutting, competitive bids and commercial bribery are related; and the extent to which they are related indicates to what extent any are to be condemned for entailing either or both of the other two.

Commercial Bribery

Excessive zeal and eagerness to enlarge sales have led some business men to engage in the questionable practice of commercial bribery. Inasmuch as the profit motive and the desire to "get the business" are justifiable in themselves, there are apologists for direct solicitation of a competitor's customers, extensive advertising, price inducements, and even false statements and commercial bribery. It is only by an examination of actual cases, however, that the line of ethical demarcation in such situations can be accurately judged. In the matter of commercial bribery, for example, it is possible to discover cases ranging from the most flagrant and direct forms, easily condemned, to subtle methods that may upon examination prove to be either harmless or all the more insidious because of their innocent appearance. Furthermore, only by a careful examination of cases is it possible to discover the incidence of any wrong or injury involved. It is not only the bribe-giver or the bribe-taker who pays the bill, economic and otherwise; frequently the major harm is to the competitor of either who desires to run his business fairly both as regards economic soundness and quality of goods and services; and society eventually pays the bill.

In England the situation has been met by an Act of Parliament, following upon the Report of the Special Committee of Secret Commissions of the London Chamber of Commerce in 1899.[7] The public support of this Act is intensified by the activities of the Bribery and Secret Commissions Prevention League, which is constantly on the alert to discover violations and to prosecute them in the courts. Germany and other continental countries similarly have leagues against bribery. There is no Federal law on the subject in the United States, only sixteen states have legislation on the subject, and in those few there is little evidence of enforcement except for five or six cases in the state of New York.[8] This difference between Europe and America may seem peculiar to those who think that America is generally over-legislated, but we are at present concerned with the facts rather than with explanations.

The situation as regards commercial bribery in England may be still further contrasted with that in the United States. One of the most prevalent forms of commercial bribery in England is connected with the purchasing of food by butlers and stewards of the wealthier families. The seasonal migrations of these families spread the practice over the whole of England, each new or temporary location becoming the center of a festering social-economic sore that spreads to all the servants and shopkeepers in the vicinity. On the other hand the national and municipal governments are singularly free from the types of petty and large

[7] Crew, A., *The Law Relating to Secret Commissions and Bribes.* London and New York: Isaac Pitman and Sons, Ltd., 1920.

[8] Stevens, W. H. S., "Some Economic Consequences of Commercial Bribery," VII *Harvard Business Review* 2, January, 1929, on which this chapter has drawn freely for a number of points. The first case in which a Federal court held that commercial bribery was an unfair trade practice, occurred October 16, 1929, *Grand Rapids Varnish Co. v. F. T. C.* The American Paint and Varnish Manufacturers Association and National Association of Purchasing Agents assisted the Government in this case.

graft so common in the United States.   True, the organ of the League[9] is continually printing cases of corruption of policemen, city magistrates, customs officers and the like, but these are practically all that occur and they are small indeed in comparison with conditions on this side of the water.   The situation as regards ordinary commercial transactions is as difficult to determine for one country as it is for the other.   In England, the practice of soliciting a bribe before an order is placed is known as "twisting"[10] and is as commonly practiced in some trades in England, notably in the marketing of coal, as it is in the United States.   The main distinction between the two countries lies, however, in the fact that in England legislative cognizance has been given to the situation, whereas in this country the Federal Trade Commission, an administrative body, has been practically the only governmental agency that has attempted to control the practice.

Professional Analogies

Inasmuch as this book is mainly concerned with the problem of business self-regulation, no proposal for legislative or judicial action in regard to commercial bribery will be considered.[11]   In order fully to understand the business situation, however, it may again be desirable to follow the method already relied upon elsewhere, namely, to see what experience some of the older professions have had in this matter.   The medical profession wrestled a long time with the analogous practice of "fee-splitting."   A general practitioner would advise a special type of treatment or a major surgical operation which he himself was incapable of performing.   He thereupon recommended a specialist.   Instead, however, of charging for such a service, analogous to the advice of an investment counsel, the doctor would expect his fee to come from the specialist to whom he recommended the patient.   The specialist, owing to the pyrotechnics usually accompanying a major operation, could usually charge the gaping patient enough to have a surplus which he would "split" with the general practitioner on the basis of a ratio that was mutually

[9] *Prevention of Bribery*, 22 Buckingham Gate, London, S. W. 1.

[10] In the United States this term is used to designate the substitution of one insurance policy for another in order to increase an agent's commission.

[11] The Hofstader-Moffat Commercial Bribery Bill of New York State went into effect September 1, 1930; it "puts teeth" into a former law by granting immunity to either party that turns state's evidence.

satisfactory to the doctors. This is one of the dark pages in the history of medical practice, and the eradication of the practice cost many a courageous doctor and teacher his professional head or reputation. In a number of states the local medical associations have succeeded in securing laws prohibiting the practice. It is doubtful, however, whether the enforcement or threat of enforcement of these laws has had as much effect in eliminating fee-splitting as has the attitude which developed in the profession and which gave rise not only to official condemnations in the Medical Code but also to combined and individual activities among the leaders of the profession against those who persisted in it.

The situation in medical practice is essentially the same as it is in business. No man can serve two masters. The doctor who accepted a split fee was unquestionably influenced as regards his advice by the relative generosity of various specialists. His service should have been concerned solely with the patient's welfare. It is true that few patients were willing to pay a fee commensurate with such valuable advisory service, but no amount of apologizing for the public will explain away the fact that the doctor who accepted a part of his pay from the fee-splitter was guilty of a violation of professional trust. And this condemnation of the more direct forms of the practice applies equally to the indirect methods; such as, for example, the general practitioner's perfunctory "assistance" at an operation. Where there is a possible basis for a division of fees, the doctor is obligated to disclose to the patient or to a relative or friend of the patient the exact nature of the arrangement.[12]

The following situation is a case in the field of teaching. The letter and the reply thereto, which are published without giving the names of the writers, show the importance of eternal vigilance if the practices of school teachers are to be kept on the highest ethical and professional plane.

Dear Sir: At first thought the proposition we are about to make to you may appear to be a fake, and especially under present doubtful business methods used by some. But we want to assure you that we are absolutely sincere in the matter and guarantee that we will carry out our agreement to the letter.

We are very anxious at this time to ascertain changes to be made in your school or those in your locality of which you may have knowledge; in the

---

[12] *Principles of Medical Ethics*, Chapter II, Article VI, Section 3. See also Chapter II, Article I, Section 5, which condemns rebates.

hope that we may recommend teachers who (*sic*) we know to be well qualified for the positions. We do not ask you to put forth effort in obtaining this information and imparting same to us gratis but will be very pleased to compensate you for same to the extent of $10 for each vacancy referred to us which we are enabled to fill. Needless to say we will put forth every effort to fill every vacancy of which we have knowledge and also that we are in a position to fill most any vacancy as our listings are great and will become more so as the present season comes to a close.

In furnishing this list kindly give us all qualifications obtainable along with salary same will pay and to whom application must be made.

We would like to have the pleasure of mailing you a check for at least $100. Will you cooperate with us in this matter?

Thanking you in advance and awaiting receipt of list of known or anticipated vacancies for 1928–29 we are, Yours very truly, ——— ———, Manager.

The superintendent of schools who received the letter sent the following reply:

Dear Sir: I have your letter offering me ten dollars for each vacancy of which I notify you and which we fill with your nominations.

If I knew of any way of having you prosecuted, I would gladly institute proceedings against you. In my opinion such practice is most damaging to the profession. I for one shall never betray the trust by using my office for personal profit in any such manner. Very truly, ——— ———, Superintendent of City Schools.

Commercial Bribery in Business

The most difficult problems of commercial bribery arise in connection with government contracts, especially those entered into by municipalities. So prevalent are certain types of such "graft" that some respectable firms do not make any attempt to secure the business of certain municipalities; one of the large steel companies in the country[13] began to make large-unit water pumps but found the situation so saturated with graft and corruption that they closed up that part of the business. In order that the reader may appreciate the situation, before going on with reading a description and analysis of specific cases, let him decide what he would do, for example, in case he were selling cotton waste, had secured an order of several carloads from a municipality after submitting a competitive bid, had shipped the waste, and then was told by his local agent in that municipality that the local fire chief had refused to accept the waste until he should receive in cash an amount which was approximately equal to 10% of the profit and threatened to report the waste as not

[13] The name cannot be disclosed.

coming up to specifications unless the required amount was forthcoming. Remember that the waste has already been shipped and that a refusal of the fire chief's demands would necessitate reselling or shipping charges back to the home plant. Whatever the right or wrong of the situation, the fact of the matter has been that, in situations of this sort, business men have submitted and paid the required sum. In many cases the act is not so bald and crude as this: "competitive bidding" is frequently substituted as a blind; it is, however, a farce, neither the reliability of the firm nor their compliance with specifications nor even the lowest bid determining its award.   The successful bidder is often the man who can assure the "proper" official or purchasing agent the "proper" bribe, and the vendor often is permitted to "pad" his bill sufficiently so as to relieve him of the obligation to pay the bribe.   The following case presents a concrete example of the situation.

The Hadel Manufacturing Company,[14] a Minnesota corporation located at Minneapolis, was engaged in the manufacture and sale of road machinery and similar products. A large part of such products were sold to municipal and county governments. The company did its dealings with firms or corporations which included one or more public officials among their members, and effected sales by paying commissions to these officials through a commission contract entered into for the sale of its products. Also, where the public officials of a community were engaged in the sale of machinery, the Hadel Company was in the habit of retaining such officials for the sale of its products in that community. The Hadel Company, by such means, was able to sell its product to the governing body of which the official was a member.

After a sale had been completed, the Hadel Company then paid the official the regular dealer's commission for such services. The duties of the official so retained were to purchase or recommend the purchase of road machinery offered for sale by the Hadel Manufacturing Company and its competitors. The effect of this practice was to secure for the Hadel Company a number of contracts for their machinery which they might not have obtained otherwise. The result was to cause Hadel's competitors to use similar practices in order to protect their trade and as a means of preventing Hadel from obtaining the business generally shared by them. In most cases, the commissions were paid directly to the officials as individuals, but in some cases these commissions were paid to their relatives or friends.

[14] Fictitious name.   V F. T. C. D. 77, 82, 86 (3 cases), 87; VI, 69.

The bribery of public officials is frequently condemned solely on the basis of breach of trust. This probably explains the inertia which generally characterizes the public attitude and that of business toward bribery. The individual citizen or buyer has come to look upon his government as he has come to look upon the large corporation: as an impersonal agency to which he owes no ethical obligations. This attitude is exhibited in various ways: people will lie about the contents of a mail package in order to save a few cents of postage and they will ride on a street-car or railway train without paying for the service if the conductor happens to overlook the matter. Similarly, the individual portion of the loss to the individual taxpayer in any single case of official bribery is generally regarded as of such a small amount as not to warrant the energy necessary to help eliminate the practice. Therefore, it is doubtful whether "civic consciousness" can be relied upon to control the bribing of public officials.

In the Hadel case, the cost of the practice undoubtedly fell on the community in the form of higher taxes. But a significant factor in the situation was that the chief conscious injury was felt by the competitors of the Hadel Company, who either faced a loss of business by refusing to bribe the officials, or were forced to meet the competition of the Hadel Company by engaging in similar practices. The former alternative is chosen by far more business firms than is generally recognized. Where the latter alternative is chosen and the public continues to pay the bill, the trade suffers morally from the prevalence of a disreputable practice, but it also suffers tangibly as the result of a general rise in the level of prices with no commensurate profit. When this situation becomes serious and is recognized to be such, the trade group is apt to assume its prerogatives in controlling the interests of the trade.

Most of the cases of public bribery involve large-sized units. This makes particularly difficult any attempt at control, not only because the size of the contract or unit makes bribery particularly tempting but also because each act of bribery is a separate act, continuity of practice not being necessary to effect the result.

The following case shows, however, that the size of the unit may be very small, and that the object and method of giving the bribe may vary considerably.

The General Distilling Company,[15] a Wisconsin corporation located in Milwaukee, was engaged in the manufacture and marketing of compressed yeast. For three years prior to 1918 this company systematically contributed sums of money amounting to several hundreds of dollars to the funds which were raised by numerous associations of operating bakers to defray the expenses of periodic conventions held in various parts of the United States. The purpose of the General Distilling Company was by such means to obtain and retain the patronage of the members of these associations.

The General Distilling Company also systematically furnished entertainment to the bakers and dealers attending these trade conventions, such entertainment consisting in the distribution and furnishing of cigars, drinks, meals, theatre tickets, auto rides, and other forms of amusement. The result was to induce purchasers and prospective purchasers to refrain from dealing with the competitors of the General Distilling Company.

The General Distilling Company, furthermore, systematically gave gratuities—liquors, cigars, meals, money, and other personal property—to bakers and dealers using yeast, including customers and prospective customers and their employees. The General Distilling Company also gave Christmas presents and special holiday presents of cigars, liquors, silverware, money, and other personal property to dealers and their employees, and also furnished them with theatre tickets, auto rides, and other forms of amusement.

The "cease and desist" order of the Federal Trade Commission included the item "entertainment at conventions" but did not apply to the contributions which the General Distilling Company made to the convention budget. In another similar case,[16] the following was added to the cease and desist order: "Provided, however, that nothing in this paragraph shall be construed to prevent respondent from making reasonable contributions to such associations for educational and scientific purposes as relate to the use of compressed yeast." One might think that a trade association would be more conscious of the factor of self-interest than a municipal government, so as to guard against the adverse interests represented by a company which, by making a donation, desires to make profitable sales. But this factor of conscious

---

[15] Fictitious name. I F. T. C. D. 88.

[16] I F. T. C. D. 119, 136. By October 31, 1930, the Federal Trade Commission had issued 188 orders to cease and desist from unfair methods of competition involving commercial bribery—Statement of Commissioner Ferguson, *Accuracy*, October 31, 1930.

self-interest in a trade group is still undifferentiated as regards the individual members. These members must have felt in some measure that they actually and eventually paid for this donation in increased prices. Whether they did or not, the chief harm fell on the competitors of the General Distilling Company. For if the buyers paid the bill, this must have been through higher prices than otherwise would have prevailed; hence a smaller amount of business. On the other hand, if the General Distilling Company paid the bill, the increased costs and smaller profits would set the standard for the trade. The latter part of the case involves practices which make the competitive situation more apparent. If the competitors all engaged in the same practice, the net effect would be an increased cost item which would become detrimental to the selling group in proportion as it became a fixed charge on the business.

Following a number of orders of the Federal Trade Commission in the paint and varnish industries, the members of the Paint Manufacturers' Association of the United States and the National Varnish Manufacturers' Association and nearly every other manufacturer of paint, varnish, and kindred products, have required their salesmen to sign an agreement not to pay gratuities and not to use expense money for such purposes. The signing of a similar agreement is a prerequisite to admission to either of these associations. The industry also began a vigorous campaign to eradicate the evil within its own field by the organization and maintenance of an Unfair Competition Bureau. They offered a cash reward of $1,000 for proof that any salesman in the industry was violating the agreement above referred to, and this offer was placed in the hands of over 3,000 foremen. Previous to this association activity, practically every member during the course of 30 years at one time or another had to pay bribes to hold old business or to obtain new business; and most members had the choice of doing as others did and "feeling like a crook" or refusing to do as others did and losing business "like a sucker." One large company reported that the elimination of bribery had reduced selling expenses from 16% in 1913–1916 to 10% in 1917–1920, while the Baeder Adamson Company[17] was enabled to make a reduction of five cents per pound on all deliveries of shellac subsequent to March, 1921. Where higher prices were not the result of commercial bribery, substitution of inferior goods

[17] See IV F. T. C. D. 129.

frequently resulted, or goods were wasted and materials deliberately damaged, destroyed or thrown away.

The prevalence of the practice furthermore has a profound influence on the wage situation. Where commercial bribery prevails, employees will be attracted sufficiently by the bonus to disregard an apparently low wage scale; in other words, the wage schedule will not be a true index of the actual wages received. Inasmuch as a highly competitive business must calculate its costs accurately, any indefinable wage item is apt to vitiate such calculations. Furthermore, published wage scales and wage comparisons cannot afford an adequate basis for humanitarian appeals on behalf of wage-earners so long as the practice of commercial bribery introduces a factor of from 10% to 20% of the scheduled wage. The problem becomes a real one when consideration is given to the advisability of increasing the salaries or wages of men who are engaged in a trade which is considering eliminating a prevalent and existing practice of commercial bribery. The additional income afforded by accepting bribes undoubtedly attracts men who may not remain in employment at the reduced scale; the business had been bearing the full wage cost and could afford to bear a part in direct increased wages, especially in view of the fact that the added sum now comes from the employer and not from someone with an opposing interest; it is beside the point to blame exclusively a particular group of men for a practice which the trade has encouraged by years of toleration; and any attempt to deal with the matter as if it affects only the ignorant laborer fails to note that exactly the same problem confronts a bank in which the senior officers are enabled to derive an income from sources other than the bank itself while they are supposed to be exclusively in the employ of the shareholders of the bank.

The following cases are still further illustrative of the practice of commercial bribery. They range all the way from extreme and direct forms of bribery to the subtler forms of "gifts" and "entertainment."

Throughout the United States there are certain commercial establishments selling lumber and building materials through the medium and by means of yards located in various cities. These establishments, usually referred to as "regular dealers," are to be distinguished from the so-called "catalogue and mail-order houses." The regular dealers usually sell lumber and building materials in the community where they are located, purchasing and supplying their materials from manufacturers and wholesalers.

The Herring-Dine Company[18] was an Iowa corporation located at Krebel[18] and engaged in the manufacture and sale of lumber and building materials in Nebraska and adjacent states. This company had no "yards" outside Krebel, but was in direct competition with the so-called "regular dealers" for at least two years preceding January, 1919. During that time the Herring-Dine Company offered to pay local contractors, builders, and carpenters a bonus or "commission," without the knowledge of the purchaser or consumer, as an inducement to influence contractors or builders to push or favor the sale of the Herring-Dine Company's lumber and building materials.

* * * * * *

The National Color and Chemical Company[19] was a Massachusetts corporation located at Boston and engaged in the manufacture and sale of dyestuffs, chemicals, soap, and kindred products. For more than one year prior to July, 1919, the National Color and Chemical Company gave to the employees of customers and prospective customers liquor, cigars, meals, valuable presents, and other personal property, provided them with entertainment, including theatre tickets, and presented them with sums of money. In most of these cases, it is not stated whether these practices were known to the employers and were accepted by them as a part of their trade relations, or whether these arrangements were secret. The purpose of these gifts to employees was to induce them to influence their employers to purchase the National products and to refrain from dealing with the competitors of the National Color and Chemical Company.

* * * * * *

The Printers Supply Company[20] was a New Jersey corporation located in New York City and engaged in manufacturing and selling rollers for printing presses and kindred products. As an inducement to influence customers and prospective customers to purchase their products and to refrain from purchasing from their competitors, the Printers Supply Company gave the employees of such customers and prospective customers, without consideration, gratuities consisting of liquor, cigars, meals, and theatre tickets. Furthermore, without the knowledge of the employers, the Printers Supply Company made loans of money to the employees of customers and prospective customers, which loans were not expected to be repaid and which were not repaid. These loans and gifts were offered to the employees as an inducement to

[18] Fictitious name.   I F. T. C. D. 316.   See also *ibid.*, I, 488; V, 177.
[19] Fictitious name.   II F. T. C. D. 71, 77 (9 cases), 78, 81 (5 cases), 82.
[20] Fictitious name.   I F. T. C. D. 240, 277; II, 102.

them to influence their employers to purchase the products of the Printers Supply Company.

* * * * * *

The Fillwood Company[21] was a Missouri corporation located at St. Louis. It sold and distributed a shellac substitute known as Fillwood. It gave to employees who used or directed the use of shellac, and who purchased or recommended the purchase of shellac to employers, gratuities in the form of liquor, cigars, meals, and other personal property, including cash payments, as inducements to recommend their goods. The Fillwood Company acted secretly and without the knowledge or consent of the employers. During the period from September, 1919, to January, 1920, approximately $7,000 was distributed by the Fillwood Company in this manner.

During a period of three years the Fillwood Company sold glue to an amount exceeding $30,000. The Fillwood Company paid employees a commission of 5 cents per pound for all glue which an employee succeeded in inducing his employer to purchase. The Fillwood Company was able to obtain a good quality of glue at that time for 25 cents per pound. It billed this glue to its customers at 33 cents per pound. At the same time other and inferior brands of glue were purchased at from 18 cents to 22 cents per pound, mingled with the superior grades, and shipped to customers, all, however, being billed at the same price of 33 cents per pound.

Whether the size or form of the gratuity effects a difference with which commercial bribery is to be viewed, has been considered by the courts. In one case,[22] the court held that "entertainment" was not objectionable but that money payments were. The court pointed out the analogy between "entertainment" and advertising expense, and held that the Federal Trade Commission has no more jurisdiction over such matters than it did over the securing of servants from competitors by paying them higher wages. From an ethical point of view, the latter is a begging of the question, as we shall see later. The practice of giving money bribes has been discovered to be especially prevalent in the sale of varnish, shellacs, and glue;[23] and of dyestuffs and soaps.[24] It is difficult to see how non-money forms of payment are any less reprehensible than the more obvious forms. A much more pertinent distinction could be made: namely, between gifts

[21] Fictitious name. IV F. T. C. D. 65.
[22] *New Jersey Asbestos Company v. F. T. C.*, 264 Fed. 509.
[23] I F. T. C. D. 138; IV, 108, 129.
[24] *Ibid.*, I, 480, 484; II, 82; III, 313, 418, 421, 425; IV, 69, 220, 230; VI, 180.

that are accepted secretly and without the employer's knowledge and those which are known to and sanctioned by him. Under such circumstances, money payments would probably be taboo, but it may easily be that the employer would give his consent to the acceptance of certain other gifts whereas even such a practice cannot be defended as good business.

The Treadwell Manufacturing Company[25] was an Illinois corporation located in Chicago and engaged in the manufacture and sale of candy and kindred products.

For two years prior to September, 1920, the Treadwell Company offered and gave valuable premiums and presents, consisting of watches and jewelry, to salesmen of merchants and jobbers who were handling the Treadwell products. These premiums and presents were offered as an inducement to salesmen to push the sales of Treadwell products in preference to similar products of its competitors.

In order to carry out the plan the Treadwell Company issued a catalogue labeled "Incentives to Success—Our Method of Showing Appreciation to Jobbers' Salesmen for Their Efforts in Our Behalf." In this catalogue was set out in detail the list of premiums offered to salesmen, together with the scheme and plan to further the sale of Treadwell products to the exclusion of the products of its competitors.

No notice was given to the retail merchants or customers who purchased from these jobbers that the Treadwell Company was offering such premiums to jobbers' salesmen; nor did these merchants or customers know of the practice, although the jobbers were notified.

* * * * * *

The Interstate Bedding Manufacturing Company[26] was a Utah corporation located at Salt Lake City. It was engaged in the manufacture and sale of mattresses, bedding, couches, and similar products. For three years prior to December, 1919, the Interstate Company, in order to stimulate sales, gave and offered to employees and salesmen of dealers who handled the products of the Interstate Bedding Manufacturing Company and of their competitors, cash bonuses and prizes for "pushing" the Interstate products.

The point in these last two cases is that the knowledge of an employer, as to the acceptance by his employees of gratuities from other companies, may not be the only requisite for sanctioning the practice. Many a bad business practice is *known* to an employer without being recognized as such or as being detrimental to his business. Furthermore, it is not fair to the other com-

---

[25] Fictitious name.   III F. T. C. D. 25.
[26] Fictitious name.   II F. T. C. D. 185.

panies from which he buys or to his customers—whether these be consumers or merchants—to let an outsider pay a part of the wages of his employees. For in such a case the salesman has advisory functions; and he becomes involved in "double-" or even "triple-agency," for the buyer is entitled to know if the salesman represents interests other than his employer's. The following court opinion is typical of the narrow point of view adopted by the law toward such situations. The decision is given at length in order to present the point of view which is opposed to the writer's. It is nominally a judicial opinion, but in reality is a special plea for the restricted point of view which may be law but which the broader business point of view cannot afford to follow.

The rights which it is urged have been affected are the rights of other manufacturers and also the rights of the public. Unless that which petitioner did fraudulently affected some competition in which either or both were interested, then the order to cease and desist was improvidently entered. It is conceded that no manufacturer had any right to interfere in the merchant's business. It is equally true that, when any manufacturer sold to the merchant, he met, overcame, and ended any competition in which he had any interest. His interest in those goods was terminated, and when they again entered the channels of trade they entered as the goods of a new owner, along with the other goods owned by him. The new owner's problems were with other retail dealers, handling oftentimes goods identical in make and kind with his own, and competing for the favor of the buying public. It needs no discussion to show that that was wholly his competition, to be met in his own way, by his own methods, and in it the manufacturer had no part. Any plan or scheme to advance one kind of goods and to keep back another is a matter wholly and absolutely under the control of the merchant in meeting his problems in his competition, and does not constitute a fraud, nor is it unfair to anyone who does not own the goods.

Likewise the public, if it has an interest in competition has such interest only in the competition between different merchants. It has no right to demand for itself that a merchant shall set up a competition in his own house and between his own goods. The channels of trade that must be kept open for the manufacturer are those that run between him and other manufacturers, and necessarily end when he has sold. The channels of trade that must be kept open for the buying public do not run through the retailer's store, but do run between the different stores seeking the favor of the buying public.

We are of opinion that there can be nothing in the contention that some special interest in a clerk which is undisclosed to the buying public represents an unfair method of competition, because of an incentive and opportunity of the clerk to deceive the public. Undoubtedly the clerk, with the master's consent, may discriminate between the master's goods. All of the buying public, with at least ordinary knowledge and intelligence, knows that a salesman is representing the merchant's interest, and that every merchant may and very frequently does have reason for pushing the sale of one kind of goods more than another; but, if that were not true it would be little less than an absurdity to say that a salesman, who often is the merchant himself, in order to escape the charge of unfairness, must disclose to every would-be buyer his interest in the transaction in hand.   That is just what the contention, if allowed, would lead to.

Nor is it conceived that there is any danger from falsehood or misrepresentation.   A salesman, with the master's consent, may discriminate all he pleases between the goods he has to sell.   Neither a salesman having a special interest in one article, where he has many to sell, nor a salesman with a single article to sell, has any right to indulge in falsehood and misrepresentation; but there is here no evidence of falsehood or misrepresentation.

The order to cease and desist is annulled and set aside.[27]

Incidence of the Practice

The complete ramifications of commercial bribery are difficult to follow, but like many other questionable practices the incidence of the injury may be in the least expected places.   The broader phases of the situation are well illustrated in the following case. Ship chandlery and the purchase of supplies for vessels have always been a means for demanding bribes.   During 1920 and 1921, when competition for furnishing repairs and supplies became exceedingly keen, due to the slump in shipping activity, no less than 65 cases of commercial bribery were handled by the Federal Trade Commission.[28]   The following case is typical.

William Sparson[29] was an individual trader doing business in New Orleans under the trade name of Latian Machinery Works.[29]   This was a general machine-repairing plant, and Sparson was engaged in repairing and furnishing repair parts to vessels entering the port of New Orleans.   His employees boarded the vessels to install materials and repair parts and to make repairs on board as they were required by the representatives and employees of the owners of the vessels.

During the year 1920, in order to secure the business of making repairs on the vessels of a certain steamship company, Sparson entered into an agreement and understanding with the boat engineer of this line of ships to pay the latter a gratuity of 10% in cash of the total amount of all the repair jobs which were assigned to Sparson.   From June 22 to October 13 the total repair bills of this one company amounted to about $8,000.   Sparson admitted that he gave the boat

[27] *Kinney-Rome Company v. F. T. C.*, 275 Fed. 665, 669, 670.
[28] See especially Vols. III and IV, F. T. C. D.
[29] Fictitious name.   IV F. T. C. D. 97 (1921).

engineer $400 and that he intended giving the latter about $400 more as soon as the repair bill was fully paid. Sparson also gave $15 to a scaler who brought him a repair job. These gratuities were added to the steamship company's bill but did not appear on Sparson's books as such, and they were given without the knowledge and consent of the owners of the steamship lines or the employers of the boat engineer.

In some cases where no previous arrangements with the owners of the ships had been made, the captain of the ship himself was solicited, and the gratuities included not only a percentage of the purchases paid in cash but also cigars, meals, entertainments, and valuable gifts. Approximately 90% of the business, however, was initiated with the owners of ships in foreign countries through contracts made by Sparson's agents. These "contracts" were virtually "options" given to the ship owners to purchase supplies at a given rate. Upon the arrival of the ship in port and after these purchasing arrangements had been made, the captain would visit Sparson's supply store, order supplies, and then after delivery check over the bill and receive his commission. Inasmuch as the captains were clothed with a considerable amount of discretion as to the port in which they secured their supplies, where previous contracts had not been made, Sparson declared that a failure on his part to pay a commission in such cases would result in the ordering of repairs and parts and the purchasing of supplies in other ports.

Aside from the effects of this practice on ship owners and their competitors and on the competitors of Sparson, there is the far-reaching effect on port developments. Most of the cases of bribery reported to the Federal Trade Commission originated in New York City, Mobile, New Orleans, and Galveston; others were reported from Norfolk, Charleston, Savannah, Pensacola, and Port Arthur. The Commission took cognizance of the fact that the ports which did not engage in the practice were obviously at a disadvantage which they could overcome only by engaging in the practice. This situation is closely analogous to the Rochester Clothing case [30] in which a trade practice, that appeared on the surface to affect only certain obvious persons, as a matter of fact involved the valuable trade reputation and rights of a large community. This factor, involving subtle but nevertheless considerable business values, has not been recognized by the courts, and it is interesting to note that no cases subsequent to those published in Volume III have been dealt with from this angle by the Commission. The District Court for the eastern district of Virginia did uphold the Commission in an order prohibiting the

[30] See Chapter XV, p. 410.

continuance of "gratuities or allowances by a merchant to an employee or agent of the customer, without the knowledge or consent of the employer" and declaring such a practice to be unfair.[31]

Thus far, business ethics has been regarded as a matter of self-determination, the minimum standards being general trade practices. This point of view implies a variety of intrinsic ethical standards varying with different kinds of business. The question now arises: Are there any extrinsic standards to which business conduct could be directed? The practice of commercial bribery affords a good instance of the problem. In the New Jersey Asbestos case, the court said:

> We take judicial notice of the fact that the method of entertainment found (by the Federal Trade Commission) to be unfair has been an incident of business from time immemorial. It is recognized by the regulations covering the assessment of income tax.[32]

If standard business practices are to determine principles of business ethics, and if certain forms of commercial bribery are discovered to be prevalent, is commercial bribery therefore ethically justifiable?

We think not, for the following reasons. In the first place, certain trade groups themselves have condemned the practice at the same time that they have recognized its prevalence. In October, 1928, the American Wholesale Grocers' Association proposed the following resolution for the consideration of the trade-practice conference of the grocery trade, held at Chicago:

> That the giving or offering to give to a dealer's salesman, with or without the consent of the employer, of commissions, premiums, bonuses, or reward or gratuity of any character by any trader whose commodities are bought and sold or dealt in by such dealer, or the acceptance thereof by any dealer or dealer's salesmen, is an unfair trade practice.

Although this suggested provision was not accepted, the conference did adopt a resolution providing "that commercial bribery, whatever the bribe, however it is given, and whether given with or without the consent of the employer, is an unfair method of business."

In the second place, the fact that commercial bribery is not only prevalent but is also tolerated and defended in a trade, as, for example, in shipping supplies, subjects that trade to a

[31] *T. C. Hurst and Son v. F. T. C.*, 268 Fed. 874.
[32] 264 Fed. 509, 510.

comparison with other trades which have attempted definitely to eradicate the practice, as, for example, the paint and varnish trade. A pluralistic view of business ethics, by virtue of which the presumption is that each trade can set its own standards, is not defensible *per se;* it must constantly be subjected to the test of the comparative experience of various trades. The presumption that a trade practice is justifiable, if it is prevalent in that trade, is only a presumption; the experience of other trades may overthrow that presumption and present a trade, which persists in such a practice, with the burden of positively justifying it. This burden increases in proportion to the number of other trades which condemn the practice.

Finally, a practice such as commercial bribery may be condemned in spite of the fact that it may be prevalent. This attitude represents a transition from the ethical to the moral point of view, but the ethical factors are nevertheless present to the degree that the situation is analyzed into its factors and consequents. Thus, the Commercial Standards Council,[33] the aim of which is to "foster and maintain higher standards in business," took as its immediate and specific aim "the elimination of the corrupt and growing practice of commercial bribery." The prominent part taken by the National Association of Purchasing Agents[34] in this organization, as well as by the American Society of Sales Executives, gives added weight to its sweeping condemnation of commercial bribery:

The secret giving of commissions, money, or other things of value to employees of customers, for the purpose of influencing their buying powers, is a dangerous evil more widespread than is acknowledged and one which is unquestionably growing.

It is a festering sore in the commercial body of the nation; its extinction calls for a drastic use of the knife. If allowed to proceed unchecked and uncontrolled, it destroys legitimate competition, and cancels the reward of merit; it frustrates the rightful development of true progress; it defeats honest advertising and salesmanship, and stands convicted as a moral obliquity which, by the very secrecy with which it is employed, stigmatizes itself as without justification or excuse. So long as this practice continues, the hope of honest conditions of trade remains a chimerical dream. It continues to exist only because there are still some people who excuse its existence on the ground that it is employed by others, or who are too timid to take a firm stand on the side of right and justice.

[33] Located at 19 Park Place, New York.
[34] This organization is now sponsoring a Federal bill directed against commercial bribery.

It adds millions of dollars to the cost of distribution. It seriously impairs the effectiveness of advertising, prevents efficient purchasing and penalizes honest salesmanship. It is an insidious influence that makes a man, otherwise scrupulously conscientious, blind to his inmost convictions and causes him to yield to competitive pressure in the belief that to resist would court disaster.

Apart from the moral aspects involved in this commercial evil, which few will dispute, there are certain considerations of an essentially commercial character which should receive attention. A firm which gives or permits bribes should not be regarded as a good commercial risk. If the bribe is given by its employees with its knowledge and consent, it indicates a moral deficiency which does not entitle it to the confidence of those whose business it is to extend credit, while if the bribe is given by its employees without its knowledge, it indicates an incomplete oversight and control of its own activities.

Commercial bribery, no matter what form it takes, must be paid for either by the purchaser in higher prices, which may be unknown to him and which certainly decrease the volume of possible sales; or it is paid for by the vendor in increased costs and therefore decreased profits, both of which are indications of unsound business methods.

The question may arise as to the ethical blame attaching to the parties that engage in commercial bribery. The English Anti-bribery Act makes both the giver and the receiver equally culpable; but the advisability of such arrangements has been questioned, especially because collusion, which is involved, may be carried to the extent of neither party divulging any information voluntarily or under pressure. The suggestion has been made[35] that the giver of the bribe be exempt from punishment if he informs against the taker of the bribe. "As a rule, he (the informer) takes no personal benefit, and is engaged in advancing the interests of his principal. The contract is gained for his employer by the only means by which it is securable and, as often as not, under virtual compulsion. On the other hand, the recipient, apart from being usually the instigator, has betrayed the interests of his defrauded employer. Both are morally culpable, but in very different degrees, and one only—the recipient— has been disloyal to his trust."

Opposed to this position is the practical fact that the giving or offering of bribes is easier to prove than the acceptance of bribes, the ratio of convictions in England being about 5 to 1. The

[35] *News Sheet*, Bribery and Secret Commissions Prevention League, Inc., October, 1929.

immunity clause in the acts of states of the United States applies to the person giving the information, whether giver or receiver. Furthermore, to regard bribery solely as a personal problem is to view it inadequately: it is an act in which persons participate, but often as agents of others, and in all cases a transaction results. It is the successful consummation of this transaction which is central to the problem, the means and persons engaged being incidental to it. Therefore, the act should be condemned, with such provisions as will sanction the condemnation.

E. UNFAIR TRADE METHODS

The discussion of the ethics of price policies has probably approached more nearly the prevalent conceptions of the problems of business ethics than has any of the preceding sections of this volume. The reason for this is clear. Prevalent conceptions of business ethics are built upon common prejudices, one of the most deep-seated of which is the consumer-purchaser interest in a low price. But prevalent conceptions are no more to be uncritically accepted as final estimates regarding business ethics than are current trade practices. Both offer a factual presumption, but both challenge intelligent criticism. The valid nub of the general hostility to high prices or to large profits is aesthetic, and not ethical, in character. It is based on a general attitude which is closely akin to the Greek conception of "good"; in which "kalos" was joined with "agathos," and to which was opposed "hybris," the Greek concept of extremes, of "too much." Excessive prices and exaggerated profits, from this point of view, become symptoms of an undue eagerness to appropriate economic goods and values, a lack of self-restraint which often amounts to indescribably bad taste.

It is this element of business activity which becomes particularly prominent in the following three chapters. Trade piracy and appropriations, which border on stealing; misrepresentations bordering on lying; espionage, criticisms of competitors, and other vexatious tactics, which border on spying, slander, and abuse; constitute, in the minds of many people, the sum-total of problems in business ethics. Not only would such an attitude identify a study of business ethics with a catalog of business scandals, but it would analogously lead one to develop the field of aesthetics by an exclusive study of ugliness. The study of business abuses has a definitive part in the study of business ethics. The truth of Shaftesbury's position, however, that good morals may be identified with good manners, lies in the fact that his exaggerated emphasis of a factor was perhaps necessary to effect its proper consideration in a balanced view.

Plato observed, in the *Republic,* that the physical and social health of a commonwealth was indicated by the absence of doctors and lawyers. His suggestion, however, that these men be eliminated from the state was an obvious absurdity. It might have been more to the point to suggest that doctors and lawyers be prevented from writing a philosophy of society, because their experiences are liable to give them a perverted view of the whole of social realities as well as of values. The study of pathological cases has contributed vitally to the understanding of normal behavior, but the balanced view of any society is approximated more nearly by the student of normal behavior than by the pathologist.

It is necessary at this point, therefore, to call attention to the main strategy of this volume before settling down to a tactical study of certain particular problems. Price policies, as well as the more acutely unfair business methods about to be described, are the symptoms of deeper and broader structural conditions and dynamic movements underlying and constituting business behavior. And these functional activities in turn can best be understood only by studying the tremendous social struggle which Business has waged with the Law and had previously waged with the Church. It may even be that these major social values have been determined by our racial and physical backgrounds and by our social traditions, although it must be increasingly apparent to the reader that the causal connections and the particular relationships are difficult to trace. But at least it is in this whole setting that the problems now about to be considered must be studied. Furthermore, only borderline cases are presented; *i.e.,* cases in which the merits of the issue are not at first clear. Beyond these borderline cases are the many gross acts which are taken care of by the law, which in this regard becomes a social agency for controlling that minimum of social acts which are unquestionably intolerable. On the other hand, well within the field occupied by these borderline cases is the bulk of decent business behavior, which anyone versed in the facts will assume. The problems lie largely in the intermediate field.

The danger of casuistry is, of course, always present. But it is necessary only to sound a warning to the reader, that the case material here presented has been selected for the purpose of making concrete and real what could so easily be made only clear and general by resorting solely to systematic abstractions. Indeed, much that passes for casuistry quite frequently, upon further study and reflection, begins to exhibit its real virtue, namely, an attempt to make the implications of a doctrine come to grips with the direct observations of social facts. Only so does one appreciate the writings of a Seventeenth Century Richard Baxter, and of Bishop Pecock two centuries earlier; and Calvin himself was not merely spinning out detailed rules. Much of what they had to say fitted their circumstances and the conditions of their own times and cannot, therefore, be regarded as materially useful today. But their method must be taken seriously. Their failure to say the final word has perhaps made the author overly cautious in that direction and particularly anxious to describe the subject-matter rather than to outline the field of Business Ethics as it exists today.

Therefore, it is well to point out in this connection that the general point of view developed in this volume, which, it is hoped, is positive and optimistic in character, is not changed but merely qualified by the facts now to be presented. As Kant once observed regarding the relation between concepts and perceptions, a positive and optimistic view of Business Ethics without a knowledge and recognition of the facts would be empty, while to lose oneself in the study of business abuses without realizing their significance as well as their place in a wholesome and constructive view of Business Ethics would be a blind procedure. Not only has an attempt been made throughout the present section, therefore, constantly to point out the corrective social agencies and methods available, but the succeeding and final section will again revert to the positive treatment of the subject by presenting four major situations in business which have been determined largely and conspicuously by self-regulation and recognized standards of business ethics.

Most of the case material dealt with in this section is taken from the Reports of the Federal Trade Commission. This is a reflection of the growing importance of the Commission, in recent years, as a controlling government agency. It further accentuates the point made earlier in this volume, that the functional view of government control is supplanting the earlier absolute attitude of the courts. But every now and then the rumblings of the political metaphysics of the courts may be heard—in decreasing volume, however, signifying the passing of the storm.

The ability of Business to regulate itself apart from the Law, is to be judged by the number as well as the nature of the obligations it is willing to assume in that direction. The ability of Business to regulate itself in cooperation with legal agencies may be judged in part by the administrative record of the Federal Trade Commission.

CHAPTER XIV

TRADE PIRACY

The crucial point of all business lies in the field of marketing activities. After all, a man is in business to sell goods and services effectively and profitably. From the social point of view, the entire value of economic goods, of business commodities and services, depends in the last analysis on the salability of those goods in the market. This observation applies not only to the current values represented in the sale price of goods and its profit content, but also to the capital values attributed derivatively to industries supplying those goods. Since sales activities involve the general public more directly than do other management activities, such as purchasing, accounting, or financing, it is to be expected that the most acute as well as the most generally familiar ethical problems arise in the activities accompanying the marketing of goods and services.

No attempt will be made to question the right or wrong of selling, any more than we shall allow ourselves, in a later chapter, to spend much time on the justification of advertising in general. Such questions can be left to those who prefer to attack business or its problems from an extrinsic point of view. The intrinsic question for Business Ethics is: Are the methods employed so unfair to the purchaser and to the competitor and to the trade, and perhaps so detrimental to the vendor himself in the long run, as to outweigh any individual gain derived therefrom? More specifically these questions of Business Ethics become: Beyond what point are advertising activities unethical? What constitutes misrepresentation to the customer? Is the "pirating" of a competitor's business justifiable? It is this last question which shall concern us in this chapter.

There are two views in regard to the results which follow when a man extends his business or makes money. One of these views is that all individual gains or losses are compensated for by reciprocal losses or gains of the purchaser. Such a view, however, is quite superficial, especially as regards the vendor-purchaser relationship. The broader view is that all business transactions can be so conducted as to result in a mutual and even in an equal gain. This view is based on the fact that most business transactions arise because men have a surplus of certain commodities and a dearth of others, the surplus and dearth varying with different men. It thus becomes theoretically possible, by exchange, to satisfy almost everybody; and this is the ideal relationship between vendor and customer. Practically, however, this ideal situation is qualified by the fact that two or more people want to buy the same thing or are trying to sell the same or similar commodities. This means that frequently one man's gain, whether in selling or purchasing, is another man's loss, especially where competition exists between two persons to sell to or buy from a third person. It is conceivable that the third person is not affected by such a competition, and he may even gain by it. In either case, however, what one competitor gains, the other loses, and the question arises: To what extent is the successful competitor justified in exerting himself in order to gain his point?

The Problem of Trade Piracy

Most persons who interest themselves in problems of Business Ethics take the view that the incidence of unfair business methods is largely on the purchaser or consumer. Although this may be a matter of major public interest, in view of the fact that everyone is a consumer, such an analysis is not adequate. Indeed, most views of Business Ethics, and of remedial legislation and adjudication, are deficient because they take into account this single interest only. As also appears in problems concerning the broader business relationships, the interests of the competitor and of the trade should also be considered, for the values generated by a vigorous and economically sound trade group contribute to economic and social welfare. Whether these interests are more important than the consumer-purchaser interest, or are as primary, remains to be seen. At any rate, there appears in the following cases of trade piracy the same problem which will later be encountered in advertising activities; namely, that of determining, especially from the standpoint of trade-health and competitors' interests, the boundary line between justifiable selling methods and those which exhibit too great a degree of zeal. The overly zealous business man who advertises unfairly or who "pirates" his competitor's field, violates certain standards not only of good morals but also of good taste. Are the indefinable aesthetic considerations, as well as the ethical principles, ultimately incompatible with effective business methods? Is it not possible for good business to be governed as much by good taste as by good ethics?

"Trade piracy" consists in stealing another man's business in whole or in part. Inasmuch as "stealing" implies the adjective "conscious," it becomes necessary to point out that the diversion of business from one firm to another by general advertising or by other means which do not specifically intend such, cannot be regarded as a form of trade piracy; any more than our modern industrial age, or certain industries which may take men's lives, can be accused of "murder." Viewed from this angle, trade piracy presents a much more acute problem to business than does unfair advertising. Whereas most unfair advertising harms the trade in general, the incidence of trade piracy is more frequently on a particular merchant or business corporation. Although the great difficulty in unfair advertising is to discover just where the harmful effects fall, the ignorance of the members of a trade as to this fact is of a purely negative type and can be corrected by positive evidence. In the case of trade piracy, however, other members of the trade than the victim may feel that he should take care of his own troubles, and this erroneous conviction must be overcome before positive evidence as to the wrong is credited or given its due weight.

Trade piracy thus presents a problem that is more intensive in its effects than one of the most unfair of advertising methods, disparagements of a competitor or of a competing industry. Especially does this become apparent when a pirated merchant attempts to control the situation by soliciting the aid of the other members of his trade. Evidence of this situation is afforded by the fact that recourse to the Federal Trade Commission has been much more frequent in connection with trade piracy than in regard to unfair advertising methods.

A study of the problem can be made from one of two points of view: that of the pirate himself and that of the person pirated. As regards the former, a study of cases in trade piracy frequently engenders a considerable amount of sympathy for the pirate. Usually piracy is practiced by struggling young merchants or corporations that have discovered a profitable field of business, yielding relatively large returns to those who are already engaged in it and therefore correspondingly attractive to the newcomer; and frequently the persons already engaged in the business have in part achieved their position by methods which the pirate himself proposes to use.   Furthermore, the consumer-purchaser's interest, in preventing too much of the purchase price from being converted into excess profits, is safeguarded to a certain extent by the constant possibility of new competitors entering the field of production and selling.   It is difficult to see how the entrance of a new competitor in a lucrative field of business can be condemned by society.   We are not here concerned with the problem confronting a trade group when a new competitor or an old member of the group has underestimated the costs of doing business.   Trade piracy is much more specific than such activities.   It involves the definite invasion of another man's business by different or more intensive methods than are present or necessary in normal, existing competition.

From the pirate's own point of view, therefore, the question is not the same as that confronting a vigorous or courageous competitor in a general struggle for business.   The question resolves itself to the alternative between taking one's chances in such an above-board struggle, on the one hand, and on the other, of imitating a successful competitor and disguising one's own identity or the identity of one's goods in order to parade under a competitor's name.   There is no doubt that a business man who thus takes his cues from another, stands considerable chance of making a measurable success.   The question is, however, whether a man wishes to take his cue from others or prefers to stand on his own abilities and rely on his own ideas. The business man that mimics others very definitely gives evidence of an inferiority complex and trains himself to follow rather than lead.   The question is not only one of self-respect and confidence in one's abilities and convictions; every man must settle such problems for himself.   Such a problem is a moral problem, and does not fall within the province of business ethics as defined in this volume.   If a man prefers to occupy an inferior but assured position in a field of business rather than risk failure in order to be a leader, however, he must face the practical possibility, amounting to a high degree of probability, that he is thereby closing to himself the future position of leadership in his field of interest.

Similarly, the attitude of a business man who has suffered the acts of a trade pirate, may involve the broader moral considerations. If an outstanding merchant or business corporation wishes to divert its energies toward looking for pirates, these probably could very easily be found. To waste too much time in pursuing them, however, is like slapping mosquitoes during a duck hunt. A few (mosquitoes) are to be expected. Even if they become too thick for comfort, it may be better to tolerate them than to employ methods in getting rid of them that will frighten away the ducks or that may prevent a man from seeing those ducks that fly his way. Trade pirates, like the poor, we shall probably always have with us. To strike back at them in kind or in degree not only entails descending to their strategically inferior level, but practically may become detrimental to the whole trade.

How to get rid of the pirates, if such a course is necessary or desirable, or how to deal with them when they become too numerous and too troublesome, is a problem in business ethics. This requires a determination, first, of the kinds of business practice which transcend the bounds of fairness, and secondly, the selection of appropriate means of control. A few preliminary cases will illustrate the problem in various forms. It may be illuminating first to refer to the practices and standards of a profession and then to present a few typical cases involving piracy in business.

Professional Standards

In certain parts of the United States, public works such as paving, sewers, *etc.*, were done by the formation of an improvement district with commissioners in charge who appointed all employees and controlled the work. Desiring to initiate a public improvement, an enterprising individual property owner called on an engineer, A, for advice looking to the formation of a paving district. A investigated and after consulting with several other property owners laid out the district and assisted the active property owners in checking up petitions to see that a majority was had, and he did other things to help the project along.

When the petitions were properly filed and necessary notice was published, B, another engineer, interested himself in the project to the extent of visiting the active property owners, from among whom the commissioners for the district were likely to be chosen, and attempted to line up the engineering work for himself. He also enlisted the services of his friends, who "went to the front" for him and tried to have him appointed because he was a good engineer. B had full knowledge, from the date of publication of formal notice, that A had worked up the district.

The Practice Committee of the American Association of Engineers pointed out that A had no rights, in the usually accepted meaning of the word, because he was not regularly employed but took a business chance for ultimate gain. The Committee stated, however, that professional courtesy should have restrained B from injecting himself into the situation unless public interest, rather than B's personal gain, had so dictated.[1]

There were in the chain industry[2] several fairly large companies directly competing with each other. These companies could be grouped into three classes, namely, those that produced quality chain only, those that produced the same types of chain as the first group of companies but of cheaper grades, and lastly, those companies that produced both quality and cheap chain. The Knickerbocker Chain Company was in the first group. Within its class the Knickerbocker Chain Company was a low-cost producer, but this fact did not prevent the company from experiencing certain difficulties.

On certain kinds of power drives a chain of the cheaper grade would serve as well as a quality chain, for on these jobs the precision of measurement and workmanship on the chain was less important than its tensile strength. The material in the cheaper chains was almost as good as that in the quality chains, but the latter were produced with more skilled labor. It was the class of trade having power drives on which the cheaper chain might be used that gave the Knickerbocker Chain Company trouble, particularly if an installation was new.

Customers with this type of drives would ask the Knickerbocker Chain Company's engineers to develop a chain which would satisfactorily take care of the power drive in the customer's plant; the cost of this development work averaged about $20,000 a year; as much as $15,000 was spent on one job of this sort. After the chain had been developed by the Knickerbocker Chain Company the customer would frequently submit the sample of the chain to companies in group two, who made a cheaper chain, to see what price they would quote to reproduce it. The price was always slightly less than the Knickerbocker price, with the result that the Knickerbocker Chain Company stood the cost of the development work while its competitors secured

[1] Case 40, American Association of Engineers.
[2] This case, names disguised, was kindly furnished by Mr. Paul B. Coffman, Assistant Professor of Accounting, Harvard Business School.

the business. The Knickerbocker Chain Company could not avoid such situations for it could not afford to jeopardize its reputation by having customers say that it would not cooperate; at the same time it could not produce a cheaper product to compete because it did not wish to "trade down" and thereby risk its reputation as a quality chain producer.

The vice president of the company who was in charge of the accounting work was of the opinion that part of the difficulty was brought about by lack of adequate cost systems on the part of some of his competitors. Consequently, he invited all of the chain manufacturers to a meeting in which the possibilities of developing a uniform cost system for the industry might be discussed. The meeting was held, but the idea of a uniform system was coolly received; most of the manufacturers felt that their cost work was adequate and that the variations in prices were caused primarily by differences in organization and production methods between the various companies and the position each occupied in the industry.

Business protects itself against piracy through patent and trade-mark legislation, whereby the development of a product and its proper registry entitles the creator and owner to the legal right of protection against infringements. The medical profession, on the other hand, has set a very different standard by insisting that practitioners shall not employ such means of asserting property rights in surgical instruments or methods of cure that may be invented or discovered.[3] This ideal was observed in the following business situation.

The making of a combination phosphorous and sulphur match was accomplished as far back as 1680, but it was not until 1827 that the first practical friction matches were made, by John Walker.[4] The first phosphorous friction match was invented in 1831 by Charles Sauria, but it was not patented and its manufacture was pirated to a considerable extent. The first United States patent for a phosphorous friction match was granted to Alonzo D. Phillips in 1836. The great difficulty with any match made from a phosphorous compound was that workmen exposed even for a short time to the phosphorous vapors were subject to a disease called necrosis of the jaw bone and popularly known as "phossy jaw." So serious had the condition become that, in 1875, Denmark prohibited the manufacture of such matches, an act which was followed by Switzerland in 1879.

[3] See *Principles of Medical Ethics*, Chapter II, Article I, Section 5, first clause.

[4] *Scientific American*, February 11, 1911. *Survey*, December 3, 1910; January 7, 21, and February 18, 1911. XX *U. S. Labor Bulletin* 31–146.

A non-poisonous match, made from amorphous red phosphorus, was patented by Pasch in Sweden in 1844, and in 1852 the so-called "safety match" came into the market. The need for some non-poisonous compound for a "strike-anywhere" match resulted in the development of a substitute known as sesquisulphide of phosphorous. The compound was originated in 1864 by G. Lamoine of Germany, and was introduced into France later by Cahen and Sévéne, who patented the compound in the United States in 1898.

This patent was purchased in 1900 by the Diamond Match Company with the purpose of introducing this type of match into the United States. After spending over a quarter of a million dollars in the purchase of the patent and in experimental development work, the Diamond Match Company abandoned its efforts because of the seemingly insurmountable climatic difficulties. The "strike-anywhere" match which could be produced effectively and sold in Europe was handicapped by the tremendous variations in climate, particularly in moisture, in the United States.

In 1909, Mr. W. A. Fairburn became associated with the Diamond Match Company. In his experimental work he rediscovered the Cahen and Sévéne formula, which had been laid aside and forgotten, and succeeded in adapting the process to climatic conditions prevailing in the United States. In 1911, he announced his ability to make non-poisonous "strike-anywhere" matches without changing the machinery already in use and without any appreciable increase in production costs.

Shortly after this announcement a bill was introduced in Congress known as the Esch bill, which virtually taxed white phosphorous matches out of existence. The passing of this bill brought out the fact that the Diamond Match Company owned the patent which covered the only satisfactory substitute and that this company alone had the knowledge and ability to use this patent successfully.

To meet this situation, the company in 1911, at the suggestion of President Taft, turned over to the people of the United States without charge the patent covering the manufacture of non-poisonous matches, and also gave to its competitors its secret and valuable technical process and formula for using this patent in America. The effect was to enable every manufacturer of matches in the United States to operate without endangering the health of his employees or putting upon the market a substitute well known to be poisonous and disease spreading.

This case is highly significant in view of the fact that the policy of the Diamond Match Company was in accord with the traditional views of ethical behavior which regard generosity and altruism as paramount virtues. The case has been chosen because it shows that these traditional ethical virtues are not only possible in business but have been practiced as a matter of fact. The practical idealism displayed is an effective answer to those who are critical and pessimistic in regard to our industrial and commercial age; and the principle of the act rises to the plane of the finest chapter in the history of the medical profession,[5] which does not countenance the patenting of surgical instruments or of remedial medicines and curative methods. Indeed, it makes piracy impossible!

Such a general treatment of the problem will not, however, suffice to establish a working principle of business conduct. Detailed and analytical elements must be discovered, especially such as will indicate the exact incidence of the harm or benefits arising from the continuance of the Diamond Match Company in its exclusive possession of the processes and formulae, or from the alternative which the company adopted. A distinction must therefore be made between the two ethical factors which are involved: humanitarian considerations for the workmen in the match factories and also for the users of matches, and the fair business treatment of the competitors of the Diamond Match Company.

The situation whereby "strike-anywhere" matches could be produced in America only at the expense of the health of workmen had been allowed to develop through a sufficient period of years to encourage a number of companies to engage in the process of making such matches; and the drastic Esch bill, like the Prohibition Law and the Emancipation Proclamation, while justifiable in the main and on the score of humanitarian reasons, made no provision for recompensing the industries it virtually destroyed. The absence of governmental remedies for the predicament in which the competitors of the Diamond Match Company found themselves, placed a burden on the latter which the Diamond Match Company could have refused to assume. The problem which confronted the Diamond Match Company was whether the few remaining years during which their exclusive title to the new process held, and during which they could consolidate their position in the field, would recompense them for any contingencies which might result from the adoption of such a policy.

One of these contingencies was the possibility of encouraging the competitors of the Diamond Match Company to engage

[5] *Principles of Medical Ethics*, Chapter II, Sections 5, 6.

in separate research activities and competitive methods which might be more successful as regards process or economy of manufacture and sale.   The positions of the Diamond Match Company and some or all of its competitors would then be exactly reversed, with this difference, that a precedent would already have been established in the trade of taking every advantage of circumstances.   It was as much to the interests of the Diamond Match Company as a leading producer in the field to establish goodwill among the various producers of matches as it was to establish goodwill among the consuming public.   Furthermore, the loss of the goodwill of the public was quite possible in view of the fact that the public could easily confuse the effects of the Diamond Match Company's policy with the results of the Esch bill, and might think that the Diamond Match Company made it impossible for its competitors to continue business except by jeopardizing the lives of their workmen.   Such misconceptions are deplorable but they do occur and prominent business corporations must take them into account in calculating their policies.   These considerations confirmed, but did not necessarily effect, the generous decision of the Diamond Match Company.

It would appear on the face of it that the predicament of the competitors of the Diamond Match Company was sufficiently serious to warrant their making or accepting a suggestion that they pay the Diamond Match Company a price for the use of its processes or at least recompense the latter in whole or in part for its expenditures in developing the process.   For the Diamond Match Company to assume the whole financial burden and to turn over to their competitors the process and formula does appear to be a case of "leaning over backward" that cannot be accounted for by any insinuations as to the advertising benefit of their act.   A sharing of the expense by all the parties that benefited, and in some measurable degree to the extent of their relative gains, would be laying the basis for a more permanent and dependable method of adjusting business relations.   The situation has recently been almost exactly duplicated by one involving major international interests.   The virtual monopoly of large-quantity supplies of helium possessed by this country morally obligates us to furnish other countries with a sufficient supply of this gas to enable them to develop dirigible airships. But the furnishing of such gas does not ethically imply furnishing it free of charge.

Trade Piracy

The altruistic attitude displayed by the Diamond Match Company in this situation reaches the height of professional idealism. It makes piracy impossible by renouncing all possessory or ownership rights that attract the trade pirate. But the question may be raised whether such a degree of generosity was necessary to conform with the soundest ethical principles of business. Certainly it would not have been too much to ask the competitors who benefited by this generous act to share the expense which had been incurred by the Diamond Match Company. This is not intended to detract in the least from the social value of the act. But the situation presents an excellent opportunity of defining the maximum point of Business Ethics, just as other cases have been employed to determine a minimum boundary. Viewed from this standpoint, the following case presents a very practical problem as regards the exact definition of the ethical responsibilities of business.

The Balany Chemical Company,[6] a New York corporation, was engaged in the manufacturing and selling of drugs, chemicals, and pharmaceutical supplies, in interstate and foreign commerce and in active competition with other persons, partnerships, and corporations similarly engaged.

Among the commodities sold by the Balany Chemical Company was acetyl salicylic acid, a patent for which had been assigned in 1900 to the Bayer Company, a New York corporation whose stock was owned by citizens of Germany. This patent had expired on February 27, 1917. Previous to this date of expiration acetyl salicylic acid had been designated by the manufacturers thereof, and had become known to the general public, as "aspirin." This word "aspirin" had been registered on May 2, 1899, as a trade-mark and the rights thereto had been acquired by the Bayer Company in 1913. But on March 3, 1917, the Patent Office of the United States upon petition canceled the registration of such trade-mark, upon the ground, among others, that upon the expiration of the patent the word "aspirin" had become a descriptive name and was, therefore, no longer the exclusive trade-mark property of the Bayer Company. In December, 1918, the Alien Property Custodian sold the capital stock and property of the Bayer Company to the Sterling Products Company, which continued to sell aspirin and to claim "aspirin" as its trade-mark.

In January, 1920, the Balany Chemical Company made application to the secretaries of state of numerous states of the United States for

[6] Fictitious name. III F. T. C. D. 369 (1921).

registration of the word "aspirin" as a general trade-mark to be used on chemicals and medicinal preparations. Upon issuance to it by the secretaries of 33 states of certificates of registration, the Balany Chemical Company started an extensive campaign of newspaper advertising in which it made erroneous and deceptive statements concerning its exclusive right to the use of the word "aspirin" in connection with its manufacture and sale. The employment of various forms or arrangements of type was declared, in the application, not to alter the character of the trade-mark. The Balany Chemical Company asserted that "Bacco aspirin," which it manufactured, was the only genuine aspirin and that only by using its aspirin could the public secure the medicinal value for which it paid and which it expected to get. The Balany Chemical Company, furthermore, warned dealers in drugs and medicines that it would protect its property rights in this trade-mark by such means as it deemed expedient.

The cases already given illustrate the difference in attitude between business and the professions with regard to the securing of customers or clients. The professions condemn all forms of solicitation, including advertising, and especially such methods as would directly deprive another professional man of his clients.[7] The position held by the professions is that the client must seek the professional man, and not the reverse. The actual practice of the professions varies, and there are important deviations from the general principle. Thus, engineers advertise more freely than do doctors or lawyers; large law firms include men whose chief function is to make "contacts" for the purpose of extending their business; banks and accounting firms—these two classes of business men are most nearly professional—engage in both forms of soliciting business; teachers as well as doctors take advantage of news items which keep their names before the public; and engineers, as the above case shows, may "work up" a district for the purpose of developing paving, sanitary or other engineering projects.

The difference, however, between the business point of view and that of the professions lies largely in the matter of securing each other's customers or clients. Among the professions, it is unethical to attempt to divert a client to one's self. In many kinds of business, all customers are considered to be "fair game." In the medical profession patents are forbidden as unethical. The protection of a business lies largely in its patents,

[7] See *Canons of Professional Ethics*, American Bar Association, Canon 7; also *Principles of Medical Ethics*, II, I, 4.

copyrights, or trade-mark rights.[8] The right to a trade-mark, however, is "appurtenant only to the established business or trade in connection with which the mark has applied, so that a trader has no property in the mark *per se*, but only in reference to his trade, and cannot prevent another trade from applying this mark to goods which are not of the same description."[9]

The Balany case is typical of many which are constantly arising in business. A business firm becomes established as a leader in the field, identifies its products by a trade name which may or may not be protected by patents and copyrights, and then discovers that its efforts to develop goodwill, its advertising expenses, and perhaps even its trade channels and sales methods have been appropriated by a rival company. In a sense the Bayer Company should feel complimented at the attempt to imitate its methods and to appropriate its product, and the company could feel reasonably certain that any rival which so lacked initiative as to resort to such practices admitted its own inferiority and condemned itself to a subordinate place in the business field.

These satisfactions and advantages, however, were not felt by the Bayer Company to be sufficient to protect its business from the encroachments of the Balany Company or to recompense it for a possible loss of business. The difficulty was that the burden of the unfair tactics of the Balany Company fell chiefly on the Bayer Company as an individual company. If the trade as a whole had been injured, an organized effort to prevent this would have been possible. The only act of the Balany Company which concerned the trade as a whole was the use of the term "only genuine." Inasmuch as civil society has set up the courts to protect the rights of individuals, this legal agency was undoubtedly the best safeguard upon which the Bayer Company could rely, especially if its rights were in the form of patents or registered trade-marks or trade names; and this course of procedure was selected by the Bayer Company in certain other cases of infringement.

In this particular case, however, recourse was had to the Federal Trade Commission, which denied the Balany Company

[8] See *General Information about Protection of Trade-marks, Prints and Labels*, U. S. Patent Office, Department of Commerce. Revised April 1, 1928.

[9] See Beech-Nut Case, III *Harvard Business Reports* 328, especially page 344 and commentary. See also Rogers, Edward S., *Trade-marks and Unfair Trading*, New York: McGraw-Hill Book Company, Inc., 1914.

the right to use "aspirin" as a trade-mark or to assert any exclusive right to its use and which ordered the Balany Company to cease using the phrase "only genuine" as a descriptive title. Such recourses to governmental agencies indicate the failure of business completely to regulate all phases of its own conduct.

A similar case is that of the Del-Com Company, which, however, employed other sanctions.

Del-Com[10] was a mouth wash that had been discovered in Europe about 1885, at which time also the process by which Del-Com could be made soluble in water had been patented. The Del-Com Company made arrangements for registering the trade name for exclusive use in several European countries after the patent should expire.

Del-Com was first introduced into the United States in 1891. The process was not patented in this country, but the trade name was registered and the product has been nationally advertised since 1912. After the Del-Com Company was incorporated in the United States, it bought the parent company, which it now owns as a subsidiary.

The solubility of Del-Com in water is achieved by saponification. The process is generally known, but the Del-Com Company had developed a considerable market for its own product under its trade name. Del-Com differed from other mouth washes in that it was of more stable and uniform quality than other products of the same type, and of better quality than was required by the United States Pharmacopoeia. This was achieved by using an oil which was distilled off within a comparatively narrow range of temperature. The narrower this range, the more by-products resulted, and these by-products were difficult to market. Hence the cost of securing the oil of Del-Com standard was relatively high.

In 1926, reports of substitutions and infringements became so numerous and so insistent that the Del-Com Company began to make inquiries and found that substitution and infringement were becoming prevalent. The company then began a systematic search for substitutions and infringements, spending in two years some $150,000 in following up cases, prosecutions, and general publicity. Not only were old Del-Com bottles being refilled by competitors and hospitals with their own products, but all sorts of containers were filled with inferior products and labeled "Del-Com" by druggists.

The Del-Com Company was faced with the problem of choosing the most effective means of handling the situation. Articles and advertisements, warning the trade, were published in trade papers, but with no effect. The education of druggists and pharmacists by such means

---

[10] Fictitious Name.

was found to be futile. The American Medical Association would probably not have given its help in the matter because of its opposition to trade names for medicinal products. Druggists' associations, wholesale and retail, were not interested; and the pharmaceutical association indicated its preference for member-druggists' interests where they were opposed to a single manufacturing firm.

The Del-Com Company considered the advisability of forming a small association of manufacturers of distinctive products such as their own, to include manufacturers who were similarly faced with infringements and substitutions. The Del-Com plan provided for a group of 18 to 20 manufacturers, including such products as safety razors and blades, cosmetics, cough and cold reliefs, *etc.;* the establishment of a fund of approximately $500,000; the employment of a director, a pharmaceutical chemist, and counsel; and the prosecution in the courts of all substitutions and infringements on patents, trade-marks, and trade names. The Federal Trade Commission was considered as a possible resort, but was regarded as being too slow in its processes for the purpose. The courts were regarded as the best available agency for redress. The whole plan fell through, however, because a sufficient number of interested manufacturers could not be brought together.

Del-Com Company then decided to prosecute cases in the courts on its own initiative and individually. The company picked out the most flagrant offenders, those that had made repeated sales of substitute "Del-Com," the analysis of which proved their guilt beyond a doubt. Furthermore, it was recognized that in many localities the courts were amenable to political and other pressure and that it would be useless to prosecute cases in districts where druggists could influence judges by their combined and direct or indirect pressure. In all, some 127 cases were prosecuted and a decree obtained in every case. In most cases, "consent decrees" were obtained, the offender avoiding publicity and heavy damages and costs by consenting to the charge before a judge, agreeing to discontinue the practice, and paying a small amount of damages to the Del-Com Company.

Prior to the settlement of many of these cases, the Del-Com Company received a great many letters and telegrams from the parties sued, denying their guilt, and from trade associations, urging leniency or insisting upon the integrity of their members. The Del-Com Company was urged to withdraw its suits. Some letters condemned the steps the company had taken as uncalled for and unjust. In several communities the Del-Com Company launched newspaper campaigns to warn the public against unscrupulous dealers. The advertisements showed pictures of substitute packages with the offender's name obliterated, and warned the public to be on their guard. The company was charged by many persons by letter with casting aspersions on the entire profession and with doing pharmacy an irreparable injury.

After over 100 convictions or decrees had been obtained in the courts, the Del-Com Company decided to publish the fact. The question again arose whether the names of the guilty persons should be stated in the published articles and advertisements. The company finally decided to include in such articles and advertisements the pictures of bottles labeled "Del-Com" and containing substitutes, but with the names of towns and of offending druggists on the labels obliterated or made illegible. Cuts of checks in payment of damages were inserted, with similar obliterations. Also, excerpts from the court decree were included, together with the name and location of the court, but without the citation. Criticisms of this policy, similar to criticisms stated above, were again received, with suggestions that actual names be published. One of the decrees was obtained against the dean of a college of pharmacy of a prominent state university. The Del-Com Company decided to retain its policy of obliterating or deleting the names of offending parties.

Whether the self-regulation of business in matters of this sort is ever to be achieved remains to be seen. Two factors seem to be essential to such a possibility: first, the definite identification of a product and a trade name, such as acetyl salicylic acid and "aspirin," and the establishment of the business custom of recognizing the rights to such trade names or trademarks; and second, the organization of a well-defined group of distributors, dealing in a particular product, which would condemn any such invasion of business rights and which would sanction its condemnation in ways which would supplement the legal restrictions. Direct forms of coercion would be prohibited by the Sherman Law, but publicity and elimination from trade-group membership are available, while much can be accomplished by discussions of such problems within trade groups themselves. Self-regulation by business could furthermore be sufficiently extended to reduce to a minimum public ill will, with its boycotts; court action with its delays, expense and failure to appreciate particular business situations; and the legislative or administrative functions of government, which may become undesirable because of the encouragement they thereby receive to interfere unduly with business.

One of the most difficult problems in trade piracy arises when a family name becomes established as synonymous with leadership in a business field, and when another person, with the same name and either related or wholly unrelated by blood, capitalizes this reputation by engaging in a similar business. When, for example, A. S. Converse sold his rubber-shoe business, the Boston Rubber Shoe Company, to the United States Rubber Company, and the latter continued to operate the Malden plant under their own name, one M. M. Converse, who was not related by blood to A. S. Converse but who had an intimate knowledge of the distribution system of the old Converse business, set up a plant adjacent to the old Converse plant and operated it as the "Converse Rubber Shoe Company." Most of the buyers of rubber shoes did not know the difference, and a large business was built up at Malden. Should a man be prevented from using his own name in such a case? An attempt was made similarly to employ Lindbergh's name, after his trans-Atlantic flight: someone by the name of Lindbergh was induced to permit the use of his name in connection with an aircraft company; this, fortunately, was effectively prevented at the very start.

The following cases present various angles of the situation which arises when a well-known trade name is pirated.

The Diamond Rubber Company had difficulty with the "Diamond Holdfast Rubber Company," a company organized in 1919 in Atlanta, Georgia, where the Diamond Rubber Company operated a branch. The pirating company made and sold inner tubes and auto accessories in containers, upon which were placed labels featuring the word "Diamond" and closely resembling the registered labels of the Diamond Rubber Company. The organizer of the pirating company had at various times given his name as "Dimond" and "Diamond." In 1906, his application for naturalization was signed "Dimond," so likewise in 1916 to an application to be declared a bankrupt, and in 1916 to an application for registering a motor vehicle. In 1917, he obtained a life insurance policy under that name, but later changed the name to "Diamond." He was unable to prove to the satisfaction of the Federal Trade Commission that either of these names was his legal surname, and he was ordered to cease and desist using the name.[11]

A more difficult situation is presented when the grandsons of a sausage-maker attempted to employ their own name in connection with a similar business, the name, goodwill and charter of the grandfather having in the meantime been sold to other parties.[12] Sometimes the name so pirated is general or descrip-

[11] IV F. T. C. D. 235 (1922).
[12] IV F. T. C. D. 297 (1922). See also Herring Hall-Marvin Safe Company case, IV F. T. C. D. 285; also "Bernice" Anthracite Company, IV F. T. C. D. 209, and "Mary Louise" Millinery, IV F. T. C. D. 323, where Christian names were involved.

tive.[13] Sometimes the name is changed so slightly as to "lead to a deception or misleading of purchasers or to cause them to believe that the products are one and the same." Thus "Mentholanum" was the trade name adopted for a product similar to "Mentholatum,"[14] and "Vielle Montagne" zinc was declared to be a "Vieille Montagne" product.[15] Other cases have occurred in connection with such diverse products as coffee, tires, oil, bacilli killer, glue and watches.[16] The Yellow Cab Company, operating at Washington, D. C., secured a cease and desist order against a company which listed itself in the telephone directory as both "Yellow Bell Taxi Company" and "Yellow Ford Taxi Company," by which means it first caught the attention of possible customers of the Yellow Cab Company, whether the customer was looking up or down the page of the telephone book.[17]

Cases of this sort have also occurred in a number of industries such as auto and electrical appliances,[18] shoes and clothing.[19] Much of this sort of thing is so mean and petty and trifling that little attention can be paid to it except by the party immediately injured, *i.e.*, the competitor, and he himself perhaps had better disregard the matter. The whole principle of law, however, rests upon society's taking an interest in the grievances of an individual, no matter how insignificant the injury may be: in the early history of the law, in order to prevent him from taking matters into his own hands and disturbing the peace; in later years, because of a developed and generalized sense of justice which guarantees to each individual the work of his hands and sometimes the results of his thinking.

Whether business in general or businesses in particular are at present facing a situation that marked the early history of law, is worthy of consideration. For the question arises: Shall persons who are injured by unfair trade practices, such as trade

[13] Liberty Paper Company, III F. T. C. D. 13 (1920); Franklin Lightning Rod Company, III F. T. C. D. 327 (1921).

[14] I F. T. C. D. 154 (1918).

[15] VI F. T. C. D. 1 (1923).

[16] II F. T. C. D. 58; II, 216; IV, 102, and V, 92; IV, 155; VI, 506; and VI, 452, respectively. "Granola" was prohibited as pirating "Mazola," VIII, 290.

[17] V F. T. C. D. 473.

[18] I F. T. C. D. 424; II, 95, 335; III, 6, 387; V, 327.

[19] II F. T. C. D. 67; V, 24, 105.

piracy, be limited to the courts or to an administrative body such as the Federal Trade Commission for redress? These agencies are slow in action, they are expensive, and they frequently are unacquainted with trade practices; in many cases, at least, these defects discourage the victims of such practices from resorting to legal or governmental agencies for redress. One alternative is to "strike back," the result being a trade war which injures everybody in the business. It is the purpose of this volume to show, among other things, how efficacious business self-government has been and needs to be in order to approximate even the early stages of the development of the law.

When Time Is "of the Essence": Plagiarism

In the following two cases, the situation is unique in some respects, both being taken from the book-publishing business and both involving to some extent the element of timeliness. In the first case, an example is given of a commendable attitude. The fact that so many of the cases referred to in this section are of questionable forms of business practice, does not mean to imply that business is generally so conducted or that business ethics consists of a list of "business scandals." Most of the cases here presented are "on the borderline of ethics," the most fruitful field of study, or involve a situation in which an obviously unfair act has been committed but in which the ethical question resolves itself to what shall be done about it. As can be observed from the footnote references in this chapter, most of the cases here treated were referred to the Federal Trade Commission for relief. The first of the following two cases was adjusted by the publishing house itself.

The Franz Toler Company,[20] a publishing house, assigned to Merrit Flager,[20] a professor of German in a well-known American university, the task of compiling a textbook of German short stories in the original German. Flager proceeded to select such stories, obtaining permission from the authors and publishers to include these stories in his text and securing the copyrights, where this was necessary. After the book was published, the Halton Bell Company,[21] a publishing firm in competition with the Franz Toler Company, discovered that one of the stories published in Flager's text was a chapter of a book soon to be published by the Halton Bell Company. The Halton Bell Company

[20] Fictitious name.
[21] Fictitious name.

wrote to the Franz Toler Company to that effect and asserted that they were in possession of the exclusive American copyright for the entire contents of the book.

The Franz Toler Company took up this matter with Flager who sent them a letter he had received from the author, giving Flager the right to use the story on the assumption that he had the right to dispose of a part of his book. The Franz Toler Company, thereupon, without inquiring further into the assertion of the Halton Bell Company, eliminated this story from succeeding publications of the text and notified the Halton Bell Company to this effect.

*   *   *   *   *   *

Since 1899 A. N. Marquis & Company[22] of Chicago has published biennially a book containing personal sketches of leading Americans under the title "Who's Who in America," a publication which through years of usage has come to be well known to the public, and is generally known throughout the United States as "Who's Who." Data and subscriptions were solicited from individuals by circular letters accompanied by a sketch of the person addressed, clipped from the last previous publication, and requesting revision and return of the sketch and a subscription to the forthcoming edition. A blank biographical questionnaire was sent to those whose names were not included in previous editions.

The Famous Names Company,[23] an Oregon corporation, in 1909 began publishing "Who's Who in the Northwest," a second edition appearing in 1917. In 1919 they issued a publication entitled "Who's Who and Why," and in 1920 contemplated the issuing of an edition entitled "Who's Who and Why in the United States." A large number of persons were sent letters containing the biographical material clipped from "Who's Who in America," and they were requested to supply additions or corrections and to return the proof and subscriptions to "Who's Who and Why." An office was established in Washington, D. C., to receive these replies. Many persons, deceived into believing that this publication was identical with "Who's Who in America," complied with this request. A. N. Marquis and Company secured a "cease and desist" order from the Federal Trade Commission.

A particular problem of trade piracy, sufficiently different from the piracy of goods and trade names, is present in the piracy of patterns and styles. Whereas in musical or literary plagiarism or in situations illustrated by the two book-publishing cases just cited, timeliness is only relatively an important factor, in the following cases time is the essential element in the situation.

[22] III F. T. C. D. 345.
[23] Fictitious name.

A new pattern or a new style or a "first-run" moving picture has a comparatively brief existence, and fairness and equity would require that the creator or designer of a style or pattern or theme should receive the major economic benefits during that short period. There is no need for arguing the exercise of extreme sentimentalism: just as "the buyer should beware," so a minimum of business intelligence should govern a man in dealing with such precarious matters as style and design. One practical case of business foresight was exhibited by the R. H. Mallinson Company[24] when it evolved a style series under a separate name: when the style went out of fashion, the firm name did not pass out with it, and any style piracy would have affected the company only in part.

But no amount of business foresight or speed in the marketing of style goods will completely safeguard a business against piracy. In the case of motion pictures, the display of a picture by an exhibitor cannot be recalled; people have seen it and have paid their admission fee. Furthermore, the time element is present in the very production process itself, as the following case will show.

In 1917 Thomas A. Edison, Incorporated,[25] a New Jersey corporation, produced a moving-picture film entitled "Your Obedient Servant." They registered this name in the United States patent office and exhibited the picture in some 5,000 theaters. In 1918 this film and the rights to exhibit it were sold to George Kleine of Chicago, who continued to produce the film for exhibition purposes. No other name or title was used in connection with this motion picture, which was a Civil War drama featuring a horse, the name of which was suggested by Anna Sewell's *Black Beauty*, written 40 years previously and well and favorably known to the American public. In the picture, "Your Obedient Servant," the horse was named "Black Beauty," but the stories were altogether different. None of the subtitles in the picture were taken from the book.

In November, 1919, the Vitagraph Company of America decided to produce a picture "Black Beauty" which would faithfully and truthfully depict and portray Anna Sewell's story. The Vitagraph Company published announcements to this effect in news items appearing in some 2,300 newspapers and in a number of trade papers, and in circulars

---

[24] VIII *Harvard Business Review* 113, October, 1929.

[25] V F. T. C. D. 219. See also IX *ibid.* 1, for similar case involving "The Three Musketeers."

sent to a large number of humane societies throughout the country. The continuity of the photoplay was finished in January, 1920, the first scenes were photographed in July, 1920, and the last in December, 1920. The picture was released January 5, 1921, and was shown in some 1,500 theaters. A melodrama was interwoven with the autobiography of the horse, but all the principal characters, scenes, incidents, and episodes of Anna Sewell's book were faithfully and truthfully depicted and correctly portrayed. Over $200,000 was spent in the production of this picture, including an advertising expense of over $50,000. The claim to the copyright of the picture under the title of "Black Beauty" was registered January 24, 1921.

On August 19, 1920, Herman Kerowitz,[26] after witnessing a showing of "Your Obedient Servant," ordered from a representative of George Kleine five positive prints of the picture. He received these prints after paying the purchase price of $863 and after it had been mutually understood and agreed as one of the conditions of the sale that Kerowitz should use the prints for non-theatrical purposes only. Kerowitz made some minor changes in the wording and phraseology of the 53 subtitles and added 16 new subtitles, 7 of which were taken from Anna Sewell's book. Kerowitz furthermore added 200 feet of scenes depicting a mare and colt taken in the neighborhood of New York City; he also added about 20 feet of a horse-race scene. To this remade film Kerowitz gave the name of "Black Beauty" and proceeded to advertise it without making it clear that the film had been rebuilt.

On December 22, 1920, Kerowitz inserted a page advertisement in a trade paper, which had a general circulation throughout the moving-picture industry, in which he issued a warning that anyone showing a moving picture entitled "Black Beauty" without his permission "does so at his own risk," and declared that he controlled the right thereto and would prosecute all infringements. He also sent copies of this notice and warning by registered mail to the managers of the 24 branches of the Vitagraph Company. He had not registered a claim to the copyright, and he did not control the rights he asserted. In his advertisements he featured Anna Sewell's name and styled his photoplay "An American Adaptation of the World Famous Autobiography of a Horse." The Vitagraph Company secured a "cease and desist" order from the Federal Trade Commission.

Matters of this sort are more and more being taken care of by the industries themselves. The producers and distributors of motion pictures have attempted to control the "first-run" and piracy situations by establishing courts of arbitration within the industry. The persistent hostility of the courts to this

[26] Fictitious name.

method of adjudication, however, has delayed the development of a justifiable method of self-regulation in business.[27]

Style Designs and Patterns

Similar to the pirating of a motion-picture theme is the piracy of a design. The following case is particularly interesting because the very company which faced the problem of piracy had in previous years adopted the tactics of the pirate on a broader scale. In connection with this situation it is also interesting to notice complaints against American pirates which emanate from British manufacturers: the lace industry of England developed out of the imitation of Continental European hand-made lace by machine processes in the early part of the last century. Any attempt to get back to the early history of style or pattern piracy faces the difficulty that meets anyone who tries to discover the origin of the McCoy-Hatfield feud. Efforts of this sort lead merely to mutual recriminations. The problem is: What shall be done about the present situation? The following case presents the matter in sufficient detail to enable one to grasp the situation fully.

The Allernet Lace Company,[28] established in 1905 with 5 lace machines, in 1922 had 30 machines. Its product, which originally had been staple lines, in 1922 was almost entirely high-grade novelty goods. It employed about 200 men and women, many of whom were highly skilled. In addition, much of the lace, which was woven or twisted in 6-yard widths, was distributed to home workers to be separated into narrower widths. The company did all its own dyeing and finishing.

Since the Allernet Lace Company was one of the few lace-manufacturing companies in the United States that employed expert designers and draftsmen, its leadership in developing lace patterns had been established. As a result, its patterns were imitated extensively by rival companies. This pirating of lace patterns had become so serious that in June, 1922, the company made a special study of conditions with a view to remedying the evil.

It was discovered that the company's own customers were the source of samples from which designs and styles were imitated. All the company's lace had been sold through a selling agency in New York which had shown samples twice each year, in June and December, to cutters-up

---

[27] See Lewis, Howard T., "Arbitration in the Motion Picture Industry," October, 1929, printed as a separate pamphlet by the *Harvard Business Review*.

[28] III *Harvard Business Reports* 279.

and wholesalers. The wholesalers, in turn, had required samples of the patterns which they purchased to show to retailers. In many instances the wholesalers not only had permitted the patterns to be seen by other lace manufacturers, but also actually had given them samples. Wholesalers had followed this practice on the theory that by encouraging competition they could purchase lace at lower prices. The Allernet Lace Company had explained to them that since the value of a lace pattern was dependent largely on its exclusiveness, this policy often proved ruinous to their own lace business through the resultant glutting of the market. The practice of giving away patterns, however, had continued.

Designs were worked out by the company's designers after the particular kind of lace to be favored by fashion had been determined. Late in 1921, for instance, the Parisian dressmakers were featuring Spanish lace. Through its selling agent, the Allernet Lace Company received assurance that the spring lace styles in America, following as usual the foreign styles, would be Spanish, chiefly fiber silk and wool, or spun silk and wool, in black and various other colors. The company's designers immediately developed patterns suitable for that type of lace. Experience had shown that designs that had been used many years before for the same kind of lace could not be used again. From each of the designs developed, the drafting, which was the most important part of pattern creation, had to be done. This consisted of making a large drawing showing the position of each thread in a different-color ink for each movement of the shuttles in the machines. From this complicated drawing the design was coded so that the jacquard cards, which regulated the pattern in the looms, could be punched. After the pattern once was drafted, it easily could be imitated. For instance, after months of study and skilful drafting, the company's designers had produced a lace almost identical in appearance with a hand-made filet lace. Because of the low price for which it could be sold, this lace had been much in demand. This weave could not be patented, because it was itself a copy of a hand weave; hence rival mills almost immediately had imitated it and flooded the market.

Under existing laws, lace patterns could be patented at an average cost of $65 each, but two or three months' time was required from the date of application till the patent was granted. If placed upon the market during the interval that the patent application was pending, there was a risk that the designs would be imitated or the style changed before the patent was granted. The patentee could bring suit and collect damages from the infringing companies retroactive to the time when application for the patent had been made. Such legal action, however, had been considered too expensive and of doubtful benefit.

The evil of pirating styles had not been confined to the lace industry alone. A Design Registration League had been formed several years previously by representatives of practically every industry into which the element of fashion design entered. The conference committee of the organization included representatives of 21 trades, such as the lace, silk, and ribbon manufacturing industries, and 25 industrial associations, such as the Silk Association of America. The object of the league was to secure the passage of a bill by Congress which would "give to the designer and manufacturer the same adequate protection as the copyright granted to authors and their publishers."

The suggested bill provided for the removal of the subject of design protection from the patent division to the copyright division and proposed at a cost of $1 for a copyright to give economical and immediate protection in place of the expensive and long-delayed registration under the patent law. Although it was not expected that this would prevent all pirating of designs, it was expected to discourage the practice. Many objections to the bill had been raised on the ground that so low a fee would encourage manufacturers to ask for unwarranted protection which would lead to endless litigation. It also was pointed out that such legislation might work an injury to innocent infringers.

Concerning the bill, however, the chairman of the Patent Committee of the House of Representatives had said:

Many foreign countries have enacted statutes giving to authors of designs copyright protection, easily and quickly obtained at small cost. The process of procuring protection under our patent laws is necessarily slow, tedious, and expensive—the procedure under this bill is short and simple, resembling the practice in copyright cases, rather than patent cases. The Commissioner of Patents expresses the opinion that the statute will be capable of easy and effective administration, and will be helpful to the industries and commerce of the country. Some members of the Committee were at first inclined to fear that the bill might lead to excessive litigation, but the fact that the copyright law had not produced such results went far to allay their fears. We believe that the provisions of the bill are sufficient to protect registrants against actual offenders and also to discourage suits for technical and unsubstantial invasions of one's rights and make it practically impossible to bring, or to threaten to bring, vexatious actions to intimidate or oppress rival enterprises.

Although it was actively supporting this bill, the Allernet Lace Company was dubious as to the bill's efficacy. The provisions for quick action in copyrighting patterns were highly desirable, provided the fact that the pattern was protected would be a more serious deterrent to imitation than the words "patent applied for" had been. Because of the legal difficulties in establishing the fact of infringement, especially if the patterns varied in slight details, the Allernet Lace Company was convinced that even if the bill were passed, other means of preventing piracy would be necessary.

The company's product was sold by a firm of commission agents, with headquarters in New York City, to wholesalers and cutters-up.

Shortly before this question came before the Allernet Lace Company for decision, several large lace companies had adopted a policy of selling directly to retailers and cutters-up, but the Allernet Lace Company was unable to ascertain whether they had made this change for design protection or for some other reason. If the Allernet Lace Company were to adopt this plan, it would be forced to establish a New York office and display rooms with a highly paid personnel. A competent manager could not be hired for a salary of less than $20,000 or $25,000 per year, and it was stated that the company would have to employ salesmen not only to meet the retail buyers who came to New York but also to visit retail stores in all sections of the United States. Other salesmen would be required to sell to cutters-up, who after all might defeat the purpose of the change by demanding samples which they could give away. There also was the practical difficulty of adjusting the selling organization to the changed conditions each season, which resulted from the fluctuating proportion of the company's sales to cutters-up and to wholesalers. Past records showed that sales to wholesalers had varied from 10% to 90% of the season's totals, the remainder going to cutters-up. The selling agency had been able to shift its salesmen between wholesalers and cutters-up as conditions demanded. Although by selling directly to retailers the company probably would retain for itself the wholesaler's margin and the 8% commission paid to the agency, it was doubtful whether this saving would cover the additional expenses incurred. Since the wholesalers carried many novelty lines, their selling expenses were spread over many products, while for the Allernet Lace Company one line would have to bear all the selling expense.

Another factor of importance was that a substantial part of the company's product was being sold as of foreign manufacture. American consumers apparently did not have faith in the ability of domestic lace manufacturers to produce a first-class novelty line such as the Allernet Lace Company was featuring. In most cases the retailers, themselves, were ignorant of the sources of the laces which they sold, as shown by an incident which occurred in the New Jersey city in which the Allernet mill was located. The manager's wife noticed a piece of Spanish "all-over" lace in a local department store show-case, which she recognized as one made in the local mill. She was surprised when told by the salesperson that the lace was imported, since "they cannot make lace like that in this country." If the Allernet Lace Company were to attempt direct selling, it anticipated that it might encounter distrust on the part of retailers and that temporarily at least the style leadership which the line had enjoyed might be weakened when the retailers discovered that the laces were of domestic production. The company also expected that it would be necessary to maintain a representative in Europe in order to secure the style assistance previously received from the selling agency; the latest European styles were followed in America almost without exception.

The selling prices of novelty lace in which the Allernet Lace Company specialized had been fixed largely on the basis of what the traffic would bear. First, the style of garment with which the particular lace pattern would be used was determined. Then the cost of the other materials and the making of such a garment was figured. The price of the lace per yard was based on an estimate of what further expense the cutters-up or dressmakers would bear for the garment. The domestic companies could not have pursued such a policy, even with the protection of the 60% *ad valorem* tariff on importations, had not the quick changes in style made it impossible for foreign manufacturers to give sufficiently prompt deliveries. In the highest-quality laces, however, especially those requiring a great deal of handwork, which were not subject to radical changes, the domestic industry could not compete with foreign manufacturers.

In addition to the possibility of pattern protection, however, there seemed to be other advantages to be gained by the company by selling directly to retailers. The company's efforts to sell under its own trade name previously had been successfully blocked by the wholesalers, but the change would give the firm an opportunity to establish its brand with the retailers and cutters-up and thus to capitalize on the novelty-style leadership which its laces had built up under foreign-appearing brands. Despite the fact that selling expense, administration costs, and credit risks would be increased—the selling agency had guaranteed accounts—it seemed that there might be an opportunity to secure an increased profit by establishing a reputation for style leadership among consumers. As the reputation of a modiste was often the chief element in the price of his costumes, the company believed that if it could establish a high reputation for style and design with consumers, it could demand higher prices. The direct contact both with the style centers and with the retail market probably would assist in the successful interpretation of style trends.

* * * * * *

A well-known shoe made in this country by mass-production methods, is advertised as the exact duplicate of a well-known exclusive English model made by hand.[29] Photographs of the English models are shown, together with a photograph of the American reproduction. Prices of the English models were given as £4:10s and 6½ guineas, or $21.84 and $33.00; the price of the American model was given as $6.60. The

[29] See *New York Times*, September 13, 1929, and *Men's Wear*, August 21, 1929.

company so advertising had been "sending emissaries to leading boot-makers of London semi-annually, buying specimens of their product and appropriating those lasts and styles which experience had taught them would be best received in the American retail market . . . (The company) purchased forty pairs of shoes from Bartley, London, for example, and exhibited one of these shoes in a display window of each of the stores in the chain. Alongside of it was displayed the American approximation. This was done with a number of models from various British sources . . . (The company's) representative brought back with him the original last that Bartley whittled out by hand—and (the company's) last makers in America used the original as a model and turned out thousands with electric lathes."

This is indeed a borderline case. If the models are sold with the knowledge that they will be copied, no difficulty arises; and the price is circumstantial evidence that such was the case here. Furthermore, it is difficult to discover a reason for condemning such piracy, other than an indefinable reason—which, after all, may be the best kind of reason. But the immeasurable social effects of handing on the benefits of mass production and lower price to the consumer would outweigh this.

Speed in the transmission of photographs, especially by tele-photo processes, decreases the time-differential advantage which the original designer has over the pirate. Where the piracy is transoceanic, it is possible for the pirate to have his goods on the market before the designer can make a transoceanic shipment. This advantage of the pirate may be cut down by the speed of ocean steamships and by air transport. But, however small the difference may be made between communication and trans-portation, it is still in favor of the pirate, an advantage which generally neutralizes the advantage of secrecy possessed by the creator up to the time that he markets his goods.

It may be that the value of creative work, such as style design, is exaggerated in the mind of the creator, and style values are highly ephemeral from the economic point of view at least. But that these values exist, not even hard-headed business men are willing to deny. The Silk Association of America, for example, which has not regarded certain so-called "problems of business ethics"—such, *e.g.*, as commercial bribery and the weighting of silk with tin—to be important enough to cause trade concern, did in September, 1929, take cognizance of the growing problem of design piracy. The power of trade opinion was asserted by Ramsey Peugnet, the secretary of the association, to be the greatest asset in combating the evil. "Within the past year," he stated, "most members of the industry have come to recognize that a pattern designed by a manufacturer for his sole use during a given period is just as much his property as the machinery of his mill and they have no patience with those who think differently." As a practical method of dealing with the situation, the association has established a Design Registration Bureau, to which companies entrust their designs, previously guarded with the greatest secrecy and care. The bureau acts as a clearing-house to prevent unintentional duplication by other manufacturers. "Originality of design will always be questionable," continued Mr. Peugnet, "as the scarcity of really new ideas unquestionably shows. But priority of use and originality in application of designs have been established by the registration bureau, and are accepted by most of the trade. Since the organization of the bureau I have noticed a growing spirit of good faith throughout the trade, and intensive persuasion is now being used on the minority."

The pirating of Parisian styles by foreign buyers, especially by Americans, has very much concerned the French couturiers, as well it may. The French people undoubtedly have a sufficient amount of realism, as well as of humor, in their character to shrug their shoulders and smile at the indirect if gross compliment to their style leadership. But there are times when righteous indignation, prompted by an aesthetic as well as ethical offense, can and should be effectively translated into corrective action. A recent round-up (*"raffle"*), by the Parisian police,[30] of these offenders of good taste and of international goodwill, as well as of trade ethics, definitely classified the trade pirate with the criminal element to which he belongs. At the same time it must be recognized that an outstanding company, such as the makers of Dobb's hats, not only must expect a certain amount of piracy but also could well afford to disregard approximations to outright copying in view of the fact that the company itself will unquestionably benefit by the general extension and acceptance of the new design as the vogue. Not to lose sight of the advantage of riding the crest of the wave is more important than to concern oneself about those who are also being carried along in its wake.

[30] Reported in the Parisian newspapers, August 9, 1930.

CHAPTER XV

MISREPRESENTATIONS

The preceding chapter dealt with the problem of trade piracy, a direct form of invading a competitor's field of activity. This chapter will deal with a more indirect form of unfairness toward a competitor, namely, misrepresentations regarding one's own goods or functions. By regarding such misrepresentations solely from the consumer-purchaser's point of view, critics of business have failed to see what business men themselves are just learning, that by such misrepresentations a merchant achieves an unfair advantage over his competitors which is relatively as serious as is the advantage he seeks by pirating goods or by discrediting a competitor. Parading under the guise of false "affiliations," misinforming the customer regarding the source of materials or the directness of that source, misstatements as to the material content of commodities and as to their weight or quality, are all old forms of business deception. But the full incidence of the injury is a relatively recent discovery.

Indeed, the problem of business misrepresentations may consist not so much in a knowledge of their evil effects as in discovering what means can best be employed to eradicate them. Prior to this problem, however, is the necessity not only of finding intrinsic grounds for condemning and correcting the practices, but especially of discovering just what persons were injured in order that control may be properly and effectively exercised. As regards this latter point, a careful examination of the case material discloses injured parties in unexpected places; and one reason why the problem of business ethics has not hitherto been seriously enough considered is that only a fractional part of the injured parties actually know that they are being harmed and to what extent. Lying too frequently is regarded as a matter of personal concern, its chief harm being felt to be that a man is not true to himself. It is also generally recognized that lying is unfair to the man who is lied about, especially if the man is designated by terms which may include a number of other people.

402

But the full implications of lying include the loss of confidence in all statements in general. Similarly the effects on the whole trade group, by the misrepresentation of one's own business, have too seldom been appreciated.

Alleged "Affiliations"

The Federal Reserve Board recently had called to its attention an advertisement issued by a mortgage corporation containing the following statement:

Representatives of the Comptroller of the Currency, the very people who issue the national bank notes, make regular periodical examinations of the trust which secures Enhart Mortgage Corporation bonds.[1]

This statement was based upon the fact that the bonds in question were secured by mortgages pledged with a national bank as trustee.

While it is true that national bank examiners examine trust departments of national banks, they do so for the purpose of assuring compliance with the laws and regulations governing the conduct of such departments and not for the purpose of passing upon the value or adequacy of mortgages pledged with such national banks as trustees to secure bond issues. The above statement, therefore, was believed to be misleading to prospective purchasers of bonds issued by the corporation using the above language in its advertisement; and the board called the matter to the attention of the Attorney General of the United States, as a possible violation of the following provision of Section 1 of the act of May 24, 1926.

Be it enacted by the Senate and House of Representatives of the United States of America in Congress assembled, That no bank, banking association, trust company, corporation, association, firm, partnership, or person not organized under the provisions of the act of July 17, 1916, known as the Federal farm loan act, as amended, shall advertise or represent that it makes Federal farm loans or advertise or offer for sale as Federal farm loan bonds any bond not issued under the provisions of the Federal farm loan act, or make use of the word "Federal" or the words "United States" *or any other word or words implying Government ownership, obligation, or supervision in advertising or offering for sale any bond, note, mortgage,* or other security not issued by the Government of the United States or under the provisions of the said Federal farm loan act or some other act of Congress.[2]

Through the intervention of the Department of Justice the use of this misleading language in the present case was terminated.

The board desires to call this matter to the attention of all national banks acting as trustees under bond issues, and suggests that they

[1] Fictitious name. See *Federal Reserve Bulletin*, p. 638, September, 1929. See also Federal Bond and Mortgage case, VIII F. T. C. D. 194.

[2] 44 Stat. 628, United States Code, Title 12, Section 485.

scrutinize carefully all advertisements of bond issues under which they are acting as trustees with a view of preventing the use of misleading statements similar to that quoted above, not only for the protection of prospective purchasers of such bonds but also for the protection of the good names and reputations of such national banks themselves.

A somewhat similar situation was recently presented by the Bank of United States, a private New York bank. The use of such a title has, since the founding of this bank, been prohibited by the Federal statute already referred to. The difficulties of the Bank of United States in December, 1930, extended by implication to far wider areas than would have been the case if the title of the bank had indicated its private nature.

Henry Drafter,[3] doing business in Nashville, Tennessee, under the name of the Drafter Textbook Company,[3] was engaged in the business of publishing and selling textbooks, charts, lesson sheets, *etc.*, whereby bookkeeping, shorthand, typewriting, business English, business arithmetic, and other studies were taught in business colleges and in home-study courses to students in various parts of the United States.

In 1919, during the course of his business activities, Drafter published and distributed printed circulars entitled "Government Reports on Pitmanic and Gregg Shorthand Writers." These circulars contained statements and statistics, some of which purported to be reports of official organizations or bodies, proving the superiority of the Pitman system of shorthand. One of the reports declared to be a government report, was that of a private organization composed of individual high-school teachers which was not a public organization or a government agency. Some of the statistics quoted in 1919 were from the official report of the United States Commissioner of Education of 1913. Another statement in regard to the percentage of official court reporters of the United States Government using the Pitman system was not contained in any United States Government report. Another statement was to the effect that on certain blanks issued by the Government for teachers of shorthand in schools conducted by the Government the following sentence appeared, "No one need apply unless he or she teaches the Pitmanic system"; this statement was false, as no such preference has ever been given government sanction. Under the caption, "still another government report," was published a report of the National Shorthand Reporters' Association, a private organization.

Similar intimations were contained in newspaper advertising with reference to alleged "decisions of the Supreme Court." References

[3] Fictitious name. II F. T. C. D. 388. See also Civil Service School, VIII F. T. C. D. 471.

were also made to the "civil service bookkeeping set drafted by the Government," consisting of entries and problems taken from specimen entries issued by the United States Civil Service Commission and supplemented by comments and instructions drafted by Drafter himself. Claims that 85% of government employees used the training course system sponsored by Drafter, were false. A statement was made that 85% of the government official court stenographers who drew $5,000 or more per year used the Pitman system, whereas no official stenographer for any United States court at that time received a salary of $5,000 or more per year.

* * * * * *

The Belleron Soap Company[4] was an Indiana corporation, located at Indianapolis, which manufactured and sold soap. The company was organized in 1895 by William Belleron[4] and his brother, but since 1903 neither had had anything to do with the control or management of the company. Aside from the fact that an uncle of the Belleron brothers was a doctor, no Doctor Belleron was ever connected with the corporation.

In conducting its business the Belleron company advertised in theatrical magazines and other publications, soliciting orders from street vendors, peddlers, and other dealers. Exclusive sales agents were appointed for various territories in the United States. Representations of the Belleron Soap Company were to the effect that some of its soaps were medicated and possessed curative and healing properties, that they were made by a formula prepared by a physician and were prescribed by medical authorities, and that they were endorsed by a national association of physicians.

One brand of this soap was sold under the trade name of "Dr. Belleron's Antiseptic Soap." In the container was the statement "endorsed by eminent physicians throughout the land." This soap was an ordinary unmedicated soap no more antiseptic than any other soap of similar quality. It was not a high-grade toilet soap nor was it endorsed by eminent physicians throughout the land; neither did it contain medicaments prescribed by medical authorities. Other brands of soap made by the Belleron company contained upon the carton the printed statements "manufactured only by United States Medical Association," "manufactured for National Medical Association," although no such association had anything to do with the manufacture of these soaps. The national body of physicians and surgeons of the United States is known as the American Medical Association.

* * * * * *

[4] Fictitious name. VI F. T. C. D. 107. For a similar case involving the engineering profession, see Associated Drafting Engineers, IX F. T. C. D. 283.

The Specialty Sweepers Company[5] was a New York corporation selling vacuum cleaners, sweepers, and similar devices. It sold at retail some 24 different makes of vacuum cleaners or sweepers out of a total of 29 such devices then on the market and made by various competing manufacturers. Among the vacuum cleaners which were handled, the Imperial Electric Vacuum Cleaner was owned by and especially manufactured for the Specialty Sweepers Company. For a period of more than three years preceding May, 1921, the Specialty Sweepers Company made a considerably greater profit on the sale of this product than it did on the sale of any other type of cleaner advertised and sold by it.

In advertising its cleaners for sale the Specialty Sweepers Company circulated a "rating sheet" wherein it designated and named certain cleaners as "Three-Star Cleaners" as an indication of their superiority over the other devices listed in the "rating sheet." At no place did the company indicate in any manner its ownership or special interest in the Imperial cleaner.

The "rating sheet" was made up as follows:

Three-Star Cleaners		Per Cent Perfect
Imperial	First Choice	94%
Victor	Second Choice	89
Royal	Third Choice	89
Regina	Fourth Choice	87
Eureka	Fifth Choice	86
Apex	Sixth Choice	85

This list was stated to be the result of the judgment of the Specialty Sweepers Company's rating committee which met semi-monthly "to test cleaners scientifically for EFFICIENCY and comparison made on the points of SIMPLICITY and CONSTRUCTION." Statistics as to "DURABILITY" were furnished by the superintendent of the repair department and "prices were not considered at all." A cash discount of 7% was allowed on all cleaners other than those designated as "Three-Star," and of 3% on all "Three-Star" cleaners. A guarantee for a period of one year from date of sale was given with all "Three-Star" cleaners.

After August, 1919, Specialty Sweepers Company discontinued the use of this rating sheet, but thereafter published and circulated a price list of various machines or devices handled by it. In this list certain cleaners were designated by stars as those in which Specialty Sweepers Company was "especially interested" without indicating what the character or extent of this "especial interest" was.

The preceding cases illustrate attempts which are sometimes made by businesses to achieve an enhanced sale value of their

[5] Fictitious name.   III F. T. C. D. 377; see also I, 30.

commodities, by asserting an affiliation with, or endorsement by, an independent and reputable institution. In the Enhart and Drafter cases, the name of the United States Government was so used; similar cases have arisen in regard to the sale of "Army and Navy" goods, and in connection with such commodities as lumber, spark plugs, adding machines, salt blocks, motor fuel,[6] and especially paints and varnishes.[7]

In the Belleron case, the medical profession was similarly used; other cases occurring in connection with the sale of "electric" belts and disinfecting fluids.[8] The American Medical Association is quite alert in handling cases of this sort: a recent campaign for selling yeast, for example, has been featured by testimonials from European medical experts only; American doctors of equal ability and reputation would not think of lending their names for such purposes. Their professional association regards this as a mode of advertising beneath the dignity of the profession, which furthermore cannot allow the health of the public to be jeopardized by possible abuses of such practices. But the chief business injury is done to the business competitor who does not employ such tactics. This is particularly true of a situation illustrated by the Specialty Sweepers Company, where just the opposite misrepresentation occurred: an affiliation which actually existed was denied by an assertion of "independence." Similar cases have occurred in connection with seeds and fertilizer,[9] where a supposedly "unbiased" statement as to quality was advertised. The problem here involved is one of double agency, which is apparently pernicious in marketing activities; in finance and brokerage, the relative magnitude of the operations practically requires a separate treatment, and is not within the province of this volume. The closely related problem of the "testimonial advertisement" will be dealt with in a later chapter.

Sources of Materials

The preceding cases have dealt with false or exaggerated assertions or implications concerning affiliations which are claimed by

[6] I F. T. C. D. 316; I, 301; IV, 41; III, 361; III, 402; IV, 149; IV, 387; see also VII, 40, 54; VIII, 415; IX, 38, 242, 420.

[7] III F. T. C. D. 42, 130, 413; IV, 102, 144; V, 112, 253; VI, 24, 294, 384.

[8] II F. T. C. D. 335; III, 53; see also "official" golf-ball case, VII, 250.

[9] I F. T. C. D. 430; II, 427.

businesses. In the following cases, a similar form of misrepresentation occurs, but with reference to the source of the goods which the business company is engaged in handling.

The Hinkel-Krauss Company[10] was an Ohio corporation located at Fremont. It manufactured and sold shears, manicure sets, razors, and cutlery. Prior to May 1, 1919, when the company was organized, the Hinkel Company[10] and the Krauss Company[10] had been operating as separate companies competing in the same line of business.

When the Hinkel-Krauss Company was organized, it purchased from the Krauss Company a small quantity of razors which the latter had in stock. Upon these razors were printed the words "Sheffield" without any other marks, although they were of domestic manufacture. The organizers of the Hinkel-Krauss Company assumed and believed that these razors had been manufactured in Sheffield, England, and that they had been imported by the Krauss Company.

That razors of high quality had been manufactured in Sheffield, England, in large quantities for a long period of time was well known to the trade and to the buying public. The word "Sheffield," when used in connection with cutlery, had come to be understood by the trade and purchasing public in the United States as indicating that such cutlery was made in Sheffield, England, and was of good quality.

These razors were closed out in job lots within one year after the organization of the Hinkel-Krauss Company and thereafter no sales were made by them under similar circumstances.

* * * * * *

H. L. Highgate[11] was an individual engaged in the business of general merchandise brokerage under the corporate name of Highgate & Company[11] in Norfolk, Virginia. Highgate & Company purchased and sold at wholesale ground rock salt imported from Germany.

Highgate & Company,[11] through their salesmen and circulars, represented their ground rock salt as "No. 1 Star Brand Common Fine Salt" and sold it at 2 cents per 100 pounds under the market price. Other names attributed to this salt were "common fine," "fine" and "highest grade of salt obtainable."

The ground salt dealt in by Highgate & Company was not manufactured or produced by the evaporation process and was inferior in quality to salt manufactured by the evaporation process in various plants in the United States, nor did Highgate & Company disclose the fact that it was obtaining its salt from Germany.

[10] Fictitious name. V F. T. C. D. 33. See also Imported Bavarian Barley Malt, VIII *ibid.*, 250. Other Sheffield cases are found in IX *ibid.*, 116, 125, 134, 143.

[11] Fictitious name. VI F. T. C. D. 28.

Salt manufactured and produced in the United States had for a number of years come to be preferred, by the trade and the consuming public, to salt imported from Germany. Furthermore, a substantial part of the trade and the consuming public had come to understand that salt which was not marked or represented as having been imported from a foreign country was salt manufactured or produced in the United States. The labeling of Highgate & Company's products led people to believe that these products were of domestic manufacture.

A large number of manufacturers who labeled their salt "common fine salt," "common fine," "fine," and "No. 1 fine salt" manufactured and produced their salt in the United States by the evaporation process. Others who did not employ such methods or who did not manufacture their salt in the United States did not use such terms. Furthermore, a number of importers of German rock salt disclosed this fact to the purchasing public.

An interesting problem is presented by contrasting the Hinkel-Krauss and Highgate cases as regards motive. In the former case, the firm had found itself possessed of the cutlery by virtue of its purchase of another business; Hinkel-Krauss did not know that the cutlery was falsely marked; and after disposing of the lot, which consisted of only a very limited supply, the practice was discontinued. In the Highgate case, however, the deception was continuous and was knowingly practiced. From a legal or moral point of view or from the standpoint of Kantian ethics, the difference in motive would constitute a radical distinction in the cases and would call for a difference in regard to any penalties inflicted on the parties concerned.

As a matter of business practice or business ethics, however, such a distinction is not a paramount question. The problem of business ethics is to discover practices which injure the competitor as well as the purchaser-consumer, and the chief purpose of business ethics is to stop the practice without necessarily entailing any punishment on the offending party. This point of view is more closely connected with Aristotle's attitude, that a man's ethical responsibility is not bounded by his consciousness of the import of the act but extends to the consequences of his acts. An examination of the incidence of injuries inflicted by ignorant as well as by dishonest practices soon discloses the fact that there is very little difference in the degree of harm done. A "dumb" competitor is frequently as dangerous as a "crooked" one, hence the motive matters little to the student of business ethics, who is interested chiefly in the objective elements of the problem, or to the business man who is interested in eliminating the injury by stopping the practice. All the Federal Trade Commission can do in such a case is to issue a "cease and desist" order. In case redress for damage is desired, the civil courts must be resorted to; in a criminal action or in an attempt to apply moral condemnation, the motive factor assumes importance. Business ethics stresses the objective situation rather than the motive.

The following case still further illustrates the point.

Since 1850 and more particularly since 1865 clothing for men has been manufactured at Rochester, New York,[12] and the industry there has had a continuous growth in the number of factories located there and in the amount of capital invested. Besides Rochester the principal centers of the manufacture of men's and boys' clothing in the United States are Chicago, New York City, Philadelphia, and Baltimore. Three grades of clothing are generally recognized by the trade: high-grade, medium, and cheap or low-grade clothing. Compared with the output of men's clothing in the places named, that of Rochester had, in 1923 and for many preceding years, the largest proportion of high-grade clothes, the development of the men's clothing industry there having been marked by the early and progressive adoption of improved methods and conditions of manufacture. A superior type of labor and favorable labor conditions had enabled the manufacturers to apply skilled labor more profitably to the higher grade of product, increasing that class of goods proportionately.

In 1892 the manufacture of men's clothing had become foremost among the industries of Rochester. In 1895 the Clothing Exchange was organized there, the membership being made up of the clothing manufacturers of that city and the purpose being primarily to prevent labor troubles and generally to promote the interests and improve the conditions of the industry. One of the activities of the Rochester Clothing Exchange was to protect the reputation of the city as a clothing market against the use of the city's name by manufacturers elsewhere and to its prejudice. The Exchange cooperated with the Chamber of Commerce of Rochester in advertising and fostering the reputation of Rochester for the manufacture of high-grade clothing for men and boys.

Among the activities of the Chamber of Commerce of Rochester were the adoption and dissemination of the slogan "Rochester-made Means Quality" which it applied to the clothing industry as well as to others. Furthermore, in the advertising conducted by the manu-

[12] VI F. T. C. D. 259. See also Tampa Cigar case, VII, 503; Havana, VIII, 136, IX, 255; Key West, VIII, 270; Mount Olive Coal, VII, 531; Grand Rapids Furniture, IX, 304, 324, 333.

facturers of Rochester they had made conspicuous the identity of their products with the city of Rochester. This activity had the result of spreading throughout the United States and establishing, for men's clothing made in Rochester, the reputation of a superior quality and value in style and workmanship and reliability. The name "Rochester" when used on labels or tags attached to clothing for men and boys was understood generally by the trade and by the purchasing public to indicate that such clothing was made in Rochester, New York.

Henry Mollowitz[13] was an individual manufacturing and selling men's and boys' clothing, with his main office and place of business located in New York City. He operated, however, under the firm name of The Rochester Clothing Company. Attached to clothing made by him were tags or labels containing the words "trade-mark, Rochester Clothing Company—for particular men." By this means the public was deceived into believing that the products of the Rochester Clothing Company were made at Rochester, New York.

Another point brought out by this case, as well as the two preceding, is that the incidence of the injury is frequently quite wide-spread. The situation may best be presented by asking: What reason is there, in the Hinkel-Krauss case, for a United States governmental agency to take cognizance of an injury to a foreign business or city—*e.g.*, Sheffield cutlery? It is easy to see why, from a limited nationalistic point of view, a practice should be condemned if the practice is unfair and benefits a German business, as in the Highgate case, or where it injures an American city like Rochester. But why should a United States Government agency protect Sheffield, England? The answer to this query is to be found by discovering that injuries result from the act even after eliminating from consideration the rights of the consumer-purchaser and of the city of origin and manufacture, whether foreign or not. These remaining interests alone suggest the desirability of curbing the practice. There are, first, the interests of competing manufacturers in this country who label their goods honestly and who are therefore compelled to meet the sales appeal of a false statement, as to origin of goods, by a price reduction which will effect competitive equality. And, secondly, there are the interests of two kinds of sales competitors: those who sell Sheffield ware honestly, and who cannot compete, either in prices or in profits, with those who falsely assert their cutlery to be of Sheffield origin; and those who do not deal in Sheffield ware and who honestly say

[13] Fictitious name.

so, and who therefore have to compete with the sales appeal of the Sheffield mark. A similar situation has already been discussed[14] in connection with commercial bribery in securing contracts for ship supplies; those ports which have made an effort to eliminate the practice have a very definite and legitimate interest in having the practice eliminated elsewhere. These broader social-economic effects are as vital as are the more obvious injuries inflicted on the consumer-purchaser.

Morality condemns the above practices primarily because of the offender's false position, and secondarily because of the immediate harm to the purchaser. The law condemns these practices largely because of the incidence of the damage on the purchaser; but the law, except in its administrative activities under the direction of a government commission, waits for the damaged party to take the initiative in prosecuting the suit in a court. The fact that a part of the incidence of the injury is on the trade as a whole, is subordinated to other interests by morality and is practically disregarded by the law. Furthermore, constitutive law would regard the ignorance, on the part of some competitors, of the injury they were receiving, as a basic reason for not offering social assistance to relieve them of their difficulties. Business ethics more nearly resembles administrative law in that it seizes upon this fact, that a whole trade group is adversely affected, as the prime reason for insisting that the more alert members of a trade should be permitted to eliminate practices among themselves which are detrimental to fair competition and to trade health.

Direct from Grower and Mills

Browns, Stagman & Company[15] was a New York corporation located at Chicago. It sold goods, wares, and merchandise from one central office by the use of catalogues, parcel-post and express service, and other means. It owned and operated warehouses in various states in the United States and purchased large amounts of merchandise both in foreign countries and in the United States. The company manufactured some of its merchandise, purchasing the necessary ingredients and raw materials thereof.

For two years prior to 1918 Browns, Stagman & Company circulated catalogues throughout the United States containing advertisements offering for sale its teas to its customers and prospective customers and

[14] See Chapter XIII.
[15] Fictitious name. I F. T. C. D. 163.

those of its competitors and to the general public. Browns, Stagman & Company claimed in these catalogues that such teas were purchased through a special representative of the company who was sent to Japan for this purpose and who personally supervised the picking of the tea. By this method Browns, Stagman & Company claimed that it not only secured the finest and choicest leaves for its best grades of tea but also saved the middleman's profit as well. As a matter of fact Browns, Stagman & Company purchased a very large percentage of its teas from importers located in the United States and in the same manner in which teas were purchased by the competitors of Browns, Stagman & Company.

* * * * * *

Harwell Dowing,[16] under the name of Federated Paper Companies,[16] an unincorporated company, purchased paper bags and towels of manufacturers and resold these to wholesale dealers. He had offices in New York City and Chicago.

Dowing held himself out as a manufacturer of paper bags and towels, his letterheads stating that "mills" were located in New York, Pennsylvania, Wisconsin, and Massachusetts. He did not as a matter of fact own any mill, nor did he hold an interest in any mill, except two shares par value $100 in one mill from which he purchased some of his products. During 1917 and 1918, Dowing purchased practically all the products handled by him from paper mills in which he had no interest.

Dowing, furthermore, represented to the trade that the prices quoted by him were "f.o.b. our warehouses, Springfield, Massachusetts, Atlanta, Georgia, and Chicago, Illinois." He did not own any warehouses in Massachusetts or Georgia. He did, however, store stocks of paper bags there in public warehouses.

In 1919, Dowing purchased six-elevenths of all the paper bags and towels, sold by him, from mills other than the one in which he owned the two shares of stock mentioned above. From December, 1918, to August, 1919, this mill made paper bags while Dowing owned stock, during which time he handled about one-third of its output as sales agent.

In so advertising and holding himself out to the public as a manufacturer of paper bags and towels, Dowing misled the public into believing that by purchasing such products from him it was eliminating the profit of the middleman.

* * * * * *

A partnership was formed in Chicago for the purpose of trading under the name of Lake Storage Company.[17] It manufactured phono-

---

[16] Fictitious name.   III F. T. C. D. 13.
[17] Fictitious name.   III F. T. C. D. 156.

graphs resembling those made by well-known manufacturers and sold these to the general public. These phonographs were advertised in part for a "mail-order" business and in part in the classified advertising columns, offering for sale "slightly used phonographs of standard makes" of great value at abnormal and unusual reductions from the full standard resale prices. In some cases this reduction amounted to as much as one-third from an advertised price of $250. These advertisements avoided reference to the fact that the Lake Storage Company was manufacturing the phonographs, but gave the impression that the individuals composing the Lake Storage Company were householders offering for sale phonographs that had been used only a short time.

Phonographs also were advertised as having been stored for safekeeping and as being then for sale to reimburse the storage concern for unpaid storage claims. The number available was not limited, as stated in the advertisements, but was large and was constantly replenished by the factory.

A part of the campaign for accurate advertising and labeling of goods has concerned itself with statements as to the place of origin or source of the goods. The reputation which has attached itself to certain countries or cities or regions, especially for high-quality goods, has been taken advantage of by those sellers who wished unfairly to enhance sales values by capitalizing such reputations. The Hinkel-Krauss Company, previously discussed, misrepresented its goods as imported, and as coming from a city the name of which has become synonymous with high-quality cutlery. Similar cases have occurred in connection with the sale of matches, cigars, rope, and watches.[18] Highgate and Company did just the reverse; they sold inferior imported goods under a trade name which customarily designated a superior American product. The Rochester Clothing case showed how the practice may effect the reputation of many industries besides the one immediately concerned. The Chamber of Commerce of Rochester recognized the extent of the incidence of the injury as applying to the entire industrial region centering at Rochester. The apple growers of the Pacific Northwest faced a similar act of appropriation of reputation.[19]

The Browns, Stagman case is similar to the Hinkel-Krauss case, in that the source was declared to be foreign. Here, however, the statement as to the origin of the commodity is true—in

[18] III F. T. C. D., 199, 407; VI, 159, 207, 253; V, 120; VI, 101; VI, 452. See also, as regards cutlery, IV, 114, 373, 382.
[19] VI F. T. C. D. 198.

some cases, involving olive oil and condensed milk,[20] the statements have not been true—but misrepresentation occurs as regards the directness of the purchase, leading the consumer-purchaser to infer that he will benefit by an implied price reduction as the result of eliminating the "middleman." Similar misrepresentations have been made in regard to coffee and seeds.[21] So much publicity has been given to the "elimination of the middleman" that a sales value lies in appropriating the slogan. This is further illustrated by the Federated Paper case, where ownership of mills or direct access to them is falsely asserted as a sales argument. This method has been employed to sell lumber, paints and oils, check-writers, rope, coal, clothing, shoes, and hosiery.[22] Exactly the reverse of this misrepresentation is exhibited in the Lake Storage case, where the sales company did not disclose the fact that it was actually engaged in production.

In dealing with these cases, the Federal Trade Commission has kept in mind the interests of the consumer-purchaser, of the locality or industry directly affected, and of allied interests. The Commission furthermore asserted its right to order such practices stopped because of the broader element of "unfair" competition to which these practices subjected the competitors of the businesses which were guilty of misrepresentation. In the Rochester clothing case, for example, a part of the injury, by virtue of the enhanced selling power these practices gave the offender, Mollowitz, fell on those New York manufacturers who did not resort to such tactics.

Material Contents

The commonest, as well as the oldest, unfair business practice has been the sale of goods for something other than they are.[23]

[20] I F. T. C. D. 285; II, 171.

[21] II F. T. C. D., 427; III, 177.

[22] I F. T. C. D., 316; I, 285, II, 295, V, 410, VI, 294; IV, 87; VI, 101, 497; IV, 209; IV, 215, VI, 155,; I, 495; V, 245. See also VII, 35, 62, 68, 195, 200, and 370; VIII, 146, 167, 214, 223, 276, 283, 392, and 420; IX, 33 and 349. The acquisition of one-sixth of the stock of a hosiery mill by a corporation and having a single director on the board does not constitute "ownership." —3 Fed. (2d) 105.

[23] Rogers, E. S., *Good-will, Trade-marks and Unfair Trading*, New York: McGraw-Hill Book Company, Inc., 1914, has an interesting outline of items constituting "unfair competition," p. 137. Chase and Schlink, *Your Money's Worth*, New York: The Macmillan Company, 1927, contains a wealth of illustrative material.

This involves either misrepresenting the material contents of articles, introducing adulterants, or misrepresenting the quality of the goods.

The royal commission appointed in 1928 by the provincial government of Saskatchewan to investigate the grain-marketing problem,[24] discovered that, in transfer houses at Montreal and also at points in the United States, soft wheat originating in the United States was being extensively mixed with hard Canadian wheat and that the resulting composition was being sold in Europe under the certificates of the Canadian Government.

The extent to which "mixing" was being carried on among the private terminal elevators at the head of the Great Lakes was revealed in the House of Commons by a western Liberal member, who submitted evidence from the ingoing and outgoing returns of wheat at these elevators during the crop year 1926–27. They showed that the elevators took in about 60,000,000 bushels classified under the three statutory grades, Nos. 1, 2, and 3 Northern, but that they contrived to send out no less than 81,000,000 bushels of these same three grades. It was also shown that inferior types of wheat, like "Kota," had a habit of mysteriously vanishing when they reached the terminal elevators. Thus, in this particular year, receipts amounted to 886,609 bushels, of which only some 19,000 bushels emerged.

Not only were complaints arising from the Liverpool grain merchants; but the western wheat farmers were aroused by this disclosure of methods which were bound to depress prices, not only because of the apparently greater supply of higher-grade wheat but also because the reputation of Canadian wheat would suffer at every important grain center in Europe. Grain exchanges and boards of trade were also concerned over the practice.

As a remedy, it was suggested that the Canadian Grain Act be amended to require western Canadian grain to be finally inspected and graded at the ocean port whence it departed overseas and the final certificate to be issued there instead of at the head of the Great Lakes.

This situation is not peculiar to business practices; it has been discovered in connection with population problems also! Thus, if one should take the number of mulattoes resident in the United States in 1910, as recorded in the census of that year, and then should add the number born in the next decade and subtract the number dying in the same period, the resulting figure should indicate the mulatto population of 1920. As a matter of fact,

[24] *Boston Transcript*, March 23, 1929. For a similar case, see IX F. T. C. D. 365.

the Census Report of 1920 discloses a much smaller figure. Evidently there is considerable evidence for believing that a large number of mulattoes were converted into "whites" in the interval.

The differentiation of natural products of the soil and their separate identification through intensive cultivation, and the identity of minerals, especially metals, afford a basis for keeping such materials distinct as constituents of finished products. Especially is this true in the textile trade, where cotton, wool, silk, and linen each has sufficient merits to warrant its use in particular kinds of commodities. Cotton, however, has perhaps been the worst offender in parading as some other material, its abundance—cotton-goods production amounts to 15 times as much as its nearest textile competitor—cheapness, and adaptability making easy its substitution for other fabrics or the adulteration of their products. Rayon, or artificial silk, has been the latest offender. The following cases are typical of the practice of misrepresenting the material contents of goods and the processes to which they have been subjected.

Frane & Hank[25] was a copartnership with its office and business located in New York City; it engaged in the sale of hosiery at wholesale.

Frane & Hank sold hosiery in containers labeled and branded "Ladies' Silk Boot Hose." This hosiery contained no true silk but was made of cotton and animal or vegetable fibre. Dealers who purchased this hosiery sold it as labeled and branded to the general purchasing public. No other words appeared on the packages to indicate the character, kind, or grade of material entering into the manufacture of this product.

The term "silk boot hosiery" signified, to the unskilled buying public, hosiery composed of silk produced from the cocoon of the silkworm, except for the top, heel, toe and possibly the sole, which were known to be composed of some different material. Other hosiery products sold by Frane & Hank were labeled "Ladies' Art Silk Hose," a term which also signified to the unskilled buying public hosiery composed entirely of true silk.

Many of the competitors of Frane & Hank sold hosiery advertised as "silk boot hose" of which the top, toe, and heel were made of cotton. Others of Frane & Hank's competitors sold hosiery made entirely of silk produced from the cocoon of the silkworm and labeled it simply "silk hose." Other competitors sold hosiery made of cotton and animal or vegetable fibre and containing no true silk, but labeled with no words descriptive of the materials entering into the manufacture

[25] Fictitious name. VI F. T. C. D. 144.

of this hosiery. Some manufacturers labeled hosiery so made "artificial silk and cotton" and "fibre silk and cotton."

The difficulty here presented is based on an even more fundamental problem, namely, the grading of raw silk. This was evidenced by the great amount of interest shown by the hosiery trade in the second international technical raw-silk conference held in November, 1929, under the auspices of the Silk Association of America. Although a considerable difference of opinion, as well as practice, was shown in reference to raw-silk classification, especially between the Japanese and American representatives, the former were very much impressed by the difficulties arising from their methods of classification among the marketers of finished products in the important market, America. The Japanese favored merging the results of all major tests into a single percentage; the American contention was that such methods conceal certain inferior characteristics, and that such results cause most of the trouble in the processing and marketing of silk products. The Chinese and Italian delegates favored the American point of view, the Italians reporting the establishment of a silk exchange in Milan where the three grades advocated by the American National Raw Silk Exchange are observed.

The Winsted Hosiery Company[26] was a Connecticut corporation located in Winsted, Connecticut. It manufactured and sold underwear, shirts, and other wearing apparel.

It labeled, advertised, and branded certain lines of underwear as follows: "Men's Natural Merino," "Men's Wool Shirts," "Men's Natural Wool Shirts," "Men's Natural Worsted Shirts," and "Men's Australian Wool Shirts." These articles of wearing apparel were not composed wholly of wool, part being wool and part being cotton. The percentage of wool varied from 20% to 80%. The purchasing public was frequently led by retailers to believe that these articles were composed wholly of wool.

For a period of 20 years it had been the general custom and practice in the underwear business to label and advertise underwear as "Natural Merino," "Wool," "Natural Wool," "Natural Worsted," and "Australian Wool," when in fact such underwear so described was not composed wholly of wool; the percentage of wool varied among different manufacturers to meet the varying demands of the trade solicited and served. The custom and practice was general in the underwear trade throughout the United States, although there were a few manufacturers

[26] II F. T. C. D. 202.

of underwear whose products were composed wholly of wool and were labeled "All Wool." Large quantities of imported underwear followed the labeling practice of the American manufacturers.

The Federal Trade Commission issued a "cease and desist" order against the Winsted Hosiery Company, whereupon the latter carried the case to the courts. The Circuit Court of Appeals, Second Circuit, reversed the order of the Commission, holding:

In this case there was obviously no unfair method of competition as against other manufacturers of underwear. The labels were thoroughly established and understood in the trade. There was no passing-off of goods for those of another manufacturer . . . Manifestly no other manufacturer of underwear could have maintained a suit against the (Winsted Hosiery) company for unfair competition . . . Assuming that some consumers are misled because they do not understand the trade significance of labels, or because some retailers deliberately deceive them as to its meaning, the result is in no way connected with unfair competition, but is like any other misdescription or misbranding of products. Conscientious manufacturers may prefer not to use a label which is capable of misleading and it may be that it will be desirable to prevent the use of the particular labels, but it is in our opinion not within the province of the Federal Trade Commission to do so.[27]

Aside from the obvious inability of the court to get beyond the strictly legal point of view, the decision exactly states the situation. A particular trade had gotten itself into a situation where lying, by its prevalence, imposed no peculiar handicap on any particular member of the trade. Granting the view of the court, that "the Commission is not made a censor of commercial morals generally," and that "its authority is to inquire into unfair methods of competition in interstate and foreign commerce, if so doing will be of interest to the public and if such method of competition is prohibited by the (Federal Trade Commission) Act," and excluding considerations for the purchaser of the commodities, the question arises: Does the prevalence of the trade practice warrant its continuance?

Note that the basic trade appeal of Business Ethics is that the unfair merchant makes it difficult for those competitors who want to establish fair and honest standards to do so. Where a trade is thus at odds with itself, Business Ethics sanctions methods which will induce the recalcitrant members to "get into line." Thus, internecine advertising and trade piracy undermine the health

[27] *Winsted Hosiery Company v. Federal Trade Commission*, 272 Fed. 957 (1921).

of a trade and are censured by those who have at heart the best interest of the trade: its stability, its dignity, and its soundness. Now, in the Winsted case, as in many others, "everybody's doing it," but what they are all doing is condemned by other trades and in general by all those who believe that truth and accuracy are social-ethical standards that should be held as preferable objectives.

One distinction which must be kept in mind, regarding the misbranding of goods, is that the merchants are less liable to be deceived by such a practice than are the consumer-purchasers. An imitation leather was sold as "Duraleather,"[28] thus having the "tendency and capacity" to deceive the ultimate consumer into believing that it was genuine leather. The jobber or other distributor purchased it from the manufacturer with full knowledge that it was an imitation, but the ultimate customer did not see the brand. The Federal Trade Commission held that the manufacturer did not thereby escape legal responsibility, this being the first time that such a case has been so decided by the Commission. The United States Circuit Court of Appeals, Third Circuit, Philadelphia, upheld the decision of the Commission.

The practical situation confronting the manufacturers of "part-wool" underwear is that no member of the trade can at any time know how much his competitors are diluting the wool content of their products. The result is a Gresham's law of commodities: the bad drive out the good. This means that, added to the uncertainty of the situation, the trade term "wool" will gradually lose all its significance and therefore all its value. The situation is well illustrated in the following case, involving wool blankets, print cloths and sheetings.

Hampley Knitting Mills[29] was engaged in manufacturing blankets, sheetings, and allied articles. The following problems confronted the management at various times, all having to do with reducing the quality of merchandise in order to meet competition.

In the manufacture of blankets, there was the "all-wool" type which was what it was represented to be. In addition, there were in the trade various grades of "part-wool" blankets which contained various amounts of wool, averaging 4% but running in some cases to as low as $\frac{1}{12}$ of 1% and even to no wool content at all. In six samples from as

[28] See *Bulletin*, Boston Better Business Bureau, November 7, 1929.
[29] Fictitious name.

many competitors, the manager of Hampley Knitting Mills discovered two which contained 7% wool, while the other four contained none. In some samples tested by the Better Business Bureau, several had a wool content of only 2%. Several years previous to this test, "part-wool" blankets contained a greater range of percentages of wool; such that a large New York department store observed the policy of labeling its blankets "wool and cotton" if the wool content was over 50%, "cotton and wool" if the wool content was between 25% and 50%, while blankets containing less than 25% of wool were called simply "blankets." Tariff practice is that goods rate as per material content of greatest value. "Part-wool" blankets of only 20% or 25% wool content would be listed as cotton products.

The cotton which is most frequently used in "part-wool" blankets is "China" cotton, a short curly fibre, and "Peruvian" cotton, a longer fibre; both are very much like wool in appearance, cheaper than wool but more difficult to weave than either wool or American cotton, and possessing insulating qualities as high as wool; their wearing qualities, however, are not comparable with that of wool. The cotton and wool content of blankets can be detected by chemical tests within an error of a few *per cent;* and with some degree of accuracy by expert observation in good light, but with an error of from 10% to 15%.

The buying of blankets is done largely by women, who cannot detect differences in cotton and wool content sufficiently accurately to eliminate competitive abuses. That is, the competitive margin among manufacturers is so close that variations in cotton and wool content, which cannot be detected by the buyer, may "make or break" a manufacturer or seriously affect his profits. The result in the blanket-manufacturing trade has been a continuous reduction of wool content in "part-wool" blankets until the present low content has been reached. Manufacturers, therefore, are faced with the dilemma of independently maintaining their own standards of wool content and therefore of operating at a smaller margin than their unscrupulous competitors, and at an actual loss in most instances; or on the other hand, of following competitive standards and consequently being continually on the alert to meet competitive conditions, until at present the use of the term "part-wool" violates the sense of decency and fairness of the manufacturer himself and his obligations toward his customers.

A similar situation exists in the manufacture of bed sheets, in connection with the "thread count", *i.e.*, the number of threads per inch in warp and woof. The sales manager of the Hampley Knitting Mills was approached by one of his customers who asserted that the Hampley prices were too high. The customer submitted a competitor's sheeting which appeared to be of the same quality but which sold at 20 cents less than the Hampley sheeting. The sales manager showed his customer by the aid of a magnifying glass that the thread count of the competitor's sheeting was three less than that of the Hampley sheeting. Competition of this sort is difficult to meet. The thread count can be reduced sufficiently to make a considerable difference in cost without being detected by the consumer-purchaser. This means again that the competitive situation forces the thread count down gradually and continuously: starting with a count of 64 × 64, the successive stages in print cloths have been 64 × 60, 64 × 56, down to as low as 64 × 48. For sheetings they had run: 68 × 72, 64 × 68, 64 × 64, 64 × 60, 64 × 48. Several years ago the thread count may have been larger than was required for wear, opacity and appearance. But the gradual reduction of the thread count soon reached the minimum possible to maintain the necessary quality, and the quality has in recent years been lowered to a point which cannot be defended from the point of view of maintaining respectable standards.

The same situation is to be found in other fabrics. In regard to broadcloths the original broadcloths were combed with fine ply yarns, maintained high counts and were mercerized. Standard "broadcloth" originally meant a thread count of 192 × 88. It was gradually reduced on combed broadcloth to 128 × 68, and in some cases recently the count has been discovered to be 122 × 64 and 116 × 60. Not only have the combed cloths been reduced to as low as 116 × 60 but, in fact, the present standard is 128 × 68 single yarns and 144 × 76 two-ply singles.

In addition, there has been developed what is known as "carded" broadcloth which is made of carded yarn of about print-cloth numbers; this is really nothing more nor less than a print cloth woven with more threads in the warp and less in the filling, but no higher count per square inch than the print cloths. Carded numbers are sold in large volumes in counts of 100 × 60, 90 × 60, 80 × 60 and 80 × 56. These goods, being carded and not combed, have no natural lustre and are not mercerized, but are simply finished with a calender gloss which launders off in one or two washings. Burgess[30] cites a case in which the Rug Guild of Peking was faced with the same difficulty. This guild attempted to set a definite price for rugs with a definite number of threads to the inch. This attempt failed because a poor quality of wool was introduced into the rugs of many of the merchants. It is obvious that any attempts at standardizing goods must take a number of factors into account.

A third factor in the blanket situation is the gross size. From the point of view of health and comfort, more difficulty is experienced from blankets that are too short or too narrow than from those which are deficient in wool or which have a low thread count. A blanket should be 84 inches long; a blanket for a double bed should be 76 to 80 inches

[30] *The Guilds of Peking*, p. 194, Columbia University Press, 1928.

wide. And yet blanket sizes range from the full 72 × 84 through 70 × 80, 66 × 80, and even 64 × 76. Sixty inches is a minimum width for single bed, and 66 or 70 for three-quarter size. All three factors in combination have frequently reduced the gross weight of a blanket from the five-pound standard to three pounds.

One problem confronting the Hampley Knitting Mills concerns the labels. Should the Hampley Knitting Mills insist on being responsible for the proper labeling of blankets, rather than the department store; and if so, to what extent should the specifications of the blanket be printed on the label? The purchaser may be content with a label which would not protect the trade against unfair competition. On the other hand, the exact figures which would be necessary to effect standardization might be unintelligible to a purchaser. Trade terms could be used provided they had a current usage in the trade, were sufficiently exact to prevent confusion among competitors, and conveyed a sufficient meaning to the purchaser to develop intelligent buying.

The extent of such substitutions and deceptions as regards the material content of textiles may be inferred from the fact that no less than 18 cases are reported, by the Federal Trade Commission in the first eight volumes of their reports, in which cotton was parading as "silk."[31] Similarly, 30 cases involve the substitution of cotton for wool.[32] Gold, ivory and rubber,[33] oils and shellacs,[34] and olive oil and lemon juice,[35] have similarly suffered as the result of substitutions or adulterations.

Other Misrepresentations: "Mark-down" Prices

The preceding cases dealt with misrepresentations as to the material contents of commodities. The following three cases are typical of misrepresentations as to weight, quality or grade. The situation, in general, is the same in all of these cases: what appears to be an injury to the consumer alone, is discovered to be

[31] I F. T. C. D., 13, 16; II, 41; VI, 144, 422; and a large number of cases in Volume V. See also VII, 426 and 472; VIII, 230 and 361.

[32] III F. T. C. D., 1, 189; IV, 452; VI, 20, 79, 84; VIII, 407; IX, 344; and numerous cases in Volumes II and V. A trade-practice rule suggested by the Associated Knit Underwear Manufacturers of America in April, 1930, declared that "the use of the word 'wool' in advertising and labeling knit underwear is an unfair method of competition unless the percentage by weight of wool content of each garment is stated on the label."

[33] IV F. T. C. D., 51, 182, 193, 199, 305, 423, 446; VI, 97, 203, 336, 462; VII, 274. See Volume VII for a number of cases involving "rubber."

[34] Some 30 cases in nine volumes.

[35] IV, 31; V, 136.

harmful and unfair to competitors who do not engage in such practices, and is ultimately detrimental to the trade as a whole. There is no question but that even the wrongdoer partakes of the injury generally incident on his trade, but his share of the injury is less than his gain through his unfair tactics. Therefore the evil cannot be left to solve itself. There should, it may be admitted, be some reliance on the *caveat emptor* rule: society or business cannot afford to assume the full responsibility for acts that can in part be attributed to individual stupid buying. Trade control through publicity, therefore, can reduce the difficulty to an endurable minimum. But the problem is also a trade problem, and it involves the necessity of concerted trade efforts controlling to some extent the unscrupulous competitor.

Meadow Grove Creamery[36] was a Missouri corporation located at Carthage, Missouri. It manufactured butter, ice, and ice cream. The butter was sold to jobbers and retail dealers.

During 1918, Meadow Grove Creamery marketed its butter in packages or cartons of recognized standard weight of 16 ounces or one pound. In 1919, Meadow Grove Creamery put up its butter in packages or cartons, containing from one to two ounces less than the recognized standard weight of 16 ounces, and marketed such packages to purchasers. Although these packages were marked so as to show the weight of the product contained, they were similar in dress, shape, size, and appearance to the packages previously sold and containing the standard weight of 16 ounces. This standard weight had become customary to the trade and to the consuming public for a long period of years preceding 1919.

To meet the demand of the consuming public for small quantities of butter, the custom had become established in 1919 of marketing butter in four-ounce and eight-ounce packages. The butter so shaped was wrapped in unmarked wrappers and packed in marked one-pound cartons. Retail dealers in Arkansas, Texas, and Oklahoma sold such unmarked units of butter in considerable quantities. In imitation of the form of such standard and customary size and weight, the Meadow Grove Creamery shaped butter in sizes weighing approximately three and one-half to three and three-quarters ounces, seven to seven and one-half ounces, and 14 to 15 ounces. These were packed in cartons simulating one-pound cartons and sold to retailers, who in turn supplied to their customers the smaller unmarked units as four-ounce and eight-ounce units respectively. This latter practice was known to the Meadow Grove Creamery.

[36] Fictitious name.   VI F. T. C. D. 426.   See also VIII, 377.

A meeting of the butter manufacturers in Arkansas, Oklahoma, and Texas, assembled at Dallas, Texas, at the invitation of the Federal Trade Commission, denounced this method of competition. A resolution was drawn up known as "Trade Practice Submittal—Butter Manufacturers." August 1, 1920, was named as the day on which the methods so denounced should cease. Meadow Grove Creamery, however, continued its practice until January, 1922.

* * * * * *

The McKelvie Glass Company[37] was a copartnership located at Reynoldsville, Pennsylvania, and engaged in the sale of window glass. It bought window glass in carload lots from manufacturers and then shipped smaller and different quantities to dealers throughout the United States.

There were at this time four grades of window glass denoting quality or clearness: AA, A, B, and C, denoting first, second, third, and fourth grades respectively. Glass was bought and sold upon a basis of these quality grades, the prices varying according to grade. Upon the outside of the boxes in which the window glass was packed were stenciled the name of the manufacturer and the grade of the glass. Some manufacturers also enclosed inside the boxes slips of paper termed "quality slips" upon which the manufacturer's name and the grade of glass were printed to correspond with the labels on the outside of the boxes.

For two years preceding September, 1919, the McKelvie Glass Company had made a practice of buying window glass of a certain definite grade from the manufacturers and then of removing the "quality slips" from the inside of the boxes and changing the labels on the outside of the boxes to indicate that a higher grade of glass was contained therein.

* * * * * *

Check-Writing Machines, Incorporated,[38] was a New York corporation located in New York City. Ninety *per cent* of its business consisted in rebuilding secondhand and used check-writing and check-protecting machines of various makes and in selling these to customers. The remaining 10% of its business consisted in buying and selling new check-protecting machines.

The practice followed by practically all manufacturers of check-writing machines was to sell direct to the ultimate user. Distribution was effected through their own salesmen to whom they gave the exclusive rights to sell the machines, no machines being sold to dealers. Each general agent or branch manager had a definite territory and was granted an exclusive right to sell within that territory. A careful

[37] Fictitious name. II F. T. C. D. 113.
[38] Fictitious name. IV F. T. C. D. 87.

record was kept by some companies of the disposition of each machine from the day it was manufactured until it was delivered to a customer, a method which, together with other safeguards, prevented other persons from dealing in their new machines.

Through advertising circulars and the like Check-Writing Machines, Incorporated, represented to the public that they sold new and rebuilt machines. In the course of their activities they took off the name plates from machines which came into their possession and substituted thereon new name plates of their own, bearing serial numbers beginning with number 750,000. These numbers were changed at times to correspond with the serial numbers of the manufacturers of check-writing machines.

Sometimes a manufacturer's salesman would sell to Check-Writing Machines, Incorporated, a new machine, after detaching and taking with him the name and number plate thereon. After Check-Writing Machines, Incorporated, had sold the machine, the manufacturer's salesman would go to the buyer, restore the manufacturer's name and number plate, and then report the sale to the company.

The manufacturers of check-writing machines maintained service or repair departments, giving for one year free repair and upkeep service. Purchasers of second-hand or used machines from Check-Writing Machines, Incorporated, demanded this service from the manufacturers, who were then obliged either to repair the machine at their own expense or to allow the customer to continue using a machine that was not giving good service. In the latter case the purchaser became dissatisfied and disparaged the machine.

Check-Writing Machines, Incorporated, furthermore, advertised and offered for sale new machines of its competitors at prices less than its competitors. In some cases salesmen were led to believe that Check-Writing Machines, Incorporated, was being conducted by its competitors in direct competition with the salesmen.

The Check-Writing Machines case is typical of attempts to "pan off" as new goods commodities that are "secondhand." This practice is discoverable in the motion-picture business,[39] auto tires,[40] rope,[41] telephones and typewriters.[42] Granted that the practice is harmful to the customer, his interests are not the only ones which are jeopardized. The trade interest in preventing such methods of unfair competition is a factor that should be given additional weight. Just as laws against stealing or murder are obviously not restricted to the interests of the

[39] I F. T. C. D., 374; II, 11, 88; V, 219; VI, 89, 119, 191.
[40] *Ibid.*, I, 380; II, 119, 216; V, 327, 349.
[41] *Ibid.*, II, 327; V, 120; VI, 101.
[42] *Ibid.*, V, 385; I, 105, 109.

victim alone, but purpose to give society a sense of security against such acts; so, in business, the harm done to the competitor is frequently as valid an objection to unfair practices as is the immediate incidence of the wrong on the purchaser. And it is this common trade interest which justifies groups of business men themselves in eliminating unfair trade practices.

Finally, among misrepresentations in business, is to be listed the practice of misrepresenting the sales price. We have already discussed the problem of price-cutting as a business problem. What of the representation that a price has been "marked down," when as a matter of fact such was not the case?

The following cases are to be distinguished from the cases involving actual price-cutting,[43] in which the deception, if it existed, was largely self-deception. In the following cases, the customer was deceived into believing that he was receiving a price cut when as a matter of fact such was not the case.

The S. H. Nure Company [44] was an Illinois corporation located at Chicago and selling at wholesale jewelry, notions, novelties, fountain pens, *etc.*

The Nure Company sold at wholesale low-priced fountain pens at prices ranging from $17 to $21.50 per gross. These pens were packed in individual boxes or containers on which was stamped "Price, $3." Dealers then sold these pens at "marked-down" prices which even then were many times in excess of the cost price of the pens. The marked resale prices enabled the dealer to represent to the ultimate consumer that the pens were of high grade and reasonably worth the false and fictitious mark on such boxes.

* * * * * *

For two years prior to June, 1918, Browns, Stagman & Company,[45] in the course of its mail-order sales of groceries and by means of catalogues, advertised sugar for sale at 3 cents to 4 cents per pound. Browns, Stagman & Company reported that it was able to sell sugar at a price lower than its competitors because of its large purchases and quick-moving stock.

As a matter of fact, Browns, Stagman & Company was making such sales of sugar at prices less than cost, but its offers to sell sugar at those prices were always limited to a definite quantity of sugar and upon the condition that certain specific amounts of other groceries be pur-

---

[43] See Chapter XII.

[44] Fictitious name. IV, F. T. C. D. 177. See also *ibid.*, II, 377; IV, 163, 167, 172, 182, 188, 193, 199, 204; VI, 126; VII, 246; IX, 226.

[45] Fictitious name. I F. T. C. D. 163.

chased at the same time.   The price involved in the combined sale was sufficient to give Browns, Stagman & Company a profit on the combined sale including the sugar.   The company's sales of sugar during the latter half of 1915 amounted to approximately $800,000 and entailed a loss of approximately $200,000.   The circulars and advertisements offering sugar for sale at the reduced price led the trade and the general public to believe that Browns, Stagman & Company's competitors were charging more than a fair price for their sugar.   The company represented in its advertising that its competitors were not dealing justly, fairly, and honestly with their customers.

* * * * * *

The Federal Furniture Company[46] was a corporation of the District of Columbia and located at Washington.   It sold furniture and other merchandise at retail.

The Federal Furniture Company advertised, in newspapers and generally, "no extra charge for credit."   In carrying on its business the Federal Furniture Company caused all of its goods to be quoted or marked at prices which were to prevail when such goods were sold on a credit basis.   When goods were sold for cash, the company gave a substantial discount to its cash customers.

The Nure case is typical of many situations arising in various trades: *e.g.*, cutlery,[47] vacuum cleaners, lumber, paint, clothing, soap, and candy.[48]   It is particularly reprehensible in that the appeal is so frequently directed toward children.   The Browns, Stagman case is quite typical of the grocery trade,[49] where "combination orders" conceal the price which is actually paid for a particular commodity.   The Federal Furniture case is typical of similar cases in the furniture and piano trade.[50]

The Chalroth Portrait Company[51] was an Illinois corporation located at Chicago soliciting and taking orders for portraits to be made from photographs.   They made and sold these portraits.   The company was incorporated in 1893 with a capital stock of $2,500 which by 1915 had been increased to $300,000.   Some 1,000 to 2,000 agents were employed by this company soliciting orders in a house-to-house canvass.   The company sold from 250,000 to 500,000 portraits each year, which

[46] Fictitious name.   IV F. T. C. D. 330.
[47] IV F. T. C. D., 317, 334, 338, 342, 346, 351, 363, 368, 373, 378, 382; V, 33, 100, 172, 189.
[48] *Ibid.*, I, 30; I, 488; V, 112; V, 424; IV, 397; I, 186.
[49] *Ibid.*, II, 188; III, 46, 95, 103, 338; IV, 31.
[50] *Ibid.*, III, 168; IV, 333.
[51] Fictitious name.   V F. T. C. D. 396.   See also VII, 100, 287, 399.

constituted about one-third of this sort of business in the United States.

In the course of solicitations representations were made by agents of the Chalroth Portrait Company that the usual price of the standard portrait was far in excess of the prices then being quoted. Special prices were offered on the announced consideration that prospective customers would recommend the portraits and advertise the Chalroth business. "Standard" prices of $40 were thus alleged to be reduced to $10 and the "standard" price of $20 was alleged to be reduced to $5. Such sales at reduced prices constituted 75 % of the entire amount of the sales of the Chalroth Company.

Among other representations, the Chalroth Portrait Company stated that the portraits were "painted" and were "handmade." As a matter of fact prints were made by enlarging the photographs and these enlarged prints were then finished in the "medium" or style desired by means of an "air brush" operated by hand. This representation that the portrait was handmade served to give plausibility to the representation that the usual price was far in excess of the prices then being quoted.

All representations by salesmen were derived from "Sales Talks" compiled from the experience of the best salesmen as to successful sales methods. These "Sales Talks" were published by the Chalroth Portrait Company and drilled into its salesmen in room drills and at conventions. The "Sales Talks" were modified by the company from time to time and the methods were kept up-to-date by a minute organization of the sales forces.

The Chalroth case is not so important in itself as it is in reference to certain interesting questions it raises as to economic value. In an opinion dissenting from the Federal Trade Commission order that the Chalroth Company "cease and desist" from its price statements, Commissioner Van Fleet held that the purchasers of these portraits were not deceived or defrauded, because the selling talk enhanced the value to the customer.[52] This argument involves a principle which lies at the basis of the valuation of all economic goods, but especially of objects of art; a principle which is illustrated by the fact that a painting is frequently greatly enhanced or depreciated in value when the artist is identified. One would think that the picture would be valued on its merits, that the product of a great artist, for example, would be appreciated aside from his identification. Of course, the merits and characteristics of a picture frequently

[52] He was upheld by the court. 4 Fed. (2d) 759.

determine who the artist was or validate the subscribed signature. But the discovery of a great artist's sign or name has frequently determined to an appreciable degree the economic as well as the reputed aesthetic value of a picture.

Hence Commissioner Van Fleet was correct in asserting that a part of the value to the customers of the Chalroth Company was the result of the selling talk. This factor is present in the sale of all commodities, and is a justifiable part of the selling price by virtue of the fact that value, economic and otherwise, is not merely intrinsic or objective but is a function of the wants and desires that support the particular demands for commodities in specific situations. Any objection to such methods of enhancing prices must be directed alike to the salesman who misrepresents or exaggerates the merits of his commodity and to the buyer who values "handmade" goods not so much because he appreciates their merits directly in the commodity itself as because of the supposed value of such a process in any commodity.

This distinction, between representations of value and representations of fact, qualifies any attempt to determine a fixed "fair price" for a commodity which is desired by a customer on grounds that are not specific as regards the article, but general as regards the whole class of commodities to which this article may be referred as the result of expert judgment. Where the representation of facts could identify an article with a fixed and justifiable market price, misrepresentations of the facts imply the setting of an unfair price. But where the value is determined by some unique situation, such as the desire to possess a rare article or the purchase of a family portrait or heirloom, the attitude of the buyer enters as a factor into the determination of a justifiable price. In the Chalroth case the portraits had no market value, hence no public interest was involved except in so far as the cases were multiplied; but the multiplication of the cases would not increase the ratios of the factors involved, hence each case could be decided on its own merits. Therefore the final solution of the unethical practice of falsely asserting prices to be "marked down" awaits the proper education of the purchaser, especially through such publicity as can be given by agencies like the Better Business Bureau.

The same principle applies to style purchasing. If a buyer is assured that a commodity is unique and later discovers that it isn't, he has a just claim against the seller, because the latter is guilty of a misrepresentation of fact. But if a person buys an article which is really unique, he has no justifiable claim on a seller who has, by playing on the cupidity or pride of the purchaser succeeded in obtaining a high price by convincing the buyer that the uniqueness warrants the price.

The situation becomes crucial in connection with the sale of antiques and of original works of art. Only experts can determine the validity of such objects of art, and even they at times make mistakes. But the purchasers of such art objects include a much larger group of people. To what extent can their desire to own an original copy of a reputable artist or well-known work of art be justified, if with that desire there is no commensurate amount of intelligence? And what plea has such a person if he discovers that he paid an excessive price?

A more debatable case was presented by the discovery of the work of a gang of clever "antiquarians" who purchased the products of Signor Alceo Dossena, a living Italian sculptor, and then by various processes succeeded in passing off these modern replicas as historic objects of art. The victims included the Frick Galleries of New York, the Berlin, Boston and other famous museums.[53] In this case, boring disclosed the fact that the colorations apparently due to age had been recently applied. Similar deceptions in painting have been disclosed by the "needle method." The problem, however, is not one involving simple deception. It involves the broader question, what is the value of an object of art? If the deception is so well done as to defy detection, then obviously the result fulfils the function of representing a historic period of art and the result must be aesthetically satisfactory. This leaves as a sole remaining factor determining the value of an object of art, its authenticity, its originality. But what is this worth if expert opinion cannot convincingly determine it? And what is it not worth if the amateur art buyer is so presumptuous as to overvalue it?

[53] See *Boston Evening Transcript*, December 8, 1928, Part II, p. 6.

CHAPTER XVI

ESPIONAGE, CRITICISMS
AND OTHER VEXATIOUS TACTICS

Espionage and Other Annoyances

The very conditions of competitive industry and business, especially patent and copyright regulations, make the problem of espionage much more difficult than it can become, for example, in a profession like medicine. In medicine it has become a well-established principle that no remedial medicines or cures shall be patented or in any way kept secret by the inventor or discoverer. One of the brightest pages in medical history is the unselfish manner in which cures and medical knowledge have been shared among the members of the profession. This freedom of communication has contributed greatly to scientific advance, the shared knowledge being not only valuable in itself but stimulative of further research and investigation. In industry and business, however, new processes and methods have been carefully kept secret, and this attitude has been supported by patent and other legislation. Hence the temptation to spy on one's competitor is great, especially in regard to matters that cannot be protected by law.

The Eagle Chemical Company[1] was a Connecticut corporation located in New York City and engaged in the manufacture and sale of fertilizer and refined animal fats, purchasing large amounts of raw material in New York and Pennsylvania.

In order to secure control of this territory for purchasing raw materials, the Eagle Chemical Company offered prices unwarranted by trade conditions and so high as to be prohibitive to small competitors, many of whom had to cease doing business in this territory. Some of the competitors who remained in the business assigned certain trucks and automobiles to follow the trucks of the Eagle Chemical Company for the purpose of spying upon the business and customers of the latter.

In return the Eagle Chemical Company, through its employees, willfully and intentionally caused certain of its trucks to collide with

[1] Fictitious name. I F. T. C. D. 226.

the automobiles and trucks owned by its competitors and operated by its competitors' employees while the latter were following the Eagle trucks. These collisions so damaged the machines of competitors as to hinder, delay, and embarrass their employees in the conduct of their business.

* * * * * *

The Elms Company[2] was an Indiana Corporation located at Indianapolis and engaged in the manufacture and sale of radiator fans for automobiles, motor trucks and tractors. These fans were of various types: hub-driven, shaft-driven, ball-bearing, plain bearing and Timken. Its largest output was a type of fan known to the trade as the cup-and-cone fan.

By means of a detective hired for that purpose, the Elms Company secured the names and post-office addresses of the customers of a competitor and the amounts of the products shipped to each customer respectively. About 85% of the fans made by this competitor were of the roller-bearing type equipped with Hyatt roller bearings. The roller-bearing type of fan manufactured by the competitor cost approximately 48 cents more to make than the cup-and-cone type. The Elms Company, however, represented to the trade that the roller-bearing type cost less to make than the cup-and-cone type, and that the former would not work satisfactorily. The Elms Company made and offered to the trade a roller-bearing type of fan similar to that manufactured by its competitor and offered it at a price less than the competitor's price.

During 1918 the Elms Company engaged the services of a private detective agency to place its operatives in the manufacturing plant of a competitor and to make daily reports of the names and addresses of the customers of this competitor together with the amounts of the goods shipped. The purpose of this detective, according to the Elms Company, was to discover the origin of a leak in its own office of information that was being conveyed to its competitor's office.

This detective, however, at the time that he applied to the competitor for employment, asked to be assigned to a position on what was known as the "assembly" bench, and was given this position. The assembly bench was the place where the fans manufactured by the Elms Company's competitor were prepared for shipment. After the fans had been assembled they were placed on the floor a few feet from the assembly bench in the same room and there packed in boxes or crated for shipment and marked with the name and post-office address of the purchaser.

* * * * * *

The Southern Hardware Association[3] was a voluntary unincorporated association with its headquarters located at Richmond, Virginia. Its

[2] Fictitious name. III F. T. C. D. 36.
[3] IV F. T. C. D. 428.

territory was bounded on the east by the Atlantic Ocean, on the north by the Potomac River, on the south by the Gulf of Mexico and the Rio Grande River, and on the west by the western boundary of Arkansas. The Association had 150 members who constituted approximately 90% of the jobbers and wholesalers of hardware in this territory. Members of the association employed a total of some 1,100 salesmen, and their combined annual business amounted approximately to $500,000,000.

The purpose and intent of this association and its members was to dominate the wholesale and jobbing trade and to enjoin upon the trade the methods which the association and its members approved. Members refused to purchase from those manufacturers who sold to non-member customers, and this attitude of the association was made known to all manufacturers of hardware and allied commodities in this territory.

For the accomplishment of its purpose the association conducted a system of espionage upon the business of the wholesale and jobbing trade in this territory, both of members and of non-members. In many instances members and officers of the association communicated to the manufacturers, found to be selling to non-member customers, that such transactions were known to the association and its members and that they were disapproved by them, the imputation being that such manufacturers must choose between the sales to members of the association and sales to non-members.

Cases similar to the Elms Company case have occurred in connection with such diverse products as vacuum cleaners, oil pumps, lightning rods, and musical instruments.[4] Similar tactics were also employed in connection with the sale of fire extinguishers, tank cars, and pressing machines.[5] The purchase of sugar beets has been similarly involved.[6] Cases in which associations, like the Southern Hardware Association, attempted to follow the private business dealings of members have also occurred in connection with lumber and canned goods.[7] In all these cases the situation which gives rise to the abuse is the secrecy which attaches to business, a secrecy which most men would regard as necessary to the effective conduct of their own business. Espionage in business should be compared with the attempt on the part of one doctor to discover the list of patients of another and their ills and suggested remedies in each particular

[4] I F. T. C. D. 30; I, 259; III, 327; III, 124 respectively.
[5] I F. T. C. D. 459; I, 144; VI, 439, respectively.
[6] VI F. T. C. D. 390.
[7] I F. T. C. D. 60, 452, respectively.

case. This sort of thing is comparable only to espionage in war—and the penalty is especially rigorous then in view of the despicable character of the act as well as of the seriousness of its effects.

A somewhat different type of vexatious practice is illustrated in the following cases. Annoyances of this sort are most apt to encourage retaliations, but the net result is a discrediting of the trade at the mutual expense of the injuring and injured party.

In 1918 and 1919 a number of corporations, firms, partnerships and individuals known as "regular" dealers,[8] engaged in the sale of lumber and lumber products at retail, systematically, on a large scale, and in bad faith wrote to "mail-order" concerns engaged in the same line of business requests for estimates of kind, quantity and prices of lumber and building material, and for catalogues, printed matter and other special information intended only for bona fide customers. These "regular" dealers, furthermore, furnished to the editor and manager of their trade journals information which would tend, if it were published, to encourage other retail dealers to make similar requests of mail-order concerns.

These "regular" dealers furthermore used their influence with banks, which were customarily called upon by mail-order concerns to report the identity and occupations of persons suspected of making requests for information not in good faith, to induce these banks to fail to make such reports or to make misleading reports to these mail-order concerns. These "regular" dealers furthermore induced manufacturers and whole-salers of lumber materials to refrain from selling their products to mail-order concerns. They also furnished to the editor and manager of their trade journals names of such manufacturers and wholesalers as sold to mail-order concerns, their purpose being to enable the editor and manager to interfere with the free purchase of supplies by the mail-order houses. These "regular" dealers also employed other methods to hinder and embarrass mail-order houses in the conduct of their business.

* * * * * *

The Chamber of Commerce of Missoula, Montana,[9] was a voluntary unincorporated association, composed of persons, partnerships, and corporations engaged in business and industrial and professional pursuits in that city. Many of the members were engaged in selling merchandise at wholesale and retail. The purpose of the organization was to do anything possible for the betterment of general conditions in the city of Missoula and surrounding territory, especially in the way of promoting its commercial welfare.

[8] I F. T. C. D. 60, 325, 363. See also VII, 115.
[9] V F. T. C. D. 451.

The National Cloak and Suit Company was a mercantile establishment engaged in the sale of wearing apparel, dry goods, *etc.*, by means of catalogues circulated among, and correspondence with, customers and prospective customers through the mails. This company was domiciled in New York City and had a branch in Kansas City, Missouri. It had been in business 34 years and was known as a mail-order or catalogue house.

The National Cloak & Suit Company in the course of its business in 1919 circulated in the United States about 11,000,000 copies of its catalogues and pamphlets at a cost to it of over $3,000,000. In Montana alone, the company distributed about 200,000 copies of its catalogues at a cost of approximately $50,000. It had from the state of Montana alone over 50,000 customers, that year, whose business aggregated approximately $700,000. Over $11,000 of this business was done in Missoula County, over $5,000 of the business coming from the city of Missoula itself. Within a radius of 50 miles of Missoula the company had over 3,000 customers in 1919.

In January, 1919, the secretary of the Chamber of Commerce of Missoula arranged with the manager of a local motion-picture theatre to secure copies of mail-order catalogues, including those of the National Cloak and Suit Company, by admitting children to the theatre upon their presenting a mail-order catalogue instead of the usual admittance fee. The object was to eliminate mail-order-house catalogues from the city of Missoula and adjacent territory. The proposition was endorsed by the Board of Directors of the Missoula Chamber of Commerce. As a result of this arrangement several hundred catalogues were received by the motion-picture theatre the first time this program was tried, and these catalogues were then turned over to the Chamber of Commerce and destroyed. This program was repeated in September, 1920, with the result that some 250 additional catalogues were secured and destroyed. Special cash prizes were offered for the "most-thumbed" and also for the "newest and latest" catalogues.

One cannot refrain from having a certain amount of sympathy for the tactics of the mid-western lumber companies and the Missoula Chamber of Commerce. In each case, the practices resorted to were not motivated by aggressiveness so much as by self-defense. It seems a strange irony of fate that the Sherman Law and similar legislation, which was aimed ostensibly at the unfair methods of "big" business should prove to be a boomerang to small local businesses. And yet it becomes apparent on closer study that such practices as are illustrated in the two preceding cases are unfair whether the business is large or small, aggressive or defensive. The purpose, to curb the intrusion of outsiders into local markets, may be justified, but the means employed cannot be.

Depriving Competitors of Source of Supplies

Another form of vexatious treatment of competitors is to deprive them of the source of their financial, raw-material or advertising supplies. In the Utaho Sugar case, the independent companies might have had a better chance of succeeding against such powerfully intrenched competitors if they had made financial arrangements commensurate with the task they undertook. So also with the Tampa cigar manufacturers. But this sort of advice does not condone the obviously unfair practice of cutting off a competitor's source of supplies by such means. Similar cases have occurred in connection with lumber,[10] moving pictures,[11] groceries,[12] and hardware.[13]

In 1915 and 1916 Hendrik A. Johnson[14] of Logan, Utah, with the assistance of others, promoted an independent enterprise with the intention of erecting a beet-sugar factory near the town of Smithfield, Utah. This town lay in the territory which had been allocated to the Utaho Sugar Company,[14] a large sugar company, under the division of interstate territory between it and a large competitor. These latter two large companies practically dominated the field in this territory.

The independent company secured an option upon a factory site, and made a large number of beet contracts with farmers in that vicinity. They had the financing well under way, in 1916, through stock subscriptions secured from farmers and business men in the vicinity of Smithfield, and from other persons of financial responsibility in the state of Utah and elsewhere.

When the Utaho directors learned of this new enterprise, they called and held a meeting, in the vicinity of the proposed factory site, of the farmers and stock subscribers committed to the new enterprise. At this meeting the directors of the Utaho Sugar Company made statements to the effect that the independent enterprise was financially unsound, that it would not succeed, and that it was unethically invading territory which belonged to the Utaho Sugar Company. They furthermore announced that the Utaho Company would, itself, build a factory near Smithfield in the near future, and shortly afterward ground was broken as an apparent first step toward building a factory, but without the intent so to build.

[10] I F. T. C. D. 60.
[11] *Ibid.*, I, 212.
[12] *Ibid.*, II, 151; III, 295.
[13] *Ibid.*, IV, 428.
[14] Fictitious name. VI F. T. C. D. 390.

Mr. Johnson had entered into a preliminary agreement with the Hyer Company[15] of Cleveland, Ohio, for the erection of the independent factory. The Hyer Company had built and equipped 13 factories for the Utaho Sugar Company. Upon learning that this preliminary agreement had been entered into, a director of the Utaho Sugar Company protested to the Hyer Company against the erection of the independent factory, and as a result, the Hyer Company withdrew from the preliminary agreement.

Similarly the financial backers and the farmers who had contracted to grow beets for the independent enterprise were discouraged from continuing their support and broke their contracts and withdrew their undertakings of financial support, all of which resulted in the abandonment of the enterprise by Johnson and his associates. On another occasion one of the directors of the Utaho Company wrote to a bank at Rigby, Idaho, which was contemplating the financing of an independent factory, and intimated that he had knowledge of the bank's connections with the independent enterprise and indirectly threatened the bank with reprisals if it did not cease supporting the independent enterprise and work in harmony with the Utaho Company.

* * * * * *

The Cigar Manufacturers' Association of Tampa, Florida,[16] was organized in January, 1920, as a voluntary unincorporated association composed of individuals, partnerships, and corporations engaged in the manufacture of cigars in Tampa and vicinity. The 77 members of this association manufactured approximately 95% of the 400,000,000 cigars made in and in the vicinity of Tampa in 1919, although the number of manufacturers not members of the association was greater than the number of members. Each member of the association filed a bond, ranging from $500 to $10,000 in amount, which would be forfeited upon the failure to comply with the articles of the association, its by-laws, rules, resolutions and acts, or to pay all dues and assessments.

The wooden box was the standard method of packing cigars for market, and an adequate and continuous supply of wooden boxes was absolutely essential to the manufacture and sale of cigars. There were but three manufacturers of cigar boxes operating in Tampa prior to June, 1920, and they supplied all of the boxes for the Tampa manufacturers, who were practically dependent on this source of supply. In 1919 the production of the cigar-box manufacturers involved a surplus of approximately 1,000,000 in excess of the needs of the Tampa cigar manufacturers. Delays in the delivery of boxes did occur during the Christmas holidays of 1919, however, resulting in the loss of some orders to the cigar manufacturers through cancellations.

[15] Fictitious name.
[16] V F. T. C. D. 1.

The difficulties with labor which were common to all lines of industry during the latter part of 1918 and continuing into 1919 affected the cigar-making industry in Tampa. Some of the manufacturers operated their shops on an open-shop basis, employing non-union workmen or not restricting their employees to union members. Other manufacturers did, or were willing to, operate on a closed-shop basis, employing only union members. Efforts were made to unionize the industry and these efforts were resisted by certain manufacturers, some of whom then organized the Cigar Manufacturers' Association. One of the articles of the association stated:

All persons are entitled to seek and have legitimate employment without discrimination whether they belong to any labor union or association, and no discrimination shall be made for or against any person in the factory or any member of this association because of membership or non-membership in any labor union or association.

All manufacturers who subsequently became members of the association, subscribed to the policies of the open shop. Differences of policy as to the open shop among the manufacturers and between the manufacturers and their employees resulted in strikes and other disturbances of industrial conditions.

In 1919 there was an extraordinary activity in the cigar trade in Tampa, orders being far in excess of those usually received and of the ability of the manufacturers to fill. Prior to March, 1920, since there was a shortage of labor in the cigar-manufacturing industry, and with several local strikes in process, some of the members of the association conceived the idea of controlling the labor situation by securing in the association the monopoly of the sale and distribution of all cigar boxes then capable of being produced in Tampa, with the idea of cutting off the supply of boxes from all manufacturers who refused to adopt the association's open-shop policy.

Accordingly a meeting was held and attended by the officers of the association and by the officers of the three box manufacturers, at which it was agreed that the association should control the disposition of all cigar boxes made in Tampa. The price was fixed at 16 cents per box, this being an increase over the preceding price of $13\frac{1}{2}$ cents per box. Prior to December 31, 1921, these agreements were renewed for the year 1922. During the year prior to the agreement the production of the three box manufacturers was approximately 9,300,000 boxes, in the year following, 7,300,000, the association not having furnished cigar-box orders sufficient to keep the box-manufacturing plants in full operation; nor did the box manufacturers during this time receive orders for the entire number of boxes made by them.

The box manufacturers continued to solicit orders from cigar makers who were not members of the association, but such orders were subject to the approval of the association. At times their refusal to approve such sales tended to reduce the number and amount of accepted orders and sales of the box manufacturers. Thus, the association was able to control the supply of cigar boxes in Tampa and to withhold the supply from such manufacturers as refused to abide by the labor policies of the association. Some of these non-member cigar makers thereupon joined the association, while others were forced to discontinue the making of cigars.

In April, 1920, when a strike closed down some 25 factories belonging to members of the association, all of the members declared a lockout. The association then solicited orders for boxes from cigar makers outside Tampa and were selling approximately 50% of the output of the Tampa cigar-box makers to cigar manufacturers located in various parts of the United States. At the same time the local cigar makers who were non-members of the association and who operated closed shops were unable to obtain a sufficient supply of boxes. The association prevailed on a large box manufacturer in Georgia not to supply boxes to the closed-shop makers of Tampa.

* * * * * *

The Lineoperator Company [17] was an Illinois corporation located at Chicago and engaged in the manufacture and sale of apparatus used by printers in producing tabulated work.

The Lineoperator Company endeavored for a period of one year or more preceding January, 1918, to persuade certain trade journals, by letters and verbal conversations, to refuse to accept the advertising of a competitor on the ground that the latter was infringing the Lineoperator Company's patents and was financially unsound. The Lineoperator Company also falsely represented to trade journals that it had a suit pending against a certain competitor who had made practically no defense whatsoever in the courts.

Enticing Competitors' Employees

Another practice which can be listed as vexatious is that of enticing away the employees of a competitor. Obviously, the practice of securing the services of a capable employee of a competitor can not in itself be condemned. The ideal situation would be one in which the competitor would be notified of such intentions; and this certainly would be to the interest of the employee, who would probably benefit by an increase in wage or salary even if he remained at his post. It is not this comparatively simple situation, however, which causes the chief trouble in business. The difficulty arises, as the two following cases

[17] Fictitious name. I F. T. C. D. 110.

show, when an employee not only transfers his skill and ability to a new employer, but carries with him trade information and misrepresents himself to his former employer's customers as still working in that capacity.

The Vacuum Oil Company[18] had in 1922 been selling its oils under certain well-known trade names and trade-marks for a number of years and had spent large sums of money advertising its products, so that these had become well known to the trade throughout the United States. Some of these brands were registered in the United States Patent Office and certified as registered trade-marks. Among these certified trade marks were the following: "Mobiloil," "Arctic," "Zeta," and "Gargoyle." In connection with the latter name there was also registered the picture of a mythical animal which was called a gargoyle. These trade names, trade-marks and brands were stenciled on the casks, cans, barrels and other containers in which the Vacuum Oil Company sold and marketed its products. These trade names and trade-marks also appeared in newspaper advertisements, posters, pamphlets, circulars, letterheads and many other methods of advertising to familiarize the general public with the trade names, trade-marks and brands under which the Vacuum Oil Company sold and marketed its products.

E. M. Ravell, previous to 1918, had been employed as a traveling salesman by the Vacuum Oil Company and was familiar with its business and acquainted with its brands, trade-marks, trade names and the different grades of its lubricating oils. In 1918, Ravell entered the employment of a competitor of the Vacuum Oil Company where he acted as sales manager and traveling salesman. Shortly thereafter, this competitor adopted a list of trade names very similar to those of the Vacuum Oil Company, the name "Mobile A" being frequently used. The customers and employees of the Vacuum Oil Company had previously grown accustomed to pronounce the word "mobiloil" as if it were spelled "mobileoil." The competitor with whom Ravell was now connected began also to brand all of its goods with names simulating those employed by the Vacuum Oil Company.

While Ravell was in the employ of these competitors of the Vacuum Oil Company he always approached dealers by referring to his product as "mobileoil" and did not refer to the fact that the oil offered by him was not manufactured by the Vacuum Oil Company. In many instances he was questioned directly as to whether the oils offered by him were those of the Vacuum Oil Company, whereupon he stated that he had been the chief chemist of the Vacuum Oil Company for many years and that the products he was now representing were exactly the same as those of the Vacuum Oil Company, that they were manufactured from the same crudes, and that the physical tests such as viscosity,

[18] V F. T. C. D. 92.

fire, flush and cold tests were identically the same as the Vacuum products.

On other occasions Ravell admitted that the oils he offered for sale were not those of the Vacuum Oil Company but suggested to prospective customers that they buy their oils of his company, empty them into the Vacuum containers that they had on hand and offer these oils to customers as those of the Vacuum Oil Company. He stated that customers would be just as well satisfied and reminded the dealers that his products were cheaper than those offered by the Vacuum Oil Company.

* * * * * *

Broad Beam Creameries[19] was a Maine corporation operating at Washington Court House, Ohio. It was engaged in the purchasing of cream and butter fat, and in the conversion of this into butter which it then sold and distributed.

Cream and butter fat were obtained by what was known as the "station plan," whereby the small quantities of cream from numerous farms were directed to stations and from these in larger volumes to the churning plant. The Broad Beam Creameries had stations in Ohio, Indiana, and Kentucky. Contracts were made by the Broad Beam Creameries and its competitors for the sale of butter prior to and in anticipation of their cream purchases. In the station plan it was necessary to equip a building and employ there a person known as the station agent who tested and cared for the cream as it was received. One company, a competitor of the Broad Beam Creameries, had established approximately 250 stations in 18 years at initial costs ranging from $200 to $1,000 per station. Other companies had made similar investments.

On December 1, 1919, in order to prevent an unfair appropriation of the values so created, leaving at the same time perfect freedom of access by competitors to customers and producers of cream, and also leaving agents absolute freedom voluntarily to terminate any contract of agency or employment and voluntarily to seek employment of competitors, members of the cream industry had adopted in open meeting a set of resolutions known as "Trade Practice Submittal—Creamery Industry." These resolutions contained a statement regarding certain trade practices then existing, among which was the solicitation by creamery companies of the employees of competing businesses. As a result of these resolutions, the practices were discontinued after December 1, 1919; with the exception of the Broad Beam Creameries, which continued to entice agents in the employ of competitors to violate contractual relations with their respective employers.

Through its representatives the Broad Beam Creameries continued to entice agents to violate their contractual relations with their employers

---

[19] Fictitious name.   IV F. T. C. D. 55.   See also *ibid.*, VIII, 449.

in spite of the fact that the Broad Beam Creameries had subscribed to the "Trade Practice Submittal" and had thereby encouraged its competitors to abandon such practices. As many as 20 agents of one competitor were visited by the Broad Beam Creameries' representatives, some as many as four times, and offered a recompense for any loss sustained by a breach of their existing contracts. This sum, in one case, amounted to $700. More remuneration also was offered by the Broad Beam Creameries; with the result that they attracted a number of agents to their organization, who brought with them the business and patronage formerly enjoyed by their previous employers. In one case 90% of the competitor's business was so transferred when the agent entered the employ of the Broad Beam Creameries.

We have just[20] dealt with several phases of business which involve questionable conduct, situations which present ethical problems because they are sometimes difficult to distinguish from a justifiable desire to "get ahead" in business. Ambition and zeal cannot be condemned from a moral point of view, and they are certainly business virtues. The difficulty is that they lead, in the case of piracy, to stealing, and in the case of advertising, to lying, practices which can be condemned morally; and which from the point of view of Business Ethics are also to be condemned, not only because of their harmful effects on the purchaser, but especially because they also injure the competitor, the trade at large, and consequently society.

Criticisms and Unfair Accusations of Competitors

The vexatious treatment of competitors, especially in the form of threats, criticisms, and disparagements, to a certain extent defeats its own purpose, for the name of the competitor is generally given prominence and publicity and this results in an advertising asset to him. But such is not always the case, and frequently when it is the fact this is not appreciated by the business man who slurs his competitor. Hence the practice is harmful whether or not it is later successfully stopped or penalized. The following cases are presented primarily to give an accurate picture of actual practices. They include unfair and false accusations of "disloyalty" to the Government, of patent infringements and other illegal acts, of governmental prosecutions, of financial insolvency and irresponsibility, of "piracy" and counterfeiting, of inferior quality and adulteration of goods,

[20] Chapters XIV, XV; also Section D.

and of other disreputable acts. Frequently such charges and accusations are false or distort the truth, but attempts to deny or disprove them seldom overtake the charges.

The main reason for presenting these cases is not to paint a picture of "business scandals," but to indicate to business men, present and prospective, the sort of thing which reputable business firms are likely to experience. Fortunately this sort of unfair practice is declining. But it does still exist, and the greatest danger involved is that the reputable business man, against whom such an attack is directed, may jeopardize his case by mishandling it. He can ill afford to engage in retaliations of a like kind and he should be careful in selecting the best agency for handling the problem: his trade association, a Better Business Bureau, the Chamber of Commerce, the Federal Trade Commission, or the law courts. Attacks such as are pictured here are frequently indicative of the trade prominence of the company which is the object of the attack, a position which argues strongly for the adoption of a policy of handling such unfair practices in the interests of the trade at large.

Once again we resort to professional analogies in order to indicate the standards which a self-constituted group of men may set for themselves. Criticism and disparagements of fellow professional men, especially in the presence of clients, are generally condemned. Frequently such hesitancy to criticise, especially among lawyers, doctors, and engineers, is interpreted by the public as an endeavor to make the profession sacrosanct. Such a charge becomes serious only when the profession has no means of bringing such criticisms before a proper tribunal.

Physicians should expose without fear or favor, before the proper medical or legal tribunals, corrupt or dishonest conduct of members of the profession. Every physician should aid in safeguarding the profession against the admission to its ranks of those who are unfit or unqualified because deficient either in moral character or education.[21]

When a physician succeeds another physician in the charge of a case, he should make no comments on or insinuations regarding the practice of the one who preceded him. Such comments or insinuations tend to lower the esteem of the patient for the medical profession and so react against the critic.[22]

In case an engineer or firm of engineers, A, has been employed or is about to do a piece of work for which another engineer, B, has good grounds to

[21] *Principles of Medical Ethics*, Chapter II, Article I, Section 7.
[22] *Ibid.*, Chapter II, Article IV, Section 4.

believe they are incompetent, is it ethical for B, when unsolicited, to state his opinion and the facts upon which his opinion is based, regardless of whether he does or does not hope to benefit thereby?

An engineer is *never* warranted in interposing between particular clients and another engineer when unsolicited. When an opinion is asked, the situation changes somewhat, but even then the burden is on the engineer called upon for an opinion to avoid any possibility of doing a brother engineer an injustice. In the case of public work the responsibility of the engineering profession to the public would somewhat modify this conclusion . . . [23]

* * * * * *

The Lineoperator Company[24] was an Illinois corporation located at Chicago and engaged in the manufacture and sale of devices and apparatus used by printers in producing tabulating work. There were only two competitors in the business, all three companies being located in the United States.

In January, 1916, and the succeeding period the Lineoperator Company through the medium of circulars and letters began to threaten the customers of its competitors with suits for infringements of certain patents claimed to be owned by the Lineoperator Company. As a matter of fact it was not until April, 1917, that the Lineoperator Company actually instituted a suit against anyone. Two years previous to the instituting of this suit the Lineoperator Company had obtained from its attorney an opinion pointing out the legal remedy of the Lineoperator Company. This opinion had been rendered only after repeated demands and challenges on the part of one of the competitors that the suit be instituted, and after two warnings by the Federal Trade Commission that the suit be instituted or the threats cease.

These threats were declared by the Federal Trade Commission not to have been made in good faith and to have constituted interference with the competitors' business, intimidating the latters' customers and coercing them into ceasing the purchase of their goods from the competitors of the Lineoperator Company.

* * * * * *

The Herside Iron Rust Company[25] was a private company engaged in business in Philadelphia. It manufactured and sold a preparation known as Iron Rust Soap for use in removing iron rust, ink, fruit and medicine stains from clothing, marble and the like.

By means of letters, circulars and advertisements which were sent out to competitors and their customers, the Herside Company for a period of two years preceding February, 1919, represented that their competitors were infringing patents granted to and owned by the

[23] Case 25, American Association of Engineers.
[24] Fictitious name. I F. T. C. D. 110.
[25] Fictitious name. I F. T. C. D. 310.

Herside Company. As a matter of fact the Herside Company owned no such patents. They continued, however, to threaten suits for alleged infringements, the effect being to intimidate competitors and their customers.

* * * * * *

The Green Portable Conveying Machinery Company[26] was, in 1919, an Illinois corporation located at Chicago and had been engaged in the manufacture and sale of portable conveying machinery since 1907. It was represented on the Pacific coast by Mr. Shailer Mearles[26] who circulated reports among customers and prospective customers of the Green Company's competitors that the Green Portable Conveying Machinery Company was about to institute legal proceedings against its competitors for infringements on the patents which the Green Company held on its own portable conveying machinery.

Mearles stated that one of the competitors against whom a suit was pending was the Colfax Manufacturing Company of Colfax, Oregon. He declared that the Colfax Company was misleading its competitors and customers in regard to the ownership of certain patents by Eugene Green, an officer of the Colfax Company. All of these representations were made by Mearles without the Green Company's knowledge.

As a matter of fact Eugene Green was the inventor of a portable warehouse elevator, and a patent on this invention had been issued to him in 1901. Since 1912, he had been connected with and was an officer of the Colfax Company which was engaged in the manufacture and sale of portable conveying machinery.

In 1915, the Green Portable Elevator Company, a predecessor of the Green Portable Conveying Machinery Company, an Oregon corporation established in 1907, and a part of the assets of which the Green Portable Conveying Machinery Company later acquired, had instituted a proceeding in equity against the Interior Warehouse Company to enjoin an alleged infringement of the Green Company's patent. This suit had been dismissed by the court, from which decision the Green Portable Elevator Company did not appeal, nor had either the Green Portable Elevator Company or the Green Portable Conveying Machinery Company since that time instituted any other proceeding for alleged infringements on their patents.

The vexatious tactics employed by the Lineoperator and Herside Companies have been practiced in trades as diversified as gummed tape, moving pictures, sugar products, blowers, and aspirin.[27] The attitude of the trades involved and of the

[26] Fictitious name. II F. T. C. D. 143.
[27] I F. T. C. D. 44, 212, 400; II, 151; III, 137, 369; V, 219; VI, 390.

Federal Trade Commission has been that threats to sue for alleged infringements should cease until *bona fide* suits are filed. This does not imply that the actual filing of suits cannot be motivated with a desire to harass and injure. But a distinction is to be made between the actual filing of such suits on the one hand and, on the other hand, threats to do so or statements to the effect that a competitor is engaged in illegal activities that could provide a basis for action at law.

Similar unfair allegations as regards competitors are illustrated by the following cases. Charges of insolvency are frequently resorted to in order to discredit a firm among farmers: the continuation of the Broad Beam Creameries case can be matched by similar tactics employed among the growers of sugar beets.[28] The Lockton case is significant in that a trade term is used to discredit a competitor, advantage being taken of the confusion in the minds of the general public of terms which were well defined among the trade. The Bregal case is interesting in view of the fact that the practices there presented were not condemned in a Federal Trade Commission decision which did however issue a cease and desist order against certain other practices which were brought to its attention at this time.

Broad Beam Creameries[29] was a Maine corporation operating in Washington Court House, Ohio. It engaged in the purchase of cream or butter fat, converted this into butter and then sold and distributed the product. For a number of years following 1919, the Broad Beam Creameries had engaged in the practice of enticing agents away from its competitors.

Among the statements made to the agents of those competitors, in order to entice them away, were statements to the effect that the competitors of the Broad Beam Creameries were insolvent, that they had asked for the appointment of receivers for their companies, and that farmers were beginning to be afraid to accept their competitors' checks in payment for cream. The Broad Beam Creameries' representatives furthermore stated that the reputation of competitors' agents thus approached would be injured by being connected with an insolvent concern at the time that it "went to the wall," and that it would be difficult for such agents to redeem the confidence of the public if they longer remained with their employers.

In the course of such approaches by the Broad Beam Creameries' representatives, the agents of competitors were shown reprints from

[28] VI F. T. C. D. 390. See pp. 437, 442, *supra.*
[29] Fictitious name. IV F. T. C. D. 55.

newspapers and copies of newspapers containing the accounts of applications entered by the competitors of the Broad Beam Creameries for the appointment of a receiver. Such reprints and copies were also sent various agents through the mail, sometimes in plain envelopes and sometimes in envelopes bearing the Broad Beam Creameries' business card. The complaints of the competitors to the Broad Beam Creameries were persistently disregarded.

* * * * * *

The Lockton Tire and Rubber Company[30] was a California corporation with its main office located at San Francisco and with branches at Los Angeles and Oakland, California, Portland, Oregon, and Seattle, Washington. This company was engaged in selling auto tires, rims, and rim parts to wholesale and retail dealers. It acted as a distributing agent for such products in competition with a number of other companies.

The Lockton Company dealt in standard rims and parts made by rim manufacturers. They referred to such rims and parts as "standard" and "genuine." The value of the replacement service was large.

In 1919 the Henrison-MacNeil Company,[31] an Illinois corporation located at Chicago, began the manufacture of parts designed to accomplish the purpose of supplying "standard" rims for wheels. This company sold parts to wholesalers throughout the United States and competed with the Lockton Company in Washington, Oregon, and California.

After this competition had begun, the Lockton Company began the practice of collecting from dealers all boards on which their competitors at a considerable expense were displaying their rim parts. The Lockton Company destroyed all such boards and substituted their own display boards in the dealers' places of business. The Lockton Company then began a campaign of disparagement against the Henrison-MacNeil Company, in the course of which the latter was referred to in circular letters and other communications as "pirates" and the rim parts as "pirate" and "counterfeit," and the trade was warned against them. The trade was furthermore told that the use of the Henrison-MacNeil products was dangerous and would automatically destroy the rim-factory guarantee on the entire rim equipment.

The word "pirate," together with other terms, was at that time extensively used in the automobile trade to distinguish repair or other replacement parts made by firms other than the manufacturer of the original article. There was, however, no usage in the trade of the term "pirate" as applicable to the manufacturer or distributor of such parts nor of the word "counterfeit" as applicable to the parts themselves. These terms as used by the Lockton Company were in such instances

[30] Fictitious name. V F. T. C. D. 335.
[31] Fictitious name.

untrue and were calculated to deceive the dealers and the public to the detriment and injury of the Lockton Company's competitors. Dealers who were not familiar with the secondary usage of the term "pirate" were misled by it.

The Lockton Company printed on its own particular boards the following warning and guarantee:

Warning.—Beware of counterfeit imitations or so-called "duplicate" rim parts. The use of any device other than the regular genuine rim parts manufactured and sold by the maker of the rim on your car is dangerous. The use of counterfeit or so-called "duplicate" rim parts immediately destroys the rim-factory guarantee on your entire rim equipment.

Guarantee.—Genuine rims and rim parts of all makes are guaranteed by the rim factories to be free from defect in workmanship and material. All genuine rim materials must come up to the standard of the guarantee or are subject to replacement on a fair adjustment basis. The use of "counterfeit" or so-called "duplicate" rims or parts destroys this guarantee.

* * * * * *

Baking powder consists of (1) a carbonate, usually bicarbonate of soda, mixed with (2) an acid ingredient, capable of reacting with the alkaline carbonate when moistened and setting free carbonic acid gas, which gas raises the dough, and (3) a filler, usually flour or cornstarch, which tends to prevent any premature reaction caused by the moisture in the air. Baking powders are known and distinguished by the public, the trade, and the United States Government according to their respective acid ingredients. Those having for such acid ingredients cream of tartar or tartaric acid are known as "cream-of-tartar" baking powders. Those having phosphate for an acid ingredient are known as "phosphate" baking powders. Those having an aluminum compound for the acid ingredient are known as "alum" baking powders. Some baking powders, containing both compounds of alum and phosphate, are known as "alum-phosphate" baking powders.

Prior to 1915, following a difference of opinion among physiologists as to the healthfulness of inorganic phosphate in food products, a Dr. Marshall published an article in the *Journal* of the American Medical Association to the effect that inorganic phosphate was entirely unobjectionable as a baking-powder ingredient. The Bregal Baking Powder Company[32] was at this time and had been, since 1899, a corporation engaged in the manufacture and sale of baking powders in the United States and foreign countries. In 1899, this corporation acquired by purchase the entire capital stock of three other corporations then manufacturing and selling baking powders, all of them cream-of-tartar baking

[32] IV F. T. C. D. 1. Fictitious name. Other cases involving disparagements of competitors will be discussed in Chapter XVII, "Advertising."

powders; and never until September, 1919, did the Bregal Baking Powder Company manufacture any baking powders other than cream-of-tartar baking powders. Since that time, however, the company had been engaged in the manufacture and sale of "phosphate" powder, using the labels of its subsidiary which had an established reputation for "cream-of-tartar" powder.

In spite of the fact that the first chemist of the Bregal Company was convinced by Dr. Marshall's article that inorganic phosphate was entirely unobjectionable as a baking-powder ingredient, the Bregal Company continued up to May, 1919, to publish and circulate disparaging advertisements concerning baking powders containing phosphate. Among such statements were the following: that phosphate was "unwholesome and dangerous as an ingredient" and that it was "produced either by dissolving bones in oil of vitriol, or from rocks formed by the action of the excreta of birds and animals on limestone."

Previous to this campaign against phosphate powders the Bregal Company had similarly advertised extensively that the use of alum or aluminum baking powders had a harmful physiological effect. This campaign was opposed by one of the officers of the company on the ground that the war on alum baking powders would injure the sale of all baking powders, and that it would bring all baking powders into disrepute, inasmuch as it would be difficult for the consuming public to distinguish the alum baking powders from the cream-of-tartar baking powders.

The history of this case is not complete without reference to the occasion for the advertising policy of the Bregal Company. A leading phosphate-baking-powder company had previously advertised that its baking powder was more effective than others and had challenged housewives to prepare two glasses of water and then simultaneously to pour a spoonful of the phosphate powder in one and a similar quantity of cream-of-tartar powder in the other. This was an unfair test, for the action of the former, although no more effective eventually, is quicker, and a small amount of egg-powder content made the effervescence appear to be more permanent. This unfair test, implying that cream-of-tartar powders were inferior in quality, brought about the counter-charge that phosphate powders were dangerous to health. This is simply another example of the unfortunate presence of McCoy-Hatfield feuds in business; with this difference, that the counter-charge, although unfounded, was much more serious.

An interesting case of false disparagements of products, or at least false assertion of relative superiority over other products, was disclosed by the British *Medical Journal*,[33] which published the results of the investigation of the Connecticut Agricultural Experiment Station on brands of tobacco that were said to be "de-nicotinized." This investigation showed that this claim— which by implication disparaged other tobaccos—was largely without foundation.[34] Such claims furthermore draw attention away from the fact that other ingredients of tobacco smoke— ammonia gas, pyridine and carbon monoxide—are even more injurious than nicotine. This situation is typical of many cases of disparagement of a competitor's goods.

Methods of Controlling Unfair Trade Practices

In reviewing the last three chapters, dealing with unfair trade practices, the question arises: What can be done about the matter? If we consider, for example, the proposition advanced in the preceding chapter, on Misrepresentations, that goods, especially those manufactured or fabricated from natural products, should not parade under anything except their true names, several distinct stages can be discovered in which remedies for the misrepresentation of goods were attempted. The Pure Food and Drug Act was an attempt on the part of the Government to protect the consumer against substitutions, adulterations, and deterioration in quality. Similarly the Act Defining Weights and Measures dealt with quantitative variations. But the exclusive attention to this phase of the problem has two bad effects. The first is probably academic: by reducing the prevalence of the rule of *caveat emptor*, the Government lessens the educational effects of bad buying methods as regards the purchaser and thereby extends its paternalistic functions; and paternalism can be justified only in cases where the purchaser cannot be expected to know what he is buying. In the second place, a more real and serious effect is that attention is drawn away from a group of men who suffer as severely as the consumers of goods—the competitors of the unscrupulous merchant.

Hence the more recent method of remedying the situation: the endeavor on the part of trade groups or associations to establish standards and to effect their acceptance among all members of the group. Publicity, an appeal to the intelligence

[33] August, 25, 1928, and October 22, 1927.
[34] See *Bulletin* 307, issued by the Station.

and discrimination of buyers, has been resorted to; government agencies—departments, commissions and courts—have been urged to enforce the statutes and the law, and their effectiveness has been intensified by the cooperative activities of business; and non-governmental organizations, such as the Chamber of Commerce of the United States and Better Business Bureaus,[35] have positively initiated the correction of business abuses and the establishment of dignified principles of conduct.   Such endeavors enable a man to sell a product with a distinctive material content on its face value, and to engage in activities the standards of which are becoming well defined.   Not only are advertisements and tags being more carefully watched by trade associations and business bureaus with a view to eliminating misrepresentation, but indefensible business tactics are also coming more and more under the definite disapproval of business units and organizations.

During the last few years the Federal Trade Commission has introduced radical changes in its method of procedure.   Where, formerly, individual cases of unfair trade practices were tried by the Commission—a stupendous task, when it is remembered that such cases are probably as numerous as the civil and criminal cases which crowd the dockets of our entire court system— the method now consists in having a trade group determine the standards of practice which prevail among the group.   The representatives of a trade are asked to make "trade-practice submittals" as regards their trade practices and trade terms. After a common agreement has been reached, the practices or terms not necessarily being alike for all trades but common even if unique to the trade in question, the resultant resolutions are considered as binding—in the sense of a "gentlemen's agreement"—upon the industry or trade.   They are then used by the Commission as informative of conditions in the particular industry and are used by the Commission as standards for determining the fairness or unfairness of particular practices thereafter called to its attention.   This method at once establishes the concept of "fairness" on a realistic basis, and at the same time raises violations to the serious level of "contempt of

---

[35] See Richardson, John, "Business Policing Itself Through Better Business Bureaus," IX *Harvard Business Review* 69, October, 1930. *The Principles of Business Conduct*, formulated by the late Judge Edwin Parker, and sponsored by the Chamber of Commerce, has already been alluded to.

court"—a distinction which the Jew early made between the unsocial effects of certain acts, on the one hand, and the rank disobedience to God which was involved in wilfully doing such acts after they were forbidden.

Previous to 1924, the following industries had made submittals: ink, celluloid, knit goods, paper, oil, used typewriters, creamery products, hosiery, macaroni, silverware, gold knives, and watch cases. In 1924, trade-practice submittals were made by the Music Publishers' Association, by the Subscription Book Publishers' Association, and by the manufacturers of band instruments. In 1925, submittals were made by the "raised-print" industry with respect to the terms "embossed" and "engraved," by producers of anti-hog-cholera serum and virus, and by the manufacturers of mending cotton. This work in 1926 was enlarged by the holding of trade-practice conferences in the following trades: retail furniture, Castile soap, dairy products, "rayon" and "silkaline"; in 1927, correspondence schools, motion pictures, woven furniture, and insecticides and disinfectants; and in 1928, shirting fabrics, fur, sheet and flat glass, waxed paper, periodicals, hickory handles, mill work, machinery and equipment, paint and varnish, and cottonseed and edible oils.[36] These "trade-practice submittals" are not perfectly obeyed by the trade or completely enforced by the Commission, any more than any law is fully obeyed or enforced. But the formulation of the submittal has the virtue of the Ten Tables at Rome: every man could discover, more clearly than before, what he could and could not do according to the best opinion of the trade.

The Better Business Bureau of New York City took the initiative in regard to similar practices. Meetings of the members of the fur industry in July, 1926, and March, 1927, for example,[37] resulted in certain recommendations for advertising and selling furs which dealt with "predictions of future prices," "statements as to saving," "comparative prices," "guarantees," and "superlative claims," in addition to the following provisions which bear directly on the problem now under discussion.

[36] *Trade Practice Conferences*, Federal Trade Commission, March 15, 1928. U. S. Printing Office.

[37] *Bulletin*, Better Business Bureau of New York City, October 30, 1928: "Name the Hide." See also *Bulletin*, December 13, 1929, for descriptive rules regarding jewelry, especially diamonds and pearls.

1. Garments should be tagged with the name of the pelt in addition to the trade name.

2. Similar provisions in regard to advertising.

3. If garments are made of pieced skins, the advertisement should so state.

4. If a pelt of an inferior color is dyed to resemble better pelts of the same animal, the advertisement should so state.

The Tanners' Council of America made an official compilation of names, classifications, terms and other words in common use in the leather and allied industries and prepared an official "Dictionary of Leather Terminology."[38]   The Council recognized that through lack of such an official listing, improper designations were being used and generally accepted in the trade, jeopardizing the confidence of buyers and working to the detriment of tanner, manufacturer, and retailer, as well as to that of the final purchaser of leather goods.   Many leathers were known commercially or popularly by names of hides or skins of which they were not actually made, most of such names and descriptions being kept alive by trade custom.

The dictionary was therefore drawn up on the following plan:

1. Raw materials used (10 groups).
2. Kinds of leather produced therefrom.
3. Terms in general use (80 terms) giving:
   a. Origin and history.
   b. Accepted or improper use.
   c. Proper or correct use.
4. Glossary of finishes, processes, and other terms (44 terms).

This dictionary illustrates what a trade group can do to establish definite and objective standards for term usages, the abuses of which result not only from vicious motives but often because members of the trade are ignorant or not clear as to specific trade terms and proper methods.

Another phase of this method has been inaugurated by the establishment of such organizations as the Cotton Textile Institute, in which the positive and unique virtues of cotton products are being presented to the public.[39]   The abundance,

---

[38] Obtainable, 41 Park Row, New York City. See also "Book of Accuracy for Advertisers" published April, 1929, by the Affiliated Better Business Bureaus, Incorporated, containing recommended terms for over 30 commodities.

[39] Sloan, George A., *Qualities of Cotton*, Cotton Textile Institute, 1928.

and therefore cheapness, of cotton is stressed, as are also its wide range of usefulness and important re-use value, its whiteness and cleanness, its durability, its comfort as a clothing fabric, and its adaptability to artistic uses. With all of these virtues, it is difficult to see why cotton, practically alone among fibers, has been parading under other names and intruding itself surreptitiously into other fabrics. The positive policies of the Institute are highly commendable, and the general goodwill of the trade will undoubtedly be enhanced by the employment of straightforward tactics in the marketing of cotton products. The factors involved in this stage of development, the definition of trade terms by business itself and the positive discovery and advertisement of the virtues of the material contents of commodities are not sufficient in themselves to prevent misrepresentations, but they intensify the effectiveness of the self-interest of both consumer and competitor in the proper labeling of goods.

These attempts at standardizing the contents of goods and products and at defining terms descriptive of materials and processes have the practical effect of eliminating many unfair trade practices which exist and persist partly through ignorance and partly through the opportunity offered the unscrupulous by the indefiniteness of the situation. Standardization of products and definition of trade terms furthermore contribute materially to the establishment of a science of business. The phase of business science stressed by such activities is chiefly the effecting of what the logician would call "the identity of terms." Just as in a debate or argument, an opponent can avoid the issue by surreptitiously and subtly changing the meanings of certain words employed in stating commonly accepted premises; so an unscrupulous or ignorant business man can gain an advantage by "changing the rules of the game" by offering at current market prices goods which do not conform to generally accepted specifications. Business could well afford to study the attempts of the Mediaeval scholastics to define religious terms, for business at the present time is in a similar stage of development.

The science of chemistry was tremendously advanced by the discovery that there are certain basic elements which have permanent and fixed qualities and which are distinguishable one from the other. Similarly, a science of business awaits the recognition and standardization of specific raw materials, defined processes, and measurable forms and sizes.   It is largely through the establishment of such a science of business that intelligent men can hope to succeed, and only so can confidence and fair trade practices be established on an objective basis.   This does not mean that standardization of products and definition of terms will eliminate all unfair practices or all chances of an unintelligent man's success—the various chemical elements are not found in their pure state, and many phenomena occur which a scientist cannot predict.   But the establishment of such a machinery increases the chances and the probabilities of the success of intelligent and honest behavior without in any appreciable degree lessening the opportunities for individual initiative and imagination.   A similar definition of trade practices, although more difficult than that of commodities, is necessary to the proper development of Business Ethics.

F. SELF-REGULATION IN AMERICAN BUSINESS

Most of the cases in the preceding section were dealt with by the Federal Trade Commission under the Act creating that administrative body and under the Clayton Act. Some of these unfair business practices were called to the attention of the Commission by individuals and trade associations, some were discovered through the initiative of the Commission itself, and more recently such matters are being dealt with by the Commission in cooperation with various trades and industries, the Chamber of Commerce of the United States and Better Business Bureaus. Therefore it would be difficult to discover just to what extent the phrase "self-regulation of business" could be applied to such activities, especially since all court or semi-judicial activities are largely in response to the initiative of the individual who seeks redress for a grievance. It is not the concern of this volume to labor the point, which is after all an academic issue. Pragmatically, the Federal Trade Commission has served to correct many business abuses, it has sponsored the assuming of such responsibilities by business men themselves, and its activities undoubtedly have indirectly generated a consciousness of the need of self-government in business. The stressing of trade-practice conferences in recent years has certainly qualified any misgivings which business might have of undue paternalism on the part of the Government.

The following chapters deal with business activities which may be regarded more strictly under the title of "business self-regulation." No attempt has been made to work out a complete theory of self-government in business. Four different areas of business activity have been chosen as illustrative of the possibilities of self-regulation completely or in large part independent of government or law. The individual business man, the trade group, and the Better Business Bureau are represented in action in various business functions. Concrete examples are given mainly in order to draw as accurate a picture of the situation as possible, but also incidentally to indicate available methods to business men who are desirous of effecting a better control over trade practices and standards.

In the chapter on "Legitimate Trade Channels," the suggestion was made that a philosophy of business is no more difficult to conceive of than a philosophy of religion or of law or of the state. This suggestion is elaborated in the following chapters, by portraying certain factors which are necessary to any thoroughgoing doctrine of business, especially such as may be likened to the functions of civil government. In the chapter on "Advertising," business displays its executive functions, largely through the activities of its own agency, the Better Business Bureau. In the chapter on "Limitation of Production," the legislative capacities of business are exhibited in determining a business function which runs counter to the very fundamentals of common and statutory law. In the chapter on "Commercial Arbitration," the judicial activities which are peculiar to business are described, especially as they have historically emerged from the thralldom of the courts and the lawyers.

The virtues of an abstract, complete and well-organized philosophy of business have been sacrificed to a concrete, inadequate and pluralistic point of view. The pick-and-shovel work that still remains to be done will be appreciated by all those who are not yet willing to inflict business with Jeremiads or apostolic blessings, and the clarion call to further work is sounding too loudly to warrant paying much attention to swan songs or paeans of praise.

CHAPTER XVII

ADVERTISING

Advertising is the medium through which most commodities are introduced to the public and by which they are kept constantly in the focus of the prospective buyer's attention. From the standpoint of the advertising agent and of the merchant, advertising has therefore become largely a psychological problem. How best can the buyer's attention be attracted, how can it be sustained, and how can his interest be intensified so as to impel or even compel him to buy a particular commodity? In proportion to the merchant's or agent's enthusiasm for his particular objective, his advertising methods may become successively attractive, clever, insistent, impertinent, blatant, even disgusting.

Probably no other function of business so frequently raises the question of good taste, especially in the minds of the general purchasing public. Just as we personally resent being introduced to disagreeable or undesirable people, or to being unduly urged to meet people that we do not know or are not interested in knowing, so advertising has frequently been regarded with displeasure by persons who prefer to do their own choosing and buying. Nor has this attitude been confined to the consuming public. Advertising managers themselves have sensed the fact that psychological and technological skill are not the sole determining factors in advertising, but that a long-time advertising policy should be governed by standards of good taste and by certain ethical considerations which the merchant himself must be made to see. Advertising standards are also a matter of interest to the trade itself. If advertising is so directed as to disparage a competitor's goods, he may hit back in the same manner, with consequences that are unwelcome to the trade as a whole, not only as regards dignity and goodwill, but also because of a non-transferable trade expense.

No attempt will be made here to develop a science of advertising or to deal with those phases of the art of advertising which have for their purpose the efficacious application of the psychological principles of selling. The purpose of this chapter is to present the ethical problems of advertising as a part of the general problem of business ethics, and to indicate in some measure that high-powered salesmanship which results from forced-draft advertising methods can well be tempered by fairness and good taste.

The tremendous development of advertising in the United States during the last two decades may be attributed in part to the World War. The burden of excess-profits taxes, then imposed on business, was lightened considerably by diverting a goodly portion of gross profits to extension programs, including advertising. The amount so spent for advertising purposes was, of course, greater than the amount which would have been necessary for paying excess-profits taxes; but business derived at least something from the former, while it did not benefit at all from the latter. The scientific approach to the problem would probably have been to determine the point at which the net returns to the business from advertising expenditures balanced the excess-profits tax. Practically, of course, this was not done. A rough approximation to such calculations, however, resulted in greatly increased expenditures for advertising. Whether the actual business gains so obtained were at all commensurate with the expenditure is questionable. But it certainly is true that business men through this experience did learn the value of advertising. The amount of advertising which is justifiable in business probably lies somewhere between the extravagant expenditures of the war and post-war period and the insufficient expenditures of the pre-war period. No one knows even the scientific answer to this problem, let alone the ethical solution.

The Control of Advertising

This new advertising situation created responsibilities which have been recognized by advertising mediums and agencies themselves. When "billboard" advertising first became the vogue, the countryside was cluttered with unsightly signs that violated the rights, as well as the sense of propriety, of persons who regarded natural beauty as a public asset. Niagara Falls and the Grand Canyon of the Colorado were disfigured by signs that intruded themselves upon the sight-seer, while the contents of these signs were frequently not above ethical as well as aesthetic reproach. Soon the public revulsion to such methods manifested itself in the form of restrictive legislation. This reaction against billboard advertising was augmented by editorials in newspapers, the chief competitor of the billboard for advertising. Although some sporadic legislation resulted, the correction of the difficulty was effected largely through the billboard advertisers themselves. Signs were removed from conspicuous parts of scenic localities, flimsy construction gave way to well-built and attractive structures, and the character of the advertising was radically changed for the better. In order to cultivate goodwill, posters of real educational and artistic merit were displayed on certain occasions—for example, at Christmastime or just prior to Lincoln's Birthday—without any advertising appeal. The result has been, in billboard advertising, a situation which, while not ideal, at least gives evidence of more good taste and sense than could have been expected during the hectic and blatant days when advertising was first discovering its possibilities.

Advertising managers themselves were concerned over the problem of public goodwill. They associated themselves into Advertising Clubs which in 1912 formed a National Vigilance Committee, to control advertising methods in such a way as to prevent undue legislative restrictions. These "Vigilantes," like their godfathers of the lawless frontier days, literally "took the law into their own hands" in the most justifiable form of such procedure, by supplementing inadequate legal provisions with regulations sanctioned by the industry itself. The Printers' Ink model statute, which was one of the results of these activities, has been adopted by over 20 states. Much was accomplished by discussions in advertising clubs and in association meetings, but the tremendous growth of advertising proved to be almost too much for this organization to handle.

The movement, however, took a practical turn in the organization of "better business bureaus," the functions of which included the checking of all advertising, of merchandise and financial promotions, for accuracy and reliability. Supported at first by the more perspicuous advertising agencies and by bankers and prominent merchants, efforts were directed particularly toward controlling the "little fellows" whose unscrupulous competition had been as unfair as the more ruthless methods of "big business." It soon became apparent, however, that the "big fellows" also needed correction, and many of the financial supporters of these bureaus learned that the bureaus were courageously independent of the very forces that sustained them.[1] Not only have these bureaus, now located in approximately 60 cities, checked and tested the advertising of merchandise and financial promotions, but they have carried on a program of general publicity and education until the statements, "Accuracy in Advertising," and "Before You Invest—Investigate," have become bywords.

Sponsored by these bureaus and by the Chamber of Commerce of the United States, a large number of newspapers, periodicals and other advertising mediums have agreed to a Trade Practice Submittal[2] whereby the Federal Trade Commission may proceed against newspapers, periodicals, *etc.*, as jointly liable, with the agency and the advertiser, for unfair methods in advertising. In addition to this, certain newspapers, conspicuously the *New York Times*, have frankly announced an "Advertising Index Expurgatorius," containing the following specific items:

1. Fraudulent or doubtful advertisements.
2. Offers of something of value for nothing; advertisements that make false, unwarranted or exaggerated claims.
3. Advertisements that are ambiguous in wording and which may mislead.
4. Attacks of a personal character; advertisements that make uncalled-for reflections on competitors or competitive goods.
5. Advertisements holding out the prospect of large guaranteed dividends or excessive profits.
6. Bucket shops and offerings of undesirable financial firms.
7. Advertisements that are indecent, vulgar, suggestive, repulsive or offensive either in theme or treatment.
8. Matrimonial offers; fortune telling; ~~massage.~~
9. Objectionable medical advertising and offers of free medical treatment; advertising that makes remedial, relief or curative claims, either directly or by inference, not justified by the facts or common experience.
10. Advertising of products containing habit-forming or dangerous drugs.
11. Want advertisements which request money for samples or articles.

[1] See Richardson, John, "Business Policing Itself through Better Business Bureaus," *Harvard Business Review*, October, 1930; especially statement by Louis Kirstein, p. 73.

[2] *Bulletin*, Boston Better Business Bureau, December 10, 1928.

12. Any other advertising that may cause money loss to the reader, or injury in health or morals, or loss of confidence in reputable advertising and honorable business, or which is regarded by the *Times* as unworthy.[3]

The Times welcomes information from readers in aid of its efforts to keep its advertising columns clean, and offers a reward of $100 to anyone causing the arrest and conviction of a person or firm obtaining money under false pretenses through fraudulent advertising published in its columns. The announced standards and achieved position of this newspaper and a number of leading magazines need no comments.

The whole philosophy of business thus becomes involved in the questions arising in regard to the ethics of advertising, especially when one compares the advertising standards of business with those of the older and major professions. The following provisions, governing the practice of medicine and law, stand out in contrast with the attitude of business toward advertising.

Solicitation of patients by physicians as individuals, or collectively in groups by whatsoever name these be called, or by institutions or organizations, whether by circulars or advertisements, or by personal communications, is unprofessional. This does not prohibit institutions from a legitimate advertisement of location, physical surroundings and special class—if any—of patients accommodated.

It is equally unprofessional to procure patients by indirection through solicitors or agents of any kind, or by indirect advertisement, or by furnishing or inspiring newspaper or magazine comments concerning cases in which the physician has been or is concerned. All other like self-laudations defy the traditions and lower the tone of any profession and so are intolerable.

The most worthy and effective advertisement possible, even for a young physician, and especially with his brother physicians, is the establishment of a well-merited reputation for professional ability and fidelity. This cannot be forced, but must be the outcome of character and conduct.

The publication or circulation of ordinary simple business cards, being a matter of personal taste or local custom, and sometimes of convenience, is not *per se* improper. As implied, it is unprofessional to disregard local customs and to offend recognized ideals in publishing or circulating such cards.

It is unprofessional to promise radical cures; to boast of cures and secret methods of treatment or remedies; to exhibit certificates of skill

[3] *New York Times*, May 4, 1929.

or of success in the treatment of diseases; or to employ any methods to gain the attention of the public for the purpose of obtaining patients.[4]

An inquirer handed the Committee on Professional Ethics of the New York County Lawyers' Association a series of advertisements appearing in a daily newspaper in the forms hereto annexed, and asked an expression of the opinion of the Committee upon the propriety of such advertising by lawyers.

> Able lawyer, specialist family troubles, private matters, *etc.;* furnishes reliable advice; all cases handled; satisfaction guaranteed; quick results; domestic relations laws of all states explained. Call, write.   . . . LAWYER.

> For results see me; reliable, experienced, successful; accident, family troubles, all cases, consultation free. Call or write.
> . . . LAWYER.

> LAWYER (American), highest standing; consultation free; notary public . . . Sundays, evenings till 9.

In the opinion of the Committee,[5] all of these advertisements were improper.   The case of *People v. McCabe*[6] was cited:

> The ethics of the legal profession forbid that a lawyer should advertise his talents or his skill as a shopkeeper advertises his wares.

The Committee furthermore declared the first two advertisements to be additionally objectionable because they seemed to indicate a willingness to take all cases, irrespective of the merit of the cause; and that the first advertisement had the demerit of containing an impossible and therefore false and misleading guaranty of satisfaction.

This professional attitude points very clearly to at least one of two propositions: either there is a basic distinction between business and the professions or there is something radically wrong with the amount of advertising which business does. The truth of the first proposition does not necessarily invalidate the second, which, however, may be qualified by independent considerations.

---

[4] *Principles of Medical Ethics*, Chap. II, Sec. 4.   See also *Canons of Ethics*, American Bar Association, Canon 27, which is quite similar.

[5] *Questions Respecting Proper Professional Conduct*, Case 45.

[6] 19 L. R. A. 231.

The Justification of Business Advertising

The intimate way in which advertising is related to sound business principles is illustrated by the situation now confronting the textile industry and by the efforts which are being made to deal with the situation.

The Cotton Textile Institute has been organized in order to advance the best interests of the cotton-textile industry. The major problem which confronted this industry at the time of the organization of the Institute was that production was exceeding demand. This situation is relative and is not due to any absolute facts as regards either production or demand; that is, an excess of production over demand could occur whether production were too great or demand were too small. Therefore the difficulty could be met either by reducing production or by increasing demand. What an individual company can do is indicated by the following announcement:

HOMER LORING ENTERS TEXTILE FIELD

Organizes and Will Become Head of Unit Comprising Selling Houses, Finishing Plants and Mills

Boston—In March of this year, having completed four years of highly constructive work in rehabilitation of the Boston & Maine Railroad, Homer Loring retired from the road's service. Resolution of the board, accepting with regret Mr. Loring's resignation, referred to his services as having "shown qualities and yielded results which are difficult if not impossible to overestimate." His equally successful rehabilitation of the Eastern Massachusetts Street Railway and his work as head of the State Commission on Administration and Finance complete a trinity of achievements during the last ten years that have given Mr. Loring deservedly high rank among New England business executives.

Before and since leaving the Boston & Maine, Mr. Loring has engaged in an intensive investigation of conditions in the textile industry. Very shortly, it is expected, public announcement will be made of a new textile concern organized by Mr. Loring and to be actively headed by him. Kidder, Peabody & Company will handle the financing.

From his study of textile conditions, Mr. Loring has gained certain definite ideas as to the soundest principles on which to create and operate a textile organization. These principles are incorporated in the new company. Mr. Loring has started with the selling end of the business. He has acquired successful selling houses, or "converters" as the trade calls them, and will add finishing plants and cotton mills of an aggregate full-time capacity of something less than the total sales of the converters. In other words, the mills included in the organization will be concerned only with the problems of production. They will not be compelled to seek a market for their goods, and on the other hand the selling houses will be assured of quality, service and low costs.   The effect of continuous, full-time operation upon production costs can hardly be other than favorable.

A textile unit built along these lines should be able, in Mr. Loring's judgment, to operate profitably even under the depressed textile conditions at present prevailing.   Given a general improvement in textiles its profits should increase substantially.[7]

If, as has been said, the trade as a whole should attempt such a program, a serious obstacle to curtailing production arises by virtue of the provisions of the Sherman Anti-trust Act.   No group of producers or sellers could, by the interpretations of this Act, combine or agree to reduce production, because this would amount to a "conspiracy in restraint of trade."   Even where the United States Department of Commerce has attempted to standardize certain commodities and reduce the number of grades and kinds, it could not proceed to ask for an enforceable trade agreement on the matter.   Trade representatives are called together and are presented with the facts; the standardizing of commodities and reduction of grades and kinds are then left to be determined by the voluntary cooperation of the members of the trade.   Any attempt to coerce or urge members of a trade group to adopt trade policies is so delicate a matter that most trade associations have avoided the problem altogether through fear of the legal consequences.   A trade group may act only through the voluntary and independent activities of its members.

But a trade association can encourage the buying of its products through sales campaigns and organized advertising activities.   This the Cotton Textile Institute has set itself to do. The qualities and characteristics of cotton fabrics are advertised and stores and sales agents are stimulated to increase their sales, style policies are studied and style values given publicity, while expert cutters, representatives of the Institute, are placed in dry-goods and department stores to help women cut out patterns, no charge being made for the service.   This campaign of education has resulted in stimulating sales appreciably, especially in the fine-goods section, and has thereby supplied one factor in reducing stocks on hand and excess production.

The traditional public attitude toward advertising has been to condemn it because of its undue stimulus of wants and desires. When it is remembered, however, that human happiness and welfare consist not in the degree of human satisfaction, but in the degree to which justifiable wants are satisfied, it becomes

[7] *Boston News Bureau,* October 9, 1928.

apparent that the stimulus of justifiable wants, which now may be lying dormant, is as necessary to human welfare and happiness as is the degree to which wants are satisfied. This point of view is opposed to the ascetic view of life, but it is equally justifiable. And the failure to appreciate this point of view has made possible a sentimental and unclear opposition to advertising in general. The fundamental philosophy of advertising is as sound as the philosophy which underlies intelligent business management. Both are directed toward increasing the ratio of demand to supply: sound business management, by avoiding overproduction; and advertising, by stimulating demand. In this sense, advertising is an intimate part of management, and if positive creative activity is preferable to a negative economy, then advertising is probably the more important part of management.

Such considerations apply at least to "primary" advertising, which enlarges demand and acquaints the public with a commodity without directly infringing on the market of a competitor. Indirectly, of course, every sale of a commodity absorbs buying power that would be directed toward other commodities. But in this sense no particular competitor or even group of competitors is singled out for attack. Direct invasions arise as the result of "selective" advertising, which thereby raises the more acute problems of business ethics.

Disparagements of Competitors

The ethical problems of advertising then become like the rules of athletic games, which in turn presuppose the justification of athletic recreation and of a particular sport. A critical analysis of advertising presupposes the justification of business and of advertising in general and turns to the questions which arise once these assumptions have been granted. So, also, advertising may have certain rules among the professions and others in business, and various businesses may have different advertising standards. Hitting below the belt is specifically forbidden in a prize fight; any sort of "slugging" at all is forbidden in football; even to consider such a practice in tennis would be an absurdity. In tennis, a part of the game is to plac the ball close to the boundary lines; in archery, the purpose of the game is to hit the bull's eye; in baseball there is virtue in "knocking the ball out of the lot." What then are the rules of the game of advertising, granted its general validity? The question can best be answered by raising some general questions and then by referring to actual advertising practices.

Recently there has appeared in advertising a method which has given merchants and advertising agencies considerable concern: the disparagement of another product.   Sometimes this consists of assertions which reflect on the product of a competitor in the same restricted industry. Cliquot Club ginger ale affords a good illustration of this sort; the statement, "Cliquot Club has been aged six months," implies that other companies do not, while the statement, "You wouldn't eat a green apple," draws an analogy which is not complimentary to competitors, to say the least.   Milder, and yet similar, are the claims of the Standard Oil Company, that its products are the "best" in the market.   The statements may be true, and so may the inferences which naturally follow.   But any positive force of the advertising is overshadowed by the outstanding effect, the disparagement of competitors, an unfair situation and one which does not add to the health and soundness of the industry as a whole. One wonders who pays the bill, especially if the competitors of Standard Oil or Cliquot Club should take it into their heads to conduct a similar campaign.

The extent of this disparaging type of advertising is a matter of concern to the advertiser as well as to the consumer, for it is bound to lower the productive value of advertising.   On one page of a magazine the reader is urged to put in an automatic oil-burning furnace to avoid the dirt and work connected with coal-burning types; on another page one is urged to keep to the coal-burning type because the automatic types explode or fail at critical moments.   Kaffee-Hag emphasizes the ill effects of coffee; Royal Baking Powder the harmful effects of "alum" powders.   Here an electric company advises one to use street cars to avoid the worry of traffic jams and parking; there an automobile company urges the buying of an extra car to avoid the delays of the street car.   Electric refrigeration and ice companies come to grips, while dairy associations fight oleomargarine.   "Not a cough in a carload" implies that many a cough is packed in another brand of cigarette; "Reach for a Lucky instead of a sweet" has become as great a menace to the candy trade as to the wheat-products industry; and then we are urged to smoke a cool, satisfying cigar, to avoid the nervousness that comes with too much cigarette puffing.

Business competition, it must be remembered, is not confined within particular industries; it exists also among various commodities that are mutual substitutes or alternatives. The Bakers' Institute has for years been studying how best to combat the vogue of slender figures among women which has been encouraged alike by stylists, food faddists, and weight-reducing agencies; the cigar industry has leagued itself with the candy, preserves, and canned-fruit industries to combat a similar sales plea of the cigarette. These struggles are comparable to the jurisdictional disputes among labor unions, and are symptomatic of the same sort of situation that gives rise to tariff disputes; such as the fight waged by the Citrus Growers' Association for a high tariff against the importation of bananas by the United Fruit Company. There may be more virtue in "an apple a day" than in a similar diet of oranges or bananas, but such facts are not going to be proved by the relative amount or effectiveness of interested advertising. In the meantime, a tremendous economic waste results because these effects merely neutralize each other.

It may be a comfort to some people to know that the worst recent offender of good advertising practice has thrown a boomerang. An investigation of cigar factories throughout the country has disclosed very little of the practice which is being broadcast as a prevalent practice; and it was found that in one large eastern state, the only two cases reported were observed in the factory of the very company that has been responsible for such advertising. Similarly, the comparative price advertising of one large department store in New York has drawn the fire of disparaging advertising from at least two of the other leading department stores in that city; the net result being creditable to none of the three: the appeal soon wears out and it is something to look back upon with regret. It is often said that the doctor buries his mistakes and that the lawyer's mistakes are mostly put in jail, but that the engineer erects monuments to his. May it not be added that the advertiser prints his in words and pictures, shadowy perhaps, but permanent nevertheless?

The difficulty, of course, is that advertising rests for its immediate results upon appeals which are psychologically effective but which may be unwarrantable from the standpoint of ethics or good taste. Mutual disparagements of various businesses[8] may become as interesting as a dog fight, and the main purpose

[8] See section on "Criticisms," Chapter XVI.

of advertising—to attract attention—may thereby be achieved. This raises the question as to whether dog fights should be tolerated by people and whether they increase the prestige of dogs. No sanely tolerant person would advocate the setting up of a moral or artistic censorship or place the fate or the control of advertising in the hands of non-business men who have certain definite notions of social values or of social welfare. And yet it is the abuses of advertising which lead to such social boycotts and legislation, which in turn react unfavorably on the whole field of advertising, good or bad, fair or unfair.

To avoid these difficulties some control is necessary; and inasmuch as the best form of control always is self-control, responsibility rests chiefly on advertising agencies and associations and on business itself, and only secondarily on the general public or on Government.

"Bait" Advertising

Another type of unjustifiable advertising is known as "bait" advertising. Here again the difficulty arises that the practice is in the main in keeping with alleged good business management: to sell some goods as "loss leaders." "Bait" advertising has been more strictly defined by Kenneth Backman, of the Boston Better Business Bureau, however, as the advertising of an article which the merchant hopes he will not have to sell. This practice ranges all the way from the advertising of "loss" leaders to the disreputable practices of certain furniture stores and "suit clubs" of enticing customers by assertions which later prove to be grossly exaggerated. No general statement can be made regarding the practice, because its viciousness depends largely on the methods employed by salesmen when the customer "rises to the bait." One particularly disreputable form of this practice is discoverable in children's magazines, where the unfair tactics of unscrupulous advertisers are creating a general suspicion and ill will toward advertising, which advertisers well could control. The following cases illustrate the more general practice.

The Lorrick Piano Company,[9] which engaged in the sale of pianos and small organs, had stores in various cities including New York, Detroit, Boston, St. Louis and Philadelphia. This company advertised

[9] Fictitious name. See *Bulletin* 11, National Better Business Bureau, New York, September 15, 1927.

player-piano outfits at $295 each. Over 100 insertions were made in various newspapers at a cost of $25,000 during the year 1927.

When prospective customers called at the store in answer to this advertising, it was the custom of the salesmen in the Lorrick stores to disparage the quality of the advertised instrument and to endeavor to sell these customers another piano at a higher price. This was the sales and advertising custom of the Lorrick business, such practices having been continued for a considerable number of years. In 1927, only five actual sales of the type of merchandise which was advertised had been made and one of these sales was to a local representative of the Better Business Bureau who had tried out the advertisement and insisted on purchasing the advertised piano.

The defense of the manager of the Lorrick Piano Company was that the purpose of the advertising was to get people into the store in order to sell them another type of merchandise. The procedure is known as "bait" advertising, the advertised article which is praised in the printed advertisement being disparaged by salesmen in the store. In some cases "switching" was engaged in, the advertised article being sold, but before delivery the customer would be prevailed upon to change the contract already signed to one which provided for the purchase of merchandise at a much higher price.

*　*　*　*　*　*

H. L. Cardon,[10] the president of Carols Music Company, Limited,[10] a New York corporation, was formerly manager of the L. F. Eyreson Piano House[10] in Erie, Pennsylvania, and also in Pittsburgh, Pennsylvania. Newspaper advertising of the Carols Music Company, Inc., which has thus far appeared in New York City, has been of the contest type similar to advertising used by Eyreson for his stores.

Following a preliminary investigation by the New York Better Business Bureau, they were assured on October 10, 1928, by the Andrew Cylinder Agency,[10] which placed all of the Carols Company advertising, that this type of advertising had been stopped. However, complaints have begun to reach the Bureau (October 19) regarding the issuance of "Merchandise Credit Checks" which were sent to unsuccessful contestants, usually in the sum of $75. This amount was to be "accepted just the same as so much cash as part of the first payment on any piano or player in our stock (one to a customer) up to and until October 16."

L. F. Eyreson and the Eyreson Piano House of Buffalo, which had the Erie and Pittsburgh, Pennsylvania, branches, were indicted in February of this year for using the mail in furtherance of a scheme to defraud.

*　*　*　*　*　*

[10] Fictitious name. *News Bulletin,* Better Business Bureau of New York City, October 19, 1928.

The H. L. Henmetz & Son Company[11] was incorporated in 1902 as a Missouri corporation succeeding H. L. Henmetz & Son, a firm which had been doing business in St. Louis since 1856. H. L. Henmetz & Son Company conducted a retail business in men's clothing and ladies' garments and furs, its principal business being in women's wear. The store was situated in a favorable locality in a business district which was given over largely to the retailing of men's clothing and women's ready-to-wear garments, a district which was recognized by customers as given over to merchandise of a high quality and value. This company, under the trade name of "Henmetz," had enjoyed a good reputation for fair dealing and reliability for a great many years. It conducted a c.o.d. business in St. Louis and surrounding territory.

In January, 1921, H. L. Henmetz & Son Company published in various daily papers of general circulation in the locality, and advertised by means of posters and in their show windows, that they were being forced out of business by unusual conditions and by financial difficulties beyond their control. They furthermore stated that a firm of "mercantile adjusters" had been appointed with unlimited authority and with positive orders to convert their entire stock into cash at once, and that all of their goods would be sold at a special sale beginning in three days. Prices were advertised at lower than manufacturers' costs "to satisfy creditors and to wind up the business." Every article was declared to be a part of their well-known high-grade stock habitually carried on the shelves.

The "regular stock" of H. L. Henmetz & Son Company had, as a matter of fact, become depleted and was to a large extent out of fashion. A few days prior to the sale, and during the course of the sale, H. L. Henmetz & Son Company purchased large quantities of goods and merchandise which were tagged with prices far in excess of fair value, these fictitious prices being stricken out in such a way as to leave the altered mark legible, and a "sale price" added. The regular stock was similarly marked and both stocks were then intermingled and mixed. The sales force was increased from the normal number of 15 persons to 50 persons.

This sale deceived people into believing that it was only the well-known stock habitually carried by H. L. Henmetz & Son Company that was being sold. The purchases of "sale stock" amounted to $20,000; sales during the first 10 days amounted to $33,000. The sale continued to June, 1921, during which time the goods in the men's department were sold out and the department was discontinued. H. L. Henmetz & Son Company was not, as a matter of fact, insolvent or bankrupt, nor was any forced action threatened by any of their competitors, nor was the business at any time during the course of the sale out of H. L. Henmetz & Son Company's control.

* * * * * *

[11] Fictitious name.   V F. T. C. D. 424 (1923).

Mr. J. D. Lisbie[12] conducted a tailoring establishment in Washington, D. C., under the name of Hixie Tailors.[12] He solicited customers through agents or "solicitors" and offered to make and sell a suit of clothes, from cloth chosen by the customers, for $48. The offer was subject to the following terms, conditions, and representations. The customer agreed to pay $1 each week for 48 weeks. Upon the completion of the payments, Lisbie was to make and deliver the suit selected. The customers were to be grouped into "clubs" of 48 members each. As each "club" was formed and completed, Lisbie engaged to select the name of one customer for whom the chosen suit was to be made and delivered without any further payments after the initial payment of $1. Each week thereafter for 47 weeks Lisbie engaged similarly to select and deliver a suit to one of the remaining members, without further payments, until all had been supplied with suits. The customer in each case was to be selected in consideration of and in return for services rendered by the customer. Such services were to consist in the securing of other customers or in the doing of such things as were requested by Lisbie or considered sufficient by him to justify such selection. In some instances the solicitors or Lisbie himself represented that the selections were to be made by lot or by chance.

As matter of fact, Lisbie arbitrarily made his selections of customers who were to receive suits. He did not divide his customers into "clubs" as represented, but selected customers who were to receive suits from the entire group and in numbers less than the ratio promised. The majority of the customers paid the full $48 for their suits.

Whether or not the sale of musical instruments and of clothing lends itself peculiarly to this type of advertising, the practice is more common in such businesses than in others. This affords circumstantial evidence of the necessity of dealing with such problems by trades rather than from the point of view of business or advertising in general. The spirit of the practice is well expressed in the phrase: "Will you come into my 'suit club'?" says the spider to the fly.[13] In these "suit clubs," the prospective purchaser frequently finds that the suit when ready for wear is priced at a much higher figure. If he can overcome the "high-powered sales pressure" of the clothing merchant and insist on the suit for which he contracted, he is given a suit which is obviously of inferior quality and make. Often the situation is merely a lottery, although even "prominent citizens" have been attracted thereby. The effect on "one-price" furniture

[12] Fictitious name. VI F. T. C. D. 486.

[13] See *Bulletin*, Better Business Bureau of New York City, March 22, 1928.

or clothing houses that advertise honestly is apparent. The Better Business Bureau, sponsored by the latter type of merchant, is constantly on the lookout for such practices and resorts to publicity in bulletins and newspapers to stop the practice. Such publicity strikes a balance between the extremes of *laissez faire* and *caveat emptor*, on the one hand, and their opposites, government regulation and social paternalism, on the other.

A closely allied practice, namely, comparative-price advertising, may be considered here.[14] The following are the more frequent statements used in advertising:

Were $2—now 85 cents.
At one-half the usual price.
Former price $10—special price $6.
Selling elsewhere at $50—our price $30.
Saving of one-third to one-half.
Worth $10—sale price $6.
$50 values for $35.
Originally $10—now $4.50.

The problem presented by such statements is a difficult one because the situation is paradoxical: the prospective purchaser has learned to distrust such statements, hence it is difficult to discover who is injured thereby. Among the trades which are suspected, by readers of advertisements, of misstating the facts are jewelry, furs, furniture, musical instruments, radios, and tires and accessories. Certain stores with established reputations are, of course, excepted from this general suspicion. Among those trades the advertisements of which are more readily believed are groceries, shoes, and, men's and women's wear. If the prospective purchaser has learned to suspect comparative-price advertising and to show just enough discrimination in his suspicions to single out some trades from others, evidently the practice is either expensive to those who engage in it or it is unfair to their competitors who do not. The net result is a loss to economic society, either because the purchaser pays the increased bill or because the honest and fair competitor temporarily suffers a loss or is forced out of business. To see this point is to grasp the essence of the problem of ethics in advertising.

[14] See "Study of Comparative Price Advertising," July, 1928; Boston Better Business Bureau.

Impossible or Exaggerated Claims

A third type of unfair advertising consists of impossible or exaggerated claims. Businesses indulging in such practices range all the way from hog breeders who assert that their hogs are "immune from cholera," to electric belts that "will keep the feet at a moderate temperature summer and winter, will revitalize the blood, and will save doctors' bills."[15] A chemical company advertises its product to be "10 times stronger as a germicide than undiluted U.S.P. carbolic acid."[16] Similarly the use of such terms as "best" and "only" have become so common as practically to become meaningless. The following cases illustrate the situation.

The Wearforever Battery Company,[17] an Illinois corporation, made and sold storage batteries for automobile ignition and lighting. Its place of business was located at Chicago and its trade extended throughout the United States. It advertised in papers and magazines that its batteries would "last forever." A further reading of its advertisements and circulars disclosed the fact that the purchaser was to pay 50 cents per month for service charges and was entitled to a new battery as soon as the old one was worn out.

* * * * * *

The Meloflian Company[18] was a Connecticut corporation doing business in New York City and vicinity. They manufactured and sold player pianos, music rolls, phonographs, and records. Dealers were made to sign the following agreement before they were supplied with goods.

"The dealer agrees that if he handles, deals in, or sells any other type or make of phonograph instruments or records than those of the Meloflian Company, or parts and accessories of the same, he and his representatives will directly and indirectly advertise, market, promote, and sell said Meloflian instruments and any parts and accessories thereof and records, as its best and unequalled leader of any and all goods of a phonograph type."

* * * * * *

Dorb & Kyer[19] was a partnership established in New York, doing business in this and adjacent states. Although this partnership was dissolved in 1920, Dorb continued the business under the old partner-

---

[15] See IV F. T. C. D. 73 and II F. T. C. D. 335.
[16] See IV F. T. C. D. 155.
[17] Fictitious name.   II F. T. C. D. 95 (1919).
[18] Fictitious name.   III F. T. C. D. 124 (1920).
[19] Fictitious name.   IV F. T. C. D. 418 (1920).

ship name. This business consisted in buying, overhauling, selling and shipping second-hand adding machines. In the latter part of 1920 Dorb & Kyer advertised "several hundred thoroughly rebuilt Halton Adding and Listing Machines available at half list price."

Dorb & Kyer, as a matter of fact, had less than a dozen of these machines in stock and had made no arrangement or contract for any more. They were equipped to overhaul such machines but not to rebuild them. "Rebuilt" had a trade meaning which was well defined; it involved "stripping to the base, building up, replacing worn with new parts, and adding new refinements and improvements." None of the large manufacturers of adding machines sold new parts; they reserved to themselves the right to do all rebuilding. This fact was known to all the dealers in the trade, although it was not a matter of general information to purchasers of adding machines. Dorb expected to fill his orders by making any necessary purchases from an adding-machine exchange company which handled second-hand machines but did not rebuild any machines.

The difficulty with such exaggerated and misleading claims is not only that the purchaser is deceived and the competitor directly deprived of business; but confidence in the trade as a whole is undermined, and the effectiveness of advertising appeals wears out in proportion to the continued use of exaggerated statements. Advertising is no exception to the general business rule that inflated values must be viewed with suspicion, for they may give rise to plant expansions or financial commitments that will accentuate the deflation process into a calamity. In order to deal with such a situation the Associated Tire Dealers of St. Louis cooperated with the Better Business Bureau of that city in working out the following rules[20] for advertising the sale of tires.

STANDARDS TO GOVERN AUTOMOBILE TIRE ADVERTISING

1. It is recommended that superlative claims such as "Lowest Prices in the City," "Greatest Bargains Ever Offered," "Our Prices Cannot be Equaled," etc., be eliminated from advertising.

2. When tires offered are not of strictly "First" quality, the advertisement shall plainly state "Seconds." The terms, "N.F.C." "Slightly Blemished," "Will not affect wearing quality," etc., shall be entirely eliminated.

3. Mileage guarantees shall be eliminated from tire advertisements.

4. Rebuilt or retreaded tires shall be plainly advertised as such.

[20] Published by the St. Louis Better Business Bureau.

5. The name of the tire shall be prominently stated when tires are advertised in connection with quoted prices and the name of the tire spelled in full and not abbreviated.

Example:

Wrong Way—	Right Way—
OVERSIZE CORDS	Oversize Cupples Cords
	First Quality
30 × 3½ $......................	30 × 3½ $.....................

or

OVERSIZE CORDS
Seconds
30 × 3½
    Cupples $..................
32 × 4 Fisk $.................

6. When tires are advertised at a quoted price in connection with the name of the manufacturer, and such manufacturer makes two or more grades of tires, the brand name as well as the name of the manufacturer shall be prominently stated. When the manufacturer's name does not appear on the tire, then the brand name shall appear first and in larger type than the name of the manufacturer.

Example:

Wrong Way—	Right Way—
Fisk Cords	Fisk "Premier" Cords
30 × 3½ $....................	30 × 3½ $....................

Example—where maker's name does not appear on tire:

Wrong Way—	Right Way—
Goodyear	Pathfinder
	(Made by Goodyear)
30 × 3½ $....................	30 × 3½ $....................

7. No specific make or makes of tires shall be advertised by a dealer, either in connection with or without mention of price, unless such advertiser has on hand a reasonable stock of such tires or is a regular dealer in such tires.

Where a dealer has a small quantity of one or more brands of tires he desires to close out, he may advertise them by stating specifically the brand, number on hand, and size of each of such tires. However, it is wrong continuously to advertise such tires as "bait."

Example under General Rule 7:

Wrong Way—
UNITED STATES   FISK   FIRESTONE
GOODYEAR   GOODRICH   MICHELIN
OR
ALL STANDARD MAKES

(Unless advertiser can qualify in regard to a "reasonable stock" of each make advertised.)

Right Way—

(6)	30 × 3½	Cupples	$..............
(7)	31 × 4	Fisk	$..............
(2)	32 × 4	Goodyear All Weather Tread	$..............
(3)	33 × 4	Goodrich Silvertown	$..............

8. All misleading credit terms shall be eliminated. Advertisers offering a discount for cash shall not use such terms as "No interest charged," "No handling or brokerage charges," etc.

9. Illustrations of nationally known tires or treads shall not be used in connection with the sale of tires of other makes.

"Testimonial" Advertising

Another form of advertising, which has caused advertising agencies themselves no end of concern, is known as "testimonial" advertising. Some 20 or 30 years ago, the prevailing method of advertising patent medicines was to include personal testimonials as to the efficacy of the cures. "Peruna," "Lydia Pinkham's Remedies" and "Carters Little Liver Pills" were heralded throughout the country by such methods. Companies often publish testimonials from places remote from the locality in which the advertising appears. A campaign against such advertising was carried on by the American Medical Association, and success was achieved through the cooperation of newspapers and periodicals, although much along the same line still remains to be done. This was no small achievement in view of the lucrative nature of this sort of advertising to the newspapers, much of the "boiler plate" of rural papers being composed of such advertising. The claim of newspapers to the title of the "fourth estate" was in part vindicated by the courageous manner in which they cooperated in maintaining the professional standards of medical practitioners. It is quite apparent that the Fleischman Yeast Company, in its recent revival of testimonial advertising, does not have the sanction of American doctors, practically all of its testimonials being signed by European doctors who are perhaps ignorant of the attitude of the American Medical Association on this matter.

But this achievement in eliminating testimonial advertising, apparently settled years ago, cropped up again in 1928 in connection with other forms of advertising, conspicuously in the sales promotion of cigarettes, and on a far greater scale than had been practiced before. Statements endorsing this or that cigarette by moving-picture actresses, ball players, and other persons in the public lime-light, not only were shown in some cases to be exaggerated and unfounded in fact—some of these people did not even smoke—but they frequently were displayed with so little regard for the most elementary sense of propriety as to nauseate the reader of discrimination and refinement.[21] One organization was formed solely for the purpose of inducing prominent society women to endorse particular brands of goods for a consideration ranging from $1,000 to $8,000, this amount to be paid over to the woman's "pet charity." During this campaign of "testimonial" advertising, readers were bombarded with a series of blatant advertisements in order that advertisers might place their wares "before the public." Advertising agencies thereby again prostituted a method which had been abused before, which had been of some value when used in moderation—as in the case, for example, of the Borden Milk Company—but which now has become a wasted asset; while a number of misguided ladies and gentlemen have exercised their proclivity to combine benignity with notoriety in this new form of the "charity ball."

There are many other forms of questionable advertising than the four types already mentioned, namely, disparagements of competitors, "bait," exaggerated claims or the use of superlatives, and "testimonial" advertising. Some of these problems are not exclusively advertising problems; they may arise as the result of misleading labels or misrepresentations by salesmen. So, for example, in the case of representations as to materials or processes, trade-marks, sizes and colors. Such problems

[21] See "Advertising Practices of the American Tobacco Company," *Bulletin*, National Better Business Bureau, September, 1930.

have already been considered in connection with the ethics of
other marketing methods.[22]

Financial Advertising

We have been dealing thus far with the problem of the ethics of
advertising as applied to marketing of goods, and at the very
start contrasted such methods with the professional attitude.
Business is not a profession and cannot therefore be measured
by professional standards. But the fact that it must apply
its own standards does not mean that it need be any less rigorous
in its own field than the professions are in theirs. Business
can permit types of advertising which the professions could
not tolerate, without discrediting business or giving it a place
in the scale of social values lower than that of the professions.
There is, however, a phase of business which may lend itself to
standards of advertising more nearly like those of the professions:
that phase is banking.

Recent years have seen increasing amounts of financial
advertising at the same time that there has developed an increasingly general interest and participation in investment securities.
Which is cause and which is effect is relatively unimportant,
except possibly to the advertising agencies. That is to say,
financial advertising may be similar to the advertising of a
book, which is not seriously considered by a publishing house
until the book has first sold itself. Indeed, the whole advertising
situation may be of this nature, and may even justify a less rigid
set of advertising standards among the professions. But the
fact of the matter is that in the latter case it has not, and law
and medicine certainly can lay claim to a unique quality in that
their advertising standards are not the same as those of business.
Accounting firms are practically as strict in their advertising
methods as are lawyers or doctors, and investment counsel do
not advertise at all. The question arises: Are the functions of
the banker such that they might be impaired even by resorting
to such advertising methods as are quite justifiable among other
business men?

In some cases, financial advertising does not even observe the
minimum standards of merchandising advertising. "Largest,"
"foremost," and "best" are frequently employed as descriptive
terms by banks or are implied in the set-up of the advertisement.

[22] See Chapter XV.

The second of the following advertisements illustrates this and at the same time comes perilously near to the type of "testimonial" advertising which can lead to nothing but increased advertising expenses all around; for other banks will not refrain from reciprocating with similar claims. The first of the following advertisements involves a general disparagement of competitors which cannot fail to release reciprocal activities.

SINGLENESS OF PURPOSE[23]

In some Trust Companies, commercial banking constitutes the principal business, and the trust department is one of several side-shows. The —— Trust Company feels strongly that the problems of trusteeship require full time, not part time; that they call for best attention, not second best. In consequence, The —— Trust Company, true to its name, centers its activities upon its Trust Department.

By thus restricting its activities, the company is in a position to promise the constant care and undivided attention necessary for the successful management of trust funds.

HOW A CERTAIN LAWYER USES THE FOREMOST BANK IN ——[24]

As a law student he got tired of explaining exactly where the little college was from which he had graduated. And as a law student he once heard Mr. Justice —— say that with patience and industry a lawyer could rise to eminence in any branch of the profession.

He is today an eminent Corporation Lawyer in ——. He recalls the day when he was admitted to the bar, and when he opened his small checking account with The —— Bank. "Now," he said, "at least I'll never have to explain where and what that bank is!"

His first case took him to the bank—a trusteeship in bankruptcy. A bank officer gave him practical suggestions in liquidating the assets. He did the job well, and presently was appointed receiver for a large going concern.

Once more he sought the bank's business advice, borrowed money on receivers' certificates, made certain changes, and proved that the business could be profitably run. His reputation grew. So did his practice. When he was made trustee of a large estate, he at once employed the large and expert organization of the bank's Trust Department—and saved the estate money.

[23] There is no point in disclosing the names or the sources of these instances; they did appear as advertisements in prominent newspapers.

[24] This case included a cut of a man, whether real or conventional it could not be determined, thus affording a borderline "testimonial" case.

Today his manifold responsibilities and concerns touch all the 18 branches of service the bank offers. He never has undertaken to do for himself a thing the foremost bank in —— can do for him—which is why he has had time to practice law, and why he has gone so far on the path he chose.

His case is actual. It is parallel in principle to the case of every lawyer. No young lawyer who proposes to succeed can really afford to link himself with any bank less competent than the best in his community.

There is no denying the fact that the entrance of the public into the securities market on a large scale during the last few years may make necessary a revision of the ideas held by investment bankers in regard to advertising as well as other aids to the distribution of securities, and commercial bankers and brokers may see fit likewise to engage in advertising on a larger scale than formerly was thought desirable. Incidentally, the candor and frankness which characterizes the publicity of large corporations has undoubtedly afforded the basis for a more severely critical check on their value and soundness. The difficulty, however, is this: that the same situation has given rise to the advertising of all sorts of worthless securities and to the publication of various unsound "tipster sheets" that work on the credulity of people whose confidence in financial advertising has been generated by its prevalent use among respectable institutions. Can respectable and responsible banking institutions engage in advertising practices which put too great a strain on the frailties of less respectable and less responsible human beings? It is, of course, unfair to hold any group of men responsible for the abuses by others of what ordinarily would constitute legitimate functions. But compare the banker and the doctor in regard to analogous situations. The doctor, by rigorously proscribing all forms of advertising other than the equivalent of a simple business card, can very effectively proceed against improper patent-medicine advertisements and such as are resorted to by quacks and charlatans, and has succeeded, with the cooperation of publishers, in eliminating such advertising to a considerable extent.

It may be objected that a similar charge might be directed against the advertising of merchandise. But money expended for merchandise is of the scale of current expenditures, whereas money used for investment represents savings and is of the scale of capital funds. Furthermore, in merchandising practice the customer may and does return unsatisfactory purchases, and most merchants stand back of their products. Is the banker willing to guarantee his securities to this extent? It may be necessary to distinguish, in merchandising advertising, between goods that have a relatively large unit value, such as furniture or pianos, and those that do not; but any such distinction would be for the purpose of establishing more, and not less, rigorous standards for the former than for the latter. But certainly the advertising standards controlling consumers' goods of relatively low-unit values cannot be regarded as sufficiently rigorous for application to the sale of investment securities. This latter function assumes the seriousness of health and liberty, which medicine and law are primarily interested in securing to patient and client.

The New York Stock Exchange includes the following regulations of advertising among its rules:

Sec. 1. No member shall publish an advertisement of other than a strictly legitimate business character.

Sec. 2. Every advertisement of a member, unless it is in a general form approved by the Committee on Business Conduct, must, before publication, receive the approval of said Committee.

Sec. 3. Every advertisement of a member offering to make purchases or sales of listed securities, must before publication, in addition to the approval required by Section 2, receive the approval of the Committee of Arrangements.[25]

Sec. 8. . . . .

No member shall make use of wireless to transmit or broadcast market information or forecasts of business, or financial conditions or for any advertising purpose, or to stimulate interest in particular securities or in the market; provided, however, that members may supply quotations to broadcasting stations which have been approved by the Committee on Quotations and Commissions at such intervals and under such regulations as are prescribed by said Committee.[26]

The "tipster sheet" has become a prevalent form of advertising securities. Such sheets advertise securities, but they make no distinction between sound and unsound securities and they take advantage of the confusion in the minds of prospective purchasers by promoting securities in which the "editors" are particularly

---

[25] Chapter VIII of the Rules Adopted by the Governing Committee pursuant to the Constitution adopted June 10, 1925.

[26] *Ibid.*, Chapter XIII.

interested. The usual method employed by such tipster sheets is to send weekly or daily pamphlets to persons on their mailing list, which has been obtained in various ways: sometimes "sucker lists" are made out; sometimes the list of stockholders of a corporation or subscribers of papers or magazines are available. The tipster sheet then prints interesting and important financial news, including the reports of corporations, which it frequently obtains through the purchase of a single share of stock. The confidence of the readers is thereby built up. The next step is to make forecasts of stock-price fluctuations, frequently including certain stocks which the "tipsters" control and can manipulate on a market which is not rigorously controlled by law or by a responsible membership. When all is ready for the "killing," telephone, telegraph, and the mails are employed, urging subscribers to buy a certain stock, which is then unloaded at a fancy price.

The methods employed by the "tipster sheet" are of two kinds. First, there is the building-up of confidence by the publishing of accurate statements. Then, second, there is the general and specific forecasting of stock prices and the advice to prospective purchasers. Both functions are performed constantly by legitimate and reliable brokers. The probability, however, is that the second of these functions does not properly belong in a financial advertisement, any more than a lawyer or doctor may similarly promise the efficacy of his services; and the difficulty of distinguishing between reliable and unreliable free advice might be lessened by recognizing that the former constitutes a service which should bear an adequate charge—which excludes the possibility of general advertising. The first-mentioned function of the tipster sheet—to supply market information—is not objectionable in itself, and it is performed by reliable newspapers and financial journals; but its employment as a means for effecting the second function, for forecasting purposes or for financial advice, is to be condemned wherever it appears. In between these two functions is still another, broadcasting by "market-information services" and "statistical bureaus," whose charges for later individual advice are frequently large enough to make the purchaser then demand reliable information. After all, however, this function is a professional one and can perhaps be no more justified than can the broadcasting of health or legal or engineering advice by parties who are interested in gaining financially thereby, and especially if the practice encourages the quack and charlatan to capitalize the confidence so built up.

This is the crucial problem of financial advertising: can financial organizations include, in their advertising, claims which after all rest upon forecasting, and that of an interested kind? The brief for such a policy would assert that science has achieved its chief value through its ability to predict from data of past events, and that intelligent business conduct involves foresight based upon factual knowledge: the latter now being at our disposal in the form of records, and the former being a function which some men clearly possess and which they can exercise in an advisory capacity. To which it must be replied that accurate prediction is possible in science in only a restricted field, and largely regarding inanimate objects and their relations; that medicine is more of a science than business or economics, and yet doctors have seen fit to discourage prognostic promises to patients and guarantees of cures in their advertising; and finally that every act of a financial organization, to promote the sale of securities by such means, enables the unscrupulous promoter to make the same claims and to disguise his real intentions—and the unscrupulous promoter is the competitor of the sound financial organization for what after all is a limited commodity, available capital funds.

The real difficulty involved in this situation is that too paternalistic an attitude toward the investor, on the part of the Government, or of a Better Business Bureau, or even of banking organizations themselves, will develop a sense of confidence in financial advertising that may at sudden intervals be capitalized by unscrupulous promoters. This difficulty, however, arises every time there is any deviation from the rule of *caveat emptor* and is of major consideration in determining the relations between advertisers and their customers. And after all the argument is a specious one. This is not the basis from which have developed the standards of professional advertising, which are basically a matter of professional self-interest; and it is not the basis from which merchandising advertising is exclusively determined, as is evidenced by the fact that such controlling agencies as the Better Business Bureau are financed by merchants themselves and not by customers. The laws of fraud can be expected to take care of the most flagrant of questionable advertising tactics that injure the customer or client, but such laws cannot take care of the injuries that unfair advertising inflicts upon competitors and the trade.   It is on this basis that the responsibility for proper financial advertising ultimately falls upon the banker himself. And it is doubtful whether financial advertising, from this point of view, can be justifiably extended beyond professional standards. It is only when the information contained in financial advertising extends beyond the name and address of the advertiser that these problems and paradoxes arise.

Summary

The ethics of advertising is to a certain extent controlled by law, but its chief problems arise in the "domain of the unenforceable." Four parties are involved in the situation: the reader, the advertiser, the advertising agency, and the publication in which the advertisement appears.   The reader should be relied upon to exercise a sufficient degree of intelligence and discrimination to warrant a partial insistence on the rule, *caveat emptor;* but he should expect some cooperation of the other three parties in securing accuracy and reliability in advertising. And since his reactions are apt to include a whole trade or business in general rather than the reliable firms or the flagrant offenders, a part of the responsibility and interest in the problem devolves upon the other three parties.   Without attempting to apportion such responsibility among these remaining three parties in the situation, it will be recalled that the Federal Trade Commission has sanctioned the proposal of newspapers and periodicals that they be held jointly liable with the advertiser and the advertising agency for inaccurate and misleading advertising.   The cooperation of newspapers and the American Medical Association in eliminating patent-medicine advertising set a precedent for the compliance of publishers with the request for a similar arrangement in regard to all unfair advertising. This move was sponsored by the Better Business Bureau and also received the support of the Chamber of Commerce of the United States.   This achievement does not make unnecessary the particular maintenance or modifications, by various businesses or trades, of specific advertising standards to meet their own peculiar problems.   And it cannot too frequently be emphasized that the best check of advertising methods is supplied by an intelligent and discriminating public.

In concluding this chapter, the advertising situation may be summarized as follows. There is a fundamental philosophical justification for advertising in business which is not properly appreciated by those who condemn advertising as immoral or unethical. The stimulation of human wants is as essential to human progress as is the satisfaction of those wants, because the contentment which follows from the latter, and which is an important factor in progress, has a quality which is determined by the kind and amount of wants which are satisfied. Although remedial professions, such as medicine and law, do not and could not ethically stimulate a demand for their services, engineering and teaching do and should encourage the further development and use of available physical and mental energy; but even so, these two professions do not and should not approximate business methods of advertising. Business cannot take its cues exclusively from the professions, but the fact that the latter vary in their practices and standards according to the circumstances and conditions with which they deal, clearly shows that business may decide this problem of the proper exploitation and stimulation of human wants on its own merits and according to standards which need be checked not only by consideration of the general social good, but also by a proper regard for the health of the trade.

The economic justification of advertising is as fundamental as is the philosophical. The stimulation of demand is equally important with the control of production as a factor in intelligent management. There is a limit beyond which increased sales may be profitable to a business or valuable to society. But within that theoretical limit it is conceivable that society has not achieved its full measure of economic value, not only as regards enjoyment of goods, but also as regards net profits and the capital values which are ideally constructed on the basis of profits. Costs in such a situation become secondary and instrumental, and not primary factors.

Related to this major problem is the questionable practice whereby advertising agencies receive their commissions from publishers rather than from advertisers themselves. It may be presumed that the rate-schedules of advertising media include the commissions paid to agencies. But the latter receive their gross income from two sources, a situation which cannot work out to the best interests of the client. This is a situation which merits the serious consideration of advertising agencies themselves as the most difficult ethical problem now confronting the profession.

Given these general philosophical, social, and economic premises, the ethical—and aesthetic—problem of advertising is to define the limits of fairness and good taste.   The controlling agency of business advertising must, however, in the last analysis be business itself, the functions of which must complement and transcend law and government and cannot be determined by standards supplied by the professions or the church.   And the diversity of business functions and commodities is such that self-regulation in regard to advertising must extend to each trade in accordance with its own specific and characteristic problems.

CHAPTER XVIII

CANCELLATION OF CONTRACTS

There is no more stubborn fact in the business world than the general rise and fall of commodity prices, and this fact is the basis for a great part of the problem of cancellation of contracts. Whether anything can be done about this situation by some broad scheme of education, legislation or economic control, we shall not undertake to discuss. We shall deal only with the problem confronting the individual business man who recognizes the fact of market fluctuations and who desires to accommodate his activities to the situation without necessarily modifying it. There is, nevertheless, an apparent necessity and implied desirability of formulating general business policies, especially in regard to cancellation of contracts and on broader grounds than those of mere opportunism.

Moral or ethical ideas of the traditional type fail to meet the situation satisfactorily. For example, in a falling market the buyer is tempted to cancel his obligations, especially when the contract price is fixed, while the seller is heard insisting on the "sacredness of contracts"; in a rising market, however, especially when the price is "at the market," the seller is dilatory in his deliveries, while the buyer now takes his turn at emphasizing the "sacredness" of the obligation; and where the contract fixes the price, the situation may become acute. Generally the moral indictment is directed against the cancellations of the buyer, but practically "the responsibility (for cancellation of contracts) does not rest entirely on the buyer. Usage in many lines of business contemplated that a contract of purchase was not binding if it became inexpedient to keep it."[1] As conditions change, adherences to moral principles are modified or even reversed, and the interested parties quote moral phrases to suit their own purposes. Hence the necessity of reexamining the social-moral-economic situation and of dealing with the pertinent factors by examining specific case situations.

[1] James S. Alexander, address before National Association of Cotton Manufacturers, Boston, April 22, 1921.

The problem of cancellations of contracts is twofold: first, to control conditions so as to prevent cancellations, and second, to select a method of dealing with cancellations when they make their appearance. The first of these problems, to anticipate cancellations by the pursuit of policies that would largely obviate them, confronts not only the vendor, but the buyer as well. As will be shown, the vendor may anticipate cancellations by promptness in the physical delivery of goods, by sales quotas and the retaining of title and of inventory control, and by an adjustable price schedule. But the buyer must also anticipate the vendor's cancellation of a contract. One such method consists in distributing the source of supply; the abuse of this method, namely, duplication of orders, merely shifts the burden of the problem and introduces one of the most reprehensible of business practices. Finally, in business, most men are both buyers and sellers; hence, a vendor, a fabricator of goods, for example, can lessen the effects of his customers' cancellations by an intelligent policy of buying raw materials. The most serious effect of cancellations of business contracts arises from the transitive nature of business transactions, whereby the cancellation of some contracts practically necessitates the cancellation of others.

Vendors' Policies to Avoid Buyers' Cancellations

The following case illustrates the vendor's attempt to avoid cancellations by adopting a policy which had for its main purpose the safeguarding and conserving of permanent sales outlets.

In 1916, the Winnick Canning Company[2] had to decide whether or not to accept an offer from a manufacturer to make a three-year contract according to which cans should be supplied under the following conditions. The Winnick Company was to purchase from the manufacturer all the cans which it needed during the three-year period. In return, the manufacturer allowed a substantial discount which represented the saving in selling and rehandling expense made possible by the agreement. Prices were to be determined at the first of each year and were to be based upon prevailing prices of tin plate, which was the primary raw material used in the production of cans. Full allowance was to be made for price reductions made between January 1 and the date of payment. The manufacturer also agreed to take

[2] 1 *Harvard Business Reports* 264 (hereafter, these reports will be designated "H.B.R.").

back surplus cans at the end of the season. In April, the company was to supply the manufacturer with an estimate of the quantities of each size of can to be used during the season. In submitting these estimates, the company was to specify the definite quantities of cans required for each product; the approximate dates on which each crop became ready for canning were known from experience. The manufacturer, in return for the privilege of shipping the required cans in carload lots to the factory at any time after the spring estimates were submitted, guaranteed delivery prior to actual need for cans; and agreed to secure and pay for insurance policies, effective from date of delivery to date of payment of invoices on all cans delivered under these conditions. If additional supplies were needed during the season, they were to be delivered with bill of lading attached to sight draft in the same manner as previously.

The assurance afforded the Winnick company, of a supply of cans sufficient for estimated requirements, delivered in advance of the period during which they were to be used, had not previously been given when the company purchased cans during the preserving season, because many other canneries bought then, and delays in carloadings by the manufacturer and in deliveries by the railroads had occurred occasionally. At other times, crops had ripened more rapidly than usual, and cans previously ordered could not be delivered in time to meet the factory requirements. The Winnick Company had sufficient warehouse space to accommodate the promised deliveries of the estimated requirements considerably prior to the time of use; and these goods could be received and stored by the watchman, engineer, and helper whom the company employed throughout the year.

The Winnick Company used only two machines for stamping the tops on cans; these machines were rented from the can manufacturer. These machines did not accommodate satisfactorily the cans supplied by other makers. The company, furthermore, had purchased its cans from this manufacturer for several years and had been satisfied with the manufacturer's attitude in all transactions. Similar three-year contracts had been made by this manufacturer with other canning companies, with mutual satisfaction.

The principal objection to accepting this offer was that the company agreed to buy all its cans from one manufacturer over a three-year period. If the company became dissatisfied with the quality of the cans delivered or with its relations with the manufacturer, it would be difficult and unsatisfactory to break this contract because of possible extended litigation. Other producers of cans, furthermore, were unwilling to sell to canning companies which had contracts outstanding with competitive manufacturers. Since, however, the proposed contract provided assurance of an ample supply of cans at all times, the company decided that the offer should be accepted.

It is apparent from this case that the purpose of the manufacturer was to stabilize his market by securing long-term contracts with his customers, a method which effected results practically commensurate with that of "repeat orders," but more certainly. In order to secure this stable market, the manufacturer was willing to make concessions in respect to price, and to assume expenses in connection with such items as insurance, interest, and risk. The danger in this situation was that the manufacturing company might, by this form of business service, cut its profits unduly to the detriment of the can-manufacturing business, especially if a frank system of cost accounting was not in use. This, however, is not stated in the case; and, even if it were a fact, it is not pertinent to the main point illustrated by the case. We shall assume that the manufacturer could afford to perform the offered services.

The main point of course is that such an agreement stabilized business both with respect to the sales of the manufacturer and the obtaining of supplies by the canners. The more likely difficulties that might have arisen because of price fluctuations were met by an arrangement for adjusting prices. This adjustment was to be made generally at the first of each year, and specifically between January 1 and the date of payment for separate shipments. This elimination of the risk element, which so often enters largely in long-time business agreements and particularly concerns the man who conducts a small-scale business, effects the stability of relations with as nice a sense of measurable discrimination as has characterized the methods of the natural sciences. Any deviation from such adjustment factors, and any increase in the unit of time within which prices hold rigidly, are bound to introduce relatively unsatisfactory business methods.

One important factor was the possibility of a decline in the quality of the commodity contracted for over a long period of time. Declining prices might tempt the vendors to economize in materials; on the other hand, in a rising market, when the seller would not be concerned in maintaining his agreements with his customers or in insisting on their obligations to him, he might realize that specifications would not be so carefully scrutinized. The element of bad faith is, unfortunately, frequently present in such a situation: not only might the deterioration of quality be purposeful on the part of the seller who would take every advantage of his customers, but unwarranted buyers' complaints as to the quality of delivered goods might conceivably arise when a turn in the market again gave them an advantage in doing so.

Furthermore, it must be kept in mind that the severing of contractual relations, because of disagreements as regards quality of goods, is a matter of general social concern. There is, first, a public interest in the stability of business relations even though the immediate interests of both parties concerned would warrant a discontinuance of those relations. Of course the immediate interests are the controlling factors, but frequently they are misunderstood or falsely valued, and there is always the possibility of collusion. And, secondly, there is a public interest in the maintenance of the quality of goods, an interest that cannot be jeopardized by conflicting claims that may be arising ostensibly because of questions as to quality, but covertly in order to avoid business obligations.

The more obvious method available to the vendor for preventing buyers' cancellations is the adoption of a policy of "sales quotas." Such a policy appears to some buyers as nothing short of impertinence, interfering as much with the independent conduct of their own business as does a policy of resale-price maintenance. And, in justice to the buyer's point of view, it must be recognized that the policy may be abused. But the reconciliation of these apparently opposing interests must be effected, and the opposition may be merely a paradox in which the buyer does not know what his best interests actually are. The following cases illustrate various attempts at establishing a policy of sales quotas with a view to preventing a situation in which cancellations might become serious.

In the latter part of 1919, because of advanced prices for its products, the Henshaw Breakfast Food Company[3] increased the amount of credit allowed to retailers. If the existing credit limits had been maintained, the quantity of goods which a retailer was allowed to buy on open account would have been decreased. In the first months of 1920, several executives of the company suggested that the sales department should instruct the salesmen to accept orders from retailers only for their immediate requirements. As a result of the rapid increase in prices, retailers were buying in advance in order to be sure of a sufficient supply and to make speculative profits.

[3] 1 H.B.R. 40. Fictitious name.

The Henshaw Company manufactured superior foods and maintained a very enlightened attitude toward its customers, allowing them a liberal margin of profit.

The sales department decided to restrict the orders accepted from retailers to the quantity that could be disposed of during the interval between the salesmen's calls. A retailer was to estimate his needs, but the salesman, if he found on his second call that the retailer had a large quantity of the company's product in stock, was to restrict accordingly the size of subsequent orders accepted.

The executives of the company reported that the plan was thoroughly successful; little retailer opposition was met, and the salesmen were able to convince those who did protest that the arrangement was to their benefit. In the latter part of 1920 and during 1921, the company's cancellations were inconsequential; when the company reduced its prices, retailers' losses were small.

A fundamental change in business policy and practice is involved in the encouragement of smaller purchases. Although larger purchases could be justified on the ground of business foresight, there is little question but that the lure of speculative profit then has considerable weight. Any possible advantage so gained, and not neutralized by corresponding losses in a period of declining prices, would be outweighed by the advantage of decreased inventory, increased rate of stock turnover, and, in this case, the constant freshness of goods. This point is emphasized because it intensifies the main principle involved: the responsibility of the seller to the buyer who may later cancel his order. The wholesaler and manufacturer can be expected to have more business intelligence than the retailer, and their responsibilities for eliminating cancellations carry over into just such provisions as have been described in the Henshaw case.

The sales of the Clarion Phonograph Company[4] were subject to a marked seasonal variation, the peak occurring ordinarily in the months from October to January. The demand for phonographs was furthermore especially sensitive to changes in prosperity, and the types of cabinets in demand were influenced by the prevailing mode in home furnishings.

In the fall of 1920 the demand for phonographs declined, and requests for cancellations of unfilled orders were received by the Clarion Company. It was deemed inadvisable to enforce acceptance of these orders, because the distributors could not sell phonographs to retailers, and, therefore, could not make payments on deliveries. As a result,

4 1 H.B.R. 54. Fictitious name.

the company wrote off a serious inventory loss and gradually disposed of the machines at reduced prices.

In 1921, buying by consumers was curtailed, and after retailers disposed of surplus stocks they placed orders only for immediate requirements.   In 1922, in view of the experience of 1920, the wholesale distributors waited until fall before placing their orders, despite a partial revival of demand.   The company was forced to manufacture for stock and to finance the inventory of finished products during the summer.   Fall orders, however, exhausted stocks, and it became evident that the demand was in excess of plant capacity.

In April, 1923, the company decided to adopt a plan of sales quotas for distributors in order to secure early orders, to receive payment for phonographs manufactured during the summer, and to prevent shortages in the autumn.   A quota for each distributor for the second half of that year was computed on the basis of monthly sales records for previous years, together with necessary adjustments, and with reference to plant capacity.   When all orders were received by the company, the total quantity was scaled down so as to conform to the maximum production schedule.

The commentator on this case holds that the Clarion Company "followed a sound policy in permitting cancellation of unfilled orders at the time of the business depression of 1920."[5]   Note that the company subsequently also took over completely the responsibility of eliminating cancellations.   And, to illustrate further the observation that contractual relations cannot be regarded as transitive—that is, that the cancelling or fulfilling of the contract by one party does not in itself justify a similar course of procedure by the second party in other contractual relations with third parties—the commentator states:

The quota plan adopted in 1923 would not necessarily justify the manufacturing company in refusing to accept cancellations under similar conditions in the future.[6]

The justification for this view is contained in the following statement which applies the principle of the non-transitivity of contractual obligations and performances to the concrete situation in this case.

A question may be raised as to whether the stated policy of expecting the wholesale distributors to take up the seasonal slack in sales, thereby permitting the manufacturing company to even out its production schedule, was fully justified, especially since no postdatings were given during the

[5] 2 H.B.R. 390.
[6] 2 H.B.R. 390.

period of seasonal inactivity of sales.[7]   The production economies obtainable by the manufacturer were not shared directly with the wholesalers whose purchases would make possible those savings.[8]

It becomes apparent to anyone who studies the situation thoroughly that the ethical obligation devolving on a firm to regulate sales so as to avoid cancellations is particularly insistent when the sales agency is denied the privilege of competitive buying.   Conversely, moreover, where the sales agency is given an exclusive territory, the obligation to cooperate with the manufacturing company is intensified.   The use of a quota plan under these circumstances "illustrates one of the marked advantages of the close and continuous relationships between the manufacturer and his channels of distribution which are made possible under a policy of selected rather than broadcast distribution." Indeed, the Clarion case has much wider implications.   It shows the necessity of anticipating the problem of duplicate or excessive buying and subsequent cancellations by viewing the situation in its totality, in which the obligations of buyer and seller are mutual but not necessarily equal or unequal or fixed as circumstances change.   The stability of contractual relations is of course highly desirable.   It is, however, merely the matrix of the problem, about which hover many ineffable considerations.

Buying Policies of Fabricators

Men engaged in business are not only vendors; they also are buyers.   Thus, the classification of problems involving cancellation of contracts into those confronting vendors and those confronting buyers is an artificial classification.   It serves the purpose of analyzing the general problem, however.   But the real situation must not be lost sight of—hence the following case, which shows the intimate relation between the sales and buying functions of a business, especially as regards the problem of a fabricator who anticipates cancellations from his customers.

In February, 1920, the purchasing agent of the Allagash Shoe Company,[9] which was receiving the largest quantity of orders for fall trade in its history, recommended to the president that the company purchase its full requirements of leather and other raw materials at once, inas-

[7] Recall the Winnick case, 1 H.B.R. 264, referred to supra, p. 490.
[8] 2 H.B.R. 390.
[9] 1 H.B.R. 38.   Fictitious name.

much as these materials were rising constantly in price and were becoming increasingly difficult to obtain.

For several months prior to 1920, shoe factories throughout the United States had operated at full capacity and had sold their stocks readily to retailers. Retail distribution, although excellent, had not been sufficient to justify the abnormal volume of production. Excess stocks of merchandise, therefore, had accumulated in the retail shoe stores. Prices had been rising steadily for several seasons, and consequently retailers had not felt the normal pressure to dispose of their old stocks before ordering new.

Because the president believed that shoe prices were inflated excessively, and that a decline in the near future was probable, he considered it unwise to purchase more than a small proportion of the company's requirements of raw material during the spring of 1920. The situation was a complex one, involving admittedly conflicting elements and opinions. The president, however, instructed the purchasing agent to restrict his purchases to 25% of the quantity of raw material required to fill the total number of orders.

This policy was adhered to during the spring of 1920, in spite of the protests of the other executives and particularly of the sales organization. By early summer, the period of deflation which the president had foreseen set in. Conditions in the shoe industry became extremely unfavorable, and there was a universal tendency for retail shoe dealers to request the cancellation of orders.

It is conceivable that a social-economic situation in which a completely mobile set of transitive relations holds, might absolve the Allagash Shoe Company of any consequences of placing large orders for raw materials. For then the cancellation of orders for shoes would be held to justify the company in cancelling its orders for materials. Whether such a system of relations would be an improvement over our present system is not the question. Responsibility for contracts cannot be made implicitly to rest on the satisfactory culmination of other contractual relations, and only seldom are they explicitly so entered into. The fact that the Allagash Shoe Company was both a buyer and seller did not relieve it of responsibilities in regard to the former function simply because the latter function might have involved it in losses due to the cancellation of orders by other purchasers. The locus of responsibility thus comes to be fairly fixed in the individual firm. This responsibility involves restricted buying in the face of rising markets, a policy which contributes to permanence and stability, the essential material conditions underlying credit and a good name.

The question now arises, to what degree does this individual responsibility for non-cancellation of orders extend beyond the self-restraint in buying exhibited by the case of the Allagash Shoe Company? Obviously it includes the responsibility attaching to the seller of commodities to restrain the buyer from excessive purchasing. Certainly an adequate view of the situation requires that both vendor and purchaser contribute to general trade health by the intelligent restriction of business transactions to such contracts as may reasonably be expected to be performed. The Allagash case presented a situation involving the obligations of the *buyer*. The Henshaw case would imply that the *seller* should in turn assume the obligation to restrict his sales to a point which would result in reducing later cancellations to a minimum. Four possible situations may thus arise: (1) the most desirable one, that in which society has the greatest interest, the performance of the contract with mutual satisfaction to the immediate parties concerned. (2) The cancellation of the contract, a result which may be socially and economically undesirable, even though mutually satisfactory to the immediate parties. (3) The desire of one party to the contract to accept his obligations, a desire not reciprocated by the other party, especially if the latter has himself already suffered from a repudiation of his contracts with a third party. Thus, the performance of contractual obligations by one party may increase the obligation of the other party; but does it completely necessitate it? (4) The desire of one party to the contract to cancel his obligations, although the other party wishes to keep his, including such as are owed to third parties. Here, again, the non-performance of one party may to some extent justify the non-performance of the other, but not fully. The obligations involved in a contract are, from a broad point of view of policy distinct and not transitive, *i.e.*, they are not contingent on the actions of others; but the proper distribution of all such obligations among buyers and sellers may result in allocating such obligations relatively more to the latter than the prevailing point of view would sanction. Such a re-allocation is necessary to effect the soundest ethical business situation.

Buyers' Policies to Prevent Vendors' Failure to Deliver

The previous situations have to do largely with vendors' policies in anticipation of cancellations of contracts. But it is not only the vendor that needs to fear cancellations; the buyer also is obligated to exercise foresight with respect to the sources of his supplies. Business has in recent years been characterized, in this respect, by an approximation to the professional relationship in which the business transactions between particular firms are exclusively and intensively developed. Better is it, according to this attitude, to develop a single dependable source of supplies—much as one has a family doctor, or a single lawyer, who has been tried and found not wanting—than to depend on the vicissitudes of opportunistic and constantly changing relationships. The dangers of such a policy of permanent relationship, however, are apparent; they appear in the following cases.

Between 1919 and 1923, the production of the Martel Shoe Manufacturing Company[10] dropped from 10,000 to 5,000 pairs of shoes per day. The inventory of raw materials maintained by the firm in 1923 was held at from one to two months' supply. Purchases of materials were but a small fraction of their former size. In his search for lowest prices consistent with desired quality, it was the purchasing agent's problem to decide whether to continue to concentrate his purchases among a few sources of supply, or to distribute his orders more widely. On the basis of orders sent in five months previous to the date needed, the management estimated production for the ensuing six months. Purchasing of raw materials was also made on a six months' delivery basis.

In March, 1920, when inventories and prices on raw materials were at their maximum, consumer demand and prices of raw material declined rapidly. The company, rather than repudiate its agreements, as was done freely by many manufacturers, adopted a policy of receiving deliveries as contracted. Purchasing up to that time in the findings and supplies department had been made consistently from a few standard sources of supply which had rendered satisfactory service, had given preferential terms in many cases, and which were known for standard quality.

When the decline in prices came, in March, 1920, shoe manufacturers, in order to dispose of surplus raw materials, created a style demand for oxfords, and the demand thus created developed into a desire for freakish styles. The Martel Company was unable to sell boots and was compelled to follow the style trend of production. As the styles became more varied, experience proved that purchases had to be made only for immediate use, and by November, 1923, the buyer of findings and supplies was committed definitely to this policy.

[10] 1 H.B.R. 268. Fictitious name.

In 1923, with inventories at their lowest and a policy of retrenchment imperative, the purchasing agent inquired the prices for materials from other sources of supply, and learned that his established sources were abusing their standing through a sense of assurance of the company's orders and were holding their prices above the competitive market. By distributing his orders, the purchasing agent discovered that he could secure lower prices. He knew that conditions had changed from a "seller's" to a "buyer's" market, and he saw that by letting it be known that he was in the market, he could obtain even better service than before. A policy of refusing materials not equal to specifications overcame the consequences of quality variation, and these changed methods of purchasing often resulted in lower quotations from the former sources.

The commentary on this case recognizes the three factors determining the change in business policy: the transition from a "seller's" to a "buyer's" market, which affected the Martel Company in two ways: the relatively high prices persisting in their source of supply, and the development of a policy of increasing the number of styles in order to stimulate purchasing:

A depression in general business or in an industry, with the resulting change from a seller's to a buyer's market, necessitates the purchasing of supplies more frequently and in smaller quantities . . .

The transition from a seller's to a buyer's market evidently had not been recognized by this company's established source of supply. An assurance of orders as a result of a long period of past patronage might have caused a neglect of service on the part of some vendors. More forceful purchasing tactics should serve to bring such vendors into line without distributing purchases to untried sources of supply . . .

A style trend in production not only diversifies the type of supplies required, thereby reducing the quantities purchased, but also makes accurate predetermination of material requirements less possible . . .[11]

This case illustrates clearly the normal temptation facing the buyer, in a falling market, to distribute his purchases sufficiently to obtain the best prices. It is easy to see how this temptation would involve business confidence if an agreement—in this case it was merely a trade habit—had previously been entered into to buy exclusively of one firm and at prices which were not adjustable. The decision of the Martel Company not to repudiate its agreements represented a situation in which the good name of the company was maintained at considerable expense, while the absence of a price-adjustment clause worked to their dis-

[11] 2 H.B.R. 472, 473.

advantage and to the advantage of the suppliers of raw materials. The failure on the part of the seller to adjust prices to a stable customer, however, proved to be unwise in addition to being unfair. This abuse of the permanence of relationship between buyer and seller is the possibility feared most by the former, and effectively prevents business relations from becoming satisfactorily stabilized.

We now turn from diagnosis to prognosis. The events related in the preceding case justified at least the adoption of a temporary policy of distributing purchases. Certainly it seemed to be compatible with the revolutionary but prevalent emphasis on rapidity of stock-turn and on close buying, which has so characterized business during the last few years. When purchases are made, they must be made quickly, and supplies must be had no matter what the source.

The purchasing agent knew that if another period of shortage and difficulties in deliveries were to occur, the probability of his receiving preferential treatment under the new system was slight. Previously, when production was high and six months' supplies were purchased at one time, the mere quantity often resulted in unusual service because the sources knew that they had the entire order; and they knew also that to obtain future orders they must quote reasonable prices. Purchases in 1923 were made in thousands of dollars, however, whereas previously they were made in tens and hundreds of thousands of dollars. The arguments of quantity purchasing, therefore, were less effective to secure either confidential price or service.

Furthermore, concentration of supply with a few companies was dangerous. Twice the purchasing agent had had to make expensive rush purchases to cover a delay occasioned by strikes in the plants which had contracted to fill orders. Transportation conditions also were a factor against concentration.[12]

In spite of these objections, and they are serious ones, the feasibility of the more stable, and therefore preferable, business relationship, can be established. Delays due to strikes and transportation conditions affect the purchaser seriously only in case he insists on buying, or is compelled by the seller or trade conditions to buy, on short-time orders. The Winnick case showed that a method could be devised whereby orders would be filled far enough in advance largely to obviate such difficulties.

[12] 1 H.B.R. 268.

Furthermore, such purchases could be made compatible with the prevalent emphasis of stock-turn and close buying, by the seller's assuming the obligations assumed by the manufacturer in the Winnick case. Recent practices as to stock-turn and close buying are matters, not of physical transportation of goods, but of invoicing. And the buyer could, as in the Winnick case, have a sufficient supply of goods physically available without necessarily assuming immediate property relations other than such as are implied in the agreement to assume property rights as dates of delivery are arranged. The burden for instituting such an arrangement falls largely on the seller, which means that it will in most likelihood be assumed by him in a period of rising prices. If he is willing to make provisions for intelligent and satisfactory price adjustments, applying also to a falling market, he will undoubtedly secure the confidence of the buyer in such an arrangement and his consent to enter into such an agreement.

As the commentator points out, the determination of the new policy by the Martel Company failed to distinguish between the transfer of purchases to *other* companies and the distribution of purchases among numerous sources.

On the assumption that the standard sources of supply were as well equipped to fill small orders as the other sources available—and in general increased importance is attached to small orders during poor business conditions—there would appear to have been no impelling necessity for changing to new sources . . .

The decision appears to have been based largely, therefore, rather on the necessity of purchasing supplies from numerous sources because of a variation in the types of supplies desired, than on failure of the policy of concentrating purchases with a limited number of sources to remain effective under changed business conditions. The presence of unusual conditions related to the change in style of product qualifies the value of the decision as a business precedent.[13]

The Martel case affords a good example of the situation confronting a buyer when the transition is from a seller's to a buyer's market. Inasmuch as the Martel Company decided immediately to honor all its contracts for purchasing, the problem they faced was largely one of the expediency of continuing their purchases from one source or of distributing their purchases more widely. The following case presents the additional factor of a failure to meet specifications.

[31] 2 H.B.R. 473.

In October, 1923, the Ballou Stove Company[14] received a month's supply of gas cocks which did not meet specifications. This shipment was next to the last one due on a yearly contract which had been placed with one firm. A letter to the supplying company brought the response that no mechanical alteration could be made on the lot delivered and that a replacement order of gas cocks could not be given preferential delivery. Attention was focused, therefore, on the Ballou Company's established policy of concentrating purchases of each type of material at one source of supply.

The events leading up to the consideration of changing the policy were as follows: On his appointment, in 1919, the purchasing agent of the Ballou Company continued the company's established policy of concentrating purchases of each type of material at one source of supply. Each of these companies had offered satisfactory service and prices. The purchasing agent's experience, during the periods of intensive manufacturing in 1919 and 1920, apparently proved the wisdom of such concentration of orders.

A unique item in the manufacturing of the Ballou stoves and heaters was the type of gas cock required, which had to be made to order according to rigid specifications. In 1920 the purchasing agent ordered a year's supply of gas cocks from one company; deliveries were made monthly as produced. Service proved satisfactory that year. Although the price of the article was increased arbitrarily beyond a point deemed reasonable by the purchasing agent, the contract was renewed in 1921, and renewed again in 1922.

During the period from January, 1920, to October, 1923, union influence upon labor conditions had caused the service of the majority of the plants with which the company had contracts to become increasingly unsatisfactory. During 1923, moreover, the prices quoted by these companies frequently were higher than could have been secured by receiving bids in the open market. When the shipment of defective gas cocks arrived in October, 1923, the Ballou Company had 1½ months' supply in stock. Final shipment on the contract was to be made in one month.

The concentration policy had in general obtained adequate service prior to 1920, and later, when the market was less stable, the policy had resulted in confidential terms and special service from several firms. On the other hand, concentration of orders for gas cocks had inconvenienced the company and had created a shortage in the supply of a material which, because of the particular specifications, could not be replaced immediately. The Ballou Company, moreover, had accepted a price higher than was necessary.

The purchasing agent observed that buyers for some companies usually divided all orders between two sources of supply and established

[14] 1 H.B.R. 270. Fictitious name.

relations with one or two other companies which at any time might be requested to furnish materials. By this policy, competitive prices and maximum service were secured from the two supply companies. The purchasing agent of the Ballou Company decided that whenever the quantity of material to be ordered was sufficient, it was advisable to place orders, for the year and for spot delivery, with two or more companies.

A commentator on this case says, in part:

The conditions relating to the failure of the company supplying gas cocks to render satisfactory service make it evident that this experience could be of little value to the Ballou Stove Company in determining the wisdom of its purchasing policy. Past renewals of contract at increased prices, the lower prices that could be secured elsewhere, and the fact that the contract had only one month to run give no indication of the underlying reason for the supplying company's hostility. Too great importance, therefore, cannot be attached to the relationship existing between the two companies in a consideration of the policy of concentrating purchases.

Special circumstances involved in the purchase of unique supplies manufactured to rigid specifications do not warrant the adoption of methods in effect among other companies, without differentiating factors.[15]

This point is well taken, but must be clarified. There are two considerations involved and these must be differentiated. The first is this, that any case method is handicapped by not having available all of the facts. The law courts are constantly bewailing this difficulty, and considerable energy has been expended on procedural rules and rules of evidence in order to "get at" all the "real" facts, and even then the description of a situation is always at variance with actual occurrences.[16] But such a description, observing the "law of parsimony" by including only the pertinent factors, is the necessary medium between the "real" facts and their interpretation. The danger lies, not so much in the process of description, as in the attempt to apply implications and inferences derived therefrom to other situations. And it is this second consideration which calls forth the warning of the commentator in the second paragraph above. Policies which might be justified in certain situations are not necessarily warranted in other situations only remotely similar, or in hypothetical situations that might be suggested. The attitude of our courts could well be adopted here: that interpretations of situations

---

[15] 2 H.B.R. 474.

[16] See "The Logic of the Case Method," XXV *Journal of Philosophy* 253, May 10, 1928.

apply solely to the case under review. Every case must be dealt with on its own merits, unless its similarity to other cases is so close and obvious as to recall the precedent. From the point of view of logic the method may be stated thus: that the "universe of discourse," to which any general principle derived from a particular case applies, is the field of cases so closely identical in their important factors as practically to be indistinguishable one from the other.

With this methodological point in mind, the remaining observations of the commentator may be considered:

Concentration of purchases involves the risk of delayed production through the failure of one vendor to deliver in accordance with his agreement. Delay or default in delivery usually is caused by transportation difficulties or unsatisfactory conditions at the vendor's plant.

Transportation conditions can easily be overemphasized. Embargoes and traffic congestion occur infrequently. Emergency deliveries by truck, when feasible, often are depended upon as insurance against delayed delivery. A fairly large supply of the materials carried in stock should, in most instances, constitute an adequate safeguard.

Unsatisfactory labor conditions may be of general nature or restricted to a particular plant. If the risk is uniform throughout an industry, a wider distribution of purchases is warranted. A careful selection of vendors should assist in carrying out a policy of concentrated purchases.

It is apparent that a decision to spread purchases might well vary with the degree to which the material or supply was a special article, the importance of quality, the quantity to be purchased, the conditions surrounding the operations of the vendor's plant, and other factors.[17]

This case bears out in two respects the anticipations and fears which readily occur to practical business men: unsatisfactory labor conditions and transportation difficulties jeopardized the prompt delivery of goods; while manufacturers were taking advantage of firms which purchased exclusively from them, by maintaining a schedule of prices above that of the market. Both these situations, however, were satisfactorily met in the Winnick case. It is difficult to see how the situation was much improved by the adoption, on the part of the Ballou Company, of a policy of buying from two or more companies. If the Ballou Company wished to be certain of its supplies, it would have to contract for the whole amount anyway. If the year's purchases were definitely contracted for, then difficulties with transportation facilities or with labor conditions might be distributed but not necessarily lessened or overcome. And

[17] 2 H.B.R. 474, 475.

the failure of any company to deliver would require the same procedure as if an exclusive manufacturer had failed to deliver. The chances are increased, by the new policy, of knowing what the market price is, but no more so than if the purchaser inquired constantly of other supply houses. There is, of course, the possibility of ordering from two or more manufacturers more than it is anticipated will be used, and then later of cancelling a part of the orders, a practice which is not foreign to purchasers but which cannot be sanctioned by sound business policy.

The distinctive item introduced by the Ballou case is the possibility of the buyer's terminating the agreement to purchase exclusively, on the pretext that goods received are not fulfilling specifications, especially as regards quality. Such a pretext would not occur to a purchaser if deliveries and prices were satisfactory, which again emphasizes the virtue of the principle observed in the Winnick case. Such ideal conditions, however, do not always obtain.

Duplication of Orders

The question arises: disregarding these two elements of price and delivery, just what significance can be attached to the danger of a cancellation of contracts on the pretext that specifications are not met in the quality of delivered goods? The facts presented in the Ballou case do not warrant the assertion that the company had a bad motive in attempting to refuse deliveries, or that any attempt was being made to find some pretext for dissolving the agreement. The following cases show very clearly, however, that such a possibility can occur.

The Lewis Treller Company[18] operated a large dry-goods and ladies'-garments store in Chicago. For two years prior to 1920 the buyers of the Lewis Treller Company were repeatedly urged by travelling salesmen of supply houses to order increasing quantities of goods, the argument advanced being that prices were rising. For a year prior to 1920 the Lewis Treller Company was repeatedly solicited for orders for goods in excess of the amount required for sale on the ground that full orders could not be delivered and that the ratio of deliveries to orders practically required that excess orders be placed if the desired amount was to be obtained.

In 1919 the Lewis Treller Company began giving orders to salesmen in excess of its requirements and greater than it expected to be delivered.

[18] Fictitious name.

In some cases two or three times the amount of goods necessary were ordered. In addition, duplicate orders were given salesmen of other companies so that in the case of some sales units, five times as much goods were ordered as could be sold.

When prices ceased rising in 1920 and then began to fall, the Lewis Treller Company cancelled all orders except such as would be warranted by the buying demands of consumers.

* * * * * *

The "specific-job contract"[19] was a form of contract in common use in 1923 by manufacturers of cement whereby cement was sold for future delivery for use in a specific piece of construction which was described in the contract. Contracts were made "whereby a manufacturer is to deliver, in the future, cement to be used in a specific piece of work, such as a particular building or road, and the obligation is that the manufacturer shall furnish and the contractor shall take only such cement as is required for or used for the specific purpose." These contracts had, by universal practice, been treated by cement manufacturers as, in effect, free options customarily made and acted upon on the understanding that the purchaser was to pay nothing until after the delivery of the cement to him; that he was not obligated in any event to take the cement contracted for unless he chose to; that he was not held to the price named in the contract in the event of a decline in the market price; whereas the manufacturer might be held to the contract price if the market advanced and might be held for the delivery of the full amount of cement required for the completion of the particular piece of construction described in the contract. The practical effect and operation of the specific-job contract therefore was to enable contractors who were bidding upon construction work to secure a call or option for the cement required for the completion of that particular job at a price which might not be increased, but might be reduced if the price declined. It enabled contractors to bid for future construction work with the assurance that the requisite cement would be available at a definitely ascertained maximum price.

The apparent one-sidedness of this arrangement can be explained on the basis of trade conditions. Obviously a tremendous competition existed at the time among the manufacturers of cement, due either to an excess supply of the commodity or to a restriction of building activities. In any contractual relationship, some fair and mutually satisfactory obligations should be expected to hold between the two parties. It is difficult to see how the cement manufacturer benefited by any

[19] *Cement Manufacturers' Protective Association v. United States*, 268 U. S. 588, 594.

such arrangement as the "specific-job contract," other than on the assumption of the business integrity of his customers.

In view of the option features of the contract referred to, the contractor is involved in no business risk if he enter into several specific-job contracts with several manufacturers for the delivery of cement for a single specific job.[20] The manufacturer, however, is under no moral or legal obligation to supply cement except such as is required for the specific job. If, therefore, the contractor takes advantage of his position and of the peculiar form of the specific-job contract, as modified by the custom of the trade, to secure deliveries from each of several manufacturers of the full amount of cement required for the particular job, he in effect secures the future delivery of cement not required for the particular job, which he is not entitled to receive, which the manufacturer is under no legal or moral obligation to deliver, and which presumably he would not deliver if he had information that it was not to be used in accordance with his contract.

The Cement Manufacturers' Protective Association, the defendants, is an unincorporated association, its members being engaged in manufacturing and shipping Portland cement in interstate commerce. The activities of these defendants complained of were directed toward securing the above information and communicating it to members, and thus placing them in a position to prevent contractors from securing future deliveries of cement which they are not entitled to receive under their specific-job contracts, and which experience shows they endeavor to procure especially in a rising market. Members are required to make to the secretary of the association prompt reports of all specific-job contracts, describing in detail the contract and giving the name and address of the purchaser; the amount of cement required, the price and delivery point; also the date of expiration of the contract; together with all changes in the contract, including additions and cancellations. The association also employed "checkers," whose business it was, by actual inspection and inquiry, to ascertain, as far as possible, the amount of cement required for specific jobs referred to in specific-job contracts, and whether cement shipped under specific-job contracts is actually used or required for use under such contracts.

There is abundant evidence to show that there were actual cancellations of deliveries on the ground that contractors were not entitled, under the terms of their contracts, to receive such deliveries. In 1920,

[20] Witness the situation during the 18 months preceding August, 1920, when "customers who ordered (steel) on the basis of tonnage contracts to resell had become accustomed to place orders with several steel manufacturers for perhaps three times the quantity of steel that the customers expected to need, in order to obtain sufficiently prompt deliveries from some source to meet resale requirements."—1 H. B. R. 242.

of 1,392 contracts investigated by the association and found to be "padded" to the extent of more than 3,500,000 barrels of cement, 978 were partially cancelled to the extent of over 2,000,000 barrels.[21]

Evidently the practice of "padding" orders has obtained. The method suggested for the correction of this trade abuse is indicated in the formation of the Cement Manufacturers' Protective Association, and in its activities in securing the necessary information and in preventing the abuses. Aside from the legal points that may be raised, there is the question whether the prevention of the abuse is worth the expense and trouble obviously occasioned the trade association. This is, of course, a matter of business policy, and must be judged on its merits. Business men cannot expect their rights to be protected, however, without the display of some initiative and energy among themselves. "Eternal vigilance is the price of liberty," and of other rights and privileges as well. The organization of a protective association and its capable management are necessary to the safeguarding of present-day business interests.

The question arises, granted the justification of forming associations from the point of view of business policy, how far may such a trade association go without falling afoul of the law, particularly of the Sherman Anti-trust Act? Note that the Cement Manufacturers' Association was an unincorporated association. Suit was brought against it by the United States Government, probably at the instigation of the contractors whose practices were being curbed by the association. The government counsel asserted the above-described activities, together with others, such as exchange of information concerning freight rates, credits, and other statistical information with which we are not here concerned, to have as their purpose the control of the price of cement, a charge with which we furthermore are not here concerned. The court held as follows regarding the legal consequences of the defendants' activities which prevented duplication of orders.

We do not see in the activity of the defendants with respect to specific-job contracts any basis for the contention that they constitute an unlawful restraint of commerce. Unless the provisions in the contract are waived by the manufacturer, demand for and receipt of such deliveries by the contractor would be a fraud on the manufacturer, and in our view the gathering and dissemination of information which will enable sellers to

[21] *Cement Manufacturers' Protective Association v. U. S.*, 268 U. S. 588, 595.

prevent the perpetration of fraud upon them, which information they are
free to act upon or not as they choose, cannot be held to be an unlawful
restraint upon commerce, even though in the ordinary course of business
most sellers would act on the information and refuse to make deliveries
for which they were not legally bound.[22]

The significance of this case and another just previously
decided, *Maple Flooring Manufacturers' Association et al. v.
United States*,[23] is that the court clearly recognizes a sphere of
activity within which such decisions may be arrived at by considerations of sound business policy. It recognizes the trade
association, whether incorporated or not, as an acceptable social-
economic group exercising such functions as will more intelligently
direct and control business policy and practice than is possible to
an unorganized society or one not organized along such lines.
Such functions and activities cannot be allowed to violate the
law, but they are largely supplementary to the law, which must
be administered uniformly and cannot be expected to function
differentially in the diversity of activities now so characteristic
of economic agencies. Such recognition by the court does
not necessarily imply that any permissible business policy or
act is positively expedient. The court recognized, however,
that the attempt to stabilize industry was highly compatible
with sound public policy, and that the chief instrumental agency
in securing such stability is the acquisition of knowledge in regard
to economic facts. "It was not the purpose of the Sherman
Anti-trust Law to inhibit the intelligent conduct of business
operations." And the court assumed that the purposes of
business men were socially and ethically satisfactory unless
otherwise specifically proved. The range of opportunity to
initiate and control economic activities is far greater than is
indicated by such legal decisions. Individual enterprise, especially as magnified and intensified through corporate or association activities, still remains the well-spring of our economic
society.

Hence, the problem: granted the justice and expediency of
these policies, what sanctions may be resorted to that they
may be prevalently accepted or enforced? The law has its
means of enforcement, and conscience and spiritual forces,

[22] *Ibid.*, p. 603.
[23] 268 U. S. 563. The broader significance of these "Trade Association
Cases" has already been discussed, Chapter X.

however unreliable, are referred to in the moral realm. What corresponding but distinctive sanctions can operate to effect ethical principles? These are to be found largely in the effects on economic values. A firm must retain its goodwill, which frequently may appear in assets, particularly at the time of sale. Furthermore, a balance sheet which discloses inflated credit items necessarily depreciates capital value; and potential cancellations are more derogatory to a sound business statement, and often more dangerous, than accounts actually written off. Finally, depreciation write-off is an inevitable accompaniment of market conditions which tempt men to cancel orders, and the firm which assumes the responsibility of controlling sales in order to forestall cancellations, and which adopts a liberal but just policy in actually permitting cancellations, is prompted to this method by the knowledge that such a price will inevitably have to be paid anyway if the business is to continue. The credit disturbances that arise from the depreciation of stock vitally affect the distributor. Indeed, it may be to the interest of a distributor to prevent even a competitor from suffering such loss, because of the ill effects of a consequent depreciation in the market value of the competitor's plant and goods and because of the eventual possibility of a new competitor in the purchaser of this low-cost plant. To say that such sanctions do not operate to prevent all merchants from avoiding these mistakes is as irrelevant as to say that laws and policemen do not prevent all murders. These sanctions are operating for that increasing number of men who are conducting their business intelligently.

Legal Enforcement of Contracts

The preceding cases have illustrated various methods, employed by individuals and by trade groups, by which the cancellation of contracts may be prevented by anticipating the circumstances which might encourage such cancellations. The following cases illustrate the methods employed by merchants after the cancellation of contracts has actually occurred. Most of these cases occurred during the period of declining prices in 1921.

Inasmuch as a contract is a legal act and involves legal enforcement, the obvious redress in case of breach of contract is the courts. But a more important matter even than the delegating of enforcement to the law is the question as to whether or not such a method should be employed at all. The alternatives

are to permit the cancellation or to resort to methods of persuasion that do not include legal processes.   These alternatives
are prompted by a desire on the part of the merchant to avoid
establishing a reputation of resorting too freely to the law, a
reputation which is apt to frighten away even such customers
as do not contemplate the cancelling of contracts.

Even though a company which finds itself faced with the
cancellation of contracts decides to resort to law to enforce
them, various methods may be employed.   A company may
decide to enforce all contracts irrespective of size or circumstances; or it may decide to prosecute only a few test cases,
whereupon the question must be decided whether to prosecute
the smaller offenders first in order to establish a precedent and
to show the larger offenders what is in store for them, or to
direct the legal attack against the strongest and largest offenders.

In the spring of 1920, prices of both raw materials and finished shoes
were unusually high.   The Randolph Shoe and Leather Company[24]
had foreseen for several months that a drastic decline in retail and
wholesale prices was probable.   The salesmen of the company were
instructed to take orders only for immediate requirements and not to
accept orders for future delivery.   Customers were advised by the
company to reduce their orders and also their stocks of shoes.   The
salesmen discovered, however, that retailers were confident of continued prosperity and purchased in as large quantities as their credit
standing would permit.

In May, 1920, there were definite indications of a general business
depression, and shoe retailers discovered that consumers were unwilling
to purchase shoes at the prevailing high prices.   Under these conditions
retailers requested permission to cancel orders at a rate which indicated
that fully 90% of the company's total sales for the season would be
affected.   In numerous instances, retailers who had large stocks of
shoes which they were unable to sell met maturing obligations by
returning the merchandise instead of by payment for it.   Since the
company was receiving repudiations of unfilled orders and returns of
rejected shoes, the president was urged by the junior executives to
adopt a policy of forcing customers by lawsuits to honor their contracts.

The president concluded that suits should be instigated against a small
number of the most flagrant offenders.   In this way the company should
secure at minimum expense the benefit of test cases useful in pointing
out its legal rights under these circumstances.   Following this decision,
the company sued three customers for losses caused by repudiations

[24] 1 H.B.R. 244.   Fictitious name.

of their orders, and in each case it eventually secured a favorable verdict. One suit, which was appealed, was for $700, and the legal cost was approximately $1,600. Another suit, for a loss of $400, involved an expense of $900. Each suit was subjected to many delays, and several executives were required to make three or four trips to the courts to testify.

Early in 1923, when orders for the fall season again reached a high point, each customer was notified that the company did not want any orders which the customer did not intend to accept. In previous years numerous shoe retailers had repudiated orders whenever the price of leather declined even slightly. In the summer of 1923, however, although the price of leather had dropped materially below the price in February of that year, the company had no repudiation of contracts by customers.

One consideration, which weighed heavily with the company, may be questioned.

The repudiation of orders had a demoralizing effect upon the (junior) executives in charge of purchasing, planning, production, and sales. They were discouraged, because nearly all the orders which had been secured and filed had been repudiated by customers with inadequate excuses or no excuses at all. If the company permitted this condition to continue without definite attempts to correct it, the morale of the entire organization was likely to be harmed. To these executives it seemed obvious that the company should have recourse to the law courts to secure redress.[25]

The difficulty with these executives was that they could not see the woods for the trees: they were so engrossed in the internal mechanism of the company and in the showing of the sales department, that they failed utterly to regard the problem as including the broader phases of policy of the company as a whole. Instead of allowing their reaction to the irritating situation to take the form of sentimentality and emotional warmth, they might have anticipated the difficulty by adopting a coherent and far-sighted policy. Morale is an important consideration in all such circumstances, but it is apt to become colored by self-pity to the detriment of intelligent action. No suggestion had previously been made by these men that sales be curtailed, nor were they able to anticipate the consequences of their own suggested policy: "They were (eventually) encouraged by the favorable verdicts, but had had enough of

[25] 1 H. B. R. 244, 246.

court proceedings to realize that the losses resulting from repudiations would have to be borne by the company." It is questionable whether such considerations of morale should be weighed in determining business policy in the face of cancellations.

A much more drastic policy with reference to legal redress was pursued in the following case. Here the percentage of cancellations is not indicated, although it clearly was increasing rapidly, and to a dangerous degree, and amounted to 15% after a warning had been issued that legal action would be taken. The company "stood pat" completely on legal enforcement, with modifications indicated in the case. This case presents the further difference, however, of a company caught between cancellation of sales and definite commitments to purchases, a situation similar to that occurring in the Martel case.[26] This latter element could be regarded as a sufficient warrant for the extreme policy resorted to by the American Sugar Refining Company.

The American Sugar Refining Company[27] refined about one-quarter of the sugar consumed in the United States. In May, June, and July, 1920, contracts were made with its customers on a basis of 22½ cents per pound for granulated sugar to be delivered between July and the end of the year. After the sudden decline in prices of raw and refined sugar during the latter part of the summer of 1920, customers attempted to cancel or repudiate their contracts. The Company previously had purchased a supply of raw sugar to fulfil the contracts it had entered into with its customers. Confronted with an inventory loss that might prove disastrous if customers did not meet their obligations, the management considered the adoption of a policy of strict enforcement of all contracts by recourse to the courts when necessary.

It was not the usual policy of the American Sugar Refining Company to sell for more than 30 days' deferred delivery. The primary reason for departure from this policy in May, June and July, 1920, was the insistent demands from the trade for definite assurance of a supply of sugar for the remainder of the year. In April the demand, regardless of price, was beyond any apparent possibility of supply from the usual refining sources.

Beginning May 24, 1920, refined sugars based on purchases from unusual sources were offered to customers at a uniform basis price of 22½ cents per pound, less 2% cash discount, for delivery in the month in which the sugar was expected to arrive. The price was from 1½ to

[26] 1 H. B. R. 268.   See p. 499, *supra.*
[27] 1 H. B. R. 248.

3½ cents per pound lower than the competitive prices of refined sugar for similar deliveries which prevailed at that time. After the loss from refining was deducted, the 22½ cent price left the company a margin of about 1½ cents per pound for operating expenses and a small profit. The public and manufacturers were thus assured of a supply at prices below the prevailing market. Customers quickly took the tenders of sugar, and in most instances it was necessary to accept orders for less sugar than the quantities desired.

Under the stimulus of direct purchases of sugar from foreign producers, sugar which had not been included in the statistics of the world's supply, became available, and under the pressure of these efforts, the market weakened and broke in August; the most violent price decline ever recorded in sugar followed. Customers were as anxious to cancel or repudiate contracts as they had been to secure them. On August 24, the American Sugar Refining Company withdrew from the market and employed its facilities in the completion of the contracts already made. The company honored all its contracts for the purchase of raw sugar which were the basis of its commitments to its customers, and therefore was justified, the management believed, in requiring its customers to fulfil their contracts. Because of the prevalence of cancellations in the fall of 1920, it was expected that a policy of strict enforcement adopted by one of the leading companies in the sugar industry would emphasize the inviolability of contracts and aid in the stabilization of conditions in other industries.

Although further business relations with a few of the customers who attempted to repudiate contracts were not desired, the most serious objection to the enforcement of contracts was the loss of goodwill. Another obstacle was the weakened financial condition of many customers who were unable to pay for deliveries under contracts. Suits might force a portion of these into bankruptcy. The difficulty could be, and later was, obviated by extension of the time of payment. The management decided, accordingly, to enforce all contracts and to resort to suits at law for damages whenever customers refused to accept deliveries of sugar.

On October 13, 1920, it sent letters to its 25,000 customers, notifying them to this effect. On December 24, 1920, it sent letters to all customers that had not availed themselves of this offer of deferred payments, setting the date, January 1, 1921, as the final date for acceptance of their plan. On February 4, 1921, a letter was sent to all customers explaining the whole sugar situation and the policy of the company and requesting a compliance with the contractual obligations.

Of the total amount of contract sales, 15% were repudiated, involving $30,000,000. The company instituted 750 suits. A large number of cases were settled out of court, after suit was brought. In order to set an example for customers who had made contracts for small quantities of sugar, contracts which involved the largest amounts were prosecuted first. The management extended every aid to customers who recognized their obligations, but allowed no exceptions and brought suit against all who persisted in their repudiation of contracts. In May, 1923, the president summarized the preceding statements and the company's position, closing with the following statement: "We ask the support of all of our customers in our effort to uphold the sanctity of contracts, on which the stability of business depends."

Whether the moral gesture contained in the last part of the president's statement was either justified or expedient, may be questioned. As a matter of fact, the contracts were not treated as "sacred," or they would have been enforced to the letter. They were regarded as symbols of a complicated business situation and were modified considerably in order to make the proper adjustments to a real situation, and the subsequent passing of company dividends is evidence of this procedure. The real contribution of the American Sugar Refining Company, as in the case of the Martel Shoe Company, was to interpose itself in what could have become an endless chain of cancellations, by assuming its own purchasing obligations. It is conceivable that the company could have requested accommodations and adjustments from those persons from whom purchases of raw sugar had been made. That it did not do so was probably due more to its recognition of the value of its goodwill and its financial ability to meet its obligations—which are to be regarded as elements in business ethics—than to any sentiment in favor of an intangible "sanctity" of contracts. This ability to stop the transitive effects of cancellations[28] is fundamental to the solution of the problem, and represents the real ethical contribution of the American Sugar Refining Company to the situation. An additional sound contribution is to be found in the practical adjustments made with its customers, in which the previously determined contractual relations were modified so as to fit the situation and be acceptable to most of the parties concerned.[29]

Although the company was able to show by later developments that it had to make considerable sacrifices—common dividends were suspended for several years in order to conserve the cash resources of the company—their treatment of the situation in its entirety was not altogether above reproach.

[28] See discussion following Martel case, p. 500, *supra*.
[29] For the legal points involved, see 2 H.B.R. 468, Commentary.

The extended situation of the sugar industry before the crash in 1920 was, in the main, the result of the difficult readjustments incident to a change from governmental control of prices to a competitive régime. The difficulties of these readjustments were multiplied because the transition occurred during a period of credit inflation. But the company officers seem to have been blind to what was occurring in their industry and in general business, and their failure to analyze the situation actually proved expensive both to the company's customers and to its shareholders. Instead of expanding operations in 1920, they should have curtailed their activities and built up a strong cash position.[30]

Indeed, as a commentator points out, a forecast of the approaching period of sharp readjustment had been made early in 1920.[31] Unfortunately, however, the forecasting of business events cannot be relied upon as a dependable factor in the solving of the problem under consideration.

Business Adjustments to Cancellations

A somewhat similar situation arose in the following case. Although this case occurred in 1920, the situation seemingly was not brought about by a general price trend; the difficulty was local and specific. The case is presented in the form of letters addressed to the legal department by the collection department of the Bartelle Company and by the legal firm to which the claim was given for collection. The facts are substantially as follows:

A balance of approximately $12,000 was due the Bartelle Company[32] on April 16, 1920, for materials that it had delivered under contract to the Fulton Fertilizer Corporation. The total amount of the contract was $139,000, 10% having been collected upon the execution of the contract, 75% of the remainder to be paid at the time the goods were shipped.

The $12,000 balance represented the 15% due on shipments already made. In addition, approximately $49,000 worth of goods was ready for shipment to complete the contract. Although the Fulton Corporation was not in a position to receive the shipments of this balance, the Bartelle Company endeavored to collect 75% of this amount according to the terms of the contract.

[30] 2 H.B.R. 476.
[31] Harvard University Committee on Economic Research: *Review of Economic Statistics*, Preliminary Volume II, p. 29, February, 1920. Cited: 2 H.B.R. 384.
[32] See 1 H.B.R. 255 for letters on which the statement of this case is based.

On March 18, 1920, the general manager of the Fulton Company promised to settle the balance of $12,000 between that date and the end of the month, but later explained that he was unable to do so as he was awaiting money from the engineering firm which was backing the enterprise. The bankers who were selling the stock of the Fulton Corporation declined to advance them any further money until they were able to procure a refund of the money advanced to the engineering company. This company had valuable assets which they were, however, unable to realize on quickly.

The Bartelle Company desired, on August 25, to apply to other more urgent orders some motors manufactured for the Fulton Corporation, especially if the latter was unable to accept them. The legal firm advised that this be not done without the Fulton Corporation's consent. They advised, furthermore, that this matter be kept distinct from the collection of the amount already due on shipments made, a confusion which was present in the mind of the general manager of the Fulton Corporation.

The legal firm, on September 20, succeeded in securing a certified check for the $12,000 overdue, but was not able to arrange for the withdrawal of some of the undelivered material from the contract. When they suggested the latter arrangement, the customer demurred and wanted to enter into some sort of manufacturing agreement which would have the effect of excusing any default in his then obligation to accept and pay for material. Furthermore, the customer seemed to the legal firm to be using the matter of release or extension of delivery date as a reason or excuse for withholding the payment for goods already received, and it seemed best to the legal firm to cease negotiations in regard to diverting orders and to stand on the demand for the check.

The matter of payment for the balance due on goods already delivered was rightly separated, by the legal firm employed by the Bartelle Company, as a distinct problem of adjustment. It is pertinent to recall, however, that resorting to the law, in this case as well as in the American Sugar Refining case, is a matter of business policy. As the commentary on the Bartelle case says:

It is not always good policy to exercise one's legal rights or use all one's legal powers against a legal opponent . . .

The case illustrates the difference between the *science* of knowing one's legal rights and powers and the *art* of using them under precarious conditions.[33]

With the legal points, discussed in the commentary, we are not here concerned.

[33] 2 H.B.R. 469, 470. Italics mine.

The second major problem in the Bartelle case was that concerning the refusal to accept, or the desire to postpone acceptance of, the materials called for by contract but not yet received. The possibility of diverting these materials to other urgent orders was a matter of policy dependent, as the legal firm pointed out, on the agreement of the Fulton Corporation to such a procedure. Their unwillingness to agree is questionable from the view-point of business ethics, but the discussion of this problem would lead us astray from the main point. It is, however, a factor in the situation. The fact, however, that they did not agree, confines the problem to the policy of the Bartelle Company under such circumstances. The case gives no inkling as to their decision in the matter. A similar situation, however, is presented in the following case, which furthermore contains the necessary facts to such a prognosis.

On August 9, 1920, the Harrison Steel Corporation[34] received a request from the Tyler Warehousing Company for the cancellation of the unfilled portion of a sales contract, dated May 10, 1920, which called for the delivery to the Tyler Warehousing Company of 500 tons of structural shapes monthly for a period of six months, specifications for the shapes to be given by the purchaser each month in anticipation of delivery two weeks later. Two of these monthly installments had been shipped by the Harrison Steel Corporation and accepted by the Tyler Warehousing Company. The third installment was in process of manufacture under the specifications. The Tyler Warehousing Company was ready to receive this third installment, but requested that the remaining three shipments be cancelled because of lack of orders on the company's books to take up the steel if manufactured and shipped.

It had been the custom in the industry for several years to grant cancellations of these tonnage contracts in whole or in part almost without discussion, provided cancellation was requested before specifications for the steel had been given by the purchaser. The basis for this custom was that the manufacturer could not start to make the steel until definite specifications, as to size and quality of steel, and other necessary instructions had been given.[35] The full amount of the contract was carried on the books of the manufacturer, however, as an

---

[34] 1 H.B.R. 242. Fictitious name.

[35] One clause in the contract form is pertinent to the situation. "A buyer's failure to furnish specifications may at the seller's option and without notice to the buyer be treated and considered as a refusal to accept and receive the unspecified portion of the goods."

unfulfilled order, and general production plans as to size of labor force, expansion, and general overhead expense were determined primarily on the basis of the quantity of the unfulfilled orders on the company's books. Cancellation of these contracts, therefore, affected the manufacturer.

If the Harrison Steel Corporation insisted upon the Tyler Company's fulfilling its part of the contract, the Harrison Steel Corporation would be adopting a policy which ran counter to that followed in the past by the industry and the probable future policy of other independent steel companies. The corporation, therefore, permitted the cancellation requested by the Tyler Company, and decided that although such cancellations of tonnage contracts were detrimental to the industry, refusal to allow them should be made by a group of independents acting together rather than by one company.

Here there is no evidence of any particular or acute difficulty presented to the seller by the buyer's cancellation. The difficulties are explicitly stated to be "general," involving unfulfilled orders on the books, general production plans as to labor, and general overhead expense. The Harrison Corporation is not faced with the necessity in turn of cancelling specific orders for raw materials or of storing them. This is not to deny the fact or possibility of a loss, especially of expected profits, but it is intended to distinguish between a loss which is probable and which can be distributed over the whole of the company's activities on the one hand, and on the other of a loss which is actual and which is specific in its incidence, such as was discovered in the American Sugar Refining case.

Summary

In the present inquiry two elements have been arbitrarily excluded from the ethical consideration of the situation presented by trade cancellations: the moral and the legal. The clash of business interests always is accompanied by a clash of emotions and sentiments which assume a moral tone but which frequently are actually determined by the character of the conflicting interests. In a rising market, as has already been stated, the buyer becomes righteously indignant over the delay in deliveries, while the seller explains and rationalizes. In a falling market, the reverse is true; one then hears much of the "sanctity of contracts." And it is only because the latter situation is usually the more acute that the problem of cancellation seems more important than that of the failure to deliver. Even where this righteous indignation over cancellations could be justified by the buyer's bad faith, his behavior cannot be regarded as a sufficient basis for reciprocal action or unqualified condemnation on the part of the seller. Morally, all contracts should be held inviolate; but ethically, adjustments to general as well as to particular conditions should be taken into account, provided such an attitude does not unduly encourage the unscrupulous. Granted this point, the question arises, just what conditions have given rise to the situation, what distribution of responsibility can be determined—and in this matter, the whole of the responsibility is seldom that of the buyer—and, finally, what adjustment will secure to seller, to buyer, and to society a maximum of benefits under the circumstances? The analogy of these business cases to the problem of German reparations and Allied debts is obvious.

In the second place, this inquiry is not a substitute for judicial opinion. The law of contracts has had too long a history to be interfered with by analyses such as these, while statutory legislation in regard to the matter is so diverse as to require that each case which develops to the point of litigation be handled by lawyers and judges who are conversant with the situation.[36] It may be that ethical considerations will eventually affect laws or judicial decisions, but such is not the immediate concern of this analysis.

Although specific questions as to the law of contracts are not included in this volume, business policy does involve the question of the expediency of resorting to law in order to enforce compliance with contracts. That is, there are two questions to be considered: a legal question, as to *what* the law is on the matter, a question outside the problem we are considering; and, in addition to the policy problem, an ethical question, distinctly

[36] Section 145 of the Personal Property Law of New York, which is part of the Uniform Sales Act, states that when a buyer repudiates a contract, he shall be liable for no greater damages than the seller has suffered up to that time. Sometimes such damages can be minimized by completing the manufacture of the article, as for example where the article is a standard product for which there is a ready market, or where suspension of manufacturing would result in the loss of perishable materials. The ethical solution of this problem would involve a wider area of obligations, although this area would not necessarily include the moral obligation of complete fulfillment of the contractual obligations

within the province of this volume, as to *whether* the law should be resorted to at all. Business men realize that satisfactory business relations cannot be built up if there is much resort to legal proceedings. Forcing customers into bankruptcy kills the goose that lays the golden eggs. Customers look upon lawsuits as unfair means of securing an advantage, especially during a period of wide-spread depression, and they are prone to develop an antagonistic attitude which is detrimental to a company's future sales. Furthermore the expense and time involved in conducting lawsuits are often prohibitive. On the other hand, the failure on the part of business men to resort to legal suits in cases which are grossly unfair to themselves, is a practice which is difficult to defend from the point of view of public policy, and frequently exhibits an ignorant fear and marks a certain loss of self-respect.

Most of the preceding cases dealing with cancellations of contracts arose during the depression of 1920–21, when dealers' shelves were packed with goods and companies' books contained inflated inventories; and when further purchases or acceptances of goods already ordered would have meant bankruptcy, especially at the then prevailing high prices. After the experience of that period, retail merchants completely altered their buying methods and began what is now known as "hand-to-mouth" buying. Inventories were reduced tremendously, especially in retail stores—although it is doubtful whether manufacturers have followed or are able to follow this practice—direct buying was resorted to, and quicker turnovers resulted. It may be that such developments prevented the recent business depression from becoming a major calamity; at least there is not the prevalence of cancellations that marked the 1920–21 depression, and the present relative lag in the decline of retail prices probably indicates the relatively better strategic position of the retailer over the wholesaler and manufacturer as regards stocks on hand. If this is the case, then the lessons learned by the retailer during the 1920–21 debacle are still to be learned by the wholesaler and manufacturer. It may also be that the "hand-to-mouth" buying of the retailer during the past ten years has contributed to the present situation; "overproduction," for which the present situation is blamed, may be merely a relative term. But such an observation borders on the speciously academic, as do all considerations of hypothetical propositions.

Similarly, recent buying methods practically question the moral virtue of "foresight" which too frequently in the past has been identified with overloaded shelves.   Therefore, it would probably be more to the point, in considering the problem of cancellations of contracts, to study the situations which actually occurred. The cases dealt with in this chapter have been selected as typical of the most important of such situations.

CHAPTER XIX

LIMITATION OF PRODUCTION

The production of an amount of goods in excess of demand will normally result in a lowering of the price of the commodity, to the benefit of the consumer-purchaser. When such a tendency is gradual, it may involve no serious effects among producers: they will have time to adjust themselves by reducing costs, the lowered price may induce sufficiently increased buying to neutralize or delay still further the downward course of prices, and this increased buying will aid in maintaining profits by reducing unit costs. But whenever the price drop is sudden, or the saturation point in consumer demand is quickly reached, the producer will be injured, perhaps irrevocably, and perhaps to a degree which is not compensated for by the increased and immediate benefits to the buyer. For, although everyone is a consumer, consumer interests being practically identical with the public interest, no social or economic organization should tolerate a sudden cataclysm which affects the whole or even a considerable part of its producers: the intrinsic rights and values of producers and owners should be recognized and protected, and the indirect effect on subsequent purchasing power, especially where laborers are involved, may seriously affect the whole consuming public. Therefore, wholesale condemnations of business men who try to protect themselves against falling prices are not justifiable. Only when such protective measures are unfair to business and to the consumer, can they be condemned. The question arises: Is limitation of production, by concerted action, such an unfair method of preventing abrupt or excessive price declines?

In considering the problem of limitation of production, certain distinctions must be made. To begin with, limitation of production as it affects raw materials is to be differentiated from that which is attempted by manufacturing and commercial organizations. And in the second place, inert raw materials—such as minerals—which are already in existence, in the form of stocks on hand or natural resources known or available to discovery, must be distinguished from renewable materials such as farm crops which are subject to seasonal periods and which thereby involve both seasonal lags and fluctuations.

So long as the curtailment of production is motivated merely by a desire to increase prices, the consumer-purchaser has a legitimate complaint that the public interest is jeopardized. This complaint could certainly be directed against the destruction of materials already produced;[1] it has less force but may be equally legitimate when directed against monopolistic concerns or trade agreements effecting an excessive limitation of production. Complaints against the maintenance of prices by concerted efforts may also be justified. But they cannot be raised against the voluntary and individual curtailments by producers who conclude, following the publication of figures regarding production, stocks on hand, and sales, that the market is over-supplied; and there is a positive interest in the curtailment of production of natural resources which are being seriously depleted.

Limitation of Production of Coal and Lumber

The three commodities which best illustrate this latter consideration are coal, lumber, and oil. The conservation cry has been raised, at one time or another, in regard to each of these three natural resources, and a considerable amount of public sentiment and emotion has been enlisted in behalf of one or more of these sources of national wealth. As a matter of fact the only one of these three commodities which is in serious danger of depletion is oil. Any extravagance in the use or production of coal which is encouraged by current price levels does not dangerously deplete our natural resources; rather, the current price levels are endangering the solvency of the producers, a competitive problem.[2]

Increased efficiency in the extraction of coal together with increased use of substitutes and greater efficiency in the employment of coal for power production have combined relatively to reduce the market for coal all over the world, but particularly in

[1] For example, the dumping of fish by members of the San Francisco market justifiably resulted in a statute prohibiting the practice. See also *U. S. v. American Coal Products Co.* Consent Decree, March, 4, 1913.

[2] See *The Menace of Overproduction*, a group of essays edited by Scoville Hamlin, New York: John Wiley & Sons, Inc., 1930. See also *Monthly Letter*, The National City Bank, New York, August, 1930.

the United States. Relative overproduction was an inevitable consequence, a condition which is evidenced not only by the chronic excess of approximately 200,000 coal miners in the United States but also by the presence of a large number of marginal mines, dramatically called "snowbirds" because they begin to operate whenever the price goes up slightly during the winter months. These marginal mines represent the relatively less efficient high-cost mines which can operate only at relatively high prices, prices which in turn would otherwise enable the permanent producers to recoup for the months during which prices were relatively low. The public, of course, is interested in some such "safety-valve" as these "snowbirds" provide against excessive prices, but the coal industry is in a depressed state as the result of this situation, and most of the acute as well as chronic labor problems of the industry may be attributed to this basic difficulty. This is not to say that management in the industry is blameless, or that ownership has met with universal bankruptcy; but the complete picture cannot be drawn without laying due emphasis on the fact of overproduction.

The following case illustrates the status of the industry at the beginning of the century, especially as regards the legal prohibitions of concerted attempts to control production and distribution. Whether the proposed association plan might have led to excess limitation, to the economic detriment of the industry as well as of the consumer, cannot, of course, be stated. But the metaphysical emphasis on "competition" in the face of apparent trade difficulties is strikingly characteristic of the earlier interpretations of the Sherman Law by the courts.

The Chesapeake & Ohio Fuel Company was incorporated in 1897 in West Virginia. It contracted with some 14 companies engaged in mining coal and manufacturing coke, to purchase and sell their entire output for a period of five years. These companies, located in the Kanawha District of West Virginia, produced a little more than one-half of the coal and coke mined and made in this region. Under the agreement, monthly reports of production and shipments were made, together with the average price of each grade of coal or coke. The Fuel Company was to receive a gross profit of not to exceed 10 cents a ton; all amounts in excess of this were to be paid back to the members of the coal association. The executive committee of the association determined each month the percentage of the total product of each class and grade of coal and coke which they deemed should be shipped by each member of the association. Membership in the association was left open to any of the companies in the district, a provision which the court seized upon as increasing the possibility of monopoly control.

This case was first prosecuted in the Circuit Court, Southern District of Ohio, Southern Division, where an injunction was granted and the combination ordered dissolved.[3] The minima of coal and coke which the fuel company was required to take and pay for, were in excess of production during the preceding year; the facilities for placing coal and coke on the western market were increased by the operation of the contract; prices, under the contract, were not materially increased or diminished; and the monthly payments by the fuel company relieved the operators from losses by bad debts and furnished the means for promptly paying employees. In spite of these alleged public benefits, however, the court held that the policy of the law looked to competition, and not combination, as the best and safest method of securing these benefits. The combination was held to enter the western markets clothed with powers which enabled it to "exercise a large influence" in regulating the supply and the prices of coal and coke; and the provisions of the contract were held to be in restraint of trade, to tend to monopoly, and to render the contract illegal.

This decision was sustained by the Circuit Court of Appeals, 6th Circuit, which held that the courts were not concerned with the policy of the Sherman Law, but rather with its enforcement.

It is not for them to inquire whether it be true, as is often alleged, that this is a mistaken public policy, and that combinations, in the reduction of the cost of production, cheapened transportation, and lowered cost to the consumer, have been productive of more good than evil to the public . . . In the exercise of its constitutional rights, Congress has declared for that policy which shall keep competition free, and leave interstate commerce open to all, without the right to any to fetter it by contracts or combinations which shall put it under restraint.[4]

In the present case, if the scheme of this combination shall prevail, until nearly all of the operators in this district have availed themselves of the opportunity contained in the contract and become parties to it, the effect upon dealers who have not its large facilities, and may be unable to compete for the contracts and meet the prices fixed by the committee, cannot be otherwise than disastrous. And when the small dealer has been driven out, the combination is one step nearer to the power to control the market.[5]

[3] *U. S. v. C. & O. Fuel Co. et al.*, 105 Fed. 93 (1900).
[4] *C. & O. Fuel Co. v. U. S.*, 115 Fed. 610, 620 (1902).
[5] *Ibid.*, p. 623.

In contrast with the above-described concerted efforts of coal dealers to control the situation is the more recent endeavor of the Consolidation Coal Company to restrict production among its own mines individually and voluntarily, with the purpose of encouraging other independent operators to pursue a similar policy.

Early in 1928, the Consolidation Coal Company, owned by the Rockefeller interests and the largest producer of bituminous coal in the world, announced the policy of closing its high-cost mines with a view to concentrating on the more efficient mines. Plans were made for transferring workers and for paying wages above the low minimum then prevailing in many parts of the industry. It was expected that the example set by a single large producer in the industry would encourage other large producers voluntarily to join in thus "rationalizing" the industry and in eliminating the cutthroat competition that prevailed. Ten mines in the Fairmont, West Virginia, field were shut down as a part of this policy, which at the time was hailed as "a constructive contribution to a sick industry."

After a two-year trial of the policy, the Consolidation Coal Company announced the failure of the plan.[6] A "steady disintegration of standards" in the Fairmont field was reported, with many companies defaulting from a month to three months in wages, some companies actually being forced into bankruptcy. The Consolidation Coal Company declared itself unable to maintain a wage differential of 15% to 25%, and announced in May, 1930, a wage reduction of 12% to 14%, affecting some 3,000 miners, "in order to meet competitive conditions."

Thus ended the attempt of the Consolidation Coal Company to stabilize conditions in the coal industry in somewhat the same manner as the United States Steel Corporation has stabilized conditions in the iron and steel industry. The experiment shows that any naive faith which one may have in the ability of business to govern itself through voluntary action, even among the larger producers, must be tempered; the pressing needs of the coal industry and its admittedly depressed condition were not sufficient to force a salutary policy upon its inert or unintelligent managers.

In the anthracite field, the remedial measures proved to be excessive. At the request of the operators, the State of Pennsylvania passed a law providing for the equivalent of an export tax in order to maintain prices on what was regarded as a monopoly product. The results were the importation of coal, par-

[6] *New York Times*, May 24, 1930.

ticularly Welsh coal into New England, and the greater use of substitutes, especially gas and electricity, with almost disastrous temporary effects on the Pennsylvania industry. This experience showed clearly that taking advantage of a supposed monopoly control,[7] whether by limitation of production or by increase in price or both, does not necessarily lead to the consequences so feared by the consuming public. The industry itself is probably jeopardized more, by the development of competitive alternatives, substitutes and the opening-up of new productive fields, than is the consumer endangered by high prices or restricted output. The conservation of coal as a natural resource will probably be adequately taken care of by economic factors; declining supplies will result in increased prices and in restricted demand. A conservation policy in the interests of the industry itself, however, will have to be worked out somewhere between the two extremes represented by the bituminous and anthracite industries respectively.

The situation as regards the lumber industry is somewhat different from that facing the coal industry. True, both are natural resources that should be conserved, and the deforested hills of northern China point as graphic a lesson in conservation as do the narrowing coal seams of England. But not only does the deterioration of forest timber in the United States because of the age of the trees represent a wastage of tremendous proportions, but timber is replaceable to a far greater extent than is coal. It is doubtful whether the current cutting of timber for use is keeping up with the rate of normal decay. Of course, one should condemn such depraved and ruthless policies as characterized the operations of many lumber mills in the past: culls, branches and trimmings were allowed to accumulate in the cut-over areas and facilitated forest fires that inevitably spread to tremendous areas, killing all the new growth, and thus also contributing to rapid run-off of surface water, with consequent floods and droughts. But these are methods that can be and have been to a large extent controlled by direct methods; attempts to control the situation by ineffable "conservation" policies have turned people away from a legitimate use of timber products. The major problem which underlies our public policy, and the real difficulty confronting the lumber

[7] See "Anthracite Is No Longer a Natural Monopoly," by Theodore G. Joslin, *Boston Evening Transcript*, January 2, 1929.

industry, consists, not in conservation, but in encouraging a sufficient use of lumber to keep pace with the natural deterioration of the standing timber. Like the man who fell on the highway and was surrounded by a deeply concerned group of "helpers," the lumber industry is the victim of misplaced sentiment: "Give him more air," said a policemen to the crowd; "Air?" said the wayfarer, "Air's all I've had for three days; that's what's the matter with me!" The lumber industry has been the victim of an overly zealous cry of conservation; what people need to learn is that a greater rather than a smaller use of lumber would be good alike for the industry and for the nation. The only practicable limitation program so far worked out has been directed at some of the fabrication stages.[8] Even so, and inasmuch as the limitation of production is only a relative term, the promotion of sales is probably the best strategic move of the industry toward accomplishing the same purpose.

Limiting the Production of Oil

The problem of limitation now seriously confronts the oil producers.[9] In order to understand the ethics, as well as the policy involved, it is necessary to examine the facts which pertain to the commodity itself. Petroleum is probably not now being naturally produced in the earth to any great extent, certainly not to the extent that it is being consumed, hence the problem of conservation assumes greater importance than with a commodity which, like lumber, is being naturally reproduced. Second, the available supply is not accurately known, but the estimates seem to indicate that the supply is likely to be exhausted, at the present rate of consumption, in a few decades; in this respect, oil differs from coal. How much such observations should be qualified by the possible development of new and refined extractive processes, particularly such as might utilize vast quantities of shale deposits, is a matter of conjecture; and it is a conspicuous

[8] See Trade Association cases, already referred to, pp. 270 ff. The National Lumber Dealers' Association has been very effective in eliminating the wastes which formerly were regarded as nuavoidable in the milling processes, and has, under the direction of its efficient secretary, Mr. Wilson Compton, been fully conscious of the major problems of the industry. The chief difficulty seems to be the inertia of some of its members and the misplaced sentiment of the public.

[9] See Logan, Leonard M., Jr., *Stabilization of the Petroleum Industry,* Norman: University of Oklahoma Press, 1930.

fact that no commodity has ever been exhausted or has ever been threatened with excessive depletion without some substitute being found or made. The inevitable advance of science is a plausible set-off to any possible exhaustion of supply. These two considerations are matters of prime social and public interest.

Of more concern to the industry, however, are the practical situations which it faces. Here again, certain distinctive facts must be recognized. First, oil production is an "all-or-none" proposition; that is, a well which strikes oil is immediately pumped "for all it is worth," especially in view of the fact that it may tap a reservoir which a competitor miles away may also be drilling toward or already pumping. The chief cause of overproduction, therefore, is the new oil well rather than any increase in pumping energy devoted to the wells already producing. And the drilling of new wells is determined, not so much even by fluctuating prices of crude oil as it is by the money available for speculative drilling of wells. The source of this money is the general investing public which wishes to speculate in oil stocks. In the case of cotton and sugar, the bankers have been no less liberal in the furnishing of funds. The remoteness of this real inducement to overproduction from the operating activities of the producers themselves shows how futile is any reliance on price declines or even producers' agreements to curtail the production of crude oil. The withdrawal of government and state lands from exploitation is perhaps the only appreciable solution of the problem, and even this solution is qualified by the fact that wells just outside the boundary of the withdrawn lands may draw oil from them.

The value of crude oil has been greatly enhanced by the use of gasoline for the automobile, especially in recent years when use outstripped production. But even more recently, due to the speculative situation outlined above, production has so far outstripped consumption as to result in increasing stocks on hand and in price-cutting. The technique of marketing oil and gas has become complicated and refined in proportion as the necessity arose for disposing of increasing stocks; and most of the ethical problems arising in the marketing field have similarly resulted from the tremendous pressure from the direction of the sources of supply. These ethical problems—price-cutting, substitution, "bootlegging" in competitors' normal markets, and the like—have led the larger companies to attempt to get at the supposed source, overproduction. Some of their efforts have been wholly misdirected, such as the seeking of a tariff on imported crude oil, a method which will simply make more profitable the high-cost wells and encourage additional drilling. Other methods have been characteristic of the hypocritical adherents of "business ethics:" the plea for conservation of natural resources. Still other methods have been neglected: the curbing of speculative oil-company ventures. While still other methods have aimed directly at a basic, if not the basic difficulty, namely, restriction of output at the wells or fields.

The general strategy of controlling the output of crude petroleum would, of course, include limitation by the national Government; this was one of the purposes of ex-President Coolidge's appointment of the Federal Oil Conservation Board. But the industry is suspicious of such governmental control, because of the fear of further extensions of its control over the industry. Furthermore, a practical difficulty lies in the fact that production is centered largely in certain states, especially California, Texas, Oklahoma and Kansas, and is therefore not strictly a national problem. The Petroleum Institute discovered that its own attempt at a nation-wide non-governmental control of oil output was less practicable than separate control schemes for the various producing areas, in spite of the fact that the competition among these areas provided a basis for increases in one area as soon as restriction was attempted in another.

In March, 1929, the leading oil producers of Oklahoma agreed, under the supervision of the Oklahoma Corporation Commission, to restrict the crude-oil output of that state to 650,000 barrels a day. Daily production in the huge Seminole field was prorated to 75% of its potential capacity, the St. Louis pool to 73%, and the Maud-Mission area to 69%. Provision was made for adjusting the ratios monthly. The potential capacity was determined by allowing producing wells to flow wide open from 7 a. m., March 1, to 7 a. m., March 2; all drilling wells reaching the top of sand in the first half of March were to be shut down for eight days, exclusive of ordinary shut-downs. By confining the agreement to the producers of a single state, the jurisdiction of the Sherman Law was avoided, and a sympathetic attitude of the state itself enabled the producers to act in concerted fashion. But, even so, the region would still be open to competition from other non-regulated areas. The much-heralded Santa Fe

Springs agreement, applying to the California district, enrolled 80% of the oil production of the region, but was not put into effect because of the provision that 85% enrollment was necessary, based on September, 1928, production.[10] A later agreement was attempted covering a wider area; in addition to the Santa Fe Springs region, the Signal Hill, Seal Beach and Ventura Avenue fields were included. But the United States Government did not at first look with favor upon such agreements, and a more practicable control now seems to be offered by state legislation. Thus the California law,[11] based on the police power, is directed against the "unreasonable" waste of gas and oil.

In June, 1930, Congress and the Federal Oil Conservation Board endorsed the "unit plan of operation," by which all the operators tapping a single pool agree upon the total output to be taken from it and then allocate this total among themselves in some equitable manner. The Board recognized as a basic consideration the fact that, once a pool is tapped, it virtually becomes common property, and asserted that voluntary cooperation had not been strong enough to prevent overproduction and huge wastes, especially of gas. The first region in which this experiment is to be tried is the Kettleman Hills Oil Field.

Limiting the Production of Agricultural Products

The conspicuous fact in connection with the production of agricultural commodities is that a whole year is necessary to

[10] See *Articles of Incorporation*, Santa Fe Springs Gas Conservation Association, Los Angeles, December 1, 1928.

The following is the substance of the plan:

Whenever gas production at Santa Fe Springs exceeds usage in field demands of gas companies and repressuring demands and storage projects, and a genuine excess exists, production of all wells producing in the field shall be cut a definite percentage every 30 days.

Any new well completed during the 30-day period shall be permitted to flow full for five days. Average production of the last two days shall be taken as potential production and same cut shall apply on that well and the well allowed to flow until the next general test of wells in the field.

At end of each 30-day period potential production tests shall be made by permitting full flow for two or three days and new prorating on basis of the next test. However, actual production of any well at end of a 30-day period shall be taken in lieu of opening up the well to establish new potential production. Percentage of cut for succeeding 30-day period shall be established at least five days in advance of time of test to establish potential production.

[11] Chapter 718, and particularly as amended in 1929, Chapter 535.

affect production figures. There are some two-season crops; and, as in the case of sugar, ignorance of available far-distant stocks on hand may pave the way for transporting these stocks so as to effect a result comparable with a "bumper" crop. But these exceptions do not vitally alter the basic agricultural situation, which—in contrast with minerals, rubber and lumber—is determined by the fact that there is a seasonal lag in production and that each succeeding seasonal crop vitally affects the stocks on hand many months after the original inventory is taken and after individual growers have based their policies on the inventory. The result too often is that, as is well known, although a crop failure may ruin. the growers, a "bumper" crop may depress prices so much that the grower loses most of the money value of his crop. California orange growers netted a larger income this year than last, although the volume was 25% less. To refuse the grower the right to statistical information on such a subject would, of course, be absurd. To deny a farmers' organization the right to gather and disseminate such information, would be equally absurd. Neither of these possibilities, however, seriously interferes with agriculture, although statistical information is sadly lacking.

The difficulty arises in connection with the grower's use of such information as is now available. It is conceivable that the very knowledge which is intended to help him, may as a matter of fact be his undoing, even when he reacts individually and voluntarily and apparently intelligently to his knowledge of the facts. For a large crop with low prices may discourage him from repeating his experience, just as it may discourage others; whereas it is possible that a repetition of the raising of the same kind of crop would meet better price conditions the next year; while, on the other hand, figures as regards low available stocks may encourage growers to plant so much that overproduction will result. The trouble is twofold: inferences as to the stock on hand a year hence are based on present figures and conditions, and these inferences as to general conditions are made by particular individuals whose mass reaction is not at all in keeping with the desired total reaction. It may even be that the subtle inference of a grower, that an anticipated shortage will lead to overproduction and that he should grow something else, would be repeated sufficiently to cause a large number of growers likewise not to raise that product; and if they happen to hit on the same "something else," the result would be disastrous. The law of chance operates against the ill effects of such secondary judgments, but it does not operate against the mass effects of primary judgments. Therefore, paradoxically periodic natural overproduction is frequently accentuated by mistaken foresight.

The result is that direct effective control can be exercised only by concerted activity, a method which is forbidden by law to practically all industries, except agriculture, and is without exception opposed by consumer interests. Indirect control may be exercised in various ways. Diversification of farm production would eliminate the excesses of "one-crop" policies, but the boll weevil had more influence in effecting this policy among the cotton growers of the South than did intelligent cooperation, and the recent suggestions of the Farm Board, that wheat growers decrease their acreage 10% to 15%, has not met with much response; evidently the law is not the only hindrance. Such suggestions could not be made by a trade association without legal consequences. Reduction of crop acreage is subject to two difficulties: if left to individual determination, it may result in excessive effects as indicated above; while even if it becomes a matter of concerted action, weather conditions may intensify its objective to the point of effecting a serious shortage. The more feasible plan would seem to be the control of the marketing of stocks on hand. Adequate storage facilities thereupon become necessary, and also credit machinery. It is a separate, but none the less important, problem as to whether the agency for delaying distribution shall be the "middlemen"— the commission merchants—or the cooperatives of the growers, the latter being the farming equivalent of a trade association.

Some of the most dramatic attempts at limitation in production have occurred in connection with agricultural products. Conspicuous among these products so curtailed are rubber, coffee, sugar and wheat. And the general conclusion one reaches, from considering these examples, is that such attempts have without exception been disastrous, particularly because of the encouragement to overproduction by others, the very difficulty it was intended to avoid. The Stevenson Act of Great Britain in 1922 precipitated the worst commodity-price break in rubber in years; partly as the result of encouraging the production from new areas, partly because of the consequent intensive production of the already existing Dutch interests, and partly because of the utilization of old rubber by improved processes. And this in spite of the fact that approximately 8 years are necessary to bring new fields into operation, a fact which differentiates rubber and lumber from most agricultural products. In the case of sugar, the price inflation of 1920 encouraged and stimulated sources of supply that were previously unknown; and the valorization plan of the Cuban Government merely added fuel to the flames. The fact that consumption of sugar is stable, regardless of price, indicates that the problem of the industry is to limit production. The so-called "Chadbourne plan," of withdrawing raw sugar from the market, has not yet had a pragmatic test. In the case of cacao, an unexpectedly rapid deterioration of the bean destroyed the accumulated supplies. Just recently the Japanese Government announced a policy of stabilization for the silk industry, in the face of increasing competition of rayon and cotton.[12]

In view of the predicament now facing American farmers, especially growers of cotton and wheat, it may be more to the point first to present the situation that has developed regarding a temperate-zone product. And since the Canadian Wheat Pool has developed its policies over a longer period than has the Federal Farm Board, the Canadian situation can be dealt with in larger perspective. The early developments of the situation[13] are particularly illuminating in view of the more recent disasters to the growers. The Canadian Wheat Pool represents a type of control which is intermediate to the limitation of production of agricultural products and a limitation in the field of manufacturing: it attempts to control the flow of products to the market.

In a double sense the Canadian Wheat Pool Movement arose out of conditions induced by the World War. On the one hand it represented the organized effort of more or less desperate grain growers to substitute collective for individual marketing as a means of countering the drastic post-war decline in wheat prices which fell from a monthly average of $2.78½ for September 1920 to 97.7 cents for October 1923 on the Winnipeg cash market. On the other hand it represented an attempt to reproduce on a voluntary basis the system of centralized pooling associated with the operations of the Government Wheat Board which had handled the entire 1919 wheat crop of the Dominion. In contrast

[12] See The Annalist, May 16, 1930, p. 1054, article by Bernhard Ostrolenk.
[13] Information supplied by A. Cairns, Statistician of the Canadian Cooperative Wheat Producers, Ltd., Winnipeg.

with the contemporary United States Grain Corporation which had been established as a government-financed agency, to make effective by its participation in the open market whenever necessary the minimum price of $2.26 guaranteed by Congress, the Canadian Wheat Board had operated as the exclusive and compulsory selling agency for all wheat producers in the Dominion. Under the latter system each grower had received on delivery a scheduled cash payment together with a participation certificate which when finally redeemed had yielded an average return of $2.63 per bushel (basis, No. 1 Northern, lakehead position).

When the demobilization of the Wheat Board at the end of the 1919–20 crop year was followed by the abrupt decline in wheat prices, which set in with the advent of the 1920 crop, and with the discontinuance of governmental buying abroad, the western grain growers initiated an agitation, continued through four successive years, for the reestablishment of the Wheat Board as an emergency measure. The circumstances which prevented the grain growers' demand from being realized, despite the enactment of enabling legislation, were too involved to be discussed here. Suffice it to say that when the impossibility of obtaining relief through a compulsory, governmental marketing agency was finally recognized, the western farmers' provincial associations determined to create a pool-selling agency of their own on a voluntary contract basis. While the Canadian Council of Agriculture was demanding a government wheat board and the American Farm Bureau Federation was endeavoring to organize a nation-wide cooperative grain-marketing agency, the United Grain Growers proceeded to organize a cooperative interprovincial wheat pool. The Canadian Wheat Pool came into being in the same year (1924) in which the first McNary-Haugen bill was introduced in Congress.

In seeking to create a voluntary, contract pool as a cooperative alternative to a government wheat board on the one hand, and to the speculative grain-exchange system on the other, the grain growers of Western Canada were not entering a field in which they were without experience. At the end of the War, indeed, the two largest companies on the Winnipeg Grain Exchange were the two farmer-owned concerns, the United Grain Growers, Ltd., and the Saskatchewan Cooperative Elevator Company, which between them handled from 20% to 25% of all the grain marketed in Western Canada.

The United Grain Growers, Ltd., was an amalgamation formed in 1917, of the Alberta Farmers' Cooperative Elevator Company with the pioneer Grain Growers' Grain Company, which had been established as a farmer-owned grain-commission agency on the Winnipeg Grain Exchange as far back as 1906. The Saskatchewan "Co-op" had been created five years later under a unique plan combining governmental financial aid with cooperative ownership and responsibility. Where a sufficient number of farmers in any locality of the province applied for the establishment of a cooperative elevator, and subscribed for stock in the company to the extent of its cost, the Saskatchewan Government advanced 85% of such amount to the company in the form of a mortgage loan repayable in 20 annual installments. This permitted elevator construction on a 15% paid-up stock basis. Under this plan 435 cooperative elevators, operated as a unified system, had been established in Saskatchewan by 1924, while the United Grain Growers maintained some 385 houses throughout the three Prairie Provinces. Around these elevators the 35,000 shareholders of the United Grain Growers and the 28,000 stockholders of the Saskatchewan "Co-op" were organized into shareholders' locals, each electing its delegate to the annual meeting of its company. Since the companies, in addition to their country "lines," also controlled nearly two-fifths of the terminal storage capacity at the head of the Lakes, and maintained export offices at New York as well as at Winnipeg, they were able to handle the farmers' grain from initial delivery points to the seaboard.

Although the earnings of these farmer-owned companies had permitted the regular distribution of large dividends as well as the accumulation of extensive reserves, and although their service and competition had done much to improve the conditions of grain marketing in Western Canada, they had come to be regarded by a good many farmers—in the critical light of post-war depression—as capitalistic rather than truly cooperative in nature. No matter how extensively a farmer might patronize a cooperative elevator, he did not, unless he was a shareholder, share in the company's earnings.

On the other hand, a shareholder who put his grain through some other elevator, or who had retired altogether from farming, could continue to draw dividends. Operating as they did along the established lines of the speculative trade, the farmers' elevator companies failed to provide the pooling method which, the growers' experience with the Wheat Board led them to believe, would not only permit greater market control, but also insure distribution on a purely patronage basis. Wheat-pool organization in Western Canada, it will thus be seen, marked not the beginning of cooperative activity by grain growers, but merely a new phase in a strongly established movement of producer-controlled marketing.

While the pools were organized by the Provincial Farmers' Associations of Alberta, Saskatchewan and Manitoba quite apart from the cooperative elevator companies, their initiation was very appreciably facilitated by the latter through organization loans, through preferential arrangements for the handling of pool wheat through their line and terminal elevators and through the transfer of experienced officials. Indeed, but for the assistance rendered by the United Grain Growers and the Saskatchewan "Co-op" in the early stages of pool activity, and but for the experience gained by western farmers through the extended participation in the grain trade by these companies, it may well be doubted whether the Canadian Wheat Pool would have attained its later enviable position.

While the provincial pools attend to the securing and execution of growers' contracts within their boundaries, and finance and operate their own elevator systems, none of them does any selling of grain. With a view to concentrating market supply and reducing marketing costs, they have from the first delegated this important function to the Central Selling Agency, on whose directorate each of the provinces is equally represented, although Saskatchewan contributes more wheat than Alberta and Manitoba combined. Thus the 140,000 members of the three provincial pools market their combined crops through a single agency which they themselves control, as was not the case under the war-time Wheat Board.

In 1928, about two-thirds of the wheat acreage of the Prairie Provinces was signed up to the respective pools. In Saskatchewan and Manitoba, where subsidiary coarse-grains pools (for oats, barley, rye and flax) are also operated, about 43% of the acreage devoted to these crops was also under pool contract. A grower may make delivery of his grain to his pool in one of three ways. He may load a car directly from his wagons over a loading platform and consign it to the order of the pool office at Winnipeg or Calgary (east or west); he may deliver it to one of the 1,000 or more country elevators now owned and operated by the provincial pools; or, where there is no pool elevator, he may deliver it to one belonging to the United Grain Growers or regular line companies, practically all of whom have signed handling contracts with the pools. In all three cases the grower receives an initial payment, in accordance with a schedule which for the four years preceding 1929 had been on a basis of $1 a bushel for No. 1 Northern, Fort William or Vancouver. As under the Canadian Wheat Board, he also received a "participation certificate" entitling him to a *pro rata* share in whatever might be realized from the sale of the indicated grade of grain through the Central Selling Agency. Under the regular method of the trade the grower either sells his grain outright "on street" or "on track" to the local elevator or other dealer at the buyer's price, or else has it stored pending sale on the open market when he judges the price to be most favorable—provided his creditors do not press him for immediate realization. Under the pool system he may make delivery at his convenience, without having to worry about whether or not it is the best time to sell. His initial-payment basis remains the same whenever or wherever he makes delivery, and he is assured of participation in the average price realized for the season.

As the grower makes delivery to his provincial pool, the latter forwards the grain to the terminals, where it is turned over to the Central Selling Agency. Although this body has its seats on the Winnipeg and Vancouver Grain Exchanges, where it makes sales in the same manner as other members, its policy has been to sell as much of its holdings as possible directly to eastern millers and foreign millers. To this end 27 agency connections have been established with wheat-importing houses in 15 countries in four continents. An overseas office for supervising its European business has been recently established at London, where the Pool has acquired membership in the London Corn Trade Association. During the three years prior to 1929 the proportion of direct sales was about 75%. Its policy is to make sales on the Winnipeg Exchange only when prices there are at least as high as it might realize by selling directly in final markets. Private exporters are interested in buying wheat at as wide spreads as possible below world prices. Larger operators indeed may resort at times to more or less concerted short selling with a view to temporarily depressing Winnipeg prices, on which farmers' returns are directly based. The Pool, on the other hand, does not have to buy on the exchange, and by selling on it only the smaller part of its holdings, and then only when the market is favorable, it tends to keep prices there both more stable and closer to world values. In so doing it benefits, of course, non-pool farmers as well as its own members.

Controlling, as it does, more than half the wheat reaching Canadian primary markets, the Pool is in a position to realize appreciable savings in its unit marketing costs. For the two years prior to 1928 the overhead expenses of the Central averaged only a fifth of a cent per bushel handled. The volume of its direct shipments, moreover, permits it to charter shipping tonnage on somewhat more advantageous terms than smaller exporters can obtain. For the purpose of chartering space and supervising loading and insuring of cargoes, the Pool maintains offices at the head of the Lakes and at Vancouver, Montreal and New York.

Since the Canadian Pool cannot exercise any control over the volume of wheat production, and since it must sell whatever supply is delivered by its members in competition with the surplus wheat crops of the world, it is not in a position to determine the ultimate price, as evidenced by the marked decline in wheat quotations beginning in July and August, 1928. What it can do, however, is to adjust its day-to-day sales to demand conditions, based on the fullest attainable market information, and to secure for its members an averaged participation in the actual prices obtainable in final markets. Possessing an assured supply, without having to purchase it outright or hedge its deliveries, it is in a position to hold off the market when prices are temporarily weak and to sell freely when demand is stronger.

The Wheat Pool does not buy grain; it acts as unrestricted selling agents for the growers, securing for its members the average price of wheat for the year. The Pool borrows money from the banks at 6%, giving as security the warehouse receipts of wheat as delivered. An initial payment is made to the growers for wheat delivered at a margin of at least from 15% to 20% below prevailing market quotations; this arrangement has been acceptable to the banks which lend the funds. Further payments are made to the growers as the wheat is disposed of, and, as the selling price of the entire crop becomes determined, final payment is made.

In order to discover the advantages to the grower of the ordinary method of selling wheat over the pool arrangement, representatives of the grain trade outside the Pool added together the daily closing quotations of wheat and divided the sum by the number of days. These figures show a substantial advance over the ultimate price paid pool members. The Pool management pointed out that these calculations ignored the fact that the volume of grain sold at different times of the year varied considerably and that no consideration was given the cost of storing, insurance, and interest charges which amounted approximately to 1½ cents a bushel per month.

In private marketing of grain it has always been regarded as necessary to "hedge" daily on the volume of that day's purchases. Since banks must supply most of the cash for such transactions, they hold as security not only bills of lading but also the certificates of the hedges. This protection involves financial operations requiring great skill and expensive technique. The Canadian Wheat Pool does not hedge any part of its huge holdings. The question arises whether hedging would be desirable to overcome a possible price disadvantage incurred by those growers who belong to the Pool.

The position of the Pool is that one of the underlying principles of the Pool is to secure for the members the average price for the year. They feel that if they were to hedge their receipts in the future market they would derive no benefit from possible higher prices later on in the year— the hedging pressure would tend to depress values. By distributing the risk of fluctuating market values over 150,000 farmers, the Pool members are alleged in effect to carry their own insurance against low prices and at the same time receive the benefits of rising prices.

One of the most spectacular achievements of the Canadian wheat pools has been their building-up of the world's largest unified elevator system within the space of a few years. At the outset the pools were entirely dependent on handling contracts with the cooperative and private-line elevator companies. Experience early demonstrated, however, the desirability of acquiring their own country as well as terminal elevators. One of the impelling considerations was the advantage of having permanent representatives at local shipping points in the form of pool-elevator operators who could deal directly with members and look after both their personal interests and those of the pool headquarters in a way that the agents of contracting, and at the same time competing, companies could not be expected to do. It was also felt that a system of pool elevators would permit a better-controlled flow of pool grain to terminals and increase growers' net returns by reducing handling costs.

Acting under these considerations, the pools began in 1925 to build or buy elevators at points not served by either the Saskatchewan "Co-op" or the United Grain Growers. Extended negotiations were carried on at this time between the pools and the farmers' companies for the acquisition of the elevator facilities of the latter, with a view to establishing one unified, farmer-owned grain-handling and marketing system. An agreement was finally reached for the sale of the 451 country elevators and the four big terminals of the "Co-op" to the Saskatchewan Pool at an arbitrated price of $11,059,310. A joint offer of the three pools to purchase the elevator system of the United Grain Growers was rejected by the shareholders of the latter, however, primarily on the ground that it was desirable to preserve its facilities for the use of farmers who did not see fit to sign pool contracts, as well as for members. Meanwhile the pools extended their system until at the end of 1927 they had 937 country elevators in operation in three provinces, equivalent to nearly one-half of all those licensed in Western Canada. Some 200 more were in process of being added in 1928. At the head of the Lakes, at Buffalo, and on the Pacific coast the pools in 1928 controlled eleven terminal elevators, having a combined capacity of 32,500,000 bushels.

The financing of this immense program of elevator acquisition, involving an investment of nearly $20,000,000, has been accomplished without any government loans or bond issues. It has been financed entirely by the unique method of deducting a maximum of 2 cents a bushel on elevator-reserve account from each member's final annual payment. The cumulative magnitude of these seemingly minute deductions has been a revelation in cooperative finance. While the system reduces the member's direct cash returns from his crop, it constitutes a form of contractual investment, since he is allowed 6% interest on the amount of his elevator-reserve deductions, payable out of elevator revenue. Thus the grower's investment interest rises automatically and proportionately to the amount of his pool deliveries. Not only is all the interest paid on account of capital invested in pool elevators thus distributed to farmers, but the net earnings of these elevators also accrue to members on a patronage-dividend basis. For the year 1926–27 the surplus earnings of the Saskatchewan Pool country and terminal elevators amounted to $1,375,000, equivalent to a rebate of 1¾ cents a bushel on all grain delivered. Expectations held in certain quarters of the Pool's power to control prices have not been realized, it is true, and there are many farmers who prefer to retain their individual freedom of marketing rather than commit themselves to pool contracts. Three out of five prairie-grain growers, however, are satisfied that while the Pool cannot of itself create prosperity, it does insure that its members can count on receiving all that consumers will pay for their product, less the actual cost of getting it to them.

Since these initial activities, the difficulties facing wheat growers have increased. Last year the extraordinarily large harvests of Germany and France were adverse to American growers, the Argentine and Australian crops added to the difficulty, and the increasing supplies from Russia are menacing more because of their uncertainty than because of their size. In the meantime, Continental and British millers have delayed purchases as long as possible, hoping for even further price drops. In spite of the early endeavors of the Canadian growers to avoid governmental interference, they have had to accept the aid of the provincial governments of Manitoba, Saskatchewan and Alberta, and are looking hopefully toward the Dominion Government for help. The banks are beginning to feel the pressure of the pool policy of advancing $1 per bushel on wheat while the banks attempt to keep credit extensions down to 85% of the value of the wheat. And most menacing of all is the precarious position of certain independent elevators, with the prospect of still further unloading of wheat on an over-supplied market.

Although attempts at pegging prices were the more direct methods employed by the various industries already mentioned, curtailment of production was also involved; in either case the great dangers of an inelastic buying power, of substitutes, and of consumer hostility are met with. And although, in most cases, the method employed has been that of government fiat rather than trade agreement, the results are much the same, and in most cases the government action was supported by the trade.

For several years prior to 1902 the price trend of #7 Brazilian coffee[14] had been downward; at that time the low price of 30 francs for 50 kilograms was reached, which was generally admitted to have been below the cost of production. During this period of declining prices various private as well as governmental plans had been considered as a means of furnishing relief to the coffee-plantation owners. The plans suggested had varied all the way from government purchase and sale to the actual destruction of the coffee by burning or by dumping it into the Atlantic Ocean. None of these plans, however, was adopted. Coffee plantations deteriorated, and the revenues of three Brazilian

[14] This statement is abridged from a case prepared by Professor J. A. De Haas. See also *The Annalist*, October 25, 1929, article by George E. Anderson.

states in which the majority of the coffee plantations were located became seriously affected. In 1906 and 1907 Brazil unexpectedly produced a "bumper" crop of coffee, estimated production at that time being 20,190,000 bags. Demand was estimated at about 17,108,000 bags. The result on prices, if this flood of coffee had reached the market would have been disastrous, so the Cabinets and Representatives of Sao Paulo, Rio de Janeiro and Minas Geraes conferred to arrange an emergency relief plan. From this conference the first coffee valorization plan was evolved. Its proponents hailed it as a notable display of economic foresight, while opponents condemned it as an unexampled attempt to form a world monopoly of a staple product.

At the time this valorization plan was adopted, Brazil was producing about 80% of the world's supply of coffee, and Venezuela, Mexico and Hawaii the major part of the remaining 20% of world produce. Coffee plantations in all of these countries became of importance, from a production point of view, the fourth and fifth years after planting.

Proponents of a relief plan believed that a "bumper" crop generally was followed by two or three short crops which would permit the adoption of a plan for the purchase of the crop surplus in years of big production and of distributing it slowly over the years when the production of coffee had been low. Because the consumption of coffee varied little from year to year, it was hoped that a control plan for the carrying of coffee over a period of years would be successful.

A coffee valorization plan was adopted before the 1906–1907 "bumper" crop reached the market. The state of Sao Paulo started buying coffee with the proceeds of loans issued from banks in New York and London. By 1908 the state had purchased and stored 8,475,000 bags of coffee; the price in the intervening period had risen from seven to twelve francs per bag of 50 kilos. Attempts from time to time to unload the large accumulated stock met with little success, however, and it was not until 1908 that the Government succeeded in lowering the stock to approximately 3,000,000 bags. At that time the state showed a large unrealized profit on its stock of coffee. Differences of opinion still existed in all coffee centers concerning the success of the plan. Many argued that the artificial inflation of prices would prove to be fictitious and ephemeral.

In 1906 the "Convention of Taubate" in substance provided that the states of Brazil maintain the minimum price of 55 to 65 gold francs per bag of 60 kilos for American type #7, the first year; other types and prices for later years were scheduled in relation to this base type price. The enforcement method consisted in an embargo on exports and credit arrangements under the jurisdiction of the Brazilian states affected— Rio de Janeiro, Minas Geraes, and Sao Paulo.

In 1911 members of the coffee trade forecast a serious shortage of coffee. At the time the forecast was made, the American Government as well as the public was much interested in curbing national trusts. The American public consumed about 40% of all coffee used at that time in the world. The combination of these different situations focused the attention of the Department of Justice of the United States on the Brazilian coffee-valorization plan.

The only good points in the plan, from the standpoint of the American public, were possibly the two following:

(1) It steadied the market and prevented useless, reckless speculation. Whether the steadying and fixing of the market was a good thing is a question. The theory in this country is that the market should be open and unsteady, inviting free and open competition . . .

(2) It has probably improved the average quality of coffee.

The net result of valorization in 1918 appeared to be:

1. Large profits to the financiers.

2. Some net profits to planters.

3. None to the state: rather a loss because of the amount of revenue . . . and while the state's coffee was going up in price yet it was probable that the interest, storage and commission charges would eat that up before the end of the valorization scheme January 1, 1919.

4. The addition and piling-up of all of these costs and advances on the coffee consumers.

5. The restraint in trade caused by the carrying-out of the plan.

6. The enhancement of the price of the great article of common use imported chiefly from Brazil—coffee.

There was substantial restraint, and an attempt to enhance the price:

1. By curtailment of production.

2. By systematically engaging in a campaign at big expense to make an increased demand in the face of restricted production.

3. By restraining exportation from Brazil under a heavy export tax.

4. By restraining exportation from Brazil by a levy of an extra tax on all exports over a given quantity.

5. By holding the valorized coffee out of the open market.

6. By holding coffee even when the price was above the declared government maximum price . . . [15]

The Government on May 18, 1912, filed suit against the agents of the valorization plan which had been in operation from 1907 to that time. The Government based its suit on the fact that the syndicate had been holding back from the American market large quantities of Brazilian coffee and had been selling its holdings only at set and arbitrary prices. The complaint particularly stressed the point of the contract between the bank syndicate and the Brazilian Government, providing for minimum sales and minimum prices at the sales or auctions of the syndicate, the equivalent being 14 cents and 15 cents per pound in the

---

[15] *Senate Document* 36, 63d Congress, 1st Session, Volume 6535.

United States, whereas the prices during the seasons preceding the adoption of the valorization plan had been much lower.

During 1912 the Department of Justice and the Brazilian Government reached an agreement whereby the entire stock of so-called valorization coffee held in New York amounting to 951,000 bags and valued at approximately $77,000,000 was to be sold to jobbers and roasters throughout the country. In consideration for this, the Department of Justice withdrew its suit to break up what was termed the "coffee monopoly." There were still left, however, 3,300,000 bags of Brazilian coffee stored in European countries, which formed collateral for the Sao Paulo bonds that had been issued to provide the fund to keep the coffee from the market in order that prices might not be depressed.

The following announcement appeared in the July 3, 1913, issue of the *New York Times*.

Retiring Sao Paulo Bonds

The action of the Stock List Committee in ordering yesterday an end to trading in 5% bonds of the State of Sao Paulo reflected in a way the operations of Brazil's coffee-valorization plan. The bonds, $20,000,000 of them, were ordered to be retired recently following the liquidation of the security back of them. This security was coffee. The bonds were part of the series issued in 1906 to finance the accumulation of thousands of bags of coffee, and provision was made for them to be paid off from time to time as the valorization committee decided. The amount listed on the local stock exchange was originally $35,000,000 to mature in 1919 . . . except for such as should be retired under the provisions mentioned.

The outbreak of the World War disorganized completely the European coffee market and, in 1915, it became necessary for the Brazilian Government to adopt a new scheme of valorization based to some extent on a large issue of paper money.

Because of an exceedingly short crop in 1918 and 1919, the coffee stored was sold under favorable conditions. With funds thus secured the State of Sao Paulo repaid the Brazilian government the entire sum advanced plus its share of the proceeds. In 1920–21 there was another "bumper" crop; this time a loan of £9,000,000 was secured in London and 4,500,000 bags of coffee were purchased. Again the surplus was marketed successfully and the loan liquidated.

In 1922 the establishment of a plan for a permanent defense of coffee was authorized by act of the Brazilian National Congress. In 1924 the entire organization which had been established under the Federal Government régime was taken over by the State of Sao Paulo, and an organization called "Institute for the Permanent Defense of Coffee" was organized. On the board of this Institute were individuals selected from the commercial and agricultural groups, and also the Secretary of Agriculture and the Secretary of Finance of the State of Sao Paulo. A great deal of power rested in the hands of the Secretary of

Finance by provision of the law which gave him veto power over any acts adopted by the Institute. Much dissatisfaction existed in the coffee trade with the plans carried out by the Institute. Consequently in 1926, a new law was passed which placed the control of the coffee trade under the exclusive control of the Secretary of Finance. This still was unsatisfactory, and finally on December 14, 1927, the Federal Government of Brazil took over the exclusive control of the defense of coffee.

In 1927, there were two chief ways in which the defense committee supported the price of Brazilian coffee.

1. It limited the quantity of coffee sent daily to the Brazilian ports for export.

2. It supported the market price of coffee by buying coffee futures on the Santos Bolsa.

At the beginning of 1927, stocks in the interior amounted to approximately 5,000,000 bags; by the end of the year this amount had increased to 13,000,000 bags. During 1928 there was no appreciable change in interior stocks, but by the end of 1929, this amount had increased to approximately 18,000,000 bags. The stocks in ports were maintained during this entire time at about 1,000,000 bags. In the meantime, coffee groves elsewhere were beginning to bear, about five years being required for crop-bearing trees to mature. Coffee prices were falling throughout the last quarter of 1929 and first quarter of 1930.

Inasmuch as approximately $7.20 per bag is the amount at which the Institute is attempting to finance coffee, the difficulty of financing the carry-over becomes apparent. To finance themselves for a period of two years, the growers would need some $300,000,000, and a good or bumper crop in the meantime would require that much more. The fact that coffee is the chief crop of so large a territory makes the situation a precarious one indeed.

Limiting Production in Manufacturing

The failures which have conspicuously marked attempts at limitation of production of raw materials have directed attention to the possibility of limitations in the course of storage, transportation or fabrication of materials. Goods in transit present little opportunity for any such program, especially in view of the fact that increased railroad operating efficiency in recent years has reduced the amount of goods in transit appreciably. Storage has been employed as a method of dealing with the situation, especially in connection with grains. The storage facilities of the Canadian Wheat Pool have increased greatly in the last few years. Attempts on the part of the United States Federal Farm

Bureau and farmers' cooperatives to encourage the storage of wheat, corn and wool on individual farms, at least during periods of market excess, have contributed incalculably toward smoothing the curve of supply. These products are bonded, the bins and elevators are locked and sealed, and an advance payment is made to the grower with warehouse receipts or bond certificates as collateral. The method is as old as the days of Joseph and Pharaoh, with few apparent improvements. The stakes are sufficiently large and precarious to warrant calling the method a gamble. And yet some such procedure is necessary if the raw-material market is to be stabilized; and without stabilization the grower will have to face periodic crises.

In the fabrication level, oil and cotton have been most conspicuous among the products in which limitation of production has been attempted. But it must be remembered that every success in the limitation of production in the fabrication stage throws just that much more of a burden on the raw-material field. This is as it should be, because blind and unrestrained production, without reference to the demand, is the root of the difficulty. If those interested in raw materials cannot appreciate the fact now, they will have to do so in an even more intensive fashion when the fabricators learn to gauge their production to consumer demands.

In the cotton-textile industry an annual production capacity of 9,000,000,000 yards is to be contrasted with actual shipments of 8,000,-000,000 yards, showing an excess capacity of over 12%.[16] The annual consumption of cloth in the United States is approximately $8\frac{1}{2}$ billion yards, with an annual increase in recent years of approximately 150,000,-000 yards, although annual fluctuations may amount to many times that figure. The difference between domestic demand and shipments is made up by the excess of imports over exports. But even so, actual annual production has amounted to approximately $8\frac{1}{5}$ billion yards, an excess over shipments of over 2%, a figure which may appear small, but which is sufficiently large to cause much of the trouble in the industry.

Concerted efforts at limitation of production are forbidden by law. That limitation has taken place, either through voluntary restriction or through market necessities, is evidenced by the fact that for the last five years there has been a net decline of approximately 700,000 spindles in operation each year. Inasmuch as "active" spindles are a more

[16] See statements of Leavelle McCampbell, Association of Cotton Textile Merchants of New York, June 3, 1930.

significant index of the situation than "existing" spindles, and since the recent development of full day-and-night schedules has tended to double the production of "active" spindles, the best index figure is that of "active spindle hours." The Bureau of the Census gives the following figures (in billions of spindle hours) for the years ending July 31:

1922	89.3	1926	93.9
1923	101.9	1927	102.6
1924	84.4	1928	96.5
1925	91.1	1929	99.6

Some of this increase in spindle hours in recent years is undoubtedly due to operating in double shifts, inasmuch as the running time in hours per active spindle has gradually increased from 1924 on at the rate of approximately 120 hours per spindle per year. The support of humane labor laws by the selfish interests of industry is interesting. The industry, especially through the Cotton Textile Institute, has now begun vigorously to sponsor programs of shorter working hours, especially for women and at night.[17]

This program involves not only an attempt to secure the enforcement of existing laws limiting hours of work, but also to secure additional legislation along the same line. Labor may well rub its eyes at the spectacle of industrial leaders sponsoring a limitation of working hours, especially if there is no curtailment or relative curtailment of wages. It is a phenomenon that is to be matched only by the endeavor of our large bankers to secure a reduction in tariff rates, and similar in its significance. Not only have the ramifications of American business assumed extraordinary and intricate proportions, but the consciousness of the full significance of business policies has apparently kept pace with the growth of American business.

The General Problem of Limitation of Production

The limitation of production, whether in the raw-material or fabrication stage, seems to be a necessity to the health of an industry or a trade. Its menace is no longer feared as a means of creating a shortage or of increasing prices, because the economic penalties of a misguided or extreme policy are even greater than are signified by existing legal restraints. These economic

[17] See "The Cotton Textile Institute," by Edward S. Mead, *The Annalist*, October 4, 1929.

penalties, especially of subsequent overproduction or of the encouragement of substitutes or of the loss of consumer goodwill, are unfortunately too often delayed so long as to give unscrupulous or unintelligent producers an opportunity temporarily and individually to gain at the expense of the permanent soundness of the industry. The hopeful phase of the situation is that such conditions arise more probably as the result of a lack of intelligence rather than from the baser motives. Hence there is an opportunity for the trade intelligently to handle the situation.

The Bureau of Agriculture has, through its representatives, warned fruit growers against unrestricted production, and is even going so far as to point out the inadequacies of local restrictions, *e.g.*, in the control of the citrus industry by California alone. For even where a state such as California contributes over 40% of the total carload shipments of fresh fruits and 15% of the carload shipments of vegetables, cooperation with the growers in other parts of the country is necessary.[18] Foreign countries are not subject to anti-trust laws even in non-agricultural industries, hence their methods may be much more direct than would be permitted here. The newsprint manufacturers of Ontario and Quebec agreed to production schedules of approximately 80% of capacity; in Canada, even agreements as to minimum prices are not taboo. The British Tin Producers' Association recently agreed that smelters hold back about 10% of the ore delivered to them, the Association agreeing to compensate them temporarily for ore not smelted, while the metal to be marketed was to be sold at a price to be determined by agreement between the smelters and the Association. A comprehensive international scheme for the regulation of supply to consumption was also to be prepared, in which the cooperation of the Dutch and Bolivian interests was to be invited.

It would be strange indeed, and yet it seems quite within the realm of probability, if economic considerations are discovered after all to be more potent arguments than legal restrictions in avoiding excessive programs of limitation and of price-fixing. The European cartel has been conspicuously unsuccessful— whether because badly planned or because voluntary agreements, paradoxically sanctioned by governmental intervention, are not adhered to, it is difficult to say. The ability of American

[18] Speech of Nils A. Olsen, December 4, 1928, before Fruit Growers' and Farmers' Convention, Riverside, California.

producers to cooperate in such matters[19] has not been fully tested since the enactment of the Sherman Law; instances in which the agreements have been effective have either remained secret or have been stopped by the courts. But the circumstantial evidence points in the direction of a greater degree of ability along the line of production control here than has been evidenced abroad. It may easily be that intelligent planning of production by an industry would keep well within the limits of what would be regarded socially and legally as a sufficient supply of goods and a fair schedule of prices. In the meantime the practical method for achieving this end in the United States must be sought in each industry by the voluntary reactions of individual producers to the trade situation as disclosed by such figures as the trade is able to secure. The sponsoring of a cartel system by our Government would perhaps be disastrous, and even more unwelcome to business than have been governmental restrictions on methods that are necessary to business health and social well-being.

Limitation of production, a method generally associated with the dangerous features of monopoly control or of trade agreements, and more recently identified with governmental policies, no longer can be judged as a purely social-consumer menace operating for the benefit of business alone. Experience has shown that it carries its own penalties, that business itself suffers most severely from the effects of its abuse and that only the most intelligent business policies will avoid its cataclysmic results. This is a situation which challenges indeed our much-vaunted social or business intelligence. Society and law have been preventing business from engaging in activities that supposedly affect the customer-consumer adversely. The relation between this class of persons and the producer has too frequently, however, been assumed to involve only one ethical obligation: that of the latter to the former. Recent experiences in connection with the limitation of production would seem to indicate that a growing awareness, by business men, of the dangers of excessive and unwise policies of limitation provides a sufficient check against unfairness to the consumer to obviate most of the fears the latter may have of the consequences of limitation on price. Especially is this true where the limitation is the result of individual volition on the part of independent producers. Business, and not artificial, competition and the law of chance are sufficient checks

[19] See Chapter III, 76 ff.

on intelligent attempts to provide the necessary adjustments. And any marginal or residual problems can certainly be left to their determination by the buyer and seller—otherwise a free market price would be denied to both.

The chief point in the problem of limitation of production consists in shifting a part of attention away from the concern for the consumer to a concern for the trade health of the producers. Intelligent control of production, on the part of producers, is as much an ethical right as is that of the consumer to an abundance of goods at low prices. The producer's right can best be safeguarded by his avoiding the two extremes: under- and overproduction. The former has the more disastrous if less appreciated effect on business, for the resulting price increases encourage undue expansion and invasion of the market by others. Although business men are more fully aware of this fact than is the general public, it must be recognized even more generally by both; otherwise, society will act through the law to control the situation. The other extreme, overproduction, can best be overcome by an intelligent recognition of the problem and by the courage to insist on the proper method of handling it. These requirements consist largely and practically in an intelligent control of inventory and of sales promotion among individual distributors, and the employment of statistical figures by the seller to a degree commensurate with the use of such figures by intelligent buyers. Until recently, business men have shown little evidence of either requirement, and many a trade association, formed for this very purpose, has allowed its chief and most valuable function not only to lapse into "innocuous desuetude" but also actually to become an additional and powerful weapon in the hands of the buyer.

CHAPTER XX

COMMERCIAL ARBITRATION

Advantages over Legal Settlements

As a method of adjusting business disputes, commercial arbitration has three conspicuous advantages over proceedings in the law courts: speed, economy, and the due recognition of trade practices. The delays attending legal suits, no matter how much they may be explained by lawyers and judges, generally practically prohibit the use of the courts by business men; almost always because time is of the essence in settling disputes involving a market of changing prices, and especially where it would be necessary to hold perishable commodities pending the decision of a case. The expenses of court litigation are no less deterrent: not only do such expenses frequently largely neutralize any awards made to the successful litigant, but many cases involving minor amounts cannot economically be brought to the courts at all for adjustment; but they can be economically settled in a court of arbitration. And the time and trouble involved in litigation are frequently more "expensive" than the money outlays.

The most important factor, however, which renders court decisions in business cases undesirable, is that the judge is an amateur as regards business problems, just as the business man is an amateur as regards the law. The result of such a situation is that business issues become lost in legal technicalities, a difficulty which can be avoided by placing the matter before a board of business men who are acquainted with prevailing trade practices. An engineer, for example, may be much better qualified than a judge to render a decision on a dispute involving purely technical matters.[1]

No one would refer a shipping dispute to a person who is not quite certain how a charter-party differs from a tea-party, and the law courts, therefore,

---

[1] See *Metropolitan Tunnel & Public Works, Ltd. v. London Electric Ry. Co.* (1926) 1 Ch. 371. See also *Bristol Corporation v. John Aird and Co.*, 1913 A.C. 241.

have to defer the really essential points of a commercial dispute to commercial men who are brought with much trouble and expense into the witness box; and after their expert evidence (which in legal circles is looked upon as the intensest form of terminological inexactitude) has been duly discredited, the dispute is settled on legal-technical grounds which neither of the parties to the quarrel is able to understand.[2]

The method of selecting judges and juries in our legal system, largely on the ground of their disinterestedness and ignorance of the issues, respectively, is a principle of legal procedure that has evolved out of exactly the opposite method: judge and jury and advocates were originally, in the early days of legal development, not distinct, and judgment was rendered by those who knew most about the situation from personal acquaintance with the litigants and the circumstances of the case.[3] We are not here concerned with the legal or social principles which led to a differentiation and complete reversal of procedure; as regards business disputes, however, commercial-arbitration procedure follows very closely the earlier method of trial[4] and can employ such methods to better effect than the methods of modern legal procedure.

It might appear that the facility with which commercial arbitration is handled might be conducive to more disputes, but experience does not bear out this fear.   Business experience in England has there led men to believe that a man who would not hesitate to take a dispute to court to be decided by a jury of non-technical men will often, realizing that he does not have a just claim, be reluctant to go before an arbitration tribunal where the case will be decided by men who are experts in the field within which the case falls.   Certain technical explanations which would be barred from court proceedings are not only admitted but expected.   Each one of the disputing parties presents his case to men who are fully capable of understanding the exact point at issue.   This is bound to reduce disputes to those which really involve a debatable point.   And while

[2] *London Chamber of Commerce Journal*, 1928.   Statement by W. J. Clark, Secretary of the Dried Fruit Trade Association, 98 Great Tower Street, London, E.C. 3.

[3] See Starkie, Thomas, *Trial by Jury*, II *Law Review and Quarterly Journal of British and Foreign Jurisprudence*, 370.   Reprinted, Boston, 1880.

[4] An arbitrator may even be called as a witness before an umpire reviewing the same case after it had not been accepted.   *Bourgeois v. Weddell & Co.* (1924) 1 K.B. 539.

commercial arbitration probably does increase the number of *hearings* of disputes—that indeed is its function—this should not be confused with the possibility of increasing the number of *disputes* themselves.

The New York Credit Men's Adjustment Bureau has been unusually successful in settling by "friendly action" hundreds of cases involving bankruptcy. This method observes the spirit of commercial arbitration. Eighty *per cent* of the money realized from the sale of assets of insolvent estates, settled out of court by the Bureau, is received by creditors.[5] Similar results have been achieved in other cities, as disclosed by Colonel William J. Donovan's nation-wide investigation into bankruptcy conditions. One conspicuous success in the Bureau's activities is the large percentage in the recovery of "accounts receivable," which in ordinary bankruptcy administration frequently represents a dead loss. Speed, and the ability to handle small as well as large cases efficiently, are the outstanding procedural virtues of the method.

The International Chamber of Commerce has published brochures[6] on the arbitration laws of Switzerland, Italy, Holland, France and Germany; others are now in preparation for Great Britain, Belgium, Sweden and the United States.

It has been stated that commercial arbitration resembles the early period of law before the various judicial functions had been analyzed and separately established and before procedure had become formalized. It can also be established that law and business arbitration were at one time inseparable. Arbitration clauses were included in contracts prior to 1400, and the guilds were using arbitration at an early period.[7] The *Rôle d'Oléron* and the *Laws of Wisby* regulated the Hansa trade; the *Ordonnances*, the trade of France; while the Levant trade was regulated by Genoan, Venetian and Florentine codes, the latter dealing especially with corporate obligations and contracts. Napoleon's *Code de Commerce* and Lord Mansfield's English *Law Merchant* represent a later stage of this incorporation of the recognized

---

[5] See *Report* of T. C. Billig to the Bureau, November, 1928.

[6] Available at the Paris office of the Chamber and at the offices of the American Arbitration Association, 521 Fifth Avenue, New York.

[7] Julius Henry Cohen, *Commercial Arbitration and the Law*, New York: D. Appleton & Company, 1918. Clarence F. Birdseye, *Arbitration and Business Ethics*, New York: D. Appleton & Company, 1926.

practices among merchants into Civil and Common Law. A history of this development is admirably worked out by Julius Henry Cohen in the book referred to in the footnote.

What is of interest here is the present development of that part of commercial arbitration which is separate and distinct from the law, and the likelihood of its approximating legal methods and procedure as has already happened in the case of the Law Merchant and Equity. It is generally recognized that the Common Law has not met the situation.

History of Arbitration in England

Commercial arbitration was introduced into legal practice by statutory enactment; in England in 1889, and in New York State in 1920. The reason for this tardy recognition of an obviously justifiable business practice is to be found in an early law case, known as *Vynior's Case*, and its subsequent misinterpretation by the courts. The rule, as well as the error, established over three centuries ago, has rested like a blight on all subsequent attempts to establish an independent system of commercial arbitration. The common-law rule was carried over into American jurisprudence, where it followed the history of so much of our legal philosophy by persisting even longer than it did in England itself. The case[8] is sufficiently important to be made a matter of record.

A written bond, dated July 15, 6 Jacob 1 (1609), was evidence that William Wilde owed to Robert Vynior £20, which Vynior claimed was unjustly retained. The bond contained the following condition:

The condition of this obligation is such, that if the above bounden William Wilde do and shall from time to time, and at all times hereafter, stand to, abide, observe, perform, fulfill, and keep, the rule, order, judgment, arbitrament, sentence, and final determination of William Rugge, Esq., arbitrator indifferently named, elected, and chosen as well of the part and behalf of the said W. Wilde, as of the part and behalf of the above-named Robert Vynior, to rule, order, adjudge, arbitrate, and finally determine, all matters, suits, controversies, debates, griefs, and contentions heretofore moved and stirred, and now depending between the said parties, touching or concerning the sum of two and twenty pence, heretofore taxed upon the said W. Wilde, for divers kinds of parish business within the said parish of Thermilthorpe; so as the said award be made and set down in writing, under the hand and seal of the said William Rugge at or before the feast of St. Michael the Archangel next ensuing after the date of these presents, that then this

[8] VIII *Coke's Reports*, pp. 80ff.; Trin. 7 Jac. 1 Rot. 2629.

present obligation to be void and of no effect, or else the same to stand, abide, remain, and be in full force, power, strength, and virtue.

Vynior in due course of time asked for judgment, *i.e.*, the payment of his debt and damages. Wilde demurred that Vynior's plea was insufficient and that Vynior be barred from action. Wilde's plea was that the arbitrator had made no award, within the time and according to the conditions specified; "whereupon he prayeth judgment if the aforesaid Robert ought to have his action aforesaid against him, *etc.*" In answer, Vynior submitted that Wilde, on August 22 (*i.e.*, before the feast of St. Michael) "revoked and did call back all the authority whatsoever" he had given Rugge, the arbitrator, "and then altogether disallowed and held void, and all and whatsoever the aforesaid William Rugge . . . should do to (for) him in and about the said arbitrament . . ."

Judgment was awarded Vynior, but the court argued the case in such a way as to jeopardize for centuries the value of commercial arbitration. The court held that Wilde might countermand the agreement to abide an arbitrament,[9] on the ground that "a man cannot by his act make such authority, power, or warrant not countermandable, which is by law and of its own nature countermandable." The court pointed out two analogies: "If I assign auditors to take an account . . . " and "If I make one my factor . . . ," and drew therefrom its conclusion. It is, of course, difficult to see how the court could isolate the provision for an arbitrator from the other parts of the contract—*e.g.*, the obligation to pay!—and assert that such a factor was *contra vires*. What probably happened was that the court sensed the possibility of a loss of legal power of the courts to arbitrators, a feeling that may have been justified by the relative lack of responsibility of the latter to the social sanctions which basically controlled the courts. However, the precedent was set, that an arbitration clause in a contract was revocable, thus practically making it void.

As for the rest of the case, the court was, of course, not so silly as to tolerate Wilde's plea; by the countermand the bond was declared forfeit. What is most interesting, however, is that in the argument of the court on this point there is discoverable evidence that the court did not intend the strict interpretation, previously given, to become the precedent. The obligee shall

[9] Citing *Clapham v. Higham*, 1 Bing. 89 S. C. 7 B. Moore 403; also, *Milne v. Greatrix*, 7 East. 611, and *Marsh v. Bulteel*, 5 Barn. and Ald. 507 S. C. 1 Dow. and Ryl. 106, S. C. 2 Chit. 317.

take benefit of the bond, argued the court, because the obligor had broken the words of the condition—"to abide"—"which words were put in such conditions, to the intent that there should be no countermand, *but that an end should be made, by the arbitrator*,[10] of the controversy, and that the power of the arbitrator should continue until he had made an award; and when the award is made, then there are words to compel the parties to perform it . . . " The recognition by the court of the validity of commercial arbitration is inescapable. The implications to that effect continue, furthermore, in the remainder of the court's argument. "The obligor has by his own act made the conditions of the bond (which was endorsed for the benefit of the obligor, to save him from the penalty of the bond) impossible to be performed, and by consequence his bond is become single, and without the benefit or help of any condition, because he has disabled himself to perform the condition." The further analogy then follows: "If one be bound in a bond, with condition that the obligor shall give leave to the obligee for the space of seven years to carry wood, *etc.*, in that case, although he give him leave, yet if he countermands it, or disturbs the obligee, the bond is forfeited." Certainly this analogy is no less strong than the direct observation of the irrevocable nature of the payment of the bond itself.

In spite of the Gordian knot with which commercial arbitration was bound, by virtue of the fact that the strict construction of a part of the judgment in Vynior's case became precedent, the Alexandrine function of statutory legislation was available, however tardy its use. The case well exemplifies the extremities to which the legal control of business may go, and unfortunately it is not to the credit of the law itself that legislation should have had to serve as a corrective in this situation. The practical effect of this exercise of the "dead hand of precedent" has been twofold: to make statutory enactment the basis for legal cognizance of commercial arbitration in both England and America, and, especially in the United States, to encourage the development of a completely independent extra-legal system of commercial arbitration.

[10] Italics mine. This phrase describes one of the most important attributes of arbitration. The case is now being followed on the basis of Brownlow and Goldesborough's *Reports* (1675), 62 and 290; in the latter citation the case is reported under "*Vivion*" *against Wilde*, an error which until recently prevented identifying the case.

The Tribunal of Arbitration of the Manchester, England, Chamber of Commerce has had almost half a century of successful experience. The following forms will indicate to some extent the method followed:

TRIBUNAL OF ARBITRATION
OF THE
MANCHESTER CHAMBER OF COMMERCE.

To the REGISTRAR,

89, *Fountain Street,*

Manchester.

Strike out the words which are inapplicable.

$\frac{I}{We}$ hereby apply for the hearing and determination by the Tribunal of a case between $\frac{myself}{ourselves}$ and whose address is

The dispute $\frac{arises}{does\ not\ arise}$ under a Contract or other instrument in writing which contains a submission to arbitration by the Tribunal of Arbitration or a Court thereof, or by the Manchester Chamber of Commerce. The document is dated the and a copy of it is enclosed.

The claim or dispute arises in relation to

Insert: "A sale of " (mentioning the class of goods) or "an order for dyeing," or "an order for calico printing," or "a custom of the trade," or as the case may be.

The quality or condition of goods $\frac{is}{is\ not}$ in question.

Signature--

Address--

Date--

TRIBUNAL OF ARBITRATION
OF THE
MANCHESTER CHAMBER OF COMMERCE.
NOTICE OF APPOINTMENT OF ARBITRATOR

In the matter of an Arbitration between

and

under   made on the

19

which contains a submission to arbitration by the Tribunal or a Court
thereof, or by the Manchester Chamber of Commerce.

I hereby give you notice that upon the application of

a party of the above-mentioned   and in pursuance
of the Rules of the Tribunal, the President of the Manchester Chamber
of Commerce has appointed Mr.   as sole Arbitrator

to constitute a Court of Arbitration for the hearing and determination of
the disputes and differences between the parties.

A concise written Statement of the material facts of the case, and of
the question or questions in issue, should be supplied to me by you in
compliance with the Rules within seven days after the receipt of this
notice.   See notes on the other side.

Due notice will be given to you of the time fixed for the hearing.

Registrar,

89, Fountain Street, Manchester.

19

AN AGREEMENT made the

day of   19

Between

of the one part and

of the other part.

The parties may name their Arbitrator or Arbitrators, or leave the President of the Chamber to make the appointment. WHEREBY they mutually agree to refer to the arbitration and decision of a Court of Arbitration of the Tribunal of Arbitration of the Manchester Chamber of Commerce consisting of*

The unnecessary words must in each case be struck out. or of such person or persons as shall be appointed for the purpose by the President of the Manchester Chamber of Commerce, certain disputes which have arisen and are still subsisting between them, *viz.,*

†*The parties may erase these words.* †and all other matters in difference between them† subject to the Rules for the time being of the Tribunal of Arbitration of the Manchester Chamber of Commerce,‡ except in so far as the same are hereby expressed not to apply or to be varied, *viz.:* Rule shall not apply to this Arbitration.

‡Notice. A copy of the Rules of the Tribunal can be obtained at the Offices of the Chamber, or from the Registrar, 89, Fountain St., at a charge of sixpence, and attention is specially called o Rule 7 (*o*).

As witness the hands of the parties:—

Signed by

in the presence of

Witness's { Signature
            Address
            Occupation

Signed by

in the presence of

Witness's { Signature
            Address
            Occupation

TRIBUNAL OF ARBITRATION OF THE MANCHESTER CHAMBER OF COMMERCE.

THE AWARD made in the matter of an Arbitration between

under   made on the

which contains a submission to Arbitration by this Tribunal

the Arbitrator

in pursuance of the Rules of the Tribunal to constitute a Court of Arbitration for the hearing and determination of the disputes between the above-named parties **Do hereby** make and publish this   Award of and concerning the matters so referred to   having first duly weighed and considered the allegations and evidence of both parties

Arbitration clauses are written into approximately 80% of the contracts made in Manchester; the number and percentage are increasing. Conditions at Manchester encourage as well as necessitate arbitration: the "horizontal organization" of the cotton industry involves a great many transactions between business firms—separate companies doing the spinning, weaving, dyeing and bleaching, printing, warehousing and packing, respectively, while import and export houses are also separate—which would be eliminated by "vertical integration." The mildewing of goods in warehouses or the spoiling of cotton goods by oil gives rise to typical cases, and time is too much of "the essence" in settling disputes to permit the courts to handle such cases.

The whole position of arbitration in England was strengthened by the case of *Collier v. Stevenson*[11] in which the former made a claim which included the loss of profit he suffered by a delay for which the latter company was to blame. The arbitrators included the amount of the lost profit in the award, although they recognized the fact that an important precedent was being established. The case was appealed to the Courts of King's Bench, where the decision was reversed by the judge, who sensed and emphasized the reluctance of the arbitrators to recompense Collier for lost profit. On a further appeal to the Court of Appeals, however, the court sustained the arbitrators' award on the ground that after the interval elapsing between the signing of the contract and its cancellation, a market for disposing of the goods elsewhere was not available. This support of the Manchester tribunal by the court in such an extreme case has encouraged the tribunal to feel that its awards will be generally validated by the courts.

In *Danish Bacon Co., Ltd., v. Food Minister*,[12] a "reasonable profit" allowed by the arbitrator was accepted by the court, although the resulting price was not identical with the market price. It has long been held in England that the decree of an arbitrator on the construction of a contract, if within his powers as designated in the arbitration clause, cannot be set aside by the courts.[13]

[11] About 1925 or 1926, according to information given by the Secretary of the Manchester Chamber of Commerce; I cannot find the case in the reports.

[12] (1922) 91 L. J. K. B. 743.

[13] *Kelantan Government v. Duff Development Co., Ltd.*, 1923 A. C. 395. See also *Re King and Duveen* (1913) 2. K.B. 32, and *Adams v. Great North of Scotland Ry. Co.*, 1891 A. C. 31.

The party who receives an adverse arbitral decision in England must have "stated his case," as regards legal points, before a court within a specified time (usually 14 days) after the case has been submitted to an arbitrator; otherwise he has no redress at law.   On one occasion,[14] when one party threatened to "state his case" if he received an adverse decision, the arbitrator delayed his decision 14 days.   The party refrained from "stating his case" in the meantime, fearing to face the expense of a lawsuit in view of the possibility of his winning the award.   The delayed award was then announced.   This sacrifice of speed in order to effect finality of decision was a questionable procedure, but would probably be employed only in such cases as disclosed a party's hostility to the spirit of arbitration.

The Refined Sugar Association, of London, issues from twenty to forty arbitration awards each year.[15]   Among these decisions are the following:

Sellers are responsible under Rule 87 on c.i.f. contracts for sugar damaged by rain while discharging into lighter.

Demurrage was allowed for sugar sold for delivery f.o.b. first half of month when no vessel was available until the second half of the month.

It is the buyer's duty to obtain the release of bills of lading on c.i.f. contracts.

Type samples of various marks of sugars from various countries are deposited with the Association for reference.   In 1924, the regulation that arbitration samples must be sealed and drawn from not less than five *per cent* of the bags, a regulation which had always been in practice, was officially recorded in a rule (No. 46) of the Association.   Because of trouble encountered with ice during the preceding winter, the Ice Clause was given consideration in 1924 with a view to alteration.   Speed in adjusting the rules and standards of practice in the refined-sugar trade, has been the chief consideration encouraging arbitration in this industry.

Early Developments in America

Commercial arbitration was employed quite early in America. The following letter was found among the "Hancock Manu-

[14] Information supplied by the Secretary of the Manchester Chamber of Commerce.

[15] See *Annual Reports*, issued August 31 from the headquarters of the Association, 39 Great Tower Street, London E.C. 3.

scripts" in the Baker Library of the Harvard Business School. It was written by Thomas Hancock, of Boston, to Messrs. Sword and Bell, of Philadelphia, on August 25, 1762.

Boston Augt. 25th 1762

Gent^n.

I rec^d your fav^r. of June 26 by Capt. Smith with Bill of Lad^g and 50 bb Pork & yr acct Curr^t. am^t. to £258. 3. 4½ for wch. you Drew Bill on Messrs. Kilby a Barnard & in which you did Right.—

I am now to acquaint you that on Recg. the Pork from I opened five $^{\text{or one in ten}}$ Barrells, but Contry. to my Expectation, the Pork Look'd Rotty. I weyd them & ye por fell Short some 10 14 to 20. in a barrell, the weather then was very hott & I did not Care to Expose ye pork to ye Heat $^{\&\ sun}$, so put them into a Cold Cellar till heat of ye weather was a little over, $^{\text{(or you Should have heard of this before)}}$ which did not happen till ye 23^d Inst. when I had every Barrell opened Surveyd & wey'd, by men on oath & I am Sorry to Tell you the pork proves very ordinary, some very Bad & Rusty, well Pack'd, ^{but} in the middle a good Deal of Large salt & short in weight. Inclosed is the Packors Certificate Sworn to, & Acct. of ye Charge attending the Same. which I have Debted you for in acc^t. with the pork short & Two Barrells, Pork, & Two of Cuttings, I propose to Ship to you $^{\text{for first oppy.}}$ in the same Barrells I rec^d them that you may obtain satisfaction of whom you bo^t. them.—

I am very happy in not sendg. this Pork to ye garrison & I assign't it $^{\text{without examination as}}$ I am sure it would have been Condem'd.—

I am sorry for this misfortune but am very Sensible it was not yor. fault but those you bought it of. and that you will bee thot I have Justice done me.—

I am Gent^n.
Your most obed Hble Servt.
(Signed) Thos. Hancock

Messrs. Sword & Bell.
(From *Hancock Mss.*, Baker Library)
Attached to this letter was the following attest.

These Certify whom it may Concern, that we the Subscribers Coopers, & Packers of Provisions in the Town of Boston, have, by the order of The Honble. Thomas Hancock Esqr. Open'd, Weigh'd & Repack'd Fifty Barrells of Pork, which said Hancock inform'd us he Rec'd from Philadelphia in the Sloop Fox Gideon Smith Master, Shipt by Messrs: John Bell & William Sword, some of which was Branded Burlington, but not all—That we Carefully Weigh'd & Survey'd every Barrell Single, that there was but Two Barrells held out weight, & one more weigh'd Two hundred & Thirty four pounds which had in it Twenty four Legs, that there wanted in the whole to make it Fifty Barrells, Two hundred & Twenty pounds to a Barrell, Eight [hundred] & Seventy three pounds, Including the Ears, Hucks of Legs, Snouts & Rust, which were Cutt off, not being Merchantable, which weigh'd Three hundred & Sixty one pounds, & is Included in the Eight hundred & Seventy three pounds, and that the whole of the Fifty Barrels of Pork made out but Forty four Barrells & Seven pounds over, that was Merchantable That there was Four Barrells Loss in Weight & Two Bad makes the Fifty-Vizt-Barrells Pork

44 & 7 good
2   Bad
4   Short of Weight
—
50

Given under our Hands at Boston, this Twenty third day of August 1762

Joshua Pice
Humphry mullans

(*Hancock Mss.*, Baker Library)

A similar situation is indicated in the following letter from Thomas Williams, of Annapolis Royal, to Benjamin Gerrish; a copy also having been sent to Woodford, an Englishman who was acting through Thomas Hancock and furnishing supplies sufficient for 500 rations per day to the English troops. Hancock usually cooperated with the government officials in picking men to survey the Nova Scotia supplies for Woodford.

Annapolis Royal 23 Sept[r] 1762

I yesterday received your Letter of the 11th Instant, in answer to which, I must acquaint you, that I have again Examin'd the bread in store, and am of opinion, that about the 4th. part of it, may be deem'd not fitt for use, but there is no forming an Exact judgement, as the whole lies in bulk, and the good and bad blended together. Another survey being Called, I fear will not only be attended with difficulty, but may perhaps prove a disadvantage to the Contractor for as all Accounts of provisions are gone to England, and in all probability, are Setled agreable to the Valuation put upon the[m], I apprehend it will be no Easy Matter for Mr. Woodford to recover payment from the Treasury for what may be Condemn'd hereafter, however,   I shall be guided Entirely by your determination, and if you think a survey can be Called again, in behalf of the Contractor, with any propriety, I shall make application for one, Accordingly—a new Survey may Condemn Some, that passes Now in the Issues—and as I have found Means of Satisfying the people, by setting aside a small quantity of the Worst, in Serving it on to. I think I may as well Endeavour to make the best of it, which I shall do with as little loss to the Contractor as possible—as we have a large proportion at this place I wrote very pressingly to M^r. Hancock to have some of it Sent to the other Garrisons in order to have it Served out as soon as possible, but he informs me that Cannot be done as they have already their quantity.

I am, &c
Thos Williams

(*Hancock Mss.*, Baker Library)

In these early cases it appears that arbitrators were rarely secured by mutual agreement, the slow methods of communication making it impossible to reach such an agreement in the necessary time; one side picked the men and the other was expected to accept the choice. Where business men were not separated by any great distance, however, it was possible to develop a system of commercial arbitration in which the arbitrator was selected by mutual agreement. Thus, the Chamber of Commerce of the State of New York[16] appointed a committee of arbitration at its first meeting at which it was:

Resolved and Ordered: That the following gentlemen are appointed a Committee, until the first Tuesday in June next, for adjusting any differences between parties agreeing to leave such disputes to this Chamber, and that they do attend on every Tuesday, or oftener, if business require, at such places as they may agree upon, giving notice thereof to the President:

James Jauncey	Samuel Ver Plank
Jacob Walton	Theopy. Bache
Robert Murray	Miles Sherbrooke

The influence of Continental trade practices, especially those current in Holland, which itself was largely interested in maritime trade, is unquestionably indicated by the Dutch names of merchants located in "New Amsterdam." Commercial arbitration is extensively employed today in Holland.[17] The origin of both systems undoubtedly had much in common.

The first meeting of the Arbitration Committee of New York was held May 3, 1768; thereafter, and monthly, for many years the Chamber appointed a Committee of Arbitration. But while the Chamber holds in its archives complete minutes of all its

[16] *Arbitration Records of the Chamber of Commerce of the State of New York, 1779–1792.* Printed by the New York Public Library, 1913.

[17] Cf. *Arbitrale Rechtspraak*, edited by W. Nolen, containing records of cases since 1919. Boekhandel Vh. Gebr. Belianfante, 'S-Gravenhage. Also: W. Nolen, *Handleiding voor Arbiters*, Second Edition, 1927.

regular meetings since the date of its organization, unfortunately it possesses no record of the proceedings of these early arbitration committees, and it was not until comparatively recently that any record was known to be in existence. Several years ago, however, some minutes comprising the period from July 6, 1779, to November 1, 1792, were discovered, in which were recorded disputes regarding shipping matters, especially such as related to the terms of employment of masters and men. The cases tried were often submitted to the Chamber by the police authorities of the city. Inasmuch, however, as such matters are more properly designated "industrial arbitration," we shall indicate merely a few cases of strictly "commercial arbitration."

John Ponsonby agt (against) Thomas Ludlow
The 8th Octo. 1779.

JOHN PONSONBY demands on THOMAS LUDLOW £1106..18..10 the Value of 175 Firkins Butter which he says was sold him in September last.

In answer thereto THOS. LUDLOW asserts he only bought the Butter conditionally in case he liked it when examined, but on examination it did not prove what he expected and told JOHN PONSONBY he would not have it. The Committee on hearing the Assertions from Both parties and on evidence to the bargains prevailed with three Merchants (judges in Irish Butter) to examine the Quality &c. who returnd for answer that the Butter was ordinary and not of the best sort as mentioned in the Bill of Parcels on which J. PONSONBY gave up his demand.

The Committee returnd the following answer to the Police. At the request of the Police The Committee of the Chamber of Commerce took into consideration the dispute between. JOHN PONSONBY and THOMAS LUDLOW. It appeared by evidence that the Butter pretended to be sold THOMAS LUDLOW for the Best Rose Butter (as p JOHN PONSONBYS bill of Parcells) was of an inferior quality on which JOHN PONSONBY gave up the matter in dispute.

Signed by the Committee

George Holmes agt Hugh & Alexander Wallace

Capt. GEORGE HOLMES of the Ship Hope was recommended to the Committee, by the Police for their opinion on Primage on a Bill of lading for Goods shipped at Dublin, addressed to & received by MESSRS HUGH & ALEXR WALLACE the Bill of Lading being filled up in the common way, *Primage & average* accustom'd.

The Committee gave it as their opinion that the custom of this Port did not pay any primage, unless the Sum was specified in the Bill of

Lading, But if any primage was intended by the Shippers tho' neglected being specified, it ought to be paid at Dublin by the Shippers.

22d Octor 1779

John Semple agt Ricd Denniston

RICHARD DENNISTON had sold a quantity of Ozenburgs to JOHN SEMPLE to be delivered sound & Merchantable. the quantity was delivered without any sight of damage and was paid for by JOHN SEMPLE Who delivered them to the order of Coll. CLARKE on whose account he purchased them without a commission.—some Weeks after, when the pieces were opend some of which proved so much damaged as to be unfit for service on which he demanded satisfaction. RICHARD DENNISTON alledged that so long time was elapsed that he had got his Certificate made for the other damage & sent home that by their not being return'd sooner he had lost the benefit of Insurance. The Committee returnd the following answer to the Police.

The Committee of the Chamber of Commerce on examining a dispute between RICHARD DENNISTON and JOHN SEMPLE are of opinion that MR. SEMPLE ought to return the damaged oznaburgs to MR. DENNISTON he repaying the money.

We recommend to MR. DENNISTON to apply to the Port Wardens for a new Certificate for the damaged pieces which they ought to give gratis as they overlooked the damage in their first examination.

30th Octor 1779

William Maddock & Isaac Burk agt Peter Alexr Allaire & John Mott

The Commandant referred to the Committee a memorial of WM MADDOCK & ISAAC BURK against PETER ALEXR ALAIR & JOHN MOTT.

JOHN MOTT lent a mare (the property of MADDOCK & BURK) to PETER ALEXR ALLAIR to go in a chair to Kingsbridge.—The mare could not perform and was left by Capt. ALAIR on the way under the care of a Soldier which mare at his return was not to be found She was lent by MOTT contrary to the order of the owner after examining all parties & evidence the Committee gave the following answer.

The Committee of the Chamber of Commerce having at the request of the Commandant taken into consideration the dispute between WM MADDOCK, ISAAC BURK and PETER ALEXR ALAIR & JOHN MOTT. are of opinion that PETER ALEXR ALAIR pay to WM. MADDOCK & ISAAC BURK Ten Pounds for a mare lost in the service of the said ALAIR, and that the said WM. MADDOCK & ISAAC BURK should allow PETER ALEXR ALAIR one pound being the hire he received for the said mare, and that JOHN MOTT should allow PETER ALEXR ALAIR one pound eighteen for his expences in taking care of the Horse & hiring another.

Price & Salmon Agt Ben: Davies

PRICE & SALMON demand payment of £1000 being the Proceeds of sum goods & Effects left in the hands of MR DAVIES by COLBORN BARRILL to secure the Sum of £1000 Sterling to MESSRS PRICE & SALMON as Attorneys for BROUGH MALTBY & SON—

2d July 1781

MR DAVIES says the Goods are not Yet Sold, and that he has directions from MR BARRILL not to push a Sale to his dissadvantage

The Committee report as their opinion the MR DAVIES should give PRICE & SALMON good Bills for £294..14—Sterling within 21 days from this date, being the Amount of Goods Sold that he should be allowed Two Months to finish the Sale, but should any remain unsold at the expiration of that time that they should be sent to Vendue, that he should not sell the goods on Credit but account for them as soon as sold—and pay the Proceeds of those sold at Vendue as soon as the sales are completed

That MR DAVIES should account for so much of the other effects left in his hands by MR BARRILL, as will with the Proceeds of the goods, make up the £1000 Sterling, within Three Months from this date—provided the goods & other Effects amount to that Sum after paying the necessary expences—

Statutory Developments in America

Because of the early date of the establishment of the Chamber, and because of the high standing it has held in the life of the community during all these years, the State of New York has passed certain laws directly concerning the Chamber in its work for commercial arbitration.[18]   In 1874 a law was passed creating a Court of Arbitration in connection with the Chamber.   Under the law, the Governor appointed the arbitrator.   He also appointed as clerk of the Court whoever had been elected to that office by the Chamber.   The Chamber was to furnish necessary facilities such as rooms, stationery, clerical assistance, *etc.* Provision was made that the arbitrator should receive a salary of $10,000 annually, and that the clerk should also receive compensation.   Subsequently another law was passed repealing the provision for payment on the part of the State to the arbitrator and clerk, but placing the responsibility for the remuneration of these officers upon the Chamber.

[18] See Birdseye, *op. cit. supra.*

Under this system, the Court functioned for a number of years with the late Judge Enoch L. Fancher as arbitrator. The Secretary of the Chamber was Clerk of the Court. While Judge Fancher was arbitrator, he dealt with cases submitted to him largely as is done by a judge or referee—that is, the briefs were submitted to him and he rendered his decisions accordingly. It was felt by many that this system could be improved, and, upon Judge Fancher's death, the office of arbitrator was not filled for a number of years, and no definite steps were taken toward another system of arbitration until the year 1911.

The matter was again taken up at that time and a standing committee of the Chamber formed to deal with the question of arbitration. This Committee, after making a careful study of all the steps that had been taken, devised a plan which has since been operating in a very satisfactory manner. The procedure of the system as devised by this Committee is carried on under the provisions of the law of the state for arbitration of commercial disputes.

Only matters having to do with commercial disputes are handled. There are three methods which may be adopted by those seeking arbitration.

First: Each party to the dispute may select whomever he may desire as an arbitrator. These two arbitrators then select a third from the "List of Official Arbitrators," maintained by the Chamber's Committee.

Second: Both parties agreeing to the arbitration may submit their difference to one arbitrator selected from the list above referred to.

Third: The question in dispute may be referred to the Chamber's Committee as a whole. This method is intended for exceptional cases only, and thus far it has been found necessary to use it but seldom.

The official list of arbitrators consists of several hundred members of the Chamber, in various lines of business, who have volunteered to serve as arbitrators when called upon. This list is classified as to trades and business, the belief being that the disputes should be tried by men familiar and thoroughly acquainted with all the customs and trade usages of that particular branch of business.

It is, of course, necessary that both parties agree voluntarily to arbitration. Having once done so, and the formal arbitration having commenced, the parties thereto cannot withdraw. When the decision or award has been handed down by the arbitrator or arbitrators, it can, under law, be entered in any court in the state and then has legal effect precisely as would be the case in a judgment secured in such court.

As time went on, the Chamber's Committee found that there were certain injustices involved in the practice of arbitration in this country as compared with that of other countries—notably Great Britain. In the latter country the courts had decided, many years ago, that, in a contract, an agreement or clause to submit any differences to arbitration was irrevocable. In this country the courts held—following the error in interpreting Vynior's case—that even though such a clause in the contract had been agreed to, either party to the dispute might refuse to arbitrate if he so elected, the theory being that under the law every man is entitled to his "day in court." Believing that this did not work creditably to the merchants of this country, on the ground that, if a man is competent to enter into a contract whereby he agreed to fulfill certain requirements, he is also able to determine whether or not he is willing to submit to arbitration, the Chamber undertook to have the laws in the State of New York changed, making such clauses in contracts irrevocable. After a campaign lasting seven years, the Legislature of the State of New York in 1920 passed a law making arbitration clauses in contracts irrevocable. This law has since been sustained by the higher courts of the state.[19] The Chamber's Committee has, for many years, been in communication with governors, members of legislatures and commercial bodies in other states of the Union urging that a similar law be passed. Likewise, through the efforts of the Chamber's Committee, a Federal law, similar to the New York State law, was passed in 1925.

The history of commercial arbitration in England and America is therefore similar to the history of "privileged communications," the rule of legal procedure which exempts certain individuals from testifying in court. For medical practitioners, the common-law principle, that the State is entitled to every man's evidence, took precedence over all considerations of the confidential nature of the doctor's knowledge and over the necessity of maintaining the inviolability of that knowledge in order to facilitate the patient's disclosures. Certain states of the United States, however, have set aside the common-law rule by statutory legislation which even forbids a doctor to testify regarding information received by him in the course of his professional activities. Some states, conspicuously in New England and in the South,

[19] See *New York Law Journal*, June 17, 1924; July 29, 1925; November 29, 1929.

retain the common-law rule, which also prevails in England.[20] In the case of commercial arbitration, the general theory underlying our judicial department, that "every man may have his day in court," has similarly been modified by statutory legislation providing for arbitration clauses in business contracts and making the arbitration awards irrevocable.

The interest in arbitration has greatly increased in the last few years and many trade associations and chambers of commerce have established arbitration committees. In 1926 the American Arbitration Association was formed. It is doing a broad educational work, disseminating knowledge, fostering the principle of arbitration and working for enactment and improvement of arbitral laws through the arbitration committees of mercantile and other organizations.[21]

The present system of arbitration as conducted by the Chamber has met with the most gratifying results. While a large and increasing number of formal arbitrations is held, the vast majority of the cases coming before the Chamber are settled before the formal arbitration is called. This is due to the careful and painstaking work done by the Chairman and members of the Chamber's Committee on Arbitration in bringing the parties together to learn the facts before proceeding to arbitrate. In the majority of cases, as stated above, when the parties to the dispute have reached the point where they will sit around the table with a disinterested third party and discuss the case, they agree then and there to a settlement.

The Chamber's system is not limited to its members nor is it confined to persons or firms resident in New York. As a matter of fact, a number of cases have been held in which one of the parties has been a citizen or resident of a foreign land, and in several cases a foreign government has been officially represented as one of the parties to a dispute. In the few exceptional instances when the arbitration has been referred to the Supreme Court of the state, the award in each case has been upheld by the court and the decision of the arbitrators approved.

In all the recent work of the Chamber's Committee on Arbitration, they have had the hearty cooperation and assistance of the legal profession generally, and especially of the Bar Associa-

[20] "Should the Doctor Testify?" XXXVIII *International Journal of Ethics* 401, July, 1928.

[21] See *Yearbook*, American Arbitration Association.

tion of the State of New York.   The latter Association appointed
a committee to work jointly with the Chamber's Committee on
Arbitration in the preparation of a pamphlet entitled "Rules
for the Prevention of Unnecessary Litigation." This pamphlet
has had wide circulation, and is regarded as helpful to business
men, and to individuals generally, in pointing out mistakes to
be avoided, and in giving advice as to proper procedure in the
making of contracts and other legal instruments.

The outstanding facts in the Third Annual Report of the
American Arbitration Association just issued, July, 1930, are
the linking-up of trade associations in a unified national arbitration system, more than 300 such trade bodies being listed as
participating in the work, and the increased use of its Tribunals
by attorneys, 290 law firms having used its services.   Listed
among the organizations participating in the educational work
of the Association and identified with the arbitration system
are the American Bankers Association, American Manufacturers
Export Association, American Society of Certified Public
Accountants, Bankers Association for Foreign Trade, National
Association of Cost Accountants and the National Association of
Credit Men.   Also associated with the Arbitration Association
are the American Institute of Accountants, National Association
of Purchasing Agents and Association of Stock Exchange Firms
of New York City.

Mr. Eastman's presidential report of 1930 lays particular
stress upon the necessity for a careful preparation of arbitration
agreements and calls attention to the number of appeals being
made to the courts to vacate awards because technical requirements are not observed.   The Association has issued a "Warning
on Arbitration Clauses" calling the attention of business men to
the losses and inconvenience which result from vacated awards,
and more than 60,000 of these warnings have been distributed
throughout the country, together with instructions as to correct
procedure for the guidance of the parties and the arbitrators.
The records of the Association indicate that in 1929, in its New
York City tribunals alone, 344 cases were submitted to arbitration, and in only four of these cases were appeals made to the
courts to have the awards of the arbitrators set aside.   In
three of the cases appealed the courts upheld the arbitrators'
awards and one case is still pending.[22]

[22] See note 19, *supra*.

There is a resemblance between these cases of commercial arbitration and the appointment of a "master" by a court of chancery or a referee in bankruptcy, but with this difference: the authority of a master is restricted to a designated case and his powers terminate with the settlement of that case, whereas, in commercial arbitration, the usual procedure is to have a relatively permanent "panel" of arbitrators from which are chosen the particular men who are best fitted to deal with such cases as may arise.   When Judge Fancher acted as arbitrator, he virtually exercised the functions of a master, except that he dealt with all cases which were referred to him.   But, although speed and economy may have resulted from this particular method, the third virtue of commercial arbitration might be sacrificed unless the community were fortunate enough to have a Judge Fancher: it is as difficult for a single arbitrator to know intimately the details and practices of all particular businesses as it is for a judge.   The present practice of the Chamber is to have a sufficiently representative body of men on the "panel" to enable merchants to select a man who is engaged in the business in which the transaction in question has occurred.

A lawyer, on being asked what he thought of commercial arbitration, replied that as a man he regarded it as an excellent method of settling trade disputes but that as a lawyer he was not enthusiastic about it.   Obviously, commercial arbitration has reduced and will continue to reduce litigation; hence it must be regarded with favor by business men and by society at large, even though it may operate to the disadvantage of the legal profession.   This latter implication is doubtful, for it is quite conceivable that crowded court dockets and resulting delays are of slight benefit to the lawyer, and they are unquestionably bringing the law into disrepute.   At any rate, the American Bar Association must learn, and has indicated its appreciation of the fact, that, like the American Medical Association in its campaigns for public-health legislation, a professional organization may well at times pursue policies that involve elements of professional suicide.

General Factors Governing Arbitration

The outstanding material factors which limit the necessity and use of commercial arbitration are the standardization and definition of goods and processes.   This proposition has been developed elsewhere (in the chapter on Misrepresentations), in connection with the possibility of a metaphysics of business, stabilizing industry and conserving the energies and intellects of men for irreducible and unavoidable contingencies. The point becomes especially significant in connection with commercial arbitration, for this method of adjusting disputes is particularly applicable to situations in which the unknowns and variables are relatively important: trade practices and methods are subject to change, while the quality of commodities, such as the natural products of the soil and goods that are subject to deterioration, is constantly changing. One hears little of commercial arbitration regarding such commodities as gold or cement; where food products or textiles or building operations are concerned, commercial arbitration is continually necessary.

As regards building operations, a Form of Agreement and Schedule of Conditions for Building Contracts, such as has been worked out by the Royal Institute of British Architects, establishes an exact and detailed and standardized contract, variations from which may be inserted, but in conspicuous writing or different type, such that many disputes, otherwise liable to occur, are eliminated. This is not to say that a standard contract will eliminate all disputes, for it is obvious that the actual operations of a building contractor are much more complex than can be adequately or accurately stated in a contract; just as the standardization of cement may eliminate most disputes as regards the cement itself, without reducing appreciably the disputes that might arise regarding the quality of the concrete poured into a foundation—with the variables of sand, water, temperature, and mixture ratios contributing to the uncertainty of the product.

Big building operations have often been held up for months while trivial details of a building contract (not to mention the serious difficulties attending jurisdictional disputes, which are frequently referred to Industrial Arbitration) were being disputed. Builders have frequently capitulated when a dispute arose, rather than face the prospect of idle machinery and an incomplete building during the course of court action. If the arbitrators receive no salary, and if the room where the proceedings are held is donated by a chamber of commerce, expenses are reduced to little or nothing, and a dispute involving $2,000 or less may be settled for as little as $10. The American Institute of Architects, through its standard documents, regulates the arbitration of disputes arising between owner and contractor or sub-contractor, the architect acting as informal arbitrator; if his decision is not accepted, another arbitrator is chosen. This procedure has been approved by practically all the leading organizations in the building industry, one of which, the New York Builders' Congress, with a membership of 1,500, maintains its own tribunal and panel of arbitrators and handles hundreds of cases each year.

The Informal Method of Arbitration

In the case of food products, it is evident that contracts to purchase before the crop is harvested are liable to two contingencies: a crop shortage or surplus with consequent effects on price, and quality variations with similar effects. The following cases give a "run of the mine" picture of the situations which are handled by the Arbitration Committee of the National Wholesale Grocers' Association, and indicate the type of adjustment which characterizes the informal type of arbitration awards.

Packer and shipper.............................Ontario, N. Y.
Broker...Philadelphia, Pa.

Regarding brokerage on undelivered #10 Apples sold to retailer on September 10, 1924.

In accordance with established custom of many years' standing in the trade, our decision is that the broker is not entitled to a brokerage on undelivered goods and we, therefore, decide in favor of the packer. Cost of arbitration, $15, to be paid by broker.

* * * * * *

Shipper..Everett, Wash.
Consignee......................................Somerville, Mass.

Regarding quality of delivery of 3,000 cases #2½ Choice Bartlett Pears, as per purchase confirmation of the consignee, #261, dated July 10, 1925.

Twenty-four cans taken from twenty-four cases from the thousand-case-lot now at Springfield, Mass., and twenty-four cans taken from twenty-four cases from the lot now in warehouse at Boston, Mass., were carefully examined and we declare the delivery to be a good one and the rejection of the consignee is not sustained.

It is our understanding that the thousand-case lot has been paid for and we find that the invoice for the two thousand-case lot is due and payable at once, net.

The costs of this arbitration are assessed on the consignee.

* * * * * *

Seller...Clinton, N. Y.
Buyer...Jersey City, N. J.

Buyer purchased from seller, from the 1919 pack when made, 10,000 cases fancy corn.

Representatives appeared from both buyer and seller, the arbitration agreement having been duly signed by both parties, but not certified to by a notary, this having been waived by mutual agreement.

Seller's representative stated the circumstances attending the sale and that 1,000 cases of the corn under buyer's label had been shipped to Boston, 2,000 cases to Jersey City, 1,000 cases to the Bronx, and the balance, 6,000 cases, was held in their warehouse. The 4,000 cases shipped had been paid for, the 6,000 cases had been charged but not paid for. He claimed that the corn delivered was of fancy quality, Evergreen variety, New York State pack.

Buyer's representative stated that he bought Fancy New York Evergreen Corn, but that he did not consider the quality as described. By mutual agreement, 24 cans had been drawn from the 1,000 cases in New Jersey, with the understanding that it did represent the entire lot of 10,000 cases. The arbitration committee examined all of the 24 tins— they found it to be strictly fancy corn as described in the contract, in consistency, flavor, color, tenderness and uniformity. It was as fine a lot of New York State Corn as they had ever seen.

The decision was therefore rendered in favor of the sellers, the cost of the arbitration to be paid by the buyer.

* * * * * *

Shipper...Los Angeles, Calif.
Consignee...Bridgeport, Conn.

Regarding size of 300 bags of Diamond Brand #1 Soft Shell Walnuts, 1925 crop.

Sample containing 871 Walnuts were carefully examined as to size by being passed over a one-inch metal screen, which has been duly certified by the Inspector of Standards of the Commonwealth of Massachusetts.

Eight per cent of these walnuts passed through this screen, and allowing for a tolerance of 2%, we find that consignee is entitled to an allowance of $6/10$ cent (six-tenths cent) per pound on the entire shipment.

The costs of this arbitration are assessed against the shipper.

* * * * * *

Shipper...San Francisco, Calif.
Consignee...Boston, Mass.

Arbitration regarding delivery of 1,200 cases $5/10$ solid pack Spinach as per contract.

Twelve tins taken from 12 different cases were weighed, cut and carefully examined, and it was found that 8 cans were as called for in the contract, namely solid pack. The remaining 4 cans were decidedly sloppy, and arbitrators found that consignees were entitled to an allowance of $17\frac{1}{2}$ cents per dozen from the contract price, on the entire lot.

* * * * * *

Sellers..Crowley, La.
Buyers.......................................Pine Bluff, Ark.
Brokers......................................Pine Bluff, Ark.

Arbitration regarding shipment of three hundred (300) packets of new crop, fancy Blue Rose or Early Prolific Rice for each of the above parties as covered by sale tickets of brokers, dated August 23 and August 25, 1919, respectively.

Seller contended that this sale should be construed as Government grading. Buyers contended that the Government is not controlling grade or the price of rice and that they are entitled to an interpretation of this sale as being based upon the standard for fancy description prior to and since government control.

After a careful examination of samples taken from fifteen (15) bags from each lot of the rice shipped the above parties, the arbitrators found that, inasmuch as the sale was made and no contracts other than broker's sale tickets were passed, and the said sale tickets, as given, call for fancy Blue Rose or fancy Early Prolific Rice of the crop of 1919, they unanimously agreed that the shipper had not delivered fancy rice in accordance with the sale and further agreed that the buyers were entitled to a quarter $(\frac{1}{4})$ of a cent per pound allowance.

* * * * * *

Packers......................................Eastport, Me.
Brokers......................................St. Louis, Mo.
Buyers.......................................St. Louis, Mo.

Regarding a car of sardines purchased from packers by brokers. Brokers contended that, inasmuch as the sardine market had declined before the car in question was shipped, they should receive the benefit of the decline, and requested that draft be reduced $250; also requested that buyers should receive same benefit of decline on twenty-five (25) cases quarter $(\frac{1}{4})$ oil sardines billed direct to them.

Packers refused to reduce the amount of draft, submitting the case for arbitration.

After a careful examination of all correspondence submitted, arbitrators found that brokers placed an order, by wire, for a car of sardines on July 14th, 1919, time of shipment not specified; additions to car were made on July 23rd, when order for buyers was mailed, also on July 28, when brokers requested an increase in their specifications, and asked that car be shipped immediately upon receipt of letter under that date.

Shipment of car was made on August 5th, which was agreeable to brokers. In this transaction there was no mention of the prices being guaranteed against decline—and as the sardines were purchased at a fixed price, arbitrators unanimously agreed that packers had complied with their part of the contract, and the contention of brokers was not sustained.

* * * * * *

Shipper...Los Angeles, Calif.
Broker...New York City
Buyers...New York City

Shipper sold buyers, through broker, 1,250 cases Standard No. 2½ Apricots. They delivered 500 cases on this contract, which on arrival were rejected by the buyers because they discovered on examination that many of the tins contained too large a percentage of soft fruit and that some of the tins were dark in color.

Nine (9) sample tins were submitted to the Arbitration Board, said to be taken from different cases—five of the nine were very soft, the fruit being practically pulp and two of the five were very dark in color, evidently from overprocessing. The syrup was full standard, in fact better than standard.

The rejection was sustained because of the condition of the fruit. The cost of the arbitration was paid by the sellers.

* * * * * *

Other typical cases involved disputes regarding the shipment of strawberries and also of pineapples: the quality having been found equal to contract specifications, decision was in favor of the shipper and fees assessed on the consignee; of white beans: delivery not being in accordance with sale agreement, the buyer was awarded an allowance, while the shipper was ordered to pay all demurrage and arbitration expenses; and of kraut and also of white beans: quality not being up to standard, the rejection of the buyer was sustained and, in the case of the kraut, shipper was ordered to supply consignee with goods specified. Where two shipments of stringless beans were rejected, the committee sustained the buyer in one transaction and the seller in the other, and assessed one-half of the fee on each. Where rain-damaged prunes were delayed in delivery and not properly iced in transit, the committee sustained the rejection of the consignee; and later, on request that the case be reexamined, sustained its previous decision by referring to even more specific reasons than before. Where canned peaches were sold by sample, and not by grade, shipper was upheld against complaint of consignee that goods were not up to standard grade; but the consignee's broker was censured for marking the goods "Standard" rather than "As per sample submitted."

Arbitration committees of this grocers' association are established in some 25 different markets throughout the country, and their services are at the command of its members. In 1927, some 27 arbitrations were held, practically all of them in connection with canned goods. Fifteen of these cases were decided in favor of the buyer, and 12 cases in favor of the seller. Many disputes arising under contracts containing arbitration clauses are settled by direct agreement without recourse to arbitration. The arbitration clause has often been regarded as the most valuable part of the contract.[23]

The Formal Method of Arbitration

This informal and strictly arbitrary method of commercial arbitration is to be contrasted with the more formal method of procedure.[24] The latter is well exemplified in the arbitration decisions of the Arkwright Club of Boston and the New England Cotton Buyers' Association. These two organizations in 1911 issued the first "New England Terms for Buying and Selling Cotton." There are two Boards for deciding appeals. If a buyer of cotton finds that cotton is not up to what he bought in grade or staple, he rejects it, whereupon the seller has the right to ask to have it arbitrated. Samples are then sent to the Classification Committee, which passes on the questions as to whether the cotton is up in grade and staple. The decisions of this committee are final. The Board of Appeal decides on questions of allowance and the interpretation of the Terms and whether the shipment conforms to the Terms of a sale "except as to actual grade or staple." Although the Board of Appeal consists of three men, one member of the Association, one manufacturer, and a third to be selected by them, the preparation of

[23] *Report of Arbitration Committee*, National Wholesale Grocers' Association, Austin L. Baker, Chairman. *Bulletin*, September 17, 1919. A pamphlet on Arbitration is obtainable at the Association headquarters, 6 Harrison Street, New York City. See next page for form of award.

[24] See Isaacs, Nathan, "Two Views of Commercial Arbitration," XL *Harvard Law Review* 929, May, 1927.

The National Wholesale Grocers' Association, the National Food Brokers' Association and the National Canners' Association.

FINDINGS AND AWARD OF THE ARBITRATION BOARD

In the matter of a controversy between   ————————————————

————————————————————————   In regard

————————————————————————

and

————————————————————————

————————————————————————

The undersigned, constituting a duly authorized Board of Arbitration of the National Wholesale Grocers' Association, the National Food Brokers' Association and the National Canners' Association, to whom were voluntarily submitted matters in controversy between the parties named, by an agreement in writing, duly signed and attested, have fully considered the proofs and allegations of the disputants and do hereby make their findings and award as follows:

————————————————

————————————————————Arbitrators

————————————————

the decisions of the Board has fallen largely to the lot of the Secretary, William F. Garcelon, whose continuity in office for almost a score of years has developed a consistent and integrated policy.

No decisions were rendered prior to the First Edition of the Terms, which therefore may be looked upon as a constitution. From the point of view of methodology and of social philosophy this is an important point. The Terms are not empirical in the strictest sense of the word; for, although they have been modified in conformity with the necessities imposed by successive arbitration cases and decisions, the original terms were a fairly complete set of general rules. Like the Constitution of the United States, however—and like the Ten Commandments—they did not represent something "struck off at a given time by the brain and hand of man," but represented the general conclusions of men of experience and expertness and may therefore be regarded indirectly as empirical generalizations. Furthermore, although a second, revised, edition of the Terms appeared in 1912 before any arbitraments were made, successive subsequent editions very clearly show the successive effects of arbitration decisions on the more general rules.

Some dozen or more revised editions of the Terms have since appeared at intervals of two or three years. The first decision of the arbitration board was rendered April 16, 1913. Five decisions were made in that year, 10 in 1914, 12 in 1915, 10 in 1916, and so on, until May 3, 1921, when 162 decisions were published in the first printed volume. Each subsequent year a supplement has been published, containing the decisions for the year ending September 1, approximately 25 cases being contained in each Supplement. About 300 cases now constitute the record of the Board. In each annual publication attention is also called to the changes that have been made in the Terms; hence, a very interesting, even if limited, study of the operation of the case system in business can be made of these records. Here is a veritable Doomsday Book of business, repeating in miniature the history of the Constitution of the United States, with original framework, and amendments and practical interpretations of actual situations that could not in detail be anticipated in the original draft, but which can be set as minor premises to the major premise in the Terms, in order to draw a conclusion which will settle a business controversy.

As regards the content of the arbitration cases, the following situations and decisions were selected at random. Where cotton was burned in shipment, *e.g.*, the loss—which was small—was apportioned, 55% to the shipper and 45% to the buyer.[25] A buyer may refuse a shipment which has been delayed by an embargo unless the seller furnishes an affidavit.[26] When delay occurs in shipping instructions, the buyer is liable for interest and insurance.[27] A mill is not responsible for loss in weight of cotton in its possession after it has rejected the cotton.[28]

Two important procedural problems were settled early in the history of the Board: the Board decided not to state hypothetical questions,[29] and the decisions of the Classification Committee were declared to be final.[30] Two legal problems were practically restated: the seller is bound by his agent's act;[31] and written instruments are not to be regarded as varied by any oral understandings unless all parties are in accord as evidenced by additional documents.[32] "Samples" are to be regarded as more specific than "types."[33] Where rejected cotton is taken at an allowance, "there seems to be no rule covering the point; the Board understands that it is the custom of the trade that charges for interest, handling and storage are not made."[34]

This "run-of-the-mine" picture will indicate, in a fragmentary way, the type of problem that is presented to the Board. Certain outstanding factors may be illustrated in the following cases. To show how the Board relies on precedent, the following case is presented.

CASE NO. 133

DECISION RENDERED OCTOBER 14, 1921

On an order for 500 bales of cotton, 100 bales, weighing 52,721 pounds, were shipped. The seller contended that he should be credited with

[25] Case CC.
[26] Case 17 (March 8, 1917).
[27] Case 4.
[28] Case 84.
[29] Cases 112 and 113. See however Case 91, *infra*, patently hypothetical.
[30] Case 171.
[31] Case 252.
[32] Case 256.
[33] Case 137, and Case 142, where the same problem arose in connection with the resale of the same cotton.
[34] Case 197.

107 bales of the average weight of 490 pounds, this shipment to be applied to the 500-bale order.

Question: What credit in bales should be given to the seller on this invoice of 100 bales?

Decision. Rules 27 and 29 read as follows:

"27. All sales, unless otherwise specified, shall be on the basis of 50,000 pounds for 100 bales with a variation of 2% either way.

* * * * * *

"29. If the number of bales shipped does not make the minimum weight, as above provided, the shipper may be required to add a sufficient number of bales to bring the total weight of the cotton delivered up to the weight required on the above basis; or if a less number of bales than the number sold will give the maximum weight as above provided, the purchaser may require that the number of bales delivered shall be reduced accordingly.

"Written notice of any dissatisfaction with respect to shipping weights under this section must be given by the purchaser not later than three days after receipt of invoice."

The Board decides that settlement of weight should be made on the basis of each separate invoice. In this case, the seller shipped 100 bales, weighing 52,721 pounds. Under Rule 29 the buyer had the right to require that the number of bales should be reduced to bring the total weight to 51,000 pounds, and, if he so desired, should have notified the seller not later than three days after receipt of the invoice. If he did not so notify the seller he accepted the shipment as 100 bales.

The seller in making shipment had the right to ship less or more than 100 but could be required by the buyer to keep within the limits provided in Rule 27, namely, 49,000 to 51,000 pounds. Having elected to ship 100 bales, weighing 52,721 pounds, it remained with the buyer either to accept said shipment as a shipment of 100 bales or to require that the number of bales be reduced and the poundage reduced to 51,000. If the buyer made no objection to the weights as invoiced, the seller still owes the buyer 400 bales on the 500-bale order.

SUPPLEMENTARY DECISION NO. 1

DECISION RENDERED NOVEMBER 9, 1921

In response to further questions the Board refers to three decisions which have been rendered, as follows:

"DECISION NO. 52, JANUARY 24, 1919

"Under date of January 14, 1919, the interpretation is asked of Rules 28 to 30 inclusive, of the New England Terms, specifically inquiring whether a delivery of any number of merchantable bales weighing between 49,000 and 51,000 pounds is a fulfillment of a contract for the sale of 100 bales.

"The Board decides that under Rules 28 to 30 a shipment may vary 2% from the basis of 50,000 pounds per 100 bales, and that a shipper is not required, as formerly, to ship the exact number of bales required in the contract. Of course merchantable bales should be delivered."

"DECISION NO. 91, JANUARY 23, 1920

"The case as presented to the Board follows:

"DELIVERIES ON SALE OF 100 B/C

1	95	B/C	weighing	51,000 lbs.
2	95	B/C	weighing	50,000 lbs.
3	95	B/C	weighing	49,000 lbs.
4	105	B/C	weighing	51,000 lbs.
5	105	B/C	weighing	50,000 lbs.
6	105	B/C	weighing	49,000 lbs.

"Q. 1. Which of the above has seller a right to deliver to complete contract?

"Q. 2. Which of the above has purchaser a right to demand?

"The Board decides that all of the above-cited cases are good deliveries. The purchaser has a right to demand a delivery of a sufficient number of bales to bring the poundage within the limits as provided by Rule 28."

"DECISION NO. 123, JANUARY 22, 1921

"A sold to B 100 bales of cotton and shipped 100 bales weighing 45,765 pounds, being less than the required weight under the New England Terms. The seller claims the right to ship additional bales to bring the weight within the required weight. The purchaser refuses to accept the additional bales.

"*Decision:* The seller could have originally shipped any number of bales to bring the weight within the weights required under Rule 27. Not having done this, he cannot ship additional bales, unless required to do so by the buyer."

In accordance with these decisions the seller may ship a less number of bales than 100 (on a 100 bale order) provided the total weight comes within 49,000 to 51,000 pounds.

You ask this question: If cotton which is available for him to ship is running in an exact average of 490 pounds per bale, can the seller ship such larger number of bales than 100 as would be obtained by dividing 51,000 by 490 or must he ship just 100 bales weighing 49,000 pounds?

The answer to this question is contained in Decisions 52 and 91 quoted above.

SUPPLEMENTARY DECISION NO. 2

DECISION RENDERED NOVEMBER 15, 1921

A second inquiry affecting Decision No. 133 is made as follows:

We ship 52,721 lbs. and claim credit for 107 B/C because the poundage is sufficient to make 107 bales of 490 lbs. each. Messrs. XXXXX Co. maintain that we can only claim credit for 103 B/C because the poundage is only sufficient to make 103 bales of 510 lbs. each.

In order to clarify the situation a little more, we may explain that we are compelled by Messrs. XXXXX Co. to show on our invoices the number of "representative" bales, as well as the number of actual running bales, under threat of having our drafts dishonored if number of representative bales is omitted.

Our contention is that under our agreement and under the Rules 27–29, we can ship anything between 49,000 lbs. and 51,000 lbs. and call it 100 B/C, quite irrespective of whether the actual number of running bales is 80 or 100 or 120. Messrs. XXXXX Co. contend that it is optional with them to apply our shipments on the basis of bale minimum or bale maximum poundage.

Reply:

The seller has the right to ship 50,000 pounds in a 100-bale invoice with a variation of 2% either way, at his option. If there is an agreement between buyer and seller that the seller must show the number of "representative" bales on each invoice, then that invoice shall constitute the number of bales so represented, provided they come within the 2% variation on the basis of 50,000 pounds to 100 bales, and neither buyer nor seller has any further option in the matter.

The following case illustrates the manner in which the Board defines its jurisdiction and also discloses the effect of certain changes in successive editions of the Terms.

CASE NO. 234

DECISION RENDERED MAY 6, 1926

A sold to B, October 1, 1925, 200 bales of cotton equal to type MARTHA. All bales were rejected. Arbitration ensued.

On October 26, B notified A that arbitration showed only 13 bales equal type MARTHA. A shipped 50 bales as replacements October 27.

All these were rejected upon arrival. Arbitration of this shipment followed.

On December 2, B notified A that arbitration showed only 9 bales equal to the contract.

On December 5, B notified A that replacement rights had expired.

Many telegrams were exchanged between the parties from October 22 to December 6. These referred to the disposition of the rejected cotton, to the arbitrations, to settlement of differences, *etc.*

A claims that B's telegram of November 18 was a consent to a delay in replacing.

B's telegrams to A of November 18, as they relate to the question at issue, follow:

"Mill rejects 50 bales for staple . . . This is a very serious situation and drastic steps must be taken at once to get the mill their cotton . . . "

"Be quick with your investigation as according New England Terms mill has right to buy in the rejected replacements at once, regardless of whatever type used for staple . . . "

The parties present the following questions:

1. Has seller lost replacement rights on 150 bales, it being admitted that replacement rights on 41 bales are lost?

2. If so, when were these replacement rights lost?

3. If seller's replacement rights had expired, what was the fair market value c. & f. New Bedford for cotton of Strict Middling grade and equal type MARTHA in character and staple on such date?

Decision: This case comes under the *Ninth Edition, Corrected,* of the New England Terms, effective September 24, 1925.

A replaced 50 bales within the time limit. Of these, only nine were declared equal to the contract.

Under Rule 77, A lost any further right to replace the 41 rejected bales.

There is no evidence of other replacements.

The Board finds no evidence of an agreement made by B for an extension of time for the replacement of 137 bales for which, according to the evidence presented, replacements were never shipped.

These replacements should not have been delayed over 14 days from the date of notification of the decision of the Classification Committee, *viz.,* 14 days from October 26.

It is not within the province of the Board of Appeal to decide the third question.

In order to show how certain concrete situations seemed to warrant a change in the Terms, the following case is of interest.

CASE NO. 129

DECISION RENDERED AUGUST 15, 1921

The buyer received from the seller 75 bales and tested the first 10 bales taken out of the car. The buyer then filed a claim for excess tare of 167 pounds, figuring the excess tare as follows:

Invoice weight of 75 B/C..................	38,515 lbs.
Gross tare of first 10 bales................	252 lbs.
Gross receiving weight of same bales........	4,815 lbs.
Percentage tare on 10 bales (252 ÷ 4,815)...	5.233%
Tare allowance under rules................	4.8%
Excess tare (being the difference between the above)................................	0.433%
Excess tare in lbs. (38,515 × .00433)........	167

The seller contends that the excess tare is 41 pounds, figuring it as follows:

Invoice weight of 75 B/C................. 38,515 lbs.

Actual tare for 10 B/C tested............. 252 lbs.

Proportionate tare on 75 B/C $\dfrac{(252 \times 75)}{10}$ .... 1,890 lbs.

Guaranteed tare on 75 B/C (38,515 × .048). 1,849 lbs.

Difference or excess tare for 75 B/C........ 41 lbs.

Decision: In accordance with Rule 55 of the *Sixth Edition*, the allowance for tare should be 4$\frac{8}{10}$% of the invoice weight and any excess tare shown by the bales set aside for tare should be settled proportionately on the number of bales in the mark; and the buyer should be reimbursed for tare in excess of this average at the invoice value, less 2 cents per pound.

In the instance stated the allowance should therefore be made as in the second clause of the matter of appeal. The excess tare figures 41 pounds.

The change which this problem effected in the *Seventh Edition* of the Terms is indicated as follows:

CLAIMS—TARE

Rule 55 of the *Sixth Edition* was changed by substituting for the words "two cents" in the last line the words "one-half cent" so as to read as follows:

"55. The allowance for tare shall be four and eight-tenths *per cent* (4.8%) of the invoice weight, and any excess tare shown by the bales set aside for tare, as per Sections 52, 53 and 54, shall be settled proportionately on the number of bales in the mark; and the purchaser shall be reimbursed for tare in excess of this average at the invoice value, less one-half cent per pound."

This record represents the more formal type of commercial arbitration. The very recording of the cases differentiates it at the start from the more informal types of arbitration where no records are kept; or where if they are kept, they are not used as precedents. This tendency of the more formal method toward systematization and toward the recognition of precedent is regarded as a serious defect by those who point out the essentially arbitrary character of arbitration. On the other hand, even the more formal method of arbitration has not come anywhere near an approximation to legal methodology, which arbitration is intended to avoid: it is not so complex, it is confined to a particular commodity, and the decisions are given by technical experts.

It represents one of many degrees of differentiation ranging from the strictly behavioristic activities of business on through to the other extreme of legal metaphysics, the "dead hand" of which touches but does not always grasp the realities and necessities of business. Just where business, or various businesses, will find themselves in this range of social methodologies, it is difficult to say. Certain types of arbitration procedure have been made a matter of record in this chapter in order to show that there is more than one type and that business men may select such as they deem best fitted to their own problems— if they wish to do anything about the problems that require adjustment.

Summary

The victory of business men, represented by the statutory provisions for commercial arbitration as an exception to the common-law rules, would be but a Pyrrhic victory, however, if commercial arbitration developed, as did Equity and the Law Merchant, into a formalized system, with rigorous procedure and *stare decisis* engulfing the flexible character intended by the proponents of arbitration. Two views are now in process of development.[35] According to the one view, the method should be kept flexible and informal, with a minimum of records so as to avoid the difficulties attending *stare decisis;* the chief exponent being Charles Bernheimer, whose personality has been a powerful factor in New York business circles and whose name ranks with that of Judge Fancher as a proponent of conciliatory methods of arbitration. The other view, sponsored by Judge Grossman, and followed to a considerable extent by the American Arbitration Association, holds that commercial arbitration can be institutionalized and made into a rival of the common-law system, with procedure and records and rules exactly formulated so as to reduce the variables to a minimum.

The spirit of the former of these views is indicated in the following excerpts:

There are certain things which an arbitrator or arbitrating body should keep in mind. It is required that an award shall cover all the matters contained in the submission and must not deal with matters which have not been submitted. An award must be final, and not leave anything to be decided later, either by the arbitrator or by others. It must also be certain; but this does not mean that it may not give an option: there is no uncer-

[35] Isaacs, Nathan, *op. cit. supra*, note 24.

tainty when a magistrate awards forty shillings or a month. If evidence is required beyond what is put before him, the arbitrator should let the parties obtain it, and must be careful that, if one party does so, the other party has an opportunity to refute it. After an award is published, it may not be altered (except for clerical errors) and fees should be collected before it is published, the award stating by whom they are to be paid. Above all, an award should give no reasons for the decision, for, although the decision may be good, the reasons will probably be bad. The ideal award is in the form: A shall pay B ten pounds.

It would seem that a man engaged in a trade is bound to have a subconscious bias one way or the other on any dispute arising in that trade. But the subconscious bias is generally neutralized by a conscious feeling that he must err, if at all, on the other side. There are, however, two faults which may beset the commercial arbitrator.

The first is what is usually called having a legal mind. To have a legal mind that has not been thoroughly disciplined by legal training is not so bad as kleptomania or dipsomania, but is even more oppressive to other people, although a source of great joy to the possessor. The arbitrator who is afflicted in this way is never satisfied with what is put before him, but wants more. He calls for documentary evidence of facts which are not disputed; and wants to drag into the dispute things which are entirely outside it; above all things he enjoys a discussion with the disputants, forgetting that an arbitrator should say little and think the more. Generally speaking, he wants to be not only judge and jury, but counsel for the prosecution and counsel for the defence, and is like the amateur actor who insisted on playing the part of the hero and the part of the villain, and when these two had to fight a duel, wanted to play the part of the man who rushed in and struck up their swords.

The other fault to which an arbitrator is prone is impatience. It must be borne in mind that one of the hardest things in the world is to make a statement on any subject without introducing extraneous matter. It is more difficult than playing the violin. People take lessons and practise diligently, yet first-class violinists are scarce; but nobody ever takes lessons in the art of saying what is relevant to the matter in hand, and omitting all the other things he knows which have no bearing on it. Therefore, the matter that is put before an arbitrator is more likely to be excessive as to quantity than as to quality; everything will be said at least twice, and much of it a third time, in case it has not been sufficiently stressed before. An arbitrator who is interested only in settling a case, and, unlike a lawyer, has no inducement to spin it out indefinitely, is tempted to put a stop to this, forgetting that a disputant is entitled to say all he can on his side, and that the other disputant is entitled to say all he can on the other side. If, as usually happens, they say too much, and weaken their cases, that is their lookout. An arbitrator must put up with this sort of thing. He must learn to suffer fools gladly, and be content to listen to, or read, a quantity of unnecessary verbiage, in the hope of getting some grains of useful information, like the gold-miner who sifts a ton of gravel in the hope of getting a few grains of gold.[36]

[36] Clarke, W. J., *op. cit.*, note 2.

As regards this "realistic view," as Isaacs calls it, involving a deliberate change in the substantive rights of contracting parties—as distinguished from the "legalistic view" which confines commercial arbitration to the realm of adjective law—little can be *said;* its virtue lies in the realm of delicately adjusted *activities* that constitute the successful arbitrator. The word "arbitration" may not be strictly derived from the same stem as is the word "arbitrary," but the latter connotation has practically become identified with the desirable character which the award is intended to have: the decision is to be given *without reasons or arguments.* The very publication of arbitral awards introduces an inaccuracy into the description of the business activities involved, and at the same time is bound to lead to their treatment as precedents, which is just what the opposing view advocates. The distinction between the judicial functions of the arbitrator and his semi-fiduciary character is indeed what the realistic business man wishes to avoid; but if he has to choose between the two, he prefers to dispense with the judicial functions and to regard the arbitrator as a common agent—an attitude which the legalistically minded cannot comprehend.

The test of commercial arbitration would seem to consist in the appeals which are made from it to the courts—not necessarily the mere *power* of the courts to review arbitration awards. The statement of Isaacs on this point is significant:

One of the most successful arbitration committees (that of the Chamber of Commerce of New York) and certainly the oldest in the country, consistently with its interpretation of its function, with its informality, with its readiness to substitute mediation and compromise for adjudication, with the general atmosphere of its hearings (even the architecture of the arbitration room can suggest a trial or the determination to avoid trials), with its opposition to the presence of lawyers, with its refusal to consider its decisions as precedents, opposes successfully every suggestion of appeal to the courts.[37]

[37] Isaacs, *op. cit.*, p. 934.

INDEX

A

W